ELIZABETH I

Elizabeth I

David Loades

Hambledon and London
London and New York

Hambledon and London

102 Gloucester Avenue
London, NW1 8HX

175 Fifth Avenue
New York, NY 10010
USA

First Published 2003

ISBN 1 85285 304 2 ✓

A description of this book is available from the
British Library and from the Library of Congress.

Typeset by Carnegie Publishing, Lancaster,
and printed in Great Britain by Bath Press.

Distributed in the United States and Canada
exclusively by Palgrave Macmillan,
a division of St Martin's Press.

Contents

Illustrations

Text Illustrations

Princess Elizabeth as Mary Magdalene, from John Bale's edition
of Elizabeth's translation from Marguérite d'Angoulême,
A Godly Medytacyon of the Christen Sowle (1548)   61

Title-page of the Bishops' Bible (1568). Elizabeth, who represents
Hope, is between Faith and Charity   125

Elizabeth I at the kill. From George Turbevile,
Booke of Hunting (1575)   207

Illustrations Acknowledgement

The author and publishers are grateful to the National Portrait Gallery for
permission to reproduce the illustrations in the plate sections.

Preface

Elizabeth died four hundred years ago, after a lifetime which had seen almost as many changes as those which we have ourselves witnessed over the last seventy years. She fascinated her contemporaries, and has preoccupied historians, particularly those writing in the nineteenth and twentieth centuries. Her reign has been studied in depth, and from every conceivable angle; many of her ministers and servants have been placed under the analytical microscope. Because she was a personal monarch, in a sense the whole political life of later sixteenth-century England was a part of her life. The documentation is vast and bewildering in its complexity, having been created for many different purposes, and on many different agendas. By contrast, her formative years, down to her accession at the age of twenty-five, are patchily recorded, and subject to much retrospective invention.

The writing of a balanced biography has therefore presented problems; too much material in some places, too little in others. In writing of her early life, I have often been constrained to interpret documents that were written for other purposes, or long after the event. In writing of her reign, my intention has been to concentrate upon those developments and events in which I have seen the queen's hand most visible; not only her marriage negotiations and the swings and roundabouts of the court, but her encouragement of maritime enterprise, and the subtle use of the royal prerogative. Above all, I have concentrated on her unique reinterpretation of the commonwealth in an imagery of partnership. Some of this thesis is based upon my own research; more upon the research of others. In doing this, I believe that I have a contribution to make to the understanding of this extraordinary woman, and the developments over which she presided.

My thinking about Elizabeth has been developed by illuminating conversations with many colleagues in seminars and conferences over the years. I would particularly like to thank Christopher Haigh, Simon Adams and Susan Doran. I would also like to thank Tony Morris of Hambledon and London for responding so positively to the original suggestion of a biography of Elizabeth, and Martin Sheppard for nursing it through its formative stages. Michael Cox read the proofs thoroughly and efficiently.

Above all my gratitude is due to my wife Judith, who has not only offered constant encouragement and perceptive criticism, but has also filtered out many gratuitous errors.

Burford   July 2002

Introduction

In 1599 John Dekker wrote in *Old Fortunatus*:

> Are you then travelling to the temple of Eliza?
> Even to her temple are my feeble limbs travelling. Some call her Pandora; some Gloriana: some Cynthia: some Belphoebe: some Astrea; all by several names to express several loves: Yet all those names make but one celestial body, as all those loves meet to create but one soul.
> I am of her country, and we adore her by the name of Eliza.

Even experienced historians are prone to read history backward; to seek in the tangle of past events for the roots of present problems, and to isolate themes which appear to have a contemporary resonance. The late Sir Geoffrey Elton compared the writing of such history to the sin against the Holy Ghost, because it was addressed to the writer's own agenda rather than to the evidence which was being used.[1] It is one thing to denounce such malpractice, another to avoid it. It is impossible for a modern scholar to write the history of England in the second half of the sixteenth century without being keenly aware of what Sir Roy Strong has called 'the cult of Gloriana'. It was, after all, a contemporary phenomenon, as Dekker's words make plain. We have to remember, however, that Elizabeth was not always Gloriana, let alone the Virgin Queen. These were images of her mature years. How far she chose them for herself, and how far merely accepted what was conveniently created for her, is not easily resolved. Nor was this kind of idolatry the whole story, important though it was. In the last few years of her life her servants knew perfectly well that they were dealing with a withered, capricious and sometimes bitter old lady, even as they were producing the standard flattery that was expected of them. Elizabeth was a very difficult person to deal with. She was also a spent force, politically, some years before her death, and amidst the theatrical lamentations for her passing in 1603, there were audible sighs of relief.[2]

Nevertheless, Elizabeth had changed England. It would never again be the unimportant island which her father had ruled, let alone the continental power of Edward III or Henry V. By the time she died, the English saw themselves as a seapower, whose future wealth was likely to come from trade. When the peers of *Iolanthe* sought the origins of England's greatness, it was rightly with 'Good Queen Bess's Glorious Days' that they chose to begin. Gilbert and Sullivan's own contemporaries, living in the reign of another long-lived queen, certainly traced the origins of their imperial achievements in the careers of Hawkins, Drake, Frobisher and Raleigh. When Britain appeared to be threatened from the Continent, the 'Armada Spirit' could be invoked, in much the same way as the 'Dunkirk Spirit' was invoked during the Second World War. The myth of Elizabeth plagued her immediate successors, and inspired more distant ones; but it was a phenomenon in its own right and needs to be carefully disentangled from the life and actions of the real queen.[3]

Nobody can claim that she is a neglected subject. There are many biographies, and numerous studies of her reign (or specific aspects of it). Many of the latter, however, are straightforward political narratives, in which the queen's role is largely taken for granted, and many of the former were written with modern agendas. There are old-fashioned 'praise-songs', 'feminist perspectives', and myth demolitions. Two of the more recent examples, by Wallace MacCaffrey and Christopher Haigh, make the point.[4] The former, although its title suggests a biography, is really a history of the reign; the queen's life before her accession is handled briefly and conventionally. The latter is a deliberately provocative attempt to represent Elizabeth as a confused and ineffective woman who enjoyed a remarkable run of good luck. The most recent biography, by David Starkey, does address some real problems of the queen's personality and is specifically concerned with her early years. It was, however, written to accompany a television series and is consequently both anecdotal and unreferenced.[5]

Elizabeth was probably the best-educated member of her family, and almost certainly the most intelligent and pragmatic. Sophisticated evasion and circumlocution had become a natural method of defence to her before she had ceased to be an adolescent, and little that she ever said or did was quite what it appeared to be. The flowery rhetoric of her letters, even the very early ones, is sometimes intended to flatter, sometimes to obfuscate, but hardly ever to convey straightforward information or opinion.[6] Elizabeth never lived a normal life, even by the standards of the sixteenth century. From her very earliest years she was a symbol as much as a person, and was aware of that almost as soon as she was aware of the people round about her. She is often described as having been a consummate actress, and keenly aware of her image. Both those things are true, as far as they go; but an actress is aware that she is assuming an identity and can change it as necessary. Elizabeth only ever played one part, and it is almost impossible to distinguish the artificial *persona* from the real woman. There are, however, places where the speculative probe touches hard rock. She was always keenly aware of her gender, and sexual stereotypes played a large part in her life. It was brought to her attention very dramatically in 1548 that she was physically attractive and had a strong effect upon men. This is something which many girls discover at that age, but Elizabeth was also aware of her royal status and its attendant responsibilities. Watching her sister struggle with the unresolved conflict between sovereign lady and dutiful wife, she evolved her own strategy to turn her sex to advantage. Her mother's rise to power had been based upon consummate skill in the game of courtly love. Elizabeth's own situation as a queen in her own right was very different, but it is tempting to see the maternal talent emerging in the manner in which she chose to conduct herself as queen.[7]

Elizabeth was well aware, both by observation and by practical experience, that women need to manage men. As a queen, you had to set the agenda. Mary never learned this. She was not successful at managing the men in her life, least of all her husband; but she did perform one invaluable service by confronting the legal issue of female sovereignty head on. In a statute of 1554, parliament declared that her authority was identical with that of her predecessors, 'kings of this realm'.[8] This exacerbated rather than solved the problem of Mary's relations with Philip, but it gave Elizabeth an advantage. Unless or until she married, doubts about the extent of her power were strictly off limit; and she was free to rule from a position of strength. This was not easy. She wanted to be her father's daughter; 'remember good old king Henry' as someone had shouted (probably by prior arrangement) during her coronation entry. She wanted to be 'a Godly Prince', and her Protestant subjects conveniently saw her as Deborah, Judge of Israel. Finally she wanted to be the Queen of Hearts, served by her adoring knights and councillors. These roles were only tangentially related to the practical problems which she had to solve on her accession. They were more a question of style than substance. Nor were they entirely compatible. To bring a divided country together, she needed to be popular; to re-establish its sense of identity, she needed to distance herself from her sister; to gain political credibility, she needed to be sober and discreet; to gain the maximum advantage from her gender, she needed to be aloof and fascinating, with a hint of coquetry. The question of marriage brought all these disparate elements together in one problem of fearsome complexity.

Without a marriage, there could be no direct heir, and the dangers of that were too obvious to need emphasis. To marry within the realm meant disparagement and faction; to marry abroad would bring undesirable foreign interference, as Mary had just demonstrated.[9] Moreover, as even Mary had felt bound to point out, a queen was a woman and needed a compatible partner, who might (or might not) be politically convenient. Scholars have struggled long and hard over Elizabeth's attitude to marriage, but it is not necessary to assume that she ever made up her mind in any conscious sense. If she had been a simple gentlewoman, she would almost certainly have married Robert Dudley after his first wife's death. Their long, and sometimes stormy, relationship has all the marks of sexual fascination; but it was almost certainly never consummated. The effects of this frustration on the queen's attitude to other issues run like threads through the politics of almost thirty years, providing clues to some unexpected decisions. Elizabeth's other courtships, which were numerous, have been studied recently and in some detail by Susan Doran,[10] but understanding can always benefit from a revisit. Did she ever seriously intend to marry a Habsburg archduke or a Valois prince? Or were these simply examples of a woman trailing her petticoat for political advantage? The evidence, which is plentiful if somewhat contradictory, suggests that all these were serious proposals, and that the last (and most improbable), with François d'Anjou, was pursued by the queen with some personal enthusiasm.

As Elizabeth grew older, the sexual imagery of her self-presentation was intensified rather than diminished. The Accession Day tilts, which had her presiding like some pagan goddess over the allegorical conflicts of her self-styled warriors, were developed by Sir Henry Lee in the late 1570s, when the queen was in her mid forties. She did not even begin to become the Virgin Queen until after 1580. There had been hints of such an idea before, usually linked to images of marriage to the realm, but it was only after all marriage negotiations had been given up that the concept began to be seriously exploited.[11] As the reality of her physical attractiveness withered, the flattery became more explicit and intense. Vanity was always a sin to which Elizabeth had been prone, and the way in which she demonstrated it during the last twenty years of her life tells us more about her personality than any number of political intrigues or decisions. The nature of the flattery changed, however. Her beauty became imperishable, and her sexuality more distant and allegorical. The Fairie Queen could not be expected to sully herself with mere human relationships. Virginity, of course, could be synonymous with power, in a man as well as a woman; and, as the myth of her heroic achievements grew to counteract the war-weariness of the 1590s, that became increasingly important. Nor did it elude her more astute publicists that virginity could also be powerful by analogy. This was a theme which required careful handling, because although the Virigin Mary was no longer the Queen of Heaven in the Anglican calendar, too explicit a comparison would still have been considered blasphemous by the great majority of Elizabeth's subjects. So the statement was implicit; quietly replacing one female principal with another. As the numerous feasts of the Blessed Virgin disappeared, or were discontinued by edict, the queen's accession day and Armada Day emerged to take their place. Little was said, or even written, on this subject, but after her death the following tribute is revealing:

> She was and is, what can there more be said,
> In earth the first, in heaven the second maid.[12]

How far the queen herself encouraged this association, or was even aware of it, is unclear, as is Elizabeth's personal attitude towards the image-building which went on around her and in her name. Every public appearance was accompanied by studied gestures, designed to encourage loyal demonstrations by the onlookers. We also know that in December 1563 a proclamation was drafted prohibiting unauthorised portraits of the queen.[13] This is supposed to have reflected a personal sensitivity in the wake of her smallpox attack, but we cannot be sure that that was the reason for it; we cannot even be sure that it was ever issued. It is tempting to see Elizabeth herself as driving the image factory, because she clearly understood its importance; but caution is needed. The queen did not call herself Deborah or Constantine, both of which names were applied by the triumphant Protestants at the start of her reign. It seems likely that classical allegories were more to her taste, particularly those implying unattainable beauty and mystery; but there is no record of her ever making such a suggestion. Sensitive (or self-serving) courtiers, with an ear to the ground, were probably alert to what would be acceptable, and were quick to oblige.[14]

We have to remember that the English justifiably spent most of the period from 1560 to 1600 in a state of chronic anxiety. They were worried about the Catholic threat, at home and abroad; they were worried about the succession; about who the queen would marry; and about her personal safety. Some were also worried that they (or the queen) were not doing enough to earn the divine favour which they so desperately needed. The execution of Mary Queen of Scots, and defeat of the Armada, went a long way towards changing this. By 1588 there were no longer worries about an unsuitable marriage, and the sharp-eyed could already see that the succession problem might solve itself. There were justified fears of Spain, and of continued Catholic conspiracies, but only the ultra-godly now feared the withdrawal of divine favour. Elizabeth and her government had passed the crucial test when God blew upon her enemies, and scattered them.

By 1590 the English were beginning to have a good conceit of themselves. This was not always a pretty sight, but it did produce some marvellous writing, and it also added a new dimension to the queen's image. *Eliza Triumphans* was a post-Armada phenomenon.[15] In 1589, when he abridged

Foxe's *Acts and Monuments*, Timothy Bright wrote (going well beyond Foxe's terms of reference):

> Her Royall Maiestie, our most gratious Soveraigne, the very Maul of the Pope, and as a mother of Christian princes; whom the Almightie long preserve over us. Englande, the first that embraced the Gospel, the onely establisher of it throughout the world; and the first reformed.[16]

It would not have occurred to any member of his father's generation that England was in a position to establish anything 'throughout the world', or that any queen could lay claim to such an exalted title. Unlike her sister, Elizabeth ended her reign on a high note, and the fanfares which accompanied her funeral went on echoing down the centuries.

Eliza Triumphans, however, was more than half myth: a *coup de théâtre* to boost the country's spirits through a long war and the economic hardships of the last decade of the reign. The reality was a good deal less triumphant, but the queen was equally central to it. The problems changed with the years, and so did the supporting cast, but Elizabeth's application to business was consistent. She was blamed at the time, and has been blamed ever since, for near fatal prevarication, for indecisiveness, and for an unpredictability which was constantly wrong-footing her unfortunate servants.[17] Even those who knew her best, like Lord Burghley and the Earl of Leicester, found her baffling and at times infuriating. Yet she frequently did the right thing, or chose the right person for a particular responsibility. In this connection we have to remember that all her ministers and acknowledged advisers, and virtually all those who wrote first-hand comments upon her methods, were men. They were loyal subjects, and had no doubts concerning the lawfulness of their mistress's authority; but they were not accustomed to a woman exercising official responsibilities, least of all in such a direct way. Although none of them would have dared to say so publicly, privately their view was often that the queen should be a focus for loyalty, but leave the serious business of government to them. This was also a discreetly hidden reason for so many of them to press her to marry. Unlike being decorative, or bearing children, government was a man's job, and they would have felt much more comfortable dealing with a man, even if he had to be a foreigner. Elizabeth, in contrast, felt no need of a man for that purpose. Unlike Mary, she did not even pay lip service to the idea of a distinctively female role for herself. She was not only going to be the queen, she was also going to be the master in the most direct managerial sense; and even her loyalest and most intimate servants found that hard to accept.[18] When her servants commented upon her methods, they were therefore commenting as much upon what they perceived as what actually happened.

They were men observing disparagingly a woman's way of doing business. They saw chronic indecisiveness when perhaps they should have seen a prudent caution. Elizabeth's extreme reluctance to go to war was similarly perceived by some as mere female timidity.

It was not as simple as that. She lacked neither strategic intelligence nor physical courage; but leading armies herself was a taboo which she felt unable to break. War consequently meant a degree of power-sharing with the men who had to wage it, and that she regarded with deep reluctance. Luckily for her there was no invasion. In spite of fighting Spain for eighteen years, she never fielded a royal army of the kind that her father had led, and the issue of overall responsibility did not have to be faced. The relatively small forces which fought in the Netherlands, Brittany and Ireland posed no threat; and the navy, which did most of the actual fighting, never had a political presence. The only situation which could have posed a threat was the massive musters held in the summer of 1588. In order to impose her presence there, Elizabeth went to Tilbury and made (or possibly did not make) her celebrated speech.[19]

Elizabeth made mistakes; but usually they were her own mistakes. She positively enjoyed receiving divided counsel, because it increased her freedom of action. The kind of unanimous pressure which finally forced her to dispose of Mary Queen of Scots was most unwelcome, as her reaction on that occasion showed. Ironically, but perhaps significantly, one of her worst mistakes was her intervention in France in 1563; and that came about because she listened too attentively to a man, Robert Dudley, who had gained her favour for other than political reasons. If she needed any urging to trust her own instincts rather than male advice, that fiasco provided the lesson. Money was another factor. She could not afford the kind of war in which she found herself after 1585 and preferred to retain the goodwill of her subjects rather than seeking to relieve them of their cash, even by lawful methods. She consequently acquired a deserved reputation for parsimony, but it was a perfectly defensible attitude, and certainly should not be attributed to some female quirk. From whichever angle one approaches the politics of the reign, the queen was the central and determining figure. This was natural in a personal monarchy, but many did not expect it when the ruler was a woman. Mary, in spite of her diligence and the decisive role which her conscience played in so many policy decisions, did not have the same ubiquity. She played very little part, for example, in negotiating her own marriage treaty, or even in reconciling her church to Rome. For months after the collapse of her 'pregnancy' in the summer of 1555, she was virtually *hors de combat*, and never showed much personal interest in naval or financial administration.[20] Elizabeth, however, would let nothing go by default; nor did she ever take refuge in feminine illnesses. When she was ill (which happened from time to time), there was nothing specifically female about her ailments. In some respects Elizabeth ruled like the king she would probably have preferred to be, but her style was uniquely feminine; and no woman, not even Catherine the Great, has ever wielded the weapon of sex more effectively.

Until comparatively recently, the received wisdom was that Elizabeth was not a particularly religious person. She was prepared to act a godly part when it suited her, but her real priority was the maintenance of her own power.[21] Such an attitude was consistent with a generally pragmatic approach to government, in which she had been schooled by witnessing the dire effects of ideology upon her sister. Recently such a perception has been largely abandoned. As a child she had been brought up in the pious humanism of her father's court, being particularly influenced during his later years by his last queen, Catherine Parr, and her circle. She was thirteen when Henry died, and, like her brother Edward, seems to have made a seamless transition from humanism to Protestantism. Edward thought well of her piety; unlike her half-sister Mary, she was *persona grata* at his court. That did not, however, prevent him from seeking to exclude her from the succession on the grounds of illegitimacy. The effect which that rejection had upon her has never been seriously examined, but it does not seem to have driven her closer to Mary, except in a very superficial and temporary sense.[22]

Throughout her sister's reign her position was extremely precarious, and much of the mettle which she was later to show was forged in the fire of those five years. Her perception of herself at that time is difficult to recover. She was very conscious of being the 'second person', but how her religious faith was affected is hard to know. In the traditional interpretation that was hardly a problem; she simply conformed because she had no real incentive to do anything else. That should now be doubted. Elizabeth's conscience was deeply troubled by the contortions which it was forced to perform. She became a Nicodemite, one who came to Christ by night, not because she did not think that it mattered, but because she had little choice. She could not leave the realm, partly because of her position and partly because of a long period of imprisonment. If she refused conformity, there was no one to protect her in the way in which Mary herself had been protected under Edward. Moreover, she wanted to be queen, and genuinely believed that it would happen. John Foxe, who was normally severe on Nicodemites, had no words of criticism for her actions in this respect.[23] Instead, he glossed them over with an elaborate and circumstantial tale of her sufferings, and of the life-threatening crises which she had endured before her accession.

Not even the most godly of her subjects ever reproached her with her conduct; but she may well have reproached herself.

As queen, her piety was almost as idiosyncratic as her father's had been, but quite different. Her pragmatism appeared, not in an indifference to the refinements of doctrine, but in an ability to distinguish her personal faith from the church for which she was responsible to God. She had, for example, no opinion of the clergy, particularly bishops; disliked clerical marriage, and distrusted zealous preachers. Nevertheless the Church of England retained an episcopal form of government, allowed its clergy to marry and developed a powerful evangelical tradition. The queen's private prayers express a total reliance upon the sacrifice of Christ, and show no interest in either the sacraments or any form of intercession:

> For thou art the God of compassion, and long-suffering. Justice is Thine, O Lord, and mercy and propitiation; but mine is confusion upon my face on account of my iniquities. Restore Thou my love for thy Holy Name. Grant me a penitent heart, O Thou who dost disregard the sins of men on account of their penitence. Say unto my soul 'I am thy health'.[24]

Both her biblicism and her sense of a direct relationship with God placed her firmly in the Protestant tradition, but her sense of responsibility also extended to her Catholic subjects – at least at first. One advantage of episcopacy was that it retained a traditional structure agreeable to conservatives, no matter what scriptural arguments might be advanced against it. Elizabeth preferred to exercise her authority by royal commission, because there could be no dispute about where the commissioners' authority came from; but the ambiguity of an episcopate was an advantage in the fluid situation which appertained at least down to 1570. Similarly, there is nothing in the record of the queen's piety which would suggest an enthusiasm for ornaments. The controversial appearance of a cross and candlesticks upon the altar of the Chapel Royal was probably another calculated gesture to placate her own conservatives and to confuse foreign observers.[25] Once they were challenged, however, they became an issue of authority and Elizabeth was bound to insist on her right to them, whether she cared much about them or not. It is clear from a number of her prayers that she took her responsibility to God with immense seriousness. Her failure to respond to evangelical pressure was consequently not the result of indifference, much less of crypto-Catholic sympathies; but rather of a keen awareness that she needed to keep as many people on board as possible, for as long as possible.

Three great crises in Elizabeth's life, shaped her mature character. Two of these took place before her accession. The first was her deeply disturbing encounter with Lord Thomas Seymour, the Protector's brother, when she was fifteen. The second was her arrest after the Wyatt rebellion in 1554. The third was her relationship with Robert Dudley.

Seymour not only taught her the disorientating effects of sexuality, but also the extent of her own vulnerability. Whatever her feelings for him may originally have been, she came to see him as a ruthless man, exploiting her for his own purposes.[26] The shock of this realisation hit her hard, and she had to fight a long and painful battle to recover her good name and self-respect. It is unlikely, as some have claimed, that this experience gave her a lasting aversion to any sexual relationship, but it certainly made her extremely wary, even devious, in her private life. It also taught her the arts of dissimulation, which later did her yeoman service as privacy became increasingly impossible.

Her arrest and imprisonment in February 1554 came as a great physical and psychological shock. To what extent it was justified by her own actions is unclear;[27] but the danger was real, and she seems to have thought that it was even more real than it was. For several months she went in almost daily fear of trial and execution. Only she knew what disclosures there were to fear, and in that respect her reaction may be seen as suspicious; but she also knew that reasons of state might be enough to dispose of her, however innocent she may actually have been. Even after that danger receded, she seems to have gone in fear of the privy assassin, aware how convenient her death would have been to some, and how vulnerable her circumstances made her. This experience affected her political *persona* as much as the Seymour encounter had affected her private one. The lessons were very similar. Do nothing in haste or on impulse; cover your tracks; watch your back; and trust as few people as possible. She also learned the hard way the dangers of being a 'second person', and this undoubtedly affected her attitude to Mary Queen of Scots.

Her relationship with Robert Dudley, at its simplest, was a raw conflict between personal desire and public duty. As a woman she wanted him; as a queen she knew that she could not have him.[28] For about two years she struggled to find a way out of this cruel dilemma. In spite of her later reputation, and carefully constructed image, the young Elizabeth was a woman, as passionate as she was intelligent, and the debilitating effects of this struggle should not be underestimated. Eventually public duty won, at least to the extent that she gave up any possible intention of marrying him; but their relationship continued in a different form and had its effects upon public policy for nearly thirty years.

Elizabeth went through many other painful, and some exhilarating, experiences in the course of her long life. Her emotion when the news of her half-sister's death reached her was palpable, and it was not grief. There was the elation of her coronation entry; the trauma of Mary Stuart's execution; and the deep sadness of Robert Dudley's death. Like most people, she became if not more resilient at least less affected by emotional stress as she became older. The most formative of these experiences took place before she was thirty, and the effect which they had upon her conditioned the ways in which she related to her servants, her councillors, and those whom she considered to be her friends.

To Conyers Read it was Sir William Cecil who was the constructive driving force behind the achievements which pass under Elizabeth's name.[29] To Sir John Neale it was the parliamentary gentry, with their new power and innovative enterprise (an enterprise which the queen did her best to restrain).[30] To Wallace McCaffrey she was a largely reactive politician, very much at the mercy of events, whose main skill lay in doing as little as possible as late as possible. There are almost as many Elizabeths as there are historians who have studied her, but the four hundredth anniversary of her death is surely an appropriate time for a fresh look. The state of the Anglican Church is now a matter of little concern except to the minority who belong to it; and certainly not a barometer of national well being. The Catholic threat was consigned to history over two hundred years ago. The myth of Elizabeth is an historical phenomenon in its own right, and we are no longer obliged to start by either endorsing or repudiating it. We are, however, in a good position to judge the extraordinary extent of the changes which took place during her reign. The issues of the Reformation were largely resolved; the orientation of commercial policy was significantly altered; and foundations were laid down for social provisions which were to last for over two hundred years.[31] A great war was fought, and a disastrous colonial policy pursued in Ireland, both of which had important long-term consequences. It was a period which saw the flowering of the English Renaissance, and the consolidation of political and constitutional changes which had begun in her father's reign. Above all, it was a period of national self-determination. At the centre of all these developments stands the person of the queen. It has always been fashionable to call her an enigma, but that is to say no more than that she was a woman normally viewed and assessed by men. Elizabeth may have claimed to have 'the heart and stomach of a king', and certainly had a king's authority, but she had a woman's mind as well as a woman's body. No whit less powerful, perceptive or well-trained than a man's, but different. If we start from that understanding, we can not only get behind the traditional myths, we can also get behind the modern myths of capriciousness and irresponsibility. Elizabeth enjoyed her share of good fortune, most particularly in living for nearly seventy years, but we do her a grave injustice if we attribute her achievement to that alone. As the only *femme seule* ever to occupy the English throne, she was in several respects unique.

1

The King's Marriage

Although the bland words of the chronicler do not suggest it, the circumstances of Elizabeth's conception made her one of the most problematic royal children of the sixteenth, or any other, century; and her birth was gratifying and disappointing in equal measure.

> The seventh day of September [1533], beyng Sunday, betwene three and foure of the clocke at after noone, the Queene was delivered of a fayre Lady which daye the Duke of Norfolke came home to the Christnyng, and for the Queenes good deliveraunce, *Te deum* was song incontinently.[1]

It was gratifying insofar as it demonstrated the fertility of both her parents. This was not to be taken for granted, as Anne Boleyn had almost certainly been a virgin before the conception, and Henry had not fathered a child for fourteen years. The king was forty-one, and the queen probably thirty-two.[2] It was disappointing in that Henry not only wanted but desperately needed a legitimate son.

The origin of the crisis which had arisen over the English succession went back to about the time of Anne's birth, when in 1501 a sixteen-year-old Spanish princess had arrived in England to marry the Henry VII's fifteen-year-old son. She was Catherine, the younger daughter of Ferdinand of Aragon and Isabella of Castile, and he was Arthur, prince of Wales. Their union was the result of a long, and at times difficult, negotiation, and represented a triumph for the king. His parvenu dynasty, which had only just become fully accepted in England, had now been recognised by the house of Trastamara, one of the oldest and most prestigious of Europe's ruling families. The fact that Arthur died less than a year later, in April 1502, did not diminish that success, but meant (or appeared to mean) that there would be no ongoing consequences. Catherine stayed in England, however, partly because of an undignified squabble over her dowry, but more because Ferdinand wanted to maintain the English alliance.[3] Arthur's death was a severe blow to his parents, but it was not a dynastic disaster because they had a younger son, Henry, the ten-year-old duke of York.

There were immediately discussions about transferring Catherine to the younger prince, and both families petitioned the pope to grant the necessary dispensation from consanguinity, which Julius II duly did in 1504.[4] By that time it was clear that the princess was not carrying any posthumous child of her husband's, but unclear whether the marriage had been consummated. Arthur's adolescent boasting had created a strong impression that it had; but Catherine denied it, and the normal resort to a discreet physical examination by 'sober matrons' does not seem to have been made. Perhaps the princess refused; perhaps the subject was considered too indelicate even to be raised; or perhaps it was not thought to matter very much. It was clear that Arthur had not left her pregnant, and the pope's dispensation had covered full consanguinity (that is, a consummated marriage), just to be on the safe side. However, no second marriage took place. That had nothing to do with Henry's youth, which would have been a bar only to cohabitation, not to marriage. It was partly caused by the fact that by the end of 1504 both Isabella of Castile and Elizabeth of York, Henry VII's queen, had died, leaving their respective widowers with different but equally pressing problems. Henry considered remarrying, but was uncertain whether he wished to continue the Spanish alliance. Ferdinand was struggling to obtain some kind of control over his wife's kingdom (to which he had no right) and did not want his daughter complicating the issue.[5] Consequently, Catherine stayed where she was, in an uncomfortable limbo, with few friends, insufficient money and very uncertain prospects. Not surprisingly, she turned for companionship to her remaining Spanish servants, and for support to God. In the course of doing the latter she became convinced that the Almighty intended her to marry Henry, and was causing obstacles and delays merely to test her sense of purpose.[6] No one else shared her confidence, certainly not Henry, who had first written encouragingly, but then had repudiated the arrangement when he reached the age of fourteen, both on the instructions of his father. Thereafter he seems not to have given the matter another thought. Catherine's was to be a durable but eventually most inconvenient conviction.

In the short term, however, her optimism was triumphantly vindicated. Within a few weeks of his accession, in April 1509, Henry VIII announced to his astonished council that he would marry his sister-in-law. He alleged that this was in accordance with his father's dying wishes, but that was probably a pious fiction. Whether there was any element of political calculation about the decision, or whether it was simply an emotional or chivalric impulse, we do not know. In spite of what was to happen twenty years later, at the time it was a sensible move. Catherine still represented a desirable foreign alliance, made all the more desirable by the fact that Henry was hankering after a war with France.[7] A domestic marriage, had one been in prospect, would not have carried anything like the same advantages. Doubts about the legitimacy of a union with Catherine, and about the outstanding financial problems, were simply swept aside; and at first the marriage was a success, both politically and personally. Catherine conceived promptly and Ferdinand appeared only too keen to join in the projected attack on France. The queen miscarried of her first pregnancy, but that was a routine misfortune and she soon conceived again. After that, however, the clouds quickly gathered. In 1511 their first son died after a few weeks, and the following year Ferdinand double-crossed his son-in-law and made a separate peace with France.[8] Catherine, who earnestly desired to keep her father and her husband friends, was deeply chagrined by both these misfortunes; she was not solaced by the fact that Henry found consolations elsewhere in the court.[9]

By 1514 there were rumours of a breakdown in the marriage, but they were premature. The relationship was patched up. In 1516 Ferdinand died, and Catherine bore a healthy child, albeit a daughter. Henry was greatly cheered by the birth of Mary, and called her a 'token of hope' and a good beginning. Catherine, after all, was only thirty-one, and Henry twenty-five. Four pregnancies in six years had aged her, however, and her physical attractiveness had waned. In 1518 she conceived again, but the child was born dead, and the warning signs were clear to see. By this time the king had a serious mistress in the person of Elizabeth Blount. In 1519 she bore him a healthy son, who was acknowledged and named Henry Fitzroy.[10] The queen's reaction was resentful, and close to despair, but there was nothing which she could do about it. Although Elizabeth Blount was married off, a new mistress took her place, Mary Boleyn, the daughter of Sir Thomas. No more children were born, and it appears that Henry continued to sleep with his wife, but she did not conceive again.

By 1524 it was clear that a crisis was approaching. At some point during the summer of that year, Henry gave up on Catherine. There was no public rupture but they ceased to sleep together. It was by then clear that the queen would bear him no son, and he had to consider his options. He could, of course, simply accept what God appeared to have decreed, and prepare for Mary to succeed him. She was by this time eight, and had been betrothed for about three years to the twenty-four-year old Holy Roman Emperor, Charles V.[11] This was an ambitious but unstable arrangement. Mary was not a well grown or precocious child, and there was little prospect of her being ready for the marriage bed at the minimum canonical age of twelve. Charles could not afford to wait another five years, at least, for his prospective bride to grow up; the surprising thing is that he waited as long as he did. Whoever the bridegroom, however, an early marriage for Mary represented one answer to her father's problem. If she could produce at

least one son in Henry's lifetime, the succession would be secured, whether
or not she ever wore the crown herself. Such a solution required both faith
and patience, but in this connection the king did not have much of either.
There was also the possibility of legitimising his existing son, Henry Fitzroy.
This would have been feasible but difficult, and would always have been
liable to challenge; it did not offer the security which was his main requirement.[12] The third option was to get his marriage to Catherine annulled,
and to remarry. This also required an ecclesiastical judgement, but since
Catherine had never misbehaved herself in any way that would not be easy.
Even so, there were precedents.

We do not know when Henry made his choice – it probably wasn't a
sudden decision. In June 1525 he created Henry Fitzroy duke of Richmond
and Somerset, and lieutenant of the North. The six-year-old duke was then
equipped with a council and a viceregal household, and despatched to
Sheriff Hutton in Yorkshire. At the same time the nine-year-old Mary was
established in Ludlow, with responsibility for the Welsh Marches. The signals
(if they were signals) were totally ambiguous. Richmond was a royal title,
but there was no word of legitimation; Mary was placed in the position of
a princess of Wales, but not given the title.[13] These moves probably had
nothing to do with the succession, being simply intended to improve Lord
Chancellor Thomas Wolsey's administrative hold over the remoter parts of
the kingdom. It was perhaps not until the winter of 1526–7 that Henry
finally concluded that the other options would not work, and that Catherine
would have to go.[14] Charles V had finally repudiated his contract with Mary
in 1525, and negotiations commenced for a French marriage. In the course
of the discussions, the French representatives allegedly raised the question
of the princess's legitimacy, in view of the original scruple about her parents'
marriage. Probably this was a fiction, although we do not know whether
Henry's 'scruple of conscience' preceded or followed his decision. The king
was conventionally pious, indeed superstitious, and may well have been
fretting for some time that he must have offended God to be left without
a male heir. At some point between 1525 and 1527, this unease turned into
a total conviction that his first marriage had offended against the Law of
God, as laid down in the Book of Leviticus. The text was not, in fact, a
perfect fit.[15] It referred to a man marrying his brother's wife, not his widow
(quite possible in the polygamous society of the Old Testament), and
declared that the offending couple would be childless, which Henry and
Catherine were not. Nevertheless, Henry convinced himself that he was
suffering from the 'Levitical curse'. Although this conviction was certainly
linked to his desire to free himself from Catherine, it was unconnected to
any plan for replacing her.[16]

Anne Boleyn's intrusion upon this scene of domestic disharmony was almost coincidental. She was the younger daughter of Sir Thomas Boleyn, first comptroller and later treasurer of the royal household, and she had grown up from the age of twelve for about eight years in European courts; first that of Margaret of Austria at Mechelen, then briefly in the household of Henry's sister Mary Tudor, queen (for about four months) of Louis XII; and finally in that of Queen Claude, the consort of Francis I.[17] With war looming between England and France in 1522, her father had recalled her and placed her in the entourage of Queen Catherine. She was, by general agreement, a remarkable young woman; quite different from her pretty but somewhat vacuous sister. Mary Boleyn was at this time just finishing her stint as the king's mistress (without, it would appear, any hard feelings on either side). She was married to William Carey, a gentleman of the privy chamber. Although there were persistent rumours that the first of the children whom she bore to her husband (Henry, later Lord Hunsdon) was really the king's, he was never acknowledged as such. Anne, partly by instinct and partly by training, was an accomplished flirt – a sexual entertainer in the manner of a Japanese Geisha. She was not particularly beautiful, but she had tremendous allure and was highly skilled in music, dancing and seductive body language. Observers also commented upon her luxuriant hair and magnificent eyes, about which one smitten poet wrote;

> eyes always most attractive
> Which she knew well how to use with effect,
> Sometimes leaving them at rest,
> And at others, sending a message
> To carry the secret witness of her heart,
> And, truth to tell, such was their power,
> That many surrendered to their obedience.[18]

Among those who so surrendered were, it would seem, Henry Percy, son and heir to the earl of Northumberland, and the elder Sir Thomas Wyatt. Percy probably wanted to marry her, and secured her agreement, but important matches of that kind needed more than the consent of the parties, and the betrothal (if it ever existed) was firmly squashed by the earl, in alliance with Cardinal Wolsey.[19] Rather surprisingly, there seem to have been no orthodox negotiations for Anne's hand during these prime years of her life. Given that she was highly intelligent, independent in spirit and with absolutely no taste for domesticity, it is possible that eligible young men found her as alarming as she was fascinating. In the light of what happened, it is tempting to think that she was playing for high stakes throughout, but there is absolutely no evidence for that.

Anne's *forte* was the fashionable game of courtly love. This was played enthusiastically in the antechambers of Westminster, Richmond and Greenwich, and the rules were relatively simple. Every male player pretended to be desperately in love with one of the female players; he sent her love letters, poems and small gifts, professing undying devotion. She responded as the mood took her; now encouraging her lover with small tokens and coy glances, now rebuffing him with disdain. There was no formal scoring system, but skilful players were those who could keep up the pretence longest and most convincingly. Those with a gift for penning amorous verses, especially those whose social status was too low to enable them to be players, were much in demand to supply the deficiencies of ardent but tongue-tied aristocrats.[20] These jousts were not, or were not supposed to be, genuine sexual encounters but – human nature being what it is – some developed in that direction. It is very difficult for the observer, particularly at such long range, to discover when this was happening. The most important slide from make belief into reality was that which occurred between Anne and the king.

As the acknowledged champion, she naturally set her cap at the highest ranking man. Henry, who was himself a skilled and experienced player, responded in kind. This dalliance began early in 1526, and the court gossips were soon busy about it, but it should not be assumed that there was any serious intent at that stage. The chronology is very hard to reconstruct, but it appears that Henry reached a decision about his marriage before his pursuit of Anne turned from play to earnest, and there may at first have been no connection between the two processes.[21] Wolsey, who had been the king's ubiquitous adviser and *alter ego* for more than a decade, certainly did not connect them. He cannot have been ignorant of court gossip, but the fact that he was talking seriously of a future French marriage for the king, and even putting out feelers in France, is sufficient indication that he did not take Anne seriously.

At Easter 1527, however, before he made the breakdown of his marriage public, Henry began to press Anne to become his mistress, not in the platonic courtly sense, but in reality. Her reaction probably surprised him. Unlike her sister, she was not compliant but insisted upon marriage. Whether or not she knew about Henry's intention to seek an annulment of his existing union is not clear, but it can hardly be coincidence that he made his first explicit, albeit secret, moves in that direction only a month after she had made her position clear. Whether his new found ardour confused him, or he was simply betrayed by his oversized ego, the king then made a fatal mistake. Catherine knew as well as he did that her childbearing years were over and that she had failed in the primary duty of giving him a son. A woman of exemplary piety in such a situation might reasonably have been expected to step aside gracefully and take the veil. Henry had, however, by this time worked himself up into a state of right-eousness indignation. Instead of the gentle approach which might have been expected towards a spouse of eighteen years standing, he simply confronted her with the bald and harsh announcement that they were not, and never had been, truly married.[22] Catherine was shocked and outraged; not merely by the insensitivity of the method, but also by the content of the message. She knew that their marriage was valid in the eyes of God; how could Henry utter the blasphemy of such a direct contradiction? Not only was he mocking God and ruining her honour, he was condemning their only and much loved daughter to bastardy; it did not bear thinking about. Consequently, instead of seeing the justification behind her husband's action, and realising that a voluntary withdrawal would protect both her own reputation and Mary's legitimacy, Catherine vehemently repudiated the whole suggestion, declaring that she would fight for her marriage through every spiritual court. As her nephew Charles V was the Holy Roman Emperor, and he was equally outraged by the king's actions, Henry started his quest for an annulment under a crippling handicap.[23] At this stage, in June 1527, there is no reason to suppose that the queen knew that she had also been supplanted by another woman; although, if she did, it can hardly have sweetened her temper.

Tangled and frustrating negotiations began in Rome in the summer of 1527.[24] For about three years Henry pleaded his case in an orthodox way. When this failed he resorted to blackmail, threatening the English clergy with punishment under the old law of *Praemunire*, which forbade the exercise of any ecclesiastical jurisdiction without the king's licence, and then tried to limit the papal jurisdiction to doctrine only, before resorting to a complete break. In this development one or two things need to be borne in mind. First, Henry had a respectable case in canon law. Those who claimed at the time, and have repeated since, that he was only supported by men who had been bribed, bullied or cajoled, were, and are, wide of the mark. It was a matter of doubt whether the Levitical prohibition covered Henry's circumstances; whether or not it was contradicted by other scriptural precepts; and whether or not it should be seen as divine law. At the same time the legal and theological disputes served to conceal the hard political reality that the emperor was strong enough, and sufficiently motivated, to prevent Pope Clement VII from giving the king of England what he wanted.[25] The sack of Rome by a mutinous imperial army in May 1527 was not a decisive factor in the long term. For a few months it made Clement both helpless and very angry. As his fear subsided before his indignation, this created a brief window of opportunity, during which Henry might have got his desire from a pope who was anxious to get his own back. The king, however, was in no position to grasp the opportunity. He could not supply the substantial amount of money which Clement needed, and probably did not understand the position until it was too late. By the end of 1528, when both fear and indignation had evaporated, the pope had calculated that his interests would best be served by allying with the stronger party in the Franco-Habsburg conflict. He announced that he would live and die an imperialist, and there was consequently no further prospect of Henry getting his will as long as Clement was alive.[26]

This straightforward situation was concealed by a great deal of rhetorical fog, as the king set out to find a way out of the impasse, and the pope strove to deflect him. It appears that Henry and Anne agreed to marry in the summer of 1527, conditional upon the king's existing marriage being annulled; although neither of them can have realised what they were embarking upon. Catherine probably, and Charles certainly, hoped that the king would weary in the face of constant frustration, take other mistresses and eventually forget about his plans for a second marriage. It was Anne's skill, and extraordinary tenacity, which kept Henry's interest (and appetite) alive for six long years, and prevented this from happening.[27] There was at first no public awareness of the king's new relationship. When the sweating sickness broke out in September 1528, Anne withdrew from the court to stay with her mother at Hever Castle; but this was taken to be no more than a sensible precaution, not betokening any special solicitude on the king's part. Catherine knew perfectly well that there was more to Henry's scruple of conscience than he had admitted to her, even if it was genuine, which she doubted. She could have deduced, even if she did not know, that he planned to remarry; but it appears that she had no idea of the determination which he had reached. Relations between Catherine and Anne continued for the time being to be correct.

It had not, however, been in the queen's interest to make the breakdown of her marriage public knowledge. It was not until Henry unburdened himself to a special meeting of councillors, courtiers and London aldermen on 8 November 1528 that any wider reactions began to appear. To the king's chagrin, they were almost uniformly unsympathetic:

> To see what countenance was made amongest the hearers of this Oracion it was a strange sight, for some sighed and said nothyng, others were sory to heare the kyng so troubled in his conscience. Others that favoured the queene much sorowed that this matter was now opened.[28]

Catherine was popular, and every married woman in England empathised with her predicament, a fact which most men could not afford to ignore. No one was going to raise a rebellion on the queen's behalf, but to the implacable opposition of the emperor and the pope was now added the hostility of many of Henry's own subjects. Early in 1529, however, it seemed as though Wolsey might have found a formula to break the deadlock, and rescue his own career.

He managed to secure what was ostensibly a referral of the case to a legatine court consisting of himself and Cardinal Campeggio, the Cardinal Protector of England, which would be held in England.[29] When Campeggio arrived, the two cardinals waited upon Catherine, and begged her to withdraw into the cloister. This reasonable request, however, came far too late to be acceded to. Full of conscious rectitude, not to say self-pity, the queen was digging in for a fight, and the cardinals therefore had no option. They convened their court on 18 June 1529, at Blackfriars.

Campeggio knew, and Wolsey must have suspected, that this was a mere façade, and that there was never any chance of a judgement, least of all in the king's favour. After a show of taking evidence, the court was adjourned and the case revoked to Rome, where the outcome was a foregone conclusion. Henry was furious and vented his wrath on Wolsey, who was deprived of the great seal and exiled to his archbishopric. On 29 October he was replaced as chancellor by the London lawyer and humanist scholar Sir Thomas More. For about a year Wolsey continued to hope that he would recover the king's confidence, and was unwise enough to keep open his communications with Rome. As a result he was accused of treason, and died on 29 November 1530, on his way to face trial.[30] The frustration was not all loss to the king. For the first time he began to find significant political support for his position, and the disappearance of Wolsey gave the opportunity for other influences to make themselves felt. The most obvious of these was Anne herself and her family. Like Catherine, but unlike any of Henry's earlier mistresses, Anne was a woman of political intelligence and commitment. Her fascination for the king may have been sexual, but Anne was not a body politic in that sense only. Her new position was confirmed by the widely held, but probably erroneous, belief that she was responsible for the cardinal's fall.[31] By the end of 1529 a new situation had been created. Catherine was simply sidelined. Henry could not get rid of her, and she remained the queen, in possession of her lands and prerogatives, but he did not consult her, keep her informed, or share her company except on a few formal and public occasions. Sir Thomas Boleyn was made earl of Wiltshire on 8 December, and the duke of Norfolk became president of the council; but as the French ambassador wrote 'above everyone, Mademoiselle Anne'.[32] The king's new lady thus took centre stage, assuming many of the functions normally associated with a consort, but she did not share his bed.

There then followed a protracted stalemate, which lasted nearly three years and tried everyone's patience to the limit. Much of our information about the tensions and infighting of these years comes from the despatches of diplomats who were unsympathetic to the king and Anne. They consequently need to be treated with caution. From late 1529 until July 1531 there was an uneasy *ménage à trois*, in which Henry could easily be made to look ridiculous. Whenever he was in Catherine's company, she took the opportunity to berate him for his neglect and inform him that it was only his wilful obstinacy which prevented him from accepting what everyone else knew to be right. Anne, however, was equal to that sort of challenge:

> Did I not tell you that when you disputed with the Queen she was sure to have the upper hand? I see that some fine morning you will succumb to her reasoning, and that you will cast me off. I have been waiting long and might in the meantime have contracted some advantageous marriage ... but alas! Farewell to my time and youth spent to no purpose at all.[33]

Caught between two such sharp-tongued and pertinacious women, Henry looked anything but the great king. Whether these outbursts were calculated or spontaneous on Anne's part we do not know, but they had the effect of increasing the king's infatuation rather than diminishing it. This was just as well, because nobody else found them particularly attractive. Anne was a very unusual woman, who not only had a shrewd political brain but took no pains to conceal the fact, giving her royal lover unsolicited advice upon all sorts of subjects, from patronage to foreign policy.[34] Established councillors eyed her warily and assessed where her influence was likely to lead before taking up their own positions; she made them uncomfortable and they therefore disliked her. This was a situation which seems to have intrigued Henry. He may even have enjoyed allowing her to bait them in this fashion. It was a high risk strategy for Anne, because it depended entirely upon maintaining her ascendancy over the king, but it worked. Men who detested her, and whose wives detested her even more, found themselves compelled to take her seriously. She was unashamedly pro-French. Both her own background and the logic of her position made this inevitable, but it was a winning hand unless or until Charles relented of his opposition to Henry's 'Great Matter', something which he showed no sign of doing. She was also sympathetic to the new learning, something much more difficult to assess. Many years later, during Elizabeth's reign, the grandson of one of Anne's admirers wrote:

> The more I have looked and entered into the vew of the reports of her times I

have found ever the bright beames of her cleerenes more and more to shine out in every part of it, even the blacke mistes of malice and darke clouds of foule and hatful railings helpinge muche therto, of thos that taught and had their tounges instructed to cover and over shaddow her glory, with their most blacke and venomus untruithes, which Hel it self could and did no doubt power out, as against her, so especialy to cloude the blessed splendor of the Gospel beginninge then againe to shew her golden luster upon our world.[35]

By then much water had passed under the bridge, and Catholic polemicists had long been accustomed to blame 'that whore Nan Bullen' for the afflictions of the Catholic Church in England; but in truth the contemporary evidence is ambiguous. That Anne should have promoted Henry's ecclesiastical supremacy to the best of her ability was inevitable, but that did not make her a 'gospeller', any more than it did Stephen Gardiner, the conservative bishop of Winchester or his like-minded colleague Cuthbert Tunstall of Durham, both of whom also supported the supremacy. She favoured and employed as chaplains men who were later distinguished Protestants, such as Thomas Cranmer and Mathew Parker, and appears to have favoured preachers who at the time were considered radical.[36] She possessed a vernacular New Testament, but it was in French and not in English; and if she did bring *The Obedience of a Christian Man* to Henry's attention, that proves no more than that she had an eye for a useful political idea. Whatever they may have been later, neither Cranmer nor Parker were Protestants in 1530 – indeed the term had barely been invented. Even Anne's numerous enemies did not accuse her of heresy and, when her own time of trial came, her piety was exemplary in its orthodoxy.

It seems most likely that Anne simply had a lively and inquisitive mind, was interested in new ideas, and that she promoted humanist scholarship to the best of her ability. Both these were characteristics which the king at the time found attractive, but that does not necessarily mean that they were assumed for that purpose. In her intellectual interests, as in so much else, Anne was her own woman. Nevertheless it was through the New Learning that a way ahead was found after the infuriating frustration of the Blackfriars court. Thomas Cranmer, a Cambridge don who was already on the fringes of royal service, suggested that the issue was not one of canon law but of theology, or more accurately of scriptural exegesis.[37] If the king consulted biblical scholars instead of lawyers, 'then his Highness in conscience quieted may determine with himself that which shall seem good before God, and let these tumultary processes give place unto a certain truth'. This of course echoed the king's existing convictions about the Book of Leviticus, so it was not an entirely new idea. Henry, however, had totally failed to persuade the pope of the primacy of that text, and what was new about Cranmer's suggestion was that the Bible could create a theological imperative which was superior to, and independent of, ecclesiastical interpretation.[38] Unfortunately, this was dangerously close to the Lutheran heresy of *sola scriptura*, and Henry, who was not ignorant in such matters, would have known that. What Cranmer had encouraged him to hope was that an exposition could be found which would bring his case indisputably into the field of divine law, without having to fall into the contamination of Lutheranism. The king was sufficiently interested in this approach to commission Cranmer to write his thoughts at length, and to instruct him to reside with the earl of Wiltshire while he did so. It was almost certainly at Durham House that Cranmer first became acquainted with Anne. The treatise which he wrote does not survive but we know that Henry was pleased with it, so it must have answered his requirements. At the same time other of the king's servants, notably Edward Fox and Nicholas del Burgo, were putting together a collection of arguments for the autonomy of national churches, now known as the *Collectanea satis copiosa*.[39] Under relentless pressure from Anne and her friends, but also driven by his own desires, Henry was moving steadily towards the idea of declaring at least a limited independence of Rome and was using a variety of unorthodox ideas to justify his course; but he would have been horrified by the suggestion that either he or Anne were dabbling in heresy.

In 1531, as the king moved against his clergy over their alleged *Praemunire*, and began to signal his new jurisdictional claims, Anne secured a significant success in her cold war against Catherine and her supporters. For over two years Henry had sustained a formally correct relationship with his queen, which deceived nobody, but which continued to give Anne cause for unease. Early in 1531, and again in April, there were lovers' quarrels. Henry is alleged to have begged Anne's relations to intercede for him, and to have complained to Norfolk about her haughty and domineering attitude. Whether these tantrums were spontaneous or calculated, they again had the effect of intensifying the king's infatuation. Chapuys observed correctly, 'as happens generally in such cases, their love will be greater than before'.[40] Perhaps as a result, in July Catherine was dismissed from the royal presence. Her status remained unchanged, but she was no longer allowed to see the king or to accompany him on formal occasions. Such communication as they had was in writing, brief and bitter. By Christmas everyone was miserable. Catherine was sidelined. She had plenty of support, but it ameliorated neither her position, nor the pain of Henry's conduct.

Anne, in spite of her victory, could not afford to be complacent, and was keenly aware how widely and intensely she was disliked. Henry had still not screwed up the courage to take the radical action which he now knew would be necessary, clinging instead to the rags of a futile negotiation in Rome.[41] A breakthrough, however, was now on the horizon. In 1531 an elderly common lawyer, Christopher St German, had published some additions to his earlier work *A Dialogue betwixt a Doctor of Divinity and a Student in the Laws of England*, in which he said (among other things) 'The king in parliament is the high sovereign over the people, which hath not only charge on the bodies but also the souls of his subjects'.[42] In other words, all the functions of the church should be subjected to the processes of temporal legislation. This was the missing stone in the arch of argument which the king's supporters had been constructing for a solution to his problem. By early 1532 Thomas Cromwell and Thomas Audley, both lawyers who had entered Henry's service from Wolsey's, were drafting Bills to put this policy into effect. The king still hesitated, but significant moves were now being made on his behalf. The 'Supplication against the Ordinaries', presented to parliament, was almost certainly Cromwell's work; and the clerical reaction was sufficiently provocative to sting Henry into action.[43] He demanded that they surrender their jurisdictional independence, and allowed a Bill to be introduced to strip the church of its powers. On 15 May the clergy surrendered, and that opened the way for the settlement which could then be planned. Thomas More resigned the chancellorship in protest against the implications of this surrender and was replaced by Thomas Audley as keeper of the great seal. Anne's position was dramatically changed as erstwhile enemies and critics hastened to make their peace. The king was now talking openly of marrying again, and everyone knew who the new queen would be.

For the time being, however, there were no steps in that direction. Henry, anxious to build up support for the showdown with pope and emperor which was inevitable, set up a meeting with Francis I in October. In preparation for this he created his bride marquess of Pembroke – an unusual but not unprecedented move to give her the necessary formal status.[44] For a few months Anne was thus a major peer in her own right, and her existing attendants and servants could be reconstituted into a great noble household. There was still the little matter of Henry's first marriage to be tidied away, and he was anxious to use at least a form of 'due process' to achieve that. Fortunately the aged and obstructive archbishop of Canterbury, William Warham, died on 22 August. Although no replacement was named immediately, the way was open for the appointment of an amenable prelate who could be relied upon to do what was required. When Henry and Anne took ship for Calais on 11 October, they both knew that in the not too distant future they would be married. With that assurance, it appears that they at last slept together. It can only be hoped that they enjoyed the experience so long delayed, because at some time between 11 October and 12 November when they returned to England, Elizabeth was conceived.

Before they set off Thomas Cranmer, then on a diplomatic mission to the emperor, was recalled to be the next archbishop of Canterbury.[45] He was only archdeacon of Taunton, and the call must have been totally unexpected. It was also unwelcome, because in addition to an aversion to the responsibilities of high office, he had also contracted an illegal marriage and probably knew that not even the king's most advanced views encompassed a toleration of married clergy. Refusal was impossible, however, and he was back in England by late January. By then, indeed probably before Christmas, both Anne and Henry knew that she was pregnant, and this probably derailed the intended timetable. The order of events should have been to install Cranmer at Canterbury; give time for his court to declare the marriage of Henry and Catherine null and void; and then (after a brief but discreet interval) to solemnise the new union. Instead of which the king married Anne in a secret ceremony the date of which is uncertain, but was probably about 25 January. It is not even known who celebrated the marriage, but it was certainly not Cranmer.[46]

Anne's coronation took the place of the public wedding she never had. The timing was tight, because although he had not scrupled to marry her while his first marriage was still (in a sense) in being, Henry was reluctant to acknowledge the fact in public. On 23 May Thomas Cranmer, using his own authority as metropolitan and *legatus natus*, declared that Catherine was not, and never had been, the king's wife. On Whitsunday, 1 June, Anne was crowned with great pomp at Westminster Abbey. It was a unique gesture, required by the extraordinary circumstances. Henry did his best to make his new queen's triumph a memorable and joyful occasion. Hans Holbein designed some of the pageant scenery, and Anne's badge of the white falcon was prominently displayed:

> Honour and grace be to our Queen Anne
> For whose cause an Angel celestial
> Descendeth, the falcon as white as a swan,
> To crown with a Diadem Imperial!
> In her honour rejoice we all.
> For it cometh from God, and not of man.
> Honour and grace be to our Queen Anne.[47]

Although Henry had a celebratory account published shortly afterward,[48] no carefully disciplined rejoicings could conceal the general lack of enthusiasm. The duke of Suffolk, a fierce critic of the marriage, was constrained to be present as high constable, but nothing could enforce his wife, the king's sister, to do honour to this pretender. The crowds were large, and impressed by the magnificence as they were intended to be, but it was not only the jaundiced Chapuys who believed that the celebration was hollow. Anne, who was visibly pregnant by this time, sat through as much of the pageantry as possible, and considering her condition stood up to the ordeal well. If she noticed the significant absentees, or any lack of spontaneity in the applause which greeted her, she was wise enough not to comment. Considering how controversial her rise had been, and how much sympathy Catherine retained, the king's agents did extremely well to lay on four days of lavish entertainemnt, involving a very large proportion of the court, with no visible or audible dissent. The coronation itself was as solemn and symbolic as that of a ruling king. Anne was both anointed and crowned; accepted by both God and the realm of England. No toehold was left for any critic of her legimtimacy, short of repudiating the Tudor monarchy itself. A contemporary observer calculated that the four days had cost the king 100,000 ducats (£23,000) and the City of London twice as much.[49] As these two sums together would have amounted to nearly half the crown's ordinary revenue for a year, they are clearly exaggerated; but they do give an accurate picture of the impression which such lavishness made upon the spectators. As she left Westminster Hall at the end of the banquet, the queen turned to the kneeling company and said 'I thank ye all for the honour ye have done me this day'. Whatever reservations may have remained, Henry had good reason to think that his money had been well spent.

In the summer of 1533 the only thing that was needed to complete Anne's triumph was for the child she was carrying to be a son. At the end of July, the queen began the elaborate and traditional ritual which preceded a royal lying-in, withdrawing into the specially prepared apartments at Greenwich. Catherine's former chamberlain, who had much experience in such matters, sent a set of instructions to Cromwell to be passed on to the queen's officers. The ex-queen herself was less cooperative, refusing point blank to hand over the elaborate christening robe which she had originally brought from Spain, saying that she would give no 'help, assistance or favour, directly or indirectly, in a case so horrible as this'.[50] In the circumstances it is astonishing that Henry should have been so insensitive as to have demanded it. Anne's pregnancy may not have gone smoothly, or the king may simply have been over-anxious, because he cancelled his usual summer progress and voiced a number of concerns about her safety. Childbirth was a dangerous time, however, and Anne was a mature age to become a mother for the first time, so his anxiety was perhaps no more than natural. Anne eventually had an easy labour, and both mother and child were well – but the child was a girl, Elizabeth.

Because she was not a boy, her arrival had settled nothing, and Anne was still vulnerable to counter-attack. This would now come, not so much from Catherine herself, but from those who supported, and would continue to support, her daughter. Before the end of September an impostor appeared in Lincolnshire claiming to be Mary, and alleging that 'upon displeasure she was put forth into the broad world to shift for a living', and that it was her intention to go to her uncle the emperor.[51] Far from being 'put forth', however, the real Mary was being kept under close surveillance. By the middle of October she had resorted to open defiance, telling her father's commissioners that the title of princess was hers by right, and that she could not in conscience surrender it. The imperial ambassador, Eustace Chapuys, was delighted by this stand, believing (as he always did) that it would be a signal for rebellion. 'It is impossible to describe the love these people have for the Princess', he wrote. He had already informed Charles that 'the holy bishop' (John Fisher, bishop of Rochester) had requested him to urge the emperor to intervene with force, and that the majority of English people were of the same opinion.[52] Neither Charles nor his council were impressed by such exuberance. He was still, as he had been since 1527, willing to defend his aunt against Henry's claims for an annulment, but he was not going to commit scarce resources to a civil war in England. With a wary eye on Chapuys and his friends, Cromwell, now the king's secretary, toyed with the idea of ignoring Mary's stand and simply leaving her alone, but neither Henry nor Anne could afford to be complacent. Elizabeth's status had to be protected, and indeed promoted; and Henry could not afford to allow his authority to be openly flouted. In November, using the convenient fiction that her familiars were really responsible for her attitude, the king dissolved Mary's household and placed her under virtual house arrest in the establishment created for her supplanter.[53] On 16 December Elizabeth's new household was despatched from the court to the old palace at Hatfield; and a few days later Mary, with one or two remaining servants, joined her under close guard.

The protests, both from Mary's dismissed officers and from Chapuys were theatrical but ineffective. Catherine applauded her daughter's decision to share in her own martyrdom, and told Mary it was a sign of divine love. In fact, Mary was far worse off than her mother, who continued to be supported at Buckden by a household which was costing the king nearly £3000 a year – as much, if not more, than Elizabeth.[54] We do not know to what extent Anne was responsible for the king's severity towards his elder daughter, although she would have had good cause to urge it. After being the main focus of attention, both for good and ill, for about six years, after September 1533 Anne faded into the background. There is no reason to suppose that Henry regarded her with any less favour than before, and indeed she was pregnant again before the end of the year, but she was now a normal part of the court. In February 1534 the king was happy, and confident that this time the queen would have a son; and in April, when her condition was obvious, he ordered an especially ornate cradle from his goldsmith, Cornelius Hayes.

In July Anne miscarried. The disaster was extremely well concealed, and did not become known outside the court until September, but the complacency of the early summer was destroyed, and never returned.[55] As has been pointed out, there are very good reasons for doubting the stories of an actual estrangement between Henry and Anne in the autumn of 1534; not least because they all come via Chapuys from sources hostile to the queen. There are, however, reasons to suppose that the climate had changed from that which had prevailed during their prolonged courtship. Then Henry had had eyes for no other woman, but by 1534 he had reverted to his earlier habits of playing courtly love with other attractive damsels. Names are occasionally mentioned, but upon investigation all these 'infatuations' turn out to have been mere passing fancies. Anne was disturbed, because she was not accustomed to challenges of this kind, and may not have remembered how ephemeral they could be. She was also made anxious by her failure to bear a son, and perhaps remembering that she was already older than Catherine had been when she had conceived for the last time.

The fact seems to have been that Anne did not adjust successfully from the role of mistress to that of wife. A queen was expected to put up with this kind of casual dalliance (and far more) on the part of her husband. Catherine had done so for years, which is one reason why she had not immediately recognised a serious challenge when it arose. Anne reacted quite differently, and the lovers' storms, tiffs and quarrels which had punctuated their courtship continued into married life.[56] Gradually Henry began to find this tedious and unnecessary, and occasionally he became very angry: his wild words filtered through to imperial or Italian diplomats, to be used as evidence of terminal breakdown. For over two years, in fact, these were false alarms; but they were an ominous sign. Henry and Anne were in love, not in any measured or dutiful sense but passionately and physically; and it is the nature of such a relationship to fluctuate wildly. This was very unusual in a royal marriage, which is why their behaviour was so often misunderstood and misrepresented. Anne also became angry; sometimes with her husband but more often with the dangerous and threatening Mary. The two women detested and feared each other, and for good reason; but whereas Mary dealt in studied insults, Anne responded with wild threats.[57] Henry recognised the peril which Mary represented, but continued to love her in an oppressive, patriarchal kind of way; consequently the royal couple did not see eye to eye over her – if Anne could have persuaded her husband to put her to death, she would probably have done so. Mary, for similar reasons, concentrated her hostility on Anne, and was later absolutely shattered to discover, after the queen's fall, that the source of her trouble was really her father.[58] Unfortunately for her, it was not only Mary who used Anne as a scapegoat. Henry's policies continued to be unpopular; particularly the executions of John Fisher and Thomas More in the summer of 1535 for the treason of 'maliciously' rejecting the Act of Supremacy. There was also widespread opposition to his taxation (when there was no war to provide a traditional justification), and unjustified fears that he intended to restructure the church from the bottom up. All this could be conveniently, and plausibly, blamed on his second marriage. In fact by 1535 Henry had convinced himself that the Royal Supremacy represented the will of God, and had nothing to do with his desire to marry Anne; but, as time was to show, that was not much help to the queen.

Nor did Cromwell's activities on the king's behalf in any way ease the pressure on her. The Succession Act (25 Henry VIII, c. 22) and the Treason Act (26 Henry VIII, c. 13), both of 1534, required an oath to support the Boleyn marriage and extended the definition of treason to words defaming the king.[59] It was generally assumed that the queen was behind such measures, and was encouraging the king in the kind of brutality shown against the London Carthusians, who were executed for treason at Tyburn on 4 May 1535. The secretary's support was a very mixed blessing; in addition to attracting the opprobrium for many of his measures, she also bore the brunt of his falling out with the duke of Norfolk.[60] At the same time, Anne did not help her own cause by being politically active. This was a habit which she was quite incapable of breaking. She continued to give Henry the benefit of her views on a variety of matters, whether he asked for them or not. As she was highly intelligent, well informed and had views on most subjects, this was far from being cosmetic. In many ways she was better suited to the council chamber than to the boudoir. Before her marriage, when her position had been irregular to the point of being unprecedented, the king's normal councillors had been forced to treat her with a wary respect; because they could hardly advise the king about how he should treat his mistress. Now, they felt more confident in advising Henry that his wife had no right to interfere in their deliberations; and there is some evidence that he also found her strong opinions intrusive.[61] Her natural commitment to good relations with France were also a hostage to fortune. Whatever the king might be up to, the French were not popular in England, and deep and ancient suspicions inevitably rubbed off on her. Nor did her commitment necessarily bring much advantage. When a French embassy arrived in November 1534, the ambassador brought a proposal for a Habsburg-Valois settlement, which would also involve a marriage between Mary and the dauphin. This was almost certainly an imperial ploy to get Mary reinstated, but Anne was horrified that it should be delivered with a French endorsement, and was even more put out when a counter-proposal for a marriage with Elizabeth was elaborately evaded. Although this episode cooled Anne's enthusiasm for France, and led to several months of chilly detachment, it did not permanently reorientate her loyalties. The main reason for this was that she was deeply, and justifiably, suspicious of Charles V and all his agents, whom she was quite convinced would bring about her downfall if they were able to. She was bound to try and influence Henry against any *rapprochement* with the emperor. By the later part of 1535, however, Thomas Cromwell was taking a different view. Catherine's health was declining and he believed that, when she died, the king would be able to renegotiate his relations with Charles, which would be very much to his benefit.[62] Anne, however, was an obstacle, both for her views and for what she represented. If Henry accepted his minister's advice, she would have to change her views, retire from politics, or be removed.

In October 1535 Anne became pregnant again, after an interval of about fifteen months. Whether the delay was the result of an intermittent relationship, as many contemporaries wished to believe, or of the king's erratic virility we do not know. Accusations later levelled against the queen suggest the latter, but the evidence is highly suspect.[63] Early in October the French ambassador, at that point the bishop of Tarbes, informed Francis I that Henry had 'new amours', but this appears from other evidence to have been just another courtly game. The later story that Henry's involvement with Jane Seymour dated from a summer visit to Wolf Hall near Marlborough has been dismissed on the grounds that there is no evidence that she was there at the time.[64] In any case Jane was well known at court, and the king had shown no previous sign of interest. By the time that Anne's condition became obvious in December, however, there were also signs that support for Mary was mounting. There were trade disputes both with the Hanse and with the Low Countries, and rumours of war with the emperor were pervasive. The death of the duke of Milan on 1 November intensified these problems. The chances of renewed war between France and the empire increased; and Anne returned to her urgings of a French marriage alliance for Elizabeth. Unfortunately Francis I was only interested in Mary; and the pope was inevitably trying to stave off the war by urging both the potential combatants to combine against Henry. The tangle of disinformation in December 1535 is impenetrable. Then on 7 January 1536 Catherine of Aragon died at Kimbolton. The reaction at court was one of huge relief. Anne and Henry shared a common joy, but for significantly different reasons. The king now believed that 'we are free from all suspicion of war', thinking optimistically that it was only Catherine's situation which had provoked the emperor's hostility.[65] The queen and her family took the view that this represented only half of what needed to be achieved, and wished the same fate on Mary. Elizabeth was ostentatiously paraded, and Henry even danced with her in his arms; but it was the unborn child who was now the real focus of attention.

In one respect Henry's optimism was justified. In the same month Francis overran Savoy; it was clear that another war was imminent, and in the wake of his aunt's death Charles made it clear to a frustrated Chapuys that he had no interest in fomenting rebellion in England.[66] This strengthened Cromwell's position rather than Anne's, and by the end of January it must have dawned upon the queen that Catherine's death had actually weakened her position rather than strengthening it. She was indeed the 'sole queen'; but, now that there was no possibility of her husband returning to his first wife, Henry was under less pressure to support his second. There then followed two dramatic events. On 24 January 1536 Henry had a heavy fall in the tiltyard and was unconscious for over two hours. The danger was palpable. He was forty-three, and although he recovered completely, he did not joust again. It must have been obvious to him that the sporting career, in which he had taken intense pride, and had invested so much of his manhood, was over. More seriously, on the 29th Anne miscarried of a son. Much later it was alleged that the foetus was deformed, and that Henry was thereby convinced that he could not have been responsible for its conception.[67] There is no suggestion of that in contemporary evidence, but what is clear is that Henry was not only deeply disappointed, he was also deeply troubled. He had been through this before, and the last time he had convinced himself that his marriage had offended God. In the circumstances of February 1536 there was no shortage of people with an interest in reviving such fears.

What passed between the couple when they first met after this disaster has been befuddled by hindsight and invention. Some have Anne berating her husband for his unkindness, claiming that he had taken advantage of her condition to pay his attention to another woman (Jane Seymour being implied); some have her lamenting the fact that the sudden news of his accident had precipitated the miscarriage; some have him leaving her in high dudgeon 'with unkind words'.[68] None of these tales need be taken at face value. Henry was upset, and his officious conscience was troubling him; Anne was upset because she had failed him, and cared deeply about it, but also because it was borne in upon her just how vulnerable she really was. If her hold over her husband faltered, or could be broken, there was now nothing to protect her. The temptation of an unchallenged third marriage for the king was strong, not least because it offered the opportunity to discard the unpopular baggage of the Boleyn connection. By March Henry's interest in Jane Seymour was real, and she was being subtly promoted by two different groups. Her brother, Sir Edward Seymour, was high in the king's favour, and had just been appointed to the privy chamber. The more effectively Jane's charms could be deployed, the better for him; although it was most important that she should not succumb to the temptation of becoming another royal mistress.[69] At the same time Mary's supporters, who had no interest in promoting the Seymours, saw in Jane the perfect lever to dislodge their prime enemy. By April both these groups were screwing up the tension as hard as they could. Since the whole outcome depended upon the king's emotional state, it is not surprising that the end came quickly.

Hard as Jane may have been trying to undermine her, and logical as the weakness of her position may have been, there are perfectly clear signs as late as the middle of April that the queen's position was unshaken.[70] The negotiations with the emperor via Chapuys were even discussing the possibilities of an imperial marriage for Elizabeth, and consequently a delayed recognition of Henry's second marriage. As late at 18 April reports of this possible agreement were filling Mary's supporters with alarm and despondency. In the event the decisive factor was the political judgement of the powerful secretary, Thomas Cromwell. Cromwell had promoted Anne's cause since first entering the royal service in 1531, but he had never been her dependant. In most respects her ascendancy had suited his reforming programme very well and, in spite of their differences over foreign policy, they had remained allies. By April 1536, however, she was becoming a serious liability. With the detached view which he could afford to take, Anne no longer looked a good prospect to produce an heir; she was thirty-five, and her miscarriage may have had more to do with advancing years than with any other circumstance. That had been true of Catherine at a younger age. Simply from a dynastic point of view there was a good case for replacing her, if only the king's erratic fascination could be finally broken. Moreover, he had good reason to suppose that the imperial interest in Elizabeth was not serious politics.[71] If Henry really wanted to mend his fences with the emperor, then the removal of Anne was a *sine qua non*. Consequently Cromwell began to move, cautiously at first, to an anti-Boleyn stance. This meant mending his fences (to an extent) with Mary's supporters, who were still numerous about the court.[72] It suited them to believe that he was a convert to their cause, but this was never the case; they were merely, and temporarily, pursuing the same aim. What Cromwell brought to the anti-Boleyn coalition was not so much power as an intimate knowledge of the king's psychology. He knew that the deployment of rational political arguments, even about Anne's advancing years, would have no effect and might even be counter-productive. The basis of Henry's relationship with his wife was not rational, or even practical, but emotional and physical. Such relationships were and are subject to wild fluctuations of mood, but fierce quarrels did not signify breakdown, as had been proved over and over again in this case.

Henry, however, had two significant weaknesses: he was incurably vain; and he was superstitious. It was acceptable for him to amuse himself with other women, if he felt inclined. After all, he was the king. His wife, however, had to be free from any suspicion of similar activity, because the paternity of their children must not be in doubt. Catherine had always been exemplary in that respect, which was one reason why it had been so hard to get rid of her, but Anne was a very different kind of woman. She had behaved with great discretion over the previous ten years, but her overt sexuality had invited accusations almost from the beginning.[73] Henry had never listened to such slanders before; so why did he do so now? Amid the torrent of sordid gossip which was subsequently released, there was one telling story. In the supposed security of her privy chamber Anne had, in an unguarded moment, mocked Henry's virility; he was often, she alleged, unable to perform the sexual act.[74] Whether the story was true or not is irrelevant; the barb would have touched the king because he knew that it was accurate. For a man who had always prided himself upon his virility, it would have been an unthinkable humiliation for such knowledge to become public. Whoever brought that story to Henry's attention, or invented it for his benefit, knew the king very well, and Cromwell is the obvious suspect. At the same time, there was a straightforward explanation available for the king's long infatuation, and his blindness to Anne's weaknesses, deceits and betrayals. He had been bewitched. To the modern mind such an allegation borders on the ludicrous, but that was not how Henry would have understood it. To him it may have come as a terrifying revelation; and one, moreover, which had the special advantage of absolving him from all blame.

Charges of plotting to poison Mary, and even the king himself, suddenly became plausible.[75] Under this barrage, Henry suddenly and dramatically changed his mind; over a few days towards the end of April 1536 his long infatuation with Anne disappeared, to be replaced with an equally irrational fear and loathing. Almost overnight his treasured and exciting companion, for whose sake he had risked so much, became a witch and a serial adulteress. Anne was shattered by both the suddennesss and the injustice of these charges. A dozen words and gestures, which in their proper context were perfectly innocuous, now became damning evidence of her guilt. Even apart from the witchcraft charges, which were never pressed, none of this would have stood up for a moment in a modern court; but that is not the point. Although he was a stickler for legal propriety, the only person who needed to be convinced in this case was the king. Once he had made up his mind, and had made it clear that he had made up his mind, the rest was a formality. It was made easier by the fact that she had so many enemies. The only person who attempted to stand up for her was her old protégé, Thomas Cranmer.[76] Normally the king listened to his archbishop, and respected his opinion, but this time he brushed him aside. Henry was not merely angry and disillusioned, he was vindictive. There was no substance at all in the charge of incest between Anne and her brother Lord Rochford, but the king was geared up to believe anything, and needed no prompting to destroy not only his queen but her entire family. The explanation is that Henry was afraid. This was not a rational fear of war or rebellion, or even of assassination, but an irrational belief that he had been unmanned by a diabolical harpy.

Anne's vigorous sexuality, her brains, her tantrums, the tiffs and reconciliations, all those things which he had found so fascinating, now fell into place as part of a plot. He had been cheated and betrayed; and, in spite of everything, still had no son. There could be no question of putting Anne aside. She would have been too dangerous. In any case the adultery of a queen (even with one man) was a capital offence. On 9 May her alleged accomplices were tried at Westminster and found guilty. After that her own fate was sealed, in spite of her 'wise and discreet answers'. At her trial she defended herself with dignity and intelligence, but to no avail. On 19 May 'the Queene was with a Sworde beheaded within the Tower'. She was thirty-five, and age had had no chance to wither her.

Even death, however, was not sufficient to assuage the king's wrath. A few days earlier, and quite unnecessarily, he had had the marriage, for the validity of which he had moved heaven and earth, declared null and void.[77] With Anne's death there was no obstacle to his remarriage; and, since Catherine had also gone, there was no obstacle to negotiations with the papacy either. Paradoxically, Henry stood by the consequences of his second marriage, while denying that the marriage itself had ever taken place. It was a judgement which reflected no credit either on the king who demanded it or on the archbishop who delivered it. It meant, however, that the daughter who had been welcomed as a token of hope less than three years before now joined her twenty-year-old half-sister in limbo as 'the king's natural daughter'. Elizabeth was no longer princess, or the heir, but just another bastard. Unlike Mary, however, she presented no threat to anything which Henry might want to do in the future. Whether that would turn out to be for the good remained to be seen, but for the time being Henry did not even want to be reminded that he had a second daughter. Just two months later his son the duke of Richmond, a promising youth, died at the age of seventeen. There was nothing for it but to start again, and on 30 May 1536, the king did just that by marrying Jane Seymour. It was widely (and naturally) believed at the time that the brutal despatch of Anne had been occasioned by nothing more calculating than Henry's inordinate lust for her successor. That would be to assume that his irrational fury against his second wife had been largely or wholely feigned, which the evidence does not support. In executing Anne, Henry had been exorcising his own demons.

2

The Infant Princess

When Anne had gone into retreat in July 1533, Henry began to plan the elaborate tournament which normally greeted the arrival of a royal prince. When the news of Elizabeth's birth reached him on 7 September, he was in a sense relieved, but he promptly cancelled plans for the tournament. Anne had had an easy labour, and too much should not be made of their disappointment at the sex of the child. The celebrations were low key, but the king immediately caused his heralds to proclaim the birth of a princess. The Chapel Royal sang *Te Deum*, and a christening ceremony was ordered for 10 September which would leave no spectator in doubt as to the child's legitimate status.[1]

In the background, Chapuys, the imperial ambassador, mocked. On the day of the christening (a ceremony which he would not have dreamed of attending), he reported to the emperor that the king's mistress had been delivered of a bastard daughter, which was causing great hilarity at the expense of all those who had confidently predicted a son.[2] He was not alone in his reaction. It was already treason to deny the lawfulness of the king's second marriage, but some could not resist the temptation to deride the new heir; and Cromwell was already investigating such reports by 13 September.[3] In reporting the christening itself, the chronicler Edward Hall waxed lyrical:

> All the walles betwene the kings palace and the Friars, were hanged with arras, and all the way strawed with greene rushes;the Friers Church was also hanged with arras. The Font was of silver, and stode in the middes of the Church, three steps high, which was covered with a fine cloth, and divers gentlemen with Aperns and Towels about their neckes gave attendance about it.[4]

The dukes of Norfolk and Suffolk, even Catherine's friend the marchioness of Exeter, all played their allotted parts in this great ritual of unity; which in its way was more effective than Anne's coronation. Chapuys inevitably struck a quite different note:

> The daughter of the lady has been named Elizabeth. The christening has been like her mother's coronation, very cold and disagreeable, both to the court and to the city; and there has been no thought of having the bonfires and rejoicings usual in such cases.[5]

The imperial ambassador could not admit that anyone was happy, or impressed by such goings-on, and he got his information exclusively from the most disgruntled sources, but up to point he was right. Elizabeth's christening was a major political event, and all the elite were there, but the real issues had merely been postponed. The king himself did not attend by custom, and the royal family was conspicuous by its absence. Henry's elder sister, Margaret, was out of reach in Scotland, and had just gone through a second divorce, to the king's somewhat hypocritical disgust. His younger sister, Mary, had died during the previous summer; and nothing would have forced either Catherine or Mary to attend. The duke of Richmond, Henry's illegitimate son, was at Sheriff Hutton, and his attendance was not required. The chronicler's account goes on to elaborate the impression which the christening was intended to create:

> First the citezens two and two, then Gentlemen, Esquires and Chapeleins, next after them the Aldermen, and the Maior alone next the Maior the kinges Counsaile, the kinges Chapell in Copes; the Barons, Bishops, Erles, then came the Erle of Essex, bearyng the covered Basons gilte, and after him the Marquess of Exceter with the Taper of Virgin waxe, next him the Marques Dorset, bearyng the salt, behind him the Lady Mary of Norffolke bearyng the Cresom, which was verye riche of pearle and stone, the olde Duches of Norffolke bare the childe in a Mantell of purple Velvet.[6]

The dukes of both Norfolk and Suffolk escorted the dowager duchess, supported by all the officers of arms, and a long list of other named peers and their ladies. The godparents were the archbishop of Canterbury, the dowager duchess of Norfolk and the dowager marchioness of Dorset. According to the custom then prevailing, immediately after the baptism Elizabeth was confirmed, the marchioness of Exeter serving as an additional godmother. Lavish gifts were then bestowed upon the new princess, and the whole company processed with an escort of five hundred torchbearers from the friars' church, where the ceremony had taken place, to Greenwich Palace. There Elizabeth was returned to her mother, who by custom if not by necessity, had remained in her chamber. It hardly needed the heralds' proclamation to announce that this was the new heir to the crown of England. Outside England, however, no one acknowledged her; and Chapuys, sneering and fuming in the background, was the authentic voice of the Catholic Church.[7] Even Martin Luther, who had no liking for the pope or his pretensions, regarded Henry's matrimonial manoeuvres with undisguised contempt. Elizabeth started her life as a gesture of defiance, or 'singularity' as contemporaries called it. Although she can have had no consciousness of the fact, it was also an appropriately prophetic beginning.

We know virtually nothing of how the new princess was cared for in the
first weeks of her life. There would have been at least one wet nurse, and
several other designated female servants, but we do not know who they
were; perhaps they were drawn from the ranks of the queen's existing
household.[8] At the beginning of December, however, the king decided to
give his daughter her own establishment; which was another gesture acknowledging her status. On 2 December the council noted that the lady
princess was to be conveyed to Hertford in the following week 'to remain
with the family assigned to her'.[9] Chapuys, whose geography was always
shaky, reported that she was to be sent into Norfolk, accompanied by both
dukes, and several lords and gentlemen.[10] This may have been correct as a
description of her rite of passage, but when she got to Hertford her establishment was a good deal more modest. It was presided over by Sir John
Shelton as steward, with William Cholmely as cofferer. Both Sir John's wife,
Anne, who was the queen's aunt (being her father's sister), and Lady
Margaret, the mother of Sir Francis Bryan, a gentleman of the privy chamber
and favourite companion of the king, are described as having been responsible for the child's personal well being.[11] What the relationship between
the two women may have been, and how the responsibility was divided,
we do not know, but there is no evidence of friction between them. Margaret
had held a similar position in the first household set up for Princess Mary,
and was clearly trusted by Henry, while Anne's family connection placed
her close to the queen. It is possible that Margaret was introduced shortly
after the initial establishment, when it was decided that Mary would join
her sister in the hope of easing the situation. If that was the thinking, the
plan failed.

When he moved on at the end of March 1534, Cholmely accounted for
the period between 10 December 1533 and 25 March 1534, a period of about
four and a half months.[12] During that time he had received from Sir Brian
Tuke, the treasurer of the king's chamber, £750, and had spent on council,
officers and servants £791 0s. 8½d. The balance, and a little more, was made
up from the revenues left at the winding up of Mary's household. This
level of provision over a full year would have given an income of about
£2200, which is approximately what might be expected for a royal child
who did not yet require an expensive education.[13] As Elizabeth had no
estate to run, it can be assumed that her 'council' would have been minimal,
but she would have had a chamber staff of nurses, rockers (cradle minders),
ladies and gentlewomen, as well as a few gentlemen, yeomen and grooms.
Being physically separated from the court, she would also have required a
full set of household departments – not on the same scale as the king's,
but approximating to that of a major peer. There would have been perhaps

twenty posts 'above stairs' and a hundred 'below stairs'; a fair amount of patronage. At a similar stage of her life, Mary had had a chamber staff of ten, but she had not been separately housed.[14] These offices would have been in the king's gift rather than the queen's, but we know nothing about how the holders were selected. Apart from an indeterminate number of personal servants (two ladies and at least two men are mentioned) who remained with Mary, her only contribution to this establishment was the residue of cash and victuals which Cholmely took over.[15]

For Mary, the former Princess, this was the beginning of a wretched period, as she would neither say nor do anything which might compromise her mother's cause. On being informed that she was to join the household of 'the Princess', she professed bewilderment as to who that might be, for 'the daughter of Madame de Pembroke had no such title'.[16] It is not difficult to see why her father decided to treat her harshly. Whether there was more to her disaffection than mere words is hard to tell. She was supposed to have no communication with her mother, but we know that that ban was evaded, using loyal servants as messengers. In March 1534 Sir William FitzWilliam reported to Cromwell that he had caused her servants to be searched 'upon suspicion', but suspicion of what is not specified; it may well have been the carrying of these very messages.[17] In the same month Chapuys reported that one of Elizabeth's senior officers had been dismissed for 'showing the Princess [Mary] too much affection'. The officer in question may have been Cholmely, who departed soon after; but in view of Chapuys's jaundiced view, not to say his prejudiced sources, it should not be assumed that his report was correct.[18] Mary was determined to make a martyr of herself, and was encouraged in that determination by her mother, who informed her that it was God's way of testing her virtue and resolution. This was all very well for Catherine, whose own sufferings were a good deal more theoretical. Although neither Buckden nor Kimbolton were particularly salubrious residences, her establishment as Princess Dowager of Wales was still costing her estranged husband a great deal of money, and she was surrounded by a household which was conspicuously loyal to her, the majority of whom she had probably chosen herself.[19] Moreover, by October 1533 she had obtained a favourable verdict in Rome, whereby Henry was commanded to return to her within a year under pain of excommunication, and to proclaim his new-born daughter illegitimate.[20] Whether she seriously expected this to happen or not, towards the end of 1533 Catherine had a number of grounds for satisfaction – not least that her supplanter had borne a daughter and not a son. Mary, however, was under virtual house arrest, and without any resources of her own, nursing her grievances with a bitter consistency which seriously undermined her health.

Having decided to make his new heir as conspicuous as possible, Henry could not afford to allow anyone to accuse him of neglect. Whether she kept the Christmas of 1533 at court or in her own household is not clear. Both 'the princess' and 'the Lady Mary' appear in the New Year gift list for 1534, as giving and receiving; but, as there are no entries for the items exchanged, we do not know whether this represents any more than an unfulfilled intention.[21] By the middle of January Elizabeth and her household had been long since settled at Hatfield, a house which at that stage still belonged to the bishop of Ely, and was presumably leased by the crown for the purpose.[22] As Henry had many residences of his own in the London area, this one must have been regarded as particularly convenient or commodious, or both. In 1538 the king obtained it by exchange. It is about seventeen miles from London, which would have been a comfortable day's ride. References to Henry and Anne visiting their daughter are scattered casually through the diplomatic correspondence, but we do not know whether all their visits were recorded. On 17 January Chapuys noted that the king had been 'recently'; and on 25 February another imperial agent, Dr Ortiz, reported what must have been a further visit, commenting sourly that Henry had refused to see his other daughter 'although she is in the same house'.[23] Anne's visits are even more casually noted, partly because Chapuys did not demean himself by describing her doings, unless he considered them to be particularly outrageous. On 7 March he commented that the king's 'amye' (one of his more flattering ways of describing her) had been to see her daughter; and we know that she wrote occasionally to Margaret Bryan. Any more detailed reconstruction is impossible.[24]

Elizabeth's household made a routine move to Eltham at the end of March 1534. This was, and had been for a long time, a royal residence, and the move had no particular significance beyond the need to clean and air Hatfield at the end of the winter. Mary, who had spent the previous three months badgering her father to provide her with more clothes, and driving Anne Shelton to distraction with claims that she was about to be poisoned, celebrated the move by refusing to budge until, or unless, she was addressed by her proper title.[25] The exasperated Lady Shelton had her lifted into a litter and carried off, still volubly protesting. This time even Chapuys was anxious that she had overstepped the mark and would provoke her father to further severity;[26] Henry, however, appears to have ignored the outburst. Queen Anne could not afford to be so indulgent, and it seems to have been while Elizabeth was still at Hatfield that the first of several recorded clashes between the women took place. In what was intended to be a conciliatory gesture, Anne offered to mediate between Mary and her father, in return for an acknowledgement of her own status. Mary responded with predictable abrasiveness that she knew no queen but her mother – but if the king's mistress wished to intervene, she would be properly grateful.[27] Anne's immediate response is not recorded, but the savage threats which she is alleged to have made against the younger woman's life are understandable. The queen made one further attempt at reconciliation while Mary and Elizabeth were at Eltham in the early summer of 1534. When that was rebuffed with almost equal incivility, she appears to have given up. It was a conflict in which Mary was eventually the winner, because when Henry turned on his second wife at the end of April 1536, one of the charges against her that he appears to have believed was that of scheming to poison both Mary and himself.[28] Needless to say, there is not a shred of evidence that Anne ever had any such intention.

Meanwhile, Henry and Anne were both at Eltham on 18 and 19 April, when, as Sir William Kingston enthused to Lord Lisle, 'they saw my Lady Princess, as goodly a child as hath been seen and her grace is much in the king's favour, as a goodly child should be; God save her!'[29] His description was not mere cooing, because a royal princess was on the marriage market as soon as she was born, and it was extremely important that she should be without any physical blemish; especially as those who believed, like Chapuys, that she was misbegotten were prepared to attribute to her all sorts of secret deformities. It was no doubt with that in mind that a slightly bizarre ritual had been performed during the week before the royal visit. About 10 April the French ambassadors visited Eltham, and then Elizabeth 'was shown to them first in very rich apparel, in state and triumph as a princess, and afterwards they saw her quite naked'. It was a very neat demonstration of her significance, and fortunately at seven months she was far too young to be embarrassed by it all.[30] Henry was certainly at Eltham again towards the end of July, and may well have paid other unrecorded visits. At the end of August the princess's household moved to Greenwich, an event which provoked more scenes from Mary, who in the course of about twenty-four hours appealed three times to Chapuys for advice. He feared, not without justice, that she was becoming unhinged, perhaps as a result of having been studiously ignored by her father since the spring.[31]

The visit to Greenwich may have been no more than a brief sojurn at court, because on 20 September Sir John Shelton wrote anxiously from Hunsdon, acknowledging an instruction from Cromwell that Elizabeth should be relocated to either Langley or Knebworth. He did not know, he confessed, what state either of these houses were in, or whether 'they be mete for her grace'.[32] She probably went to Langley, which was a royal residence; she was certainly there for a while in 1535. Langley was far away in Oxfordshire, however, and there are no reports of the king having gone there at this time. Probably, having satisfied himself that she was healthy and in good hands, Henry felt that there was no need for frequent visits. There are no reports of Elizabeth ailing as a small child, so his confidence seems to have been justified. Anne may well have visited more often: her affection for her only daughter is well testified, and she spent lavishly on fine clothes for her, but no one was particularly concerned to note her movements. Nor is there any way of reconstructing Elizabeth's itinerary in any detail. She appears to have been at Richmond early in 1535, because John Husee noted, on 24 March, that when the king arrived there to keep Easter his daughters were promptly moved on to Hunsdon.[33]

In October 1535 came her next rite of passage, when Sir William Paulet solemnly wrote to Cromwell that, after due consultation with Lady Bryan and other of the princess's officers (but not, apparently, her mother), the king had decided that Elizabeth should be weaned.[34] Anne wrote to Lady Bryan on the subject, which suggests that they had had no chance to talk about it. The same letter also decreed another move – back to Langley, which may have been considered more private for these domestic mysteries. Elizabeth was now more than two years old, but that tells us more about contemporary notions of child care than it does about this particular child.

Whatever affection Henry may have felt for his young daughter, she was primarily a piece to be moved on the political chessboard. In the circumstances of 1534 that meant primarily as bait for a French alliance. Relations between Henry and Francis were unstable. Although each in a sense needed the other, there was no cordiality, or mutual trust.[35] The English need for support against the pope was, however, probably more significant than any of the other contributory factors, and this was something of an embarrassment to Francis. In October 1534 the English drew up a draft declaration, inviting the French king to maintain the validity of the Boleyn marriage, and to recognise Elizabeth as legitimate.[36] Francis, however, was not to be drawn, and in November proposed a general settlement which would have involved a marriage between Mary and the dauphin. This shocked Anne, and revealed to Henry how little he could count on Francis's goodwill; he nevertheless responded obliquely rather than directly by offering instead a marriage between Elizabeth and the third son of the French king, Charles of Angoulême, a child of twelve at that time.[37] He may have been intending to do this anyway, and the two offers may not have been directly connected. By 28 November Chapuys knew that such a proposal had been made, but was not in possession of any details.[38] On 5 February 1535, when Palamedes Gontier, one of the French agents in England reported, he gave the impression that real progress was being made. Henry would have to confirm that Elizabeth was his sole heiress, so that (if he had no son) the crown would come to her on his death; but that was not likely to be a problem.[39] At the same time, Francis himself was now suggesting that 'some means ought to be found to deprive the Lady Mary of any occasion or means of claiming the Crown'. Such a step would have been a logical corollary to Elizabeth's marriage but represented a major shift in the French position since the previous November.[40] If Anne was aware of this development, she must have been highly gratified. Chapuys believed that Henry was trying to use such a marriage as a means of circumventing the papal verdict against his own union with Anne. The ambassador calculated that Francis would not agree without papal approval, and if the pope recognised Elizabeth as a princess of England, it would mean reversing his predecessor's decision. He admitted that he did not much trust his informant, but he was probably right in thinking that Paul III was willing to consider such a concession in return for a formal submission.[41] There is no evidence that Henry ever had such an intention, but it may have featured in French thinking.

By March the English king believed that his 'good brother' had agreed to the marriage in principle and started haggling about details. Francis had apparently demanded the remission of all pensions due from France to England under earlier treaties, 'as things most odious to the realm of France'. Henry metaphorically threw up his hands at such 'dishonourable conditions', pointing out that his daughter was 'of most certain title, without remainder of quarrel to the contrary', and that the revenues of the crown of England, which she would inherit, stood at 200,000 marks sterling (about £135,000).[42] Such protests, however, were a ploy and should not be taken seriously. At the same time, the king was appointing ambassadors to negotiate, taking the opportunity to claim that the original proposal had been made by the admiral of France, Philippe de Chabot, during a visit the previous autumn.[43] It is possible that this claim was true. Rumour, as always, moved ahead of the actual events, and as early as 16 March it was believed in some parts of the imperial camp that a deal had already been struck, and that 'the French king will send M. d'Angoulême to England, and promise him as a husband to that *puttina*, so that England will be sure of France'.[44] The same writer, a month later, believed that Henry had now despaired of a son, and was mortgaging his kingdom to France to keep it out of the hands of the emperor.[45] On 17 April Chabot himself wrote to the king of England, confirming that his master had indeed agreed the union in principle, and had also appointed ambassadors to negotiate the details. Francis would send to the pope, requesting the revocation of Clement's decree, but did not suggest that the outcome of the negotiation would depend upon the response.[46] In May the duke of Norfolk and Thomas Cromwell were issued with formal instructions for a meeting to take place at Calais. They were to demand that the marriage be solemnised when Elizabeth reached the age of seven (that is, in September 1540, more than five years away). In the meanwhile the young duke of Angoulême was to complete his education in England, as befitted its future king.[47]

The negotiations failed after reaching that point, and it is consequently impossible to be sure whether either or both parties entered into them sincerely. The stumbling block, unsurprisingly, was the English demand that the duke of Angoulême should be sent immediately to England. It was a sensible enough requirement if Charles was going to be the next king, but anathema to Francis's sense of honour that his son should be educated as anything other than a French prince. As a compromise, Chabot offered to allow the prince to come to England as soon as Elizabeth was old enough to marry.[48] As we only have this report from an imperial source, it is not quite clear what was meant. Elizabeth could have married in a formal sense immediately, so presumably the admiral meant until she was old enough to consummate the marriage – which would have meant a wait of at least ten years. By that time Charles would have been about twenty-two and his formative years would have been passed. Norfolk rejected the suggestion, and Chabot then began to find other reasons to break off the talks. His master would do nothing against the Church; nor would he recognise Henry's second marriage. The latter was a particularly odd statement, and again the source is suspect.[49] If Francis was not prepared to recognise Elizabeth as legitimate, why had he ever contemplated marrying her to his son at all? Such goodwill as there may have been at the start quickly evaporated, and few weeks later Francis was allegedly denouncing the king of England as an impious and unstable madman, who would soon be an open enemy 'according to the custom of that country'.[50]

Whatever actually transpired at Calais, the imperialists were quick to attribute the breakdown to the influence of Anne Boleyn, because 'all business passes through the hands of people who depend on the new Queen'. It was allegedly she who had insisted that Angoulême must come to England at once.[51] This is intrinsically unlikely, because Anne had everything to lose from the breakdown, and nothing to gain from such intransigence. Nor would Henry have been ruled in such an important matter by his wife. However, imperialists such as the bishop of Faenza, from whom the report comes, took great delight in representing him as hag-ridden by 'the concubine'. A more plausible explanation is hinted at by Chapuys, who on 7 March reported a conversation with Cromwell, in which he claimed that the minister had raised the possibility of a match between the prince of Spain (Philip, then aged eight) and 'this bastard whom they call princess'. 'Seeing my looks', the ambassador continued virtuously, 'he said no more.'[52]

Six months later, however, Cromwell returned delicately to the same point, and this time was not so abruptly brushed aside.

Cromwell favoured an understanding with the emperor, and had taken advantage of an alleged ailment not to attend the Calais meetings; so it is reasonable to suppose that he was a good deal less distressed by their failure than Anne was.[53] There is no reason to suppose that he sabotaged an agreement with France, but he did nothing to assist it, in a situation where his influence could have made a difference. Meanwhile, he was sowing seeds which might germinate in due course. Francis may have renounced all interest in an English marriage after the failure at Calais – or he may not. Imperialist reports of his extravagant language need not be taken too seriously, and early in October the French ambassadors paid another call upon the infant princess, much to the chagrin of Chapuys and his friends.[54] Such visits were not made out of idle curiosity. The purpose may have been to gratify the queen, who was still an influence to be reckoned with, rather than because any new negotiation was in mind. There appear to have been no consequences, but a gesture of that kind would not have been accidental.

Less than a month after Cromwell had dropped his second hint to Chapuys, Catherine of Aragon died, subtly changing the political landscape. She appears to have had a heart attack, or more likely a series of heart attacks, at her residence at Kimbolton in Northamptonshire. There were the inevitable rumours of poison, but not even Chapuys took them seriously. Henry's first reaction was one of undignified relief and joy. He appeared 'on the following Sunday clad all in yellow from top to toe' and the young Elizabeth was 'conducted to mass with trumpets and other great triumphs'.[55] Anne, who was pregnant again after a fairly long interval, seems to have shared Henry's reaction, believing that her estate was now secure from any challenge.[56] When she suddenly miscarried at the end of January, however, Chapuys was quick to seize upon the most derogatory rumours he could find. It was being said, he alleged, that Anne had never been pregnant at all, and had faked her miscarriage; more significantly, that she was actually unable to conceive at all, and that Elizabeth was really another woman's daughter.[57] He did not say that he believed these rumours, and indeed they were sufficiently extravagant, but they do perhaps indicate that Cromwell's hopes for a Habsburg marriage for Elizabeth were not making much progress. Instead, it is possible that a French match was back under consideration, because on 3 March the bishop of Tarbes took the trouble to write to Francis, reporting that the duke of Norfolk still favoured the Angoulême marriage, and was now (almost a year after the failed negotiation) saying how annoying it was that it had broken down for such comparatively trivial reasons.[58]

At the end of April 1536, all these insubstantial speculations were blown away by the dramatic fall of the queen. Henry's sudden reaction can only be described as paranoid, but it arose from the whole nature of his relationship with Anne Boleyn, which had been emotional, passionate and subject to violent fluctuations. This time, instead of ending with a demonstrative reconciliation, his revulsion was deep and lasting enough to be fatal. Anne's sex appeal, which had fascinated him for nearly a decade, suddenly became a thing of evil. This turn of events could hardly have been more ominous for Elizabeth, as Anne realised with despair when she wrote to the king on 6 May, begging him not to vent his displeasure on their innocent daughter.[59] The rumours were dense and confusing, with Chapuys relaying them more or less as they reached him. At one moment he was writing to the emperor that Lord Rochford had been charged with spreading reports which called Henry's paternity in question, implying that these reports were known to be untrue. The same day, however, he informed Cardinal Granvelle in the Netherlands that Cranmer, in annulling the king's second marriage, had declared that 'the concubine's daughter was the bastard of Mr Norris, and not the king's daughter'.[60] Neither of these reports was accurate. The first appears to be a distortion of the fact that Rochford was accused of making jokes about the king's sexual prowess; and the second was without any foundation whatsoever. In spite of the fact that he was executing his wife for adultery, Henry wanted his marriage annulled, not dissolved, and that, of course, could not be done on the basis of misdemeanours which had taken place after marriage. So Cranmer annulled the marriage on the basis of the pre-contract created by the king's earlier relations with Anne's sister Mary. This verdict was aimed exclusively at Elizabeth. It could no longer affect Anne, who was on the point of execution, except to deepen the despair of the last days of her life. After the queen's death, the sordid rumours continued: on 2 June one correspondent believed that the child had been 'taken' from poor parents; on the 10th another claimed that the council had 'declared that the queen's daughter was the child of her brother'.[61]

The king's vindictiveness did not, however, extend to his daughter. In spite of all that had been alleged about Anne's sexual peccadilloes, and the price which she had paid, Henry had no intention of renouncing Elizabeth. In terms of legitimate offspring, however, he had wiped the slate clean and was about to start again. Charles V hoped that Henry would now marry a Habsburg princess; Francis hoped he would find a bride in France.[62] Each preferred that he should marry at home rather than ally with the rival European camp. Both hoped that he would mend his fences with the papacy. In fact Henry's mind had been made up, even before Anne's head was off, as would have been known to Thomas Cromwell, and to anyone else close to the king. Apart from the indecent haste of their marriage, on 30 May, Jane Seymour was an excellent choice. She was the fifth child, but eldest daughter of Sir John Seymour, an experienced courtier who had placed her in the service of Catherine of Aragon, and adroitly switched her to Anne when the political wind changed. She was twenty-seven years old, came of a fertile family and had no known enemies. She was alleged to be intelligent, but there is no surviving evidence of that; and neither she nor her brothers at this time had any commitment to the pro- or anti-papal parties at court.[63] Mary's supporters welcomed her as a friend, and so she was, but not to the extent of crossing the king's will, or being antagonistic to Elizabeth. Sir John Russell appears to have been right when he wrote, shortly before the king's third marriage, that he 'hath come out of hell into heaven, for the gentleness in this, and the cursedness and unhappiness in the other'.[64]

In June a hastily convened parliament tidied up the legal situation with a new Succession Act, vesting the crown in the heirs of the king's new marriage, and confirming the illegitimacy of both Henry's existing daughters. This did not go far enough to satisfy Chapuys, whose hatred of Anne had not been assuaged by her execution. On 8 July he wrote to Granvelle

> The statute declaring the concubine's daughter princess and legitimate has been repealed, and she has been declared a bastard – not as being the daughter of Master Norris as might have been more honourably said, but because the marriage between the king and the concubine was invalid.[65]

His bile was largely the result of disappointment. Like Mary herself, he had been convinced that Henry's repudiation of his elder daughter had been mainly, if not wholly, the work of 'the concubine'. Now it was clear that that had not been the case. There was to be no penitent reinstatement for Mary, and no reconciliation with the papacy. Even the loophole, that Mary had been conceived in good faith (*bona fide parentum*), and therefore might be deemed legitimate even if her parents' marriage was subsequently disallowed, was not to be taken advantage of.[66] After more than a month of fierce pressure, both from her father and Cromwell, in the course of which threats of high treason had been uttered, on 22 June Mary surrendered and accepted both the ecclesiastical Supremacy and her own bastardy.[67]

It will probably never be known whether her change of heart was genuine, as her behaviour for the rest of the reign would suggest, or feigned, as Chapuys wished to believe. Her rehabilitation was immediately signalled in a number of ways. On 6 July the king and queen visited Hunsdon, where the establishment of both daughters was situated. This time there was no question of ignoring Mary, who was greeted with favour and affection.[68] The possibility of her marriage again began to be canvassed, and her full chamber establishment was restored. This amounted to some thirty servants, both male and female, some of whom had been with her during even the darkest days, and a radical reorganisation of the Hunsdon establishment.[69] Instead of being Elizabeth's household, into which Mary was reluctantly incorporated, it now became genuinely double. Sir John Shelton remained the steward, and accounted for both sides in a single account, but Mary seems to have moved independently, sometimes being at court, sometimes in a separate house; so there must have been two sets of 'below stairs' departments, as well as chambers, rather like the king's side and the queen's side in the court, which gave the consort the opportunity to move separately if circumstances required. On 28 August Henry issued a warrant to Sir Brian Tuke, the treasurer of the chamber

> to pay or cause to be paid unto our trusty and well beloved servant Sir John Shelton, knight, steward of the household of our children, the sum of four thousand pounds in advancement of the charge of the said household for one whole year.[70]

This was almost twice the provision which had been made for Elizabeth's household, even in 1534–35 after Mary had joined it, and indicates the radical nature of the changes which were taking place. Tuke grumbled, and protested that he could not find so much money, but his lamentations appear to have fallen on deaf ears. As he had done for Catherine before her death, Henry was making 'honourable provision' for his daughters, whether he recognised their legitimacy or not.

Two lists of Elizabeth's servants survive from this transitional period. Neither is precisely dated, and the relationship between them is not clear; but, since one contains thirty-two individuals and the other sixteen, it might be deduced that they represent before and after her demotion.[71] Neither the Sheltons nor Margaret Bryan are mentioned, although Sir John Shelton at least remained in office and Margaret was still responsible for Elizabeth in August 1536. Both lists appear to be of normal chamber staff, and therefore exclude the higher officers of the household. Lady Shelton may well have been dropped from active participation after her niece's disgrace. She is no longer alluded to. The first list is headed by a group of five, styled ladies and gentlewomen; then follow two female chamberers, two gentlemen, a chaplain, two grooms of the chamber, two yeomen, a laundress a woodbearer, and a number of others of unspecified duties.[72] The second list starts with four gentlewomen, followed by two chamberers, two gentlemen ushers, a chaplain, two grooms of the chamber, a wardrobe keeper, a laundress, a woodbearer and (rather oddly) two grooms of the stables. Making due allowance for somewhat random spelling, two of the gentlewomen (Catherine Champernowne and Elizabeth Garnet) appear on both lists, as do the two chamberers (Alice Huntercombe and Jane Broadbelt), two of the gentlemen (Richard Sandes and Robert Parker), the chaplain (Ralph Taylor) and the laundress (Anne Hilton).[73] Apart from the reduction of scale attendant upon Elizabeth's loss of status, there seems to have been no particular plan behind these changes. Probably the two women who would have had daily charge of the child were the chamberers, and they were unchanged. If the little girl was in any way distressed by what had happened, no one commented upon the fact; and the story that her mother sought to soften her father's heart by carrying her into his presence appears to be apocryphal.[74] How much Elizabeth would have remembered of her mother is highly uncertain. She was less than three years old at the time of Anne's execution. Although she must have seen her fairly frequently, they had never spent long in each other's company. In later life she was very aware of her mother's fate but seems not to have been emotionally affected by it. By the time that she was old enough to think about such things, she knew that it was her father who mattered – who was still there.

The person who seems to have suffered most was Margaret Bryan. At some point during the August following the king's third marriage, she wrote to Cromwell a long letter, full of unhappiness and complaint.[75] 'When your lordship was last here you bade me not mistrust the king or you, which gave me great comfort, and encourages me to show my poor mind.' Her 'poor mind' was burdened with a sense of responsibility. Now that Elizabeth was 'put from that degree she was in', she had no idea how to order her, or the grooms, or herself. Nobody had given her any instructions, and she only knew about the changes by hearsay. 'Mr Shelton says he is master of this house', but she had no idea what sort of a house it was to be, or how it was to be ordered. As Shelton had been steward since the creation of the household, this protest sounds a little disingenuous, and Margaret's real grievance was probably that she had not been consulted over the new arrangement, as she thought that her status required. She had also fallen out with Shelton about Elizabeth's eating arrangements. According to her story, he wanted the child to 'dine and sup every day at the board of estate', a regime which she considered quite unsuitable for a child not yet three. 'If she do, I dare not take it upon me to keep her grace in health', because of the unsuitable food which she would be forced to consume. Shelton clearly believed that the extra cost of providing special meals and service was unjustified, but on this point he was defeated, because on 16 August he also wrote to Cromwell, acknowledging the king's instruction that the child should 'keep her chamber'.[76] He did not, however miss the opportunity to point out that £4000 a year would be 'little enough', if such extravagance was encouraged. It was his job to keep the books balanced, but it was Margaret's job to ensure that Elizabeth was 'well seen'. 'I beg you to be a good lord to her and hers', her letter went on, 'and that she may have raiment.' She had neither gown, nor kirtle nor petticoat, and no linen for smocks, or sleeves or kerchieves. What had happened, one is bound to wonder, to the three pairs of sleeves, the kirtles of yellow satin and tawny velvet, the orange velvet gown and the black partlet, for which William Lok had billed her mother no longer ago than the end of April?[77] They could hardly have been outworn or outgrown in four months. Unless they had never been delivered, it looks as though Margaret Bryan was improving her tale.

Elizabeth was teething, and this was causing her much pain and misery. 'I trust to God and her teeth were well graft to leave her grace after another fashion than she is yet', Margaret added piously, 'For she is as toward a child and as gentle of condition as any I saw in my life, Jesu preserve her grace'. Her affection for her charge was genuine, but somewhat thoughtlessly expressed. She won her battle with Shelton, but Elizabeth was no longer 'her grace', and Margaret Bryan's enthusiasm could become an embarrassment. How much longer she continued in post after this outburst is not clear, but she does not feature again in the surviving documents, until she was appointed in the following year to a similar custody of Prince Edward. Although she had also looked after Mary as a child, her affection seems to have transferred to the younger girl. It was to be transferred again to her new charge in due course. Mary, who was now in good favour with her father, would not have looked kindly upon such a painful reminder of the situation which she had now happily escaped. Whatever she may have felt about her half sister previously, by August 1536 she had no particular cause to resent her; they were both in the same situation, and she had a long advantage of years. Shortly before Margaret Bryan launched her jeremiad, Mary had written to her father that 'My sister Elizabeth is well, and such a child toward, as I doubt not but your highness shall have cause to rejoice of in time coming'.[78] Whether her words were inspired by any genuine affection or not, the experiences of the summer had taught her to talk carefully, and to say the right thing when required. In spite of all that she had said about Anne Boleyn in the past, and in spite of the opportunities created by her fall, at this time Mary made no attempt to deny her kinship with her half-sister.

3

The King's Daughter

One of the young women who entered Elizabeth's life during the changes of the summer of 1536 was to exercise a profound influence over her for nearly thirty years. This was Catherine Champernowne, better known by her married name as Kate (or Kat) Ashley. On 10 October Catherine wrote to Thomas Cromwell, thanking him for promoting her to her position. It is clear that she belonged to that circle of educated humanist gentry whom the secretary was introducing to the court. Her father was a scholar with antiquarian interests, who debated family history with John Leland, and in 1538 her sister Joan, who also seems to have been something of a scholar, married Anthony Denny, a member of the privy chamber and soon to be its principal gentleman.[1] Catherine's position seems at first to have been honorary, because in the same letter she asked Cromwell to prompt the king to give her 'some yearly stipend', without which she felt unable to serve to the king's honour. She was, she declared, loth to charge her father, 'who has much to do with the little living that he hath.' Not much is known about Sir Philip's circumstances, but he had a reasonable estate in Devon, and it may have been a desire for independence rather than genuine need which prompted Catherine's request. For the time being she was simply one of Elizabeth's gentlewomen, and it was not until Margaret Bryan assumed responsibility for the new-born Edward in October 1537 that she became lady governess, and began to take her charge's education and training in hand.[2] Many years later, Elizabeth paid tribute to Catherine's 'great labour and pain in bringing me up in learning and honesty'. Catherine should be given the main credit for that precocity, both in scholarship and behaviour, which was to be such a characteristic of the girl as she grew up. The bond between them was deep and lasting; and it seems to have been Catherine more than anybody else who gave Elizabeth the emotional security which she needed in the hazardous world which followed her mother's disgrace and death.[3]

In the period of a little over a year between the reconstitution of the joint household and the birth of Edward on 12 October 1537, not much is known about Elizabeth. Servants of the household are occasionally alluded to, going about their business, or getting into minor trouble; and it seems that the establishment 'below stairs' was treated as a single unit, unlike the chambers, which were distinct. In August 1536 Sir John Shelton was constrained to sue for a new assignment, which was apparently done on an annual basis, and Sir Brian Tuke again appealed to Cromwell not to make it upon the chamber.[4] It seems that his appeal was ignored, because he was still trying to scrape together money for the joint household in the following May.[5] A report sent to Cardinal du Bellay at the end of October, mainly about Mary's restoration to favour, indicated that the infant Elizabeth was still 'keeping her chamber' at meal times, as Cromwell had decreed, although the king was 'very affectionate' towards her.[6] In April 1537, when the pregnancy of the new queen was apparent, and hopes for a secure succession were again rising, the council addressed itself to the question of the king's natural daughters, and how they could best be made to serve the king's honour. 'The king has two daughters', ran a memorandum of business,

> not lawful but the king's daughters, and as princes commonly contract amity and things of importance by alliance, it is thought necessary that these two daughters shall be made of some estimation, without which no man will have any great respect to them.[7]

The author was mainly concerned with Mary, who at twenty-one was fully ripe for marriage, and recommended that the king should 'advance her to some certain living, decent for such an estate', without which no foreign prince was likely to be interested. Mary already had a personal allowance of some £450 a year, paid not out of the chamber but out of the privy purse, but that was not the kind of 'estimation' which the writer had in mind.[8] The idea was to use Mary for Henry to 'provide himself of a present friend', of which he always had need; and then to set up Elizabeth in a similar manner 'hereafter to get another friend'. The matter was debated in council on 3 April, but no action was taken.[9] Whether Henry was unconvinced by the arguments, or uncertain what sort of status to give his daughters, is not known. Perhaps he was waiting to see whether Jane was carrying a son or another daughter before he made up his mind. There was no question of either of the girls being out of favour. In terms of the king's domestic circumstances, the year 1536–7 was one of the happiest and most relaxed of the reign. A rebellion, the Pilgrimage of Grace, made sure that it was not politically relaxed, but because she behaved sensibly even the fact that some of the rebels used Mary's name did not damage her restored favour.[10] This harmony was largely due to the new queen. Although both her brothers were political figures of significance, she was not. She had no ideological agenda, and led no party. Henry obviously found her attractive, but her sexuality, like everything else about her, was subdued. When the king began to pay attention to her, before Anne's disgrace, she had responded with self-conscious rectitude; and where Anne's professions of chastity had been mocked, hers were taken seriously. Apart from Catherine of Aragon, she was the most conspicuously virtuous of all Henry's queens, and seems also to have been the most amiable. The king married her in almost indecent haste, and took the odd precaution of getting Cranmer to issue a dispensation from the third degree of affinity. There was a remote kinship, going back six generations to Lionel, duke of Clarence, but they were nothing like as close as second cousins, so the need for this dispensation remains mysterious.[11] Perhaps Henry had taken one of Jane's cousins as an unrecorded mistress.

The new queen is not known to have had any enemies, but that was partly because her political influence was insignificant. Shortly after her marriage, she had begged the king to take Mary back into favour, probably in response to the clamour from her supporters, and apparently unaware of what a minefield she was traversing. Henry made uxorious noises and ignored her request; he had no appetite for more political pillow talk.[12] This rebuff, if such it was, left the queen unruffled, and Mary's submission soon gave her the chance to play the peacemaker more effectively. Chapuys was delighted, and ignored the fact that her affection extended equally to Elizabeth. The queen's association with the fall of the Boleyns made her an ally in the eyes of the imperialists, and even Reginald Pole, who was soon to be Henry's arch enemy, wrote from Italy expressing his pleasure 'that in place of her of whom descended all disorders, God hath given you one full of goodness'.[13] The one thing that Jane's friendship did do for Mary was to quieten her officious conscience, and persuade her to accept her new situation with a good grace. In September 1536 both the king and Cromwell sent her small gifts, and in October it was noted that Madame Marie was second at court after the queen.

None of this directly touched Elizabeth, because she was too young to respond in the way her sister did; to her Jane was a surrogate mother rather than a sister. We do not know how often Jane visited the child, or caused her to be brought to court, but it is clear that she was well cared for; and Mary's frequent absences at court may have benefited her in terms of attention. In spite of their illegitimacy, both Mary and Elizabeth were accorded precedence over their legitimate cousins, Frances and Eleanor Brandon, the daughters of Henry's sister Mary and Charles Brandon, duke of Suffolk: a clear sign of the direction in which the king's mind was moving.[14] Meanwhile, Jane's star continued to rise. In spite of her popularity, no good Catholic could recognise her marriage to Henry as lawful, because the realm was in schism. Catherine's death had rendered the papal sentence of 1533 inoperative, but Henry had indicated no willingness to surrender his ecclesiastical supremacy, and so his excommunication still stood. In spite of this, he referred to Jane openly as his first 'true wife', and provided for her lavishly, with a jointure of over a hundred manors in nineteen counties, producing an income well in excess of £3000 a year.[15]

By February 1537 matrimonial tranquillity was duly rewarded, and Jane was known to be pregnant. Henry had intended a lavish coronation for her, possibly to make up for the fact that she was of relatively humble birth, but there was not the same need as in 1533, and in view of her condition the plan was quietly dropped. In May and June, while the execution of the leaders of the Pilgrimage reassured the king of his political security, the untroubled advance of the queen's pregnancy was equally comforting. At the end of June it was announced that the child had 'quickened'; *Te Deum* was sung in St Pauls, and bonfires were lit all over London. Fervent prayers for a prince began to appear in public worship, and the university of Oxford sent a loyal address, congratulating the king on three achievements. He had rescued his realm from the tyranny of the bishop of Rome; he had defeated the traitors in the north, and 'our most excellent lady and mistress Queen Jane is great with child'.[16]

In spite of all this, Henry was anxious. On 12 June he cancelled a progress which he had been planning to the north, to consolidate his victory over the rebels. The council had advised him not to leave the queen too long alone, and he may have welcomed this excuse not to embark upon an arduous journey. He may also have remembered that Anne had blamed her miscarriage eighteen months earlier on anxiety for his safety. Bearing in mind the late queen's reputation for imperiousness, Henry was quick to reassure the duke of Norfolk, whose activities would have been adversely affected by his decision, that Jane had not pressed him to remain, but rather 'that she can in all things well content, satisfy and quiet herself with that thing which we shall think expedient and determine'.[17] Astrologers were again forecasting a prince, as they had done before; but if that put any pressure on the queen she gave no recorded sign of it. She retreated into the customary seclusion at Hampton Court at the end of September, and went into labour on 9 October. After an easy pregnancy, the birth was hard, and anxious intercessions were offered as the child obstinately refused to appear. It took two days and three nights, and left Jane exhausted; but on the eve of the translation of Edward the Confessor, 12 October, the long expected prince finally appeared. Then 'was great fires made through the whole realme and great love made with thankes gevyng to almightie God whiche hath sent so noble a prince to succeed to the croune of this Realme'.[18]

The child was healthy and perfect, and was christened at Hampton Court on 15 October with a magnificence not seen since the baptism of the ill-fated Prince Henry in January 1511. He was named, it would seem, partly for his paternal great grandfather, Edward IV, and partly for the proximate saint. His godfathers were the archbishop of Canterbury and the duke of Norfolk, and his godmother the Lady Mary; the duke of Suffolk was his godfather 'to the bishop'. This was not only an event of immense political significance, it also symbolised the unity of the royal family after so many divisive traumas. Elizabeth, just turned four, was too young to be a godmother; and in any case only one was needed for a boy. Instead she was given the almost equally important role of bearing the chrisom cloth, which was wrapped around the infant's head to prevent the escape of any of the holy oil.[19] For most of the ceremony she was herself carried in the arms of Edward Seymour, Viscount Beauchamp, the queen's brother. Decorum would have required her to attend the baptismal feast, but her attendants probably removed her before the unaccustomed diet could do any harm. The only shadow over the proceedings was an outbreak of plague in the vicinity, which limited the attendance of servants and hangers on; so there was probably no torchlight procession such as that which had followed the christening of Elizabeth herself. Jane was well enough to sit in the antechamber to the chapel during the ceremony, and to receive the congratulations of the company afterwards.

The queen, however, did not survive her triumph long. After appearing to recover well, by 18 October she had become seriously ill; by the 23rd she was delirious, and late on the 24th she died. Henry was devastated. As the chronicler recorded:

> of none in the Realme was it more heavelier taken than of the kynges Maiestie him self, whose death caused the kyng imediately to remove into Westminster, wher he mourned and kept himself close and secret a great while.[20]

Jane was buried at Windsor on 12 November. By custom Henry did not himself attend, and Mary was the chief mourner, whose grief was almost as profound and genuine as that of her father. It is unlikely that Elizabeth was present; it would hardly have been a suitable occasion for a child, and there was no symbolic point to be made. As with the loss of her own mother, we have no idea what effect Jane's death had upon her; she was a year and a half older, but still very young.

The court spent the Christmas of 1537 in mourning, and it was not until 2 February that the king declared the public grief ended. Meanwhile Jane's personal jewellery had been carefully inventoried, and a fair proportion of it distributed among her ladies and female friends.[21] The queen's death had been unexpected, and she had left no will, so this was probably done on the king's orders. Both Mary and Elizabeth received a number of items, but none of their servants. The new year gift list from 1538 does not survive, but there is a note to the effect that Elizabeth received a gold brooch at that time, in common with a number of other ladies of the court. Mary's servants received 53s. 4d. between them by way of reward, and Catherine Champernowne the sum of 10 shillings, perhaps in recognition of her growing importance.[22]

Even before the period of mourning was over, his council were pressing Henry to marry again. There was now a male heir, but life was uncertain and the king at forty-seven was well advanced in middle age; the realm would benefit greatly from the birth of a duke of York. Strongly urged by Thomas Cromwell, the king began to look around for a diplomatic marriage, to 'win him friends' as the council advice of the previous year had put it. By the middle of February the French ambassador was reporting to Francis I in some alarm, that an elaborate plan for multiple Anglo-Habsburg marriages was under consideration. The king himself was thought to favour either the infanta of Portugal or the emperor's niece, the widowed duchess of Milan; at the same time there were proposals for Edward to wed 'the Emperor's daughter' (either Mary or Joanna), to match Mary with Dom Luis of Portugal, and Elizabeth with 'the son of the King of Hungary' (Maximilian).[23] The existence of part, at least, of this scheme is confirmed by Henry's own correspondence with Sir Thomas Wyatt, then his resident with Charles V. Another possibility mentioned for Elizabeth was the young duke of Savoy. On 2 March Chapuys reflected the new climate of Anglo-imperial relations by reporting to Mary of Hungary that he had been to see 'Madame Isabelle' (no longer 'the little bastard'), probably at Hatfield.[24]

Nothing came of these negotiations, and the truce of Nice later in the year between Francis and Charles alarmed Henry with the prospect of complete diplomatic isolation. He feared a Franco-imperial crusade, and Cromwell began that search among the Lutheran and non-aligned princes of Germany which was to result in the Cleves marriage. As early as June 1538 Chapuys believed that there would be a double marriage with the duchy, involving both Henry and Mary.[25] The treaty of Toledo in January 1539 between the king of France and the emperor appeared to confirm Henry's worst fears; the pope rejoiced, and the king began a frantic pro-gramme of fortress building on the south coast. It was a false alarm; all the warlike preparations were in England, and by May it was being reported in Rome that the Anglo-Habsburg negotiations were on again.[26] That was not true either, because Cromwell was pursuing a Cleves marriage for Henry with some urgency; but the second proposed match, between the duke's heir William and Mary was not proceeded with. Instead, by December 1539 the latter was being actively pursued by the Lutheran Philip, duke of Bavaria, the heir to the Elector Palatine, who came to England apparently for that specific purpose. Because of careful chaperoning, this was the nearest thing to actual courtship which Mary was ever to enjoy. The French ambassador, Marillac, reported happily that not only had they met, but that the duke had even ventured to kiss her 'which is an argument either of marriage or near relationship'.[27] Mary was unenthusiastic; however much she may have wanted to marry, she did not want a Lutheran. She professed herself willing to do her father's bidding, and Marillac believed that an agreement had been sealed; but, like many such negotiations, this one also came to nothing. By this time Elizabeth had dropped out of consideration entirely, and the only result of over two years of hectic matrimonial diplomacy was the short-lived union between Henry and Anne of Cleves, which took place in January 1540.[28]

For the first six months or so of his life, Edward appears to have been cared for on an *ad hoc* basis by Lady Margaret Bryan and her assistants; sometimes at court, sometimes elsewhere in the vicinity, particularly at Havering in Essex, a house which had formed part of his mother's jointure. This did not argue any lack of interest on the king's part; indeed his concern for his son's health and well being was almost obsessive. A suitable establishment required thought, and Henry was not only distracted at first by the death of Jane, he was also mindful of the fate of his first-born son twenty-seven years earlier. It was not until March 1538, a month after the end of court mourning, that a new establishment was created for the prince.[29] Sir William Sidney was appointed chamberlain, Sir John Cornwallis steward and Richard Cox (later Edward's tutor) almoner; Lady Bryan continued in charge of the vital nursery, and the suitably princely sum of £6500 per annum was allocated for the expenses of the new household.[30] This large establishment was normally settled at Hampton Court, where extensive improvements were made to 'the prince's lodgings'; but Edward himself and his immediate attendants went wherever the king's whim might dictate. In May 1538, for example, Henry took him to his hunting lodge at Royston in Hertfordshire where 'with much mirth and joy' he is reported to have cradled him in his arms 'a long space', and to have held him up at a window, to the great gratification of the crowds assembled outside.[31]

From 1538 until August 1543 there were two households for the royal children, costing between them over £10,000 a year. As no accounts survive from this period, our knowledge of their personnel and organisation is scrappy. Mary was no longer a child, and increasingly went her own way, but her servants continued to be paid by the king through the joint

household. Shelton appears to have continued as steward until the reorganisation which followed the king's last marriage; but the chamber
structure is obscure. Mary had her own gentlewomen, and their names
are known, but apart from Kate Champernowne we do not know who
served Elizabeth at this time. We do know, however, that positions in her
chamber, like any other posts connected with the court, were much sought
after. In June 1539 John Hussee reported regretfully to Lady Lisle that her
ambition to place her daughter Mary Basset in Elizabeth's household was
unlikely to be realised, as 'one or two gentlewomen of older years have
applied, and the king answered that he would have none so young'.[32]
Unfortunately we have no names for these mature ladies. In April 1539
Cromwell revoked one 'Lady Kingston' from what must have been a
senior position in the household.[33] This was Mary, the wife of Sir William
Kingston, the controller of the royal household, but we do not know what
title of appointment she held. At the same time Sir Edward Baynton and
his wife were appointed, probably as vice-chamberlain and governess,
but we do not know how long they served, or what effect their appointments had on Kate Champernowne's position. Edward's steward, Sir John
Cornwallis, died at Ashridge in 1541, but the remainder of the prince's
household appears to have continued unchanged until 1544.[34] The new
arrangements of August 1543 were therefore essentially practical. Mary
had spent most of her time at court during her father's marriage to
Catherine Howard (1540–41), by his wish rather than hers as she did not
like the new queen. After Catherine's arrest she had been sent away for a
while while Henry nursed his battered ego.[35] However, when he married
Catherine Parr in July 1543 she was not only recalled but 'retained to be of
the Queen's side'. This meant that Mary's chamber staff became part
of the main court, and the joint household was dissolved. Rather than
maintain a separate establishment for Elizabeth, the king then decided, as
Chapuys reported, that she should be 'sent to be with the Prince his son'.[36]
This does not seem to have coincided with any major restructuring of
Edward's household, so probably the Bayntons' appointments came to an
end at that point, and Elizabeth's chamber was absorbed at Hatfield in the
same way that Mary's was at court. As Henry was by that time at war on
two fronts, and very short of money, this would have appealed to him as
an economy measure, if for no other reason. Elizabeth was almost ten and
Edward almost six. Serious thought had now got to be given to the training
of the heir to the throne; and this merger consequently spelled an opportunity which was to transform a bright and precocious little girl into one
of the best educated young women of the age.

A number of tributes survive to the young Elizabeth's talents. On 1 January

1539, when she was rising five and half, she presented to her infant brother as a New Year gift 'a shirt of cambric of her own making'.[37] Kate Champernowne's sister Joan had married Anthony Denny at some time in 1538, and that union had brought the Champernowne sisters into contact with Anthony's university friends, particularly John Cheke, and Cheke's favourite pupil, Roger Ascham. Ascham was quick to appreciate Kate Champernowne's abilities as a teacher, but advised her rather pompously not to push her young charge too hard.[38] Kate knew Elizabeth better than he did and ignored his advice, with excellent results. When Thomas Wriothesley reported to Cromwell after a visit to her in December of the same year, he wrote that she had responded to the king's message of greeting 'with as great gravity as if she had been forty years old'. 'If she were no more educated than she appears', he went on enthusiastically, 'she will be an honour to all woman-hood'.[39] A few weeks later she gave Edward 'a braser of needlework of her own making'; she was a year on from cambric shirts. The real change, however, did not come until Henry decided to go campaigning in France in July 1544. In making the arrangements for routine government during his absence, he took the opportunity to reshape his son's establishment. Sir Richard Page was appointed chamberlain, Sidney becoming steward; and most of the nursery staff were pensioned off.[40] Edward now emerged from 'among the women', and had his own establishment of privy chamber gentlemen, headed by Sir Jasper Horsey. Richard Cox, who had been his tutor since 1540, was now joined by John Cheke, the regius professor of Greek from Cambridge; and his serious training in the classical languages began just as he passed his seventh birthday. A schoolroom was set up for the young prince, so that he would not have to endure his lessons in solitude, and boys of about his age, such as Henry Brandon (the son of the duke of Suffolk), Robert Dudley (the son of Viscount Lisle) and Barnaby Fitzpatrick were recruited to join him.[41] Exactly how Elizabeth benefited from this injection of academic talent and endeavour is not clear, but she certainly did. Her first tutor was William Grindal, a pupil and friend of Ascham's, which suggests that she was taught separately, as would become a somewhat older child. However, neither Grindal nor Cheke believed that it was necessary to segregate boys and girls, when both were doing the same thing. There are hints, which are not quite certainties, that Jane Grey, the eldest daughter of the marquis of Dorset, who was the same age as Edward, also shared his lessons; so it is likely that for some purposes Elizabeth and her brother were taught together.[42]

Grindal may have been starting from scratch on instruction in Latin and Greek, but the quality of the foundation which Kate Chapernowne had laid is apparent from two letters which Elizabeth wrote during 1544. The first

is in Italian and written in an immaculate italic hand. It is addressed to
the queen (Catherine Parr), and dated 31 July. It begins

> Inimical Fortune, envious of all good, she who revolves things human, has de-
> prived me for a whole year of your most illustrious presence, and still not being
> content with that, has robbed me once again of the same good: the which would
> be intolerable to me if I did not think to enjoy it soon.[43]

The extreme formality of this epistle to her stepmother (and the language;
there is no evidence that Catherine could read Italian) indicates a schoolroom
exercise, written under the supervision of her tutor. It also calls in question
Catherine's reputation as a motherly reconciler of the royal family. At the
time when it was written the queen was at Hampton Court as regent, Henry
being then in France, and Elizabeth at St James's. It is now recognised that
Catherine was not responsible for the educational provision made for either
of the royal children, but it also seems clear that, however close they may
have become by the end of the reign, there was no intimacy at this
stage.[44] Beneath the ornate language, there is a sense of neglect. In 1544
Catherine was much closer to Mary; perhaps she did not know quite how
to deal with a very bright and self-possessed eleven year old. The second
letter (in English) was written at Ashridge on 31 December, also addressed
to Catherine. This is similarly extremely formal, and nothing can be gleaned
from it about the real nature of their relationship. It was written to accompany a New Year gift; no longer a piece of needlework but a translation
into English of Marguerite of Angoulême's *Miroir de l'âme péchereuse*, which
had been published in French in 1531.[45] The covering letter is full of self-
deprecation, and worthy remarks about the spiritual value of academic
diligence. It is also addressed to the queen's 'fervent zeal' towards 'all Godly
learning', which may have been slightly tongue-in-cheek because in truth
for all her zeal Catherine was a mere beginner as a scholar, no more advanced
than Elizabeth herself. This translation was a considerable achievement for
an eleven year old, and Catherine was sufficiently impressed to make some
additions and amendments of her own before passing the manuscript to
the ex-Carmelite reformer John Bale, who eventually published it in
1548.[46] It may well have been the evidence of this work which began to draw
Elizabeth and Catherine together. They were drawing their education from
the same pool of reforming humanist talent, and forming similar religious
views, which were eventually to emerge as explicitly Protestant.

That, however, lay in the future. During 1539 Elizabeth hardly appeared
in the public records at all. During November Thomas Cromwell debated
with himself, and no doubt others, whether it would be appropriate for
Mary and Elizabeth to attend the reception of Anne of Cleves; in the event,

they both did, and were suitably decked out for the occasion.[47] In December, as we have seen, Elizabeth made a favourable impression on Thomas Wriothesley. Early in 1540, when the king was coming to terms with the failure of his fourth marriage, his thoughts naturally turned again to the succession. Edward was a strong child, but as one of the queen's ladies somewhat snidely observed, under present circumstances there was little prospect of a duke of York. Cromwell began to inject into his correspondence with ambassadors abroad some mild hints that the king was considering his options. To Sir Ralph Sadler in Scotland there was a slight suggestion that the king of Scots himself might be included, if he behaved himself; to Sir John Wallop in France the more obvious thought that the king's daughters would have to be considered.[48] The broader the hints in that direction, the more valuable they would become on the marriage market. In this connection Duke Philip had been an unrewarding prospect, which was probably why his suit had come to nothing. If Henry was again fishing in the big pool, it was October 1540 before there was any hint of a response. By then the temporary amity between Francis and Charles, which had so alarmed the king in the previous year, had clearly evaporated.[49] The queen of Navarre (Francis's sister, and the author of the *Miroir*) asked for portraits of all Henry's children; a request which she pressed again in December.[50] On the 2 June 1541 Francis instructed Marillac to return again to the question of an English marriage for the duke of Orleans. His letter refers only to 'a daughter who is held legitimate'; and, as this was not true of either Mary or Elizabeth, it is not clear which of them he was interested in.[51] In August, however, Marillac reported that he had discussed this proposal with the duke of Norfolk. The duke was at this point in high favour, having successfully disposed of Thomas Cromwell in 1540, and engineered the king's fifth marriage, to his niece Catherine Howard. He advised Marillac to go for Mary, who was a more suitable age, and who (in his opinion at least) was closer to being legitimate. Norfolk then elaborated at some length on the disadvantages of any union with a daughter of Anne Boleyn, pointing out fairly enough that, if both remained technically bastards, the elder was always to be preferred.[52] There was then a silence of several months. We do not know whether the matter was discussed with the king or not. By the time that it surfaced again in a privy council minute of 3 March 1542, the queen's fatal indiscretions had consigned Norfolk to the political wilderness, and Henry's mood had become decidedly morose. Correspondence with Sir William Paget, then in Paris, refers to a negotiation for Elizabeth's hand in some detail, including financial provision, but refers in the past tense, as though the issue was by then dead, which was probably the case.[53] In June 1542 Henry moved decisively in the direction of a new imperial alliance, and became increasingly hostile to both the French and the Scots. After James had failed to honour an agreement to meet Henry at York during the progress of 1541, there were no more hints of his inclusion in the succession; and in September English commissioners presented the Scots with a set of demands which were intentionally provocative.[54]

Between 1540 and 1542 we can catch only glimpses of Elizabeth going about her daily life. In May 1541 she used the queen's barge to go from Suffolk Place to Chelsea, at a cost of 16d. In December 1540 her servants received a Christmas gratuity of 20 shillings; and in November 1541 she received a few trinkets from the jewels of the recently disgraced Catherine Howard.[55] However, on 8 July 1542, at the same time as Henry sent Thomas Thirlby to the emperor, Chapuys in London reported a new initiative for the hand of Elizabeth; this time the proposed groom was the prince of Piedmont, and the ambassador frankly conceded that the girl's illegitimacy would be ignored if the marriage 'would set the king more strongly against the French'.[56]

At the same time Paget reported a rumour in France that the widowed emperor himself would marry Mary, and 'a son of King Ferdinand' would take Elizabeth. There appears to have been no foundation for this. Having got his imperial alliance, Henry did not pursue any matrimonial negotiation purposefully. Instead, he began to deploy his younger daughter in discussions with Scotland. There his heavy-handedness had eventually had the desired effect, provoking James into launching an invasion at the end of November 1542. If Henry had calculated the outcome, he could hardly have judged it better. The Scots were heavily defeated at Solway Moss, and many of their nobles were captured; James, already a sick man, died soon after, leaving his throne to a week-old daughter, Mary.[57] The earl of Arran became governor, and Henry set out to exploit his advantage by proposing a marriage between the new-born Scottish queen and Prince Edward, by then aged five. Arran was in a difficult dilemma, because he knew that such a union would be ill-received in Scotland, but he was in no position to resist English pressure. In order to settle his mind, in April 1543 the English ambassador Sadler was instructed to offer the earl a marriage between his young son (then aged about four) and the king's younger daughter, in return for his agreement to the main proposal.[58] On 6 May two of the Scots lords taken at Solway Moss, the earl of Glencairn and Sir George Douglas were given credence by Henry and sent home to negotiate for Elizabeth's hand. In August the king even offered to make Arran 'King of Scotland beyond the Forth' in return for the two proposed marriages.[59] The earl warmly expressed his appreciation of the honour done him, but confessed that he was unable to accomplish either. Henry eventually secured the treaty of Greenwich,

agreeing to the match between Edward and Mary; but of Elizabeth's union
we hear no more. Neither marriage took place.

Other proposals were made in a desultory fashion over the next four
years. In October 1544, after Henry had returned from the successful siege
of Boulogne, the council at Calais reminded him that Granvelle, the emperor's chief minister, had raised again the question of Elizabeth's marriage
while they were still celebrating the fall of the town.[60] The rupture in
Anglo-imperial relations which followed the truce of Crespy in September
ensured that no further action was taken in that direction. Henry's bitterness
against Charles, and the continuing war against France, meant that the
king was again reduced to fishing for allies. In January 1545 he sent agents
to the Lutheran Duke Maurice of Saxony, effectively inviting bids for both
his daughters, but nothing came of the initiative.[61] Three months later the
same agents had moved on to Denmark. Christian III apparently favoured
a deal, but pointed out that both his brothers, who were being solicited,
were grown men and would have to answer for themselves. It appears that
neither was keen, and Francis I was later told that 'the Englishman was
dismissed with good words'.[62] By October Henry had either overcome his
chagrin or was facing up to the failure of his alternative policies because
the Habsburg negotiation was back on the agenda. By then England had
fended off the threat from France, and an end to the war seemed to be
in sight; on the other hand, in Scotland the treaty of Greenwich remained
a dead letter, and the earl of Arran had joined the pro-French party, to
Henry's disgust.[63] On 23 October two commissions were issued to treat
with the emperor. The first, to Stephen Gardiner, Thomas Thirlby and
Edward Carne, was for general amity; and the second, to Gardiner and
Thirlby alone, for an ambitious package of marriages. The first of these
was a revival of the earlier project for union between Mary (now twenty-
nine) and Charles himself (forty-five); the second between Charles's
daughter Mary and Edward; and the third between Prince Philip (eighteen)
and Elizabeth (twelve).[64] The ages of the parties were reasonably compatible,
but it is doubtful whether Henry seriously expected any of this to come
about. At one point he instructed his commissioners that the marriage 'of
my lord prince is to be most advanced'; but it seems likely that the main
objective was to alarm the French into concluding peace on favourable
terms. In that it succeeded. By December Francis was getting twitchy,
and on 6 June following the treaty of Camp was concluded, whereby
Henry retained both Boulogne and his freedom of action in Scotland.[65]
Consequently both Mary and Elizabeth reached the end of their father's
reign unwed and uncommitted. Whereas the former was deeply chagrined
and frustrated by this, the latter was probably young enough to remain

indifferent. If she had any views about her use as a conventional diplomatic pawn, she kept them to herself.

Elizabeth was, however, firmly established in the line of succession. After long thought, and some discussion, Henry had secured another Succession Act in the summer of 1543. Edward was, as everybody knew, his heir; and after him any child lawfully begotten between the king and his present wife (Catherine Parr); failing such a child, or any child lawfully begotten by Edward, the crown was next to pass to Mary and her lawful heirs; and then to Elizabeth and her lawful heirs.[66] By this statute, consequently, both of Henry's illegitimate daughters (who remained illegitimate) were preferred before the legitimate line of Scotland (represented by Mary Stuart) and the equally legitimate descendants of the king's younger sister, Mary (Frances and Eleanor Brandon). This peculiar demonstration of the power of statute also authorised the king to confirm or alter these provisions by the terms of his last will. When the time came, he confirmed them. The Act has to be seen against the background of war, the unsatisfactory nature of the situation in Scotland, and the king's desire to enhance his daughters in the marriage market. It is highly unlikely that he, or anyone else, expected it to be his last word on the succession question. Henry fathered no more children, however, and Edward died without reaching his majority. Although Mary did not admit it, the success of her claim in 1553 was to depend upon this statute; and Elizabeth was to be acutely aware for the whole of her long life that the legitimacy of her position rested upon secular law, not upon any ruling of the church.[67]

As she passed from childhood to adolescence, Elizabeth's life was focused, not upon these somewhat unreal negotiations, which scarcely touched her, but upon her education and her personal servants. Her chief mentor and friend, Kate Champernowne, married at some time in 1544 or 1545. This must have been a notable occasion in the small household, but unfortunately it has left no record. Her groom was John Ashley (or Astley), the eldest son of Thomas Ashley of Melton Constable, Norfolk.[68] His mother was distant kin to the Boleyns, and it may have been that connection which first brought him to the court. John had been born in about 1507, and is alleged to have been in the royal service from the age of twelve, although the first record of him is as a gentleman waiter to Prince Edward in 1543. It was probably this appointment which first brought him into contact with Kate, as the two households were merged at about the same time. John was a friend of Roger Ascham and a man of culture and scholarship, which suggests at least a short period of residence in Cambridge, although the university records contain no trace of him. What is clear is that he fitted comfortably into the intelligent humanist atmosphere of the 'junior royals', a group composed of Kate Champernowne herself, Roger Ascham, William Grindal, Richard Cox, John Cheke and Jacques Belmain, the prince's French tutor. There is no suggestion that John Ashley was involved in any way with Elizabeth's education, a function for which he was unqualified, or even that he had much direct contact with her at this stage; but the impression of a cohesive group of like-minded men and women is very strong. Although Grindal was officially her tutor, we know that Kate went on teaching her, particularly the exquisite handwriting which was already evident by 1544 and which was to be one of her trademarks in later life. Ascham also taught her, and so did Jacques Belmain, although it is not clear who was responsible for her early mastery of Italian.[69] Following what had become her custom, on 30 December 1545 she sent an example of her work to Queen Catherine as a New Year gift. This time it was a translation into English of the first chapter of John Calvin's *Institution de la réligion Chrestienne*, which had been published in Geneva in 1541.[70] The covering letter, florid and formal as usual, was in French. This time she also plucked up the courage to send a similar gift to her father: no less than a translation into Latin of Catherine's own 'Prayers and Meditations'! The covering letter, also in Latin, is her only known writing to the king.[71]

In case he should think that she was losing touch with womanly accomplishments, she also embroidered an elaborate cover for the manuscript. It is probable, but not certain, that in preparing this gift Elizabeth also used the source upon which Catherine herself had drawn, Richard Whitford's translation of the third book of Thomas à Kempis's *Imitatio Christi*, which had been published in about 1530.[72] By this time she was three months past her twelfth birthday. It is not surprising that everyone who came in contact with her was impressed by her intellectual accomplishments. Her choice of material is also significant. That may have been dictated by one or other of her tutors, but it is also indicative of the learned and pious climate in which she was growing up. If Elizabeth ever indulged in the kind of rebellious tantrums to which Mary had been prone, particularly between 1533 and 1536, we have no record (or even hint) of them. The impression is always that of a young lady who had herself very much under control.

Both Mary and Elizabeth were members of that select group who witnessed their father's final wedding in July 1543, having been introduced to the new queen at court in the previous month.[73] This time there had been no hasty rush to the altar, and the former Lady Latimer had been given plenty of time to assess the magnitude of the task which she was undertaking. Mary was based at court soon after, and although she continued to move independently, her attendance there was frequent, but often unremarked. Elizabeth and Edward moved around, now at Hampton Court, now at

Ashridge, now at Hertford; usually together but sometimes separately. Neither seems to have seen very much of their father or stepmother. In June 1544 their presence at court was especially noted in the formal arrange- ments for a royal banquet, but Catherine seems not to have been present on that occasion.[74] In September the junior household was quarantined, along with the court, because of plague. During the same month, rather mysteriously, payments were made out of the queen's privy purse to a Mr. Cornwallis 'gentleman usher to the Lady Elizabeth' for riding on an errand which appears to have nothing to do with his mistress, and to various gentlemen and grooms for attending upon her.[75] Why Catherine should have made these one-off payments is not clear; perhaps the servants were on loan for some unrecorded purpose, or perhaps the junior household was short of cash – a situation that seems to have arisen from time to time. Towards the end of 1545 another change appears to have taken place in Elizabeth's circumstances. It is not clear whether she was formally withdrawn from the joint arrangement with Edward, or whether she was simply spending more time at court. In November warrants began to be issued from the great wardrobe for 'stuff and apparel for my Lady Elizabeth and her graces women'.[76] The following April she received more 'apparel and necessaries', and then further apparel and 'stuff for saddles'. In November the material for the Christmas celebrations was issued from the same source; and the ordinary of the court for 1546 lists both Mary and Elizabeth among the 'Queen's ordinary accustomed'.[77] When an inventory of the royal wardrobe was taken after Henry's death, in February 1547, the wardrobes of both the king's daughters were included, but not Edward's. By this time she was thirteen, and had obviously parted company with the prince's schoolroom. The effect upon her education was not obvious; both Kate Ashley and William Grindal accompanied her, and Ascham clearly remained in contact. She was now also regularly in touch with the learned circle which Catherine had gathered around herself, and no momentum seems to have been lost. As if to emphasise her departure from him, in December 1546 the young prince wrote twice to his sister.[78] Both were school exercises (he was now nine) but his expressed grief at her going appears genuine enough; they were not only fond of each other, but forming similar opinions under the same influences. She had clearly written to him, and his letters are responses, but her own letters do not survive, so we cannot tell whether she adopted a less formal style when writing to a child. As he thanks her for her 'good exhortation and example', perhaps she was playing the big sister; but, if so, he did not mind. He was as well schooled as she was.

The Christmas of 1546 must have been tense and difficult. In a final burst of energy during December Henry had destroyed his old servant the duke of Norfolk and his son the earl of Surrey on charges of treason which were exaggerated and distorted rather than invented.[79] During the festivities both were in the Tower awaiting execution. After this final effort, the king himself had collapsed, and was dangerously ill. In an effort to maintain a show of normality the usual New Year gifts were exchanged, but the record does not survive; and because Elizabeth was now resident at court, it was no longer necessary to write covering letters. The king died on 28 January, and Edward succeeded without fuss or trouble; so that one of Henry's greatest desires was fulfilled. The emperor expected Mary to challenge Edward's title, but she did no such thing, and in due course he himself accepted the new ruler.[80] In doing so, however, he metaphorically held his nose, because the council which now assumed regency powers was made up of those reformers who had gained the king's ear during the last months of his life, and whom the imperialists did not hesitate to label heretics.

Elizabeth had retired to Enfield after Christmas, and Edward to Hertford. The leader of the regency council, the earl of Hertford, did not immediately announce Henry's decease; not for any sinister reason but simply to enable the necessary arrangements to be made with decorum. On 29 January he rode to Hertford and collected the young prince, but without explaining why. They then proceded to Enfield, where he broke the news to brother and sister together.[81] Tradition has it that they both wept inconsolably, but no contemporary actually says so; both were thoroughly conditioned to control their emotions, and the news can hardly have been a surprise. Edward was then swept off to his coronation, and to the magnificent hazards of a royal minority. For the time being Elizabeth and her servants stayed more or less where they were, in the household of Catherine, now the queen dowager, and apparently a good friend and protector. But it soon transpired that it was Catherine herself who needed protection; and the death of her powerful father exposed Elizabeth to danger from an unexpected quarter.

4

The King's Sister

Henry VIII lay in state at Westminster until 14 February, when his body was conveyed by easy stages to Windsor, where it was interred on the 16th with great solemnity. By custom, none of his immediate family attended this ceremony. Edward was proclaimed over his father's grave, but he was not present, the chief mourner being Henry Grey, marquis of Dorset.[1] Dorset was no blood relation, nor was he one of the handful of powerful men who were busy assuming control of the kingdom; but as the husband of Frances (née Brandon), the late king's niece, he was close enough to justify his selection for this duty. Stephen Gardiner preached on the text 'Beati mortui qui in domino moriuntur'. The widowed queen watched the obsequies from 'the Queen's closet above', an enclosed part of the chapel gallery, but it seems that neither Mary nor Elizabeth was with her; at least no account mentions them.[2] The great wardrobe issued Elizabeth with eleven yards of black velvet 'for the cover of one saddle and one harness', which suggests that she played some part, perhaps in the procession which had escorted the cortège. The whole household was required to go into mourning after so momentous an event, and the same account records the issue of black liveries to no fewer than 205 servants and attendants.[3] The fact that Sir William Sidney appears as steward and John Ryther as cofferer, posts which they also held in the household of Edward as prince, suggests a formal continuation of the joint arrangement after Elizabeth began to be normally resident at court. In fact the appearance of this whole list under Elizabeth's name may be no more than the result of bureaucratic convenience. Those who should properly be identified as her servants numbered only thirty-two, ten ladies and gentlewomen, five gentlemen, eight yeomen, four grooms and five grooms of the stable.[4]

Elizabeth's ladies were theoretically led by Lady Herbert of Troy, but 'Lady Troy' makes no further appearance until she was remembered for a gift in 1552; so her service was probably part time and may have been temporary.[5] Catherine Ashley and Blanche Parry, listed second and third, were her real and favoured companions. Her chaplain was still the otherwise unknown Ralph Taylor, and her 'schoolmaster', as we have seen, was William Grindal. For the time being Elizabeth remained resident with the queen dowager; she was thirteen, and her main occupation was still in study, at which her progress continued to be remarkable. By the terms of her father's will she had been allocated a 'portion' of £3000 a year, with a further sum of £10,000 on her marriage.[6] In early 1547 there was no immediate prospect of the latter, but the former commitment was honoured at once. The council probably intended from the start to cover this with the grant of a landed estate, similar to that which was provided for Mary during the summer of 1547. This did not happen for some time, however, and in the interim the bills continued to be paid on an *ad hoc* basis, rather than by a general assignment on the chamber as had been done a decade earlier. On 6 and 9 April 1547 warrants were directed to Sir Edward Peckham, the treasurer of the mint, to pay £100 and £200 to Richard Sandes, a gentleman of Elizabeth's chamber, who was presumably acting as her cofferer.[7] On 17 April the cofferer of the king's household, was instructed to pay a number of her bills: £39 9s. 7d. to her tailor; £41 5s. 0d. to her embroiderer; £74 13s. 4d. to her robemaker, and two other accounts to a total of about £40. On 15 May £200 was issued from the exchequer, and a further £400 on 24 June. Two months later the treasurer and chamberlains of the exchequer were instructed to pay Elizabeth £600 'for her half year's rent', which suggests that a regular arrangement had been made for what might be termed her 'ordinary' expenses – although how they were defined is not clear.[8] On 1 September a further £200 was issued from the same source 'for provision of horses and other things', presumably not covered by the 'rent'. The last such warrant recorded was for £351 9s. 1d., dated 8 May 1548, for 'my Lady Elizabeth Grace's necessaries for her household and stable'.[9]

Some warrants appear to have been specifically recorded, others not, for reasons that are unclear. At this stage in her career, however, Elizabeth was costing her brother's government £1200 per annum, plus occasional payments of about half as much again. This was well short of the £3000 intended, but then she did not have a fully independent household. At what point she again became independent is not specifically recorded. She left Catherine's household under a cloud in the summer of 1548, as we shall see; and the absence of council warrants suggests that some regular arrangement was made at that point. She went at first to Sir Anthony Denny's house at Cheshunt, and later set up her base at Hatfield, with a household of some 140.[10] The patent for the grant of her landed estate was not dated until 17 March 1550, but the grant had at least been notified by December 1548, and issues were assigned from Michaelmas 1546.[11] Most of what we know about Elizabeth in the first two years of her brother's reign, however, relates not to her housekeeping, nor to any part which she may have played

The Conclusyon.

At all tymes God.is with the iuſt/
Bycauſe they put,in hym their truſt.
Who ſhall therfoꝛ, from Syon geue,
That helthe whych hāgeth,in our beleue?
Whan God ſhall take,frō hys the ſmart,
Than wyll Jacob,reioyce in hart.
Prayſe to God.

Imprented in the yeare of our loꝛds
1548. in Apryll.

Princess Elizabeth as Mary Magdalene, from John Bale's edition of Elizabeth's translation from Marguérite d'Angoulême, *A Godly Medytacyon of the Christen Sowle* (1548).

on the international marriage market, but to a fundamental rite of passage. The discovery of her sexuality.

By adroit political manoeuvring, Edward Seymour, the brother of Henry VIII's third queen and consequently the uncle of the young king, had secured control of the minority government, with the titles of Lord Protector and duke of Somerset. He also constituted himself governor of the king's person, and thereby greatly annoyed his own younger brother, Thomas, who felt that the position should have gone to him, as being no less Edward's uncle. Thomas Seymour, who was the agent of Elizabeth's self-discovery, was a man approaching forty, who had also built a successful diplomatic and military career on the back of his sister's marriage to Henry VIII in 1536, and on the achievements of his rather more talented elder brother. He was already a gentleman of the privy chamber and a councillor before Henry's death, and at the outset of the new reign he became a baron and lord admiral.[12] He was unmarried, but it was generally, and probably correctly, believed that he had been on the point of marrying the widowed Lady Latimer when she had been snatched up by the king in 1543. He was a man of considerable charm, and considerable sexual appeal.

No sooner was Henry buried than he again laid siege to the widowed queen. Whether he really found her attractive, or was drawn by her status and wealth as queen dowager, we do not know, but she found him irresistible. After a passionate and clandestine courtship, they married secretly in the early summer of 1547. This union outraged the Lord Protector; not least because he had been outwitted. Thomas knew perfectly well that he could not marry Catherine without permission, but the question was, whose permission? He should, of course, have applied to the Protector and council, but he knew which way the wind blew in that quarter, and instead went directly to the nine-year-old king. He was the boy's uncle, and well known to him; and by distributing largesse in the privy chamber he was able to come and go more or less as he pleased. The subsequent confession of his main agent, John Fowler, gives a splendid insight into his methods:

> He paused, and asked me if I had communication with the king soon, to ask him if he would be content that he should marry, and if so, whom. I agreed, and that night when the king was alone I said I marvelled that the admiral did not marry. He said nothing. I asked him if he was content he should do so, and he agreed. I asked him whom, and he said Lady Anne of Cleves, and then he said no, but he should marry his sister Mary, to turn her opinions. Next day the admiral came again to St James, and called me to him in the gallery. I told him all the king had said. He laughed and asked me to ask the king if he would be content for him to marry the queen and if he would write in his suit. I agreed and did so that night. Next day the admiral came to the king; I cannot tell what

communication they had, but the king wrote a letter to the queen, and the admiral brought one back from her.[13]

Catherine was obviously a willing accomplice in this plot. Having obtained Edward's explicit approval, they went ahead and married. However much the duke of Somerset might dislike it, he could hardly overrule the king in a matter which was not one of public policy. Somerset had been so busy consolidating his authority over the council that he had taken his eye off the privy chamber, perhaps thinking it of little significance during a minority, and had been circumvented. In August 1547 he appointed his brother-in-law, Sir Michael Stanhope, as chief gentleman; but by then the damage had been done.[14]

Mary left Catherine's household in April 1547, before the queen married but not before Thomas Seymour's amorous presence had become both obvious and embarrassing. She received seisin of her own estate, granted in accordance with the terms of her father's will on about 15 August, and thereafter was an important magnate in her own right.[15] Elizabeth, however, stayed where she was; perhaps by her own wish, but more likely by that of Catherine; and she continued there after the queen remarried. Amid the confused babble of confessions which were uttered eighteen months later, there were allegations that Thomas Seymour had originally intended to marry either Mary or Elizabeth, but had settled for Catherine as being both willing and available. There is, however, no evidence of that from the first part of 1547.

Elizabeth was not without company of approximately her own age, because Thomas Seymour inveigled the marquis of Dorset into sending his eldest daughter, Jane Grey, to live in his household also.[16] Jane was four years younger than Elizabeth, but intellectually precocious, and they may well have shared their lessons, because, of course, Thomas and Catherine had no children of their own. Thomas seems to have persuaded the marquis by claiming that he could arrange a marriage between Jane and her young friend the king. If he made such a claim, it is a sign that his success with Catherine was going to his head. By 1548 he was also becoming paranoid about his brother. This had started with a grumbling discontent that Edward Seymor had become a duke while he had received a mere barony, but he also believed, probably rightly, that Edward VI would have found him more congenial than his brother as governor of his person. There was also a rumbling quarrel over the jewels which Henry had given to Catherine, and which she claimed as her own, but which the Protector had retained on the grounds that they were the property of the crown.[17] For all his charm and plausibility, Thomas Seymour was volatile, and could easily become both

dangerous and irresponsible. It was probably that very combination which
Catherine found so attractive. After two unsatisfactory marriages to elderly
and ailing husbands, she wanted sex, excitement and children. Seymour
certainly provided the first two, and by the early summer of 1548 his wife
was pregnant for the first time. Whether there was any connection between
this development and his relationship with Elizabeth we do not know,
because the chronology of events is not clear. Elizabeth, however, was a very
attractive and perfectly normal adolescent who turned fourteen in September
1547, and Seymour was exactly the kind of man to scatter a girl's wits.

There was a good deal of horseplay of a fairly obvious nature. Thomas
would appear in her room first thing in the morning before she was up,
half dressed and promising to leap into bed with her. He never did so, and
seems to have confined himself to 'giving a greeting' (perhaps a kiss). He
slapped her on the back, and even across the backside.[18] These commonplace
familiarities were observed by the servants, and may well have been innocently intended, but not only was Elizabeth an impressionable young girl,
she was also (in all but name) a royal princess. Such behaviour on Seymour's
part should have been unthinkable. Not only ought her status have made
her untouchable, but he was also her guardian, and she was a guest under
his roof. Far from objecting, however, Elizabeth clearly found this rough
and tumble as enjoyable as it was unsettling.[19] Unlike virtually every other
over-protected princess of the century, she was given some of the rudiments
of a sexual education. One wonders what effect a similar experience might
have had upon the fiercely repressed sexuality of her elder sister. At first,
Catherine saw no harm in all this, and even joined in the fun. On one
occasion she held Elizabeth, who was probably not struggling very hard,
while her husband reduced the girl's dress to shreds.[20] The line between
such romps and serious impropriety was a thin one.

'I do remember', Thomas Parry later admitted,

> that she told me that the Admiral loved her but too well, and had done so a
> good while; and that the Queen was jealous of her and him, in so much that
> one time the Queen suspecting the often access of the Lord Admiral to the Lady
> Elizabeth's grace, came suddenly upon them when they were alone (he having
> her in his arms) wherefore the Queen fell out both with the Lord Admiral and
> with her grace also.[21]

Elizabeth was probably deceiving herself, being too young and inexperienced
to tell the difference between casual lust and real love; but at least she had
the satisfaction of being taken seriously as a rival. She also convinced herself
that, if her father had only lived a little longer, Seymour would have taken
her to wife rather than Catherine. Not surprisingly, soon after this episode

'they parted asunder their families'; probably in June or July 1548. Catherine relinquished her charge with some solemn words to Elizabeth about the dangers of hazarding her reputation; the charges were well founded, and Elizabeth knew it, but she had enjoyed herself a great deal.

As yet she had no house of her own to go to, but it seems that a financial arrangement was cobbled together in anticipation of the estate she was to receive, and when she went to the Dennys' house at Cheshunt she was adequately provided for. As we have seen, Joan Denny was Kate Ashley's sister, so the arrangement was probably a comfortable one. It was at this time that Thomas Parry was appointed as her cofferer. No list survives of Elizabeth's servants after January 1547, and apart from Parry the evidence is scrappy and inconclusive.[22] Rather surprisingly, after a few weeks apart, the friendship between Catherine, now heavily pregnant, and Elizabeth resumed. They clearly liked each other, and as the dust settled the queen dowager was no doubt more willing to blame her husband for what had occurred. In July Elizabeth sent a warm message of good will, in the name of all the household at Cheshunt.[23] Unfortunately, their prayers for a safe delivery were only partly answered. On 30 August Catherine was safely delivered of a healthy girl; but she was taken ill of puerperal fever a few days later, and died on 7 September. It is hard to tell whether Thomas Seymour was more distressed or annoyed by this turn of events, and some of Catherine's friends later blamed him for neglect.[24] He had regarded his wife as a major piece to be moved in the political game which he was now playing in earnest against his brother; and his loss was consequently political as much as personal. Even after her remarriage, Catherine's status had been protected by an estate worth more than £4000 a year. Inevitably, this now came to an end, but Seymour did not dismiss her inflated household. He no longer had the custody of Elizabeth to justify such extravagance, but he did manage to persuade the Greys to return their daughter to his care, after she had been withdrawn in the wake of Elizabeth's departure. This was some sort of an excuse to continue a royal household, but the admiral's real intention seems to have returned to Elizabeth, now fifteen and apparently as infatuated as ever with his dash and charm.

Seymour was now playing a very dangerous game. It had been bad enough to marry the queen dowager behind the backs of the council, and to flirt with the king's sister. But the latter had been in his wife's lifetime; now she was gone, any further relationship with Elizabeth was bound to set him on a collision course with the Protector.[25] Moreover, Somerset was alert to the methods by which Thomas had outflanked him before, and had taken steps to increase his control over the privy chamber. Exactly what the admiral was planning to do is a matter of dispute. He was certainly receiving some at least of the profits of Sir William Sharrington's malpractices at the Bristol mint, and he was alleged to have been using this money to pay and arm his retainers.[26] This may have been so, but he was equally in need of money to maintain the inflated household which he had kept on; and the distinction between servants and retainers may not have been very clear. He was also canvassing support, which was a natural political activity for a man with his ambitions. More tangibly, there is evidence that he was planning an attack on the Protector's position in parliament.[27] Since Somerset's patents of appointment had never received statutory approval, this could be regarded as a shrewd line of attack; much of what we know about Seymour's political activity in the latter part of 1548 supports such an interpretation. He was not particularly discreet in soliciting support, and the Protector was perfectly well aware of what was afoot. If Seymour could have persuaded enough peers and members of the House of Commons to pass an Act annulling Somerset's patents, it would have been perfectly lawful and the Protector would have had no defence.[28] On the other hand, to back such a campaign with a show or threat of force would be treason. At the same time, to marry Elizabeth without the consent of the council, or indeed to take her without marriage, would also have been treason. She may not have been a legitimate princess, but she was a king's daughter and, more importantly, second in line to the throne. Consequently, when Seymour was arrested on 17 January 1549 in order to forestall whatever attack he may have been planning on his brother, it is not surprising that every effort was made to prove him guilty under both heads.

Seymour's intentions towards Elizabeth became the object of intense scrutiny. Sir Robert Tyrwhyt testified, as did his wife, and Kate Ashley and Thomas Parry.[29] The first thing that emerges from these examinations is the closeness of the bond which existed between Elizabeth and Kate Ashley. It was alleged that the latter was fiercely possessive, 'and could abide nobody there but herself', having been given that responsibility, she claimed, by King Henry. She had contrived to get rid of both Lady Troy and Blanche Parry because they appeared to threaten her position; but Elizabeth would hear no ill spoken of her.[30] It also seems that Kate had fallen under the lord admiral's spell no less than her mistress – and with less excuse. As she later confessed, she knew quite a lot about the flirtation which had been going on at Sudeley and elsewhere in the early part of 1548, and had done nothing to discourage it.[31] When she admitted this, it was with tears and pleas for forgiveness, but at the time she may well have felt it was a relatively harmless way for her charge to learn some of the facts of life. That was not something which she could disclose to an indignant council, and it would have been a risky strategy at the best of times.

What actually happened after the queen's death did not, however, get the inquisitors much further. Kate Ashley obviously favoured Seymour, and teased Elizabeth about the prospect of marriage: 'she told her that her old husband, appointed at the king's death, was free again, and she might have him if she wished'.[32] They joked about his attractiveness, and Elizabeth became coy when she 'drew him in play' – apparently a sixteenth-century version of *Happy Families*. When it came to the point, however, the girl showed a streak of common sense more obvious than that of her mentor. She would be quite willing to marry him, but only with the king and council's consent; a qualification with which Catherine, according to her own testimony, hastened to agree.[33] Elizabeth had even hesitated to send a letter of condolence to Seymour after his wife's death, 'lest she be thought to woo him'; a caution eloquent of her state of mind. There was obviously an acute nervousness in Elizabeth's household about her relationship with Seymour, and a shared unwillingness to discuss the matter. Seymour himself had done nothing to arouse suspicion. He had offered Elizabeth the use of his London house when Durham Place was unavailable, a courtesy which could only be misinterpreted with a good deal of ingenuity. Nevertheless, the rumours persisted. About a fortnight before Christmas, when Kate Ashley returned from London, she told Elizabeth (according to the latter) that 'the voice went there that my Lord Admiral should marry me. Then I smiled at it and said it was but London news'.[34] Somebody was clearly keeping such speculation alive, and it may have been Elizabeth's servants, intentionally or otherwise; but in view of what was shortly to transpire, it may equally have been Seymour's enemies, determined to put a treasonable face upon his ambitions.

Elizabeth was a more or less helpless spectator of these events. There is no suggestion that she was personally threatened, but on 21 January, four days after Seymour's arrest, Thomas Parry and Kate Ashley were committed to the Tower. There, at the beginning of February, the hapless Kate related a series of trivial hints and alarms, including a falling out with her own husband, but absolutely nothing of substance.[35] On 23 January John Ashley was committed to the Fleet 'for the matter of the admirall'.[36] On the 22nd and 23rd Sir Robert Tyrwhyt reported to Somerset on his conversations with Elizabeth, who was 'marvellous abashed' by these dramatic events.[37] Although she 'wept very tenderly a long time', and admitted that she had asked Seymour to 'be a suitor' for her to obtain Durham Place, 'in no wise she will not confess any practice by Mrs Ashley or the cofferer concerning my lord Admirall'. He added somewhat sourly, 'I see by her face she is guilty, yet she will abide more storms ere she will accuse Mrs Ashley'. In that he was right; although she admitted that they had often spoken of

Seymour and his intentions, she never admitted that her friend had been guilty of the slightest impropriety. The council must have been hoping for something more conclusive, but in the event only one of the thirty-three articles objected against Seymour made any reference to Elizabeth, and that was unsubstantiated. Article 19 ran:

> It is objected and laid to your charge that you have not only before you married the Queen attempted and gone about to marry the King's Majesty's sister, the Lady Elizabeth, second Inheritour in remainder to the Crown, but also being then let by the Lord Protector and others of the council, sithence that time, both in the life of the Queen continued your old labour and love; and after her death by secret and crafty means, practiced to achieve the said purpose of marrying the said Lady Elizabeth; to the danger of the King's Majesty's person, and peril of the state of the same.[38]

Thomas Parry's 'practices' with Seymour were almost certainly about Elizabeth's desire for a London house; and the rest of the speculation about marriage was little more than girlish chatter. Given the chance Seymour would probably have asked her, and, if he had asked with the council's blessing, she would have accepted eagerly. It can only have been with that in mind that Seymour was asking cautiously in December whether her patent (that is for the grant of her estate) had been sealed or not.[39] When it came to the point, all that could be proved was that there had been an indiscreet flirtation, and that Elizabeth had talked about Seymour in the way that any girl might who believed that she had attracted the attention of a much older man, both dashing and married. Seymour was, nevertheless, condemned in parliament by Act of Attainder on a variety of charges, which collectively had considerable impact, but individually would hardly have stood up in court; which may be why he was not tried in the normal way.[40] He was executed on 20 March.

Elizabeth had been bullied and cajoled into admitting words and feelings of which she probably felt ashamed, but she also had her own sense of grievance. On 28 January she wrote to the Protector, repeating much of what she had already told Tyrwhyt, but adding:

> Mr Tyrwhyt and others have told me that there goeth rumours abroad which be greatly against both mine honour and my honesty, which above all other things I esteem, which be these; that I am in the Tower and with child by my Lord Admiral. My lord, these are shameful slanders.[41]

She had been disturbed and badly frightened by this experience; but she had also learned a great deal. She had the power to attract men, although she did not yet know how to use that power; and she had also suffered the destabilising effects of her own sexual desires. It is highly unlikely that her relations with Seymour ever amounted to more than a few surreptitious kisses and cuddles, but at fifteen that was more than enough to set the hormones racing, to encourage excited chatter, and to arouse an enjoyable sense of guilt. She also knew her worth, however, and had been thoroughly drilled in the female virtues – of which chastity was the chief. For the first, but not for the last time, the struggle between nature and breeding had been intense.[42]

Apart from Seymour himself, the other victim of this domestic tragedy was, at least temporarily, Kate Ashley. Her conduct had certainly not been above reproach, but had rather shown that kind of human weakness which would have been endearing in less unforgiving circumstances. She favoured Seymour, and if not attracted herself, at least had no difficulty in understanding Elizabeth's feelings. She had turned a blind eye to some of his indiscretions, and reproved others in a manner which he must have found less than intimidating.[43] Once the queen was dead, she had encouraged speculation about marriage in a manner which she clearly found enjoyable; but it seems unlikely that she had any direct encouragement from the admiral himself. In short, she behaved more in the manner of a girlish confidante than of a responsible guide and mentor; a fact which those interrogating her did not hesitate to point out. She was plainly terrified and intimidated by her imprisonment, and probably disclosed, during a series of interrogations, all that she knew. This was not much to the purpose as far as the case against Seymour went, but she may have remembered the fate of Lady Rochford, who eight years earlier had lost her head for aiding and abetting the infidelities of Catherine Howard. Her final deposition, on 4 February, concludes with an anguished plea for mercy.

> I remember no more, and would not hide it if I could. Pity me, and let me change my prison, for it is so cold that I cannot sleep, and so dark that I cannot see by day, for I stop the window with straw as there is no glass. My memory is never good, as my lady, fellows and husband can tell, and this sorrow has made it worse. Move my lord's grace to pity me, and forgive my great folly in speaking of marriage to such a person as she. I have suffered punishment and shame. I trust my lord will not deny me for this first fault, and if I were with her grace again (which I do not look for) I would never speak of marriage. I told my lord his boldness in her chamber was complained of to the council, but he would swear, asking what he did, and wishing they all saw. I could not make him stop, and at last told the queen, who made little of it.[44]

On 7 March Elizabeth petitioned the Protector for her release, on the grounds of her long and good service, and of her husband also 'bicause he is my kinsman'. They were soon after discharged.[45] As she had anticipated, Catherine was removed from Elizabeth's service as an undesirable influence and replaced by Elizabeth Tyrwhyt. The latter was in an invidious situation. Although she had been a loyal servant of Catherine Parr, and shared the reformed intellectual interests of her circle, she was not Kate Ashley. Elizabeth's loyalty to her former governess, and unwillingness to hear any ill spoken of her, was common knowledge. She greeted the hapless Lady Tyrwhyt with a storm of rage and a prolonged fit of the sulks; 'she wept all the night, and loured all the next day', as Sir Robert Tyrwhyt unhappily reported.[46] Somerset appears to have restored the faithful but ill-advised Kate to her mistress before 2 August 1549, when she wrote a letter on Elizabeth's behalf to William Cecil, and she remained there until 1554, when her mistress was sent to the Tower. She was to be restored a second time in 1555, and then to suffer further imprisonment and interrogation on Elizabeth's behalf in 1556, when she was removed for the third time.[47] In 1558 she returned again, and was to remain with Elizabeth until her death in 1565, aged about fifty.

Meanwhile Elizabeth was too resilient, and too sensible, to fret overlong about a situation which could not be amended. No further action was taken against John Ashley, and he was certainly at Hatfield in 1552, although probably not in Elizabeth's service. Somerset also responded positively to the princess's complaint of defamation, at least to the extent of agreeing to punish any tale tellers that she might name. He declined, however, to issue a formal proclamation, and she obviously thought that his offer was disingenuous. To take such action herself, she thought, would engender 'an evil name of me that I am glad to punish them, and so get the evil will of the people, which thing I would be lothe to have'.[48] It was typical of Elizabeth at this early stage of her career to intersperse comments of such political maturity with fits of petulance and self-pity.

Thomas Seymour was beheaded on 20 March, but if anyone expected her to betray herself in a storm of grief similar to that which had greeted the news of Kate's dismissal, they were disappointed. Her alleged comment, 'this day died a man with much wit and very little judgement', is probably apocryphal, but she did not have herself so well under control that the death of a man for whom she had felt genuine affection would have produced no sign of grief. The only hint we have of her real feelings is a comment by Tyrwhyt that she could not bear to hear the admiral discommended, which may have meant no more than common courtesy to the dead.[49] The fact is that Seymour had been a fascinating and unscrupulous rogue, upon whom she had had a crush. The flirtation, and then the prospect of marriage, had been only too exciting at the time; but they were not deeply rooted and by the time of his execution her prevailing emotion may well have been one of relief. She had had a narrow escape in more ways than one.

By April 1549 the assignment of Elizabeth's lands had taken effect; indeed it had probably been made by 18 February, when William Cecil had notified the foresters of Collyweston, Northamptonshire, that they should now account to her.[50] A cancelled memorandum in the council records notes the issue of a warrant to Peckham on 16 March for £351 19s. 7d. 'to William Cantrell for the use of the Lady Elizabeth, in full satisfaction of the land allotted her'.[51] Cantrell was probably her temporary cofferer until Thomas Parry returned to her service later in the year. The total value of these lands was £3106 13s. 4d. a year, and this income replaced the portion originally allotted to her out of the royal revenues. The assignment was made for life, or until the council should make an alternative arrangement on her marriage; and it made her the equivalent of a powerful nobleman.[52] Unlike Mary, however, she did not immediately become a magnate in her own right. Although in certain respects she might be deemed to be of age at sixteen (she could not, for example have been married without her own consent), she did not appoint her own officers or have an identifiable affinity. When a commission was issued in April 1549 to collect the first instalment of the parliamentary subsidy, only eleven men were taxed via her household, and two of those were the commissioners themselves, Sir Robert Tyrwhyt and Robert Oxenbridge. What position Oxenbridge held is not clear. None of her female attendants were taxed, and Thomas Parry was still in disgrace.[53]

Once the Seymour scandal had subsided, Elizabeth retreated again behind the screens, and can be only occasionally glimpsed over the next year or so. Her first tutor, William Grindal, had died young in January 1548, and Elizabeth had managed to secure the appointment of Roger Ascham in his place.[54] Ascham had already some experience of teaching her, and she obviously liked him; so her will was allowed to prevail although Catherine and Seymour apparently had someone else in mind. For about two years Ascham remained very close to Elizabeth, and his friendship was perhaps the main support which enabled her to cope with the trauma of early 1549, when everyone else around her seemed to be compromised. Ascham remained with her on a full time basis for about two years, returning to his official duties in Cambridge in or slightly after January 1550.[55] Thereafter he continued to guide her studies, but not on a day by day basis; perhaps by then she felt able to manage for herself. Ascham's praise for his pupil, written admittedly after she had come to the throne, was lavish and heartfelt: 'Ex anno decimo sexto non nihil excessit, tanta in hac et aetate gravitas, et celsitate comitas, inaudita est.' (From the age of sixteen she was unsurpassed in gravity for her age, and in a cheerful alacrity of mind that was wonderful to behold).[56] She had, it is clear, a very acute mind, a retentive memory, and an appetite for learning. Perhaps she did not have very much else to do, having been warned off vulgar intrigue by her recent experiences, but it was very much to her credit that she should have occupied herself in this way. She was probably the nearest thing to a trained academic ever to occupy the English throne, and it was an occupation which won her universal praise, both at the time and afterwards.

She also absorbed, from the same influences, a similar form of Protestantism to that of her brother. In February that stern unbending critic of the unrighteous, John Hooper, wrote to Henry Bullinger:

> Not only does she know true religion, but she has become so strong in latin and greek that she is capable of defending it with the most judicious arguments and dextrous ability, so that she is victorious over almost all adversaries she encounters.[57]

A jewel among women! It was a fashion among the sons and daughters of the high nobility to display their piety and erudition. Both the young duke of Suffolk and Jane Grey received similar encomia, and of course the king himself was buried in praises which sound suspiciously like flattery. But John Hooper was not easily deceived, and was certainly no flatterer; his praise was a serious commendation. Ascham fell out quite seriously with Elizabeth's favoured servant, Thomas Parry, and that may have been one of the reasons why the former returned to Cambridge in 1550. It seems as though Parry was jealous of the tutor's influence, but Elizabeth continued to favour them both impartially, a skill which was to stand her in good stead in years to come.

Thanks to *The Scholemaster*, published in 1570, which is actually Ascham's memoirs, we know a great deal about his methods, and about the routine which Elizabeth followed between 1548 and 1550.[58] The day started with the Greek New Testament, and proceeded to Isocrates and Sophocles, which were studied both for their pure diction and for the loftiness of their moral precepts. Ascham believed that exalted sentiments, whether moral or theological, could only be expressed in the most elegant style, and therefore placed much emphasis upon the study of St Cyprian, and also of Melanchthon's *Commonplaces*. Language was at the very heart of Elizabeth's study programme, and Ascham taught it by the standard contemporary technique of double translation. The pupil would translate a passage from the original into English, and then, after a suitable interval to remove the clarity of memory, translate the passage back into its first language. Elizabeth was trained in this technique with Latin, French and Italian (in all of which she was fluent) and also Greek (in which she had less facility).

At this stage of her life, her written style, although intensely formal by modern standards, was reasonably simple. According to Ascham, she preferred a style:

> that grows out of the subject; chaste because it is suitable and beautiful because it is clear, and her judgement is so good that in all Greek, Latin and English compositions there is nothing so loose on the one hand and so concise on the other which she does not immediately attend to.[59]

This is borne out by her surviving letters. Of those to her brother the king, there are four from between February 1547 and the autumn of 1548. All are in Latin, congratulating him upon his accession, or upon recovery from illness. They are stiff, carefully crafted schoolroom exercises, but they show no sign of the excessive ornateness which Elizabeth was to favour in later life.[60] Over the same period, she also wrote in English to Queen Catherine, to Protector Somerset and once (briefly) to Thomas Seymour. None of these give much away in terms of personal feeling, although those to Somerset in early 1549 are diplomatic exercises showing a high level of skill and maturity: 'I am sorry that there should be any such [rumour] aboute me', she wrote on one occasion,

> bicause that thogh the people wil say that I deserved throwgh my lewde demeneure to have such a one, and not that I mislike anything that your lordship and the Counsel shal thinke good; for I knowe that you and the counsel are charged with me, or [until] I take upon me to rule myself.

On 15 May 1549 she wrote to Edward, unusually, in English, sending him her portrait.[61] This was a not very subtle reminder that, in the wake of the Seymour affair, she was not getting many invitations to court.

> I shall most humbly beseech your majesty that when you shall look on my picture you will witsafe to think that as you have but the outward show of the body afore you, so my inward mind wisheth that the body itself were oftener in your presence.

That was both elegant and straight, and confirms, up to a point, that she was being a credit to her teacher.

Accomplished as she was, Elizabeth's education was by modern standards extraordinarily lacking in information content; or at least Ascham placed no emphasis upon it. Theology she certainly studied, and the politics and history of the ancient world via approved classical authors; but whether she ever read any modern history, let alone mathematics or cosmography, is much less clear.[62] If she did, it was probably with other teachers. She was, according to contemporary testimony, a skilled musician (like most of her family) but 'took little delight' in it. Ascham also believed in simplicity of dress, as becoming the Protestant bluestocking into which he was turning her; and surprisingly enough to anyone remembering the elaborate costumes in which she later luxuriated, during her brother's reign she was noted for the sobriety of her virtuous example.[63] In other respects she was not particularly puritanical, enjoying hunting and dancing, just as Edward enjoyed 'war games' and circus acts. To what extent this restraint was due to Ascham's influence, to a desire to ingratiate herself with her brother, or to repair a reputation somewhat besmirched by her supposed relations with Seymour, we do not know. Whatever the motive, it still has a calculated air about it. Perhaps it was no more than a desire to distance herself from her sister Mary, whose flamboyant taste in dress was as notorious as her religious conservatism.

Elizabeth's active political role was negligible at this time, but she was certainly restored to favour by the end of 1549. If there was an element of calculation in her behaviour, it worked. After Thomas Seymour's execution her relations with the Protector seem to have been correct rather than amicable. The council wrote to her formally on 9 October, detailing the circumstances of his overthrow, but she was in no way involved, and her reaction to the news is not known.[64] Whereas François Van der Delft, the emperor's ambassador, kept in regular touch with Mary, and reported his contacts, no one did the same for Elizabeth. On 19 December, however, Van der Delft himself reported that Elizabeth had arrived at court 'the other day', had been received with great pomp and triumph, and was 'continually with the king'. 'It seems', he went on, 'that they have a higher opinion of her for conforming with the others and observing the new decrees.'[65] She probably spent the Christmas of 1549 at court. If she had ever been seriously out of favour, this was the time of her rehabilitation. John Dudley, now earl of Warwick, who had led the recent *coup* against the Protector, and at this point was just emerging successfully from a power struggle with his former allies, the conservatives on the council, may have identified her as a useful ally. In February 1550 the council instructed the chancellor of the court of augmentations 'to assign to the Lady Elizabeth the supplement of the lands assigned to her'. Her patent was finally sealed on 17 March.[66] This may not have made much practical difference to her income, but it signalled another step along the road to independence, and it was followed up in June with a similar friendly gesture from Warwick.

Hatfield was Elizabeth's favourite house, and she had lived there, for the most part, since at least January 1549. It was a crown property, having been obtained by Henry VIII in 1538, and Edward had used it as prince. How or when it had come into the hands of the earl is not clear, but on 22 June, in response to a request from her, he made it over to Elizabeth in exchange for other lands.[67] As Van der Delft had observed, they were in some respects two of a kind. In time, this friendliness was to lead to a

1. Queen Elizabeth I, unknown artist. (*National Portrait Gallery*)

2. King Henry VIII, after Hans Holbein, *c.* 1536. (*National Portrait Gallery*)

3. Anne Boleyn, unknown artist. (*National Portrait Gallery*)

4. Catherine of Aragon, *c.* 1530, unknown artist. (*National Portrait Gallery*)

5. Thomas Seymour, unknown artist. (*National Portrait Gallery*)

6. Queen Mary I, by Hans Eworth, 1554. (*National Portrait Gallery*)

7. Edward VI, *c.* 1547, unknown artist. (*National Portrait Gallery*)

8. Henry VIII on his deathbed and Edward VI. (*National Portrait Gallery*)

bizarre misunderstanding. Van der Delft was replaced in May 1550 by Jehan Scheyfve, a less able man who was kept at arm's length by the council as they tried to build up good relations with France. In January 1551 he reported to Mary of Hungary:

> I have heard from a safe source that my Lord of Warwick is about to cast off his wife and marry my lady Elizabeth, daughter of the late king, with whom he is said to have had several secret and intimate personal communications.[68]

Scheyfve's 'safe source' was presumably one of Warwick's numerous conservative enemies, who were regularly in touch with the imperial camp.

Elizabeth was indeed back on the marriage market by that time, which was hardly surprising as she had turned seventeen. In November 1550 an anonymous Danish envoy had arrived in London, presumably to feel out the ground, and in the following month Sir John Borthwick was accredited to the Danish court 'with privy instructions for marriage of the Lady Elizabeth' to the Danish king's son. This prince was Frederick, later King Frederick III, and some particulars of Borthwick's instructions survive.[69] He was to take the initiative, stressing the commercial and religious bonds between the countries, and the learning, piety and beauty of the princess. He was not, however, to admit to being authorised to negotiate on behalf of the king of England. The idea, clearly, was to establish some sort of common ground without running the risk of a formal rebuff. For some reason the negotiation, if there was one, petered out, although it was still being spoken of in June 1551. This was, however, no reflection on the attractiveness of the proffered bride, who was by contemporary accounts a very striking girl. She was not particularly tall, but had her father's red hair and her mother's pale complexion. Her features also took after Henry to some extent, and it was remarked that her hands were particularly beautiful, perhaps because they were the only parts of her body which were regularly visible!

In January 1551 Elizabeth paid another visit to her brother, who was then at St James's, 'with a great suit of gentlemen and ladies, escorted by a hundred of the king's horse'.[70] Scheyfve was probably right to see this as a calculated demonstration. She was, he reported 'most honourably received by the council', in order to demonstrate to the people 'how much glory belongs to her who has embraced the new religion, and become a very great lady' – in contrast, of course, to Mary. By the summer the marriage rumours had shifted, first to the duke of Enghien, the brother of Antoine de Bourbon, king of Navarre, and then to a brother of the duke of Guise.[71] Whether or not such moves were contemplated, no actual negotiations seem to have taken place, and by November Scheyfve was reporting another approach to the king of Denmark, although he had to add 'it is said'. The ambassador was neither very well regarded, nor very close to the court, so all his reports have to be taken with a pinch of salt; and there appear to be no other records of such an approach. In August 1551 both Mary and Elizabeth were summoned to court at the end of the king's progress. Whereas it is clear that Mary was under suspicion and the council wished to keep an eye on her, there were no similar reasons for Elizabeth's presence; perhaps Edward simply enjoyed her company.[72] The absence of letters between them from May 1549 to April 1552 suggests frequent personal contact, and there may well have been more visits than were recorded.

In April 1551, for reasons which are not clear, Elizabeth surrendered her patent of March 1550, and was granted a new one. The new grant appears to be virtually identical, except that the total value is some £50 a year less, and the reserved rent about £3 more.[73] Such adjustments can hardly have made much difference, but there may have been some technical defect in the first patent which a dispute had revealed. How this estate was run, and who ran it, is now largely conjectural. The Tyrwhyts' regime seems to have ended before October 1549, when the duke of Somerset's overthrow changed the political landscape. Both Kate Ashley and Thomas Parry had been reinstated by August, at Elizabeth's earnest request, and the Tyrwhyts may well have left at that point. The names of individual servants are recorded from time to time, going about their mistress's business; but apart from Parry, the officers are mainly unknown. When the second instalment of the subsidy was collected in 1550, the eleven who paid through the household were headed by Sir Walter Bucler and Thomas Parry. The list shows several changes from 1549, and neither Bucler nor Parry were commissioners.[74] By 1552 Sir William Cecil was her surveyor, inaugurating one of the most famous political partnerships in English history, but exactly when he was appointed, or what his duties involved, is not clear. The nineteen-year-old princess was not at liberty to appoint whoever she chose, although she was consulted. She was not yet legally of age, and it appears that the council intervened occasionally in routine matters of estate management. For example, in November 1552 the chancellor of augmentations was instructed to inhibit the sale or grant of reversion of the manor of Blackesley in Northamptonshire, in spite of the fact that it was 'parcell of the lands granted by the king's majestie to the Lady Elizabeth'.[75] It is possible that the lack of information about Elizabeth's estate management is actually the result of the fact that the lands continued to be managed by the court of augmentations during her minority, and that the court simply paid the revenues to one of her officers, although the accounts show no sign of such transactions. Her wishes may well have been respected, when they were expressed, but had no legal force.

Parry's accounts survive for the year 1551–2. Although they do not resolve all the problems, they do provide a number of indications.[76] Elizabeth's income was theoretically a little over £3000, but in that year he showed an expenditure of £3725 and an income of £5791. Of this sum, £4760 was received 'by her Grace's own hands', and at the end of the account he delivered again the balance of £1507. Such figures do not make sense if we imagine local receivers and stewards paying their balances to Parry, or to someone on his behalf. In fact 'vendicions and foreign receipts' (which he did receive directly) account for a mere £207. It has been suggested that the £4760 represented a surplus accumulated during something like three years of living largely at other people's expense.[77] That may be so, and Elizabeth may have been managing her own money during the months while Parry was in the wilderness (or in prison), but she was a tender age for such a responsibility. The fact seems to be that her establishment was settled gradually over many months between the summer of 1548 and March 1550, and that the payments for her upkeep were similarly shifted from an *ad hoc* to a regular pattern during that time. If she had the equivalent of a privy purse, and began to receive her income into that account while she had no cofferer, then the payment to Parry in 1552 can be seen as the regularisation of a situation which had been allowed to get out of hand. On the other hand, the account suggests that this was a normal practice. A privy purse account would have been held by one of her chamber servants, just as the king's privy purse was held by the groom of the stool. That money was described as 'in the King's hands', but it did not mean that he was stowing the coin away under the bed. Such an explanation is possible, but does not entirely account for the fact that Elizabeth appears to have been handling such large sums herself. She may have been receiving her main income direct from the court of augmentations into her privy purse, while Parry was receiving the minor estate income as it became available. What is clear is that Elizabeth was living up to every penny of her income, but she was not spending much on jewellery or on building. 'Reparations' account for only a few hundred pounds. The scale of her housekeeping, on the other hand, was enormous. It was often commented upon, and in 1551–2 'the House' accounted for £2850, of which only £434 was spent on wages. Her chamber expenditure over the same period (including wages and fees) was a reasonable £875. Most of the names of those with whom she dealt mean little now, but it is interesting to note that she purchased a Bible for the substantial sum of 20 shillings from one Edmund Allen. A man of the same name, described as a miller of Frittenden in Kent, was burned at the stake in 1557, accused of heresy and holding conventicles. When his house was searched, several bibles were discovered, and it seems that he ran a supplementary trade as a bookseller.[78]

These accounts also provide a number of clues to the way in which the household was structured. The only officers referred to are the chamberlain, the cofferer and the auditor. When the final instalment of the subsidy was collected in 1552, Bucler and Parry received nineteen certificates of assessment for men paying through the household, and there must have been more as neither the chamberlain nor the cofferer were represented.[79] It is known that Cecil was surveyor during this period, but he is not mentioned, and how he was paid is not clear. Sir Henry Parker, who died on 8 January 1552, is referred to as 'late Chamberlain' in the payment of an arrear of his livery, although he had not featured in either of the earlier subsidy returns.[80] He was replaced by Sir Walter Bucler, who had been in the household since at least 1550, although it is not clear in what capacity. Bucler was to be removed on the council's instructions in March 1553, and replaced with Sir Nicholas Strange, but it is not known why.[81] Kate Ashley received a number of sums to be spent on Elizabeth's instructions; and Blanche Parry, 'Mrs Slannyng' and 'Mrs Qwrtnaye' (Courtenay?) received each the modest fee of £5 a year as gentlewomen of the chamber. The auditor was Thomas Benger, and some of the other names which appear in large numbers were servants, tradesmen or other people's servants; it is often hard to tell. Whereas Parry meticulously recorded his expenditure, and that small proportion of the income which came directly to him, on most of the income he is unenlightening. This curious feature, together with the apparent absence of either a steward or a controller, which were both normal offices in aristocratic households, confirms that the estate officers were not accounting to the household. Somehow or other the money was arriving in Elizabeth's 'own hands' and being passed on by her to Parry for disbursement. As an under-age heiress would normally have been in wardship, this may have been an improvised alternative. Theoretically she was in wardship to a brother who was himself a minor, so the council set up this unusual compromise, but unfortunately did not make any specific record of it. It would also have meant that her whole position was extremely vulnerable to the council's displeasure.

Elizabeth's relations with her brother continued to be good, although correspondence was infrequent, and mostly concerned with the health of one or other of them.[82] The ambassadors only commented upon her visits to the court when they involved coming to London, or when some significant negotiation was suspected. They seem to have visited each other frequently on an informal basis and to have exchanged New Year gifts. There are no records of these between 1549 and 1553, only references to them, so we do not know what she gave; her previous practice suggests some work of learning or piety in her own hand. The fact that there are no covering letters probably indicates that they were delivered personally at court during the holiday. When Mary of Guise, the queen mother of Scotland, passed through England on her way north at the end of October 1551, the council wrote to both Mary and Elizabeth to advertise them of her coming, although the account of her reception which Edward wrote down in some detail does not contain any mention of either of his sisters.[83] As we have seen, her relations with the earl of Warwick, John Dudley, were also good; at least until the last six months of the reign. Robert Dudley, Warwick's son, later claimed to have known Elizabeth from the age of eight. He married Amy, the daughter of Sir John Robsart, in June 1550, and there is no suggestion that he ever lived in the princess's household; but their friendship seems to have been continuous, and he was a regular attendant at court.

Speculation about Elizabeth's marriage continued in a desultory way. At the end of March 1552 Scheyfve had picked up a rumour that the widowed earl of Pembroke (a man of about forty-five) was entertaining such ambitions 'but she refuses her consent'.[84] According to Robert Dudley, she was averse to the whole idea of marriage, but that may have been only sour hindsight. Probably the king's youth and the uncertainty of England's international position (to say nothing of the scarcity of Protestant bridegrooms) are more likely explanations for the lack of action than any particular feelings of Elizabeth herself.

Early in 1553, when Edward's health first began to give cause for concern, there was speculation about the succession. Scheyfve's not particularly sensitive nose began to sense plots. On 5 May he reported to the bishop of Arras that Elizabeth was shortly expected in town, and that there were rumours that John Dudley the younger (earl of Warwick since his father's elevation to the dukedom of Northumberland in November 1551), would put away his wife in order to marry her. This, he admitted, did not look very likely.[85] He repeated the report a few days later, however, adding that there were again rumours that Northumberland himself would abandon his duchess, to marry Elizabeth and 'secure the Crown'. He also noticed a secret French mission, but prosaically ascribed that to an intention to invite Elizabeth to be godmother to 'the new princess of France', rather than to any plot against the succession of Mary.[86] In fact there probably was no such plot until the king's health suddenly deteriorated early in June.

Plot or no plot, Edward had already made up his mind, long before the situation became real and urgent, that he did not want either of his half-sisters to succeed him should he die without natural heirs.[87] The main focus of his concern was Mary, whom he had come to dislike and distrust as her religious conservatism became more obvious and assertive. Her religious proclivities, however, did not make a good case for exclusion. Not even his more advanced Protestant advisers would at this stage have suggested that ungodliness was a reason for altering a lawful succession. On the other hand, it was quite possible to argue that a statute could not set aside the bar of bastardy. By 1553 precedent was against such an argument, but not conclusively so. Henry VIII had been authorised by parliament to decree the succession in his last will 'signed with his own hand'; and he had done so, laying down that if Edward were to die without offspring, the crown should pass first to Mary, and then, on the same terms, to Elizabeth. If, however, either the will or the statute were set aside as unlawful, then the heir would be the young Mary of Scotland,[88] granddaughter of Henry's elder sister, Margaret. Mary had been ignored, both in the will and the Act, as being an alien, born outside the realm, but it was not entirely clear that that was lawful. Put simply, either the will was valid, in which case Mary Tudor was the heir; or it was not, in which case Mary Stuart was. Neither of these solutions, however, was acceptable to Edward as he brooded on the problem in January 1553. He wanted a male heir, and tried ingeniously to limit the crown to hypothetical boys of the royal kindred who had not yet been born.

Nobody took this seriously, but when his health collapsed, and death became not merely certain but imminent, some solution had to be found. Edward, it is clear, was firmly convinced that both his half-sisters were bastards, and in a sense he was correct. His letters patent, by which he sought to limit the crown, spoke rather vaguely of

> severall divorsements, ratefyed and confirmed by authority of diverse actes of parleamente remaininge in their full force, strength and effecte; whereby the saide lady Marye as also the saied lady Elizabeth to all intents and purposes are and clerely be disabled, to aske claime or challenge, the said imperiall crowne.[89]

If parliament had the power to bastardise, however, then it also had power to determine the succession. Of course the legitimacy of Henry's second marriage depended entirely upon parliament. If the power of statute should be called in question in this fashion, it could be argued that his first marriage was lawful, and Mary legitimate; but the same did not apply to Elizabeth. Consequently, even if Edward had wanted to exclude Mary in favour of Elizabeth, there was no way in which he could have done so.

The solution eventually adopted, whether by the king's initiative or by that of the duke of Northumberland, was to intrude Jane Grey, the granddaughter of Henry's younger sister, Mary. A pretext could be found for this, but only by using the same will which was in its main provisions being rejected.[90] Edward's eventual decision to bequeath the crown to her was a legal and logical mess. Not even the Protestants, who were most suspicious of Mary's intentions, generally accepted it. Elizabeth made no recorded comment, and took no action. She was as suspicious of Mary as any other Protestant, but equally well aware that their causes stood or fell together. If Jane Grey were accepted and became established, her own prospect of the crown would disappear, and her status would be that of an illegitimate daughter of the ruler before last. When it came to the point, Elizabeth's good relations with her brother, and with the Dudleys, and even her conspicuous Protestant virtue, counted for nothing. Mary's swift success in July 1553 must have been a great relief to her; but the rules of the game had now changed. For the time being she was the second person in the kingdom rather than the third, but it remained to be seen how she would fare under the regime which now seemed likely to follow.

5

In Danger

Elizabeth appears to have played no part at all in the dramatic events which followed the death of Edward VI on 6 July 1553. William Camden, writing many years later, claimed that she declined promises of land and money from the duke of Northumberland in return for her support, but there is no contemporary evidence of such offers.[1] He might have calculated that if she could be induced to surrender her rights to Jane Grey, it would have strengthened the latter's hand, but Elizabeth reputedly pointed out that she had no rights to surrender as long as her elder sister was alive. That both Mary and Elizabeth were unmarried was used as an argument against them by Jane's supporters, on the grounds that either might marry a foreign prince 'and bring the realm into subjection'. This was precisely the reason why first Henry and then Edward had been so concerned about a male heir; and in Jane's favour it could be said that she was already safely married 'within the realm'. One of the strongest reasons for supposing that the plot to exclude both Mary and Elizabeth had been hastily improvised is that neither of them had been pressed to marry. Mary, with the emperor's support, would have been in a strong position to resist such pressure, if it had been applied, or to have insisted upon a Habsburg marriage which would have been unacceptable to the council; but Elizabeth would have been much more vulnerable. Northumberland was at one point reported to be planning to marry her to the son of the duke of Ferrara, and there was talk of the duke of Enghein and the duke of Aumâle. There was a negotiation of sorts with Frederick of Denmark, and even rumours that Northumberland would marry her himself, but nothing was pressed with any determination.[2] Elizabeth would almost certainly have resisted such pressure if it had been applied, but, if the council had been resolute, she might have had no option. Jane Grey, after all, had been forced into a marriage with Guildford Dudley which she certainly did not desire.

During the crisis itself Elizabeth took refuge in diplomatic illness, and it is a matter of dispute whether she encouraged her servants to make any gesture on her sister's behalf.[3] Like many others, however, she hastened to declare her loyalty once the matter was resolved. She wrote to Mary almost at once, congratulating her upon her success, and asking for guidance on the question of court mourning. She actually reached London ahead of Mary, on 29 July, with what can only be described as a substantial military escort.

> The sam day cam rydyng thrugh London my lade Elssabeth grace, and thrugh Fletstrett, and so to my [lord of] Somerset place that was, and yt ys my lade grasys with iiM [two thousand] horse with speres and bowes and gunes, all in gren gardyd with whytt welvett saten taffety.[4]

Such a force could not have been raised and equipped overnight, but it could well have been called together after the confrontation was over. The real purpose of such an unnecessary show of strength is uncertain. It might have been a gesture of loyalty to her sister, or it might have carried an implied warning. Two thousand horsemen constituted an enormous retinue, far in excess of the honorific attendance which the circumstances required. Nor did anything in Elizabeth's recorded past suggest a capacity to raise such an affinity. She was still not yet twenty, but her brother's death seems to have turned her into a different kind of political animal. On 31 July she went out of London again to meet her sister. This time her escort was only half the size, and no doubt much smaller than the numbers accompanying Mary, estimated at ten thousand, but the symbolism of the meeting again looks calculated.[5] If the queen noticed, however, she paid no attention. She was exalted by her triumph, and convinced that God had called her to a healing ministry in England. If she felt threatened by Elizabeth, she gave no sign of it. Their meeting was cordial, and according to eye witnesses accompanied by much embracing. The general atmosphere seems to have been one of spontaneous elation.[6] Beneath this apparently calm surface, however, there were rocks.

Mary immediately began to use religious observance as a test of loyalty; and Elizabeth did not go to mass. By the middle of August the queen had done what she was to do repeatedly over the next few months: she consulted the imperial ambassadors. They discouraged her from making an issue of religion, on the grounds that she should rather capitalise upon the consensus which had brought her to the throne than stir up unnecessary divisions. Although it was clear that no one had much sympathy for Northumberland and his henchmen, the ambassadors believed that 'the heretics' were strong and should not be unnecessarily provoked.[7] Following this advice, and probably that of her council as well, on 18 August Mary issued a conciliatory proclamation, declaring her own position and expressing the pious hope that all her loving subjects would 'charitably embrace the same'. She had no intention, she declared mendaciously, of coercing anyone's conscience; not, at least, until 'due order' had been taken. By this a parliamentary settlement along the lines of 1535–36 was generally expected.[8] It was not widely known that she had already told her council of her intention to restore religion 'as far as the pope's authority'.

It may have been this issue to which the ambassadors somewhat cryptically alluded in their despatch of 16 August, but is also clear that by then they were worried about Elizabeth. They believed that she adhered to the 'new religion' out of policy, in order to create a political following from among people who were bound, sooner or later, to become hostile to the regime. She 'might out of ambition, or being persuaded thereto, conceive some design and put it in execution, which would be difficult to prevent, as she is clever and sly'.[9] There was a debate about the desirability of her continued presence at court. She had already caused embarrassment by refusing to attend the requiem mass which Mary had privately ordered for the repose of her brother's soul. It was a measure of the new queen's total lack of sensitivity that she should have considered this intensely controversial gesture to be a meritorious duty on her part, instead of a calculated insult to Edward's memory. It was better that Elizabeth should remain at court, however, in spite of her defiant behaviour, rather than withdraw to her estates and start weaving plots. So she stayed, and was immediately subjected to overwhelming pressure to conform to the conservative (but still schismatic) regime which her sister had imposed. As late as 3 September Elizabeth refused all blandishments to attend the mass which followed the creation of Edward Courtenay as earl of Devon; and when the reintroduction of mass at St Paul's was accompanied by riots and demonstrations, she was suspected of complicity.[10]

The similarity of Elizabeth's position to that of Mary herself three or four years earlier would have been obvious to anyone except the queen. Elizabeth's reaction, however, was very different. She had no Holy Roman Emperor standing behind her, threatening war if she was coerced. Elizabeth may also have realised that her sister had not a scrap of political sensitivity in her make up. Although it would not have occurred to her to compromise her own principles when she was under pressure, Mary could see no principle in Elizabeth's reluctance, only time-serving duplicity and deceit.[11] There was only one true path in religion, and those who could not see it were either dupes or criminals, or both. Elizabeth was aware of this implacability; if she wished to live to inherit the crown, she would have to give way. She did so, with tears which must have owed more to rage and frustration than to penitence or guilt. About 4 or 5 September she begged time and instruction. If Mary was gratified, she did not show it, but insisted that Elizabeth attend mass on the Feast of the Nativity of the Blessed Virgin, 8 September. Elizabeth complied, but was theatrically unwell.[12] Whether this was a genuine illness produced by stress and humiliation, or one skilfully feigned for the occasion, we do not know. There was a deafening silence about this surrender among the princess's fellow Protestants. Not even the most rigorous follower of Calvin or Bullinger took her to task. That John Foxe should have been forgiving in the circumstances of the 1560s is not surprising; but no one in 1553 knew how the dice were going to fall, and yet it seems clear that nobody believed that she had really changed her mind. Mary may not have been deceived either, but she had now no pretext for further action. Ostensibly good relations were restored, and Elizabeth took her due place at the coronation celebrations on 1 October.

The imperial ambassadors, however, and particularly the new resident, Simon Renard, were not reassured. Unless or until some decisive action could be taken, the princess was the heir to the throne; or rather, she was generally accepted as such. As far as the ambassadors themselves were concerned, they agreed with Edward VI. Elizabeth was a bastard and inca-pable of inheriting, no matter what any statute might say. Of course Mary was Henry's legitimate daughter, so the rest of Edward's argument did not apply. They were wise enough to realise, however, that owing to the pecu-liarities of English law, even the majority of Mary's council did not see the situation in that light.[13] Had they done so, and had that view prevailed, the princess would not have been a danger. The ambassadors identified four groups as actually or potentially hostile to the regime: the followers of Northumberland; the Protestants; the agents of Henry II of France; and an amorphous secret cabal of 'great men'. The last three they associated with Elizabeth.[14] It was part of their peculiar world view that anyone hostile to the emperor must favour the king of France, yet there is no trace of evidence that Elizabeth at that time had any secret contacts in that quarter. Even the pathologically suspicious Renard did not associate her with any surviving followers of the fallen duke; but the other two fears were not unreasonable. After her coronation Mary considered dismissing her sister to the country; Renard would have preferred to have had her placed under house arrest. In the event neither course was pursued and Elizabeth remained at court, in a curious limbo between favour and disfavour.

Meanwhile the queen embarked upon a longer-term solution to the prob-lem by negotiating her own marriage. She was thirty-seven, and a realistic appraisal of her medical record would have suggested that it was already too late to produce an heir. No such thought was allowed to obtrude – at least not in public. There were only a handful of possible consorts. The emperor Charles V was a widower, and they had been betrothed over thirty years earlier; but he was now over fifty and in poor health. His son, Philip of Spain, was also a widower and aged twenty-six; there was Dom Luis, the younger brother of the king of Portugal, a man in his forties; and there was the newly restored earl of Devon, Edward Courtenay.[15] Many Englishmen, including Mary's chancellor Stephen Gardiner and a number of her council, would have preferred her to marry 'within the realm', for obvious reasons. Unfortunately, Courtenay was not a very good candidate. He was twenty-seven and reputedly a Catholic, but had spent most of his life in prison, and had quickly become derailed by unaccustomed liberty and money. His dissolute behaviour, if nothing else, ensured that the queen showed no interest in him. No matter what others might argue, or believe, there is no evidence that Mary ever had the slightest intention of marrying him. There was also the little known, but real consideration that Mary had long since sworn that she would never marry without the emperor's advice, declaring that she regarded him as her true father – a statement which she had repeated to his ambassadors early in August.[16] This understandable but totally improper commitment determined the outcome. Charles disclaimed any ambition himself, declaring that he was too old; but he studiously blocked the candidacy of Dom Luis (who would probably have been the best choice), and promoted that of Philip. His reasons for doing this were entirely concerned with his own interests and those of his family; they paid no attention to Mary's happiness or to the interests of her kingdom. Charles had tried very hard to obtain the reversion of the imperial succession for Philip, but he had failed because the diet rejected a man who was generally (and rightly) regarded as being an entirely Spanish prince.

To redeem this situation in 1548 the emperor had juggled with the imperial constitution in order to settle both Milan and the Low Countries on Philip, instead of upon his imperial heir, his brother Ferdinand. He had done this by means of imperial decrees, called pragmatic sanctions, which had constituted Milan as an imperial vicariate and converted the seventeen provinces of the Low Countries into the Burgundian Circle, which was exempt from imperial law.[17] This had created bad blood between the brothers, and by 1553 Charles was worried lest on his death or retirement (both of which he had very much in mind), Ferdinand would overturn his settlement. An English royal marriage for Philip provided the perfect solution, giving him a power base in northern Europe from which to protect his interests in the Netherlands. There was also the additional, but secondary, consideration that such a marriage would complete the encirclement of France. It is not surprising that Charles quickly instructed his son to disengage himself from his negotiation for a Portuguese bride and begin to show enthusiasm for his ageing aunt.[18] Philip, for whom England was a remote and barbarous island, full of heretics, was dutiful and obedient – although it is clear that his desire was for an ancient and prestigious crown rather than a problematic wife. Having at first instructed his ambassadors to deny any intention of seeking to control the queen's marriage, Charles eventually did just that. Acting on new instructions, by 8 September Renard had insinuated the name of Philip into the discussions which were going on at that point, and had begun to establish that confidential relationship with Mary which was to prove so fruitful. By 5 October Renard could report that the queen was persuaded that she should marry for the sake of the succession, and on 10 October he formally proposed a union with Philip.[19] Meanwhile the French ambassador, Antoine de Noailles, had picked up rumours of what was afoot. In fact his rumours were well ahead of events, but not inaccurate. On 7 September he wrote to Henry II of France that, if the reports were true, he would be in for 'perpetuelle guerre'; and urged him to take whatever steps he could to inhibit the match.[20]

On 5 October, parliament met. Having passed three Acts redefining treason as the basic crime of 1352 (again) and restoring the Courtenay family in blood, it was promptly and rather mysteriously adjourned. Some interpreted this as an endorsement of the earl of Devon's matrimonial prospects, but that was clearly not the queen's intention. The Houses reconvened on 24 October, when their first act was to declare the marriage of the queen's parents lawful and to repeal all statutes to the contrary.[21] This was a clear statement of how Mary saw her claim to the throne, but, as Renard quickly perceived, it did not solve the problem of Elizabeth. She might be even more emphatically a bastard, but until Henry's last Succession Act was repealed, her claim to the throne was unaffected. 'I believe', he wrote optimistically, 'that [the queen] will easily assent to have both will and statute annulled for the sake of avoiding all the difficulties which Elizabeth would make if she were able'.[22] Renard was wrong. Mary was pressed, not only by the emperor, but by several of her own servants, including Gardiner, to take some action to bar Elizabeth from the succession; but she did not do so. This was not out of any regard for her sister, whom she both distrusted and disliked. She made it clear on several occasions and in different contexts that she did not want Elizabeth to succeed her; and yet she did nothing decisive to prevent it.

In the autumn of 1553 it was not unreasonable to suppose that the problem would solve itself. The queen would marry, not immediately but soon; and she was confident, in spite of the risks, that she would have children. Moreover, Elizabeth was popular. Much as she disliked the thought, Mary was shrewd enough to see that. Perhaps she hoped, by forcing her into religious conformity, to destroy something of her appeal. Renard, however, was right; Elizabeth was a threat. She may or may not have been involved in plots against the regime, but her mere existence posed a problem, unless or until death, a foreign marriage or a statutory bar removed her from the political scene. Even the last might not have been effective if the queen had no other heir, and that may have been one of the reasons why it was not tried. But the situation was one of tense and unresolved conflict which was to last for the whole five years of the reign.

On 29 October, in a scene of emotional exaltation, Mary solemnly swore on the sacrament that she would marry Philip of Spain.[23] The whole negotiation had been conducted in secret, and we only know about it through the detailed reports which Renard made to his master. Noailles, and no doubt most of Mary's council, knew what was going on; but the only councillor directly involved was Lord Paget, who was known to favour the match. Noailles, inevitably, attempted to spread alarm and despondency, and was in touch with several disaffected groups.[24] The councillors were in a much more difficult position. Many of them disliked the proposal and were deeply distrustful of Renard, believing his influence and confidential position to be improper. When the House of Commons presented a petition to the queen to marry within the realm, she lost her temper with them, and blamed Gardiner for this unwelcome initiative.[25]

When the news of her decision became public, late in November, all her councillors, including Gardiner, accepted it with the best face they could. After all, it was up to the queen to decide whom she would marry; nor could they quarrel with her judgement, however much they may have disliked the way she had reached her decision. Noailles was almost certainly wrong in claiming that there was serious disaffection within the council at this point. Courtenay, however, was deeply chagrined, and foolish enough to show it. His mother, the dowager marchioness of Exeter, who had been close to Mary in the first weeks of the reign, lost favour in consequence, and the family so recently restored to honour, passed under a cloud.[26]

Just when the earl's name started to be linked to Elizabeth rather than the queen is not clear. As early as 19 September the imperial ambassadors reported rather mysteriously that they had been approached by an agent acting for both the princess and Courtenay. The subject of the enquiry was innocuous – a matter of protocol connected with the coronation – but the juxtaposition is curious. On 31 October, immediately after Mary's matrimonial oath, and some time before it entered the public domain, Renard had written 'it now only remains to decide what should be done with Courtenay, and some are of the opinion that he ought to be married to the Lady Elizabeth'. One of those who appears to have favoured this course was Renard's ally, Lord Paget.[27] Reporting a conversation with Paget on the subject of the succession, which took place about 3 November, he wrote:

He says that although parliament has willingly declared the marriage of King

Henry and Lady Catherine his first wife to have been legitimate, and the heirs born of it legitimate, and has repealed an Act of parliament to the contrary, and tacitly declared the Lady Elizabeth to be a bastard, yet she has been called to the succession by the consent of parliament if the Queen dies without issue, and it would be difficult to deprive her of this right without giving rise to trouble, especially as the duke of Suffolk's children have been found to be bastards because of his betrothal *per verba de praesenti* to the earl of Arundel's sister before taking the Lady Frances to wife.[28]

Because this would leave the queen of Scots as heir, it would be much better to confirm Elizabeth's position on the condition that she marry Courtenay. On the 28th of the same month the ambassador reported at length on a similar conversation with Mary herself, in which the queen had come to a very different conclusion. She admitted that the queen of Scots had the best right by descent, but she could be excluded both on the grounds of having been born abroad, and because she was married to the dauphin of France. The duchess of Suffolk had never been properly married, the queen declared, because of the precontract, to which Renard had alluded. 'As for the Lady Elizabeth, the queen would scruple to allow her to succeed because of her heretical opinions, illegitimacy, and characteristics in which she resembled her mother.' Anne Boleyn had caused great trouble to the kingdom, and Elizabeth would do the same, and 'she would imitate her mother in being a French partisan'.[29] If God were to call her without giving her heirs, Mary had continued, the Lady Margaret Douglas, countess of Lennox, the daughter of Margaret Tudor by her second marriage to the earl of Angus, would be the best person to succeed. Nobody else appears to have shared this view, for the perfectly good reason that the countess of Lennox was almost unknown. Paget, for one, was unconvinced. There was no danger that Elizabeth would favour the French; she knew her fellow countrymen too well for that; and it would be very difficult to repeal Henry's Succession Act.[30]

Consequently, no official statement was made. The emperor gave the matter serious thought, and early in November sent a special representative to interview both Elizabeth and Courtenay. A few days later it was being rumoured in Brussels that the negotiations for the queen's marriage were also including discussions for the betrothal of Elizabeth to Philip's son, Don Carlos. The latter rumour was probably unfounded, but Charles eventually vetoed any suggestion of a marriage between Elizabeth and the earl of Devon. As Courtenay was of the Plantagenet royal blood, any such union would have strengthened Elizabeth's pretensions, rather than diminishing them. He was a Catholic, but he was also a weak character who would be dominated by such an able wife. Whatever decision Mary might make about the succession was up to her, but no marriage between Elizabeth and Courtenay ought to feature in it.[31]

The marriage treaty between Mary and Philip, concluded at the end of December, avoided the issue altogether. As has often been pointed out, this was extremely favourable to the English, for the simple reason that Charles was not very interested in how England was governed, as long as his son was recognised as king. Philip was to exercise no authority in England, except in conjunction with the queen. He was not to take her out of the country without her own consent, and was not to employ his own servants in English offices. If there were issue of the marriage, whether male or female, that heir would inherit England and the Low Countries but have no claim on Spain. If Mary should predecease her husband without heirs, then his interest in the kingdom was to end.[32] Significantly, Philip himself played no part in these negotiations. When he discovered what had been agreed in his name, he was very angry, considering his proposed position in England to be dishonourable. He was particularly baffled by his father's willingness to allow England to stay out of the current war with France, which to his mind destroyed one of the main purposes of the treaty. Charles was unmoved, not choosing to confess that he did not trust his son's ability to establish himself in the Low Countries without such a base. He may also have considered that, once Philip was accepted as king, nobody would be in a position to uphold that clause of the treaty against him. Philip eventually agreed, confining himself to a secret disclaimer; but it was a worm in the bud of this marriage from the start.[33]

Renard meanwhile wrote a great deal about Elizabeth, but had very little evidence of what she was actually doing, or to whom she was talking. His suspicion of her, and conviction that she was up to no good, is reflected in every despatch; but apart from the obvious reluctance of her religious conformity he had no tangible information to go on. There was tavern gossip reflecting hostility to the Spaniards, and scepticism about the durability of the Catholic restoration, but little more. Noailles was certainly doing his best to encourage this sort of talk, and was in touch with a conspiracy to derail the marriage.[34] Renard did not know this, and his suspicion of French intrigue was based partly upon a hunch, and partly upon knowledge of how hostile Henry II was to the marriage. His distrust of Elizabeth similarly seems to have been based upon rational deduction rather than knowledge. If anything were to happen to the queen, 'the kingdom would become entirely heretical, and Catholics would be persecuted'. The nearest thing to tangible evidence he retailed on 29 November; a story of what the queen had told him that Lord Paget had told her. According to this third-hand tale, two of Elizabeth's 'principal supporters' had been to Paget and told him that, although they were old and familiar servants of the princess, they acknowledged a prior duty to the queen; over the last month Elizabeth had excluded them from her confidence and had been acting in secret. She had been talking to 'a priest who was said to be a Frenchman and a preacher at the French church in London'. If she was doing anything against the queen, they did not want to be blamed.[35] Given the febrile atmosphere of the court while the marriage negotiations were going on, and the growing evidence of popular opposition to the idea, this does not add up to much; but it helps to explain Renard's continued preoccupation with Elizabeth's 'intrigues'. The council was divided, and Paget had threatened to confront the French ambassador with his knowledge of these dealings – which probably amounted to no more than the story which the queen told Renard.

At the beginning of December, Elizabeth asked for leave to withdraw from the court and go home, presumably to Hatfield or Ashridge. Mary, as usual, asked the imperial ambassador for his advice. He replied with conscious rectitude that she should consult her council, but he regarded the timing of the request as suspicious. Parliament was about to rise, and the statutes which had been passed would come into force, including that restoring the mass. If the heretics were going to cause trouble, it would come then, and he feared that Elizabeth wanted to be in a position to take advantage of such unrest.[36] He advised that she should be detained. On this occasion, however, Mary did not heed his counsel, and by 8 December the princess had left for St Albans. 'She very courteously took her leave', Renard wrote, 'and the Queen also dissembled well.' He then, apparently, took it upon himself with Mary's permission, to go and lecture Elizabeth upon the error of her ways. Both she and the French ambassador were being watched. Noailles knew about this surveillance, but he was used to it, and at this point there was little enough to discover. He had been feeding arguments to the agitators against the Spanish marriage, but there had as yet been no approach from the conspirators, and of Elizabeth there is scarcely a mention. Noailles claimed contact with Courtenay, and some knowledge of his intentions, but beyond retailing a rumour that he would marry the princess and carry her off to 'Dampshire', he had nothing to say of her activities.[37]

On her side, the princess seems to have decided to create a diversion. She knew that the idea of a marriage with Courtenay was popular in some quarters (although no longer in the council), but neither she nor the earl desired it. On the other hand, pressure upon her to make a match acceptable to her sister was bound to grow and she therefore decided to take an initiative. About the beginning of December, probably before she left the court, she sent her cousin Henry Carey to pay a call upon the duke of Savoy.[38] Emmanuel Philibert had suceeded his father Charles III earlier in the year, but he was a prince without a land, because Savoy was under French occupation and its duke merely a general in the service of the emperor. Whether Elizabeth's approach was seriously intended may be doubted, but it was a shrewd move, given her circumstances. Emmanuel was a Catholic, and *persona grata* with the emperor. Even if he regained his inheritance, he would be a minor prince, who in the event of Elizabeth's succeeding to the crown could reasonably be expected to give England priority. This made him acceptable to the English; or at least to such of the nobility as were privy to the move. As usual, rumour at court ran well ahead of the truth. It was said that the duke was coming a-courting, and that Carey's report had been so favourable that it had 'awakened feelings of love and hope in the Lady Elizabeth', who must have been badly in need of both at that point.[39]

Needless to say, there was no sign of Savoy as the year turned, and the princess presumably spent Christmas with her household at Ashridge. By the end of January the threatened storm had broken with a vengeance, in the form of Wyatt's rebellion. The queen's marriage plans had caused great resentment, and her way of going about them more still. Most of what we know about actual developments, as opposed to rumour, has to be pieced together from statements made later, often under pressure. Although there was a good deal of discontent within the council, Renard's suspicions of treasonable conspiracy at that level were unfounded. The initiative for action seems to have come from a number of members of the House of Commons particularly affronted by Mary's reception of their petition on 16 November: Sir Peter Crew, Sir James Croftes, Sir Nicholas Arnold, Sir William Pickering, Sir Edward Rogers, Sir Thomas Wyatt and Sir George Harper.[40] There were also others involved, such as William Winter and William Thomas. These were not negligible men. Carew, Croftes, Arnold and Wyatt were among the leading landowners of Devon, Herefordshire, Gloucestershire and Kent. Winter was surveyor of the navy, Pickering had been Northumberland's ambassador in France, and Thomas clerk to the privy council.[41] Most of them had visible connections with the Edwardian regimes, but none had held high office or been conspicuously in favour, with the possible exception of Thomas, who was nevertheless a comparatively minor figure. Carew, Pickering and Thomas were obviously Protestants, but the others seem to have conformed to 'the queen's proceedings' in that respect without protest.[42] A conspiracy among these men existed in some form by the end of November; and at about that time they established contact with the earl of Devon and the duke of Suffolk. Unfortunately, these two noblemen were politically very different. Courtenay, who was a Catholic and who had no quarrel with the religious regime, seems to have been inspired by no more than a rather childish desire to 'get his own back' on Mary for having rejected him. Suffolk, who remained a Protestant and who had been very fortunate to escape the fate of Northumberland during the summer, may have been hoping to secure the release of his daughter and son-in-law. None of these men were servants of Elizabeth, even in the broadest sense, or known to have been close to her, although both Sir Nicholas Arnold and Sir Nicholas Throgmorton had visited Ashridge.[43] By Christmas the French ambassador was also aware of what was going on, and was encouraging it, although he had no authority to offer his master's support.

The purpose of the conspiracy has never been clearly established, largely because it was the object of deliberate misrepresentation on both sides. After the event the conspirators themselves claimed that their objective had never been other that to force the queen to abandon her marriage plans. 'We mind in no wise to touch her grace', as Sir Thomas Wyatt claimed, even in the midst of action.[44] Stephen Gardiner and his supporters on the council, on the other hand, claimed that it was a heretic plot to restore the Edwardian religious settlement. The queen also appears to have believed this, but that was largely because she did not want to face up to the real unpopularity of her marriage. Gardiner, moreover, had a private agenda. He wanted to minimise the involvement of Courtenay in the plot, because he was religiously orthodox, if nothing else. He also wanted to regain the influence with the queen which he had lost by opposing her marriage in the early stages of negotiation; and a religious interpretation would have best favoured an ecclesiastical remedy.[45] If Gardiner was broadly correct, then the conspirators were obviously aiming to depose Mary. Both Renard and Gardiner believed that the plot was in favour of Elizabeth; but whereas the former believed that part of the conspirators' agenda was to marry her to Courtenay, the latter would accept no such thing. In the event the involvement of the duke of Suffolk, and the fact that Jane Grey and Guildford Dudley were conveniently in custody, already condemned for treason, offered a way out. The official story thus became that this was a religiously motivated plot to restore 'Queen Jane'; and Jane, Guildford and Suffolk were all executed in consequence.[46]

Renard, whose influence was still greater than that of any councillor, and probably increased during the rising which followed the conspiracy, was not satisfied with this. He did not reject the religious explanation, because he had been expecting a 'heretic plot', but he had no time for the theory of a Grey and Dudley restoration. To his mind the French were the moving spirits, working upon the genuine discontent which existed, and Elizabeth was their chosen agent. He had already listed 'the Lady Elizabeth's intrigues, the activities of the French and the state of mind of the people' as the three main obstacles in his path; and the emperor had accepted his view, declaring just before Christmas that the Lady Elizabeth's marriage ought to be delayed, in case it should give the malcontents a leader around whom they might rally.[47] Given his religious priority, Gardiner had no quarrel with that; and together or separately they strove to move the queen and council against Elizabeth. What actually happened is not in much doubt. Having rejected a proposal to assassinate the queen as a 'horrible deed', the conspirators planned a triple rising to take place about Easter. The duke of Suffolk would raise the east midlands from his seat at Bradgate in Leicestershire; Sir Thomas Wyatt would raise Kent from Allington Castle; and either the earl of Devon or Sir Peter Carew would raise Devon. This last proved to be the weak link, because Gardiner succeeded in either frightening or cajoling Courtenay into revealing what he knew.[48] This was garbled and inconclusive, but a sufficient warning. At the same time Renard also picked up what he thought were significant signals, and independently sent an urgent message to the queen to take steps to protect herself.[49] These disclosures quickly became known to the plotters, who had to decide whether to act long before they were ready or run for their lives. They chose the former course, and about 18 January 1554 began to put their hastily formed plans into effect.

On 14 January the council had proclaimed the terms of the marriage treaty, which had just been concluded. This was a very unusual step, but then the marriage of a ruling queen was an unprecedented event. Given the hostile reception which the special ambassadors had received from the London crowd, it was probably also intended to placate opposition by drawing attention to the unexpectedly favourable terms of the treaty. If that was the intention, it seems to have been successful, at least in London. Renard's warning had already been sent, on about 7 January, so the council's action may also have been in response to that. Although Noailles also knew what was going on, and had by this time secured Henry II's promise of support, events were moving far too quickly for him to have any significant impact. On 20 January word reached London 'that Syr Peter Carowe with dyverse others, were uppe in Devonshire resysting of the Kinge of Spaines comyng'.[50] On the 25th the duke of Suffolk and his brothers moved up to Leicestershire, apparently one step ahead of arrest. The same day

the councell was certyfied that ther was uppe in Kente Sir Thomas Wiat, Mr Culpepper, the Lorde Cobham, who had taken his castell of Coulyng, and the lord warden who had taken the castell of Dover, and Sir Herry Isley in Meddestone, Sir James Croftes, Mr Harper, Mr Newton, Mr Knevett, for the saide quarrell in resystyng the Kinge of Spaine.[51]

On 26 January, Elizabeth wrote to Mary from Ashridge, congratulating her upon her forthcoming marriage, but complaining of a heavy cold. The letter is significantly preserved among Renard's papers.[52] On the same day the queen wrote to her 'Entirely beloved sister', summoning her to court. The ambassador commented, 'If she does not come, there will be no doubt that she is the cause of all the trouble.' There were rumours that Ashridge was being fortified.[53] By that time the marquis of Northampton and Sir Edward Warner were already in the Tower, and a hastily mobilised force of Londoners had been sent down into Kent to confront the rebels.

Elizabeth did come; and it is perfectly clear that, whatever she may have been up to, she had not been involved in any kind of hostile mobilisation. Given that she had been accompanied to London by 2000 horsemen the previous July, this is not without significance. The details of what happened thereafter are not clear, or rather there are three versions. A contemporary chronicle declares:

> At this tyme [19 February] or a litle before, the ladye Elisabeth was sent for of the quene by Sir John Williams, with a great nombre of men to come upp to the court immedyatly. And she saying she was very sicke desyred the said Sir John Williams to depart, and that she woulde most willinglye in as spedy a manner as she colde for her sicknesse, repayre to the quenes highnes with her owne company and folkes only.[54]

Another version is the later and apologetic account of John Foxe. According to him Sir Richard Southwell, Sir Edward Hastings and Sir Thomas Cornwallis arrived at Ashridge at ten o'clock at night (date unspecified), and forced their way into the princess's sickroom. Behaving themselves with the barest minimum of courtesy, they informed her that she must accompany them to the court at nine o'clock the next morning. Both she and her servants protested that she was too sick to travel; but the messengers had clearly expected this. According to Foxe they called for two doctors, Wendy and Owen. As these were the queen's own physicians, the implication is that they had brought them with them. They pronounced her fit to be moved 'without danger of life'.[55] Reading between the lines of Foxe's indignation, it is clear that he believed she had been placed under arrest. The choice of agents, who were all councillors of lower rank and staunch Catholics, constituted a calculated disparagement. Accompanied by a small number of her own servants, none of whom are named, the following morning Elizabeth was unceremoniously deposited in the queen's litter, and borne off. Foxe makes the most of her illness, declaring that she was 'ready to swound'. Having secured her person, the councillors were then in no hurry. The twenty-seven mile journey to Westminster was allowed to take five days; first to Redbourne, then to St Albans, then to 'Mymmes' (South Mimms), then to Highgate, and finally to the court.

These two accounts are in some respects contradictory, and it is likely that neither of them is quite accurate. Elizabeth clearly obeyed the queen's summons, but tried to use illness as an excuse for delay. Southwell's involvement seems to have been invented by Foxe, because, according to the third source, a short contemporary letter, it was Lord William Howard who accompanied Hastings and Cornwallis, which puts rather a different complexion on the mission as Howard was sympathetic to the princess.[56] According to Howard, Elizabeth's servants and council were cooperative, although he confirms the involvement of the physicians; and it was presumably he who escorted her to London. Perhaps Williams had already retired rebuffed, which would account for the peremptory tone of Howard's mission, or perhaps he was simply named in error. In the circumstances, it seems unlikely that she would have been allowed 'her owne company and folkes onely', and Howard's testimony certainly does not suggest that. As to the timing, Elizabeth was summoned on 26 January; Howard reached Ashridge on 10 February; she left there on the 12th, and arrived about the 18th, a schedule which allows time for the slow journey, much as Foxe described it.[57]

As they awaited her arrival, the council strove to confront a situation in Kent which seemed likely to get out of control. On 29 January, the duke of Norfolk had been defeated by the rebels at Rochester Bridge, and Wyatt was rolling up the loyalist forces in Kent.[58] There was, however, no movement in Essex or Hertfordshire to join the rebels, and when the crowds turned out to see the princess pass, they knew that the rising had already collapsed. Whether they were as sympathetic to her plight as Foxe claims, we do not know; but no demonstrations caused Howard and his colleagues, or whoever was escorting her, any qualms. On Thursday 1 February, Mary made her stirring and successful appeal to the loyalty of the City of London, and on Saturday, the 3rd, Wyatt's forces entered Southwark.[59] This was a dangerous moment, but the Kentishmen found London bridge held against them, and Wyatt seems not to have known quite what to do next. The same day news reached London that the earl of Huntingdon had captured the duke of Suffolk without a fight. The council began to feel that the worst was passed.

Wyatt, now knowing that the others in his conspiracy had been defeated, made his last move on Tuesday, 6 February. Quitting Southwark, he went up river to Kingston bridge, and marched on London along the north shore of the Thames, arriving early on the morning of Wednesday, 7 February. The best surviving account of what followed, written by the same chronicler already quoted, makes curious reading. Royal troops, under the command of the earl of Pembroke, were waiting for the rebels, but made no attempt to confront them. There was an exchange of gunfire and a skirmish, but no serious fighting. Sir John Gage, the lord chamberlain, had a thousand men at Charing Cross, but they fled after an exchange of fire; and the Kentishmen proceeded via Temple Bar to Ludgate 'going in no good order', and crying out that the queen had granted their requests.[60] She had, of course, done no such thing, but the failure of Pembroke's men to engage is very hard to explain. Wyatt clearly expected the City gate to be opened to him, but when he arrived he found it commanded by Lord William Howard, who ensured that it remained closed. There is no reason to doubt Pembroke's loyalty to the queen, but it is possible that he narrowly avoided the fate of the duke of Norfolk at Rochester bridge. Whatever the true explanation, Wyatt's failure to gain access to the City was critical. Seeing what had happened, Pembroke's men attacked briskly and the rebels, out-numbered and dispirited, were soon overpowered. 'Then was takyng men on all sides.' A small contingent had broken away from the main rebel force and gone down to Westminster, causing panic in the court. When Wyatt surrendered, they tried to cut their way out but were also overpowered.[61]

By the evening of 7 February the rising was over, and Wyatt and his lieutenants were in the Tower. Arrests continued over the next two weeks, and on 12 February Edward Courtenay earl of Devon was returned to the prison which he had left only six months earlier.[62] Courtenay had actually been with Pembroke outside London, but presumably, with the danger over, Gardiner was no longer willing, or able, to protect him. He had certainly been close enough to the rebels to justify his arrest; but whether the same can be said of Elizabeth is more doubtful. For about two weeks after her arrival at Westminster, no one seems to have paid much attention to her. The captured rebels and conspirators were closely interrogated, and some tortured, in an attempt to incriminate her; but nobody seems to have questioned the princess herself. More remarkably, no one questioned her officers either. When she had been in trouble five years earlier, Kate Ashley and Thomas Parry had been quickly arrested, and interrogated with menaces about what she had been doing. This time, there was silence. As Foxe's story unfolds, there are numerous references to her servants and the gentlemen of her household, but they are not named; and none of them were arrested or questioned. Sir William St Low, who was arrested on 25 February, was a dependant of the princess, but not close to her. Wyatt also admitted having written a letter to Elizabeth during the rising

that she shulde gett hir asfar from the cyty as she coulde, the rather for her saftye from strangers; and she sente him worde agayn, but not in wrytyng, by sir William Seyntlowe that she dyd thanke hym for hys goodwil, and she wolde doe as she sholde se cawse &.[63]

St Low had actually been rash enough to appear in company with Sir Henry Isley at Tonbridge, but he admitted nothing in respect of Elizabeth. That was almost the only evidence which was forthcoming.

There was confusion at the time over whether Wyatt himself had, after his conviction on 15 March, drawn up a full statement in writing, accusing both Elizabeth and Courtenay. Lord Chandos later testified in Star Chamber that not only had he done so, but he had also repeated that confession just before his execution on 11 April. However, on the scaffold Wyatt denied the fact: 'yt is not so good people, for I assure you neyther they nor any other now in yonder hold of durance was privie of my rising'.[64] Nor, in spite of Chandos's testimony, was the 'statement in writing' ever produced. A copy of an otherwise lost letter from Elizabeth to the queen turned up, suspiciously enough, enclosed with one of Noailles's despatches which had been intercepted, but that also disappeared.[65]

Had any of the princess's immediate servants been present in the rebel army, they would certainly have been noticed; and it seems reasonable to suppose that Elizabeth had done nothing to further the rebel cause. Apart from anything else, she was under surveillance before the rising began, and the rumours of military preparations at Ashridge were demonstrably false. On the other hand, we know that there were letters and messages. Sir James Croftes had visited Ashridge on his way to Herefordshire at some point in mid-January, and had urged her to move to Donnington. Francis Russell also admitted having carried a letter from Wyatt to her.[66] She herself committed nothing to writing, but she must have known something of what was afoot. If she had decisively distanced herself from any move against the queen, the rebels would not have had anywhere to go, and might well not have embarked upon their enterprise. That she was in contact with Noailles seems entirely likely, and would account for the 'French preacher' who was alleged to have visited her. It is equally likely that she kept these contacts from her own officers. Experience in 1549 would have taught her that what they did not know they could not testify to. Had someone thought of interrogating Kate Ashley under duress they might have learned more; but those who would have known that were not in Mary's confidence.

Elizabeth knew perfectly well that everyone who disliked Mary's policies, for whatever reason, looked to her for remedy; and it was an awareness which she was to remember keenly many years later when she was on the throne.[67] To that extent she was guilty in the queen's eyes, no matter what she did or did not do. She also knew that her mother had been executed on charges not much more substantial than those which could be brought against her now, careful as she had been. It is not surprising that she was frightened.

The council, however, was divided about what should be done with her. Renard was insistent that both Elizabeth and Courtenay should be put on trial, with a view to removing them both by execution.[68] Gardiner had no love for the princess either, but believed that the ambassador's campaign could backfire, not only upon himself but also upon the prince for whose security he would be partly responsible. Most of the council were even more equivocal, realising that, unless or until the queen had a child of her own, Elizabeth represented the only secure and acceptable succession. While they debated the issue, Elizabeth was kept in comfortable but nerve-racking isolation at Westminster, where she saw 'neither King nor Queen, nor lord nor friend'. At length, on 16 March, the chancellor decided to try bluff; accompanied by an impressive array of nearly twenty fellow councillors, he descended upon the princess and charged her roundly with complicity, not only with Wyatt but also with Sir Peter Carew's abortive efforts in Devon. The implication was that, if she confessed her fault and submitted, the queen would be merciful.[69]

Elizabeth, however, was far too shrewd to fall for such a ruse. If she confessed to having offended the queen at all, it could be used as a confession of treason. Perhaps Mary intended to pardon her in return for such a submission – or perhaps not. Neither then, nor throughout the ordeal which followed, would the princess admit to having been an offender in any way. Disappointed of his purpose, Gardiner then made his next move: he proposed to send her to the Tower. There was considerable opposition to such a move within the council; she was a king's daughter, and nothing had been proved against her. The chancellor, however, had the answer to these scruples; if one of the lords of the council was prepared to accept responsibility for her safe-keeping, he would drop his proposal. No one was prepared to take such a risk, and on 18 March she was committed to the Tower.[70]

The scenes which followed have become part of the fabric of English folklore, but both the main sources are in substantial agreement. When the marquis of Winchester and the earl of Sussex arrived on the 17th to escort her to prison, she begged permission to write to her sister. The marquis demurred, pointing out that they would miss the tide at London bridge, and declaring that such a letter was likely to do more harm than good. Sussex, however, disagreed, and Elizabeth duly wrote:

> I am by your council from you commanded to go unto the Tower, a place more wonted for a false traitor than a true subject ... And to this present hour I protest

afore God (who shall judge my truth whatsoever malice may devise) that I never practiced, counselled, nor consented to anything which might be prejudicial to your person any way or dangerous to the state by any mean.[71]

There was a good deal more in the same vein, concluding 'I humbly crave but only one word of answer from yourself'. Whether Mary ever saw this letter we do not know; she certainly did not respond. Whether Elizabeth really expected a reply, or was mainly concerned to play for time, we do not know either.

Winchester was right, in that they missed the tide; but it did not make any difference, and the following morning she arrived at the Tower by barge. A large crowd had assembled, and she seems to have been genuinely intimidated, as was no doubt the intention. It was also her first great histrionic opportunity, and one she obviously took; perhaps as much by instinct as calculation.[72] At first she refused to leave the barge, on the grounds that she was no traitor to be brought to such a place. When it was pointed out to her that she did not have any option, and that in any case it was beginning to rain, she gave way. Then, putting aside the proffered cloak 'with a fine dash', she crossed the drawbridge to where Sir John Gage was waiting to receive her. According to Foxe, there were emotional scenes of men falling on their knees and crying out 'God save your grace', 'who the next day were released of their cold coates' (that is, dismissed from their positions).[73] The Tower chronicler says nothing of this, but both agree that she made another impassioned speech, declaring her innocence and the injustice of her treatment, before entering the prison. So far, honours were about even, but the council had no idea what to do with their captive. Towards the end of March it was still realistic to hope that some of the rebels and conspirators who had been caught would testify against her. Renard's hostility was implacable, and he was prepared to believe any story to her discredit. On 19 February, reporting the execution of Jane Grey, he also retailed the familiar scandal that Elizabeth 'lived loosely like her mother, and is now with child', although he did not venture to name the putative father.[74] On 8 March he reported that she had been interrogated by Gardiner, Arundel and Paget, and that her fate would hang on the result, but nothing transpired; and a few days later he blamed the chancellor for conducting affairs so slackly, and for keeping everything in the hands of his own men.[75] On 13 March he wrote to Philip that both Courtenay and Elizabeth would be put on trial; and then, believing that he had won his point, he began to pressure the council to get the trials completed (and presumably the executions carried out) before Philip's arrival.[76] He also knew, however, that the council was deeply divided on the issue, and continued to be jittery about 'heretic plots'. In fact the attitude of the earl of Sussex seems to have been representative. He probably did not weep as copiously as Foxe alleged, but both at Westminster and at the Tower he was very careful to warn his colleagues against exceeding their commission:

> Yt is saide that when she was in [the Tower] the lorde trezerer and the lorde chamberlaine began to lock the dores very straytlye, then the erle of Sussex with wepinge eies, saide What will you doe my lordes? What meane ye therein? She was a kinges daughter and is the quenes syster, and ye have no suffycient commyssion so to do.[77]

Such an attitude was common prudence in the circumstances, particularly as the queen's real intentions were unknown, but Renard found it deeply frustrating. As far as he was concerned, Sussex was in league with the heretics, and he named Hastings, Cornwallis and his erstwhile ally Paget as being in the same case.[78] By early April the ambassador's attitude was verging on the paranoid, and he found himself in alliance with Stephen Gardiner, of whom he had recently been so suspicious. Nor was the emperor a great deal of help. Having issued what he revealingly described as his 'instructions' as to how the offenders were to be dealt with, he then reminded Renard that it was the queen's responsibility to 'proceed with Elizabeth and Courtenay as she shall think best for her own security.'[79] A few days after her arrival at the Tower, Gardiner had questioned her 'of the talk that was at Ashridge'. Elizabeth was confronted with Sir James Croftes, but neither of them made any admission of significance, and the princess's protest against the manner in which everyone was questioned about her was spirited and to the point.

Failure to extract any usable evidence from Sir Thomas Wyatt himself probably marked the end of this investigation, although not of the suspicion which had inspired it. Having at first been denied the liberty of the Tower gardens, by the middle of April that privilege had been conceded. Foxe's story of the child who was thought to be carrying messages between Elizabeth and Courtenay dates that episode to when she was at liberty to walk; but the point is merely to emphasise the unreasonable strictness of Sir Thomas Bridges, the lieutenant of the Tower, rather than to suggest that there really was a clandestine correspondence.[80] By 17 April even Renard had given up. He was still firmly convinced of her guilt, but had to accept the lawyers' opinion that by English law there was insufficient evidence to convict.[81] He did not stoop to observe that such trivialities had not stopped Henry VIII.

What was to be done with her? It would not be safe to let her follow the court; perhaps she should be sent to the far north 'where the people are good Christians'; or perhaps she should be married overseas. Both Dom

Luis of Portugal and the duke of Savoy were mentioned as possibilities.[82] Simply to do away with her without law would provoke rebellion, in which many lords would join; if she were released unconditionally, the heretics would probably proclaim her queen. By about 5 May it had been decided to send her away to house arrest in the country, but not to press any marriage plans. The council did not share Renard's alarmism; and if Gardiner was still 'gaping after her blood', he was restrained. According to Foxe, the chancellor had tried to short-circuit the judicial process, presumably after 11 April, by issuing on his own authority a writ for Elizabeth's execution. He had been frustrated by the vigilance of Sir Thomas Bridges, who would not act without the queen's sign manual; when he sought it, the fraud was exposed.[83] There is not a scrap of supporting evidence for this, and it is inconceivable that a man in Gardiner's position would have taken such a risk; or that he would have kept his office if he had. Elizabeth's situation during these three months or so was certainly dangerous, but not as dangerous as Foxe was anxious to make it appear in support of his vision of a protective Deity.

None of the steps were taken which would have been usual against one about to be charged with treason. Even when Elizabeth was committed to the Tower, her estates were not sequestered and her goods were not inventoried. The disruption to her household should not be underestimated, but it was not deprived of the means to function. Nor, as far as we know, were any of her officers or other servants displaced. There are references to her council and her officers collectively, but they are never named. Presumably they remained at Ashridge, managing her affairs as best they could. According to Foxe, she was accompanied to the court by some of her own ladies and gentlemen, but neither their number nor their names are given. A person of her status under arrest would normally have been allowed between six and twelve attendants, and although she was kept in seclusion at Westminster, meals and all other services would have been provided from the court.

When she moved to the Tower, the situation inevitably changed. A prisoner was expected to live at his or her own cost in confinement, but that would normally have meant paying a fee to the gaoler for provisions. Elizabeth was not treated in that way. For some time, again according to Foxe, her 'diets' were brought into the Tower by a team of her own servants, who had presumably set up a kitchen somewhere nearby.[84] There arose over this an altercation between the princess's gentlemen and the garrison soldiers who appeared to receive the provisions from them at the gate. On appealing to the constable, they were told that, as Elizabeth was a prisoner, she would be served by his own men, and that the princess's council had no business appointing them to that function. If they persisted, they would find themselves imprisoned as well. For some undisclosed reason, however, the queen's council did not back him up, with the result that a team of Elizabeth's servants, cooks and others were allowed to prepare her food separately in one of the Tower kitchens. This inevitably led to further strife, but the constable was unable to dislodge his unwelcome visitors, who went on serving their mistress as long as she was there.[85] The implication is that she paid handsomely for this unusual privilege. Where they lived while they were performing this service is not clear, but it was certainly at Elizabeth's expense. Some at least of the princess's servants seem to have feared a 'privy conspiracy' against her, or perhaps that is just the way Foxe makes it appear. At least they had the means to ensure that nobody poisoned her.

Towards the end of April the council appears to have decided that such close confinement could no longer be justified, or at least that it was no longer producing any dividends. On 4 May Bridges was relieved of his responsibilities as constable of the Tower, and replaced by Sir Henry Bedingfield.[86] Bedingfield was a man with no experience of office, but he was a substantial landowner in Norfolk, devoted to the queen, and perhaps most important of all, a loyal Catholic. He was appointed to serve with a hundred of his own men, and Elizabeth apparently believed that this was a move intended to do away with her. According to Foxe, she enquired anxiously whether Lady Jane's scaffold had been removed. She need not have worried; although there was an elaborate exchange of memoranda between Bedingfield and the council about the exact extent of his duties, his stay at the Tower was brief, and was intended to be so. His main job was not to run the Tower but to guard Elizabeth, and on 19 May she left that prison under his escort, bound for Woodstock in Oxfordshire.[87] Renard believed that her eventual destination was to have been Pontefract, but that seems to have been mere wishful thinking. Foxe was extremely rude about Bedingfield's men, calling them rascals and rakehells, and implying that they were all desperate to do the princess some injury, but there is no reason to suppose that they were anything other than ordinary soldiers.

They proceeded in a leisurely fashion, via Richmond and Windsor to Wheatley and Kidlington, before arriving at Woodstock about four days later. Bedingfield was nervous and intensely conscientious, reporting at length to the council at least once a day during the journey. Comparing his letters with Foxe's account produces what is recognisably the same sequence of events from two different points of view.[88] Foxe claims that the people turned out in droves to see the princess pass, with many shouts of 'God save your Grace!'; and that Bedingfield was intensely displeased,

ordering the imprisonment of some hapless villagers who had rung their
church bells to honour her. His own letters confirm the latter story, and
include such comments as, 'betwixt London and these parts [Windsor] men
be not good and whole in matters of religion, the noblemen and gentlemen
be fully fixed to stand to the late abolishing of the bishop of Rome's
authority'.[89] Having encountered 'a very protestant', of whom he had sought
directions, he 'enquired of Woburn and Wickham market, which for the
most part be of the same opinion'. Between Windsor and Wickham there
had been 'much gazing', and 'the wives had prepared cakes and wafers,
which at her passing by they delivered into the litter', until they threatened
to swamp it, and Elizabeth had been forced to ask them to stop. 'Item,
passing by the town of Wheatley, there all the people awaited her passing,
with God save your Grace'. So in this respect, Foxe did not exaggerate, and
Bedingfield had every reason to be pensive, if not alarmed.

Woodstock had been an important residence in the days of Henry VII
and of earlier kings, but Henry VIII had used it very little, and Edward VI
not at all. The council had ordered some kind of preparations to be made,
but Bedingfield was alarmed to discover on arrival that only four rooms
had been made properly habitable, and that only three doors in the entire
house could be locked.[90] He took what steps he could, and settled down
uneasily for an indeterminate vigil. Elizabeth herself was difficult enough;
bored and frustrated, she constantly took out her ill humour upon her
'gaoler', as she insisted upon calling him. He was not her equal in wit,
education or intelligence, and was constantly driven back upon his orders
in justifying some refusal to grant what looks like a reasonable request.
There were numerous altercations about what books she was to be allowed
to have.[91] On one occasion he refused her demand to be given an English
Bible, and was then overruled by the council. At another time she requested
the company of one John Picton, whom she claimed had taught her languages in the past. She was getting out of practice and wanted such
conversation to help pass the time. The request was refused on the grounds
that no one knew who John Picton was.

There were constant battles over her walks in the grounds, and on more
than one occasion the situation undermined her health. Bedingfield reported
these ailments with a straight face, but the council obviously suspected her
of malingering, and refused her request for one of the royal physicians,
referring her instead to a doctor in Oxford.[92] Her servants were the real
nightmare. She seems to have had about three or four ladies, a similar
number of gentlemen, and perhaps half a dozen yeomen and grooms. They
were constantly changing, either because of illness, or because Elizabeth
dismissed them, or because Bedingfield decided that they were up to no

good and got rid of them himself. Elizabeth Sandes was so dismissed, much
to the princess's annoyance, and her request to have the attendance of
Dorothy Broadbelte and Elizabeth Norwich was refused.[93] The council
obviously vetted everyone who had regular access to her, but their names
do not mean much in a wider context. Although she was paying them, it
cannot be assumed that they were her servants in any proper sense. There
is no mention of the Ashleys, and Kate Ashley's attendance, if not her
service, must have been suspended for the time of Elizabeth's imprisonment.
Thomas Parry, on the other hand, was very much on the scene. This was
largely because Elizabeth was constrained to pay the bills not only for herself
but also for Bedingfield.

Sir Henry was still constable of the Tower, although not in residence,
and his hundred men were paid by the council; but his own expenses, and
those of twenty servants, were paid by the princess.[94] This meant that Parry's
presence, however distasteful to Bedingfield, was necessary, and the council
rescinded its original decision to send him away. He set up an 'office' in
the nearby town of Woodstock, and from there fed regular sums of money
to the palace, not without disagreements and recriminations. He also provided lodgings for Elizabeth's real servants, as they came and went about
her lawful business. Her estate still had to be run, and her house at Ashridge
maintained. Bedingfield regarded these comings and goings with the deepest
suspicion, but was unable to prevent them. There is no doubt that, in spite
of his vigilance, the princess managed by this means to keep open her
communications with the outside world. Some messengers were detected
and frustrated; a few were even briefly imprisoned. We do not know what
got through, or what difference it made; probably very little, except to give
Elizabeth the satisfaction of scoring the occasional point. The strain of this
hostile relationship took its toll on both of them. On 7 July Bedingfield
was licensed to be absent from his post during the day, provided that he
left a sufficient person in charge, and returned each night.[95]

Mary's suspicions of her sister were undiminished. When Elizabeth occasionally got permission to write to the queen, with Bedingfield standing
over her, she always took the opportunity to protest her innocence, and her
loyalty. Mary obviously found this liturgy as tedious as it was unconvincing,
and either ignored her letters, or replied via Bedingfield:

> the copies of her secret letters to us were found in the packet of the French
> Ambassador, and divers of the most notable traitors made their chief account
> upon her. We can hardly be brought to think that they would have presumed
> to do so unless they had more certain knowledge of her favour towards their
> unnatural conspiracies than is yet by her confessed.[96]

The deduction was natural, but not valid. The council had received, and was to go on receiving, reports of people in all walks of life expressing support for Elizabeth who were not conspirators, and who had no known connection with her.[97]

Bedingfield's surviving correspondence with the council comes to an end in November 1554. Letters were becoming less frequent by the end of August, or it may be that he simply stopped recording them. It is also possible that Mary's supposed pregnancy, which was revealed at that time, had the effect of diminishing interest in Elizabeth. It is alleged that she spent the Christmas of 1554 at court, on Philip's initiative, but there is no contemporary allusion to that, and she was certainly at Woodstock soon after the New Year.[98] Bedingfield's ordeal finally came to an end on 17 April 1555, when the council decided that Elizabeth should be brought to court for the dangerous time of the queen's lying in. He was responsible for escorting her there, but kept no record of the journey, and thereafter seems to have been discharged. Throughout the period of his custodianship, he conveys the impression of a most conscientious man, slightly out of his depth. Elizabeth, in spite of her real fear and anger, played games with him, and enjoyed causing him as much confusion and distress as possible; it was her way of exacting a small revenge. She did not do anything dangerous, such as refusing to go to mass; indeed on one occasion Bedingfield reported with obvious satisfaction that she had received the sacrament of the altar most devoutly; but she did enjoy making him sweat. Foxe makes him appear something of a buffoon, with more than a streak of cruelty, but that has more to do with Foxe's agenda than with Bedingfield's real behaviour.[99] He was to follow Sir Henry Jerningham as vice-chamberlain in 1557, so Mary obviously found no fault with his service.

Just as Foxe was concerned to make Sir Henry appear malicious, when in fact he was just being conscientious, so we should take his stories of the princess's perils with a pinch of salt. According to Foxe there was an attempt to set fire to her room; one of the park-keepers called Paul Peny was suborned to assassinate her; and a servant of Gardiner's named James Bassett turned up in the vicinity with twenty thugs, but was foiled in his purpose by the loyal subordinate whom Bedingfield had left in charge in his absence.[100] These stories are very much like that of the chancellor's abortive execution warrant and should be seen in the context of Foxe's attempts to demonise the Catholic clergy. It was they, he declared, who were constantly insisting to the queen that she should secure a formal submission, and when frustrated 'looked blacke in the mouth, and tolde the Queene that they marveiled that she submitted not herself to her majesties mercye, considering that she had offended her highness'. Apparently even some of

Elizabeth's friends thought that this would have been a prudent course, but she herself disagreed, saying

> that she would never submitte her selfe to them whome she never offended. For (quoth she) if I have offended and am giltie, then I crave no mercye but the law, which I am certaine (quoth she) I should have had ere this if it coulde be proved by me.[101]

Hard as it was, she held to this uncompromising line, striving, as Mary realised perfectly well, to convince the interested onlookers that she was being unjustly victimised. It was in this spirit of defiance, bordering on bravado, that she left (Foxe claims), her famous inscription at Woodstock:

> Much suspected by me
> Nothing prooved can be
> Quoth Elizabeth prisoner.

A few days after Elizabeth's removal to Woodstock, on 25 May, Courtenay was sent to a similar confinement at Fotheringhay.[102] The evidence against him had been rather stronger, but he did not represent a similar threat and was in any case regarded as something of a fool. Renard's panicky letters in January and February always linked him with Elizabeth, and with the French. On one occasion the ambassador had even claimed that Anne of Cleves and her brother the duke of Cleves were in the plot, although he always alleged that 'the king of France was the prime mover', a claim now known to have been unjustified.[103] As the imperialist clamour for Elizabeth's execution subsided during March and early April, Courtenay faded from the scene. Efforts to incriminate him had always been indirect attempts to get at the princess; as those attempts failed, interest in him also waned. The long-term problem of what to do about Elizabeth remained, however, and her rustication to Woodstock was not an answer. When Paget fell out of favour for opposing Gardiner's religious plans in the parliament of April 1554, Renard suddenly became convinced that he, too, was intriguing with the princess. This was apparently on the basis of his having had a long conversation with Sir Philip Hoby, 'who is a heretic and deeply devoted to Elizabeth'. The ambassador even went to the extraordinary length of persuading the queen to have Paget's correspondence intercepted to secure evidence of his seditious activities.[104] This sedition was entirely imaginary, and that the queen should have complied is an indictment of her lack of political sense. Paget's attitude to Elizabeth was entirely pragmatic: she was the heir to the throne and her position was a great deal stronger than Mary (but not Renard) was prepared to acknowledge.

On 29 July, after Philip's arrival and when he himself was no longer quite so close to events, the ambassador reported with weary frustration that a decision about Elizabeth's future had still not been taken. If she should be set at liberty, she would renew her plotting; if she was kept in confinement, it would offend her sympathisers within the council, of whom the admiral (Lord William Howard) and the earl of Arundel were the chief. The latter was alleged to be hatching a sinister plot to marry his son, Lord Maltravers, to the princess, with an eye on the crown.[105] Perhaps she should be sent to the queen dowager's court at Brussels. In November 1554, and now distinctly out of touch with events, Renard reported that Elizabeth was of less account now that the queen was pregnant, and might be married to some minor German prince – the margrave Charles of Baden was being discussed as a possibility.[106] On 5 December the duke of Savoy made his long delayed appearance in England, and there was renewed speculation about a marriage with him; it is possible that she was brought to court at that time to meet him; if so, nothing came of it.[107]

Instead, and surprisingly, Paget, now fully restored to favour, seems to have revived the possibility of a Courtenay match. Nothing came of that either, apart from an attempt by some malcontents in Hampshire to use it as a pretext for rebellion. In March 1555 the emperor instructed Renard, via the bishop of Arras, to secure the despatch of Courtenay to Rome and Elizabeth to Brussels, where it was intended that she should reside with Mary of Hungary until a suitable marriage could be arranged for her.[108] Courtenay was indeed sent to Italy in May, but Elizabeth remained firmly in England. If the queen should miscarry, it was not only the princess herself who wanted her to be on the spot.

Elizabeth was brought to court soon after. Suprisingly, Foxe attributed this improvement in her circumstances to the friendship of Philip's Spanish courtiers. It may be that Philip himself had decided that it was in his interest to hold out a hand of friendship to the heir; or it may have been the result of a mysterious initiative by Lord Williams of Thame. Williams requested permission to visit the princess at Woodstock, partly on the grounds that he could persuade her to abandon 'the new religion' and thus recover the queen's favour, and partly to encourage her to ask permission to leave the country.[109] Bedingfield, Renard reported, had monitored their encounter closely, and knew that they were plotting, but could not find out what. As Elizabeth had already ostensibly abandoned Protestantism, and it is hard to see why Williams should have wanted her to go abroad at that juncture, the whole episode remains unresolved. The report may have been a garbled misunderstanding; in the same letter, as further evidence of the princess's plotting, the ambassador declared that she was in the habit of speaking secretly to her 'purveyor' and 'treasurer' (presumably Parry) 'but she is too clever to get caught'.[110] Elizabeth remained at court throughout the painful fiasco of Mary's non-delivery; but once it was clear that the queen was neither going to die nor have a child, on 4 August, she was quietly allowed to withdraw to Ashridge, from which she had been so unceremoniously removed eighteen months before.

Her position as heir had been neither rejected nor confirmed, but it did not require a sensitive political intelligence to realise that Mary's misfortune had significantly shifted the balance of power between the sisters. As Elizabeth reassembled a normal life, and her scattered household hastened to rejoin her, the emperor's servants took council to resolve her future for her, without reference to Mary. A servant of Ferdinand, king of the Romans, the emperor's brother and heir, wrote to his master on 29 September, that as there was now no prospect of issue from the marriage between Philip and Mary, the question of Elizabeth's marriage was urgent. The English council would not discuss the matter, as too dangerous, but he could see three possible solutions. The best 'in the interest of your Majesty' would be a match with his own son, Prince Ferdinand; 'if he were to give up whatever he might be entitled to as your son, he might go to England and never leave that country, which is what the English desire'.[111] After this dig at the recently departed Philip, he went on that a second possibility would be a union with Don Carlos (Philip's son); and the third the duke of Savoy, in spite of his 'reduced circumstances'. No matter what they might think, however, neither Ferdinand nor Charles had the disposal of Elizabeth. For the next few months she either lived quietly at Ashridge, or began a fresh round of feverish plotting, according to your point of view.

The year 1555 was a bad one for Mary. It had started well enough with the final completion of the reconciliation with Rome. The queen had been forced (mainly by Philip) to make more concessions than she had wished, but England had rejoined the Catholic Church, to sounds of rejoicing throughout the Habsburg lands.[112] The queen was also ostensibly, and visibly, pregnant, and Philip had agreed to defer his urgent business elsewhere until after her lying in. However, as early as February things had started to go wrong. With a proper ecclesiastical jurisdiction back in place, the time had come to deal with the heretics who were cluttering up the prisons. There were at this stage no disagreements between the three people mainly responsible for dealing with the situation. Cardinal Reginald Pole, whose legatine jurisdiction was the chief agency, was not an enthusiastic persecutor, but he knew his duty. Neither Mary nor Gardiner took Protestantism seriously as a religious movement. They believed that reformed doctrine was simply an excuse to plunder the church and diminish its power. The imprisoned heretics were therefore simply a dispossessed political party;

and their so-called 'constancy' was merely a skin-deep pretence to gain them some credibility. The threat of death by burning, which could now be used, would be more than sufficient to expose them for the timeserving hypocrites they really were.[113] Unfortunately for the government, this turned out to be a serious miscalculation; by the time that about a dozen leading preachers had gone to the stake with unflinching courage in February and March, Gardiner had realised that. By the summer, with the death toll steadily mounting, and the preponderance of humble lay victims becoming very noticeable, he tried to call a halt. The religious credibility of Protestantism was growing by the day, and there were worrying signs that hostile propaganda was beginning to find an audience. Neither Mary nor Pole, however, saw persecution as a policy, which might succeed or fail; to them it was a duty, and there could be no question of halting or turning away. The chancellor's reservations were brushed aside.

In July came the disaster of Mary's miscarriage – or whatever it was – when the trappings of pregnancy were removed, and it was admitted that there was no child. Within a month a regime that had seemed to be establishing itself solidly, with good long-term prospects, became fragile. With hindsight it is easy to argue that that had always been the case, and that, given Mary's age and medical history, the prospect of an heir was always remote. That was not how it appeared in the early part of 1555, however, when the doubters appeared to have been confounded; and her supporters were eager to point out how good God had been to their virtuous queen.[114] By the end of July it was the sceptics who had been justified. Mary was shattered, physically and emotionally. Her piety refused to allow that God had turned his back on her, and she continued to believe, in the face of all the evidence, that she would have a child; but only the most ideologically committed shared her conviction. Neither at home nor abroad did serious politicians now believe that Mary would have an heir of her body. Worse still, there must be serious doubts about the state of the queen's own health. She recovered slowly, and by October was discharging business more or less as usual; but she had become prone to fits of depression and her energy was noticeably diminished.

On 26 August Mary was well enough to accompany Philip as he set off on his long-delayed journey to his father in the Low Countries, but that parting, and what it implied, lowered her spirits still further.[115] By the end of September Philip had taken over responsibility for the government there and the main burden of the ongoing war with France. At the same time the anti-Habsburg pope, Paul IV, was being seriously troublesome in Italy; then in January 1556, Philip received the remainder of his inheritance, the crowns of Spain. His political centre of gravity had shifted finally and decisively away from England. There were many reasons for this, but one was his conviction that he would not now father a future king or queen of England, and that that kingdom in consequence represented a purely temporary asset.

The summer of 1555 was wet and cold, and the harvest failed, threatening food shortages and high prices. In November Stephen Gardiner, the lord chancellor, died. He had been a cross-grained and difficult man, who had not always seen eye to eye with either Henry or Mary; but he was a statesman of first-class ability and the queen was unable to replace him.[116] In September Simon Renard also left. He had played little part in the events of the year, being distrusted and disliked by Philip. With the king's departure he might have recovered some influence, but Charles V decided to post him elsewhere; another sign, perhaps of England's diminishing importance in imperial plans.

It is impossible to overestimate the importance of this turn-around from Elizabeth's point of view. Whereas she had been heir to the throne since Edward's death, that position had been precarious. We know that Renard had wanted to secure her execution in order to safeguard Philip; and we do not need to believe Foxe's atrocity stories to accept that Gardiner also wanted her (at least) excluded from the succession. Now both had gone. Gone also was any realistic prospect of an alternative heir. Margaret Douglas was a non-starter; Mary Stuart was unacceptable both to Mary and Philip; so was Catherine Grey, Jane Grey's sister, suspect both for her religion and her connections. Not only the failure of Mary's pregnancy but the manner of it was significant. An ordinary miscarriage might have been regarded as a routine misfortune, of no great importance; but this was not an ordinary miscarriage. It appears to have been a phantom pregnancy induced partly by an intense desire for a child, but also partly by a physical condition which was shortly to prove fatal.[117] No one could have been sure of that at the time; but the omens for long life were not much better than the omens for successful childbearing.

With Philip deeply committed in Europe, and having no legal claim to the throne in the event of Mary's death, it became a question of not whether but when Elizabeth would become queen. In a sense she remained vulnerable. Mary could, at any time, have had her framed on a charge of treason, or forced her into a foreign marriage; but her council would have been solidly against the former solution and divided over the latter. Moreover, Philip's attitude, which still counted for a great deal with Mary, had also changed. As long as he hoped for a child of his own, Elizabeth was more of a threat than an asset; but when that hope disappeared, she became the best prospect. This increased the possibility of her being forced into marriage, but virtually removed any remaining chance of a plot against either her life or her legal rights.[118]

A new conspiracy which was to extend the energies and imagination of Mary's council began in the dark days of August 1555, at just about the time when Elizabeth returned to Ashridge. The council had already moved to break up what it regarded as a suspicious gathering of gentlemen in London during July, when they should have been about their business in the country. Renard, who reported this move, described them as 'partisans of Elizabeth'; and they may have been a group of her servants and adherents who, having got wind of her impending release, were waiting to escort her back to Ashridge.[119] If so, it was an ill-considered gesture. In order to emphasise the danger which he thought this gathering represented, Giovanni Michieli, the Venetian ambassador, claimed that the Dudleys were among them, although it is not clear whether he meant the surviving sons of the duke of Northumberland (Ambrose, Henry and Robert), or their cousins (Henry, John and Thomas).[120] The former were enjoying favour from Philip, which they would not have wanted to jeopardise, but all could be described as friends of the princess.

At the same time Edward Randall, who had escaped abroad after the failure of the Wyatt rising, turned up in London and approached Noailles with a fresh proposal. A group of English gentlemen, he told the ambassador, had sworn to 'recover their liberties' by the end of August. Would the French king be willing to help? Montmorency, to whom Noailles referred this enquiry, instructed him not to be drawn.[121] The queen's misfortunes seem to have stimulated a groundswell of discontent. Much of the surviving evidence was testified later in different circumstances, and it is difficult to know how seriously to take it all, but there was certainly a good deal of talk. Much of this focused on persistent rumours that Philip was trying to force Mary into crowning him as king. Although strictly speaking this would have made no difference to his position, it was widely interpreted as a move to secure the crown for Philip if Mary should 'miscarry'.[122] The rumour was well founded, because the king did indeed attempt to put pressure on the queen for that purpose; but the interpretation was probably exaggerated. Other evidence suggests that Philip already believed that he would have to fight for the English succession, and was not prepared to do so. His aim may well have been more limited: to strengthen his position during Mary's lifetime, and particularly to make it easier for him to draw on English military and naval resources. He was thought, however, to be threatening Elizabeth's rights, and all those who were building their expectations upon her succession were worried and alarmed. When parliament met, on 21 October, the storm signals were set. There was opposition to the subsidy which it was known that the queen would demand; there was opposition to the expected proposals to return first fruits and tenths to the church; and it was feared that some measure would be introduced to facilitate the king's crowning 'by force or fraud'.[123]

It is an exaggeration to suggest that the House of Commons in this parliament was in any general way opposed to government policy; but, for the first time in any Tudor parliament, we have some evidence that there were organised opposition groups, meeting outside the House to concert their tactics; we also know that they were in touch with the French ambassador.[124] In the event, they did not achieve very much. The subsidy was passed without too much difficulty, and the restoration of church revenues was pushed through on a division, which was itself unusual. Their one tangible success was to frustrate a measure to confiscate the property of those who had left the realm without licence. As these were mainly religious refugees, this has been interpreted as a crypto-Protestant objection, but the chances are it was more concerned with protecting property rights against arbitrary interference.[125]

The queen also declined Philip's request for a coronation, on the pretext that parliament would not allow it. Whether this really influenced her decision we do not know. The king pointed out indignantly, and rightly, that such a crowning was none of parliament's business, but Mary did not relent and relations with her consort deteriorated. As had happened two years earlier, the meeting of parliament threw up a conspiracy which involved some of the members. Although the queen was intensely annoyed by the recalcitrance of the Commons over the 'Exiles Bill', and the ring leader, Sir Anthony Kingston, was briefly imprisoned when the session ended on 9 December, neither she nor her council seem to have connected this demonstration with the rumours of sedition which were circulating.[126] In which case they were a shade complacent, because not only was there a real plot involving the French ambassador, but Kingston was deeply involved.

The Dudley conspiracy was fundamentally an attempt by the French to use English malcontents to destabilise the pro-Habsburg government. At least the aim was to keep that government unsettled and busy at home so that it would not enter the war on the emperor's side; at most it was to depose Mary and replace her, either with Elizabeth or with Mary Stuart. The intention of the plotters as they got together in November and December was to set up an invasion by a force of English exiles from France, supported by French money and mercenaries; that invasion was then to be greeted by a sympathetic rising among the gentry of the south west and the Welsh marches.[127] Such a plan was not ridiculous. It was, in fact, very much the sort of action which had got rid of Richard III in 1485; and nobody knows whether, if the invasion had come, Mary would have proved any stronger than Richard.

In the event, the invasion did not come, and the conspiracy exists mainly in the papers of the investigators who tried to get to the bottom of it in March and April 1556. The main reason for this was that Henry II, having secured a truce in his war with the emperor at Vaucelles in January 1556, turned against provoking Philip into renewed hostilities. Henry Dudley and his colleagues, who had been 'entertained with fair words' before Christmas, were sent away with fleas in their ears, and Noailles was instructed to disengage.[128] The latter was easier said than done, and the ambassador was eventually expelled for his encouragement of sedition.

In the meantime the conspirators had to decide what to do following the withdrawal of this crucial support. They appear to have decided that what they had really needed from Henry was money, but if they could get that from another source, then their plan could proceed. They may have been led to believe that they would be able to recruit mercenaries in France, so long as the French king did not provide them himself. A subsidiary plot was therefore developed to relieve Nicholas Brigham, one of the tellers of the exchequer, of £50,000 in silver bullion which was in his custody.[129] The conspirators gained access to the vault, and had a ship waiting to remove the silver, when they were betrayed and arrested. We do not know whether this detection was last minute bad luck, or whether the plotters had been under surveillance for some time, so it is very difficult to assess their real chances of success. If, however, they had got away with £50,000, they would have had more than enough to hire three thousand men for three months, which was approximately what they had intended. At the same time, with only some three or four hundred English exiles to call upon, the ability of such a force to overturn Mary's government would have depended entirely upon the scale of their support within England, as against the queen's ability to mobilise against them.

Such events inevitably drew attention to Elizabeth, and the question of whether she had any involvement in them. Her name was automatically in the mouth of anyone who hoped to benefit from Mary's discomfiture, and the withdrawal of active French support meant that there would no longer be any pressure to intrude Mary Stuart. Nor did anyone any longer even pretend to believe that a demonstration in force could compel the queen to change any aspect of her policy. The Dudley conspiracy was therefore intended to overthrow Mary and replace her with Elizabeth.[130] As the imprisoned conspirators fell over each other to confess and incriminate each other, they hardly bothered to conceal the fact. As they almost invariably linked that intention with the purpose of marrying her to the earl of

Devon, we are entitled to wonder how much they really knew of the purposes of their true leaders, who were never named, much less caught. Courtenay was in Italy, and although it is known that messages were sent to him, there is no evidence at all that he was actually involved. The queen later wrote to him to reassure him that she held him guiltless of the innuendoes.[131]

There is similarly no evidence that Elizabeth countenanced any plans made on her behalf – least of all any that involved marrying Courtenay. As an unnamed councillor wrote to Sir John Mason, probably in July 1556:

> There are letters appointed to be written to Lord Devon for his comfort, and for taking away any such conceit as upon rumours in those hurls he might conceive, against whom doubtless there was nothing intended nor believed, nor yet of Lady Elizabeth, for everyone thought them both of too much wisdom and respect to duty to be party to such matter. Who can prevent knaves to say we hope this of the Lord Devon, of Lady Elizabeth, of this lord, this man etc.[132]

Such an attitude may, however, have been a shade complacent. We can probably discount the remarks which Christopher Ashton and Lord Bray were alleged to have made about how they expected to benefit from Elizabeth's triumph; that 'jolly, liberal dame', as Ashton described her.[133] He was certainly an admirer of hers, and a man of substance; but he was also a wild character, who was not in her service and whose contacts with her seem to have been sporadic. He fled into exile, being last heard of as a Channel pirate. Lord Bray was a neighbour who undoubtedly knew the princess personally, but again had no formal connection. More serious was the undoubted involvement of one of her gentlemen, Francis Verney, whose brother-in-law, Henry Peckham, was in it up to the neck and was eventually executed.[134]

When Henry II wrote in February 1556 to instruct Noailles to back off, he added 'and above all make sure that Madame Elizabeth does not begin, for anything in the world, to undertake what you have written to me'.[135] It is doubtful, however, how much Henry really understood of what was happening, or likely to happen, in England; he may simply have been making the same assumption as everyone else. It is inconceivable that Elizabeth would have taken any initiative against her sister, whatever her attitude may have been to those who claimed to act on her behalf. Nevertheless, at the end of May, having collected an enormous variety of testimony, much of it garrulous and more or less useless, the council moved against the princess. Sir Henry Jerningham and John Norris arrived at Ashridge with a troop of horse; not, this time, to arrest Elizabeth herself but to detain several members of her household. Four of her ladies, including Kate Ashley, and her Italian tutor Battista Castiglione, were removed to the Tower.[136] Perhaps someone remembered from eight years before that Kate was easier to intimidate than her mistress, and would almost certainly know all there was to know, because of their confidential relationship. What they actually got was promising, but not conclusive. They all knew about the plot, but by the end of May that must have been true of everyone with court connections; none admitted to any wrong doing, either on their own behalf or their mistress's. The most damaging disclosure was made through a search of Kate's rooms at Somerset House, which revealed a quantity of anti-government and anti-catholic propaganda.[137] It could not, however, be proved that Elizabeth knew about this, strong though the suspicion must have been.

Unlike the situation of two years before, Mary's reaction this time seems to have been almost resigned. The offending servants were removed from Elizabeth's household, and seem to have been kept in prison for a while. Kate Ashley was released in October, but barred from her mistress's service.[138] It was probably also at this time that Sir Thomas Pope and Robert Gage were placed in charge of the princess's house, although under what titles is not known. Foxe's confused chronology makes it appear that this had happened the previous summer, but Pope can hardly have been in control when these arrests were made without being called to account, and his date of appointment appears to have been 8 June 1556.[139] He was not particularly hostile to Elizabeth, but he was Mary's man and a reliable servant. He remained in charge for about four months, after which the princess was again left to her own devices.

Instead of taking further measures herself, Mary referred the case to her husband. Of course that option had not been open in the spring of 1554, and it may be that she expected Philip to be more severe than she would have been herself. If so, she was disappointed, because the king's attitude to Elizabeth had been changed completely by the events of July 1555. He advised – 'instructed' would perhaps be a better word – that all further enquiries were to be dropped, and that the princess was to be reassured that it was understood her servants had acted without her knowledge. They had abused her name for their own purposes. On 6 June the queen duly despatched her reassuring message, accompanied by the present of a valuable diamond, and removed the guard which had been placed around Ashridge two weeks earlier.[140]

Later in the month there was another hare-brained Courtenay/Elizabeth conspiracy in Suffolk. It came to nothing, but it gave a chance for the council to write to Elizabeth again on 31 July, pointing out that her name had been abused once more. On 2 August the princess wrote a grateful letter to her sister, full of biblical and classical allusions, concluding 'like as I have been your faithful subject from the beginning of your reign, so shall no wicked persons cause me to change to the end of my life'.[141]

It is unlikely that Mary was impressed, or that her affection for her sister was much enhanced, but there was little that could be done. Elizabeth was beginning increasingly to look like the queen's nemesis; but Philip already knew, and Mary was learning, that to antagonise her further was to increase the risk that at some stage in the future she would deliberately demolish everything that Mary had striven to build. By the summer of 1556 there was no chance that parliament would repeal Henry's Succession Act, and a substantial risk that any serious move to disinherit the princess would result in civil war. Mary was not seriously or noticeably ill, but she was a lot older than Elizabeth, and if at any time in the future she should become pregnant, the result might well be fatal. There were only two possible courses: to woo her sister with favours and affection, and hope that her hostile mind might change; or to marry her safely to a loyal Catholic and imperialist.

Philip favoured the latter course, and put his weight behind the duke of Savoy as prospective husband.[142] As we have seen, this course had been proposed before, and at one time Elizabeth had appeared to favour it. Now she resisted all overtures, and for that she paid a price. During the autumn of 1556, relations between the sisters appeared to improve. On 18 September Courtenay died in Padua, and that may have helped. In October Sir Thomas Pope's surveillance was withdrawn, and at the end of November she was licensed to come to London. Perhaps Mary was trying the second option, either as a means to the first, or as an alternative. We do not really know what Mary thought of the Savoy marriage. It is usually assumed that she was backing Philip's plan, but the evidence for that is indirect. At the beginning of December 1556 Mary received Elizabeth for the first time in over three years.[143] If this was the same meeting as that recorded by Foxe, it was polite rather than cordial; but that was a major step forward. Cardinal Pole was equally polite, and that was taken as a portent.

Then, for some unknown reason this budding *entente* collapsed; within a couple of days Elizabeth was on her way back to Hatfield, accompanied by her two hundred horsemen; a move so unexpected that it appears to have taken the whole court by surprise.[144] There was no imperial ambassador at this point, with his ear to the ground, and neither the Venetian nor the French envoy were in the council's confidence; so we can only speculate about the reasons for the rupture, if rupture there was. It may have been that Elizabeth had categorically rejected the Savoy marriage; but that seems an unlikely explanation for such a sudden reversal. Several weeks of sustained pressure would have been more rational, because such a rejection would not have been unexpected. It seems to have been a personal rather than a political quarrel, because the council took no steps against the princess in consequence; nor was there any revival of the gossip of the previous year that she would be sent (however unwillingly) to Brussels. As Elizabeth spent this brief visit not at the court but at Somerset House, it is possible that it was never intended to be more than a flying visit. Nevertheless, something which Elizabeth had done or said appears to have caused serious offence; so serious that there were fresh rumours that she would be declared a bastard and incapable of succession.[145] As there was no parliament in session, nor any plan to summon one, and the council made no move, it all sounds like Mary losing her temper. Indeed, Savoy marriage or not, it is highly unlikely that Philip would have countenanced so potentially disruptive a move when he was bending all his energies towards getting England involved in the war which had now broken out again.

Elizabeth was not the only person who disliked the idea of the Savoy marriage. Faced with the indefinite hostility of an England in which the duke would hold the crown matrimonial, Henry II threatened to obtain a papal censure against the princess if the match went ahead; a move which would, of course, have made Mary Stuart the heir after Mary Tudor. François de Noailles, who had taken over the embassy from his brother the previous year, considered trying to contact Elizabeth during her brief visit to London to convey this warning, but decided it would be too dangerous.[146] The princess's relations with the younger Noailles at this point are highly problematical. According to a letter which he is alleged to have written about fifteen years later, Elizabeth sent the ex-countess of Sussex to him in disguise, to enquire about the possibility of her escaping to France.[147] Anne Radcliffe was a troublesome eccentric who had a history of brushes with authority, and who had been divorced by the earl in 1555. She was not formally in the princess's service, but could have been acting as an agent. She certainly went to France in January or February 1557 with a few servants, and was arrested and interrogated on her return in April; but it is not clear that this had anything to do with Elizabeth.[148] According to Noailles, he warned the countess that, if she fled, the princess would sacrifice all her prospects; a warning which so astute a woman would hardly have needed. The whole story is out of character. If Elizabeth had ever contemplated flight, it would surely have been in the spring of 1556, when the Dudley conspiracy was being broken; not a year later, when her position was stronger and war with France was obviously brewing. Perhaps Noailles's memory was at fault, but more likely the countess was acting on her own initiative, without the authority, or even the knowledge, of the princess.

It is also clear that Mary was less enthusiastic about the Savoy marriage than Philip; indeed she was torn between her desire to please and obey

him, and her instinctive aversion to the whole idea. When she was particularly displeased with Elizabeth, Mary had been known to observe that her
alleged half-sister bore a much closer resemblance to Mark Smeaton, one
of Anne Boleyn's alleged paramours, than she did to King Henry (which
was manifestly untrue).[149] She did not say that explicitly to Philip, but she
did reject his claim that she had a duty in conscience to promote the match.
In response, Philip was blunt: if the marriage failed to take place, it would
be Mary's fault.[150] Their relationship was under severe strain, and Mary
replied that, in the face of such a threat, 'I shall become jealous and uneasy
about you, which will be worse to me than death; for I have already begun
to taste [of such] too much to my great regret'.[151] If he was so anxious to
secure the marriage, let him come and arrange it himself.

In March 1557, Philip came. He had three objectives: to repair his relations
with his wife; to secure England's entry into the war; and to secure Elizabeth's
marriage. In the first two he succeeded, and in the third he failed. It was
probably to help in the latter project that he brought two female cousins,
the duchesses of Lorraine and Parma, with him. Their appearance was so
remarkable and unexpected that there were immediate rumours of a plot
to kidnap Elizabeth and bear her off to her matrimonial doom.[152] She was
warned of this threat by François de Noailles, using another female go-
between, Elizabeth Parr, the rejected marchioness of Northampton. Like
Anne Radcliffe, Elizabeth Parr seems to have gravitated towards Elizabeth
as a kindred spirit rather than an employer.[153] The king's real intention was
almost certainly less dramatic and lay in the powers of example and persuasion.
Nothing, however, would move the princess, who refused to compromise
either her rights or her independence. By the summer of 1557 Mary was
openly and equally opposed to the idea, so that, when he returned to the
Low Countries in July, Philip had an English army but no bride for his ally.
Thereafter the idea was abandoned; and the king, who was too busy, and
had too much self-belief to lament a setback, proceeded to his alternative
plan of making friends with this formidable young woman. Whether they
ever met face to face is unclear. Elizabeth was at court in the summer of
1555, when they were both awaiting the outcome of Mary's supposed pregnancy. They might also have encountered one another during this second
visit in 1557, although the princess is not known to have been at court during
that time. It is most probable that they met during the earlier period;
although the story that Philip was smitten by his attractive sister-in-law is
a romantic fiction, it does suggest that he knew what she looked like.

In the summer of 1557 Elizabeth was temporarily forgotten. The country
was at war, and there was no French ambassador to complicate the situation.
Mary was again dispirited after Philip's departure, but her health was no

worse than usual, and there was as yet no sense of imminent change. When Michieli went to a new posting in February 1557, he wrote (as was customary) a lengthy appraisal of the country and court to which he had been accredited; and in it he included some interesting observations upon the queen and her sister.[154] Mary, he wrote, was in poor health, unpopular with her people, and consumed by desire for her absent husband; 'she is, moreover, a prey to the hatred she bears my Lady Elizabeth'. She would have dearly liked to bar the latter from the throne, but could find no way to do so. By contrast, Elizabeth gave the impression of being in control, because 'all eyes and hearts are turned towards [her] as successor to the throne'. She has, he wrote, concealed her religion and 'comported herself like a good Catholic'; and like a wise woman, he might have added. He also noted that Elizabeth was protected against her sister's malice by the friendship of Philip, in spite of the fact that her name was always on the lips of plotters and conspirators. Simon Renard, by then in Brussels, expressed a very similar view in a memorandum to Philip on the English succession probably written in May 1557.

> It must not be forgotten that all the plots and disorders that have troubled England during the past four years have aimed at placing its government in Elizabeth's hands sooner than the course of nature would permit.[155]

Renard similarly added that she was popular, everyone was looking to her as the future, and nothing short of all-out war could deprive her of the succession.

By the spring of 1558, the queen's fortunes were in terminal decline. The war had started well with a victory at St-Quentin in August 1557, in which the English had served with credit, albeit at Philip's expense. The army had been withdrawn in October, however, and an undergarrisoned Calais had been brilliantly taken by the duke of Guise in January 1558.[156] The English sulked, blamed Philip for their setback, and lost whatever interest they had originally had in fighting. The parliament which met soon after was subdued, but not particularly difficult; the succession was not mentioned. The bad harvest of 1555 had been followed by another in 1556, and although that of 1557 had been better, general malnutrition had by then encouraged an influenza epidemic which was one of the worst of the century. Cardinal Pole's legatine commission had been withdrawn, and relations with the papacy had become frosty.[157] The religious persecution ground on, its victims now being mainly artisans and husbandmen, despatched in groups with minimal process.

Elizabeth spent another week at Somerset House at the end of February, and had a courteous but chilly audience with the queen.[158] At the end of

March Mary made her will, not because she was seriously ill but because – extraordinarily enough – she believed herself to be about to give birth. Philip had left in the previous July, and nothing had been said (or noticed) of this alleged condition, which nobody seems to have believed in except the queen herself.[159] Her will named no heir beyond 'the issewe and frewte of my body', but went into elaborate detail in respect of specific bequests, particularly for pious purposes. In April an embassy arrived from Sweden, with a proposal of marriage between Elizabeth and the king's son, Eric. Ignoring protocol, they went straight to Hatfield. Mary was furious at the implied insult, but calmed down (according to Philip's agent, the count of Feria) when Elizabeth disclaimed all desire to marry and the ambassadors excused themselves by ignorance.[160] At the end of May Feria visited the princess on Philip's instructions, and afterwards reported that their discussions had been very satisfactory, although he did not say what they had covered.[161] The king dutifully informed his wife of this instruction, but clearly feared that it might have caused offence.

In September Mary became ill. At first it was thought that this was no more than one of her periodic ailments, but by the middle of October it was obviously serious and by the end of the month her life was despaired of. How Elizabeth reacted to this news we can only deduce, because there is no direct evidence; but from what happened immediately after her accession we can form some view. From the speed and efficiency with which she established her council and filled offices, it is clear that what would now be called a 'shadow cabinet' had been meeting at Hatfield for some weeks. Also from the orders which were issued countermanding musters, it would seem that some sort of mobilisation had taken place in case her right should be challenged. This was, of course, no more than Mary herself had done before Edward's death, and was no fanciful precaution because at the beginning of November the rapidly declining Mary was still obstinately silent on the subject of the succession. The only concession which she had made was to issue a codicil to her will, admitting that the 'fruit of her body' was now uncertain, and that the crown should pass to the next heir by law. Elizabeth was not named, and it is not even certain that she was meant.[162] Finally, in what must have been a heartbreaking scene to anyone who knew Mary well, or shared her hopes and ideals, on 7 November the Queen named Elizabeth as her heir; knowing full well that the differences which had soured their relationship for years would now be fully revealed. On 17 November, she died. When the news reached Elizabeth, she is alleged to have thanked God for this wonderful consummation.

6

The New Queen

Parliament being in session, Elizabeth was proclaimed in the Upper House later the same morning, 17 November, by the lord chancellor, Nicholas Heath. When she came to the throne, the whole theatre of Elizabeth's life was transformed. For five years she had played the suffering and innocent victim – now she had to play the queen. In a sense she was at last free to please herself, but at the same time her position was constrained by political realities and the expectations of others. The choice of her supporting cast was therefore of great importance. Not only did she have to reward earlier service, she also had to assemble a capable team, and to signal the directions in which she was intending to move. Elizabeth's early appointments to state and household offices therefore provide many clues, both to her sense of purpose and also to her sense of obligation.

Her household, nevertheless, remains hard to decipher, largely because her position during her sister's reign had been so ambivalent. We know that Thomas Parry, her cofferer, served throughout those five years, but only one of his accounts has survived, and apart from his dealings with Bedingfield in the spring and summer of 1554 there is no record of his activities. Kate Ashley had also served as principal gentlewoman until she was displaced by the council in May 1556. Sir Thomas Pope was her chamberlain for about four months in the same year, but we do not know whom he displaced, or who replaced him. It has been suggested that Sir John Bridges occupied that position at the time of her arrival in London in July 1553, but that is based upon a misreading of the source, which merely says that he accompanied her.[1] The 'Mr chamberlayne' who is there referred to should have been Sir Nicholas Lestrange, who had been appointed in May, but there are no references to him by name in that office. An approximate nominal roll of those who were with her at Woodstock can be compiled from the references in Bedingfield's letters, but not much can be concluded from it, except that some of them were more resolute in their Protestantism than their mistress.[2] Elizabeth Sandes was dismissed for that reason, and according to Foxe later fled to Geneva, although no trace of her has been found there.[3] In what sense such *grandes dames manquées* as the countess of Sussex and the marchioness of Northampton were in her service remains doubtful; it is highly unlikely that they were on any official payroll. Castiglione would have been on the payroll until his imprisonment in 1556, and he survived to become a groom of the privy chamber, and to receive an annuity in 1559, but we do not know whether he had been allowed to return to Elizabeth after his release.[4] Nor do we know how many of her official household were of her own choosing, and how many were placed there by the council. Even at Woodstock she clearly had some of her own people, and some who were in the queen's confidence.

With a few exceptions, therefore, we should not even attempt to look at the service household after her accession for an indication of her earlier political position as 'leader of the opposition'. The important people were among those who in an earlier generation would have been called her 'well willers'. It has been suggested that the financial difficulties which she suffered, and of which there are some indications, were the result not of diminished income nor of an extravagant lifestyle, but of the payment of retainers to a number of such people. This may be one reason why all her accounts for the period have vanished. It should, however, be added that one of the few pieces of evidence which we have for such transactions points in the opposite direction. Elizabeth later admitted to having borrowed money from Robert Dudley during these lean years, when he was certainly not a rich man himself.[5] The identity of these 'well willers' can be partly reconstructed from the suspicions of Renard and Feria, partly from the allusions of the Noailles brothers, and partly from the pattern of appointments at the beginning of her reign. The man most consistently mentioned as a favourer and protector of the princess was William, Lord Howard of Effingham, and his immediate appointment as lord chamberlain after her accession confirms that. The other man who had certainly earned suspicion for the same reason, William, Lord Paget, was on the other hand excluded by the new queen. His health was poor, but that was a mere pretext; and he claimed himself that he had been rusticated for his lack of sympathy with the religious settlement.[6] To add insult to injury, his post as lord privy seal was left vacant for over a decade. The earl of Arundel, whom Renard believed had been scheming to marry his son to Elizabeth, retained the office of lord steward; and the pragmatic marquis of Winchester stayed on as lord treasurer.

Shortly before Mary's death the count of Feria described to Philip what he thought the shape and tone of the new regime would be.

> She [Elizabeth] is a very vain and clever woman. She must have been thoroughly schooled in the manner in which her father conducted his affairs, and I am very much afraid that she will not be well disposed in matters of religion, for I see

Title-page of the Bishops' Bible (1568). Elizabeth, who represents Hope, is between Faith and Charity.

her inclined to govern through men who are believed to be heretics, and I am
told that all the women around her definitely are. Apart from this, it is evident
that she is highly indignant about what has been done to her in the queen's
lifetime. She puts great store by the people, and is very confident that they are
all on her side, which is certainly true, there is not a heretic or traitor in the
kingdom who has not joyfully raised himself from the grave in order to come
to her side.[7]

She was not at all inclined to be grateful to Philip for promoting her
succession, and the existing councillors were very much afraid of her.

I shall now tell your Majesty [he went on] of the persons with whom she is on
good terms (according to what I heard from her), together with those with whom
she is not, and it seems to me that she knows who is who in the kingdom, at
least among those of rank.[8]

Of the existing council, he considered her to favour the chancellor,
Nicholas Heath, Paget, Sir William Petre, the recently retired secretary, and
Sir John Mason – particularly the last. Others whose chances were positively
assessed on the same evidence were Dr Nicholas Wotton, Lord Clinton,
Lord William Howard and Lord Grey, at that time a prisoner in France.
The most negatively assessed were the lord chamberlain (Sir Edward Hastings), the controller (Sir Robert Freston), the secretary (Boxall) and Cardinal
Pole. Slightly less negative were the earls of Arundel and Pembroke and
the bishop of Ely (Thomas Thirlby). Moving on to more circumstantial
evidence, he thought that the earl of Bedford, Lord Robert Dudley, Sir Peter
Carew, John Harrington and Sir William Pickering were likely to be favoured. He also had good reason to believe that Sir William Cecil would
be the new secretary, and that 'two other old men who run her household'
would be promoted. These are identified as the cofferer and controller; the
first was clearly Thomas Parry, and the second would appear to have been
Sir Ambrose Cave, although this is the only reference to him serving
Elizabeth as princess.[9]

Feria's judgement was shrewd, and well informed up to a point. His
positive expectations were certainly correct for Cecil, Mason, Clinton, Howard, Dudley, Petre, Parry and Cave; less certainly for Wotton, Grey, Carew,
Pickering and Harrington, who were favoured, but not conspicuously; and
clearly wrong for Heath and Paget. His negative judgements were correct
for Hastings, Freston, Boxall and Thirlby, but not for Arundel and Pembroke. His assessment of Pole was right but irrelevant as the cardinal died
within forty-eight hours of Mary.[10] Feria clearly did not expect to have any
rapport with the new regime – and he was right. He described his own
reception on 14 November as being like that of 'one who bears bulls from

a dead pope'. Cecil he identified as a friend of Paget, an able and virtuous man, but a heretic. After Elizabeth's accession he confined himself to the business of the peace negotiation, except for his delayed marriage to Jane Dormer, a lady of Mary's former privy chamber, on 29 December. He left England in May 1559, and his household thereafter became a refuge for English Catholic exiles.[11]

Elizabeth's policy in respect of the senior offices of state was pragmatic. The great seal remained with the queen, although the duties of the office were discharged by Sir Nicholas Bacon as lord keeper. She had no particular animus against Nicholas Heath, the archbishop of York, who appears to have been an amiable man, but was clearly determined to send a signal to the church.[12] The privy seal office likewise remained unoccupied, although again Bacon seems to have discharged the function, without any official appointment. Winchester continued as lord treasurer, in spite of his lack of sympathy with the religious settlement; Lord Clinton continued as admiral; and Sir Henry Sidney as lord justice of Ireland.[13]

The conspicuous new appointment was Cecil, who quickly restored the office of secretary to the kind of omnicompetence that it had enjoyed in the early days of Thomas Cromwell. Cecil had risen to prominence under Protector Somerset, whose personal secretary he had originally been. After the Protector's fall he had successfully transferred his allegiance to the earl of Warwick, and became king's secretary in September 1550.[14] Under Mary he had for the most part kept a low profile, although he was identified as one of those who caused embarrassment to the government in the 1555 parliament.[15] As we have seen, he became Elizabeth's surveyor as soon as her estate was confirmed; and although that office did not in itself confer a high degree of intimacy, it seems that in this case it did. Cecil has been tentatively identified as one of those who were sending money abroad to support the Protestant exiles, and seems to have given refuge to the fugitive printer John Day on his estate in Lincolnshire.[16] Like Elizabeth herself he was a Nicodemite, and like her avoided subsequent reproach.

The queen's council showed a similar pattern. Apart from Winchester, Arundel and Clinton, who were retained in their offices, the queen also continued the earls of Derby, Shrewsbury and Pembroke, Lord William Howard, Sir John Mason, Nicholas Wotton, Sir William Petre and (briefly) Nicholas Heath. Over two thirds of Mary's last council were therefore dispensed with; a greater turnover than Mary herself had achieved, and far greater than that between Henry and Edward. This was partly the result of a substantial reduction in size, from over thirty to twenty, a reduction which probably reflects the new queen's confidence in her own judgement as much as any governmental strategy.[17] Of her new appointments, only Cecil, Parry and Cave had been anticipated by Feria. Bacon became a privy councillor as lord keeper. William Parr, restored to his title as marquis of Northampton, Francis, earl of Bedford, Sir Edward Rogers and Sir Francis Knollys had been conspicuous anti-Marians, and both Bedford and Knollys had been religious exiles.[18] Sir Richard Sackville, like Bacon, had had his career checked by Mary's accession; like Knollys he was a kinsman of the queen by marriage.

Once Heath had departed, early in 1559, there were consequently nineteen councillors; ten of whom might be described as 'conservative Henricians' in their religious views, and nine Protestants. None of those who had been conspicuous for their loyalty to the papacy, or their personal devotion to Mary, survived into the new regime. Even before the religious settlement had been broached, these appointments had signalled a policy, at least of balance, and at best of reconciliation. Doctrinal alignment was going to matter less than loyalty to the queen. It was already apparent to the conservatives that this was likely to mean a return to the Royal Supremacy; but it was less apparent to the Protestants that it was also going to mean abandoning any hankering after 'the best reformed churches'.

Elizabeth did not particularly like Arundel, Winchester, or Bedford, but she recognised their value, and particularly the experience of the first two.[19] She did like Bacon, and Cecil and Parry, who were equally experienced and more congenial in their outlook, but it was only Cecil who was marked out for special confidence:

> This judgement I have of you that you will not be corrupted by any manner of gift, and that you will be faithful to the state, and that without respect of my private will you will give me that counsel which you think best.[20]

These words, which sound so magnificent and prophetic in retrospect, were not much more than a paraphrase of the traditional councillor's oath; but they were delivered with a sense of theatre which provided a taste of things to come.

It is significant that Cecil was the queen's private secretary, as well as secretary of state, because it was within the court, and particularly in her chamber appointments, that Elizabeth revealed her real taste in company. The only officer in the household 'below stairs' who was displaced was the controller, Sir Robert Freston, although many of her more menial servants from earlier days were absorbed into the relevant departments, at first on a supernumerary basis.[21] Sir Thomas Cheney, the treasurer of the household, died less than year into the reign and was replaced by Parry, who had previously replaced Freston. In contrast, the chamber saw major changes, and the privy chamber was renewed from top to bottom. The lord great chamberlain was an hereditary office in the family of the earls of Oxford, and that was not disturbed, although John de Vere was close to neither Mary nor Elizabeth and his precedence was purely formal. Both the lord chamberlain and the vice-chamberlain (Sir Henry Bedingfield) were displaced, in favour of Lord William Howard and Sir Edward Rogers. Sir John Mason remained as treasurer, and groups like the gentlemen pensioners and the ushers of the chamber were not noticeably affected.[22] Both the almoner and the dean of the chapel royal, which were religiously sensitive posts, were replaced, but most of the staff of the chapel remained. Departments such as the great wardrobe and the music underwent little change; and the only conspicuous change in the 'outdoor' departments was the appearance of a new master of the horse, in the person of Lord Robert Dudley.

The privy chamber, the most intimate of the service departments, was completely replaced. At the time of her death Mary had been entertaining seven ladies, thirteen gentlewomen, three chamberers, and about half a dozen gentlemen and grooms.[23] Elizabeth appointed four ladies of the bedchamber, seven or eight gentlewomen, three chamberers, and just two men, one gentleman and one groom.[24] These, however, were only the fee'd staff; in addition there were seven 'ladies extraordinary', an indeterminate number of gentlewomen, and a few gentlemen and grooms. In terms of regular attendance there was probably not very much difference between the two queens, except that there were clearly fewer men around Elizabeth.

The core of this establishment was the four full-time ladies, and it should not surprise us to discover that these were Catherine Ashley, Blanche Parry, Elizabeth Norwich, and Catherine Knollys (née Carey).[25] The first, and for many years the only, gentleman was John Ashley. Catherine Ashley was usually styled the chief gentlewoman, and seems to have doubled that function with mistress of the robes, as Susan Clarencius had done before her. She did not hold the privy purse, which was in the custody of John Tamworth, the groom.[26] This had been a strictly personal account since the beginning of Mary's reign, but Elizabeth sometimes used it for political expenditure of a discreet kind. When that was done, money was drawn from the privy coffers (a fund that had survived almost unnoticed since 1552); and the privy coffers, about which virtually nothing is known for this period, were in the hands of the queen's secretary – Sir William Cecil.[27]

As queen, Elizabeth endeavoured to keep her private life and her public life as separate as possible, Cecil being almost the only link between the two sides. Although related by marriage or kinship to leading councillors or household officers, the ladies and gentlewomen were her chosen friends and companions, not her advisers. They read and prayed, and chatted and sewed, and created an illusion of domesticity, which Elizabeth clearly found congenial and relaxing. They shared an educated and liberal Protestant piety; and although they could, and did, urge petitions on behalf of their menfolk or their menfolk's clients, they had nothing like the same access to patronage that the gentlemen of Henry VIII's privy chamber had enjoyed. Indeed Rowland Vaughn, who was in a good position to know, later declared that 'these near and dear ladies never once durst meddle' in affairs of state.[28] The privy chamber was almost exclusively female, just as the outside political world was almost exclusively male.

Unfortunately for Elizabeth's peace of mind marriage represented the coming together of these two worlds in the most uncomfortable fashion. Whether Elizabeth liked it or not, marriage was high on the political agenda at the beginning of her reign, and since this was a matter of understandable and legitimate interest in the privy chamber as well as in the council, there was no way to escape it. Elizabeth was haunted by marriage and its implications for nearly thirty years. Politically, it was just another problem to be confronted; but personally it was a raw nerve, and became a dangerous subject over the needles and prayer books. Some of the queen's most uncontrollable outbursts of rage came in the privacy of her bedchamber, and on that very subject,[29] sometimes because of indiscreet words about her own marriage – or lack of it – and sometimes because of the wedding plans of others. The queen was notoriously volatile over such such plans, and sometimes reacted with blind rage when permission to marry was sought by one of her own companions. The reason for this was not far to seek, and lay in the whole anomalous position of a ruling queen. Mary in a sense had reduced the problem by securing a statute which had degendered the authority of the crown; but she had never solved the other dilemma, the priority between wifely duty and motherhood on the one hand, and public responsibility and rule on the other.[30] Elizabeth knew both by instinct and experience that a woman could have a huge advantage in using her sex to manage and baffle the men who would otherwise seek to dominate her. Marriage not only meant the surrender of that mystique, but also a religiously sanctioned duty to obey. When Maitland of Lethington declared that she had 'an high stomach', he was only echoing her own reputed words 'I will have one mistress – and no master'.[31]

In 1566, when his own prospects were past, Robert Dudley expressed the view that she would never marry. He had known her, he said, since they were both eight years old and 'he had not seen her waver in that decision'. That may have been no more than sour grapes, because no marriage meant not only personal frustration, but also no heir and no secure succession. Which was the primary obligation? It is not surprising that the agony of this dilemma sometimes seemed to tear her apart, or could result in outbursts of hysterical fury. Perhaps she had decided not to marry at an early age, a decision confirmed by her sister's unfortunate example, and all the negotiations were so much political play-acting. It has also been said that she knew herself to be incapable of bearing children, and that marriage would consequently have been all loss and no gain. There is no conclusive evidence to support either of these assertions. On the other hand, there is plenty to suggest that some of the negotiations, at least, were real; and that Elizabeth prevaricated until time foreclosed her options. It is not surprising that she sometimes lost her temper with innocent damsels who had only to chose a man and get on with it; or that she should have repeated her youthful desire to be a milkmaid instead of a queen.

Marriage was a dominant item on the early agenda of the reign, but it was not the only one. Even more urgent was the presentation of a compelling image of authority, which began with her first reported speeches at Hatfield. As Feria had shrewdly observed, popularity meant much to the new queen. This was not mere vanity. Elizabeth knew perfectly well that many of the nobility were eyeing her askance. They had accepted her because there was no plausible alternative, but they distrusted her religious views and doubted her capacity to do the job.[32] She needed the plaudits, and the cries of 'God save your Grace!'; but much more she needed to convince everyone, high and low, that she was in control. As Sir John Hayward wrote:

> Now, if ever any persone had eyther the gift or the stile to winne the hearts of the people, it was this Queene; and if ever shee did expresse the same, it was at this present [her first entry to London] in coupling mildnesse with majesty as shee did, and in stately stouping to the meanest sort. All her faculties were in motione, and every motione seemed a well guided actione; her eye was set upon one, her eare listened to another, her judgement ranne uppon a third; to a fourth shee addressed her speech; her spirit seemed to be everywhere, and yett so intyre in her selfe, as it seemed to be noe where else.[33]

Hayward was an admirer, and was writing long after the event, but the impression that he recorded was immediate and lasting. Her entry into London on 14 January 1559, in preparation for her coronation, was more of the same: a courteous attention to each of the pageants on offer; a subtle hint of enthusiasm for the English Bible; a gesture of loyalty to her father's memory.[34] Elizabeth could not afford to take anything for granted. She had seen her sister's support from both the gentry and the people at large sweep aside the uncertain opposition of Northumberland and his supporters in 1553. No such opposition faced her, but that did not alter the fact that Henry's long and tumultuous reign had shifted the balance of power away from a nobility increasingly anchored in the court and towards the gentry

– and the city of London. She needed to be the 'gentleman's queen' that Lord Bray had invoked; and she needed her brother's *rapport* with the capital. No gesture, no speech was gratuitous.

In November 1558 England was at war, and Mary's death brought a general expectation of religious change. On 20 November, three days into the reign, Sir John Mason wrote to Cecil that 'the first and principal point is to think upon the peace', and that it was a waste of time to 'stick upon Calais'.[35] Elizabeth did not appear to agree about the latter point. In appointing new commissioners to Câteau Cambrésis, she threatened to cut their heads off if they failed to secure the return of England's former possession. It was an empty gesture, and she probably knew it, but the temptation to score another point off her sister was too great to be resisted. Philip was not going to risk a much needed peace to support such a quixotic demand, and when the treaty was negotiated, leaving Calais in French hands, Elizabeth on the unanimous advice of her council, accepted it.[36]

A religious settlement, however, was far more controversial, and the queen approached it gingerly. Whereas Mary had issued a conciliatory proclamation, and then acted in the opposite spirit, Elizabeth did nothing in haste. Significantly, Mary's death stopped the persecution dead in its tracks. Men and women already condemned were reprieved and quickly released; those awaiting trial were simply discharged.[37] Whatever the Queen said, or did not say, in that respect at least immediate change was expected. Elizabeth was keenly aware that the Catholic Church which her sister had left was by law established, and there was no equivalent of 'the queen's proceedings' which had dominated the first three months of Mary's reign. Although she had duly repealed the statutes that formed her brother's religious settlement, Mary had ignored them, and encouraged her subjects to ignore them, from the moment of her accession. Elizabeth was extremely careful to observe the law and to insist that everybody else observed it. The chapel royal began to use the English litany, and the gospel and epistle in English, but otherwise the rites continued unchanged; and the zealous Protestant preachers who began to appear got rapped over the knuckles.[38] In a proclamation of 27 December all controversial preaching was inhibited 'until consultation may be had by parliament'.[39]

The visible signals were unequivocal, but carefully considered. George Carew, the new dean of the chapel royal, had been her chaplain in the heady days of King Edward, but had disappeared from view under Mary and had probably conformed. William Bill, her chaplain and almoner, had been deprived of the mastership of Trinity College, Cambridge, in 1554, and had then likewise disappeared.[40] No one seems to have doubted that they were Protestants, but like their mistress they were Nicodemites. Elizabeth famously walked out of her coronation service at the elevation of the host; but she had not attempted to prevent the mass from being celebrated.[41] It is perhaps not surprising that, although some of the religious exiles packed their bags and returned to England, as soon as they knew Mary was dead, others, and particularly those in Geneva, hung back to observe what would happen.

The process by which the queen secured her religious settlement in the parliament of 1559 has been frequently and carefully examined.[42] Her recorded prayers from this period are not controversial, but are Protestant in spirit.

> I acknowledge that Thou hast dealt as wonderfully and mercifully with me as thou didst with they true and faithful servant Daniel the prophet; whom thou deliverdst out of the den, from the cruelty of the greedy and raging lions: even so was I overwhelmed, and only by thee delivered.[43]

> Lord God of mercy, my and my people's King. I acknowledge Thy great name, for Thou hast made thyself a helper and protector to me. I will extol Thee highly, God of my salvation, who hast freed my body from perdition and rescued me from the hands of those who sought my soul.[44]

The allusions in both these prayers are unmistakable, and the implications equally clear. Although Elizabeth would never allow any explicit public criticism of her sister's government, Cecil's early memoranda for council business are full of observations about how 'the realm hath suffered great loss' by such policies as the restoration of first fruits and tenths to the church.[45] There can be no doubt that the queen wanted a Protestant settlement, similar to that of her brother; but she was equally concerned to avoid religious strife of the kind which was already disrupting France and the Low Countries. The House of Commons was amenable, both to the restoration of the Royal Supremacy and Protestant doctrine. There were objections to the latter, but they were few, and after five years of established Catholicism that is significant. The House of Lords was equally amenable to the Supremacy, though the bishops fought an unavailing rearguard action,[46] but not to the Prayer Book. In that debate a substantial number of lay peers, including some councillors, joined the bishops in resistance. Elizabeth appears to have contemplated retreat on that issue, but the convocations, meeting at the same time as parliament, had cut off her retreat. By unequivocally reasserting a full Catholic position, the clergy had made it clear that she would be unable to find a bench of bishops to staff a compromise church of the Henrician kind. There was therefore no point in compromise; and by exercising her maximum powers of persuasion, not unallied with chicanery, the queen forced the settlement through.[47]

The ceremony surrounding her coronation in January 1559 was a statement of intent in this respect. In the official account of her entry into London, written by Richard Mulcaster, the pageants are uniformly intended to symbolise a new start, and rejection of the immediate past. These involved not only the reception of the English Bible, but the pointed contrast between a flourishing and a ruined commonwealth. The crowning itself was strictly traditional, but in refusing to be escorted by the monks of Westminster, and even more in refusing the elevation of the host, Elizabeth spelled out her rejection of the old faith. It is not surprising that, in spite of having accepted her authority, and remaining for the time being in possession of their sees, the senior bishops of the English Church uniformly rejected the opportunity of crowning her. Only the junior Owen Oglethorpe of Carlisle was willing to oblige.[48]

Having thus, in a sense, given her Protestant supporters the settlement that they desired, her priority immediately returned to the attempt to recover consensus. She could not afford to be blinded by godly rhetoric, and knew perfectly well that real Protestants were a small minority among her subjects. Although she and her chosen servants were of that persuasion, her peers, and even her council, were divided. Mary's enthusiasm for the papacy had not put down deep roots, but the 'old religion' was still very popular. Outside London, a few port towns and the Home Counties, most people preferred the mass to the communion, and happily maintained the rituals of the liturgical year.[49] It therefore became her considered and long-term policy not to force issues that did not have to be forced.

Within hours of her accession, the primatial see of Canterbury was vacated by the death of Reginald Pole. This deprived the remaining bishops of their natural leader, but otherwise changed nothing. Of twenty-seven English and Welsh dioceses, seven were vacant at the time of Mary's death, although nominations had been made to two of them. A further three bishops died before the new settlement became law.[50] Of the seventeen who were confronted with the new oath of Supremacy, one accepted it, one resigned, two others evaded it by dying during 1559, and thirteen were deprived.[51] Elizabeth tried hard to persuade some of these, particularly Heath and Tunstall, but to their credit they refused to compromise their consciences a second time. This intransigence confronted Elizabeth with a similar problem to that which her sister had faced, to find new bishops, although it was a more extreme situation, because almost a third of Edward's bench had accepted reconciliation. In other respects, however, it was not at all the same. Although the deprived Marians were imprisoned, most of them were soon released into house arrest; Heath, for example, retreated to the country and lived the life of a private gentlemen for another twenty years.

Edmund Bonner, who had made himself particularly obnoxious to Protestants, remained in prison until he died in September 1569, but if zealous
reformers were looking for revenge upon their persecutors, they were disappointed. Although it became an offence to celebrate the traditional rites,
there was no counter-persecution; nor were Protestant groups permitted to
take the law into their own hands.[52] Catholic gentlemen who refused the
oath of Supremacy were removed from the commissions of the peace, but
this was not a common practice. The overwhelming majority of the gentry,
and even of the clergy, conformed. This was partly because the queen
restrained the zeal of the godly (where it existed), and much conformity
was, and was permitted to be, purely formal.[53] The subsequent history of
the enforcement of the Acts of Supremacy and Uniformity is a familiar
story; but its apparent contradictions should not be allowed to cast doubts
on the queen's own religious position. Elizabeth's piety had some unusual
features, such as an affection for modest ornaments and church music, but
her Protestantism was strong, and her theological understanding considerable. Her aversion to married clergy was much less powerful than is often
claimed, having more to do with her own tormented attitude to marriage
than with ecclesiology.

   In the church as a whole, the turnover of clergy between 1559 and 1565
was between 4 and 5 per cent; but at the episcopal level it was over 90 per cent;
and this meant a massive deployment of ecclesiastical patronage. Elizabeth
approached this task without enthusiasm. She did not much like clergy,
and did not count them among her intimates even when she approved of
their doctrine. Moreover, she had just been treated to a close and overwhelming view of clerical intolerance at its most obnoxious. Whether she
understood, or was ever willing to admit, her sister's personal responsibility
for the recent persecution we do not know; but she was temperamentally
sympathetic to John Foxe's calculated demonisation of the Catholic priesthood.[54] Her primary concern in making her new appointments was therefore
to avoid creating a mirror image of Mary's intolerant church.

   With this priority in mind, within about a month of her accession, and
well before the settlement was made, Cecil and Bacon began a correspondence with Mathew Parker.[55] Parker had been a chaplain to her mother, and
also to Henry VIII. Elected master of Corpus Christi College, Cambridge,
in 1544, he had become vice-chancellor in the following year. Deprived of
all preferments on the accession of Mary, he had thereafter succeeded in
maintaining a low profile, and was living in learned retirement in 1558.
There was no doubt about his reformed credentials, and he had a good
track record as an administrator; but he was hardly an obvious candidate
to the survivors of the heroic generation. Although Elizabeth did not write

to him directly for fear of revealing her hand too soon, there can be no doubt that he was her personal choice for Canterbury. He preached one or two sermons at court before Christmas 1558, but did not draw attention to himself by staying in residence, and it was not until the following June that he was finally and publicly nominated.[56]

Of the twenty-three other bishops who were nominated between the summer of 1559 and the beginning of 1562, not one can be shown to have had any close personal association with the queen, although some had been close to Cecil or Dudley. Fourteen of them had been at one time or another in exile for their faith; the remainder, like Parker, had gone into hiding in England.[57] They were a highly respectable team, both pastorally and intellectually; the equal, at least, of those they were replacing. As the queen's most senior ecclesiastical servants, however, and the men charged with the immensely difficult task of making her religious settlement work, they hardly broke the political surface. None of them, not even Parker, was called to the privy council, and this was unprecedented. It was not because the queen lacked commitment, either to Protestantism or to her own settlement, but it may have been a signal that Elizabeth intended to run her church as a department of state.[58] She had probably been forced to appoint more returned exiles to the bench than she would have liked. Although notorious radicals like Goodman and Knox had been firmly excluded, they were more zealous than she might have wished. It was not easy to persuade men who believed that they possessed the message of saving truth (and who had suffered for that conviction) that they were not required to force that message down the throats of a conservative, and potentially hostile, population. Elizabeth could not chose her bishops in the same way that she could chose her councillors or courtiers, and consequently never had quite the same confidence in them. She kept them at arm's length, and dealt with them mainly through Cecil, whose position on religious matters was somewhere between her own and that of most of the episcopate.[59]

How much the settlement was beholden to clerical advice is not clear. Of the eight Protestant divines who were appointed to dispute on behalf of the 'new religion' in March 1559, six were subsequently to be bishops, and it seems that Cecil was closely in touch with them while preparing the legislation for the parliament.[60] However, they played no part in bringing it about. Similarly the royal articles and injunctions which began to enforce the settlement in the summer of 1559 antedated any new episcopal appointments, and were part of the process of removing the old establishment. The visitations themselves were based upon Henrician and Edwardian precedents, but the articles must have been modified on clerical advice. The commissions which carried them out consisted of both clergy and laity, but the emphasis was entirely upon the authority of the queen.[61] In theory the demands of the commissioners were uncompromising, but in practice they allowed themselves to be satisfied with a minimum level of compliance. In Durham, for example, only the dean and two of the twelve prebendaries were deprived, although the conservative sympathies of most of the others were notorious.[62] In fact these visitations set the tone for the first decade of the reign. Open defiance or nonconformity was not tolerated, but a great deal of evasion and finger crossing clearly went on. It was years later when the queen declared that she had no desire to make 'windows into men's souls'; but she had set out in the same spirit. In spite of the ecclesiatical context, this was a purely political agenda; and it was asking too much of clergy who believed that they had the stewardship of souls to expect them to share the same priorities. When Parker and his colleagues wished to impose a more searching conformity, they had to do it on their own authority; and when convocation in 1563 began to clamour for a more throughgoing reformation, the bishops were compelled, against their inclination and on the queen's orders, to oppose it.[63]

Frustrating as this could be to individual evangelicals, it was a position perfectly capable of principled defence. If it was accepted that the visible church was an aspect of the commonwealth, then it was logical also to accept that the authority that God had conferred upon the queen to manage the latter, also extended to the former. When the bishops revised the Edwardian articles in 1562, article thirty-seven made this point explicitly:

> The Queen's Majesty hath the chief power in this Realm of England, and over her dominions, unto whom the chief government of all estates of this realm, whether they be Ecclesiastical or Civil, in all causes doth appertain, and is not, or ought not to be, subject to any foreign jurisdiction.[64]

Consequently, as far as England was concerned, divine revelation was mediated through the crown, and further reform could only come by persuading Elizabeth that it was God's will for her to undertake it. In short, the bishops were her agents or servants in ecclesiastical causes, and in the discharge of their offices had no more direct mandate from God than they did from the pope. As good Protestants, they were sceptical about all human traditions; but by accepting that it was the queen's responsibility to interpret the scriptures to her people, they could comfortably convert themselves into a 'privy council' for ecclesiastical affairs.[65] It was their duty to advise in accordance with their consciences, but it was Elizabeth's responsibility to decide. Unfortunately, they lacked immediacy of access, and most of them were constrained to deliver their counsel at second hand, usually through Sir William Cecil.

As the queen felt her way cautiously towards a consistent and workable religious position between 1558 and 1561, she was also bombarded with advice on the related issues of marriage and the succession. Given Elizabeth's age, and contemporary assumptions about the nature of women, it was the former that took precedence. At first, perhaps as a reaction to her sister's unhappy experience, her courtiers seem to have favoured a domestic match.[66] The duke of Norfolk was five years younger than Elizabeth and unmarried; the earls of Arundel and Westmorland twenty and ten years older and widowers. There is not the slightest evidence that she took any of them seriously as suitors, although there are some hints that Arundel took himself seriously. Feria thought that she was inclined to Sir William Pickering, but that seems to have been solely on the basis of the fact that he was 'a proper man', and without any regard to circumstances. As far as we know, none of these possibilities were discussed in council, and if they were discussed in the privy chamber it was probably surreptitiously, when the queen was not within earshot. Philip continued to favour the duke of Savoy, and corresponded with Feria about this possibility throughout December 1558.[67] The latter was emphatic that 'everything depends upon the husband this woman may take', and did not take Elizabeth's professed indifference to marriage seriously. The council was as hostile as the queen herself to this proposal, however, believing that if the duke became king of England he would involve the country in interminable wars for the recovery of his Italian patrimony.[68]

By the end of December, Philip had accepted defeat on this issue, and for that reason advanced his own candidature. There is no reason to suppose that he wanted to marry Elizabeth, and plenty of indication that the idea arose in the course of duty, as a 'service to God'. 'Nothing would make me do this', he wrote in January 1559, 'except the clear knowledge that it would gain the kingdom for His faith and service.'[69] He need not have worried. Elizabeth had no desire to offend her 'good brother', but was as averse to the idea as he was himself. She pointed out to Feria that they were related within the prohibited degrees, and whereas he might regard that as an ecclesiastical bar which the pope could dispense, she regarded it as a scriptural prohibition, and would recognise no exercise of papal authority.[70] Feria was persistent to the point of being obtuse, and it was not until 14 March that the queen made her refusal absolutely unambiguous. The date was significant, because she was in the midst of a struggle to get her church settlement through parliament, and more than two weeks away from signing the treaty of Câteau Cambrésis. The signal was clear; she would not sacrifice her freedom of action, or her conscience, for the security of a Habsburg embrace, literal or metaphorical.

Philip was personally relieved, but politically anxious. He paid no attention to Elizabeth's pretended pique at his marriage to Elizabeth of Valois in April, but threw his weight cautiously behind an alternative proposal from his uncle, the emperor Ferdinand, on behalf of the latter's younger son of the same name.[71] When the emperor's ambassador, Count George Helfenstein, reached London, he seems to have had no specific instructions, but this may have been a device to test the ground. According to Feria, the idea was broached to Helfenstein by 'some of those people who went to and from with him to the palace'; that is, the queen's chamber gentlemen, among whom he named Sir Thomas Challoner.[72] If he was right, they are unlikely to have acted spontaneously, although whether the initiative came from Elizabeth or Cecil is not clear. What is clear is that the proposal was welcomed when it was eventually made. A portrait of the younger Ferdinand was tactfully solicited, and there was talk of 'close amity', although Feria was honest enough to admit 'I could not tell your Majesty [Philip] what this woman means to do with herself, and those who know her best know no more than I do.'[73]

An additional reason for this uncertainty, as the same despatch reveals, was the sudden appearance of a new domestic candidate in the person of the master of the horse.

> During the last few days Lord Robert has come so much into favour that he does whatever he likes with affairs, and it is even said that her Majesty visits him in his chamber day and night. People talk of this so freely that they go so far as to say that his wife has a malady in one of her breasts, and the queen is only waiting for her to die to marry Lord Robert. I can assure your Majesty that matters have reached such a pass that I have been brought to consider whether it would not be well to approach Lord Robert on your Majesty's behalf, promising him your help and favour and coming to terms with him.

This suggestion was not followed up, and Feria left England soon after, but he had observed the beginning of one of the most celebrated relationships of the century. Elizabeth had known Robert since they were both children. While there is no indication as to why she suddenly took a fancy to him at this stage, so it was. Politically, Lord Robert was unpredictable, and all the queen's established councillors distrusted him; most particularly Cecil, whose known hostility to the favourite jeopardised his own special relationship with Elizabeth.[74] Of course Dudley's unique access to the queen brought him an army of clients, but not very much by way of serious support for his pretensions. What he did do was to guarantee rather more political support than might otherwise have been the case for a foreign match. Almost any king consort would be preferable to the maverick Dudley.

When a Habsburg candidate finally emerged in the summer of 1559, it was not the younger Ferdinand, as originally expected, but his brother Charles.[75] Feria's successor, Alvarez de Quadra, was understandably keen on this match, and rather too sanguine about it, because Elizabeth's reason for encouraging the negotiation had nothing to do with her personal feelings. Anticipating success, de Quadra wrote in October 1559 to his opposite number in Rome '[you] must take care that the French do not get at the new Pope [Pius IV] and cause him to proceed against the queen on the Scottish queen's claims. It would do much damage, both here and elsewhere'.[76]

Whether Pius was really being solicited on behalf of Mary Stuart is uncertain. Following the death of Henry II, Mary was now queen of France as well as of Scotland, and Francis II's advisers were as aware as anyone that any action by him on his wife's behalf would immediately resurrect the Anglo-imperial alliance; and perhaps even force the marriage which they so much disliked. No action was taken, either by the king or by the pope. Among Elizabeth's servants, the main supporters of Charles were the duke of Norfolk, and possibly Sir Thomas Parry.[77] Cecil was sympathetic as long as it served his purposes, and Dudley appeared to be, for quite different reasons. The most enthusiastic group were the London merchants, who saw it as a means of stabilising their commercial relations with the empire, which were becoming more important as Antwerp began to get into difficulties.[78] Ferdinand himself was not particularly keen, however, and vetoed a proposal for his son to visit England in the autumn of 1559. The negotiation finally petered out with Helfenstein's recall in May 1560. The main stumbling-block was ostensibly the failure to reach an accommodation over religion, but in fact the only person who was unequivocally enthusiastic was de Quadra, who filled his despatches with progress reports which probably give the discussions a higher profile than they really deserve.

No such problem obstructed another pertinacious suitor, who had actually appeared on the scene before Elizabeth's accession. This was Prince Eric, son and heir of King Gustavus of Sweden. Dionysius Beurreus had been resident in England on Gustavus's behalf since March 1558, and he had at first neglected to renew his credentials to the new queen. He had already been in trouble for attempting to approach Elizabeth in her sister's lifetime without proper permission, and was clearly inexperienced in the ways of diplomacy.[79] When he was finally permitted to make his proposal in due form, it was politely declined by the council on 6 May 1559. Gustavus, however, chose to regard this not as a rebuff but as a false start, and sent another, properly accredited embassy in the summer of 1559 for the same purpose. This extravagant deputation attracted a lot of attention (not all of it favourable), but made no progress in its main business.[80]

Undeterred, Gustavus then sent his younger son, Duke John of Finland, to plead on Eric's behalf. In contrast to his predecessors, John made an excellent impression, was liberal with his money, and made many friends. None of this impressed the queen, but John refused to be put off. He had arrived in September, and in December was still in London, in spite of having been told by Elizabeth that she would not marry his brother.[81] His persistence may have been prompted by some in the queen's inner circle who thought that they could read the mind behind the words, and who believed that a Protestant prince such as Eric offered the best safeguard against either a Catholic or a Dudley marriage. In December 1559 John put forward a new, and more comprehensive proposal, embracing not only marriage but also a full alliance, and providing for Eric to live in England, even if he should inherit his father's crown.[82]

Unlike Ferdinand or Philip, Gustavus clearly wanted this marriage. It is not hard to see why. Sweden was a newly established kingdom, and the Vasas were parvenus, as the Tudors had been in the 1490s. Such a union would greatly have enhanced his status, and his potential power in the perennial conflicts of Baltic politics. It was for the same reasons that Elizabeth was hostile and her councillors, in spite of John's best efforts, mostly unpersuaded. Sweden had too little to offer, apart from the prospect of an heir. In spite of religion, there was far more support for the Archduke Charles, especially among the powerful merchants of London. In April 1560 John returned to Sweden with his enthusiasm still undiminished, and in June Eric himself proposed to come and press his suit in person. King Gustavus was getting tired of spending money to no purpose but he died in September, and Eric succeeded. This removed any chance of a personal visit, but at the beginning of 1561 a fresh Swedish embassy arrived to try again.[83] This time, for reasons quite unconnected with Sweden, they received a more sympathetic hearing.

In September 1560 Amy Robsart, Lady Dudley, had died in suspicious circumstances. She broke her neck falling downstairs at Cumnor in Oxfordshire. The chances are that she succumbed to breast cancer, and that the fall was a mere accident; but Lord Robert's many enemies believed and claimed that he had ordered his servants to despatch her.[84] The queen suspended him from court and ordered an enquiry, which exonerated him. Although this was probably fair, hardly anyone outside the Dudley affinity was convinced, and his triumphant return to court was regarded with the deepest foreboding. Passions began to run high. Elizabeth refused to hear any criticism of her favourite: servants were punished for spreading anti-Dudley slanders; and councillors frozen out for refusing him their friendship. The queen resumed her indiscreet visits, and the courts of

Europe were convulsed with rumour. 'The queen of England', Catherine de Medici is alleged to have scoffed, 'is to marry her horsemaster.' Nicholas Throgmorton, in Paris, was mortified:

> one laugheth at us, another threateneth, another revileth her Majestie, and some let not to say what religion is this that a subiecte shall kill his wief, and the prince not only beare withall but mary with him, not sticking to reherse the father and the grandfather.[85]

Cecil threatened to resign, and Catherine Ashley is alleged to have besought her mistress with tears not to ruin herself with such folly. The ins and outs of this relationship have been frequently and deeply examined, but there can be no final assessment of it. That Elizabeth loved Dudley in the ordinary sense of that word seems clear; much clearer than in the case of Seymour, when she had been little more than a child. That she seriously considered marrying him for several weeks in the autumn of 1560 is very probable; but that she persisted with that intention over months, or even years, seems highly unlikely.[86] The traumatic crisis in her own mind seems to have come in November 1560, when she intended to ennoble Dudley, which would have been a necessary preliminary to marriage, and then dramatically changed her mind, slashing the patent in impotent fury. Shortly afterward her old and loyal servant Sir Thomas Parry died. Elizabeth at first intended to give his lucrative office of master of the wards to Dudley; but in January 1561 she changed her mind and gave it to Cecil instead.[87] Lord Robert received these signals, but he refused to draw the obvious conclusion. What he did realise was that his native charm unaided would no longer be sufficient. In the same month, and using his brother-in-law Sir Henry Sidney as an intermediary, Dudley approached de Quadra, offering England's continued friendship and a modification (at least) of the religious settlement in return for Philip's support for his union with the queen. It was broadly hinted that Elizabeth was cognisant of the offer and agreed to it.[88]

Elizabeth blandly turned aside de Quadra's intercession, denying that she had any intention of marrying Dudley, or anyone else – as yet. It seems, however, that other courtiers and councillors picked up rumours of what was afoot. This made conservatives such as Arundel more sympathetic to Dudley, but strengthened the hostility and distrust of Cecil and his Protestant allies. One result of this was that the Swedish negotiation was given a new lease of life at the beginning of 1561. This time Cecil and Throgmorton were positive, but not without an eye to the implications of the death of Francis II of France in December 1560; a death which was bound, sooner or later, to bring Mary Stuart back to Scotland as a young and attractive widow.[89] London began to warm towards the Swedes, and Eric again prepared to visit England in the summer. His plans were disrupted by the weather, however, and by renewed malicious gossip about Elizabeth's relations with Dudley. By the end of 1561 it was understood in London that he had gone off the whole idea, and was pursuing Mary Stuart instead.[90] In January 1562 his ambassadors were given an unmistakable cold shoulder, and when they left in April the negotiation was not resumed. If there had ever been a real chance of this marriage, it had probably come in the summer of 1561, when a merchant trading to Stockholm, named Robert Dymock, who was a friend of the Ashleys, approached them for some inside information on the queen's real attitude to Eric, and received the impression that she was 'well minded' to such a match.[91] It was a small enough indication. By the time that Dymock returned to Stokholm in 1562 the negotiation was history; but such crumbs are all that can be recovered of the bedchamber gossip.

There were other candidates. Before his death in a jousting accident in July 1559 Henry II had toyed with various ideas to deflect both the Habsburg and the Swedish suits, but the only one which showed any stamina was James Hamilton, earl of Arran.[92] This was seriously considered in the summer of 1560 as a means of cementing the recent treaty with Scotland, and for that reason Cecil was thought to favour it. It quickly became apparent, however, that such a marriage would inevitably drag England into the tangles of Scottish domestic politics in a manner that the treaty had precluded. For that reason, if for no other, Elizabeth turned the idea down flat; and, unlike others which had been similarly handled, it promptly disappeared. Dudley, in spite of numerous negative signals, showed no inclination to follow suit. This was partly because his personal friendship with the queen continued to be warm, even affectionate, and partly because he persisted in his relations with de Quadra. There was, however, a change in the latter direction. If Lord Robert had ever offered a change in the religious settlement in return for Philip's favour, by January 1562 he was doing so no longer. On 31 January the ambassador reported:

> Lord Robert has intimated to me, and has caused others to tell me that he is desirous that your Majesty should write to the queen in his favour, and persuading her to marry him. He would like this boon to be obtained for him without writing himself to Your Majesty, as he fears the answer might make conditions with regard to religion which were out of his power. He has let out in the course of the negotiations that the French are making him great offers.[93]

De Quadra made encouraging noises, but in spite of his remark about the French, Dudley had no leverage, and Elizabeth persisted in her assertions that she had no intention of marrying anybody.

In October of the same year, before any further progress could be made, there came a crisis. Elizabeth nearly died. The trauma was brief but acute. On 10 October 1562, while resident at Hampton Court, she became unwell, but decided to take a bath – something which she did much more frequently than most of her subjects. The illness turned out to be smallpox, 'and the cold caught by leaving her bath for the air resulted in so violent a fever that on the seventh day she was given up'. The anxiety was intense.[94] The council convened twice to discuss the succession;

> Some wished King Henry's will to be followed, and Lady Catherine [Grey] declared heiress. Others who found flaws in the will were in favour of the earl of Huntingdon. Lord Robert, the earl of Bedford, the earl of Pembroke, duke of Norfolk with others of the lower rank, were in favour of this. The most moderate and sensible tried to dissuade the others from being in such a furious hurry, and said that they would divide and ruin the country unless they summoned jurists of the greatest standing in the country to examine the rights of the claimants.

The marquis of Winchester led this group, although they were few as most of the others understood such a manoeuvre to be a move in favour of a Catholic heir, because it would 'give time for your majesty to take steps in the matter'. No one (apparently) mentioned Mary Stuart, or at least de Quadra was not inclined to say as much to Philip. While these anguished debates were going on 'the eruption' in Elizabeth's condition occurred, and she began to recover. For two hours she was unconscious, and her first words on coming to herself were to beg her council to make Lord Robert protector of the kingdom, with a title and an income of £20,000. She also protested at that time, that, although she loved Lord Robert dearly 'as God was her witness nothing improper had ever passed between them'. 'Everything she asked for was promised', de Quadra drily observed, 'but will not be fulfilled'.[95]

By the 25th, when the ambassador wrote, the worst was clearly over, and there would be no need to confront that awkward request on behalf of Lord Robert. It had, however, been a revealing moment. Believing herself to be in extremis, Elizabeth for once was not acting; and her political judgement was wildly astray. Even in these circumstances, however, she would not name a successor, preferring a similar expedient to that which her brother had conceived in January 1553. If she had died, her wishes would almost certainly have been ignored; but she did not die and by the end of the year the stately political dance had been resumed as though never interrupted. Dudley himself was philosophical. In writing to Maitland of Lethington on 27 October, he observed 'well this sharp sickness hath been a good lesson, and as it hath not been anything hurtful to her body, so I doubt not but that it shall work much good otherwise'. The queen, however, had not escaped unscathed. Her health recovered completely, and her intellect was unimpaired; but her beauty had suffered. She lost much of her hair, and her face was heavily pockmarked. This was nothing that a wig and cosmetics could not remedy, but such resort was a terrible humiliation to so vain a woman, who had only just passed her thirtieth birthday. In December of the following year a proclamation was even drafted prohibiting the painting of unauthorised portraits. It is not clear that it was ever issued, but it indicates the sensitivity that the issue had by then acquired.[96]

Neither the succession nor the marriage issue went away, even briefly, during this early period. In 1559, 1563 and 1566 the House of Commons petitioned the queen to marry, and the Lords did so in 1563 and 1566.[97] To each petition she replied with a speech, elegant, conciliatory and evasive. She would marry in her own good time, and in her country's interest; she would take advice; she was grateful for their loving concern – and so on; but specific commitment she would not make. Negotiations came and went, of infinite and baffling complexity. The politics of the court was deeply influenced by this uncertainty, because the court was an arena of competition and emulation, and parties formed and dissolved around the various candidates. It is sometimes said that the dominant rivalry of these early years was that between Cecil and Dudley, but that is only true over certain issues. Over the latter's matrimonial ambitions they were opponents, and they competed for some kinds of patronage; but over religion, relations with Scotland, and several other issues, they collaborated.

Nor were they the only players in the game. The duke of Norfolk and the earl of Sussex, for example, were not clients but principles, although of less influence.[98] The same could be said of the earl of Arundel or the marquis of Winchester. On balance, Dudley probably did rather better in terms of material rewards, and it was in his clientage rather than Cecil's, or the queen's, that the survivors of the Marian conspiracies, and his father's military connections, tended to surface. As Cecil himself observed:

he shall study nothing but to enhans his own particular friends to welth, to offices, to lands, and to offend others. Sir Henry Sidney, Sir James Croft, Henry Dudley, Sir Francis Jobson, Appleyard, Horssey, Leighton, Mollynex, Middlemore, Colsill, Wyseman, Killigrew (etc).[99]

His brother Ambrose recovered the earldom of Warwick on 26 December 1561, and he started to receive significant land grants from the crown at about the same time; but it was not until long after Elizabeth had decided not to marry him that he was rewarded in political terms by himself receiving the earldom of Leicester in September 1564, and being admitted to the privy council.

His most significant political influence in these years was probably exercised in favour of the English intervention in France. This was an opportunistic alliance with the French Huguenots in 1562, designed to recover Calais. Le Havre was surrendered to the English as a pledge for Calais, and garrisoned with a substantial force commanded by the earl of Warwick. However, everything went wrong. The English fell out with their allies; the Huguenots made a separate peace, and plague broke out in the garrison at Le Havre. Warwick was permitted to make an honourable withdrawal in June 1563 with what was left of his force, but Elizabeth was constrained to make a disadvantageous peace at Troyes in 1564, and to surrender her residual claim to England's last outpost.[100] This gave her a lasting distaste for continental adventures, but she never blamed Dudley for his misguided council and it did not impair their friendship.

Nevertheless, Cecil was the gainer from this debacle, and that was doubly the case because his own adventure had been so conspicuously successful. The English withdrawal from Scotland in 1550 had given an opportunity for the Scots to appreciate the extent of their dependence on France; and many of them did not like it. By 1559 the Francophile government of the regent and queen mother Mary of Guise was as bitterly resented as the English pretensions had been ten years before. In the summer the Protestant Lords of the Congregation emerged as open rebels, representing themselves as a 'patriotic' party by linking the Catholic faith to the French ascendancy. Henry II would probably not have wanted to risk the peace of Câteau Cambrésis by sending more troops to Scotland, but he was accidentally killed in July and the government of his young son was dominated by the queen regent's brother, the duke of Guise. His backing for Mary was limited, but effective, and in the autumn of 1559 the Lords, disorganised and lacking resources, were facing defeat.

Abandoning their patriotic scruples, and playing the religious card, they appealed to Elizabeth for help.[101] The appeal which actually reached the queen, however, was mediated by Cecil, with whom the Lords had been in touch for some time. He knew, as they did not, his mistress's aversion to John Knox, and her dislike of rebellion against legitimate government. Consequently the petition which arrived emphasised the Lords' loyalty to their lawful queen, and made no mention of any Protestant cause, common or otherwise.[102] Instead the emphasis was upon the misgovernment and abuses of authority perpetrated by the French, that is by the Guise faction rather than by the French crown. On this basis the secretary had no great difficulty in securing surreptitious assistance in the form of money and arms.

Open intervention, however, was a different matter, and the council was divided. Pembroke, Clinton, Howard and Parry were for a 'forward' policy; Arundel completely against; Bacon, Winchester, Petre and Mason doubtful but inclined to hostility. One of them (it may have been Arundel), wrote to the queen in the middle of the dispute:

> It may please your Most Excellent Majesty to understand that yesterday Mr Treasurer [Winchester] and Mr Secretary were in hand with me againe on your Majesties behalf for the voyage into Scotland by land. Whereupon the more I thinke, the more I do mislike it.[103]

He then gave a list of reasons why a military campaign would be a mistake.

In the middle of December Elizabeth decided to send a fleet to the Firth of Forth, but without declaring its purpose, which would have kept her options open until the last possible moment. By the 24th, however, Cecil had so far prevailed that the fleet commanded by Sir William Winter was given specific orders to intercept French reinforcements, and it was decided to send the duke of Norfolk north with a small army.[104] It was probably some firm intelligence that the French had actually sailed which prompted these decisions, because any further delay would have been tantamount to doing nothing. The French fleet was turned back by storms, but the intention to send as many as ten thousand men remained, and was known. By the middle of January Winter was on station in the Forth to prevent this, but Norfolk's orders had been temporarily countermanded. Clearly the argument in council continued, and Elizabeth favoured a minimalist strategy, containing the situation in the hope that it would resolve itself. By the end of January, however, Cecil had won over Bacon (at least) among the doubters, and persuaded Elizabeth that she was already committed. Norfolk's orders were reinstated, but he was given very careful instructions as to the nature of the agreement which he was empowered to make. Meeting with the Scottish commissioners at Berwick on 27 February, this agreement was reached and set down.[105] Nothing was said about religion, or about any English interest:

> The Queen, understanding that the French intend to conquer the realm of Scotland, suppress the liberty thereof and unite it to France, and being required thereto by the nobility in the name of the whole realm, with all speed shall send into Scotland sufficient aid of men to join with the Scots as well by sea as land, not only to expel the present power of French, but also to stop all greater forces to enter therein.

It was on this basis that the subsequent campaign was conducted. Although the Anglo-Scottish siege of Leith was a failure, Winter's presence in the Forth and increasing domestic problems in France precluded any reinforcement

for the troops already there. As long as the English and the Scots did not
fall out, there could only be one outcome, and this was hastened by the
death of Mary of Guise in June 1560.[106] When the treaty of Edinburgh was
concluded in July, it was on the basis of complete mutual withdrawal, the
ratification of all existing treaties, and the reference of outstanding issues
to the Scottish parliament. Only one clause specifically expressed an English
interest: 'The French King and Queen shall abstain from using the arms
and style of the Queen of England, and shall prohibit their subjects from
doing the same.'[107] A concession which affected the Scots not at all. This
restraint was entirely down to Cecil.

Elizabeth tried at the last minute to insert a clause for the recovery of
Calais, but was persuaded that such an attempt would sabotage the whole
delicate operation, and did not persist. In spite of this, the treaty of Edinburgh reflects creditably upon all concerned: Cecil's wisdom as a policy
maker; Winter's skill and tenacity as a seaman; and the queen's capacity to
act when necessary. Whether it was Cecil's discretion or her own scruples
which kept out such divisive issues as English claims to overlordship or the
pursuit of a confessional agenda, we do not know. The decisions, however,
could only have been the queen's, and the way in which they were reached
provide a good example of her style of government at its most effective.
Queen Mary refused to ratify the treaty when she returned to Scotland, but
the failure of her own government a few years later robbed that refusal of
any significance. Although the subsequent history of Scotland continued to
be unstable and a cause of anxiety, centuries of intermittent warfare between
the kingdoms had finally been brought to an end.[108]

By the time of Elizabeth's second parliament in 1566, she had good reason,
on balance, to be pleased with her progress. Her religious settlement, while
pleasing hardly anyone except herself, had quietened strife at home without
provoking any violent reaction abroad. Through Cecil's skill, and a timely
show of severity against Catholic nonconformists, she had managed to evade
an invitation to send delegates to the council of Trent, without making her
international situation any more precarious than it already was.[109] Both her
council and her court were working satisfactorily, although it must have
been a cause of great grief to her that both Thomas Parry and Kate Ashley
had died; the former in 1561 and the latter in 1565. Kate's death must have
taken the last of Elizabeth's childhood and youth with her, but we do not
know how she reacted. The chief gentlewoman's last recorded intervention
was typically over the matter of her mistress's relations with Robert Dudley,
and we do not know what effect that had on their friendship. She seems
to have died in her own home and not at court, but nothing is known of
the circumstances. John Ashley survived her by more than thirty years. He

married again, and kept his position at court until the end; but he features very little in the rest of the queen's life.

Politically, there had been successes and failures; and issues like marriage and the succession had neither been resolved nor gone away. Catherine Grey had been disgraced and imprisoned for her clandestine marriage to the earl of Hertford, but that had not, in the eyes of her supporters, invalidated her claim.[110] Mary, back in Scotland since the autumn of 1561, had married Henry, Lord Darnley in spite of Elizabeth's best efforts to prevent it, and in June 1566 bore a son, James. Elizabeth was bitterly distressed at being upstaged in this fashion, but resolutely refused the obvious remedy. Above all, she had created around herself stability. In spite of the competition and emulation of the court, this was not a giddy world in which favour was lightly won or lost. The same servants and companions attended her for many years; natural wastage was slow, and dismissals very unusual. The same applied to her council. Councillors quarrelled and argued; sometimes they were heeded and sometimes not; sometimes individuals attracted the royal wrath; but there was a consensual loyalty which grew greater with the passage of time. Elizabeth could not escape the buffetings of political fortune, but she had no intention of making her problems worse by sowing the seeds of dissent among her own attendants and advisers. Francis Naunton was mistaken when he claimed that she 'ruled much by faction', although his observation was intended as a compliment. As we shall see, Elizabeth never deliberately encouraged faction. What she did do was to encourage competition for her favour, and that sometimes bred quarrels; but she had no need to balance the forces of powerful men. She had more subtle ways of maintaining control.

7

Threats

In spite of her youth and theatrical style, Elizabeth's strategy was always defensive; protective of her own position and of her country's autonomy. Unlike her father, she had no agenda of personal or national prestige. Her intervention in France in 1562 was not in the interests of promoting international Calvinism, or even to increase England's weight in the game of European power politics, but simply to recover a piece of land around Calais which everyone in England regarded as an integral part of the kingdom. Her intervention in Scotland was not intended to secure the ascendancy of Protestantism, and certainly not to reassert English overlordship, but simply to prevent the French from using the northern kingdom as a base from which to attack her. Unlike her sister, she had no fixed preconceptions of where virtue and safety lay. This made her extremely pragmatic, and the council that she assembled shared that pragmatism. The disagreements, which were numerous in the first half of the reign, were thus always about means, never about ends. Before 1570 there was no question of England, with its fragile Protestant church and limited military resources, leading any kind of crusade against the Counter Reformation. It is said that Cecil's great success in Scotland was to persuade nearly all his fellow councillors of the need for action, and particularly to win over some of the more conservative, such as Clinton, Howard and Pembroke.[1] In fact the only person he had to persuade was Elizabeth herself; who, unlike her sister, was not much swayed by the consensus of her advisers. It did not appear in the summer of 1560 that the Scottish problem had been solved by the treaty of Edinburgh. Mary remained queen, and the personal link with France was intact. Nobody knew when, if ever, the queen would return; or what effect that would have on relations with England. For the time being, however, the ambitions of the Guises had been thwarted.

A similar move had been executed in respect of the papacy. Philip's ambassador, Alvarez de Quadra, was in a dilemma. As a bishop, and a man of straightforward piety, he considered it to be his duty to undermine the heretics in England and to restore the country to the true faith.[2] As a representative of his king, however, it was his job to remain on friendly terms with Elizabeth, and to prevent any English understanding with France.

The new pope, Pius IV, who had been elected to succeed the irascible Paul IV in December 1559, had already made one attempt to send an envoy to England early in 1560. However, his choice of Vincenzo Parpaglia, an ex-member of Pole's household and a strong French sympathiser, for the mission ensured its failure.[3] Parpaglia was *persona non grata* with Philip, and the king of Spain had stopped his mission before it got anywhere near England. William Camden later alleged that Pius offered to rescind the judicial verdict against the marriage of the queen's parents in return for her cooperation, and cited a letter, allegedly written to Elizabeth, in which the pope 'exhorting and admonishing your greatness (most deare daughter)', urged her to reject 'these lewd councellors, who love themselves better than you, and aime but at their private ends'.[4] It is not clear that any such letter was ever received, but the line of approach was also one which de Quadra adopted.

At the end of 1560 Paul decided to reconvene the council of Trent, in abeyance for nearly a decade, and to use this as a pretext for another attempt on England. Philip, who knew Elizabeth better than anyone in Rome, was again sceptical, but offered reluctant assistance through de Quadra. This time the envoy chosen was an unexceptionable protonotary, Martinengo, who arrived in the Low Countries in April 1561, bearing letters of friendly greeting in which the schism and heresy of the realm were blandly ignored.[5] The council was almost unanimous in opposing any initiative to admit Martinengo to England, but de Quadra's efforts on his behalf were seconded by Lord Robert Dudley (who was not a councillor), in the hope of persuading Philip to support his fading matrimonial pretensions – an illusion in which Lord Robert was to persist for over a year.[6]

In spite of the support of his colleagues, Cecil was sufficiently concerned by this unlikely alliance to spring a trap on the English Catholics which he had been preparing for some time. Clandestine masses were neither here nor there, but he needed to persuade the queen that secret Catholic sympathisers posed a security threat. A priest by the name of Coxe was arrested at Gravesend, and an investigation of his baggage produced evidence of widespread evasion, not only of the Act of Uniformity, but of the Act of Supremacy as well. The trail led to several members of Mary's privy council, and several ex-bishops.[7] There were rumours of the appearance of a miraculous cross in Glamorgan, triggering a further investigation, and a Jesuit named David Woolf was discovered in Ireland assisting the rebellious preparations of Shaun O'Neill. It was necessary, the secretary declared, to take some action 'for the rebating of the papists' humours, which by the Queen's lenity grow too rank'.[8] A policy necessary to ease conservatives into conformity could easily be taken advantage of. Elizabeth became alarmed at this evidence of subversion, and whereas in the middle of April de Quadra had been optimistic of success, on the 1 May the council unanimously agreed to refuse Martinengo admission, and the queen accepted that advice. De Quadra thereafter confined his efforts to attempts to ameliorate the condition of the English Catholics, but although he was given some limited spiritual authority himself, neither he nor anyone else was in a position to give the kind of political leadership which might have turned them into an opposition which posed a real threat.[9] In August 1563 de Quadra died, and Dudley withdrew from his flirtation as it became clear that he had far more to lose than to gain.

Meanwhile, the situation in Scotland was again giving cause for anxiety. Queen Mary had returned to her northern kingdom in August 1561, and although she had been given a chilly welcome, there was no attempt to repudiate her. While making no secret of her continued allegiance to the Catholic Church, she in her turn accepted the situation as she found it, and apart from her refusal to ratify the treaty of Edinburgh, posed no immediate threat. She was not quite nineteen years old, however, and the question of her remarriage, although not urgent, was obvious and immediate. Union with a powerful Catholic prince would both have strengthened her own position, and revived the fears both of England and of Protestant Scotland.[10]

She was also innocently anxious to secure recognition from Elizabeth of her status as heir to the English crown, and sent Maitland of Lethington to England for that purpose within a month of her return. Incensed by Mary's attitude towards the treaty, the queen was unsympathetic. Her reasons cast an interesting light on her perception of her own position:

> I know the inconstancy of the people of England, how they ever mislike the present government, and have their eyes fixed upon that person who is next to succeed, I have good experience of myself in my sister's [time], how desirous men were that I should be in place, and earnest to set me up. And if I would have consented I know what enterprises would have been attempted to bring it to pass, and now perhaps [the] affections of some are altered, men that bare me goodwill when I was the Lady Elizabeth, finding the event answer not their expectation, it may be that some could be content of a new change in hope to be then in better case.[11]

Behind the affectionate *bonhomie* of her image, there was a shrewd and cautious scepticism, and Mary was its immediate recipient. Rebuffed, the Scottish queen was doubly anxious to strengthen her hand. In 1563 her uncle, the cardinal of Lorraine, put out feelers for a marriage with the Archduke Charles, who had so far failed to secure the hand of Elizabeth. In the early summer of the same year, Maitland had contacted de Quadra about the possibility of a union with Don Carlos.[12] Philip was unenthusiastic; and Elizabeth, when she got wind of these approaches, declared that any union with a Habsburg prince would be a declaration of enmity, and would remove any chance of her recognition as heir. Both negotiations fizzled out. Elizabeth's attitude had put her cousin on the spot. A marriage acceptable to the English would do nothing for Mary's international standing, but if she got the additional strength which she desired she would have to make good her English claim by force.

At the end of 1563 Elizabeth took the initiative, and sent Thomas Randolf north with the suggestion that her cousin consider an English noble-man.[13] Mary's Protestant councillors responded favourably, but Mary was unimpressed, particularly as no particular name was being canvassed. It took Elizabeth some time to confess that the man she had in mind was Robert Dudley.[14] From the English point of view such a proposal had political logic; not least because it foreclosed more dangerous options. Elizabeth had not ceased to love Dudley, but she had decided not to marry him, and a royal bride in Scotland would be a noble compensation. In a way it was an unselfish gesture, but Lord Robert was also the only man who stood any chance of establishing a friendship between the two women, thus easing Mary's way to the English throne. If Elizabeth could not give Robert the crown matrimonial of England, perhaps the chance to father an heir to both realms was not a bad alternative. Mary was surprised, and more inclined to be insulted than flattered.[15] The negotiations went on for several months, nobody being quite sure how serious Elizabeth was, until Mary finally ended them by demanding unequivocal recognition in England as her price for acceptance. If the original offer was a bluff on Elizabeth's part, it had been called in the most obvious way. So far, Mary was winning on points, but she was about to throw away her advantage.

In the summer of 1563, in an effort to distract Scottish continental ambitions, Elizabeth had asked that the earl of Lennox and his son, Lord Henry Darnley, exiled for years in England by the vagaries of Scottish politics, should be allowed to return.[16] Darnley was the son of Margaret Douglas, whom Mary Tudor had once favoured, and had a claim of his own to the English throne. In September 1564 the earl reached Edinburgh, and in October he was restored to his Scottish estates.[17] He then asked Elizabeth for licence for his son to join him. After some apparent hesitation, the request was granted. In view of the outcome, it is tempting to suspect that the queen was setting a trap for her rival, but there is no contemporary evidence of that; nor does Elizabeth seem to have considered the possibility that Mary might marry him. The Scottish queen had hitherto shown a highly political attitude towards marriage, and had accepted cool political advice. No sooner had Darnley reached Edinburgh in February 1565 than all such caution was cast aside. Mary fell violently in love.[18] She was twenty-three, and in view of her first husband's general debility probably still a virgin. Suddenly her need for a man transcended every other consideration. Faced with a similar situation in 1561, Elizabeth had allowed her head to prevail; not so Mary. Darnley was a Catholic, of sorts, and an extremely handsome young man; but he had neither intelligence nor political experience to commend him, and he was no less Elizabeth's subject than was Dudley.

At first it appeared, however, that a counter-revolution had been wrought in Scotland. Mary and Darnley (by then Duke of Albany) were married in July 1565, and several of the Protestant lords, notably Moray and Argyll, having tried to oppose the queen's choice by force, were defeated and Moray was driven into exile.[19] Elizabeth denounced the marriage as a hostile action, and it seemed that all the work of 1560 had been undone. Appearances were deceptive; Darnley was an irresponsible fool, and the Protestant ascendancy was too strong to be eliminated by a single defeat. Although Mary became pregnant within a matter of weeks, her relationship with her husband quickly turned sour. Although he was known as the king by courtesy, he did not receive official recognition, and felt slighted and misused by his wife, who was much the stronger character of the two, as well as being queen.[20] Even before their child was born, he became involved in complex and foolish plots, one of which resulted in the murder of Mary's Italian secretary, David Rizzio. By the summer of 1566 tragedy was brewing in Scotland, and Elizabeth's piqued observation that a marriage contracted in haste would be repented at leisure was already proving prophetic.

Meanwhile, and quite unconnected with Scotland or its queen, Elizabeth began to rebuild the good relations which had existed between her brother's council and the City of London.[21] Mary had allowed Sebastian Cabot's Chinese venture to turn into the Muscovy Company, but she had done nothing in particular to promote it; and Philip had done his best to discourage any enterprise which might cross the interests of the Flemings.[22] However, at some point before Christmas 1558 Robert Dudley brought to court the powerful and mysterious person of John Dee. The ostensible reason was to get him to cast a horoscope for the coronation, but Dee had been a leading figure in Cabot's schemes, and was a natural successor to the old Genoan, who had died in 1557.[23] William Cecil had also been involved in the earlier relationship, and was now ideally placed to promote the trading and exploring initiatives which were being canvassed by such men as Stephen Borough, Richard Eden, and Dee himself. Towards the end of Mary's reign the London-Antwerp cloth trade recovered well from the crisis of 1551–52, but its stability could no longer be trusted, and some diversification was clearly desirable.[24]

Elizabeth was also anxious to shift the large debt which Mary had bequeathed her from Antwerp to London, where it would be more amenable to political bargaining. To facilitate this, she allowed the Merchant Adventurers to appeal a number of the new customs rates which her sister's council had introduced, and began to pick away at the recently restored privileges of the Hanseatic League.[25] At the same time the refugee Protestant congregations, which had fled or gone underground during Mary's reign, now reappeared, and brought their commercial expertise and contacts with them.[26] It is unlikely that Elizabeth was personally much interested in such matters, but she was very interested in the prosperity of her greatest city, and willing to listen to its expert financial advice. It is no coincidence that so many of its leading citizens were Nicodemites, like herself, and immediately began to channel money into godly causes.[27]

There was also a close connection between commercial enterprise and sea power. At the very beginning of the new reign Sir Nicholas Throgmorton wrote to Cecil:

> Bend your force, credit and device to maintain and increase your navy by all the means you can possible, for in this time, considering all circumstances, it is the flower of England's garland, your best and best cheap defence and most redoubted of your enemies and doubtful friends.[28]

He was preaching to the converted, but it was also significant that those same officers of the navy board who were close to Cecil, like Sir William Winter and Benjamin Gonson, were soon investing in the Guinea voyages being sent out by their London friends such as William Garrard and William Chester. Because of Portuguese hostility, these voyages had to be defended, and naval ships and guns were made available on favourable terms. Now English merchants were no longer constrained by the interests of a Spanish king, opportunities for profit were soon to be found. There was a chronic labour shortage in the Spanish American colonies, and the Portuguese had been running slaves across the Atlantic illegally for some time. More recently, during the war which was still going on when Elizabeth came to the throne, French ships, particularly Huguenots out of La Rochelle, had also taken to raiding those colonies, which Philip, lacking an effective ocean going war fleet, had been unable to protect.[29] In the circumstances of the new reign, and with the active cooperation of the navy board, an English consortium was formed to break into this Atlantic treasure chest.

The moving spirit in this enterprise was John Hawkins, the son of William Hawkins of Plymouth, who had attempted unsuccessfully to pioneer English trade to Brazil in the 1530s.[30] Hawkins had connections in London, and through London with some of those merchants who had gone into Spain when relations had improved after 1553. He also appears to have believed that he enjoyed Philip II's favour, although the grounds for that conviction are unclear.[31] In 1562, in collaboration with a group of London investors which included Winter and Gonson, Hawkins set up a modest expedition consisting of two small ships and a pinnace. The accounts of what happened are conflicting, but he appears to have purchased about five hundred slaves in West Africa, probably from conniving Portuguese who could not afford to admit their complicity. He then proceeded to Tenerife, where he had a contact who provided him with a Spanish pilot who took him to Hispaniola. Like the Portuguese in West Africa, the merchants there were willing to trade, but only surreptitiously to avoid their own authorities. Hawkins acquired a large and profitable cargo, and two additional ships. Presuming upon his supposed favour with Philip, he sent his additional ships and their cargoes to Spain, where they were promptly confiscated.[32] His original ships, however, returned intact and richly laden, a handsome dividend was paid, and everyone was happy except Hawkins, who spent years fruitlessly pursuing his missing cargoes in Spain.

The importance of this voyage lies less in what it achieved than in what it led to. In 1564 a second syndicate was formed, which was not only much larger, but which had a much higher political profile. Among the investors were the earl of Pembroke, Lord Clinton, the earl of Leicester and (secretly) Sir William Cecil. Most important of all, the queen herself became a shareholder. This was also done secretly, and we do not know anything of the thinking behind the decision; but it was a new departure.[33] Monarchs had traded through their own factors in the past, and had regularly hired out their ships to merchant groups. In this case, however, Elizabeth contributed a ship – the elderly but imposing *Jesus of Lubeck* – not in return for a rental but as her share of the venture capital. She also, probably, contributed guns and victuals from the navy stores. This entitled her to a handsome share of the profits (if any) and gave her a vested interest in the success of the expedition. It also compromised her in what was, from the Spanish point of view, an illegal venture. Hawkins followed much the same path as in 1562, only this time, when it was expedient to do so, he hoisted the queen's flag and described himself as her officer. He had no commission, but no one challenged him, and the Spaniards duly took note.[34]

The expedition returned to Padstow in September 1565 with all its ships intact, having lost only about a dozen men. The profit to the investors was about 60 per cent; not enormous by contemporary standards, but definitely encouraging. Meanwhile, the disturbed condition of the Low Countries was causing further problems for the Merchant Adventurers. After a good year in 1563, Antwerp's opposition to Philip's centralising plans for the government of the provinces led to a series of niggling restrictions on her trade, and in 1564 to a total ban on English cloth, imposed by the regent, Margaret of Parma.[35] This reinforced Cecil's politically motivated search for diversification. 'It is to be confessed of all men', he wrote in a memoranda at this time,

> that it were better for this realm for manny considerations, that the commodities of the same wer issued owt rather to sundry places, than to one, and especially to such one as the lord thereof is of so great power as he may therewith annoye this realme by waye of [such embargoes].[36]

The cloth staple was temporarily moved to Emden, and this particular dispute was resolved in less than a year; but the trade thereafter remained depressed, and Cecil was committed to the development of alternatives. In 1566 two relevant ventures were proposed. The first was the search for a North-West Passage to China, promoted by Humphrey Gilbert; and the other was a third voyage by John Hawkins. In the event Gilbert, not at this stage having adequate backing in the council, was frustrated by the Muscovy Company, which pleaded its own prior right to all such exploration. At the same time, Hawkins's plans fell victim to the delicate state of Anglo-Spanish relations. With France in turmoil, and Mary Stuart bogged down with her own problems in Scotland, Philip no longer had the same need for Elizabeth's friendship, and was therefore more disposed to listen to the message which his former ambassador, de Quadra, had sent him consistently between 1559 and 1563:

> This woman desires to make use of religion in order to excite rebellion in the whole world. If she had the power today she would sow heresy broadcast in all your Majesty's dominions, and set them ablaze without compunction.[37]

Hawkins's behaviour in 1564/5 had made Elizabeth's complicity in his operations clear; and the encouragement which members of her council (if not the queen herself) were giving to disaffected elements in the Netherlands appeared to confirm de Quadra's judgement. Elizabeth judged that another illegal trading voyage would at this stage be a provocation too far; and when de Quadra's successor Guzman da Silva asked her to stop Hawkins from sailing, she complied. Or rather, she partly complied; a much lower key voyage commanded by John Lovell did sail, and returned with a modest profit in September 1567; but this time neither the queen nor leading members of her council were shareholders.[38]

By the time that Lovell returned, the political situation had taken another turn. Philip had sent the duke of Alba to the Netherlands to suppress all opposition by force, and this was a development which posed a direct threat to English security. Elizabeth therefore deemed it necessary to fire another warning shot, and Hawkins was soon at the centre of a new high profile syndicate. By August 1567 he had six ships and about four hundred men at Plymouth, and two of his ships – the old *Jesus* and the *Minion* – had been provided by the queen. In spite of some attempt to confuse the issue, Philip's agents soon found out about this expedition, and where it was bound.[39] This was a high risk strategy on Elizabeth's part, and not at all consistent with her usual reputation for extreme caution and indecision. Perhaps she could simply not resist the temptation of another substantial cash bonus; but it seems more likely that she was attempting to demonstrate that there were ways in which England could make a serious nuisance of itself if its representations were ignored; in other words, to set up a bargaining position. It is also possible that the fact that Cecil, Leicester and Dee were all independently urging her in the same direction may have had some influence.

If that was her thinking, it did not work. Hawkins encountered more problems than in 1564, and obtaining his cargo cost more lives than he would have liked, but he was still on course for a profitable voyage until the old *Jesus of Lubeck* started to leak seriously. Had she not been the queen's ship, he would probably have abandoned her, but as it was he was forced to put into San Juan de Uloa on the Mexican coast for repairs. There he was caught by the new viceroy of Mexico, Don Martin Enriques. Hawkins held a strong position in the harbour, and thought that he had negotiated a safe passage, but

> the Spanyardes ment nothing lesse for their partes. The vice Roy forthwith blew the trumpet and of all sides set upon us; the *Minion* was made ready to avoide, and so leesing her hedfastes, and hayling away by the stearne fastes, was gotten out.[40]

The *Jesus of Lubeck* was abandoned, the *Minion* and the pinnace *Judith* escaped. If Hawkins had been intended to represent a threat to the New World, Elizabeth's bluff had been called. He salvaged some of his profit, but not enough to pay a dividend; and the queen had lost a ship. More important, however, both Hawkins and the captain of the *Judith*, Francis Drake, returned with a burning hatred of Spain, and the conviction that all Spaniards were treacherous and untrustworthy.

Literally days after the news of this débâcle reached England, on 23 November 1568 a fleet of Genoese galleys, bearing the money to pay the duke of Alba's army, took refuge from the weather and French pirates in several

harbours along the coast of Devon and Cornwall.[41] On the 29th de Spes
hastened to court to request safe-conduct for this money, either by sea to
Flanders or overland to Dover. Elizabeth was gracious, and pointed out
that Winter's ships had already rescued several of the galleys from French
attack. Winter, however, was about to sail for Bordeaux and would not be
available to provide an onward escort. It would therefore be safer to land
the money in England.

> the master, one Lope de Sierra, seeing the danger in which his ship was, begged
> the Governor in writing to help him to place the treasure on shore, which was
> done three or four days before Christmas, and was put into a safe place under
> the seal of Lope de Sierra himself.[42]

This, however, is the English version of what happened. According to
the Spanish version the money was taken off the ships against the will of
the Spanish officers.[43] Hearing this, de Spes sought an immediate audience
on 18 December. Being unable to obtain one, on the 21st he informed Alba
that the money had been seized by the English, and urged him to take
counter measures. It appears that, when de Spes jumped to this conclusion,
it was not actually true; but he had probably learned that there were voices
in England urging such a course. One of these was John Hawkins's brother,
William, who had just learned of what had happened in Mexico. Another
was Odet de Chastillon, the exiled Protestant cardinal, who informed Cecil
that the money was still legally the property of the Genoese bankers, and
that the Spaniards would have no claim upon it until it was handed over
in Flanders.[44] This was confirmed, apparently, by the Genoese factors
themselves.

By the time that de Spes obtained his delayed audience on 29 December,
two things had happened. Alba, not waiting for confirmation of de Spes's
report, had seized all the English shipping he could lay his hands on; and
Elizabeth had decided to borrow the money from the Genoese herself. The
delaying answer which was given to the Spanish ambassador was therefore
less than honest, but at the same time it could be represented as a legitimate
response to Alba's over-hasty action. According to Camden

> the councell made a question whether they should deliver it or no; and the
> greatest of them that sat in councell were of opinion that it should be sent into
> the Low Countries, for fear of provoking the Spaniard, who was a great Prince
> and already stood but hardly affected to England. But Queen Elizabeth, being
> assured by two of them to whom it belonged, that the merchants were only
> interested in it, the Kinge of Spaine nothing at all, she resolved to take it up of
> the merchants by way of loane.[45]

This makes it look as though the queen decided against the advice of her council, but it is reasonably certain that Cecil and his allies were urging such a course, and that the opponents were such conservatives as Winchester and Arundel. The result was a major crisis in Anglo-Spanish relations, and a profound split between those who blamed Cecil for leading the country into mortal danger, and those who believed that the only way to check Spanish aggression was to strike back whenever an opportunity presented itself.[46] Ignoring the fact that Elizabeth herself had made the crucial decisions, a group of these conservatives, in both court and council, began to conspire to bring about his downfall. For the first time since the queen's accession, there was serious dissension among her advisers.

Inevitably, given the other preoccupations of the time, this conspiracy also involved plans to settle the succession in a way which Cecil would certainly not approve, and thus cut him off from any return to major political office. In order to make sense of that attempt it is necessary to return to Scotland. The birth of the future James VI, on 19 June 1566, brought about a temporary reconciliation between Mary and Darnley. The news was received with formal rejoicing in England, although reports of Elizabeth's personal alarm are probably correct.[47] Mary tried to take advantage of this situation to press further for recognition as heir, and several members of Elizabeth's council, including Leicester and Pembroke, were sympathetic. Philip II also, contacted through various shadowy intermediaries rather than formal diplomatic channels, began to warm towards the idea.[48]

Mary had shown no sign of wishing to reintroduce French influence into Scotland, and the Guises had their hands full at home. At the same time, Leicester's unpopularity helped to keep the English situation in equipoise; and Elizabeth sent conciliatory but inconclusive signals to Scotland. Then, in the early part of 1567, Mary self-destructed in the most spectacular fashion. Darnley's behaviour had earned him many enemies. Once the euphoria over the birth of a prince had subsided, they had returned to the congenial task of conspiring to get rid of him.[49] As long as he was protected by the queen, this presented difficulties; but, as their relationship again deteriorated, he became vulnerable. By the time that James was christened with elaborate Catholic pomp on 17 December, Darnley had decided to leave for Glasgow and was not present at the ceremony. In Glasgow he fell ill, either of smallpox or syphilis according to different accounts, and although Mary had him brought back to Edinburgh with every sign of solicitude, it appears that she was already directing her favours elsewhere. While Darnley was convalescing at Kirk o'Fields, just outside the city, on 10 February he was murdered and the house blown up.[50] Who was actually responsible for this crime is not known, but suspicion was immediately cast upon James Hepburn, earl of Bothwell. No evidence supported these accusations, but it seems likely that he was already the queen's lover, and that the real target of this vilification was Mary. She swiftly set up an enquiry that vindicated him. This was probably fair, but in the circumstances it was received much as the verdict of Elizabeth's enquiry into the death of Amy Robsart in 1560: no one believed it.[51] By 1 March de Silva was writing from London: 'Every day it becomes clearer that the queen must take steps to prove that she had no hand in the death of her husband'.[52]

Elizabeth wrote Mary a sisterly letter of advice to the same effect, and common prudence would have suggested no less. Prudence, however, was not Mary's strength. What happened next, and why, is still unclear, but the upshot was that Bothwell bore the queen off to his stronghold at Dunbar, and there on 15 May he married her with Protestant rites. She had created him duke of Orkney as soon as the enquiry had exonerated him, and he had taken the precaution of obtaining a hasty divorce from his existing wife about two weeks before the 'abduction', so a premeditated and collusive move is almost certain.[53] Who was colluding with whom, however, is another matter. According to one account:

> they who absolved Bothwell of that crime, and gave consent to this marriage, took up arms as if they would have seized upon his person. But in effect, underhand they privily admonished him speedily to withdraw himselfe, for feare lest, being taken, he might have revealed the whole complot, and that from his flight, they might draw argument and subiect whereof to accuse the Queen.[54]

On 15 June, just a month after their wedding, Mary and Bothwell were defeated by the Lords of the Council at Carberry Hill, and Mary was captured. Bothwell escaped, giving some plausibility to the conspiracy theory, but his death ten years later in a Danish prison suggests the contrary. Whether she was the victim of subtle treachery or of her own uncontrollable passions, the upshot was an ignominious captivity for Mary.

> they seyzed upon her person, and intreated her so ignominiously and disgracefully, that although she had nothing on, but a very homely night-Gowne, yet they so clapt her up in prison at Lake Levin, under custody of the earl of Murray's mother, who was James the 5 his concubine.[55]

This is embroidery, although the queen's position was dangerous and humiliating enough.

Elizabeth was genuinely outraged by the news from Scotland. Mary had ignored her advice, and behaved with extreme folly, but she was still the queen; and whatever might be said about her claims on England, her legitimacy in her own kingdom was undisputed. In July Elizabeth sent Sir Nicholas Throgmorton north to make a number of unrealistic demands on the Scottish council. They ignored him, and forced Mary to abdicate in favour of her one-year-old son.[56] It is possible that she could have escaped this enforced retirement if she had been willing to renounce Bothwell and agree to the dissolution of her marriage; but on that point Mary was absolutely unyielding. Whatever the truth of his conduct, and in spite of his absence, her devotion to him was complete. When Elizabeth heard of this deposition, she displayed the full range of her royal wrath, and many expected the newly established concord between the kingdoms to break down into renewed war. As far as she was concerned, Mary's fate set the worst possible precedent for what might happen when a woman behaved like a woman and not like a queen; a situation from which she could never entirely distance herself, certainly not at the age of thirty-four.

There was no war because Mary, with indomitable spirit if little else, seized the initiative. On 2 May 1568 she escaped from Lochleven and withdrew to Hamilton Castle. There 'with the unanimous [consent] of all the Nobles who flocked thither in great numbers', she renounced her abdication, and set out to recover her kingdom by force.[57] Like much else in Mary's life, it was an heroic and futile gesture. Her 'great numbers' were an illusion, and the force that she did raise was swiftly and utterly defeated at Langside. With an endurance and courage born of sheer desperation, she then rode ninety-two miles across country without stopping or alighting, and crossed the Solway Firth into England. It was not refuge which she was seeking, but revenge.[58] Mary had misinterpreted Elizabeth's principled, and entirely self-seeking, support for her position in Scotland as a sisterly sympathy with her predicament. She came expecting England to wage war upon her rebellious subjects to restore her to the Scottish throne.

Such an expectation merely reflected that lack of political grasp that she had shown repeatedly over the previous two years. Elizabeth was quite prepared to use diplomatic leverage to persuade the Scots to restore her, upon reasonable conditions; but no conditions which might strike the Scots lords, or Elizabeth, as reasonable would have been acceptable to Mary, who seemed to be unaware how few cards she had left to play.[59] From being a Scottish problem, she had now become an English one.

What pity and commiseration soever Queen Elizabeth had of her, the Councell of England deliberated gravely and advisedly what in this case was to be done. They feared that if she remained any longer in England, having a persuasive and moving tongue, she might draw many to her partie who favoured the Title which she pretended to the Crowne of England. If she were sent into France, the Guizes her cousins would again set on foot the Title whereby she laide claim to the crown of England. And that the Amity between England and Scotland, so be-hoofefull and beneficiall, would be broken, and the ancient alliance between Scotland and France renewed.[60]

This is rather less than fair to Elizabeth, who did not need her council to tell her that she had a problem. She also had her own, somewhat devious, solution. If Mary's complicity in her husband's murder could be proved, then she should be returned to Scotland to face justice. Equally, if her innocence could be similarly established, then she should be restored to her throne. This was to take the moral high ground for international diplomatic consumption. It is quite likely that the queen knew, or strongly suspected, that neither of those positions would ever be established beyond doubt; but such a stance would then justify the third option, to retain her indefinitely in England in honourable confinement, taking advantage if necessary of the Scots legal verdict, 'not proven'.[61] Mary's possible return to Scotland did not disappear from diplomatic intercourse, but it ceased to be a real policy; instead political activity focused with increasing intensity upon her claim to the English succession. It was in this connection that Elizabeth's vivid memories of her predicament in Mary's reign became most relevant.

It was while the English and Scottish commissioners were going through the motions of failing to agree about Mary's future at York in October 1568 that the suggestion was first raised of 'persuading' her into a safe marriage. Mary's ardour for Bothwell had cooled by this time, and she was already considering the desirability of mending her fences with the Catholic Church. To do that she would have been forced to concede that her third marriage was invalid, and therefore that there was no legal obstacle to a fourth. The person first suggested was George Carey, the son of Elizabeth's cousin Lord Hunsdon; obviously considered a safe Protestant, because the suggester was Sir Francis Knollys.[62] Nothing happened, but the idea germinated. The next candidate whose name was canvassed, without Elizabeth's knowledge, was a rather different proposition. Thomas Howard, fourth duke of Norfolk was England's premier peer. Howard had actually presided over the abortive discussions at York, and it may be that it was there that the notion was implanted. Howard was not a Catholic, but he was on the conservative side in ecclesiastical debates, and he disliked Cecil as a parvenu.[63] By the time that the secretary had stirred up a hornet's nest in the Low Countries, there were already the makings of a plot to oust him, and to secure the succession for Mary. More accurately, there were two plots, and they existed side by side in a fog of mutual misunderstanding.

The Norfolk marriage plan was backed by a number of councillors, including the earl of Leicester, and was intended to persuade the queen into a radical change of policy in the interest of future security. The other was a scheme being energetically promoted by de Spes, designed to use whatever Catholic support could be mobilised, including that of the duke of Alba, to get rid of Elizabeth at once and replace her with Mary. The Norfolk marriage was merely a concession, countenanced on the assumption that he could be easily converted.[64] The common element in both these intrigues was the queen of Scots herself, who was prepared to collaborate in any plan which offered her own advancement. Alba himself was cautious, not believing that he had the resources to intervene effectively in England, and preferring a diplomatic solution to the existing stand off.[65] He saw the Norfolk marriage rather as the English councillors saw it, and was prepared to broker a return of Mary to Scotland as part of a settlement. In July 1569 he peremptorily ordered de Spes to stop interfering, as his machinations were known to the English government, and were placing the queen of Scots in danger of her life. By this time, unknown to Alba, and probably unknown to most of his English backers as well, Norfolk had negotiated with the government of Charles IX for French troops to be sent to Scotland, presumably to secure Mary's restoration by force, and thus to catch Elizabeth between a Franco-Scottish rock and a Spanish hard place.[66] How seriously the French intended intervention may be doubted, but it was a sinister development in the general confusion of plot and counter-plot.

How much the earl of Leicester knew about this dimension of the intrigue is uncertain, but by early September he had become seriously alarmed. What had seemed at first like a relatively innocent scheme to push the queen in a different direction began now to look like a danger to her state:

> And finally the earl of Leicester being at Tichfield, found himself ill (or else counterfeited the sicke) and being visited and graciously comforted by the Queene, he was seized with such feare, that her Maiestie could easily descerne it, beholding the blood and vital senses to shrinke in himselfe; which was the cause, that after he had asked pardon, and implored forgiveness with sighs and teares of the Queene, he declared unto her all the busines from the beginning.[67]

Or at least all that he knew. Elizabeth immediately sent for Norfolk and 'rebuked him sharply for having sought the Queen of Scotlande in marriage without her leave and permission'. He abased himself, but the damage was done. The queen absolutely forbade any such union, and the erstwhile plotters ran for cover. Leicester had already extricated himself, but the earls of Pembroke and Arundel were briefly placed under arrest.

Norfolk, furious and humiliated, found himself shunned at court, and in the middle of September withdrew to his estates without the queen's leave. This was an extremely dangerous thing to do, and de Spes immediately jumped to the conclusion that he had gone 'to raise his power'. That, however, was no longer an easy thing to do, even for a duke. His own affinity had no intention of rising, and its leaders advised humble and immediate submission.[68] Even if he had had the stomach for a fight, his men did not. Faced with that, the duke had no option. He wrote to the queen on 24 September, begging for her pardon; and a few days later made a formal submission. He was arrested by Sir Francis Knollys and Sir Henry Neville, and conducted to the Tower. While he still had the liberty to do so, he wrote to those of his former allies and backers who were still in a position to act, asking them to refrain from doing anything which would make his own situation worse.[69] In one quarter his message arrived too late.

In the far north both Thomas Percy, earl of Northumberland, and Charles Neville, earl of Westmorland, were disaffected. They disliked Cecil, disliked the religious settlement, and were not trusted in London. The cold wind of suspicion had already cost them a number of border offices that they considered theirs by right.[70] They also, and particularly Percy, had more command of a traditional affinity than any peer further south. They were also far enough away, both physically and mentally, to be out of touch with the twists and turns of central politics. Just what they originally intended to do is not clear. They supported the Norfolk marriage plan, would have liked to see Mary recognised, and hoped for a more conservative direction in policy generally. They probably had no intention of going beyond some kind of demonstration.

There were others in the north who were far more radical in their aims, particularly the Nortons, Thomas Hussey and Robert Tempest.[71] The elder Richard Norton had been active in the Pilgrimage of Grace over thirty years before, and he and his supporters were mortal enemies to Cecil and all he stood for: 'they relyed uppon some secret succours, which the Scots Leaguers and the Duke of Alva were to land at Herripoole [Hartlepool] within the Bishopricke of Durham as after was made mainifest'.[72] It was probably thanks to these activists, rather than the earls themselves that 'the rumour of that rebellion to be excited in the North Country was daily augmented'. The rumours could not be ignored, however, and the earl of Sussex, the queen's lieutenant in the north, summoned them to explain themselves. This they did to his satisfaction on 13 October, but the rumours did not subside and the council was not satisfied. On 24 October Sussex was instructed to order the earls to appear at court forthwith.[73]

Confusion reigned. They declined to appear, and began to mobilise their affinities, but apparently on the grounds that they had been ordered to raise their powers for the queen's service. By sowing alarm and despondency, the radicals thus got their way, because once men had taken arms they were caught in the open, even if their intentions were loyal; and once mobilised they were prey to the latest rumours. It was not until 13 November that Sussex proclaimed the earls traitors, and by then many of their followers were too committed to turn back.[74] Northumberland himself appears to have been forced into decisive action by some of his own servants, who claimed that his private enemies were laying in wait for him under cover of the general alarm.[75]

The declared objective of the rebellion was to rescue Mary from Tutbury, where she was being held, and its undeclared objective to place her on the throne. It was reasonably well supported by the Percy and Neville affinities in Durham and North Yorkshire, but not very much in Northumberland, the rest of Yorkshire or the north west.[76] At first, royal forces in the north were few and scattered. The rebels took over Durham Cathedral, celebrated mass and destroyed as many prayer books and English Bibles as they could lay their hands on. For about a week, as they advanced south into Yorkshire nearly ten thousand strong, the rebels looked threatening. They reached Bramham Moor on the 24th, still about fifty miles from Tutbury, but then their momentum petered out. This was not another Pilgrimage of Grace, and its failure to attract any significant support beyond the two affinities spelt inevitable failure.

On 25 November, the day that Mary was moved from Tutbury to Coventry, they began to retreat. By the 30th the earls were back at Brancepeth, about ten miles west of Durham. As a final defiant gesture they were able to capture the lightly garrisoned stronghold of Barnard Castle, but they could not hold it. On 15 December they disbanded what was left of their force, and fled, first to Hexham, then to Naworth, and finally over the border into Scotland.[77] Meanwhile, substantial royal armies marched up from the south, gathering the (suddenly very loyal) gentry of the north as they came.

There was an epilogue, which could have been serious, in January 1570 when a disappointed claimant to the Dacre inheritance also raised a flag of revolt. This time the threat came less from the border counties than from the sympathetic Scots who were reported to be rallying to his cause. On 20 February, however, Lord Hunsdon with a small force caught Dacre near Naworth before his Scots allies could join him. The rebels left about three hundred dead and two hundred prisoners. Dacre joined the earls in Scotland, and the queen wrote her cousin an effusive letter of gratitude:

> I doubt much, my Harry, whether that the victory were given me more joyed me, or that you were by God appointed the instrument of my glory; and I assure you, for my countries good the first might suffice, but for my heart's contentation the second more pleased me.[78]

In truth this last Tudor rebellion posed no threat to lowland England, or to the stability of Elizabeth's crown. What it did was to give an opportunity for the queen to complete that restructuring of government and power in the north which her father had begun, but which had been partly turned back by Mary's decision to resurrect the Percy earldom of Northumberland. There were hundreds of executions, many large confiscations of property, and the chapter of Durham Cathedral was belatedly purged.[79] When the dust had settled and the property had been redistributed, there was hardly a trace left of the ancient noble affinities of Percy, Neville and Dacre which had dominated the borders for centuries. If the northern earls had been tempted into rebellion by the queen herself, the outcome could not have been more favourable to her.

It also provided some punctuation of another kind. Although he had been warned off by Alba, de Spes continued his contacts with the malcontents, and probably encouraged them to look for Spanish assistance, if it was only to discourage further contacts with France.[80] About the end of November, when the rebellion was already on the point of collapse, an agent of the earl of Northumberland called on the ambassador, and was sent on by him to Alba, bearing a ciphered letter. Nothing came of these contacts, but another, made a little earlier, was more fruitful. Almost from the moment of his election in January 1566, Pope Pius V had been seeking leverage against Elizabeth. At first he had been frustrated, not only by Philip II's lack of enthusiasm, but also by the fact that the Catholic candidate for the English throne was in deep disfavour.

Mary's behaviour between 1566 and 1568 had made her almost as unpopular in Rome as in Scotland; but her fall, and subsequent detention in England, changed that situation. By the summer of 1569 Mary had made her peace with the Holy See, and was beginning to acquire something of the aura of a Catholic martyr. A rebellion in her favour was therefore a sign that God was moving.[81] Not only had one of Pius's own agents, Nicholas Morton, assured him that the English Catholics were powerful and ready to rise, but Nicholas Sander, the most energetic of the English religious exiles, had confirmed this news.[82] The only thing that was holding them back, the latter claimed, was the fear that they might be committing a sin in rebelling against a lawful ruler. The earls, or at least their agents, were aware of these views and about 8 November, before openly taking up arms, they wrote to Pius for his assistance and blessing. Even if this letter had travelled direct and by the fastest route, it would probably still have arrived too late. As it was, it did not reach Rome until 16 February, when the main rising had long since collapsed, and even Dacre's belated effort was about to end.[83] Pius acted with exemplary speed. He responded immediately, assuring the rebels of his moral and financial support; and within a few days he had signed the bull *Regnans in Excelsis*, declaring Elizabeth deposed, and absolving all her subjects of their allegiance.[84]

What this achieved had nothing to do with the rebellion which had occasioned it, but everything to do with Elizabeth's attitude to the Catholic Church. Successive popes had hitherto given no clear lead to English Catholics, but had allowed them to remain half assimilated and half dissident; a potentially dangerous nuisance, but not a specific threat. After the promulgation of *Regnans in Excelsis*, however, anyone refusing the oath of Supremacy became the adherent of a foreign power that had declared war upon the English state, and thus a traitor. The logic of this was not always pursued, and most English Catholics did their best to avoid it. But it was always there to be invoked, and played directly into the hands of the 'forward' Protestant party upon the council. There was no longer any point in equivocating in the interest of placating the conservatives. No person who took the oath of Supremacy could call himself a Catholic; and no one who refused it could call himself a loyal Englishman.

On 22 June 1570, Antonio de Guaras wrote to the duke of Alba:

> The declaration of the pope against the queen has been posted on the bishop of London's gate, which has caused great sorrow to the bad people and much delight to the godly, who are convinced that, as a consequence of it, redress for their evils will follow by the arms of Christian princes, and especially of his Majesty [Philip].[85]

Philip was less than pleased at the prospect of this responsibility, and most of the faithful were more filled with alarm than delight, but that is not the point. Elizabeth's delicate bluff had been called, indeed denounced as humbug. This bull, combined with the northern rising, spelt the end of crypto-Catholicism as legitimate politics. The practice itself continued, even within the confines of the court, but became subject to increasingly sharp sanctions. Excluded from the House of Commons in 1563, and from the privy council in 1567, no Catholic could now be trusted in public office; and recusancy had become a recognised and recalcitrant problem.[86]

The queen's personal role in all these events was decisive. However sympathetic Cecil may have been to the spirit of maritime enterprise, he could not have committed royal ships to John Hawkins's voyages without her specific sanction. His own investment he could (and did) keep secret; but the presence of ships as obvious as the *Jesus of Lubeck* could not be concealed. When Elizabeth decided that Hawkins should not sail he remained in harbour; when he left it was with her permission, although his instructions were probably drawn up by his shareholders. Equally, the decision to borrow the Genoese money was hers, not Cecil's. He may have advised it, and carried it out, but he could not have overridden those senior voices in the council who were opposed to so risky a venture. Only the queen could do that. In the spring and summer of 1569, as Alba made it clear that he did not intend his indignation to extend to actual hostilities, the secretary's position became somewhat less exposed. It was Elizabeth's support for Cecil, however, which caused Leicester in September 1569 to disclose the Norfolk marriage plot.[87] He judged that there was no realistic chance of turning the queen against her chief adviser, and that anyone caught in the attempt would suffer serious consequences; so he made his peace in his own way, and abandoned the duke of Norfolk to his fate.

How much Elizabeth was swayed by her councillors in her early dealings with the queen of Scots is hard to say. While Mary was in Scotland, she lectured her in a manner fully justified by the outcome, but which can only have caused annoyance. When James was christened, she stood godmother. When Mary wrote indignantly about her reception in England, and particularly about the detention of her agent, the bishop of Ross, at the time of the northern rising, she was met with a further lecture:

> Then followed a hard manner of dealing with me, to entice my subject and near kinsman the Lord Darnley, under colour of private suits for lands, to come into your realm, to proceed in treaty of marriage with him without my knowledge, yea to conclude the same without my consent or liking. If I should now enter into the accidents happened since flying for your succour out of Scotland into my realm, as well of your manner of coming and of your usages sithen that time, as of my benefits towards you, being charged with such heinous facts offensive to God and to the world, I have thought good to assure you that the restraining of the bishop of Ross, your minister at this time, hath proceeded of many reasonable and necessary causes, as hereafter you shall understand.[88]

There was no love lost between the women, but at this time Elizabeth's attitude seems to have been one of profound irritation, not untouched with contempt, rather than fear or anger. Perhaps she also had a slightly guilty conscience, but in the early part of 1570 Mary was still a legitimate piece on the chessboard of English politics. The tense conflict over her position came later.

Although it was Elizabeth's personal summons to the northern earls which drove them into open revolt, it is unlikely that she played any direct part in its suppression. There was scarcely time, or justification, for serious alarm in London, because less than a month separated initial defiance from final defeat, and the real danger lasted no more than about ten days.

The government's reaction to *Regnans in Excelsis* was predictably swift and angry. John Felton, the man who posted the bull on the bishop of London's gate in early June, was arrested, tried and executed as a traitor

9. Elizabeth I, *c.* 1575, unknown artist. (*National Portrait Gallery*)

10. Elizabeth I, *c.* 1588, unknown artist. (*National Portrait Gallery*)

11. Elizabeth I, *c.* 1592, Marcus Gheeraerts the Younger. (*National Portrait Gallery*)

12. William Cecil, Lord Burleigh, unknown artist. (*National Portrait Gallery*)

13. Robert Dudley, earl of Leicester, *c.* 1575, unknown artist. (*National Portrait Gallery*)

14. Mary, Queen of Scots, unknown artist after Nicholas Hilliard, *c.* 1610. (*National Portrait Gallery*)

15. Sir Francis Drake, *c.* 1580, unknown artist. (*National Portrait Gallery*)

16. Robert Devereux, earl of Essex, *c.* 1597, Marcus Gheeraerts the Younger.
(*National Portrait Gallery*)

on 25 July.[89] 'The first result of the declaration', as Guaras noted, 'has been the persecution and imprisonment of Catholics'; 'she herself', he continued, has 'answered the pope's declaration in Latin verse, scoffing at the apostolic authority, saying that the boat of St Peter should never enter a port of hers, and other heresies of a like nature'.[90] Unfortunately this particular poetic effort does not seem to have survived. Such events were pregnant with future trouble; but meanwhile those intense preoccupations of the early years of the reign, marriage and the succession, continued to occupy much of the queen's personal attention. The unfortunate Catherine Grey died early in 1568, depriving the Protestants of their most plausible candidate, and leaving Mary Stuart's claim in stark and dangerous isolation. In 1570 Elizabeth was thirty-seven, the same age as her sister had been upon her accession, and the hope of a peaceful and acceptable succession seemed to depend more than ever upon her choice of a husband.

At the end of 1565 it had seemed that the Habsburg negotiations had run into a brick wall over religion. The new emperor, Maximilian, was conciliatory at the end of November, but Elizabeth was unimpressed, and unwilling to make any concessions. The queen's council persisted; and on this issue Cecil, Norfolk, Sussex and Winchester were all in agreement.[91] Parliament was due to reconvene later in 1566. Unless some negotiation was being visibly pursued, its clamour was likely to be intolerable. In February Elizabeth agreed to send an envoy to Vienna, ostensibly to confer the Order of the Garter on the emperor, but in reality to pick up again the flagging marriage negotiations.[92] The envoy chosen was the unimpressive Thomas Dannett, and Maximilian did not take the queen's intention seriously. So unsuitable was Dannett that it is a mystery why he had been chosen, ostensibly by Cecil who must genuinely have wanted progress. It is possible that he was Elizabeth's personal choice, because she had no real desire for success; and indeed the only positive thing to emerge from Dannett's mission was his favourable report upon the personal appearance of the Archduke Charles. Undeterred, the councillors kept up their pressure, Cecil by attempting to invoke the support of Philip, and Sussex by organising pointed entertainments at court, consisting of masques celebrating the married state. Elizabeth's reaction is unknown.

As expected, the parliament caused trouble. In September the queen had asked her council to head off any pressure from that quarter because, as Cecil put it, 'the Queens Majestie is by Gods special providence moved to marriage, and that she mindeth for the wealth of her Commons, to prosecute the same'.[93] Such fair words could not conceal the fact that no nuptial agreement was in prospect; and, as soon as the session was under way, both the Lords and the Commons began to agitate. Elizabeth was furious, not least with her councillors for having failed to observe her instructions. Warned that petitions were in the offing from both Houses on the subjects of both succession and marriage, the queen determined upon a pre-emptive strike. On 5 November she summoned thirty members of each House, and forbade any further discussion of the succession:

> And as to her marriage she said she thought she had so satisfied by her answer therto that she looked rather for thanks than for request [considering] that she is fully determined to marry. And that should be proved by her deeds as soon as time and occasion should serve, if Almighty God should not take away either her own person or the person of him with whom she meant to marry. And at this present she could use no other mean to satisfy the doubtful but with the word of a prince, which being in so public a place ought not to be mistrusted.[94]

Mistrust or not, her words did not mean quite what they appeared to say, because her commitment to the Archduke Charles was very far from unconditional, and she felt constrained to add 'they (I think) that moveth the same will be as ready to mislike him with whom I shall marry as they are now to move it'. The parliament could not have both a strong Protestant priority and a Habsburg marriage; and if she failed to resolve that contradiction, she would accept the former rather than the latter. When the parliament was dissolved on 2 January 1567, she allowed her council to draft instructions for a mission to Vienna. For months this enterprise hung fire in the hope that the Austrians would make the first move; but they gave no sign, and on 29 June the earl of Sussex set off on his mission. He was a far more suitable envoy than Dannett, and the council thought that it had found a way round the intractable problem of religion.

Lutheranism had been officially accepted within the Empire since 1555, and if Sussex could persuade Maximilian that the English Church adhered (more or less) to the Confession of Augsburg, then his objections would have less logical force.[95]

> in dede no quyet Catholik may nede to forbeare to resorte to our churches and common prayers, for that ther is nothing redd or spoken other in praiers, or in the ministration of the sacramente but only the very worde of scripture.

Unfortunately Maximilian, who had access to Spanish information, understood quite otherwise, and would not even receive Sussex when he arrived. He did, however, summon Charles on the grounds that it was his scruples that had to be addressed, and by the end of October it looked as though a compromise had been hammered out.

This was reported to the council in England on 7 November, and the debate that followed revealed a deep and even division over the religious concessions which Sussex proposed, particularly the archduke's 'private' mass.[96] Thanks probably to the earl of Leicester, who was a strong opponent of the scheme, news of these debates leaked out, and there were Protestant demonstrations, both in London and in various influential pulpits. Elizabeth's caveat had been fully justified. Faced with the choice between satisfying the clamour for her marriage and retaining the trust and affection of her Protestant subjects, she chose the latter. In spite of Cecil's advocacy, she rejected the compromise, and that was effectively the end of the Habsburg negotiations.

The next initiative came from a quite different quarter. Although the divisions afflicting France were broadly ideological, and the Protestants were one clearly defined party, there were Catholics and Catholics. When a cessation of hostilities had been agreed at Longjumeau in March 1568, other political priorities resurfaced, and one of these was the conflict between the moderately Catholic Montmorencies, and the ultra-Catholic Guises. In June the duke of Montmorency and the Huguenot leader Gaspard de Coligny began to promote the idea of a marriage between Henry duke of Anjou, the king's younger brother, and the queen of England.[97] Their immediate objective was less to solve Elizabeth's problem than to wean Anjou away from ultra-Catholic influences. They told the English ambassador, Sir Henry Norris, that it was necessary to detach Anjou from a Guise conspiracy in favour of Mary Stuart; but nothing happened because civil war broke out again in France in October 1568, before any negotiation could even commence.

It was not until the Pacification of St-Germain in August 1570 brought another lull in the strife that the scheme resurfaced. This time the circumstances were more promising: the king was clearly turning against the Guises, and Montmorency and Châtillon influences were prevailing at court. One of the reasons for this was the threat presented by Alba in the Netherlands, and an Anglo-French marriage acquired the additional attraction of being a defensive alliance against the power of Spain. Both Charles and the queen mother, Catherine de Medici, also saw advantages in getting the young prince away from his Guise mentors, and preferably out of the country altogether.[98] Both were sceptical, partly because of the age discrepancy (Elizabeth was thirty-seven, Henry nineteen), and partly because Catherine did not believe that Elizabeth seriously intended to marry; however, a negotiation was proposed in October 1570.

The omens were never good, partly because the duke was a *dévot* who regarded all heretical practices with extravagant horror, and partly because the Huguenot leadership was no longer supportive, preferring a union with their own leader Henry of Navarre, which never got as far as the negotiating table.[99] The English council was keener on this match than either the French or the queen, because there had been a renewed threat in the spring of 1570 to send French (or rather Guisard) troops to Scotland to support those who were trying to resurrect Mary's political fortunes. There had even been some talk of Anjou marrying the queen of Scots, and although this could not have happened as long as Mary was in English custody, it provided sufficient incentive for Elizabeth to sanction a further negotiation. By such a marriage, Nicholas Bacon observed, 'the Q. shalbe delyvered of the continuall feare of the practizes withe the Queene of Scottes, on whome dependeth almoste the onlye prosperitie of the Q. hole liffe and raygne'.[100]

Consequently Châtillon's tentative feelers met with a more positive response than he expected or perhaps hoped; and when the French ambassador made a formal move in December 1570, Elizabeth welcomed it with apparent enthusiasm. She told him that she was determined to marry a foreign prince rather than a subject; which was no great news because the Dudley match was long since dead, and there was no other plausible candidate at home. Cecil, Bacon and Leicester were all in favour, not without an eye on the reconvening of parliament in April. It was decided to take advantage of Lord Buckhurst's attendance at the wedding of Charles IX himself to begin serious, but secret negotiations, and Anjou gave a reluctant consent for these to go ahead in February.[101] He was no less averse to heresy, but seriously tempted by a crown.

The French demands, however, when these emerged, were stiff; and Elizabeth was as unwilling as ever to offer more than a private mass by way of concession. In May 1571 it looked as though deadlock had been reached, but the queen insisted that she did not wish to break off the negotiation, and Charles and Catherine de Medici reluctantly agreed. Various compromise formulae were suggested, but none were agreed, and by July Anjou himself was alleged to have gone off the whole idea, in spite of his mother's pleas that he would at least appear to negotiate. By October he was refusing to marry Elizabeth on any terms whatsoever, but still the pointless negotiation dragged on because in fact there was a hidden agenda: a shared fear of Spain between Charles and Elizabeth.[102] In January 1572 Sir Thomas Smith and Sir Henry Killigrew made one final effort:

> when in answer to Smith's earnest demand the Queen Mother declared that the only stay of the marriage between the Queen of England and the Duke of Anjou was religion, wherein he was so earnest that he thought he would be damned if he yielded in anything. Smith replied that the matter of religion would be the most honourable to break off with, both for his Mistress and the Duke. The Queen Mother declared that they meant no breaking off and never desired anything more in their lives than this.[103]

Anjou's attitude, abetted by an almost equal intransigence on the part of the queen, killed the marriage negotiation at this point. In spite of assurances within the English council that any *rapprochement* with the French must depend upon the marriage, the agreement was salvaged, and the treaty of Blois, which was concluded in April 1572, provided for common action in case of attack, and a mutual undertaking not to assist each others' enemies.[104] At the last moment Catherine suggested her youngest son, Francis, as a replacement for Henry, but by this time Elizabeth was not interested. She had in truth probably secured the substance of what she sought at no personal cost; alone among her more significant marriage negotiations, she had shown no interest in the person of the duke of Anjou. It seems to have been an entirely political exchange from first to last, and the only emotion engaged was the paranoid revulsion of the duke. Most important from Elizabeth's point of view was the fact that she had headed off any possible involvement of the French in Scotland – at least for as long as the treaty endured. Without that support Mary's supporters in the north were a nuisance rather than a serious threat.[105]

Paradoxically, the more likely an Anglo-French agreement became, the more dangerous became the alternative courses that the Scottish queen began to adopt. Early in 1571 she began to turn back to the duke of Alba, rightly believing that his earlier reluctance had been more due to his negative appraisal of the circumstances than to any unwillingness to unseat the queen of England. The agent of her new policy was Roberto Ridolfi, a Florentine banker who had earlier been employed by Cecil. In January 1571 Ridolfi received dispatches from the papal nuncio in Paris, for onward transmission to Mary. Pius proposed that should Mary fail to secure a satisfactory settlement with Elizabeth, then he would provide money and Philip (via Alba) troops for an invasion of England on her behalf, on condition that Mary's English friends would rise and support the invaders.[106]

Mary's reaction was to instruct the bishop of Ross to contact Norfolk. The duke had made his peace with Elizabeth in the summer of 1570, and had been released from confinement; now, with extreme folly, he allowed himself to be drawn into this fresh intrigue. The queen of Scots seems to have believed that Norfolk was the key to inspiring a rising by the English Catholics, in spite of his record of religious conformity; at the same time she wanted to use him as a kind of matrimonial shield against Spanish pressure to wed her to Don John, the king's illegitimate brother.[107] Ross obeyed his instructions, and Ridolfi had two clandestine interviews with Norfolk at Howard House. The Italian's powers of persuasion must have been considerable, or else he lied through his teeth, because, according to the account which he gave of these interviews, Norfolk professed himself to be a Catholic, and agreed to raise all the friends he could 'make' to support Alba if he invaded.[108] Shortly after Easter 1571 Ridolfi made his way to Brussels, where he was received by the duke of Alba. He then wrote several letters detailing this interview in the most optimistic terms, but two of these, to Norfolk and Lord Lumley, were intercepted by the English authorities in April.[109] Ridolfi himself then proceeded to Rome and Madrid, where he received somewhat lukewarm backing for the scheme, which seems to have been largely his own brainchild. Warned in July that the English had uncovered his activities, by the end of the year he had vanished from the scene, by the simple process of returning to Florence and getting on with his own business.

Meanwhile the bishop of Ross and the duke of Norfolk's secretary had been arrested and interrogated. It soon became clear that anger and impatience had tempted the queen of Scots into folly, just as lust had done six years before. For the first two years of her confinement in England, Mary had believed that the twists of Scottish politics, and some leverage from France, would restore her fortunes. When it became clear that Elizabeth had moved shrewdly and effectively to block both those possibilities, instead of waiting for circumstances to change, as they were bound to do, she countenanced (and indeed encouraged) Ridolfi's imaginative plotting. By so doing she forfeited any claim to Elizabeth's consideration, and embarked upon a lengthy course of self-destruction. At the same time, however dangerous she might be, she was not a subject of the English crown, and could not be lawfully indicted for high treason.

The same consideration did not protect the duke of Norfolk. Why he had acted as he did remains a mystery. Having aroused the queen's anger by his ill-advised bid for Mary's hand in 1569, his conduct in 1570 is inexplicable. He was not a committed Catholic; nor was he in thrall to a beautiful woman – indeed his personal remarks about Mary were disparaging.[110] He may have been motivated by injured pride or by irrational ambition. It has been argued that he was merely foolish and confused, and that his words were much less intentionally treasonable than they were made to appear; but that is hard to sustain given the threat which the duke of Alba was believed to pose to England's security.[111] He had actually done nothing, and his unwillingness to promote any scheme for Mary's escape had encouraged her own desperate course, but the undertakings which he had given to Ridolfi were treasonable within every accepted meaning of the word. Perhaps the greatest mystery of all is why anyone should have trusted Ridolfi, a man with no proven record in diplomacy or espionage, and one whom none of the parties had previously known. The natural suspicion is that he was a double agent, but there is no evidence for such a conclusion.

While he retired harmlessly to Florence, several of those who had relied
upon him and believed in his schemes faced the consequences. Guerau de
Spes was expelled from England as *persona non grata*, a gesture which did
not signal a breakdown of diplomatic relations (and may even have come
as a relief to Philip II), but certainly did nothing to solve the Anglo-Spanish
impasse.[112] The parliament that assembled in April 1571 set up an insistent
clamour for the execution of both the duke and the queen of Scots; and
the duke of Alba, for quite unconnected reasons, was withdrawn from the
Low Countries.[113]

Norfolk was tried in January 1572. Great pains had been taken to publicise
his guilt before the trial ever opened, because he had sympathisers in high
places; but he also did himself no favours by standing upon his honour
and attempting to impugn the credit of witnesses on the ground that they
were men of no substance.[114] He did not quite claim that it was no treason
for a nobleman to behave as he had done, but that was the implication.
He was inevitably condemned, but he did not immediately suffer execution.
He was of kin to the queen, and outside of the council there were many
who were prepared to plead for him. Elizabeth hesitated, but not for long.
The parliament of 1571 had lasted less than two months, but had succeeded
in making its feelings abundantly clear; and now another was due to assemble
on 8 May.

As soon as that happened, a joint committee was set up to examine the
actions of the queen of Scots.[115] One natural consequence of this was a
clamour for the death of Norfolk, and on 2 June he went to the block. He
was attended by his old tutor, John Foxe, who had many reasons to be
grateful for his patronage, and consequently appears to have died a Protestant, albeit in the cause of a Catholic plot. Against Mary herself, however,
the queen would allow no action to be taken. A Bill passed both Houses
to provide for her exclusion and trial for treason should any plot on her
behalf against the queen's life succeed, but Elizabeth refused her assent.[116]
She had no affection for Mary, and less respect for her judgement; indeed,
she addressed her like a wayward and passionate child:

> Of late time I have received divers letters from you, to which you may well guess
> by the accidents of the time why I have not made any answer, but specially
> because I saw no matter in them that required any such answer as could have
> contented you. But now, finding by your last letter of the 27th of the last [January
> 1572] an increase of your impatience, tending also to many uncomely, passionate
> and vindictive speeches, I thought to change my former opinion.[117]

For her part, Mary appears to have shown not the slightest awareness
that she was endangering the lives of her own servants, and would eventually

endanger her own, by pursuing what she perceived to be her rights. The clearly and frequently expressed opinions of Elizabeth's councillors, and of her parliaments, to say nothing of the preachers of the English church, were just so much clamour by insignificant heretics. By 1572 the tragedy which was to be played out over the next fifteen years had entered its second act.

The era of plots had also dawned. An obscure and foolish scheme by two minor Norfolk gentlemen, Edmund Mather and Kenelm Berney, had been brought to light at the beginning of 1572. The seriousness of their intentions may be doubted, but they had talked loudly and indiscreetly about killing Cecil and the queen, and they had been in contact with the Spanish embassy.[118] If the first decade of the reign had been reasonably secure, the second and third were to be fraught with panics of this kind: some substantial, most (like this one) insubstantial. But as the queen's years advanced, and she failed to marry or name a successor in spite of all the pressure which even her loyalest servants could apply, an air of persistent paranoia developed.

The slightest sign of illness on Elizabeth's part sent quivers of apprehension through the whole political nation. The queen was defying all conventional wisdom, and apparently endangering her realm, by pathological indecisiveness. But if she had really been indecisive, she would have followed the line of least resistance; fudged her religious settlement to have retained most of the 'old religion'; held back from Scotland; and probably sacrificed Cecil to the indignation which his actions over the 'Spanish' treasure had aroused. She would also, very probably, have yielded to the pressures of her most trusted advisers, and married the Archduke Charles, even at the cost of religious concessions. Elizabeth, however, was becoming remarkably sure-footed as a politician; a woman who was determined to do things in her own way. It did not matter if rival courtiers like Leicester and Sussex decorated their followers with coloured favours, like racers at the ancient hippodrome;[119] both were equally her loyal servants, and were competing for her favours. Sometimes she took the advice which was offered her by necessary but self-important men; and sometimes not. It was her business to decide which risks to take, and which to eschew; but men, who expected all women to be indecisive, interpreted her actions to suit themselves. Edward Aglionby was MP for Warwick in the 1571 parliament, and therefore as familiar as most with the discontent of the House of Commons over the queen's apparent failure to grasp important nettles; but he was also the recorder of the town, whose duty it was to deliver the loyal address during Elizabeth's visit in August 1572. As such, he was the recipient of a classic demonstration of the royal style:

And after the mace delivered, she called Mr Aglionby to her and offered her hand to him to kiss, withal smiling said 'Come hither little recorder. It was told me that you would be afraid to look upon me or to speak boldly; but you were not so afraid of me as I was of you. And now I thank you for putting me in mind of my duty, and that should be in me'.[120]

How that duty should be discharged was not, however, for Mr Aglionby and his like to say.

8

France and the Netherlands

Both at home and abroad, the year 1572 was a significant one. In March William Paulet, the aged and long-serving lord treasurer died, and was succeeded in July by Sir William Cecil, created Lord Burghley for the purpose. Sir Thomas Smith succeeded Cecil as secretary, and was joined eighteen months later by Sir Francis Walsingham as a second appointment. In June the duke of Norfolk was executed, and just over a month later the earl of Northumberland was handed over by the regent of Scotland, to suffer the same fate at York on 22 August.[1] A few days later the St Bartholomew's Eve massacre in Paris temporarily nullified the *entente* with France achieved in the spring, removed much of the Huguenot leadership, and plunged France back into religious war. The queen of Scots had been revealed by the Ridolfi plot to be an unscrupulous intriguer against the English crown, and Elizabeth abandoned all thoughts of seeking her return to Scotland. In the Low Countries the revolt which the duke of Alba had apparently crushed sprang to life again, creating a new problem for Elizabeth which was to run for many years.

In spite of this, there was something of a lull after the storms of the previous four years. There was no immediate sequel to the Ridolfi plot, and it was not until 1574 that the first missionary priests began to emerge from the new English College which William Allen had founded at Douai in 1568. The Treasons Act and the Act against Papal Bulls had both been passed in 1571, signalling a harsher and more repressive policy towards Catholics, but little had been done to implement such a policy on the ground.[2] At the same time, the Protestant radicals marked the beginning of a new and critical phase in their campaign for further reform, the *First* and *Second Admonitions to Parliament*, the former of which was probably issued before the session ended in June 1572.[3] They were about to move their arena from convocation, where they had been frustrated in 1563 and 1566, to the House of Commons, which offered much better opportunities for political pressure.

There was a sense also in which Elizabeth's government had matured. Her unequivocal defence of Cecil in 1568, followed by his promotion in 1572, signalled the end of serious attempts to undermine him. Whether you agreed with him or not, William Cecil was a fact of life. At the same time, Elizabeth increasingly confined her search for counsel to those whom she had appointed for the purpose. Gone were the days when Lord Robert Dudley had been a powerful and unpredictable backstairs influence.[4] When Sir Thomas Heneage was observed to have long and private conversations with the queen in 1570, he was severely taken to task. The queen was, of course, entitled to talk to whoever she liked, but it was not in her interests to arouse the ire of her councillors by going behind their backs – a mistake which Mary had notoriously made with Simon Renard. When extra-conciliar advice was required on some specialist topic, or some subject of surpassing concern, it was better to get the council to make the suggestion itself. In 1568 the privy council had actually suggested the calling of a great council, but the idea was not followed up.[5] The other standard method of obtaining advice was for individual councillors to receive, or even solicit it, before passing it on, either at a council meeting or directly to the queen. Similarly a councillor who was absent from the court for any reason never hesitated to make his opinion known by letters. Sir Francis Knollys, absent in the north in 1568, recorded that he had written thirteen letters since arriving in Bolton; two to the queen, one to the council, and ten to Cecil; that would have been a normal pattern.[6] When Thomas Smith took over the secretaryship in July 1572, he took over some of this burden, but by no means all. Routine communications, for instance from ambassadors, went to the new secretary, but anything politically sensitive continued to go to Cecil. As he complained to Sir Francis Walsingham, then in France, at the end of that month 'now I am out of office of the secretary, and yet I am not discharged of my ordinary cares'.[7] So it would continue to be, because it was not the office but the man which made him the linchpin of government. Just as Thomas Cromwell had taken his role with him when he moved from secretary to lord privy seal, so did Cecil when he became lord treasurer.

Once he was no longer compelled to fight for his political life, Burghley began to face a different problem. Too much influence bred jealousy. Although this was no longer a threat to his career, it could make life difficult. Elizabeth had no desire to discourage her other councillors, or to put them out of credit with their clientage; so she not infrequently made promotions or appointments at the intercession of Bacon, Leicester or Sussex, in preference to the candidates put forward by Burghley. Nor did the lord treasurer's unique relationship with the queen guarantee that she always took his advice. He struggled unavailingly for years to persuade her to marry, and his eventual success in bringing about the execution of Mary Queen of Scots probably owed little to his persistent advocacy.[8] One of the reasons for this was Elizabeth's acute sensitivity on the subject of her prerogative. As Burghley himself ruefully observed to Sussex in 1575:

> my doynges have been interpreted as deminutions of her maiesties prerogatyve, which your L[ordship] knoweth is so gratefull to princes to maynteane, as in no thyng more may a princes displeasure be attayned.[9]

This was partly, as Burghley implied, a normal royal reaction, but it was aggravated in Elizabeth's case by her fear of male encroachment. If she made a habit of accepting the advice offered, particularly if it was always from the same quarter, she would give the impression of having surrendered control. She was well aware that this was what many of her advisers, including those most loyal to her, wanted and expected her to do. So she faced a difficult problem over just about every issue of importance. If her councillors were divided, then she could make a decision without prejudice. But if they were largely in agreement, and particularly if the advice was obviously sensible, then she had to perform a delicate balancing act. Her commonest reaction was to prevaricate, for long enough to encourage the unwary to express opinions about female indecisiveness, and then to take the offered advice, perhaps in a modified form. No doubt Sir Francis Knollys had the unintended effect of encouraging such behaviour when he took advantage of his privileged position in the royal kindred to give her a lecture on the irresponsibility of going her own way, following

> sotche affections and passions of your mynde as happen to have domynyon over youe. So yet the resolutions digested by the deliberate consultations of your most faythfull cownsayllors oughte ever to be had in moste pryce.[10]

In other words – men knew best; which was not what Elizabeth wanted to hear, especially if it was true. However, it should not be concluded that Elizabeth was playing games with her privy council; she did not deliberately set them at odds, and there was always a shrewd practical mind at work on the advice which she was given. She was naturally reactive rather than proactive, responding to situations as they arose rather than trying to control them. Her instinct was to wait, in the hope that someone, or something, would solve the problem for her; and she had complete confidence in the soundness of her own judgement.

By 1572 she had defined her position in a number of ways, and consequences had followed. Her first priority was England's autonomy, including both its distinctive religious settlement and her own prerogative. This left her on the Protestant side in the great ideological division of Europe, and with a highly ambiguous attitude towards her own marriage. The hostility of the papacy was guaranteed, and had been confirmed by Pius's excommunication in 1570. The hostility of Spain, and consequently friendship with Spain's enemies, was likely but not inevitable. The country was full of men who thought that they could make a better job of leading it; but all accepted that, for his own inscrutable reasons, God had entrusted that task to Elizabeth.

In the summer of 1572 France was an ally, and although the duke of Anjou had finally ruled himself out as a possible bridegroom, discussion of marriage was still in the air. This now focused on Francis, duke of Alençon, an unprepossessing man whose main characteristic was that his ambition, and his desire to carve an independent career for himself, were more powerful than his religious scruples.[11] 'Surely', Cecil wrote without enthusiasm, the queen

> findeth the marriage to be necessary for her, and yet the opinion of others misliking of the party for his person doth more hinder her purpose than her own conceit. I see such extremytyes on both sides as I can make no choyse, for bye noe marriage all evil is to be looked for and by marriage without lyking noe good can be hoped.[12]

Alençon was a youth of sixteen, and Elizabeth at thirty-nine was old enough to be his mother. English supporters of the match, like Sir Thomas Smith, pointed to his flexibility in religious matters, and indeed to the fact that he had many Huguenots in his service, but the queen was at first unimpressed. It was not until the end of April, with another parliament due to convene in a couple of weeks, that she began to show some signs of responding to the persistent French hints. Charles IX was sufficiently encouraged by this to instruct the duke of Montmorency, when he came to England in June to ratify the treaty of Blois, to open a new marriage negotiation.[13] Elizabeth could find little enthusiasm, but as the House of Commons was making an unwelcome clamour for the execution of the Scottish queen, as well as for a settlement of the succession, she deemed it prudent to give them some satisfaction.

As negotiations got under way, it began to look as though the religious issue could be resolved, and most of the leading councillors, including both Burghley and Leicester, came to support it. They believed, among other advantages, that it would ease the way for both French and English help to be sent to William of Orange, the leader of the Netherlands revolt.[14] On the other hand, some of the most strenuously Protestant members of the council, such as Knollys and Mildmay, opposed it on the grounds that no religious concessions at all should be made, as a matter of principle. The queen herself sent out mixed signals. She did not want to marry the duke, but equally she wanted to maintain her friendship with France, and could not fall back upon any religious intractability on his part as a reason for refusal. At one moment she was saying 'we cannot indeed bring our mind to like of this offer', the next she was suggesting that Alençon might like to visit England.[15]

This delicate, if not particularly promising, negotiation was ostensibly blown out of the water by the massacre of Protestants which took place in Paris and elsewhere on 23 August, planned and executed by the Catholic duke of Guise and his followers. There were fiercely emotional reactions in England; and a more considered fear that this would now align France with whatever Catholic position the Guises chose to take up. Nevertheless, it was precisely for that reason that the contacts were not entirely destroyed. For Charles IX and Catherine de Medici, some continuing link with England was just about the only independent gesture of which they were capable, given that their links with the Protestant party in France were now completely eradicated.

During the winter of 1572–73 a number of messages were received, from the French king, from Catherine and from Alençon himself, expressing a desire to keep the negotiation alive.[16] It seems that by this time Elizabeth had not the slightest intention of marrying the duke, but she responded politely because she had no desire to alienate the king of France, or to encourage him to become involved again in Scotland, where the remnants of Mary's party were still holding Edinburgh Castle, and looking for French assistance. This succeeded up to a point; at least no French troops went to Scotland. It encouraged Alençon a touch too far, however, in that in April 1573 he announced his intention to go to England and woo the queen in person.[17] Elizabeth was appalled, and withdrew the invitation as quickly as possible. By this time Edinburgh Castle had fallen, and the queen had been able to end her long-running trade embargo with the Low Countries, so in June she sent an envoy to France to explain, with reasonable honesty, that she could not pursue a friendly exchange with a king who was making war upon his Protestant subjects.[18]

At the beginning of July, Charles IX raised the siege of La Rochelle and signed a limited peace with the Huguenots. This was actually a result of the election of Henry, duke of Anjou, the king's younger brother, to the throne of Poland; but it suited both sides to represent it as a consequence of English pressure.[19] As a result, the comte de Retz visited England in September in an attempt to restart the negotiation. His mission was a failure, partly because the English tried to raise the stakes, and partly because Catherine was losing patience with Elizabeth's prevarications. As a result of the end of the latest religious war, the king's position in France was now a little easier, and an English lifeline less important. Now persuaded that he had no chance of becoming king of England, the duke of Alençon turned his attentions to making a nuisance of himself at home. As the king's health began to decline at the beginning of 1574, Alençon was suspected of conspiring to take advantage of Henry of Anjou's absence in Poland to secure the succession for himself, and was at court, under virtual house arrest, when Charles died on 31 May.[20]

Anjou hastened back to secure the throne, but there was no obvious role for his brother, who was distrusted by both the Guises and the Huguenots. Alençon kept up his restless intrigues, with no particular object in mind, other than to recover his freedom. The idea of packing him off to England thus began to develop a new appeal, and in September 1575 a further French mission arrived in England with a formal offer of marriage on his behalf.[21] Without waiting for a reply, however, Alençon escaped from confinement on 15 September, declared himself Protector of the Realm, and appealed to England for assistance.

Anjou, now Henry III, and Catherine de Medici persisted with their matrimonial offer, being anxious above all things to prevent English involvement in France. Alençon came to an agreement with his brother in November, but Elizabeth, rightly suspecting that he had no intention of keeping his word, began to be seriously interested in intervention. She never directly addressed the marriage offer, but started by suggesting mediation, and then in March 1576 came around to favouring a coalition of French nobles and foreign princes to force Henry III into a general pacification of his kingdom.[22] This was clearly an alternative to marriage, and her council was divided, Sussex and Burghley favouring marriage, while Leicester and Knollys took a more aggressive stance. The queen herself was probably not considering matrimony as an option; the decision was between intervention and non-intervention.

Her vague promises of assistance were never put to the test, because in May 1576 a general pacification was signed, known as the peace of Monsieur (Alençon's formal title of address) because of his presumed role in bringing it about. Elizabeth disapproved of the peace, for reasons which are not entirely clear, but possibly because she suspected that it would provide no real solution.[23] Alençon was rewarded for his efforts with the dukedom of Anjou, and the marriage 'negotiation', which in truth had never begun, was abandoned by mutual consent. At no time during the four years which these contacts lasted did Elizabeth show any real enthusiasm for the match, or any real interest in the duke. It was a purely political process, resulting partly from her desire to maintain some sort of constructive contact with France, and partly to have something with which to still the perpetual clamour at home. Even councillors like Burghley, who favoured the various initiatives, were under no illusions, so there is no reason to suppose that her various shifts and expedients were anything other than her own ideas. It was the French who wanted to conduct matrimonial diplomacy, and she was willing to play the game in her own way. The only thing which she really gained by it was the respect of Catherine de Medici, who had originally made the mistake of believing that she was dealing with a woman who was 'passion's slave'.[24]

Anjou lost interest in Elizabeth in 1576, one of the reasons being that he was fishing in the troubled waters of the Netherlands. Revolt against Spanish rule had been rekindled there in 1572 when the Protestant rebels known as *Les Gueux* had seized the ports of Brill and Flushing; but thanks to the successes of the Guises in France, no help had been forthcoming from the Huguenots. At this stage, William of Orange was not committed to an independent Netherlandish state, being only determined to defend the traditional autonomy of the seventeen provinces, and their relatively liberal religious traditions.[25] Consequently, when peace negotiations with Philip failed in the summer of 1575, he persuaded the estates of Holland and Zeeland to offer sovereignty to Elizabeth. She declined, because although there was widespread sympathy in England for the Dutch cause, she had only just repaired her fences in the Low Countries, and acceptance would inevitably have meant war with Spain. She believed that Orange should return to the negotiating table, not choosing to understand how important the religious issue had become in the Dutch agenda, or how inflexible Philip II was on that issue.

This caused William to turn his attention to Anjou.[26] The duke was sufficiently autonomous to be able to act without committing Henry III to hostilities with Spain, and powerful enough in his own right for his intervention to be significant. In May 1576 Orange arranged for the same offer which the estates had made to the queen to be made to the duke. At that particular moment he was not interested, but once he had secured a further religious truce in France in September 1577 he began to warm to the idea. One of the reasons for this change of heart was the way in which events in the Low Countries were developing. Philip, who was always under financial pressure, had effectively gone bankrupt in September 1575, and by the beginning of the following year his armies in the Netherlands were becoming mutinous for lack of pay.[27] Then in March 1576 the governor, Don Luis de Requesens, died unexpectedly, and the Spanish administration started to disintegrate. It was eight months before Requesens was replaced, and the army began to take the law into its own hands. In November it sacked the city of Antwerp, causing great destruction and loss of life, and alienating the Catholic southern provinces which had previously shown themselves amenable to Spanish rule.[28] When Don John of Austria, Philip II's illegitimate half-brother, arrived to take control in December, he therefore found a situation of great confusion, and it was this confusion which prompted Anjou to offer his intervention.

By the beginning of 1577 there were two revolts in the Netherlands, working (more or less) in collaboration. The Catholic nobles of the southern provinces did not want Orange's leadership (let alone Elizabeth's), and tried to bring in the Austrian Archduke Mathias against Don John. This might have marked the end of Anjou's pretensions, except that Don John, having got his troops back under discipline, inflicted a heavy defeat on the rebels at Gembloux in January 1578. This discredited Mathias, and caused the nobles of Hainault to turn to Anjou instead. Orange did not object, as he had already made a move in that direction, and the duke began to mobilise forces in preparation for his intervention.[29] Elizabeth and her council, however, viewed this development with mounting alarm. Once it was clear that a large-scale French Protestant intervention was not going to happen, after August 1572, the Queen kept in reserve the idea that she might have to do something herself to support Orange. In September 1572 the duke of Alba received word from London that

> if the Prince of Orange prospers, they have ready here some 7000 men who have been collected secretly to aid him; 3000 in London, 2000 in the ports on the East coast, and 2000 in the West Country. The seven Queen's ships, of which I recently wrote, are ready to carry over the 5000 here and on the east coast.[30]

The figures were probably exaggerated, and the duke's informant was mistaken if he thought that these preparations portended an official expedition. He had probably got wind of the mobilisation of some of those volunteer groups which certainly did cross to fight in the Low Countries, with the queen's knowledge, but without her official permission or support.[31] The momentum of these groups was maintained over several years, and enabled Elizabeth, up to a point, to have her cake and eat it.

Whether these forces were of much help may be doubted; but they did constitute a gesture which enabled Elizabeth to remain officially aloof and to continue to make disparaging remarks about rebellious subjects. For several years she resisted pressure from militant councillors, such as Leicester, to adopt a more open policy. This even enabled her at one point to offer her mediation, although the offer was declined. In the confusion which followed Requesens's death, she was under no pressure to do more; but as Don John recovered control of the situation, and Anjou showed signs of becoming involved in the autumn of 1577, she went so far as to offer both money and troops. In January 1578 she loaned the estates general the modest sum of £20,000, and was preparing to send a small force when the defeat at Gembloux forced a hasty reappraisal.[32] Her aid was now more necessary than ever but could not be openly offered without the risk of war. The troops were not sent, but instead Elizabeth endeavoured to hire Duke John Casimir of the Palatinate to intervene on her behalf. The estates general, understandably not impressed, pursued the alternative negotiation with Anjou with renewed enthusiasm.[33] This put the queen on the spot. Apart from the complete collapse of the revolt, the thing that she least desired was a French Catholic presence in Hainault or Brabant. Somewhat desperately, she tried to broker a ceasefire, threatening at the same time to withdraw all support from the Dutch if they came to an agreement with Anjou.

There was, however, another possibility. The earl of Sussex suggested resuscitating the long dormant marriage negotiation as a method of distracting the duke's attention. This appealed to Elizabeth. It was a lot cheaper and safer than committing additional resources to the rebels, and easier than 'travalling' for peace.[34] Sussex was allowed to approach the French ambassador in May. The move took Burghley by surprise: 'I heare the French ambassador here hath bene the cause [of the new talk of marriage] upon some conference had with hir Maiestie to me unknown', he confessed late in July.[35] Burghley had been one of those pressing for greater assistance to be sent to the Low Countries, so Sussex's suggestion may have been as much intended to circumvent him as anything else. For the first time, William Cecil was not the chief policy maker in an overseas marriage negotiation.

In foreign affairs the kaleidoscope of events was constantly changing, and the queen's responses often had to be swift; at home events were more measured and the options more limited. The *First Admonition to the Parliament*, however, signalled a new departure in ecclesiastical affairs. This was the work of men who have been called the 'Young Turks' of the English Reformation, men like John Field and Thomas Cartwright.[36] To the older generation of radicals, such as Laurence Humphrey, Thomas Norton and John Foxe, the Royal Supremacy was a *sine qua non*, and the bishops were their allies in the search for further godly reform. They were quite prepared to agitate and protest, but they knew that it was the queen whom they had to persuade, and were happy with that knowledge. They were discouraged but undeterred by failure, believing that they were doing God's work. Field and Cartwright, however, belonged to a different tradition. They did not reject the Royal Supremacy, because if they had done there would have been no place for them in the post-1559 church, but they did regard it with a certain scepticism as a means to an end.[37] And they were frankly hostile to episcopal government, regarding it as unscriptural. Their objective was to mobilise opinion, and particularly influential lay opinion, to force Elizabeth to restructure her church fundamentally on Genevan lines. Then, and only then, would they be quite happy with the idea of her as a godly magistrate. This Presbyterian programme was not subversive in the same sense as Catholic recusancy, because it did not involve allegiance to any other temporal power outside the kingdom, but it did imply a conditional allegiance, which would have made it unacceptable to the queen even if she had not been concerned to mollify conservative feelings. Paradoxically, the Presbyterian programme was also a clerical programme, concerned with issues like doctrinal heresy. Its protagonists were quite prepared to persecute Catholics as false believers, if they ever got the chance.[38] Parliament, by contrast had conspicuously failed to pass any Heresy Act since 1558, and had rejected the idea of a Test Act in 1566.

Unfortunately, Pius V's excommunication of 1570 raised the stakes, and the Presbyterian campaign took off in consequence. Many Protestant laymen became so convinced of the danger that they became willing to support a clerical programme which appeared to present the only watertight option against papistical infiltration and subversion. The queen's reaction to this pressure, although it appeared extremely negative, and deeply disappointed the older advocates of reform, was nevertheless politically sound. She chose her closing address to parliament in March 1576 to deliver some home truths on the subject:

> And as for those rare and special benefits which many years have followed and accompanied my happy reign, I attribute to God alone, the prince of rule, and count myself no better than His handmaid, rather brought up in a school to bear *ferula* than traded in a kingdom to support the sceptre. If policy had been prefered before truth, would I, trow you, even at the first beginning of my reign, have turned upside down so great affairs or entered into tossing of the greatest waves and billows of the world that might (if I had sought mine ease) have harboured and sought refuge in more seeming security?[39]

How dare they challenge her godly credentials! In 1572 the ecclesiastical commission, established originally in 1559 to hear disciplinary cases, was renewed and greatly increased in size, from twenty-seven to seventy-one. This was no doubt in realistic anticipation of increased business, but it was also a symbolic gesture intended to signify the active engagement of the crown with the process of church government.[40] The proportion of clergy appointed was not very different (from seven to twenty), and they remained a small minority. Elizabeth, or perhaps Burghley, also took the opportunity to appoint a number of influential puritans, including the

councillors Sir Francis Knollys and Sir Walter Mildmay. This can be interpreted as an infiltration of radical influence designed to make the
commission less effective against puritan agitators, but it can also be seen
as a move to divide the agitators from their potential patrons, by laying
the Royal Supremacy on the line as an acid test of unconditional allegiance.

The ecclesiastical commission was a blunt instrument, and neither able,
nor intended, to replace normal episcopal oversight. At that level *Regnans
in Excelsis* was a help because it gave to beleaguered bishops in conservative
areas a perfectly valid reason to associate Catholic sympathies with temporal
disloyalty; and very few Catholics in the traditional sense wished to be seen
as politically subversive.[41] There was, no doubt, a marked increase both in
'church papistry' and in dissimulation, but there was similarly a marked
decline in confrontational attitudes.[42] This enabled a competent bishop like
John Whitgift at Worcester to discharge his duties effectively, and to earn
the respect of his neighbours in a relatively conservative area such as the
west midlands; although it did not help the abrasive Parkhurst to cope with
Norwich, which contained both Catholic and puritan activists in unresolved
conflict.

The trouble was that the church was not in a satisfactory state, from
whichever point of view you looked at it, and these were not problems that
could be addressed at the level of first principle. As the House of Commons
pointed out in 1576,

> a great number of men are admitted to occupy the place of ministers in the Church
> of England who are not only necessarily and inseparably required to be incident
> to their calling, but are also infamous in their lives and conversations.[43]

In her response, the queen 'alloweth well that her subjects, being aggrieved
therewith, have in such sort and discreet manner both opened their griefs
and remitted them to be reformed by her majesty'; but then proceeded to
pass the responsibility back to the bishops, as being a matter 'respecting
them of the clergy'. The cake of responsibility was good to be looked upon,
but not always to be eaten. Nor, having referred the matter in this way,
did Elizabeth then allow her bishops a free hand in tackling it.

Raising the quality of ordination candidates was not for the moment an
available option, so the only remedy was to improve clerical training in
post. One way of doing this was by a sequence, or course, of clergy meetings
for prayer, Bible study and exposition, in which the educated and experienced sought to share some of their skills with the inadequate recruits to
whom the House of Commons had reacted so unfavourably. Unfortunately
the queen, alarmed by this evidence of a clerical initiative which she had
herself encouraged but not initiated, chose to regard these 'prophesyings'

as subversive.⁴⁴ In 1577, ignoring convocation, which was not then in session, she wrote directly to the diocesan bishops ordering the suppression of these exercises:

> Although we doubt not but that you do well and effectually remember our Speeches unto you, to continue and increase your care and vigilancy over your charge and God's church (a matter of no small Weight), warning you also of the dangerous Presumptions of some in these Dayes, who by singular exercises in Public Places, after their own Fancies, have wrought no good in the Minds of the Multitude, easy to be carried with novelties.⁴⁵

The reason for this response seems to have been that these prophesyings were not usually established by episcopal initiative, but rather by those 'forward' reforming clergy who were beginning to be associated with Presbyterianism. The bishops, seeing their main task as the evangelical advancement of the faith against those of a Catholic or conservative temperament, welcomed such initiatives for the improvement of clerical effectiveness, not seeing them as threats to their own authority. The queen, however, was treading a very delicate path between a clergy that was effective and one which was too independent. When it came to the point, she was not prepared to sacrifice any element of her own control in order to improve effectiveness.

Shifting the responsibility for reform onto her bishops was merely a sleight of hand. This was starkly revealed when her archbishop of Canterbury, Edmund Grindal, who had only been in post since December 1575, declined in 1577 to accept the royal order on the grounds that his first duty was to promote the kingdom of God; with the clear implication that that should be the queen's first duty as well.⁴⁶ Elizabeth's reaction to such defiance was predictable. Grindal was suspended from office, and forced into limbo for the last six years of his life. His conscience would not allow him to submit, or to resign, which would have cleared the way for a new appointment. So the clergy were deprived of their constitutional leadership for six important years, which is probably a fair reflection of where they came in the queen's order of priorities. By this clear expression of her intentions, both lay and clerical opinion was divided. Many clergy by this time had accepted that as far as the Church of England was concerned, God spoke through Elizabeth; but the most conscientious could not possibly accept such a notion, being theologically committed to the sufficiency and sole authority of scripture. Similarly, most laymen were quite happy to see the country effectively protected against clerical pretensions, or any revival of ecclesiastical autonomy. On the other hand, there were those at all levels, including the highest, who believed that it was imperative to obey God rather than man, and who feared that the Almighty would withdraw his favour from any community which abused his word in the way which the queen's actions seemed to imply.[47] By 1578 the government of the church had become an issue which was presenting many polemical opportunities to its Catholic enemies.

Catholicism presented two rather different problems, both present since 1559. As soon as the Acts of Supremacy and Uniformity had passed, a number of university-trained priests left England to continue the fight from safe havens abroad. Some of these quickly became Spanish pensioners, not because Philip II had hostile intentions at that stage, but simply because he felt a sense of responsibility for them.[48] Thomas Harding, for example, conducted a vigorous and highly polemical debate with John Jewel throughout the 1560s; and Nicholas Harpsfield's *Six Dialogues* (1566) was (among other things) a fierce attack on Foxe's *Acts and Monuments*.[49] These men were committed, first and foremost, to the restoration of the true faith, as they saw it, in England. The overthrow of Elizabeth's government was a process they were perfectly willing to contemplate, but as a means and not an end in itself. When one of them, William Allen, founded an English seminary at Douai, along the lines prescribed by the council of Trent, it was with a view to training missionary priests for this purpose. Their position was based upon the premise that England was an overwhelmingly Catholic country, led astray by a few heretics in high places. If enough of these Catholics could be persuaded to stand up and be counted, the whole heretical establishment would collapse.[50] They were highly educated men, fully abreast of the changes that had taken place in the church over the previous decade, and were in regular contact with papal agents and representatives. They were not (at least at first) looking for a military invasion of their homeland to realise their aims; but, as Elizabeth's settlement gradually grew stronger, most of them embraced it as the only realistic option. Pius's action in 1570 was thus highly gratifying to them, giving explicit recognition and leadership to their efforts.

The second Catholic problem has been dubbed 'survivalism'. Noblemen and gentlemen, particularly, accepted the Act of Supremacy, but constructively ignored the Act of Uniformity that went with it. Conniving clergy of similar mind, who had accepted the oath of Supremacy, celebrated mass and other traditional rites in their private chapels, having celebrated the Prayer Book liturgy in the parish church the same day.[51] Some conscientious priests refused the oath of Supremacy, and having been deprived of their livings, lacking either the will or the means to go abroad, moved surreptitiously from place to place, catering for the same clientele. Less well-off Catholics used the services of these priests in the same way, when they could obtain access to them. This was a situation with little logic, and little long-term future, unless the political position changed. In so far as such people had a political agenda, it was to support Mary of Scotland as the heir to the throne, and perhaps to hope that that eventuality would arrive sooner rather than later. Typically such Catholics, both clergy and laity, were increasingly out of touch with the mainstream of the church, paid lip service to the papacy, and were instinctively averse to any foreign political intervention on their behalf. Although to a strong Protestant like Foxe or Grindal there might not be much distinction between these attitudes, and even to Cecil or Bacon it might not be obvious, the queen always understood it very clearly. Unfortunately for her, the distinction was not simply between those who had gone abroad and those who had remained behind, because there were some in England who took the 'ultracatholic' position, as was revealed by the northern rising. Consequently Elizabeth was always under pressure to be 'safe rather than sorry', even before *Regnans in Excelsis*.

Logically, that bull should have discredited the survivalist position entirely; but it did not do so because people do not react logically. It did weaken it, however, and as the older generation of Marian priests died out, there was no one to replace them with a similar ambiguity of attitude. The missionary priests who began to arrive from Douai in 1574 were very different.[52] They were rigorously educated and trained in contemporary Catholic attitudes, and had no time or use for compromise. They did not have a specific political agenda, but rightly perceived the Church of England to be a political construct, and were quite at ease with the idea of destroying it by rebellion, assassination or invasion. Catholic recusancy was the achievement of these men, who often believed that they were converting heretics when in fact they were establishing the faith in its new form in the minds of some that had previously been survivalists. That recusancy was dangerous in a sense that survivalism had not been is undeniable, but it should not be assumed that the distinction was always clear-cut. The zealous recruits who flocked to Douai, mainly from minor gentry and merchant families, and who made the mission possible, were expressing a commitment which went back well before the papal bull. At the same time, the new attitudes did not sit comfortably alongside the old. Those whose attachment to the old religion did not amount to much more than custom and nostalgia were not likely to make the sacrifices which were now demanded, and defected into a rather lukewarm Anglicanism in large numbers. Even among firm recusants there were few that were prepared to accept the political logic of their confessional stance. How effective the missionary priests were in creating a church, as distinct from motivating a small number of zealots, is a subject of debate.[53]

Traditionally it was believed that the Catholic Church in England owed its entire existence to the rescue work of these missionaries, but a generation ago it began to be argued that what they actually did was to destroy the ancient *Ecclesia Anglicana* and replace it with a new commodity, manufactured abroad.[54] This antithesis is probably too stark, but it does appear that areas where popular survivalism was strong, like northern and central Lancashire, were relatively neglected in favour of more 'gentrified' regions such as the Thames Valley. Such a priority could be justified, on the grounds that gentry support in south-east England was far more useful politically than peasant zeal in the north west; and also because these were the very families which produced the best recruits for the priesthood and the religious orders. On the other hand, such arguments were a poor justification for the deployment of resources for the salvation of souls.

Whether these strictures are justified or not, the English government treated recusancy as a political threat. If there had been any prospect of Catholicism expiring gracefully as the last survivalist priests died, the mission from Douai quickly put an end to it. The statutes of 1571 had made it high treason to seek to deprive the queen of her royal title (including that of the Supremacy), to import bulls from Rome, or to reconcile any English subject to the Catholic faith.[55] They had refrained from declaring it treason to be a Catholic, because the ambiguity of much so-called Catholicism was understood. There was also no great pressure for rigorous enforcement; partly because it was optimistically thought that the problem was declining after 1569, and partly because the queen had no desire to match the pope in the business of forcing issues. However, when one of the first of the new missionaries, Cuthbert Mayne, was arrested in Cornwall in 1576, the fact that he was carrying a copy of an old (and irrelevant) papal bull was used as a pretext to execute him.[56]

By then it was clear that the recusant problem was not going to go away, and the search was on for an effective remedy. Priests, if caught, could be indicted for treason under the existing Act, because reconciling the queen's subjects to Rome was their principal, and declared, objective. The existing penalties against those who simply refused conformity, however, were relatively trivial. In 1577 John Aylmer, the recently consecrated bishop of London, who was seeking sanctions against non-conformists on both sides, proposed dramatically increasing the fines for recusancy.[57] The following year a judicial opinion confirmed that the Supreme Governor had the right to impose such penalties (which did not touch life or real property), and to use whatever agents she chose for the purpose. Walsingham promoted this verdict to a council of bishops, and over the next three years it began to be implemented, by the privy council, by high commission, and by individual bishops.[58] It remained a discretionary penalty, however, used alongside varying terms of imprisonment, until parliament imposed the standard fine of £20 a week by statute in 1581.

The actual impact of the Catholic mission in England before 1580 is debatable. It created a tough and resilient recusancy, but this never approached the position where a large-scale Catholic rising appeared likely. In Ireland, however, the situation was very different. English attempts to impose any kind of coherence upon the chaos of Irish politics since the 1530s had been bitterly resented and self-defeating. Angry, frustrated, and insensitive to the environment, successive English governments had been sucked into a cycle of rebellion, confiscation, plantation and rebellion. Irish support for English rule was never more than self-serving and narrowly focused, with the result that today's enforcer was tomorrow's rebel – and the submissive penitent of the day after. The Irish tribes lacked any sense of political or ethnic identity, and the ferocity of their rebellions served to conceal a lack of any overarching policy, beyond a bilious desire to get rid of English officials and all they stood for.[59] After 1559, however, the Protestant religious settlement in England began to change that situation, and the Irish discovered a devotion to Rome that had not previously been much in evidence. Using Catholicism as a principle of unity had the additional advantage of sweeping in most of the old Anglo-Irish families that had their own reasons for disliking the new ascendancy. A report on the condition of Ireland in 1571 makes the consequences of this abundantly clear:

> In Ulster there are two principal and powerful lords, viz. O'Neill and O'Donnell. Those under the Lord O'Neill are MacMahon, Maguire [etc] To the Lord O'Donnell are subject O'Docherty, O'Boyle [etc]. All these most ardent catholics and foremost confederates with force and hatred against the Queen of England. In Desmond is the Earl of Desmond whose deputy is James Maurice, brother of the earl and chiefest enemy of the English, who entered an agreement with the French that reserves be sent to him in that vicinity both of soldiers and ships, while they wait for the greater army from the Spanish.[60]

Every region except the Dublin Pale is assessed in similar terms, giving the impression of a massive force prepared to sweep the English into the sea. Of course it wasn't quite like that, and whoever believed that the French, let alone the Spaniards, were about to land troops in Ireland in 1571 had little grasp of the real world. Nevertheless, Thomas Stukely was being entertained in Madrid two years later in the expectation that he would be useful; [61] Irish priests and bishops were constantly bending ears in Rome; and revolts, small scale but often very violent, were endemic in Ireland itself. The queen committed very little to record of what she thought of

Ireland until much later in the reign, and it is possible that she had no very clear idea of how to discharge the government of that kingdom. The first principle of her government in England, based on the love of her subjects, was a non-starter in Ireland. Deprived of this point of orientation, Elizabeth hardly knew where to begin, and was guided mainly by swordsmen who viewed the Irish as primitive barbarians who only understood the language of force.[62] By 1575 Ireland was, in the eyes of the English council, valuable only in so far as it could be colonised; and until it was so settled a perpetual source of danger.

Scotland, by contrast, was a source of relatively little anxiety until the dramatic fall and execution of the earl of Morton in 1581. In 1572, when the executions of Norfolk and Northumberland tidied away the detritus of the northern rising, the main source of concern was that the divided and rather feeble regency of the earl of Mar did not seem to be able to eliminate the remainder of Mary's supporters who had seized Edinburgh Castle. Burghley's main concern was that Edinburgh might become a base for Franco-papal moves against James VI's position in Scotland, which would endanger the whole Anglo-Scottish *entente*.[63] Elizabeth, on the other hand, saw the existence of the 'Castillians' as an opportunity for some more constructive Anglo-French diplomacy, and in the summer of 1572 that was not an unreasonable view to take. The indecisive truce which was patched up in July did nothing very much to promote anyone's interests, and did not get the Castillians off the hook from which they were suspended.

It was St Bartholomew's Day which defeated Elizabeth's hopes. For the time being at least constructive diplomacy was not on the agenda, and Burghley's fear appeared the more realistic. The decisive event was not English action, however, but the death of the Scottish regent, the earl of Mar, in November. The earl of Morton who replaced him was a much tougher proposition. By February 1573 he had persuaded the last of Mary's aristocratic sympathisers, the Gordons and the Hamiltons, to submit to the king. He had also asked for, and obtained, English military assistance to reduce Edinburgh Castle.[64] Elizabeth had to be persuaded that this was necessary, but by April the heavy English guns were in place, and at the end of May the fortress finally yielded to bombardment. That was effectively the end of the Marian party in Scotland, and the ex-queen became thereafter an exclusively English problem. For the next few years, with the French either preoccupied at home or fishing for an English connection, the situation in Scotland seemed finally to have stabilised in England's favour. Cecil's investment of effort in the treaty of Edinburgh in 1560 had finally paid the expected dividend.

Why Mary was not executed after her incrimination in the Ridolfi plot is one of the reign's more intriguing mysteries. The Lords and Commons clamoured for her head in both 1572 and 1576. The bishops in the upper House were even more vocal than the Commons, linking such punishment, significantly, to the godly status of the church. To punish such a guilty offender, it was argued, would 'abash and damp the minds of all the enemies of God and friends of Anti-Christ'. Peter Wentworth, with irrelevant zeal, denounced Mary as 'the most notorious whore in the world'; and there was a growing feeling that the queen's failure to act in this respect was all of a piece with her failure to reform her church.[65] Even Charles IX expected Mary to die, and added unfeelingly 'I see it is her own fault and folly'.

Elizabeth had no desire to execute her rival, and both in 1572 and 1574 drew back from schemes to return her to Scotland when it became perfectly clear that the Scots would kill her and share the responsibility with the queen of England.[66] She had no particular affection for Mary. They never met, and the correspondence between them varied from the chilly and polite to the downright querulous. Privately she seems to have despised a woman who had so little control over herself, and who was stupid enough to allow her disgruntlement to be obvious and her intrigues to be detected. Perhaps she saw the Scottish queen as some kind of a hostage for the good behaviour of her Catholic subjects. There was certainly a connection in her own mind between Mary's safekeeping and the peace and wellbeing of the realm. Writing to the earl and countess of Shrewsbury, Mary's custodians, in June 1577, Elizabeth declared:

> In this acknowledgement of new debts, we may not forget our old debt – the same being as great as any sovereign can owe a subject – when through your loyal and most careful looking to the charge committed to you, both we and our realm enjoy a peaceable government, the best good hap that to any prince on earth can befall.[67]

It is probable, however, that the queen's real motivation was neither as calculated nor as subtle. There was always the chance of a deal. As long as Mary was alive, she might be persuaded to give up her faith, and her immediate claim to the throne, in return for her freedom and recognition as heir. We now know from evidence of Mary's attitude during these years that there was no chance of that; but Elizabeth could not be sure, and it was a course that would have offered advantages. The godly clamour would have been stilled by Mary's conversion, and Catholic plots would become pointless. Conversely, of course, if she remained recalcitrant the risk increased; but it is likely that Elizabeth thought the chance worth taking. Mary was also in very much the same position that Elizabeth herself had been in in 1554. If she had not found a grudging mercy then, she would never have come to the throne. The queen had no desire to shed blood without compelling reason, and she also continued to hope against hope that the prisoner could be made to serve her own purposes. So she made her decision, stuck to it with true Tudor obstinacy, and defended it with years of ingenuity and evasion.[68]

After 1572 Anglo-Spanish relations improved, in spite of the grumbling tensions in the Low Countries. Agreement in principle for a resumption of trade had been reached with Requesens in April 1573, but not ratified until August 1574, probably because of the governor's continuing unhappiness about English volunteers.[69] He had, however, to face the fact that Antwerp was suffering far more than London from the embargo, and in March 1575 the English were fully readmitted to the port, provided that they did not also visit Flushing, which was in rebel hands.[70] London cloth exports immediately recovered from 63,000 cloths in 1573 to 110,000 in 1575. It was a last flicker of that particular candle. After the 'Spanish Fury' of 1576 the London merchants finally departed, never to return; and English cloth exports settled down at about 100,000 a year – all shipped through other ports.

Meanwhile Francis Drake had begun what was virtually his own private war against Spain. He was in the West Indies in 1569, 1570 and 1571, on poorly documented expeditions that stirred up much fear and anger in New Spain, and returned a profit of over £100,000.[71] There is no evidence of royal investment, or even permission (although that must have been granted), but this was serious money and quite a bit of it found its way into the royal coffers. In 1572 Drake was back again, with a frankly piratical agenda which included a fruitless attack on Nombre de Dios and the successful seizure of a mule train of silver near Panama.[72] By 1575 he was as well known at court as John Hawkins, and much admired by the bolder spirits. It is not surprising that the friendly reception accorded to Philip II's new ambassador in London, Bernardino de Mendoza, in 1574 was regarded with scepticism in Spain.

In 1576 a major new initiative at sea was being considered, and Drake seemed the obvious man to lead it. The source of this initiative is not clear; it may have come from Hatton, Walsingham or even the queen herself. Elizabeth was certainly involved from the beginning, but did not want this fact to be known; partly because the voyage did not even pretend to be a about trade. Exploration was probably the main agenda, but whether of the coast of South America, or Terra Australis or the elusive western end of the mythical strait of Anian is not clear. It is also quite possible that annoying the king of Spain was an objective from the beginning, which would explain both the queen's coyness and the appointment of Drake to command. The sponsors were very similar to that for Hawkins's ill-fated trip in 1568. The queen contributed one ship, and the investors included the lord admiral, the earl of Leicester, Walsingham, Hatton, Hawkins and the Winter brothers.[73] Drake sailed in his own ship, christened on Elizabeth's insistence, the *Pelican*, which was probably a calculated gesture of support.

The expedition eventually left Plymouth in November 1577, and turned into one of the great epics of maritime history. Sailing by way of the Canary and Cape Verde Islands, Drake reached Cape Horn in September 1578, having taken a number of Spanish and Portuguese ships on the way, and executed one of his gentlemen adventurers, Thomas Doughty, in controversial circumstances. From the Horn he sailed north, acquiring a large booty by raiding Spanish colonies on the totally unprotected Pacific coast of South America. By April 1579 he had reached Guatulco on the coast of Mexico. It is still a matter of controversy whether he landed in what is now California before turning west across the Pacific. Eventually, sailing by way of the Moluccas and the Cape of Good Hope, Drake circumnavigated the globe, and returned to Plymouth in September 1580 with one ship and about half the men he had started out with.

He had discovered no new lands, and opened no new trade routes, but he had performed a heroic feat of seamanship, and laid down a marker of immense importance. The English had now advertised a global ambition and given notice that they had the technical capacity to realise it. The plunder alone would have been sufficient to ensure Drake a warm reception, but what actually happened must have confused him not a little:

> Queene Elizabeth received him graciously, with all clemency, caused his riches to be sequestered and in a redinesse whensover the Spaniard should reclaim them. Her Majestie commanded likewise, for a perpetual memory to have so happily circuited round about the whole earth, his ship should be drawen from the water and put aside neere Deptford on Thames, and after the Queene's feasting therein, she consecrated it with great ceremonie, pompe and magnificence, eternally to be remembered; and her Majestie forthwith honoured Drake with the dignitie of knighthood.[74]

Sir Francis must have found it a mixed blessing to be greeted with honour, and relieved of his treasure. The sequestration was more apparent than real, however, for enough remained in Drake's hands for him to offer gold and silver to 'the Chiefest of the Courte', some of who declined it, to his great chagrin. Those whose priority was to mollify the king of Spain were less than gratified by his exploits; but that did not include the ordinary people, who 'applauded him with all praise and admiration', or the queen. When Mendoza demanded the return of the money and bullion taken, he was told that it did not amount to more than a fraction of what his master had cost the queen of England, that Drake had broken no law, and that the money would stay where it was – that is in her own hands and those of the other shareholders.[75]

While Drake was away, his colleague Martin Frobisher had conducted two well-supported expeditions to what is now the Canadian Arctic. The 'gold ore' that they brought back turned out to be useless and the shareholders lost their money. But ventures of this kind were becoming increasingly popular, and it was Elizabeth herself who named the land which they had discovered *Meta Incognita*.[76]

Hostility to Spain, and increasing emulation, were also fertilising shoots of a different kind. Spain derived great wealth from her colonies, and there were discussions in London as early as the mid 1560s about the desirability of establishing an English foothold in the New World. At first the idea was to trade with the Spanish colonies, and then to attack them. For the time being nothing came of these plans, but in 1577 John Dee published a seminal work entitled *The Perfect Arte of Navigation*, in which he broached (among other things) the idea of a British empire.[77] What he meant by this embraced the British Isles and part of the North American littoral, so it was not quite as revolutionary as might appear; but it was nevertheless a new idea, as was the notion of supporting a 'Petty Navy Royal' to maintain it, supported by taxing foreign fishermen. This last idea was unworkable, but a royal navy already existed, and the close alliance between the City merchants, the privy council and the 'Navy Board Group' was beginning to set political agendas by 1580.

A symbol of the closeness of this world is provided by the career of John Hawkins. Although not a gentleman by birth, or even a Londoner, he had by the early 1560s established contacts, through London, with the court. His voyages at that time, although they met with mixed success, made him *persona grata* with the queen, and he married Catherine, daughter of Benjamin Gonson the long-serving treasurer of the navy.[78] In 1577, when Gonson retired, Hawkins was appointed to succeed him, and served until his own death in 1595. John Hawkins was a merchant, but he was also a pirate, and like several other seamen in the queen's service, he learned his fighting skills in small-scale, hit and run encounters. Pirate ships, or privateers as they became after the outbreak of war, were perforce swift sailors, heavily manned and heavily gunned. All the characteristics of Elizabethan naval warfare – nimble galleons, hard hitting culverins, skilful seamanship, and the capacity to improvise tactics on the move – were all taken over by the navy from these pirate ventures, along with the men themselves.[79]

There were drawbacks. Such captains were accustomed to being their own

masters, and their discipline was less than perfect. Sir Francis Drake was
even accused of breaking off the fight against the Armada to secure a prize
for his own purposes; but by and large the combination of private enterprise
and public service worked extremely well. When put to the test, it enabled
England to fight a protracted war which in theory it could not possibly have
afforded. The key person in this initiative was Elizabeth herself. It was the
queen's favour which enabled men like Hawkins, Drake, Frobisher and
Gilbert to trade slaves and raid Spanish colonies on the one hand, and
command the royal ships and run the navy on the other. Burghley supported
Hawkins, but he was less enthusiastic about Drake, who was more of a
'people's hero'.[80] Elizabeth, however, connived with the latter for precisely
that reason. By the 1570s, these sea dogs were a point of contact between
the queen and her subjects. Hawkins was not popular with his subordinates
at the navy board, who accused him of incompetence and corruption, but the
charges were never substantiated and Hawkins, like Leicester and Burghley
a little earlier, thrived on the queen's confidence.[81] John Hawkins, and even
more Francis Drake, who was not even born legitimate, were symptomatic
of a new kind of enterprise which began to flourish in Elizabeth's reign.
Henry VIII had been deeply interested in his navy, and in the topography
of the English coast; but Elizabeth was interested in *Meta Incognita*, and in
the topography and economic potential of distant places. The significance
of her favour towards seaman and merchants should not be underestimated.

As the queen advanced through the middle years of her life, there were
inevitably further changes among those around her. Most of these were
enforced by natural wastage, because Elizabeth was tenaciously loyal to
those in whom she had once expressed confidence. Of her councillors only
the duke of Norfolk had so far died by the axe; even the earl of Arundel
had not been excluded, in spite of incarceration for his share in Norfolk's
plot. He hardly ever appeared at court, however, between 1572 and his death
in 1580.[82] The marquis of Northampton died in 1571, the earl of Pembroke
in 1570, Lord William Howard and the marquis of Winchester in 1572, Sir
Thomas Smith in 1577 and Sir Nicholas Bacon in 1579.[83] The council was
joined in 1571 by the earl of Shrewsbury, but this was a notional appointment,
as he remained virtually leashed to the queen of Scots. In 1573 Sir Francis
Walsingham and the earl of Warwick were sworn, and in 1575 Sir Henry
Sidney, although the latter did not take his seat until he returned from
Ireland in 1578.[84] Sir Thomas Smith was replaced as secretary by Thomas
Wilson, and Bacon by Sir Thomas Bromley, who immediately became lord
chancellor. Sir Christopher Hatton joined the council as vice chamberlain
in 1577, at the same time as Henry Carey, Lord Hunsdon, the queen's
cousin.[85] During the 1570s, the council thus became slightly smaller and

slightly less aristocratic. The continuities were strong, however, and there was no sense of fresh initiatives or policies being introduced as a result of changes of personnel. Burghley, Sussex and Leicester served throughout the decade, as did Sadler, Croft, Clinton, Knollys, Mildmay and Bedford. Although still in a sense rivals, they had become accustomed to each other's methods and ambitions. At court Edward de Vere, the 17th earl of Oxford, was almost unnoticed as lord great chamberlain from 1562 until his death in 1604, but Sussex replaced Howard in 1572, and the vice chamberlainship remained vacant from 1570 until Hatton's appointment in 1577. Sir Thomas Heneage took over the treasurership of the chamber from Knollys in 1570, and served for a quarter of a century. On the household side, Lord Clinton, who became earl of Lincoln in 1572, took over the lord stewardship after a brief vacancy, while Francis Knollys began a long stint as treasurer in 1570. Similarly, Croft was comptroller for twenty years from the same date.[86] It was a question, for the most part, of reshuffling the existing cards; Howard's was the only death to enforce a change. Long service was the rule rather than the exception, Knollys, for example, serving for almost the entire reign in four different offices.

In the privy chamber, the story was the same. The ladies grew older together, the continuities sometimes masked by changes of name and status on marriage. Blanche Parry, a companion of the queen's youth, became chief gentlewoman at some point after Kate Ashley's death, and was still in post in 1582.[87] John Ashley, like Knollys, served continuously from 1559 to 1596. In spite of her theatrical tantrums, which could result in verbal abuse, and even in injury, Elizabeth's personal staff was remarkably stable; and this was not just the result of an aversion to change. The queen had an emotional need for deep and abiding affection, which she recognised in herself. She could hardly ask her council for that sort of support, although some of them provided it, but it was proper to draw on the emotional resources of those whom she had chosen as her intimates.

In the summer of 1578, Elizabeth made a progress into East Anglia. It was intended as a public relations exercise, to 'show herself' to her people, and it was carefully written up and published to enhance the effect. She made progresses most summers, often ending up at the home of one of her major courtiers, who would lay on lavish and flattering entertainments. The climax in 1578, however, was not at Kenilworth or Theobalds, but in the city of Norwich. Norwich did not see the queen very often, and it put itself out in the most spectacular fashion.

Sir Robert Wood, then Esquire and now knight, mair of the same citie, at one of the cloke of the same happy day [16 August], sette forward to meet with her

Maiestie, in this order; First there roade before him, wel and seemely mounted, threescore of the most comelie yong men of the citie, as bachelers, appareled all in black satten doublets, black hose, blacke taffeta hattes and yellow bandes, and their universal liverie was a mandylion of purple taffeta, laid about with silver lace.[88]

The queen was treated to mythological pageantry, and the 'acclamations of the people to the Almighty God for the preservation of her Maiestie', which was more to the point. The mayor delivered an oration of welcome, and so pleased was the queen with her reception that she even turned down a gift of money.

We heartily thank you, master maier, and all the rest, for these tokens of good will, nevertheless princes have no need of money; God hath endowed us abundantly, we come not therefore but for that whiche in right is our owne, the heartes and true allegiance of our subiectes.[89]

It was a significant gesture. Elizabeth knew as well as anyone that she had plenty of need for money, but if it came to a conflict between cash and popularity the latter won. There was a case for this priority, and it did not matter very much at the gates of Norwich, but her unwillingness over the next twenty years to be realistic about the need for taxation was to turn a symbolic gesture into a major problem of government.

9

The Gathering Storm

Elizabeth's last marriage negotiation was also in many ways the most complex and mysterious. By 1578 Protestant and popular opinion was against the whole idea. The queen was forty-five, and although her health was robust, there was no real prospect of solving the succession problem that way. Any match, and particularly a Catholic one, would mean compromising the integrity of both the queen and the realm to no purpose. The matter was strictly off-limits for public debate, but it was already clear to the observant that the twelve-year-old king of Scots, brought up as a Protestant, was emerging as a natural successor. Not everyone liked the idea of a Scottish king, but his hereditary claim was beyond dispute, and his faith made him acceptable. Consequently there was an outburst of what might be called 'anti-matrimonial' propaganda, thinly disguised as the triumph of chastity.[1]

This was particularly evident during the queen's visit to Norwich in August of that year. The corporation was staunchly Protestant to the point of being puritan, and the earl of Leicester was not without influence in the city. Elizabeth apparently enjoyed her visit, and lapped up the enthusiastic applause of the citizens, but she also had to take in a lot of didactic pageantry in the process. This was commissioned by the corporation and prepared by Thomas Churchyard. Both because of Churchyard's court connections, and because of the importance of the visit to the city, there must have been consultation with the revels office before any of this was presented, which casts an interesting light upon the disputes that were also going on within the court.[2] There were two broad themes to these pageants. The first was Deborah, the godly magistrate (a reference to the Book of Judges), not so much taking council for the people of the Lord as protecting them from foreign (Catholic) tyrants:

> No fraude, nor force, nor foraine foe may stand
> Against the strength of thy most puissant hand.[3]

Although this was not urging her to any specific war, the message was clear enough: the cause of God and the cause of England were indistinguishable, and as the Lord's anointed she must be prepared to defend both by force of arms. The second theme was that the queen's unmarried state signified a chastity that was becoming a symbol of her realm's inviolability.

> Who ever found on earth a constant friend.
> That may compare with this my Virgin Queene?
> Who ever found a body and a mynde
> So free from staine, so perfect to be seen? [4]

What Elizabeth privately thought of these broad hints we do not know; but she professed herself well pleased with all that had passed at Norwich. About two months later, she sent the duke of Anjou her portrait, and he sent two senior and trusted servants, Bussy d'Amboise and Jean de Simier, to London to woo the queen in his name. [5]

It appears that, although the thought of a marriage treaty had not departed from either of their minds after the unsuccessful exchanges of recent years, on this occasion it was the queen who took the initiative. The reason for this was probably political. King Sebastian of Portugal had died at the battle of Alcazar-el-Kebir in August 1578, and his successor was an elderly celibate, Cardinal-King Henry. Philip II was known to have designs on the Portuguese succession. [6] This was an alarming prospect. Although Portuguese power was not what it had been, its oriental empire was still yielding great wealth; and perhaps more important, Portugal had an ocean going war fleet far superior to anything which Spain at that moment could deploy. Although the Dutch revolt showed no signs of collapsing, it was common prudence to seek to breathe new life into the treaty of Blois. The prospect of this was aided by the fact that Henry III had found the Catholic League an extremely uncomfortable bedfellow, its power being incompatible with his responsibilities as king. [7]

The main problem from Elizabeth's point of view was one of priority. Should she agree the outlines of a new treaty before receiving the duke on an official visit, or should she stick to her previous position of saying that she could not agree to marry a man she had never seen? From his point of view, Anjou now urgently needed the English alliance. He could not afford to pay his troops in the Netherlands, where without any sign of support from his brother the king, they were deserting in numbers. For similar reasons his Catholic supporters in the southern provinces were going over to the new Spanish governor, the duke of Parma, and would shortly come to terms with Philip in the Union of Arras. [8]

Because only marriage with Elizabeth offered a way of redeeming this situation, and although he knew that the price might be high, he returned to the project with renewed enthusiasm and commitment. For this purpose, he chose his principal envoy well. Whatever his own shortcomings as a

Elizabeth I at the kill. From George Turbevile, *Booke of Hunting* (1575).

lover may have been, Jean de Simier was an accomplished courtier, and he quickly detected and exploited a vulnerable streak in Elizabeth's personality. Being extremely vain, the queen loved beautiful jewellery, and above all wanted to be courted. Simier was 'a choice Courtier, a man thoroughly versed in Love-fancies, pleasant conceits and Court-dalliance'.[9] He arrived in January 1579, and within a month had secured a unique place in Elizabeth's regard. Sir Francis Walsingham drew the obvious conclusion:

> The negotyacion of Monsieur here taketh greater foote than was at the first lookid for and receaveth no smaule furtheraunce upp[on] occasion of the decayed state of things in the Low Countryes, for that Her Majestie, foreseeing that yf the King of Spayne come once to have his will there he will prove no very good neythbour to her.[10]

Perhaps he was right, but Elizabeth was not talking to Simier about political alignments, or even about the terms of a possible agreement. She was entertaining him with feasts, dances and masques, exchanging small but expensive gifts, and indulging in a 'dalliance' which she obviously found extremely gratifying.

Although some of her ministers were baffled, and even embarrassed by this behaviour, it contains no great mystery. The queen may have been indulging in menopausal fantasies, but she had not lost her sense of political reality. She merely found herself in a position where her coquettish instincts and the demands of her job had fallen into some kind of alignment; and she enjoyed herself a good deal. Even if she had felt no personal commitment at all, it would have been prudent for Elizabeth to have put on a love-sick face.[11] Whether she wanted to marry him or not, at this stage she certainly wanted to maintain some kind of a hold over Anjou. She wanted to attract him to England before any agreement had been reached on a marriage contract – a move that he had so far resisted. She probably hoped against hope that he was not quite as unattractive as he was reputed to be, and believed with reason that the unresolved problems over religion would be best confronted face to face.[12] There were also rumours that the duke was angling for a Spanish princess. That would have been worse than a rebuff; it would have been a disaster. Consequently the queen set out to persuade Simier, not only of the seriousness of her intentions, but also of the absence of any obstacles to their union.

In fact her council was as divided as it had been before, but she contrived to conceal this fact by inveigling the earl of Leicester into professing his support in conversations with the French envoys.[13] In the face of what seems to have been a direct order from the queen, the earl did his duty, and Simier was both surprised and impressed. Leicester, however, was not a seasoned courtier for nothing. In professing to have spoken warmly in support of the match, he contrived to convey the news that not only were some Protestant councillors, such as Huntingdon and Bedford, still in opposition, but also that many of the more conservative were not particularly favourable either.[14] Although he remained optimistic, Simier did not press his employer to plan an immediate visit; and Catherine de Medici persuaded her son not to contemplate such a move until the terms of the agreement were clear.

In the face of this, Elizabeth executed a political retreat under the cover of enthusiasm to proceed, and allowed formal negotiations to commence at the end of March, without having seen a hair of her intended. Her council debated the French conditions long and hard, but were unable to come to any agreement.[15] Those who were most averse to the whole idea, like Walsingham and Mildmay, had two lines of objection. They feared that the realm would become, in one way or another, subjected to French Catholic rule, and they feared that the queen's life would be placed in danger. The first point was predicated partly upon the fact that Henry III was childless, and likely to remain so, which made Anjou the heir to the throne; the second was aggravated by the fear that the queen might still conceive, which would involve extreme risk.[16] Those who supported the marriage, like Burghley and Sussex, believed that parliament could provide adequate protection against the first danger; and that the second did not exist because Elizabeth was no longer fertile. It is possible that the queen's own enthusiasm was partly prompted by knowledge of her physical condition; but, if that was the case, she did not see fit to reassure her advisers. In the event, these protracted discussions ended up where they had started; because the only way ahead which all could agree upon was to leave the demands upon the table until the duke arrived in person.

This was, in a way, a victory for those who supported the marriage, but Simier was angered and frustrated. He got his own back in a manner typical of a Renaissance court. He found out that the earl of Leicester had secretly married the widowed countess of Essex in September 1578, and told the queen.[17] Lettice Knollys was the queen's cousin, and she was furious, both because her permission had not been sought and because the earl had deceived her. Leicester withdrew from the court under a dark cloud.[18] This did not make much difference to the balance of power over Anjou because, as we have seen, he had been forced into an ambivalent position, but it does seem to have jolted Elizabeth into issuing an invitation for the duke to visit England. According to one report, she did this 'with many tears, almost forced by those that have led this negotiation'.[19] But no one ever forced Elizabeth to act against her will, and certainly not in a case of this kind. If she was reluctant, it was not because of a divided council, but because she was perfectly well aware that her subjects were every bit as averse to Francis of Anjou as they had been to Philip of Spain twenty-five years earlier.

By the late summer, popular broad sheets and ballads attacking the marriage began to appear in large numbers. The most celebrated was the *Discoverie of a Gaping Gulf whereinto England is like to be Swallowed*, by John Stubbs.[20] Stubbs was a dependant of Leicester, and related to the Presbyterian leader Thomas Cartwright. It is not difficult to see the basis of his position, and indeed so many of his arguments were close to those that had been raised in council against the match that collusion was suspected. France was a kingdom of darkness; Anjou was likened to the serpent who had deceived Eve, and the comparison was by no means flattering to the queen's judgement. She was being 'led blindfolded as a poor lamb to the slaughter'. Had Stubbs confined himself to pointing out that 'It is natural to all men to abhor foreign rule as a burden of Egypt, and to us of England if to any other nation under the sun', he might have been tolerated as a misguided patriot, but to suggest that the queen was not in control of her own destiny was too provocative to be endured. On 27 September a revealing proclamation was issued, which started by pointing out that

> her majesty hath had so good proof of God's singular goodness in the continual preservation of her from his first setting of her in the Crown as his chosen servant to reign.[21]

It continued with a specific denunciation of Stubbs's work, not only on the grounds of the 'slanders and reproaches' offered to the duke of Anjou, but also because 'it doth manifestly appear that the only scope hereof was under plausible reprehensions to diminish her majesty's credit with her good people'.

At the end of October John Stubbs and two of his collaborators were tried under a Marian statute against seditious libels and found guilty. On 3 November 1579 Stubbs and William Page lost their right hands to Elizabeth's outraged *amour propre*; if it had not been for their powerful backers, it was generally thought that they would have lost their lives.[22] The queen lost more than she gained by this attempt at intimidation, because the ire of the godly was now thoroughly roused, and there was open defiance of the proclamation, not only in London, but also in Norwich where Elizabeth had recently been so well received.[23] By the end of 1579 opposition to the marriage was almost universal. Court poets like Sidney and Spenser addressed carefully crafted appeals to the queen's vanity, and it was at this time that the Virgin Queen first emerged as a cult figure. Plays, allegories and ballads for more popular consumption took up the same theme. It was several years later that Shakespeare wrote 'the Imperial votaress passed on, in maiden meditation, fancy free', but it was as thinly disguised criticism of the Anjou marriage that the English at this time uttered such lavish, praise of their queen's virginity.[24] Apart from the savage treatment of Stubbs and Page, the official response was muted. Very unusually, the September proclamation attempted to refute the arguments of the *Gaping Gulf* as well as banning it, but there was very little propaganda output in that vein.

Burghley was taken aback by the strength and virtual unanimity of the opposition. Since giving up the secretaryship he seems to have lost touch with public opinion. Debates in council during October became less heated as the lord treasurer began to hedge his bets. Without giving up his support entirely, he agreed that religious conditions should be imposed which he knew perfectly well that the French negotiators would reject.[25] Anjou must accompany the queen to public acts of worship; he must not openly favour recusants; also the duke 'shall publyckly kepe some Nombre of Gentillmen of the Relligion reformed, and shall direct them to be of the French church'. Even this retreat failed to win the support of the majority, and at the end of the discussions the council simply handed the decision back to the queen, with a clear indication of their reservations. Elizabeth was extremely cross, not because she doubted her own judgement, but because of the implications of what had happened. It was her business to make the decision, and a genuinely divided council, to say nothing of public opinion, would have served her purpose very well. But neither the council nor her subjects were really divided. In spite of some fudging in the former, the message was clear. Elizabeth hated having her freedom constrained in that way.

As in 1560 with Dudley, prudence and obstinacy battled in her mind. No one had the right to dictate to her; yet the consequences of ignoring such unanimity could be dire. Obstinacy won the next round. The more she was warned off Anjou, the more she was attracted to him, and on 20 November she commissioned a select group of councillors, led by Burghley, to negotiate a marriage treaty with Simier.[26] This was done in days, and the draft was modelled closely on the precedent of 1554. A lot of key issues were deferred, however, and the step forward was more apparent than real. At the end of January she informed the duke that the hostility of her subjects would be an insuperable obstacle unless he was prepared to make further concessions on religion. This time it was Henry III who put his foot down. There could be no retreat on that issue, and he began to look in earnest for a Spanish bride for his brother.[27]

Logically, that should have been the end of the matter, but it was not; partly because Anjou himself wished to persist, and partly because the international situation still pointed to the need for a French alliance. The duke made a tentative but impractical attempt to break the religious deadlock in April 1580, and then negotiations hung fire. Civil war stirred again in France, and in spite of the fact that Philip had made good his claim to Portugal in January on the death of Cardinal-King Henry, Elizabeth resisted, or rather ignored, pressure from a section of her council for a more forward foreign policy. However, news at the end of June that Anjou was again negotiating with the estates general of the Union of Utrecht goaded her into action once more.[28] Envoys were sent to France to reactivate the agreement reached earlier in the year, and Anjou, disappointed with the speed of his Dutch negotiation, welcomed them. At this point both sides were playing a political game. Anjou and Elizabeth wanted a marriage alliance while Henry III and Elizabeth's council wanted an alliance without marriage, but nothing could be done until the civil strife in France was pacified. By the end of September that had been accomplished, and Anjou had also signed an agreement with the estates general; so a new phase of negotiation could commence.[29]

From November 1580 to April 1581 both sides manoeuvred for position, each changing tactics and priorities in response to small shifts in the circumstances. By the latter date the queen appears to have given up on the marriage and accepted the priority of alliance, but being unwilling to alienate the duke was no longer being frank with his representatives. In May a marriage treaty was actually signed, but this breakthrough was again more apparent than real. It was a means of keeping the issues alive rather than a real commitment.[30] At the same time Anjou allowed bad weather to abort a proposed visit to England, signalling in his turn a mood of ambivalence. The only real progress during the summer was a shift on Elizabeth's part; she was now willing not only to accept, but even to support surreptitiously, his involvement in the Netherlands.[31] The need to do something to counteract Spain's growing power and aggressiveness had converted such a move into a relatively cheap and effective option.

In July 1581 we can gain a comparatively rare insight into the state of the queen's mind:

> she said she had rather be at the charges of a war with the marriage than without a marriage. But saieth she, I would gladly enter a league with the French King, onely with these conditions, that if I were invaded, he should help me.[32]

She would support him in turn if France were invaded.

By August the balance of mistrust had shifted, and it was Henry who was trying to pin down the elusive alliance by insisting upon a marriage. Neither side was talking about the succession, or even about Anjou's prospects in

France, but only about the immediate need to do something to curb Philip. The duke's resources were again on the point of exhaustion, and had to be rescued in September by a loan from Elizabeth.[33] It may have been that supportive gesture which finally prompted him to cross the Channel at the end of October. He was open-minded about marriage, but realised he could not face another campaigning season in the Low Countries without the queen's support. His visit was a very high profile affair, with a lot of public entertainment. The agreement which was the duke's main objective was signed at the end of November, and the English, believing that marriage was now off the agenda, were reasonably welcoming.[34] Then, quite out of the blue, Elizabeth set her whole court by the ears, entering into 'amorous discourse' with her visitor, kissing him on the mouth, and drawing a ring from her finger to present to him. Not surprisingly 'The assistants took that for an argument and assurance that a marriage was by reciprocall promise contracted betwixt them'.[35] There were rejoicings in Antwerp, and devastation in the privy council:

> Her women which were about her fell all in sorrow and sadnesse, and the terror they put her into, so troubled her mind that shee passed all that night without sleep amongst her household servants who made a great consort of weeping and sighing.

It was not like Elizabeth to get carried away by a momentary impulse, at least not in so public a manner, but she may have done so on this occasion. It seems to have been the reaction of her chamber servants rather than her councillors that poured the cold water upon this unexpected enthusiasm.[36] The very next day, while the news of an impending wedding was still on its way to Paris,

> finding the Duke and taking him aside [she] had serious discourse with him. The Duke returning himself after he left her into his chamber, plucketh off the ring, casteth it upon the ground, taketh it up againe, rayleth on the lightness of women, and the Inconstancie of islanders.[37]

Opinion about this strange episode has been divided ever since it happened. Was it a calculated trick to extract further concessions from Henry III? Was it (as the Spanish ambassador at the time thought) a device to send a disgruntled duke on his way? Or was it a genuinely unguarded gesture, quickly regretted? Anjou seems to have been as surprised as anyone, and in spite of his alleged railing, quickly digested the disappointment and returned to the questions of alliance and aid in the Netherlands. When he finally departed in February 1582 he had secured what he sought, and had formed a new alliance with Leicester and the 'war party' in the council. That alone was sufficient indication that marriage had by then been abandoned as an option by all parties. Whether it had ever been seriously intended, or had from the start been a diplomatic stalking horse, can probably not be determined.[38] Elizabeth quickly rebuilt her damaged relationship with her subjects, and appears to have embraced their characterisation of her as the Virgin Queen; at least there was no further talk of marriage to distort the political priorities.

Less happily, Philip II had not been deceived for a moment by this romantic interlude, nor by the occasional talk of improving the lot of English Catholics. He knew that this protracted and frequently convoluted dalliance was aimed at him; and that Elizabeth, as usual, was playing both sides against the middle. Within a fortnight of Anjou's departure, Mendoza warned the queen on his master's behalf of the danger of war if she intervened in either the Netherlands or Portugal.[39] Elizabeth the politician had spent years taking shelter behind Elizabeth the woman. With the end of the Anjou marriage negotiation, such an option disappeared. Intermittent flirtation had to be replaced by the power of chastity. It remained to be seen whether the queen's strength would become the strength of ten.[40]

Absorbing as it undoubtedly was, Elizabeth's fluctuating relationship with Anjou did not monopolise her energies during these years. As Francis Drake struggled around the world on his epic voyage, unflattering reports of his progress filtered back to Europe, mainly via the Spanish authorities whom he had relieved of a proportion of their wealth.[41] To Mendoza, already simmering with hatred for the people among whom he was constrained to serve, such actions were an insult to his king; but, unless or until Drake reappeared, there was little that he could do about it. Early in 1580 the queen was alleged to be so anxious about the fate of her famous mariner that she was contemplating fitting out another expedition to go in search of him. If she ever had such an intention, it was not carried out. When Elizabeth found out that he was on his way home, and that he was carrying a valuable cargo, we do not know; but his arrival at Plymouth in September 1580 clearly did not take her by surprise. She sent word that he should make his way to the Thames, where he would be well received. On his arrival, the queen came on board his ship, and not only knighted him but designated his ship as a national monument.[42]

In spite of her pride in his achievement Elizabeth was also keenly aware of how controversial his methods of guaranteeing a profit had become. To his intense annoyance, and perhaps alarm, many leading courtiers, including Burghley, declined his bounty 'as if he had not lawfully come by it'.[43] Having weighed the risks against the didactic opportunities, however, the queen was less pusillanimous. No doubt the temptation of securing the lion's share of a plunder valued at tens of thousands of pounds was not without its influence, but when the irate Mendoza 'demanded vehemently the things taken', he was answered 'that the Spaniards had provoked unto themselves that evil through their injustice towardes the English, in hindering, against the right of Nations, their negotiations'. She had indeed sequestered his cargo 'to no end but to give satisfaction to their king', but when it came to the point, she was not prepared to confirm that satisfaction. She had, she claimed, spent more money in subduing the rebels whom Philip II had moved against her in England and Ireland than Drake was worth.[44] Spain had not the slightest right to claim a monopoly of the New World trade, least of all to those areas beyond the reach of their settlements. Moreover

> he [Philip] cannot iustlie hinder other Princes to negotiate in those Regions, but they, without infringeing in any wayes the Lawes of Nations, may lawfully bring in colonies in those partes that are not yet inhabited by the king of Spain's subiectes; sith prescription without possession is of no validity.

Mendoza no doubt took this merely as an example of English bluster. It did not matter however just one's claims might be, he later wrote, the English would always make ridiculous demands – like the right to trade freely or worship God in their own way. Whether she used these actual words or not (William Camden was writing some time later), it appears that Elizabeth took the opportunity of Drake's remarkable success not only to secure a large dividend but to lay down a position on world affairs which was bound to be inimical to the king of Spain.[45] At that time she may have felt that Philip's many preoccupations offered her a measure of protection; but at such a rate she was bound to rise in his order of priorities.

Drake was an irritant, not a *casus belli*, but he did serve to remind Philip what a nuisance the English were becoming. The nub of the problem was the Low Countries, because although the Union of Arras had more or less restored the southern provinces to their obedience, the corresponding Union of Utrecht had clarified the ideological resistance of the north in a manner that was bound to increase its determination.[46] Philip riposted in March 1580 with a proscription of William of Orange that was virtually an invitation to potential assassins.[47] On 26 July 1581 the estates general of the United Provinces formally renounced their allegiance to the king of Spain, and the war entered a new phase. The new Spanish commander, the duke of Parma, was more effective and better resourced than his predecessor. Additional Portuguese wealth, and a lull in the conflict in the Mediterranean, had given Philip the chance to concentrate on the Netherlands; which made William's search for outside assistance the more urgent. In spite of the efforts of Leicester and his supporters in the council, Elizabeth continued to resist pressure for direct intervention, and her diplomatic efforts concentrated on what sort of help, and how much, should be given to Anjou.[48] By late 1581 this had ceased to be a personal matter for the queen, although she must have endorsed the grant of another loan of £60,000 in December. Anjou's relative poverty might serve more effectively than a marriage to keep his ambitions within acceptable bounds.

In January 1582 French troops, many of them Huguenots, marched into Bruges. They were reported to be unimpressive, but at least they were present on the ground, and the duke himself was warmly welcomed when he landed at Flushing on 10 February.[49] Shortly afterwards, and supported by a high-profile English presence which included both the earl of Leicester and Lord Hunsdon, he was installed as duke of Brabant. Although most of Brabant was under Parma's control, that did not affect the symbolism of the occasion. Thanks to the Act of Abjuration, the new duke was in theory a sovereign in his own right, and one recognised by Elizabeth through the participation of her servants. Inevitably, events failed to live up to expectations. Anjou's relations with his Brabant subjects, and with their neighbours of Flanders, quickly became strained; in the heartland of the revolt, Holland and Zeeland, he was scarcely acknowledged at all; and William of Orange, whose personality was vital to hold these disparate elements together, was temporarily incapacitated by a failed assassination attempt in March.[50] The duke remained ineffectually at Antwerp, and Parma won a series of victories in the field.

Finally, in December 1582 the expected French reinforcements arrived, again many of them Huguenots, with an impressive set of aristocratic officers. Unfortunately, instead of coordinating operations with his allies under the command of the estates general, Anjou attempted to use these new forces to seize control of Antwerp. There was bitter street fighting, resulting in hundreds of casualties, and the French were defeated.[51] Anjou fled, leaving many of his men as prisoners, and a period of confusion followed. Orange, himself disillusioned, made a futile attempt to heal the breach, but his Protestant followers would have no further truck with this papist prince.

Disappointment, and no doubt frustration, distorted Elizabeth's reaction to these events. She chose to see Anjou as the innocent victim of Dutch intrigues, although what source of intelligence could have given her that impression is a mystery. She ordered John Norris, commanding the small English force still serving in the Netherlands, to obey the duke rather than the estates. He evaded the order, eventually convincing the queen that she was misinformed; a service which not only preserved his own reputation, but rescued a morsel of credibility for his mistress with the estates.[52] Totally discredited, Anjou finally withdrew and returned to France in June 1583, still talking of returning, and still apparently convinced that the queen of England would back him. Elizabeth, however, had now had enough. When Anjou made the mistake of sending an agent to England in August to solicit further financial assistance, he got a blistering response:

> he [the agent, de Reaux] tired me with language which seemed very strange to me; that you desired to know what will be the aid that you will [be given] for the preservation of the Netherlands, saying to me that you are assured by the king that he will aid you the same as I do. My God, Monsieur, how unfortunate you are to believe that this is the way to preserve your friends, by always debilitating them.[53]

This letter marks the end of any lingering respect that Elizabeth may have had for the duke, either as a politician or a friend. Sir Edward Stafford, newly arrived at the French court in November, reported that Anjou was now totally discredited with all parties. He died in June 1584, leaving the childless Henry III as the last of the Valois kings, and the Huguenot Henry of Navarre as the hereditary heir. This immediately resurrected the Catholic League and with it the prospect not only of renewed religious strife in France but also of Spanish intervention.[54] A month later a second and successful assassination attempt removed the embattled Dutch leader, William of Orange, and forced Elizabeth to confront the realities of a rapidly deteriorating situation.

Throughout 1583 and 1584, Parma had been picking off the rebel held towns in Flanders one by one, and until the end of the former year the queen had done little but press for the repayment of the money which she was already owed. Although William did not give up hope of more direct support from England, relations were strained, and he was endeavouring to persuade Henry III to pick up his late brother's commitments at the very time when he was struck down.[55] In a sense, William's death concentrated minds. Unlike him, the estates had no faith in the French, and sent urgent and specific requests to London for assistance in what were now desperate circumstances. Elizabeth's response was a good deal less decisive. She sent verbal messages of support, suggested a joint consultation with the French, and declined to take Holland and Zeeland under her specific protection.[56] This was to some extent justified, because she knew that Orange and the estates had not been seeing eye to eye about the role of the French, and that Henry III now had an additional reason for wishing to thwart Philip's schemes.

The joint consultations were duly held in the autumn of 1584, but there was an absence of clarity, and perhaps honesty, on all sides. The estates offered Henry a vague overlordship; the English first objected, and then withdrew their objections when they understood that the offer was not likely to be acceptable.[57] At the same time, the Dutch were at odds among themselves, some wishing to trust in France, some in England, and some to do a deal with Philip. So serious were these disputes that it was not until January 1585 that the estates' mission arrived in Paris. Henry at first prevaricated, and finally, threatened with renewed war by the resurgent Catholic League, declined to do anything other than offer mediation with Philip.[58] Until the late summer Edward Stafford tried to stave off the full impact of this by seeking an Anglo-French intervention, but this initiative never had any real prospect of success. Elizabeth was soon to be faced with the additional dilemma of whether, and to what extent, to support the Huguenots in what was clearly going to be a new round of religious wars.

Henry III's preoccupation with his own troubles forced the English and the Dutch into each other's arms. Elizabeth wriggled hard, seeking all manner of guarantees, but was finally constrained to face the inevitable by no less a person than Philip II himself. In May, perhaps misinformed about the state of Anglo-Dutch relations, perhaps provoked beyond endurance by Drake and his like, but most likely no longer caring about the consequences, Philip seized all the English ships he could lay his hands on.[59] Elizabeth was outraged, and her council feared an immediate attack. In June she sent Norris back to the Low Countries with a further three thousand men, and a delegation from the estates general reached London.[60] There were already signs that any agreement might be too late to save Antwerp, which Parma had been besieging for months, but on 15 August a treaty was finally agreed at Nonsuch. With the benefit of hindsight, William Camden put a highly positive gloss on this last ditch agreement:

> After the Queen had seriously and carefully for some time considered the barbarous cruelty of the Spaniards towards her neighbours the Netherlanders, and their hatred against England and the Religion which she embraced (for the Spaniard was certainly persuaded that the Netherlands could never be reduced to his obedience unless England were first conquered); lest the war should be brought home to her own doors [and] also lest they should put themselves under the protection of the French; she resolved that it was both Christian Piety to relieve the afflicted Netherlanders, and good wisdom to provide for the safety of the people committed to her charge.[61]

Elizabeth agreed to provide, at her own initial expense, five thousand foot and one thousand horse, 'under a Governor General, an Honourable man', to be repaid by the estates in agreed instalments; in return for which she would receive the town of Flushing and two forts to garrison as securities. As aid went, it was not lavish, but it did represent a public commitment of the kind that the queen had always hitherto avoided, and was, to everyone's perception, an explicit act of war.[62]

All the Princes of Christendom admired at such manly fortitude in a woman which durst, as it were, declare war against so puissant a monarch; insomuch that the King of Sweden said That Queen Elizabeth had now taken the diadem from her head and adventured it upon the doubtful chance of war.

In the event, Philip had given her no option if she was to preserve England's integrity and the credibility of her own position with her subjects. Elizabeth was not averse to war, not simply because it was expensive, but also because warfare developed a logic and momentum of its own, one which it would be beyond her power to control, and which was amenable to neither cajolery nor manipulation. This outcome probably owed little to the long-standing disagreements of her councillors, and nothing at all to any ambition on her part to promote the Protestant gospel; but there comes a time when the failure to act is more dangerous than the most problematical intervention. Elizabeth judged that that time had come in the summer of 1585, and events proved her to have been right. For the remainder of her life she would be at war, but she was getting too old to learn any new style of management, and her political life continued with remarkably little change. What she did succeed in doing, for the most part, was to keep both the fighting and the men who conducted it, at arm's length.[63]

In a sense, war made government more straightforward. The pope and the king of Spain were now open and declared enemies, and this was an improvement on the game of cat and mouse which Elizabeth had been playing with Mendoza between 1579 and 1584. The ambassador was both arrogant and short-tempered. He considered the queen's convoluted negotiations with both Anjou and William of Orange to be inexcusable misbehaviour, and the reception of the Portuguese pretender Dom Antonio in England an outrage.[64] Antonio had come at the suggestion of the earl of Leicester, but although he was courteously entertained, he received virtually no support. The fleet which operated in his name, and which was defeated at Terceira in 1583 by the marquis of Santa Cruz, was predominantly French and Portuguese; the handful of English ships involved not being supported by the government.[65]

Mendoza at the same time believed that his master was perfectly entitled to take what action he chose against heretics, without being required to offer either explanation or apology. This lack of detachment exposed him to the queen's manoeuvres. Unwilling to face any more awkward questions about Drake, in October 1580 she declared that she would not receive him again until he had satisfactorily explained Spanish involvement with the rebellious Irish, and with the papal intervention at Smerwick in September.[66] With the privy council being equally obstructive, Mendoza asked to be recalled. Philip II, who by this time seems to have viewed his London embassy as a pressure point rather than a means of communication, did not respond. In June 1581 the frustrated ambassador asked for leave to withdraw without recall, but this was refused and there was a further bad-tempered exchange which caused Elizabeth to wonder aloud why Philip was bothering to maintain such a pretence.[67] The main reason was that he wished Mendoza to issue threats, either directly if he could secure access or indirectly if the circumstances required. In September 1581 Philip endeavoured briefly to head off a possible Anglo-French agreement by offering a renewal of the old Burgundian alliance; but by the time that Mendoza secured an audience on 11 October the instruction was out of date. The interview degenerated into another angry exchange of complaints, and Elizabeth banned him from her presence, this time permanently.[68] By the end of 1582 Mendoza was complaining with justice that no one in office would talk to him at all. This made him useless as a conventional ambassador, but enabled him to devote all his time and energy to plots and schemes designed to overthrow the regime which he so much hated and despised.

These were focused upon Mary Stuart. Since 1569 she had been held, securely but comfortably, at Sheffield Castle. The earl of Shrewsbury was courteous but implacable, and no one gained access to the imprisoned queen without his knowledge and permission. He was quite unable to sever her lines of communication, however, and perhaps he did not try very hard, as Walsingham had his own methods of finding out what passed.[69] The tentacles of Mary's intrigues ran all over Europe. They were frequently reckless and unrealistic, and the only consistent feature of them was her obsessive desire to recover power in Scotland, and to gain her revenge against Elizabeth. In 1579 Scotland seemed to offer the best prospects. The earl of Morton's authority as regent was in decline, and a group of his opponents, using Mary's agent in Paris as a go-between, applied to Philip for money to assist in his overthrow.[70] Mendoza, who was more objective about Scotland than he was about England, was unimpressed, realising that Morton's foes were neither Catholic nor pro-Spanish, and not even clearly determined to restore Mary. Nothing came of this approach, and Scottish politics ran its own course without outside intervention, if not without alarms.

James VI was now fourteen, and his personal preferences were beginning to matter. By the end of 1579 his preference was for his French cousin, Esmé Stuart, who became earl of Lennox in 1580 and duke in 1581. Esmé placed himself at the head of the anti-Morton faction, securing his overthrow in September 1580 and his execution in June of the following year.[71] Elizabeth and her council were deeply perturbed, seeing a revival of French influence in Scotland, and possibly the conversion of the king to Catholicism. Interestingly, they were not particularly worried about any plan to restore Mary. Although nearly a third of the Scottish nobility still favoured the old religion, English fears eventually proved groundless. Henry III had no desire to destabilise his delicate friendship with Elizabeth, and without outside help Lennox proved unable to hold on to his ascendancy.[72] In spite of the active interest of the Guise party in France, and discussions in Paris early in 1582 fronted by the Jesuits, in August 1582 a party of Protestant lords seized control of the king, and arrested several of Lennox's associates. The duke himself fled to France by way of England, and the conspirators in Paris were consumed with frustration. Scotland, they decided, was a broken reed as a weapon to use against the heretic queen. More direct action would therefore be necessary.[73]

Mary herself had already pointed the way ahead. Realising that Henry III would not help her, and that her kindred, with the best will in the world, had too many other preoccupations at home, early in 1580 she offered, through her agent in Paris, to place herself, her realm and her son under the protection of the king of Spain.[74] Philip's initial response was friendly, but non-committal. The political pieces, however, were now set in a different order. The Catholic cause, both in Scotland and in England, was now the cause of Spain; and success would involve the overthrow of both James and Elizabeth. This was a situation that appealed to Mendoza, who from early 1581 became increasingly involved in these plots, almost without reference to the wishes of his master.[75] They have a slightly surreal air, partly because Mary was losing such grasp of reality as she had ever possessed, and they were posited upon two impossible conditions: large-scale Spanish military aid, and a powerful rising by the English Catholics. Elizabeth, meanwhile, did not give up the search for some positive solution to the problem of Mary. She listened with interest to the latter's proposal for a kind of condominium in Scotland, whereby the queen would return to rule alongside her son, the implication being that the *status quo* would otherwise be observed. The advantage of such a scheme, Mary argued, would be that it would secure the recognition of James in France and Spain.[76]

Even while Elizabeth was considering this idea (April–June 1583), it is clear that Mary's real intention was, and had been from the beginning, quite different. In a letter of 28 October 1581 she had revealed that her true purpose was to secure her own return to power, and the destruction of her Scottish enemies.[77] She had also asked Philip to receive her son in Spain, to make sure that the dregs of heresy were washed out of him, a proposal to which the Spanish king had made a sympathetic response. At the same time a separate scheme was being worked out in Paris for the overthrow of Elizabeth in Mary's interest. The prime mover in this was the duke of Guise, who proposed an invasion of England supported by Spanish and papal forces. Mary's agent in Paris, Thomas Morgan, put the ubiquitous Mendoza in touch with a young Catholic aristocrat named Francis Throgmorton, whose role would be to establish the Catholic network which would support the invasion, and to provide intelligence about strong points, landing places, and the deployment of government troops.[78] Unfortunately for the conspirators, the council was already aware of Throgmorton, who was arrested and interrogated towards the end of 1583.

Raphael Holinshed recorded:

> You shall understand that the cause of his apprehension grew first upon secret intelligence given to the Queenes Maiestie that he was a privie conveier and receiver of letters to and from the Scottish Queene; upon which information nevertheless divers months were suffered to pass on before he was called to answer the matter to the end that there might some proof more apparent be had to charge him therewith directly; which shortly after fell out.[79]

His houses in London and at Levesham in Kent were searched, and other incriminating documents discovered, including a pedigree 'of the descent of the crown of England, printed and published by the Bishop of Rosse, in defence of the pretended title of the Scottish Queene his mistresse'. The declared purpose of the invaders was to secure 'a toleration in religion for the pretended catholics', but the real intention was the removal of Elizabeth.[80] The danger which Guise and his associates represented was not great. As Holinshed pointed out 'there wanted two thinges, monie, and the assistance of a convenient partie in England to join with the forren forces'. Nor was it clear how Mary could be released without danger to her person. Nevertheless, Throgmorton's disclosures achieved two things; first the expulsion of Mendoza in January 1584 and the consequent breakdown of diplomatic relations with Spain over a year before any overtly hostile action; and, secondly, the unequivocal exposure of the queen of Scots as an inveterate and hypocritical conspirator. For fifteen years Elizabeth had persisted, in the face of mounting evidence, in believing in her cousin's good faith, if not in her wisdom or discretion. She had now no further excuse for deceiving herself.[81] Even while Throgmorton and his colleagues were plotting on her behalf (and with her knowledge), Mary was professing to Elizabeth her desire to retire from active politics altogether – as though that had been an option.

The other thing that this insubstantial plot achieved was the complete healing of the breach between Elizabeth and her subjects which had arisen over the Anjou marriage.[82] With their usual skill, Cecil and Walsingham made sure that both Throgmorton's confession and Mendoza's expulsion were given the most effective exposure. There was an upsurge of loyalist enthusiasm, both anti-Catholic and anti-Spanish. The Catholic problem was by this time a long running sore, and had been aggravated since 1578 by the build up of missionary activity, and particularly by the arrival of the first Jesuits in 1580. In July of the latter year Robert Parsons had delivered himself of a broadside in the form of an open letter to the magistrates of London, accusing them of using treason as a pretext to silence the prophets of the true faith: 'certain monstrous crimes being attributed to [them], such as conspiracy, rebellion or the crime of high treason or such like. This with the sole object that [they] may be involved in the meshes of this deceit and so be less in favour with the people.'[83]

The council was sensitive to this kind of jibe, and Cecil pointed out that since Catholicism involved allegiance to a foreign and hostile power, Catholics, and particularly priests, could hardly complain of being accused of treason. Restraining the activities of the missionaries was a high priority for the parliament of 1581. The House of Commons would have been happy to have made any profession of Catholicism treasonable, and drafted legislation to that effect, but that was not the queen's intention.[84] The council's focus was upon the act of reconciliation to Rome, partly because that could only be carried out by a priest, and partly because such an action was a calculated and deliberate defiance of the queen's authority. Catholics could still be mere creatures of habit, but reconciliation involved a positive choice. Consequently,

> all persons whatsoever which have, or shall have, or shall pretend to have power to absolve, persuade or withdraw any of the Queen's Majesty's subjects from their natural obedience to Her Majesty, or to withdraw them to that intent from the religion now by her Highness's authority established within her Highness's dominions, shall be to all intents judged to be traitors, and being thereof lawfully convicted, shall have judgement, suffer and forfeit as in cases of high treason.[85]

One of the first of those caught by this new law was the Jesuit Edmund Campion, who arrived in England on 24 June 1581, was arrested on the 17 July, tried on 20 November, and executed with two others on 1 December. Campion's fate was a salutary reminder, not only of the determination of Elizabeth's servants, but also of their capacity to act effectively.[86] It was also at that point a warning to the queen herself not to tamper with her religious settlement in any possible deal with the French.

Walsingham's intelligence service was famously efficient, and Burghley also had his own independent sources, such as Francis Touker, who sent him a report of English activities in Rome in 1583.[87] This was what made the activities of Mary and her agents so reckless. Whether they despised their opponents on the grounds that all heretics must be fools, or believed that God would look after his own, they took absurd risks and were detected over and over again. Throgmorton was probably no more dangerous than several other indiscreet young men who had fallen victim to similar fantasies, but he was a timely reminder of the need for action, not only against Mendoza but also against Mary herself.[88]

Unable either to persuade or to coerce the queen, in 1584 the council tried another device, and adopted what had originally been a private initiative for a Bond of Association. This was an agreement, signed eventually by thousands of zealous Protestant gentlemen, never to accept any claimant to the throne in whose name an attempt had been made upon Elizabeth's life. Should such an attempt be successful the person concerned, far from securing the throne, would be executed as a common criminal.[89] The principle behind this bond was truly, and perhaps unintentionally, revolutionary, because it implied the right of a godly community to select its own ruler, rather than obeying the laws of hereditary succession. Even Burghley, by this time becoming cautious and conservative, accepted this principle, and drew up a scheme for managing such an eventuality.[90] During the interregnum that would result from such drastic action, parliament and the council together would exercise supreme power, and select the next occupant of the throne. This would enable James to be selected, but would not guarantee it, because his own role in such a situation could not be anticipated. It was the most 'constitutionalist' statement of political thought since Henry VIII had first had the idea of limiting the succession by Act of parliament – and probably a direct consequence of it.

Although not opposed to the Bond of Association itself, Elizabeth would have no truck with such limitations upon the succession.[91] She had always claimed that her right to the throne was that of Henry's last legitimate child, which was why she had been so vulnerable to Mary Stuart's pretensions. Had she claimed her right by her father's will, and the Succession Act which authorised it, she would have had no such problem. There could be two opinions about her legitimacy – and only one about Mary's – but neither the 1543 Act nor the king's will had recognised any Scottish claim at all.[92] By 1583 the queen had long since nailed her colours to the mast, and to have changed her mind would have been to damage her credibility. By then also she had an additional reason to stick to her position; however much scope it may have given to Mary, it also left the way open for

James. By the 1543 Act he had no claim, but forty years later he was the
only plausible candidate; Elizabeth therefore had to steer a delicate course
between excluding the queen of Scots and recognising her son. Cecil's
scheme would effectively have made the monarchy elective, and that she
was not prepared to countenance.

For that reason, the lord treasurer kept his opinions on that aspect of
the crisis away from the parliament; but the House of Commons was eager
to have the Bond of Association confirmed. The result was a clever compromise, embodied in the 'Act for Provision to be Made for the Surety of
the Queen's Most Royal Person':

> Forasmuch as the good felicity and comfort of the whole estate of this realm
> consisteth only (next under God) in the surety and preservation of the Queen's
> most excellent Majesty; and for that it hath manifestly appeared that sundry
> wicked plots and means have of late been devised and laid, as well in foreign
> parts beyond the seas as also within this realm, be it enacted and ordained, if at
> any time after the end of this present session of parliament any open invasion
> or rebellion shall be had or made into or within any of her Majesties realms or
> dominions, or any act attempted tending to the hurt of her Majesty's most royal
> person, by or for any person that shall or may pretend any title to the Crown
> of this realm after her Majesty's decease, that then by her Majesty's commission
> under her great seal, the Lords and others of her Highness's Privy Council [plus
> some others to the number of twenty-four] shall by virtue of this act have
> authority to examine all and every the offences aforesaid.[93]

Any person found guilty of collusion in such a plot 'shall be excluded and
disabled for ever to have or claim, or to pretend to have or claim, the
Crown of this realm'. Anybody found guilty by the Commissioners named
was not only to be excluded, but might 'lawfully be pursued to death'.

Nothing was said about provision for the succession in the event of that
happening, an omission that left several options open. Most of those involved
in the discussion probably believed that the commissioners appointed to
investigate the circumstances, and try offenders, would also have some say
in the way ahead, but there was nothing in this Act to empower them to
do so. The Bond of Association was acknowledged in a concluding clause,
where it was also laid down that, in case the wording of the Bond should
give rise to misunderstanding – that is to unauthorised action – it was

> declared and enacted by the authority of the present parliament that the same
> Association and every article and sentence therein contained, shall and ought to
> be in all things expounded and adjudged according to the true intent and meaning
> of this Act, and not otherwise.[94]

The parliamentary session ended on 29 March 1585. In spite of all efforts, this Act was as near as it got to taking action against the Scottish queen. By patient diplomacy, however, Walsingham and Cecil were now edging nearer to a solution. Elizabeth, apparently, did not regard the statute as retrospective, and would not invoke its provisions in respect of the Throgmorton plot.

Given Mary's reckless disregard for the realities of life, however, it was only a matter of time before she did the same thing again. To facilitate such an eventuality, in January 1585 the earl of Shrewbury was relieved of his charge, and Mary was removed from Sheffield Castle to Tutbury, and into the care of Amyas Paulet.[95] Shrewsbury had always been conscientious, but Amyas Paulet showed a single-minded devotion to duty that boded ill for the Scottish queen. He was also in close communication with Walsingham, who by the end of the year was determined to bring Mary within the scope of the 1585 Act. In December she was moved to Chartley, a manor house a few miles from Tutbury, and deliberately deceived into believing that she had discovered a secret and reliable method of circumventing Paulet's vigilance.[96] This involved smuggling letters in and out in the bungs of beer barrels. For several weeks the transcription and deciphering of these letters produced nothing of significance, but then, on 6 July 1586, a zealous but extremely incautious young man named Anthony Babington wrote her a highly explicit letter, seeking her approval for another assassination plot which had been hatched in Paris by her agents, Mendoza and the Guises.[97] Walsingham already knew something of what was afoot, because another conspiritor, a priest named Ballard, had already been arrested and had made damaging disclosures. However, from the secretary's point of view everything depended upon Mary's response. If she did not respond to Babington, or express her disapproval, he would have broken up another plot, but would be no nearer his real quarry.

Mary did not disappoint. On 17 July she wrote very explicitly to Babington, not only approving his scheme but offering various pieces of advice as to how he should set about his task.[98] By the time that the letter reached Babington on 29 July, Walsingham possessed a full transcript and was in possession of the conclusive evidence that he sought. His only anxiety now was lest Elizabeth should still refuse to see what was evident to everyone else: that Mary was incorrigible.

That was a problem for the future. Immediately his task was to arrest the other conspirators and bring them to trial. Early in August all Mary's possessions at Chartley were seized and her secretaries taken into custody. Babington and his confederates were rounded up in London. Confessing their guilt, they were executed on 20 September, amid scenes of patriotic rejoicing.[99] On 12 September Giovanni Dolfin, the Venetian ambassador in France, reported that letters had been received from London, dated

30 August outlining the details of the plot. He believed that the conspirators had been betrayed by Ballard, and he had been told by the English ambassador

> that it was understood from the examination of the prisoners that the queen of Scotland had given her consent to the attempt. The ambassador has orders from his mistress to communicate these occurrences to his Most Christian Majesty, and to point out to him that in virtue of the good relations between the two crowns it would be right and proper for him to refuse asylum in his kingdom to men of such quality.[100]

Nothing was said about the intercepted letters, but Mary's complicity was clearly indicated and Elizabeth's options were steadily being foreclosed. As a result of the war which had now become a reality, the Scottish queen was not merely a threat but an enemy agent; a Spanish puppet, now exposed by her own folly and the logic of political events.

In spite of Elizabeth's extreme reluctance to fight, the long build up of tension with Spain had given her council ample opportunity to prepare. The militia had been reorganised as early as 1573, making a distinction between the general musters and the trained bands. The latter, 'a convenient and sufficient number of the most able', were to be armed with up to date pikes and muskets at the expense of their counties, and were to be professionally drilled for a specified number of days each year. They were to be exempt from service overseas, and were clearly intended as a 'home guard' in the event of invasion.[101] The remainder were required to muster as before, and to provide their own traditional weapons, but they were not required to train. The thinking behind this system was straightforward. Men would be willing to defend their homes to the best of their ability, and even to pay to have it done more effectively. Should it be necessary to send troops abroad, they would have to be paid and equipped by the queen, and could be trained as and when necessary. The priority was clearly defensive.

The size of the trained bands varied from county to county, according to how much money the local commissioners could be persuaded or coerced into finding. It cost about £1 a year to drill each man, so a county the size of Norfolk would face an annual bill of about £500, over and above the cost of the equipment. There was plenty of grumbling, but persistent rumours of invasion demonstrated the need and prevented serious opposition.[102] By 1585 the whole basis of military preparation had shifted. Even as late as the French war of 1557–59 private retinues had formed the core of royal armies, whether they were to serve abroad or at home, and licences to retain had been extensively used by both Edward VI and Mary. Elizabeth issued very few such licences, and in 1572 a proclamation had ordered the enforcement of those anti-retaining statutes which were still on the books.[103] Thereafter even the commission of array for overseas service was used only occasionally. The council preferred to use county quotas, raised by the lords lieutenant.

Of course these lieutenants were the same noblemen who would previously have served at the head of their own retinues, and the difference may not have been very apparent to the rank and file. Nevertheless, the shift in emphasis from the private to the public concept of war was extremely significant. It reflected and continued that long and slow change from a magnate culture to a service culture in the aristocracy, and was an expression of the queen's debt to her father and grandfather.[104] The old chivalric values, which the nobility had seen as peculiarly its own, were being increasingly restricted to the tiltyard, particularly with the development of the Accession Day tilts in the later 1570s. The Virgin Queen presided fittingly over these celebrations of courtly love, which at the same time elevated and emasculated military skills. Although England was a long way behind her continental neighbours, and particularly the Spaniards, by 1585 war was increasingly being seen as a professional business rather than the sport of noblemen.

As was fitting for a maritime power, the navy was ahead of the army in this respect. Henry VIII had created a professional navy, aided by the fact that command at sea had never been an aristocratic monopoly. Although the lord admiral was always of noble family, by Elizabeth's reign most captains in royal service were of mercantile or minor gentry origins, both Hawkins and Drake being cases in point. The council for marine causes, which functioned efficiently from its creation in 1545, was the most professional system of naval administration in Europe.[105] Elizabeth, however, did not like the budget or ordinary that her sister had established, and reverted to a more *ad hoc* system of finance. She encouraged private enterprise with investment and semi-official support, and from 1579 onward allowed John Hawkins to experiment with 'bargains' or contracts for naval maintenance. These did nothing to assist efficiency, and caused furious quarrels among the admiralty officers. Hawkins was accused of negligence and corruption, and although he was officially exonerated, the system was dropped shortly after the outbreak of war.[106] In a sense these experiments were simply the result of Elizabeth's reluctance to spend money, but they were also attempts to set up a partnership between the crown and the maritime community, which was to be amply vindicated in due course by the contribution of the privateers to the war effort. Although this was reducing the navy as an expression of state power, it was actually increasing its professionalism, because it was among the privateers that skills of seamanship and gunnery reached their highest development. A survey of merchant shipping resources carried out in 1582 reveals that the council was already thinking in terms of an 'auxiliary' navy; one which would be under the command of the lord admiral, but largely self-financing.[107] Without such a system the war eventually waged at sea would have been virtually impossible. Elizabeth knew perfectly well that her resources were limited, and that she could only fight with a level of support among her subjects which had to be purchased and carefully cultivated. Significantly, she was much happier cooperating with a maritime community of merchants and gentlemen than with a military community of noblemen. Fortunately for her, the coming war was to be fought largely at sea.

By 1585 one other change had taken place, which was to be more significant for the future than it appeared to be at the time. In 1583 Archbishop Grindal died, and the church's period without effective leadership came to an end. In his place John Whitgift was translated from Worcester to Canterbury on 23 September. Whitgift was the queen's personal choice, and was to enjoy better relations with his sovereign than either of his predecessors.[108] He was already a seasoned polemicist against Cartwright and the puritan radicals. He was also a keen defender of the establishment and a skilled administrator. He was the first (and only) cleric to serve on Elizabeth's privy council, and enjoyed an amicable relationship with Lord Burghley. For the first time since 1559 there was no conflict of priorities between Westminster and Lambeth. This was to prove extremely important as the Presbyterian campaign gained momentum in parliament during the early 1580s.

10

War with Spain

In September 1583 Elizabeth passed her fiftieth birthday. No one was now talking about an heir of her body, or of marriage, and the fictions of courtly love were becoming increasingly arid. Yet a passionate young woman still lurked behind the obvious wig and the increasingly raddled face. After 1585 her foreign policy was locked into a war which foreclosed most other options. Although she continued to negotiate spasmodically with Philip II, the only way to achieve peace would have been by a total withdrawal from the Netherlands that would have left England's coast fatally exposed. Consequently any enemy of the king of Spain was a potential friend: the Huguenots, the king of France, even the Grand Turk.[1] The pragmatic opportunism of earlier years, the tortuous matrimonial diplomacy, and the spasmodic attempts at conciliation, all disappeared. In their place came strategic debates about how to fight the war, and above all, about how to find enough money to do so. Paradoxically, war diminished the Catholic threat at home, but stimulated the puritans to fresh efforts, as they saw Godly Reformation as the only way to win the divine favour now so much needed.

The first important casualty of the war was Mary Stuart. After the Babington plot the case for decisive action against her became overwhelming. Babington and Ballard had been executed on 20 September 1585, having both confessed their own guilt and incriminated the queen of Scots. Elizabeth was extremely distressed, because she found two of her deepest instincts in conflict, self-preservation and respect for legitimate rights. The former dictated, and had done for some time, that Mary should die. Quite apart from the unresolved matter of Darnley's murder, Mary had repeatedly proved herself incapable of negotiating in good faith, and had on at least two occasions explicitly sanctioned plots to murder Elizabeth.[2] On the other hand, she was a kinswoman, an anointed queen, and not an English subject. She had not been sufficiently at liberty to commit any actual offence since her arrival in England, and it was questionable whether any English court had lawful jurisdiction over her.[3] She could certainly not be guilty of treason in the ordinary sense. Elizabeth had no personal sympathy for Mary, and was no more squeamish than most of her subjects about inflicting the death penalty. The evidence suggests that she despised Mary as a woman lacking both integrity and self-discipline. Elizabeth, however, was also a stickler for the due process of law and a believer in the sanctity of monarchy. Only papists were sufficiently depraved to murder their enemies in the name of the faith.[4] Elizabeth probably did not know that the papal secretary of state had explicitly authorised her own murder in 1580, but she had the evidence of William of Orange's assassination and of St Bartholomew's Day before her eyes. Elizabeth had no desire to follow such an example.[5]

The statute of 1585 had, however, provided for just such a situation as had now arisen. It laid down very clearly and precisely exactly how a person in Mary's position was to be proceeded against; and the queen had accepted it. By September 1586 the logic of this argument, pressed very hard by her council, had finally convinced her. Early in October she appointed a commission of thirty-six peers, councillors and judges, and moved Mary to Fotheringhay Castle, where the commission was appointed to meet. On 6 October, she formally notified Mary of her decision.

> Whereas we are given to understand that you, to our great and inestimable grief, as one void of all remorse of conscience, pretend with great protestations not to be in any sort privy or assenting to any attempt either against our state or person; forasmuch as we find by most clear and evident proof that the contrary will be verified and maintained against you, we have found it therefore expedient to send unto you divers of our chief and most ancient noblemen of this our realm, together with certain of our privy council, as also some of our principal judges, to charge you both with the privity and assent to that most horrible and unnatural attempt.[6]

Mary did not attempt to challenge the jurisdiction of the court, perhaps because she did not understand the nature of Elizabeth's scruples, but conducted her defence with energy and not a little skill. She denied all knowledge of the letters which she was alleged both to have written and received. 'I would never make shipwreck of my soul by compassing the death of my dearest sister.' Unfortunately, it was not only the suspect testimony of the conspirators that was against her, it was also that of Walsingham's agents and her own secretaries.[7] She also knew that compassing the death of a heretic, sister or not, would be no jeopardy to her soul in the eyes of the Catholic Church. Elizabeth continued to be reluctantly driven by the logic of the situation. Before the commissioners delivered their verdict, she summoned them back to London and went through the whole case with them. Satisfied at last with the justice of the decision, she then allowed it to be concluded and delivered; and on 4 December it was proclaimed in accordance with the terms of the Act.[8] Mary was now lawfully debarred from any claim to the succession; but James was immediately reassured that this was *ad feminem*, and did not in any way affect his own position.

Elizabeth now had to decide what to do next, as the matter lay in her own hands. Parliament was in session, and on 12 November had petitioned in the strongest terms for the death penalty. Although convinced of Mary's guilt, the queen hesitated and would give no answer.[9] There were a number of reasons for this, and it is unlikely that feminine pity or indecisiveness were among them. Elizabeth, not for the first time 'played the woman'; but representations were being received both from France and Scotland asking for clemency, and she had to decide who it was more dangerous to upset – her neighbours or her subjects. It is also likely that she was still not convinced that she had the right to proceed to extremities against a person who was not her subject, whatever her own statutes might say.

In January 1587 London was full of rumours: the Spaniards had landed at Milford Haven; the north was in revolt; Mary had escaped. A fresh plot was discovered (or possibly invented) emanating from the French embassy, which undermined the credibility of French protests; and James made it clear that his own filial indignation was not going to jeopardise his prospects in England.[10] 'Aut fer, aut feri', Elizabeth is alleged to have said, 'ne feriare, feri' (Suffer or strike; strike in order not to be struck). On 1 February she signed the death warrant. Even after this was done, she tried to shift the responsibility onto the signatories of the Bond of Association, presumably on the grounds that they had declared their own right to carry out the death sentence against any person found guilty.[11] This did not work, but the signature on the warrant was sufficient, unless it was recalled; and Elizabeth did not attempt to recall it, which was the only thing that could have saved Mary's life. In fact, the queen did not really want to save her rival's life; she wanted to avoid responsibility for her death, which was not the same thing at all. The council despatched the warrant to Fotheringhay on 4 February, without any further reference to Elizabeth – which they were perfectly entitled to do – and Mary was executed on the morning of the 8th; in her own eyes both a tragic heroine and a martyr. She died with more dignity and panache than she had lived, in the presence of the sheriff and most of her own household, having commended her soul to God and her son to the duke of Guise.

Writing in the reign of James I, William Camden contrived to give Mary the memorial which she sought, and which has lodged firmly in the historical imagination, without directly criticising either Elizabeth or her council.

Then forth she came, in gesture, carriage and demeanour right Princely and majesticke; cheerefull in countenance, and in attire very modest and matronlike;

she wore a linnen vaile uppon her and before her face, which she discovered; at her girdle hung her rosarie or rowe of Beades, and in the hand she held a Crucifixe of Ivory. In the porch, or passage of her lodging, met her the Earles and the rest of the Noblemen, where Melvine (one of her servants) falling on his knees and pouring forth teares, lamented his unlucky fortune, that he was designed the man that should carry into Scotland the sad message of the tragicall death of his deereste Mistress: Oh weep not (quoth she) for you shall shortly see Mary Stuart at the end of all her sorrowes.[12]

The emotions were no doubt real enough, but every gesture in this scene was carefully choreographed, in a manner that Elizabeth perfectly understood. When the earl of Kent expressed scruples about allowing a number of her servants to ascend the scaffold with her, perhaps fearing a demonstration, he was treated to a response worthy of the queen of England herself:

Feere you not, sir; the poore wretches desire nothing but to take their last leaves of me. And I know that my sister, the Queene of England, would not that you should deny me so small a request. For the honour of my sex, my servants should be in presence. I am the nearest of her Parentage and Consanguinitie, grand child to Henry the seventh, Dowager of France and anointed Queene of Scotlande.[13]

It was an impressive performance: in the best traditions of political theatre, Elizabeth was totally upstaged. This she had no doubt foreseen, and it had contributed to her reluctance to allow it to take place. She could only respond by seeking to maintain the fiction of her own disengagement, disowning the action of her secretary, William Davison, who had borne the warrant to Fotheringhay. It was an unworthy gesture, and persuaded nobody. It did not have to: Davison was expendable; with Philip II she was already at war; and James VI, whose honour was most nearly touched, confined himself to verbal protests. At the same time, the gains were substantial. Most of her subjects, particularly the members of parliament who were going to have to pay for the war, were highly gratified. There was also no longer a plausible Catholic claimant to benefit from the queen's demise. That did not entirely remove the danger, but it greatly reduced it, because it also meant that no Catholic could now pretend that conspiracy against Elizabeth was anything other than an act of war in support of Spain.[14]

Although the pressure of the law was maintained and enhanced against seminary priests and Jesuits, towards ordinary Catholics, even those of some wealth and status, the attitude of the the authorities was pragmatic. On 23 April 1586, well before Mary's death, the justices of the peace for Suffolk had written to the council, explaining how they had compounded with a number of wealthy recusants for an annual payment in remission of all penalties incurred by statute. William Yaxley £40; John Bedingfield £20; Margaret Daniel £20; Roger Martin 40 marks; and so on to a total of about £320 a year.[15] This was a significant sum, and if similar action was taken in other counties would have given the crown what was in fact a 'Catholic Tax' of some £6000 or £7000 a year without any further action being required.[16] Since compounding was a way of demonstrating temporal allegiance without having to subscribe to heretical practices, or undergo the hazards of prosecution, it is not surprising that many recusants took advantage of it. At the time of the Armada crisis the government took the additional precaution of disarming known Catholics, and there was much protest from the recusant community, on the grounds that they were just as keen to fight against Spain as anybody else. The outbreak of war, and Mary's execution, made Catholic activism more explicitly treasonable than before, but the government did not make the mistake of being logical and assuming that every recusant was a Spanish agent.

By 1587 there was a consensus between queen and council as to how the Catholic threat should be confronted, but no similar consensus over how the church proper should be managed. From 1571 until 1587 the House of Commons petitioned regularly for further reform, both of the liturgy and of the recruitment of clergy.[17] In 1584 the petition 'for a learned ministry to preach the Gospel and to be resident in every parish', also asked, significantly, 'for further regulation of the Bishops, Officers and Governors of the church'.[18] This clearly reflected the rise of Presbyterian influence, because its objective was to place every bishop under the control of a diocesan synod. Clause 13 demanded:

> That no one Bishop do hereafter proceed in admitting or depriving of any Pastor by his sole authority; nor in excommunicating any faulty person; nor in absolving any person that is excommunicated; nor in the deciding or determining of any cause Ecclesiastical without the Advice and Consent of the aforesaid seniors and associates joined with him.

The queen's responses were usually courteous and noncommittal, but occasionally she forbade further discussion on the grounds that the day-by-day running of the church was a matter for the bishops, controlled by her own prerogative. A debate with some of her bishops and councillors in February 1585, while parliament was in session, reveals the nature of the divisions which then existed.

> Then said she unto the [arch]bishop, We understand that some of the Nether House have used divers reproachful speeches against you, tending greatly to your dishonour, which we will not suffer; and that they meddle with matters above

their capacity, not appertaining unto them, for the which we will call some of them to account.[19]

Whitgift, she made clear, was responsible to her, and not to the parliament, or to any part of it. She was not, however, without sympathy for some of the Commons' substantive complaints, particularly over the ordination of unsuitable ministers, and took her archbishop to task for permitting abuses.

> Then spake my Lord Treasurer, saying Truly, my lord, her majesty hath declared unto you a marvelous great fault in that you make in this time of light so many lewd and unlearned ministers.
> My Lord of Canterbury said, Well ...
> Quod her Majesty, Draw articles and charge them with it that have offended.
> I do not burden, quod my Lord Treasurer, them that be here, but it is the Bishop of Lichfield and Coventry [William Overton] that I mean, who made seventy ministers in one day for money; some tailors, some shoemakers and other crass men. I am sure that the greatest part of them are not worthy to keep horses.[20]

It is easy from this to see why the godly in the Lower House saw Burghley as an ally, and indeed the earl of Leicester as well. The queen herself was concerned with due process. If there were abuses, even among the bishops, let them be remedied in the proper manner by the archbishop, who would have her full backing. Failures in the system should be redressed by making it work properly, not by tampering with it or replacing parts of it.

At the level of first principles, her position was clear. God had entrusted His honour and worship in England to her; and her subjects had given their consent to that dispensation in 1559. It was their duty to draw to her attention whatever shortcomings they might detect, but it was her responsibility, and hers alone, to decide what to do about them. The bishops were her chosen servants and agents in this respect, and their authority was consequently hers at one remove.[21] Bad clergy dishonoured their bishops, and bad bishops dishonoured the Supreme Governor; but the remedy was between herself and God, and woe betide anyone who suggested that a woman could or should not wield such power. No member of the council would have denied that, but they differed widely as to how far to go in making representations. Some, like Christopher Hatton, had no time for godly clamour, and saw no cause for change. Others, like Burghley, were more appreciative of the scriptural priorities of the malcontents, and tried very hard to avoid a head on collision with Elizabeth's Erastianism. They were keenly aware that there was no room for ideological conflict within an England embattled against the Counter-Reformation.[22]

The issue was eventually resolved not by heroic action, or even by strenuous intellectual effort, but more or less by accident. In 1588, angered and disgusted by the failure of their petitioning campaign, and genuinely worried lest God turn away His face from the unregenerate, the Presbyterians decided to try something completely different. They attempted to undermine the episcopate by mocking individual bishops out of countenance.

They published, in 1588 and 1589, from clandestine presses, a series of pamphlets, known from their pseudonymous author as *The Marprelate Tracts*.[23] An attack on Thomas Cooper, bishop of Winchester, and entitled (with reference to the London street cry) *Hay Any Work for Cooper*, gives a fair flavour of 'Martin Marprelate's' approach:

> a briefe Pistle directed by waye of an hublication to the reverende Bysshops ... wherein worthy Martin quits himself like a man ... Printed in Europe not far from some of the Bounsing Priests ...
>
> A craftie whoresons brethren B[isho]p. did you think that because ye puritans T.C. [Thomas Cartwright] did set John of Cant[erbury]. [Whitgift] at a nonpluss, and gave him the overthrow that therefore your T.C., alias Thomas Cooper bishop of Winchester or Thomas Cooke his Chaplaine could set me at a nonplus. Simple fellows, methinks he should not ...
>
> Ha, olde Martin yet I see thou hast it in thee, thou wilt enter into the bowels of the cause in hand I perceive.
>
> ... that was far from my meaning and could by no meanes be gathered out of my woordes, but only by him that pronounced Eulojin for Eulogeni in the pulpit; and by him whom a Papist made to beleeve that the Greek word, that is to give thanks, signifieth to make a crosse on the forehead: py hy hy. I cannot but laugh.[24]

Not surprisingly, this mocking and scurrilous tone gave the tracts an appreciative popular readership; but it was not only the bishops who failed to be amused. Such a carnivalesque attitude towards authority was infectious. Today the bishop of Winchester, tomorrow Lord Burghley or the earl of Leicester, or even the queen herself. The author, or authors, and the cause for which they spoke, rapidly found themselves without those friends in high places who had given them their main weight over the previous ten years.[25] Marprelate also misjudged the popular mood. Charivari was essentially ephemeral, but what these tracts represented was not a temporary 'world turned upside down', but the imposition of a strict standard of godly learning on anyone in a position of authority. In other words a kind of theocracy that was quite at odds with conventional notions of hierarchy and subordination.[26] The assault was also ill-timed, in the sense that the defeat of the Armada, at almost exactly the time that the first of these tracts was published, was widely interpreted (and not only among the humble) as clear evidence that God was quite satisfied with England the way it was.

Strenuous, and largely successful, efforts were made to track down the perpetrators of these offensive tracts. The presses were located and broken up; suspects were interrogated and imprisoned; one, John Penry, was later executed for treason. In all this activity Whitgift enjoyed a level of magisterial cooperation which neither Parker nor Grindal had ever received, and the energy gradually ebbed out of the Presbyterian cause.[27] It did not go away, but it became less politically assertive and strenuous. By the early 1590s Elizabeth's Protestant subjects were probably better pleased with her handling of the church than at any time since 1560. In her Prayer Book of about 1582, she had written

> teach me, I humbly beseech thee, Thy Word and so strengthen me with Thy grace that I may feed Thy people with a faithful and a true heart, and rule them prudently with power. O Lord, Thou has set me on high; my flesh is frail and weak. If I therefore at any time forget Thee, touch my heart, O Lord, that I may again remember Thee.[28]

Whether she ever accepted that God could sometimes speak to her through those same subjects that she ruled in His name is not entirely clear. What is clear is that she did not believe that He usually did so, and the consistency of her approach lay largely in the fact that she saw her relationship with God as personal.

Meanwhile, there was a war to be fought. This meant primarily the emergency in the Low Countries, which required an instant response not conducive to long-term strategic planning. 6400 infantry, 1000 cavalry and £126,000 were required immediately, and the appointment of a nobleman of seniority and distinction to lead them. The earl of Leicester virtually chose himself for the latter role.[29] He had a long-standing interest in the Low Countries, was well known and respected there, and above all enjoyed the unique confidence of the queen. No one else had this combination of attributes. Yet, at the same time, he was a deeply flawed selection. He was over fifty years old, and his only military experience had been at St-Quentin, nearly thirty years before. He was a vastly experienced courtier and councillor, but had never served in embassy abroad, and had no first-hand knowledge of Dutch politics. Elizabeth was perfectly well aware of all this, and also reluctant to lose the company of so valued a friend, whose absences from court over last few years, although often stormy, had always been brief in duration.[30] She considered sending Lord Grey instead, and Leicester (who wanted the mission) became frustrated at the delay. More seriously, Antwerp fell before any relief could reach it and the tactical thrust of the expedition had to be reviewed.

Leicester did not finally leave for Flushing until the middle of December, but when he went, he went in vice-regal state that did not bode well for his mission. He had raised some four hundred foot and three hundred and fifty horse at his own expense, and was accompanied by an ordinary household which may have numbered as many as two hundred, including two noblemen, the earl of Essex and Lord North.[31] In a sense Leicester was very much the master of this operation. Most of the political and military appointments of the mission, such as Sir Henry Killigrew to the council of state and Sir Philip Sidney as governor of Flushing, were his friends and dependants. In another sense, however, he was not the master at all. Elizabeth's paranoid fear of losing control of a political situation was never more clearly demonstrated than by what followed Leicester's arrival in the Low Countries. Having put him in a position where he needed to exercise his discretion in all sorts of ways, she allowed him none. Having committed significant money and troops to a war, she then proceeded to treat her allies with contempt, and continually endeavoured to negotiate with the enemy.[32] She handled the Netherlands campaign rather as she had handled the church in the early days of her reign, and for much the same reason. The Dutch needed her, even on her own terms; and if she could force some kind of an agreement with Parma, her position would be strengthened at little cost. If the war proceeded, she could have virtually no control over the outcome. If Leicester distinguished himself, his honour would outshine her own.

Elizabeth is usually described as having again been chronically indecisive, but in fact her policy was quite consistent.[33] She had to prevent Parma from winning, for the sake of her own security, and she had to prevent Leicester from returning in triumph and upstaging her. Given the earl's limitations, and the limitations of his resources, the latter was probably never a real possibility; but the queen was taking no chances. Her personal affection for him was still strong, but she wanted him on her own terms, as she always had. A Leicester recalled in semi-disgrace and dependent upon her gracious forgiveness was a much more attractive prospect than the return of a victorious warlord.[34]

The situation in the Low Countries themselves conspired to promote this devious programme. The United Provinces were in confusion, and desperate for some strong leadership, preferably from outside. They had tried Anjou, they had tried Matthias, they had even tried Elizabeth, and had been let down each time.

Within days of his arrival at The Hague at the beginning of January 1586, Leicester was approached by the estates general and offered the governorship of all the provinces.[35] The offer was not entirely unexpected. The treaty of Nonsuch had specified that the queen send a nobleman of high standing, who was expected to serve, with two others, on the council of state. What Elizabeth intended by that was an unofficial and advisory role, but Leicester had never been happy with that kind of restriction. Without consulting his mistress, he accepted the offer and was proclaimed governor-general on 27 January.[36] He trusted, he wrote, that he would be allowed so much discretion, as it seemed to be the only way to make his mission effective.

Elizabeth was predictably and understandably furious. Her reproaches were withering: he, 'a creature of our own will', had acted in contempt of her authority and brought her name and reputation into dishonour. He was to resign his pretended office at once.[37] The storm lasted for about three months, as Hatton, Burghley and others endeavoured to calm the queen down, and to persuade her that Leicester's action represented the only viable way ahead in the Low Countries. The substance of her grievance was that he had overcommitted her, and given the impression that she had expansionist ambitions. It was the manner, however, rather than the substance that caused her most anger. He had acted without authority, and given the impression that it was his own honour which he sought, rather than hers.[38] Someone wickedly added fuel to the fire by starting a rumour that the countess of Leicester was about to join her husband and set up a vice-regal court. There was no truth in the report, but Elizabeth's reaction was revealing; she was terrified that Robert Dudley would escape from her control and set up on his own. He was hers to do with as she liked, and woe betide any woman, or any political regime, that sought to disturb such control.[39]

At the end of April Leicester was still governor general, and the storm seemed to have abated, but in May there was another tantrum, and Burghley and Thomas Heneage, the queen's special envoy to the estates general, conferred dejectedly about some positive way out of the morass.[40] The problem was not so much offending the Dutch, who were in no position to take umbrage, but the debilitating effect which the row was having on Leicester's effectiveness, to say nothing of his confidence. There was, after all, fighting to be done as well as delicate political manoeuvres to be executed. An English army was already in place under the efficient command of John Norris, but it was neither at full strength nor of good quality.[41] Leicester's chosen military assistant, Sir William Pelham, was a good choice, except in one respect. The queen had no opinion of him, and it was July before he was allowed to go over.[42] Meanwhile, Leicester and Norris proved cantankerous colleagues, probably because they were too much alike, but they managed to avoid an open quarrel that would have damaged their operations. To make a major contribution, the earl needed more men and much more money, but the queen was reluctant about both. She was extremely unwilling to provide more than the treaty minimum, partly because she was still endeavouring to negotiate with Parma, and partly because intelligence was warning her of an impending attack coming directly from Spain.[43] Soldiers were recruited, however, both in Ireland and in Scotland, until by August there were approaching 12,000 men at Leicester's disposal.

On paper this was a viable army, but in practice it was mostly a rabble, and both crime and desertion were major problems. Money arrived from England in instalments, and about £47,000 had been received before the earl reached Flushing. By February 1586 the barrel was empty, and no more arrived until April.[44] In March, and again in May, Leicester was forced to borrow from the Merchant Adventurers to keep an army in the field at all. The £32,000 that was supposed to come in July was only £20,000 when it arrived, spread over July and August. No doubt the money was inadequate, and he did borrow as he claimed, but this information comes mostly from Leicester's complaints, and his tale of woe should be treated with some caution. There were disagreements between the governor general and the treasurer about exactly how much had been received; and the accounting procedures, which were strict in theory, in practice were anything but.[45] Moreover the arithmetic of sixteenth-century clerks was notoriously erratic. Leicester claimed to have put £11,000 of his own money into the campaign, but when he died two years later he owed the crown £20,000, rather than the other way round.[46] Burghley responded sympathetically to Leicester's complaints, and negotiated a deal with the Merchant Adventurers to place more credit at his disposal, but Elizabeth had good cause to doubt that her money was being efficiently spent. Payments were made without authorisation, or even proper record, and the queen herself queried the treasurer, William Huddlestone's accounts.[47] The governor general was charged with irresponsibility, and he in turn blamed the treasurer. The whole management of the campaign was a mess, but no one individual was responsible and the queen herself was to blame mainly because she had chosen the wrong man for the job. Whatever honour might require, the day of the aristocratic amateur was over.

In the circumstances, the English forces did not do as badly as might have been expected. Although they failed to relieve either Middelberg or Venlo in June, an attack on Axel at the beginning of July was successful, and Doesburg was captured in early September.[48] Inconclusive fighting around Zutphen at the end of the season was notable mainly for the death of Sir Philip Sidney. A drawn campaign against a commander of the calibre of Parma has to be counted an achievement, but Leicester drew little satisfaction from it. He was understandably convinced that Elizabeth had no confidence in him, and that he was being set up by his political enemies at home, who would move in for the kill when he was sufficiently discredited.[49] Meanwhile he added to his own difficulties by renewing his quarrels with Norris, complaining endlessly to Burghley and Walsingham about how ill he was being used. Elizabeth did not know quite what to make of him. Although his demoralisation was largely the result of her own actions, she did not see how she could have acted otherwise in the circumstances; and as her confidence in him as a soldier and politician steadily ebbed away, her personal regard for him did not change. On 19 July she wrote:

> Rob. I am afraid you will suppose by my wandering writings that a midsummer moon hath taken large possession of my brains this month, but you must needs take things as they come into my head, though order be left behind me. And if the treasurer be found untrue or negligent, according to desert he shall be used, you know my old wont that love not to discharge from office without desert. Now will I end that do imagine I talk still with you, and loathly say farewell O O, though ever I pray God bless you from all harm and save you from all foes with my million and legion of thanks for all your pains and cares.
> As you know, ever the same. ER.[50]

If the earl derived any encouragement from this affectionate letter, it did not last. His quarrels with Norris, and with the Dutch leaders, grew worse, and by September his recall was under active consideration. Norris was not only a very good professional soldier, he also had the ear of Lord Burghley, and was consequently heard at court. He knew, and did not hesitate to say, that it was Leicester's incompetence, and his irresponsible meddling in Dutch politics, which was mainly to blame for the occasional crises in relations between the allies, and the bitter complaints of the estates general.[51] The earl was recalled, not exactly in disgrace but largely discredited, in November 1586, leaving behind a legacy of mistrust and recrimination. Within a few weeks two of the officers in whom he had reposed particular confidence, Sir William Stanley and Rowland Yorke, had betrayed their trusts and entered Parma's service. It was a fitting epitaph upon his career, and left only Norris between Elizabeth and a complete breakdown in relations with her allies.

The queen's urgent desire to limit her commitments in the Netherlands, which explains a lot of this sorry tangle, can best be understood in relation to what was happening elsewhere. The success of Drake's circumnavigation had increased enthusiasm for long-distance trade, and for several years after his return there was much talk of returning to the Pacific, and of establishing a trading post in Brazil. Voyages actually went to the Azores and to West Africa, but the queen was not an investor, and their success was modest.[52] Then in the summer of 1584, Drake was placed in charge of preparing an expedition that would sail to the Moluccas. His backers were a distinguished team, headed by the queen herself with £10,000 and two ships.[53] Drake himself ventured £7000, the earl of Leicester £3000; and John Hawkins, William Hawkins and Walter Ralegh somewhat smaller sums. For the time being these were pledges rather than cash in hand because nobody – probably not even Elizabeth herself – knew whether the expedition would actually sail. By February 1585 a fleet was being fitted out which the Spanish ambassador believed was destined for a raid on the West Indies. Whether his intelligence was particularly good, or he just assumed that any large-scale preparation was aimed against his master, we do not know.[54] By April the operation appeared to be on hold, but then Philip issued his arrest order against English ships. Elizabeth did not respond at once, perhaps to allow time for the verification of what had happened; but on 1 July she renewed Drake's commission, instructing him to proceed to Vigo and demand the release of her subjects' property.[55] At the same time general letters of marque were issued to enable the English merchants to recover the value of their goods by reprisal.[56] There was no declaration of war.

The nature of Drake's further instructions is uncertain. He may have been intended to intercept the *flota*, or treasure fleet; he may have been ordered to proceed straight to New Spain. What is clear is that his intentions were hostile. He did not, however, put to sea until 14 September; partly because his preparations had been suspended, and took time to get going again, and partly because there were problems about who should actually go. The original plans had not included soldiers, but the new ones did, and that meant finding a suitable commander. Philip Sidney had wanted the job, but with a joint overall command which Drake was not prepared to allow. Dom Antonio, the pretender to the Portuguese throne, also turned up in Plymouth bidding for a berth. Drake appears to have liked him, but thought his presence would have been a risk too far.[57] Eventually Christopher Carliell was recalled from Ireland to command the troops. All this took time. Neither hesitancy on Elizabeth's part nor shortage of money lay behind these delays, but simply practical considerations, and the fleet was as well found as anyone at the time was capable of making it. As soon as Drake had left, there was a general belief that the queen would change her mind and recall him. This, however, like a number of such rumours, seems to have been based on Elizabeth's habit of thinking aloud. She did indeed worry lest she should be leaving the realm without adequate naval defences, but there is no evidence that she had any serious intention of stopping her carefully considered gesture of retaliation.

The fleet consisted of some two dozen ships of various sizes, headed by the Queen's *Elizabeth Bonaventure* of 600 tons, in which the admiral displayed his flag. The events that followed are among the best documented of any voyage; no fewer than three expedition diaries were planned and two actually survive.[58] Drake arrived at Vigo at the end of September, having picked up some small prizes on the way. The town was unprepared for resistance, and the governor agreed both to release the Englishmen held there and to sell fresh provisions to the fleet. Whether the latter need was caused by carelessness and haste in the original loading or because Drake believed in taking on fresh provisions for a transatlantic voyage at the last possible moment is not clear.[59] There had been no need for haste in loading, but the latter was a risky strategy. The English believed, with some justification, that the governor was attempting to renege on his undertaking, and pressure was applied in the form of some small-scale but destructive raids. There was also a severe storm a few days after their arrival. Between one thing and another it took Drake some two weeks to get all that he wanted out of Vigo. Satisfaction at this success, however, was quickly tempered by the realisation that he had missed the Panama fleet, which had slipped into Seville while he tarried in the north.[60] Ironically, it was both rich and unescorted; but it is surely attributing too much to Spanish cunning to argue that he was deliberately detained.

The fleet reached Las Palmas in the Canaries on 2 November, but was greeted with effective gunfire, and did not press an attack. Meanwhile Drake and Carliell had drawn up strict orders for their men, with whose conduct at Vigo they appear to have been less than satisfied. Both were well aware that a strict account would have to be rendered, not only for their actions but also for any plunder that they might obtain.[61] In spite of appearances, this was not a privateering expedition but war, and military discipline was necessary.

> Item, for as much as we are bounde in conscience and required also in duty to yielde an honest account of our doings and proceedinges in this action and that her Majestie ... shalbe appoynted and persons of creditt shalbe assigned, unto whom such porcions of goods of speciall price as golde silver, jewells, or any other thing of moment or valew shalbe brought and delyvered, the which shall remayne in chestes under the chardge of four or five severall keyes, and they shalbe committed unto the custody of souch captens as are of best account in the Fleet.[62]

After a brief and unproductive landing on the island of Hierro, Drake proceeded by way of Cape Blanco to the Cape Verde Islands, where he landed on Sao Tiago on 17 November. This was a sizeable settlement, and the attack was pressed effectively, not yielding much in the way of valuables, but a lot of food, some artillery and at least one ship.[63] The commander also started to fall out with his officers. Thanks to the diaries, we have detailed accounts of this fracas, although probably not unbiased ones. Drake would stand no questions or criticism of his leadership, and in view of the reputation of gentlemen adventurers he was probably right. Much as his autocracy was resented, it was probably the best way to get results, and Sao Tiago was burned and plundered from end to end.[64]

By the time that the fleet reached Dominica in the West Indies on 18 December, disease had begun to take its toll. Twenty men died there; more than had been lost in action or to judicial execution put together. In spite of this, the fleet arrived at Santo Domingo on La Española on New Year's day 1586, and captured the town with a regular military operation of total success. Drake remained for almost a month in Santo Domingo, unsuccessfully demanding an enormous ransom and systematically destroying the town.[65] He eventually left with far less gold than he had hoped, but with a lot of miscellaneous plunder and several ships, including one of 400 tons. He had not won a great victory, because the resistance had been no more than patchy; but he had inflicted an humiliation on the viceroy of New Spain, who had proved quite unable to defend his territory, and left the wretched inhabitants with no more than ruins to pick over. Drake's reputation probably benefited more than his pocket from this exploit. *El Draque* was not only believed to be a fearsome pirate, but to have agents and servants all over the Spanish Main to assist in timing and directing his attacks. In fact he seems to have gained most of his intelligence from runaway slaves and other disaffected individuals on an *ad hoc* basis, as strenuous Spanish searches for his network of agents produced very little result.[66]

On 9 February 1586 he reached Cartagena on the mainland, smaller than Santo Domingo, but more important and better defended. Here there was serious fighting, described in detail by a member of the English force:

> God fought for us, for our ships could not come near the town for lack of water to batter it, and where our pinnaces should go in was but the length of two ships, and it was chained over from the castle, with sixteen pieces of ordnance [so that] we had not the length of a pike left us for passage to enter, and there were four hundred horsemen and footmen in arms and still bent against us. But God is all in all, by whose good help we made them fly into the town like sheep. We lost in this skirmish twenty-eight men besides those that were hurt, yet constrained the Spaniards to fly like sheep into the mountains.[67]

Drake, having captured the town, again became bogged down in lengthy ransom discussions lasting several weeks and again resulting in the systematic destruction of many buildings. He demanded 500,000 ducats; the bishop and governor offered 25,000. Eventually they settled on 107,000. In spite of his dramatic success, time was not on the Englishman's side. Far more than the twenty-eight men mentioned had died in the battle for Cartagena, and disease continued to take its toll. By the end of March he had only 850 men left, of whom 700 were fit for duty.[68] Inactivity took its toll of discipline also, and the officers continued to squabble among themselves. It was not until the middle of April that Drake finally left Cartagena. After some debate, he decided that they were not strong enough to attack Havana. Having taken on water at a particularly unpromising spot on the coast of Cuba, he sailed instead to St Augustin in Florida, where his fleet arrived on 27 May.[69] The incomplete and indefensible fort was abandoned at his approach, leaving weapons, tools and money behind. At almost no cost in time or effort, Drake collected about 6000 ducats, a lot of equipment and another small ship.

He remained only about two days at St Augustin, before sailing north to the fledgling English settlement at Roanoake. There he found the settlers in dire straits, thanks largely to their own incompetence. The governor, Ralph Lane, asked for assistance, and was promised tools, guns and a small ship.[70] Drake's arrival appears to have triggered a collapse of morale among the rank and file, and two days later they all sought passage back to England. Drake had no difficulty in finding room for them, and the settlement was abandoned. The augmented fleet returned to Plymouth on 28 July. Drake's first large-scale command had undoubtedly enhanced his reputation as a fighter and an inspirational leader. It had also exposed his limitations; particularly an inability to work with colleagues whom he did not find congenial, and his somewhat casual approach to the details of logistics. He was an apt leader for a straightforward fighting mission, but not so well suited to anything more complex. He had lost 750 men of the 1700 or so who had set out, and ended by paying his investors only fifteen shillings in the pound. On the other hand, he had inflicted incalculable damage on Spanish morale, particularly in the New World, devastated several important towns, and reduced the eventual cost to his mistress to about 25 per cent of her original outlay. As an act of war, it had been an unqualified success.[71]

Philip II thought so too. No sooner had the news of the sack of Cartagena reached him than he instructed his veteran commander, the marquis of Santa Cruz, to commence preparations for a massive counter-stroke against England itself. In the summer of 1586, as Hawkins patrolled the Channel and the western approaches, Santa Cruz began to put together a great fleet, which he intended to lead in the following year.[72] In December, Drake also began to plan a further voyage. His first thought seems to have been to support a bid by Dom Antonio for the Portuguese crown, a mission for which he attempted unsuccessfully to solicit aid from the Dutch. By March, however, it was clear that Santa Cruz's preparations were reaching a point

where his target for operations might be achieved, and Drake was immediately instructed to prepare a pre-emptive strike.[73] Like his raid on the
Carribbean, this was organised on a partnership basis. On 18 March he
signed a contract with a group of London merchants, whereby they would
supply a given number of ships (and pay the crews) in return for a half of
any proceeds.[74] The queen contributed four warships, fully manned and
victualled, and was to receive the other half of the plunder. Since the purpose
of this voyage was strictly military, and was known to be so, this contract
was not quite what it appeared; the merchants may have hoped, but could
hardly have expected, to recover their outlay. Drake sailed on 27 March,
and on 2 April an attempt was made to modify his instructions. This is
usually attributed to the queen's habitual second thoughts, but, since it
shifted the balance against a purely military operation and in favour of
plunder, it may well have been the merchants who were having second
thoughts and pressuring the privy council.[75] In any case, the modified
instructions never reached the fleet, which was already well on its way.

Drake's target was Cadiz, where he arrived on 19 April. There are many
accounts of the resulting action, which from a military point of view was
almost entirely successful. Surprise was complete; many of the ships in the
harbour were unmanned and unrigged. Apart from the shore batteries, the
main opposition was provided by a dozen or so armed galleys. Even in the
confined space of the harbour these were no match for the sailing warships,
and virtually everything afloat was looted, being either captured or destroyed.[76] The arrival of the duke of Medina Sidonia on the following day
with substantial reinforcements prevented any landing, but that had been
no more than a speculative objective anyway. The following day Drake left,
having destroyed about two dozen ships, and set back the Armada preparations so far that there was no prospect of it sailing in 1587. Taking
advantage of a temporary flat calm, the surviving galleys pursued him, but
it was an act of greater courage than wisdom. Even with the advantage of
mobility, they were beaten off with losses.

Having achieved his main objective, Drake then felt free to follow his
own instincts, as well as the spirit of the revised instructions that had never
reached him. He went in search of plunder. On about 6 May he captured
the village and castle of Sagres, on the coast of Portugal, and operated out
of that base for about three weeks, looking for prizes.[77] During this period
he quarrelled with one of his captains, William Borough, and when plague
began to stir on the ships, Borough's command, the *Golden Lion* abandoned
the voyage and returned to London. Unfortunately for Borough, Drake's
version of events arrived first and he was imprisoned to await the admiral's
return. Meanwhile Drake had sailed to the Azores, making what he realised

would have to be his last bid for a big prize. On 8 June he was fortunate enough to sight and capture the *San Felipe*, a large royal carrack inward bound from the East Indies with an immensely rich cargo. On 26 June he reached Plymouth with his prize.[78] According to contemporary Spanish estimates the damage inflicted at Cadiz amounted to some 172,000 ducats (£57,000), and the value of the *San Felipe* to 300,000 ducats (£100,000).[79] The latter is a speculative figure, for proper accounts were never rendered, but neither the London merchants nor the queen complained, and it is clear that Drake himself profited very substantially. His only failure was in securing a conviction against Borough, who had powerful friends as well as Burghley's support.

Drake's Cadiz voyage yielded valuable intelligence, in addition to a minor but significant victory and a large profit. 'I assure your honour', he had written to Walsingham while still at sea, 'the like preparations have never been heard of nor known as the King of Spain hath and daily maketh to invade England'.[80] He thought that an invasion force of 40,000 was intended, and was well within Philip's capability. England must look to its defences in every possible way. In fact, as we now know, he overestimated the threat. Philip's intentions were in deadly earnest, but his capability was less than Drake believed. Santa Cruz's original plan had indeed involved an army of 60,000, and about 800 ships, but long before the English raided Cadiz that plan had been abandoned as unrealistic.[81] Instead, the king intended to send an invasion force of some 18,000 men, carried in about 150 ships. This was intended to rendezvous with a second army, which would be assembled from troops already in the Low Countries under the command of the duke of Parma.

Had this worked, southern England would have been invaded by nearly 50,000 men, and Elizabeth would certainly have been defeated and deposed. It was, however, a defective plan in a number of ways. Thanks to his acquisition of Portugal, Philip now had a war fleet of some thirty large carracks, but only very antiquated and clumsy methods of recruiting the other 120 ships which would be needed.[82] They came from as far away as Ragusa and Naples, as well as from the Biscay coast; but they came very slowly, poorly manned and undersupplied. Nor did Spain have the capacity to produce enough guns for so large a fleet. The king's agents scoured Europe, ending up providing a huge diversity of artillery; enough in quantity, but of all shapes and sizes, many of them not suitable for use at sea.

The preparations advanced so slowly that many of the men originally recruited deserted, and the remainder consumed victuals faster than they could be provided. Santa Cruz was a great fighting captain, but a very poor administrator. With the additional problems caused by Drake, which put

back the sailing by many months, in December 1587 it looked as though
the whole enterprise would collapse under its own weight without a shot
being fired.[83] That did not happen because Santa Cruz died in February
1588, and the man whom Philip forced into his place, the duke of Medina
Sidonia, was his exact opposite: an uninspired and inexperienced commander at sea, but an excellent organiser. Thanks to his almost superhuman
efforts, by June 1588 the Armada was ready to sail. It had good ships,
enough guns, enough ammunition and enough provisions. Unfortunately
many of the men were raw conscripts; the soldiers were at daggers drawn
with the seamen; and much of the ammunition did not fit the guns. It
appeared nevertheless to be the most imposing war fleet that had ever put
to sea, and it cost Philip the bankrupting sum of 6,000,000 ducats
(£2,000,000).

Unfortunately, defects in the fleet were not the only problem. In the
Netherlands, Parma was obedient but unenthusiastic. He could muster
enough troops of good quality; but how was he to get them across the
Channel? The deep draft Armada ships could not get close enough to the
shore to protect his troop barges from the shallow draft Dutch warships,
which would surely blow them out of the water. Nor did he know how he
was going to rendezvous with the incoming fleet, since he did not command
a deep-water port large enough to receive it.[84] Philip knew all this, but
brushed it aside with lofty talk of doing God's work. Medina Sidonia had
no precise instructions for the rendezvous, only pious aspirations. In the
circumstances, it was very unlikely that the English would have to worry
about the duke of Parma.

That was just as well, because they had no force capable of withstanding
his veteran soldiers. Thanks to Drake's intelligence, and that from other
sources, in December 1587 Elizabeth's council realised that the Armada was
only delayed, not destroyed. They did not know of its acute logistical
problems, and began preparations for an attack in the summer of 1588.
Musters could not be held until the weather improved, but at least the
county trained bands had some arms and some discipline.

The first line of defence, however, would be at sea. The lord admiral,
Lord Howard of Effingham, was placed in supreme command, with all
England's experienced seamen serving under him as captains or vice-admirals
– Drake, Hawkins, Frobisher and Winter.[85] There was much debate about
how the fleet should be deployed, and what strategy should be adopted, but
the mobilisation was relatively rapid and efficient. The queen had about
forty ships of her own, the royal navy proper, the City of London armed
and fitted out another thirty; and between sixty and seventy other fighting
ships of various sizes were contributed by other port towns, by merchant

groups and by private individuals.[86] This was a national emergency, and the degree of cooperation achieved was almost unique.

Drake was insistent that there could not be too many ships to meet so great an attack:

> Touching my poor opinion how strong your Majesties fleet should be, to en-counter this great force of the enemy, God increase your most Excellent Majesties forces both by sea and land dayly for this I surely think; there was never any force as there is now ready or making readye agaynst your Majesty and trew religion.[87]

Significantly, on several occasions Drake wrote directly to the queen, rather than to Burghley or Walsingham, knowing that, in a crisis of this kind, final decisions could only come from her. He also pressed for a pre-emptive strike, believing that the Armada should be first encountered on its own coast. By the middle of May, Elizabeth had made up her mind, and her decision did not correspond with any of the advice that she had received. Drake was to be vice-admiral under Howard; the main fleet was to assemble at Plymouth; and a Channel Guard of forty ships under Lord Henry Seymour was to remain to protect the Kent and Sussex coasts.[88] Once assembled at Plymouth the main fleet was to follow Drake's strategic advice and proceed straight to Spain.

Contrary to what many had expected, Drake and Howard collaborated amicably and effectively, and their counter armada set out on 30 May. A week later, it was back in Plymouth, frustrated and buffeted by gales, but having learned that Medina Sidonia had left Lisbon a few days before. Twice more, on 19 and 24 June, Howard set out to encounter the Armada, both times being driven back by the weather. The same conditions had forced the Spaniards to take refuge in La Coruña, and had damaged several ships; but after hasty repairs they took advantage of a change of wind direction, and arrived off the Lizard on 19 July (which was 29 July by the Spanish reckoning).[89]

Medina Sidonia's instructions were to hold his close formation, and to proceed straight to his rendezvous with Parma, not seeking battle and not attempting to land on the English coast. These orders he followed to the letter, in the process throwing away any possible chance of success. The discipline of his fleet was excellent. Apart from one or two inadvertent stragglers, it suffered almost no damage from the persistent English attacks. When the vagaries of the wind gave him the opportunity to land a force on the Isle of Wight, however, he did not take it, but allowed himself to be shepherded back into mid-Channel.[90] Worse still, his attempts to com-municate with Parma were intercepted or failed for other reasons; and when he reached Calais on 28 July (English reckoning), he discovered that the duke would not be ready until 2 August. Calais was an open roadstead, an impossible place to remain for six days with a hostile fleet waiting to attack. The next night the English sent in fireships, breaking up the Spanish formation and scattering all but the admiral's own squadron.[91] The Spanish plan had broken at its weakest point.

The battle of Gravelines that followed was a one-sided affair. The English had the weather gauge, driving the Armada towards the Flanders banks. The Spanish ships were crowded with soldiers who could not get to grips with their elusive opponents, and the deficiencies of their sea gunnery were ruthlessly exposed. Medina Sidonia managed to recover part of his formation, saving his fleet from an even worse mauling. Sir William Winter described the action the following day:

> His Lordship [Howard] with such as were with him, did bear after the Spanish fleet, the wind being at South South West, and the Spanish fleet bearing away North North East, making into the depth of the channel; and about nine on the clock in the morning we set near unto them, being then athwart of Gravelines. The fight continued from nine of the clock until six of the clock at night, in the which time the Spanish army bear away North North East and North by East, as much as they could keeping company together, I assure your honour in very good order. Great was the spoil and harm that was done to them, no doubt. I deliver unto your honour, on the credit of a poor gentleman, that out of my ship was shot 500 shot of demi-cannon, culverin and demi-culverin.[92]

Eventually the wind changed, and the Armada moved out into the North Sea, with the English, now very short of ammunition, following. At first it was thought that they would head for Norway to regroup, but Medina Sidonia, realising how severely his ships had suffered, was bent only on escape. Once he was past the Firth of Forth, the English gave up the chase. Very few ships had actually been sunk, but many were barely seaworthy, and the casualties from the one-sided cannonade had been appalling.[93]

Ironically, the English crews were not in much better shape. Battle casualties had been light, and for once victualling deficiencies were not to blame; but plague had broken out, and an immediate return to harbour was imperative. The admiralty, which had coped reasonably well with mobilisation, and even with the supplementary supplies of victuals and ammunition, was quite unprepared for this disaster. Finance was always on a hand to mouth basis, and the fleet had not been expected to return to port for several weeks. Instead, ships were landing hundreds of sick and dying seamen all the way down the east coast. Howard wrote to Burghley on 10 August:

> My good Lord: Sickness and mortality begins wonderfully to grow amongst us; and it is a most pitiful sight to see, here at Margate, how the men, having no place to receive them into here, die in the streets. I am driven myself, of force, to come a-land, to see them bestowed in some lodging; and the best I can get is barns and such outhouses; and the relief is small that I can provide for them here. It would grieve any man's heart to see them that have served so valiantly, to die so miserably.[94]

To their credit, Howard and his fellow captains did what they could with their own resources, but it was usually too little, too late. Was the council really as callous and indifferent as it was made to appear? The problem was probably not so much carelessness as an inability to get resources (particularly money) in adequate quantities to where it was needed. Burghley knew as well as Howard that, humanitarian feelings aside, these men were a valuable asset which the country could not afford to lose. There was also the technical problem that many of the ships had been provided at private expense, and the direct reponsibility for paying and caring for the men lay with the owners rather than the crown; the council would have expected to reimburse the owners later for their outlay in the service of the state, but not to have been the first resort. Ideas of public responsibility had not been adjusted so far.

Did Elizabeth herself either know or care what had befallen? On the day before Howard wrote his heartfelt plea, when the danger was already over, she appeared in front of the army assembled at Tilbury and made, or is alleged to have made, a stirring and famous speech:

> I am come among you at this time but for for my recreation and pleasure, being resolved in the midst and heat of the battle to live and die amongst you all, to lay down for my God and for my kingdom and for my people mine honour and my blood even in the dust. I know I have the body but of a weak and feeble woman, but I have the heart and stomach of a king, and of a king of England too.[95]

Whether she used these words, we do not know, although they have an authentic, theatrical ring; nor do we know whether she had been informed that there was no longer any danger from Parma – or from Medina Sidonia.[96] Had her fleet entered the Thames in triumph, she would no doubt have been there to milk the applause; but as it is we have only traditional accounts of her joy and relief, and it is not clear just when they were uttered.

What we know of official reactions to the victory reflect no credit on either Burghley or the queen, both of whom seem to have been calculating that the more the men died the fewer there would be to pay; although by tradition every mariner should have been paid for his voyage, whether he died on it or not.[97] Howard pleaded in vain for consideration for his men, pointing out with justice that the government's failure in this respect would make it even harder to recruit men when they were needed again. Before the end of August, while the camp at Tilbury was being run down, the queen wrote to her cousin of Scotland how the Spaniards

> by God's singular favour, having their fleet well beaten in our narrow seas and pressing with all violence to achieve some watering place to continue their pretended invasion, the winds have carried them to your coasts, where I doubt not they shall receive small succour and less welcome.[98]

This was hardly a triumphalist reaction, but on the other hand there was no hint of an awareness of the cost of victory. Perhaps it was a consequence of putting the whole responsibility on God. 'Afflavit Deus et dissipati sunt' (God blew and they were scattered), the inscription on the commemorative medal, left little room for other gratitude.

An immediate counter-stroke was out of the question, as neither the men nor the ships were in any fit state for further service. Such a stroke was under consideration, however, almost before the Armada had disappeared over the horizon, and on 11 October a commission was issued to Sir Francis Drake and Sir John Norris to raise four thousand men and an appropriate number of ships, but without specifying the intended mission.[99] By the end of October the projected number had risen to ten thousand, a subscription list in London had resulted in pledges of £25,000, and the exchequer had actually delivered £20,000 to the adventurers;[100] all of which casts an interesting light on the parsimonious treatment of the Armada survivors. By the end of November it was generally understood that the objective would be to set the pretender Dom Antonio, who claimed that the country was seething with discontent under the Spanish yoke and wanting only such encouragement to rise, on the Portuguese throne. His lavish promises of rewards and commercial privileges no doubt help to explain the size and composition of the subscription list. By the end of December the estates general of the Low Countries had reluctantly agreed that six hundred horse and two thousand foot could be withdrawn from their own service for the enterprise.[101] On the 22nd Elizabeth wrote personally to Peregrine Bertie, Lord Willoughby, to thank him for his efforts in securing this concession; and it appears that she had been actively involved in the planning from the first. As mobilisation proceeded, however, in early 1589, difficulties began to mount. The money already available was quickly spent, and the estates general turned difficult. Better news was that the emperor of Morocco was offering his active support, to the tune of 150,000 ducats, although that would not be available until the expedition actually appeared.[102]

On 23 February 1589, Drake and Norris were issued with their instructions, from which it is immediately apparent that the queen's own thinking differed substantially from what was popularly supposed.

> Forasmuch as the chief and principal end of the setting forth of our army under your charge tendeth chiefly to two purposes, the one to distress the King of Spain's ships, the other to get possession of some of the Islands of Azores thereby to intercept the treasure that doth yearly pass that way.[103]

They were only to proceed to Lisbon if they were fully satisfied by independent enquiry that Dom Antonio really had a large following ready to act in his interest.

By the time that the expedition sailed at the beginning of April, there had been further financial difficulties, further negotiations with Morocco, and deep disagreement (or confusion) over the instructions. The trouble was that the queen's orders were purely strategic, but the voyage was more than half funded by private investors looking for a profit. There was no profit to be gained from destroying the remains of the Armada in the Biscay ports, and not much in the short term from seizing an island in the Azores. But much was hoped for from Dom Antonio, not least the support of Morocco.

Perhaps yielding to pressure, or perhaps following their own instincts, Drake and Norris ignored Elizabeth's orders, made no attempt to destroy the royal ships being repaired in Santander, Gujon and San Sebastian, and sailed instead to La Coruña, where there was reported to be a rich merchant fleet.[104] There was no merchant fleet. They took the town, but found little of value and the citadel held out against them. So far, they had spent time, effort and lives to no purpose. In view of which it was very unwise of the commanders to write to the queen in mid May asking for more men and money. On 20 May Elizabeth drafted a sharp rebuke, recalling them to their orders. 'We find that contrary thereunto ye have left two of the chiefest places where the said king's ships lay and passed to the Groyne [La Coruña] a place of least hurt to be done to the enemy.'[105]

It may be that this reproach never reached them, for at the end of May, having wasted their resources, and suffered a number of losses by desertion, they abandoned La Coruña and proceeded to Lisbon, thus ignoring the second part of their instructions. It quickly transpired that Antonio's claims were a fantasy; scarcely anyone joined the invasion force, which was not strong enough to take Lisbon unaided. On 2 June Anthony Ashley wrote to Walsingham, 'not above two hundred Portingals have repaired unto him'.[106] Without local support, and with no reinforcements from England, the commanders had no option but to retreat. As Ashley pointed out 'the landing at the Groyne is judged to have been the special hindrance of good success'. Disease and unfamiliar diet were as usual wreaking havoc with the English force, and there could be no question of going to the Azores. At the end of June the remnant limped home to face an enraged queen and a bitter inquisition.

At first it seems that both Elizabeth and the council were misinformed about the extent of the débâcle. Letters were drafted commending the good service of the commanders, and concern focused on the disposal of some captured cargoes.[107] It was not until October that the evidence of dereliction of duty became too strong to ignore, and the storm duly broke. It appears to have been the queen herself who insisted upon calling Norris and Drake to account. On 23 October they were called before the council to answer five specific charges of having ignored their instructions, each of which was fully justified.[108] They excused themselves as best they could, but did not plead the real reason for the failure, which was the dependence of an essentially military operation upon private and commercial investment. This was the queen's preferred way of waging war; indeed it could be argued that, in her financial circumstances, it was the only possible way of waging war. On this occasion it did not work, but Elizabeth was not inclined to blame herself for her choice of options.

Norris and Drake were more than scapegoats; they were actually guilty as charged. Norris eventually recovered favour, and was to lead campaigns in France and Ireland, but Lisbon was effectively the end of Drake's career. In 1590 Philip II was still struggling to come to terms with the failure of the Armada; he made no scapegoats, but reflected bitterly on the sins which could have caused God to punish him so grievously. In England the sense of euphoria was short-lived; the danger had not gone away, and the cost of victory had been high. But England, unlike Spain, became increasingly convinced of God's favour.

In the Netherlands also there was the beginning of returning confidence, because the failure of the Armada had been almost as much a victory for the Dutch as for the English. In France the desperate measures of Henry III against the Catholic League finally resulted in his own assassination in 1589, and the accession of the Huguenot Henry IV.[109] As a result, the country became divided in a new way. Protestants and moderate royalists accepted Henry, but most Catholics recognised the League candidate, Charles X, who was also backed by Spain. Elizabeth, inevitably, supported Henry, loaning him £20,000 in September 1589, and sending four thousand men to support him at the battle of Ivry in March 1590.[110] This drew the duke of Parma down from the Netherlands to break the siege of Paris, and led to the arrival of three thousand Spaniards at Blavet in Brittany under the command of Don Juan d'Aguila. Both England and Spain were fighting limited campaigns on someone else's soil, because neither had the means to deliver a knock out blow against the other.

Meanwhile, death continued to take its toll of Elizabeth's servants, and their replacements tended to lack the quality of the older generation. Thomas Radcliffe, earl of Sussex, died in June 1583, Sir Walter Mildmay in 1589, Sir Francis Walsingham and Ambrose Dudley, earl of Warwick, in 1590.[111] Most important to the queen herself, Robert Dudley, earl of Leicester, died in September 1588, leaving a gap in her life that could never be adequately filled.[112] Badly as she had treated him at the end of his last mission, their personal relationship had suffered no lasting damage. By 1592 only the aged Burghley remained of those who had shared her hopes in 1558, and the even more aged John Ashley, whom she can have seen but seldom. John Whitgift may have been an improvement at Canterbury, but Sir Thomas Bromley was a mediocre chancellor after the capable Nicholas Bacon, and Sir Christopher Hatton, who replaced him in 1587, died in his turn in 1591. Walsingham was not replaced as secretary until 1596, and the council dwindled in size to not much more than a dozen.[113]

11

The Earl of Essex

Elizabeth's domestic circle was a world into which men very seldom intruded. There were only two fully salaried gentlemen of the privy chamber in the whole reign; one of these was Christopher Hatton, who accompanied the position with many others; the other was John Ashley who confined himself to his duties as master of the Jewel House after his wife's death.[1] At any given time there were about six grooms – young aristocrats who ran messages and performed other relatively menial tasks. There were also a number of extraordinary gentlemen, unsalaried, who were called into attendance on special occasions.[2] It was, however, an overwhelmingly female world, and one that aged steadily with the queen. There was a steady turnover through natural mortality, but only twenty-eight women served in the privy chamber (whose normal working strength was between twelve and sixteen) throughout the forty-five year reign. Frances, Lady Cobham, Elizabeth, Lady Carew and Katherine, countess of Nottingham, all of whom died between 1595 and 1603, achieved an average service of forty years.[3] These women were Elizabeth's true *familia*. They were mostly drawn from a handful of families with kinship connections or generations of court service: Howard, Carey, Radcliffe, Stafford, Brooke and Knollys. Their loyalty was complete. There were extraordinary ladies, as there were extraordinary gentlemen, but it was with this salaried core that the queen sought refuge from the pressing and masculine world of politics. The privy chamber was not immune from political pressures, and there were ladies who favoured each of the leading courtiers – Cecil, Dudley, Radcliffe, Devereux and Ralegh – but their partisanship was low key and discreet.[4] They might prompt their mistress to favour a petitioner for some minor favour or piece of patronage; but their job was to protect Elizabeth from such pressures, when she wished to be protected, and to have allowed serious politics into the privy chamber would have been a betrayal of trust.

This stability is often attributed to Elizabeth's sheer conservatism, her unwillingness to envisage change; just as her frequent hostility to her ladies' marriage plans is ascribed to sexual jealousy and frustration. In fact both were self-protective. The world changed constantly, throwing up new and unexpected challenges that had to be confronted. Men came and went, constantly pressing her for decisions, plans, favours and promotions. She was continually on stage and, although there is every reason to suppose that she relished this most of the time, there were times when she needed to retreat, and her *familia* provided the refuge. She may sometimes have been jealous when her ladies married, but the real reason for her outbursts of bad temper was that these marriages represented a male intrusion into her otherwise secluded world. Her closest servants and friends were now proposing to share their love between her and the men who had a lawful claim upon it. In fact these potential discordances seem to have caused few problems, but Elizabeth needed to be soothed and reassured. Throughout her life, she was perfectly prepared to play the games of courtly love, but always for the purpose of gaining, or retaining, control over her 'suitors'.[5] Her relationship with Robert Dudley had been, at least for a time, a passionate one; but she had always been able, both as a woman and as the queen, to dictate how far it went. Marriage would have meant the surrender of at least some of that power, and that may have been what she meant when she professed in an unguarded moment that she hated the whole idea.

Her relationship with the earl of Essex has to be seen in a similar light, although she never contemplated marrying him. Robert Devereux had been born in 1566, the son of Walter Devereux, Viscount Hereford, who was created earl of Essex in 1572. Walter had married in 1561 Lettice, the beautiful and wayward daughter of Sir Francis Knollys. He dabbled heavily and unfortunately in Irish plantations and, when he died at the age of thirty-three in 1576, he had left an estate encumbered with debts of over £20,000.[6] Young Robert's wardship was taken over by Lord Burghley, who provided him with an excellent education in the modern humanist mode, and sent him to Trinity College, Cambridge, at the precocious age of twelve. Unlike many noble undergraduates, the young earl actually proceeded to a degree, receiving an M.A. in 1582.[7]

He was undoubtedly highly intelligent and articulate, and it was probably his aptitude for uninhibited intellectual conversation that was one of his main attractions for Elizabeth. Unfortunately, he appears to have inherited his temperament as well as his looks from his mother, and his brilliant qualities were vitiated by a total lack of self-discipline and common sense. Unfortunately also, Lettice earned the queen's undying hatred by capturing as her second husband none other than the earl of Leicester. She seems to have had little or no say in her son's upbringing, and it may well have been Burghley rather than Leicester who brought the boy to court for the first time in 1584, when he was a little short of his eighteenth birthday.[8] He was an immediate success. Not only was he very handsome, he also had excellent manners, and a fresh energy and ingenuousness which appealed to the queen. At first he was very much his stepfather's protégé, a kind of surrogate son, and Leicester may have seen him as his heir. In 1585 he accompanied the earl to the Low Countries, and raised a band of his own retainers (which he could not afford) to serve under him. He accomplished very little in military terms, and his behaviour verged on the irresponsible, but he did show personal bravery in some small-scale actions.[9] This gave Leicester sufficient excuse to knight him, and he also seems to have won the friendship of Sir Philip Sidney, inheriting his sword when the latter was killed in action.[10] He returned to England in November 1586, but had not been in a sufficiently responsible position to share the disfavour which his stepfather suffered.

By the spring of 1587 he was clearly Elizabeth's new favourite. He spent a great deal of time in her company: 'when she is abroad, nobody [is] near her but my Lord of Essex; and at night my Lord is at cards, or one game or another with her [so] that he cometh not to his own lodging till the birds sing in the morning'.[11] Essex was in demand, but he could not afford to be relaxed about this success. He was not her only favourite, although he seems to have had the upper hand at this point. Sir Walter Ralegh was always in the background, should he make a mistake. He also needed urgently to turn his favour into tangible gain, because his debts were already pressing, and had been made worse by his escapade in the Netherlands. Leicester had become lord steward of the household in 1584, and for some time the mastership of the horse was vacant. This was the office which Essex coveted. Not only was it worth £1500 a year, it was also a position of high honour, with guaranteed access to the sovereign. In the summer of 1587 he may not have stood in need of much help in the latter respect, but the office would be useful if the wind should change. On 18 June the desired promotion was granted to him; when Leicester died in September of the following year, it must have seemed as though he had been born again in the person of his twenty-two-year-old stepson.[12]

In truth Essex was a deeply flawed character, lacking the substance that Robert Dudley had had, even as a young man. He was both proud and vain: proud of his ancient lineage and vain of his talents. He accepted his success with the queen as a kind of birthright, and believed that he had the capacity to be a great soldier and statesman. He was also a slave to passionate emotions that he could neither control nor conceal.[13] He made all the mistakes which an impulsive young man could be expected to make, but never learned from them; always choosing to regard the adverse reactions which he evoked as evidence of a deep-laid personal conspiracy against him. In March 1587 he made the extraordinary mistake of writing to King James on behalf of William Davison, the unfortunate secretary whom Elizabeth had chosen to make a scapegoat for the execution of Mary Queen of Scots, and in July he quarrelled openly with Elizabeth herself.[14] He must have known that the queen could not stand his mother, but he took umbrage at some disparaging remarks that were made while the court was on progress, and then compounded his error by trying to blame Ralegh for turning Elizabeth against Lettice. The queen enjoyed tormenting her courtiers in this fashion, but Essex stormed out of the house, declaring that his affections were 'so much thrown down', and that he intended to sail straight to Flanders.[15] Fortunately for him, Elizabeth chose to regard this as an amusing tantrum, and contented herself by peremptorily summoning him back to court.

On this occasion, all was well; but Essex seems to have had no awareness of the fact that he had had a narrow escape, and that his mistress's favour could not be presumed upon in such a fashion. So much was this so that he repeated the mistake in the following year, although in different circumstances. Knowing that Norris and Drake were commissioned to 'go upon' the king of Spain, and realising that this was intended at least as much as a plundering venture as an act of war, he decided (without apparently consulting anyone) that he would join the expedition.[16] On 1 April he wrote to Knollys:

> What my state is now, I will tell you. My revenue no greater than it was when I sued my livery; my debts at the least two or three and twenty thousand pounds. Her Majesty's goodness hath been so great as I could not ask more of her. No way left to repair myself but mine own adventure.[17]

A few days later Norris and Drake were notified that Essex had left the court without licence, and that it was the queen's pleasure that he should return immediately. Unfortunately, he could not be found, and it was feared that he was already at sea in the *Swiftsure* – one of the queen's ships.[18] After a panic lasting several days, he was located and ignominiously returned to London.

Incredible as it may seem, he had apparently intended to carve an independent command for himself out of the forces which Norris and Drake were assembling, and to operate on his own behalf without reference to them.[19] Such an ambition almost beggars belief, but it may have sprung as much from the freebooting atmosphere of such expeditions as from his own lack of judgement. For all his intelligence, charm and courage, he had a boy's head, stuffed full of dreams of adventure, plunder and derring-do. In the circumstances, this was a dangerous combination; but again his charm and skills as a courtier averted the wrath that might have been expected. If Elizabeth could see the warning lights that were now flashing, she paid no heed to them. In 1590, after he had returned to pleading his

financial cause, she granted him his stepfather's monopoly for the import-
ation of sweet wines, which unheroic operation brought an income of £2500
a year and transformed his circumstances.[20]

Burghley had seen such favourites come and go, and so far he had not
taken this pretty youth very seriously. The manner of Essex's proceeding
so far suggested that he might destroy himself at any moment. By 1590
Burghley was an old man, become somewhat saturnine and suspicious, but
unrivalled in experience and in the queen's confidence. The tentacles of his
influence were everywhere; in the court, the council, and even the privy
chamber. He knew well enough, however, that he did not have, and never
had had, a monopoly of counsel. The queen would please herself. So when
Sir Francis Walsingham died in April 1590, and Burghley advised his immediate replacement, his advice was ignored.[21] The main reason for this
appears to have been that the only plausible candidate was Burghley's own
son, Robert Cecil; and for the time being at least Elizabeth did not want
it to appear that the lord treasurer could place her ministers to suit himself.

Burghley drew up a scheme for sharing out the work among the existing
members of the privy council, but ended up doing most of it himself. Or,
at least, that was the official situation. Unofficially Robert Cecil did most
of it, and rapidly became an indispensable agent, although one employed
by his father and not the crown.[22] It may, or may not, have been a factor
that Essex was pressing for the reinstatement of William Davison.[23] The
earl's influence in government could not touch that of the lord treasurer;
but his rescue from debt and his continued success – indeed his charmed
life – at court made him a man with an ambitious following. Robert
Cecil was appointed to the privy council in 1591, in what was probably a
compromise arrangement; and Sir John Puckering on his appointment as
lord keeper in 1592.[24] Puckering was a Cecil ally, if not exactly a client, so
the treasurer was probably satisfied that his grip upon public affairs was
unshaken.

There was a war going on, however, and although the council remained
overwhelmingly civilian, the advice of military men could not be ignored;
and it was as a military man that the earl of Essex saw himself. By the end
of 1590, as the situation in the Low Countries became somewhat easier,
that in France became both more pressing and complex. Elizabeth had a
clear interest in supporting Henry IV, but either could not or would not
understand the difficulties of the situation that he faced in conflict with the
Catholic League.[25] At the same time, while he pressed the queen for further
aid, Henry could not afford to make too many concessions to English
interests for fear of upsetting his own subjects. Early in 1591 Elizabeth
committed a small force under Sir John Norris to Brittany, where it enjoyed

a moderate success. When it was doing well, the queen tended to leave it to its own devices; when it was in danger of collapse she would send modest reinforcements – and even some money. John Norris did extremely well in such circumstances to maintain a holding operation, until the arrival of Spanish forces at Blavet forced Elizabeth to give his efforts a higher priority.[26] The other theatre of operations was Normandy, and again the queen began to filter in small forces in the spring of 1591, establishing a presence but satisfying neither Henry nor her own officers.

It was this campaign which Essex identified as his big opportunity. After a lot of hard pleading, in June 1591 he was appointed general of the queen's armies in France.[27] He landed in Normandy in August with about seven thousand men, by far the largest commitment that Elizabeth had so far made. Presumably his commission should have included Brittany, but Essex wisely refrained from trying to give orders to the experienced and hard-pressed Norris. His energies were concentrated upon the seige of Rouen, and in frantic diplomatic efforts to persuade Henry IV to give Normandy a higher strategic priority.[28] Essex was not without experienced officers, but his own amateurism was swiftly and painfully exposed. He visited Henry, on the latter's invitation but without the queen's authority, and nearly got caught in a Leaguer ambush on the way back. Although he established a good *rapport* with the king, Elizabeth was deeply displeased by this exercise of initiative.[29] The earl had made the mistake of taking seriously a campaign which was intended mainly as a gesture. When the queen in high dudgeon ordered him and most of his forces home in September, his anguished protests were supported by Leighton and Killigrew, his seasoned advisers, who agreed that such an action would destroy every prospect of success in Normandy and make the capture of Rouen an impossibility.[30]

Elizabeth's rage, however, was occasioned less by what Essex had done, or failed to do, than by the fact that he had acted without permission, like Leicester in the Low Countries. Imperfectly informed, she also appears to have thought that, like Leicester, he had overcommitted her by following his own agenda. Wiser councils prevailed. Within a week of arrival back in England, Essex was again on his way to France, his relations with his mistress once more repaired. The campaign that followed was a failure; less because of defeat than because no opportunity for victory ever presented itself. Foul weather, disease and desertion reduced Essex's command to no more than fifteen hundred effectives. Henry was constantly diverted, and Elizabeth refused to commit more men or money until the king arrived to campaign in Normandy in person.[31] The earl, characteristically, believed that he was being deliberately exposed to failure and ridicule by his enemies at home: 'I was blamed as negligent, undutiful, rash in going, slow in returning, undiscreet in dividing the horse from the foot, faulty in all things because I was not fortunate to please.'[32]

Essex had made the mistake of expecting his command to be a high-profile campaign – a chance for glory – which it might have been if Henry IV had played his cards differently. As it was, it turned into a grinding and demoralising holding operation in very adverse circumstances. That is, however, the nature of real warfare, and it was a reflection of Essex's limitations that he was unable to see that, seeking rather a scapegoat for his lack of success. In January 1592 he was recalled, leaving the remains of his army under the command of Roger Williams, a seasoned professional with no illusions. Elizabeth was displeased, not so much by his failure, which had its compensations in her eyes in that it made him more than ever dependent upon her favour, as by the fact that he had dubbed twenty-four knights, more than she had herself done in a decade. Although as a commander in the field he was perfectly entitled to take such action, in a campaign that had been by any standards a miserable failure, this was excessive.[33] She rightly suspected that he was trying to buy himself supporters among the second-rank military men.

By October he had wheedled and flattered his way back into grace, but it was an open question how long he could continue these violent ups and downs. The answer was made more urgent by the fact that Burghley was beginning at last to take him seriously. Debt no longer made Essex vulnerable, and when Sir Walter Ralegh disgraced himself and ended up in prison for getting one of the queen's maids with child in the summer of 1592, he was without a serious rival at court.[34] It was only a matter of time before he turned his ambitions to affairs of state. He probably did not covet either the secretaryship or the lord chancellorship for himself, but he now had talented and ambitious clients, like the Bacon brothers, and his continued credit would depend upon his ability to place them. The treasurer's own position was not at risk, but the career of his son could be very adversely affected if rising political talent began to look to Essex rather than Cecil for patronage.[35] As if to confirm the reality of this threat, the earl himself was admitted to the privy council on 25 February 1593.

If in a sense Essex had now arrived, it was less clear what he had arrived at. He had no office, and no access to the official intelligence operations, which were firmly in the hands of the Cecils. This sense of exclusion, combined with the fact that his own followers bombarded him with good advice about how to overcome his personal defects and consolidate his position, preyed on the earl's mind.[36] He set up his own alternative intelligence network, run by Anthony Bacon. In order to demonstrate its effectiveness, he brought about the trial and execution of Dr Rodrigo Lopez in February 1594. Lopez, a Portuguese Jew who had sought refuge in England in 1559, was a talented physician frequently consulted by Elizabeth herself. Towards the end of 1593 Essex claimed to have evidence that Lopez was conspiring to poison the queen. She did not believe him, dismissing the charges as malicious fabrications (which they almost certainly were).[37] After sulking furiously at the rebuff, Essex flung himself into a hectic round of interrogations, and came up with enough of a case to get the unfortunate doctor and two associates convicted of high treason. As this was due process of law, Elizabeth did not interfere; nor, in spite of her doubts, did she grant Lopez a pardon. Whether there was any substance in the charges remains a matter of controversy, but it seems clear that the real purpose of the whole tragedy was to demonstrate the earl's solicitous care for his sovereign's safety and the incompetence of the official network run by his rivals.[38]

This was a success of a kind, but it was an isolated example. Try as he might, Essex was unable to secure the promotion of his clients, or to turn on the golden tap for anyone except himself. This was partly because he did not choose very promising clients. Having failed with William Davison, he tried to secure the secretaryship for Thomas Bodley. Bodley was worthy but undistinguished, and the queen was not at all inclined to appoint him; not least because the earl was foolish enough to let it appear that his main purpose was to exclude Robert Cecil.[39] Francis Bacon, for whom Essex tried in vain to secure the office of attorney general, was a similar case. Undoubtedly very able, he had become a man marked for disfavour by speaking strongly against the 1593 Subsidy Bill in the House of Commons. The queen regarded him as a brash young troublemaker; but that did not deter Essex from staking his credit on securing his promotion.[40] By 1595 Essex was becoming paranoid. Completely unable to see any weaknesses in himself, he attributed all his failures and frustrations to the Machiavellian scheming of the Cecils. When Robert expressed straight-faced surprise that he should seek to push so flawed a candidate as Bacon for the attorneyship, Essex stormed: 'the attorneyship for Francis is that I must have; and in that I will spend all my power, might, authority and amity, and with tooth and nail defend and procure the same against whom soever'.[41]

Unfortunately for him it was the queen, not the lord treasurer, who had to be moved, and on this point she would not budge. Essex was quite unable to comprehend why his mistress, who continued to be forgiving and generous towards himself, so consistently ignored his clients. He either could not or would not grasp the fact that she enjoyed keeping him on the leading string of her favour, and had no intention of allowing him to become a power in his own right.

Nevertheless, in 1596 he enjoyed one of the things that he coveted most, military success. Early in April the Spanish army in the Netherlands, which had been losing ground since the death of Parma in 1593, suddenly turned its attention south and seized the port of Calais.[42] This dramatic setback focused the minds of the queen's advisers on a counter-stroke. An expedition of some kind had been under discussion for months, but neither its objective nor its command structure had been decided. Drake and Hawkins had both died on a fruitless voyage to the Caribbean in the previous year, so it was now decided that the lord admiral himself should command the fleet.[43] In a secret meeting at court on 11 April it was also decided that Cadiz should be the objective, and that Essex should command the land forces. Inevitably Elizabeth changed her mind, or appeared to change her mind, several times before these decisions were finalised, so in the end there was need for haste.[44] The complex comings and goings involved in assembling a force of this size (over a hundred ships and some twenty thousand men), to say nothing of rendezvousing with the Dutch ships which were to form part of the expedition, are well recorded and show a high degree of professional efficiency.

On 1 June the fleet set sail, and on the following day Essex and Howard issued rendezvous instructions to their captains, in the event of the fleet being separated by bad weather. No such misfortune occurred, and on 20 June the fleet reached its target, which was inadequately defended and taken completely unawares. Apart from having to restrain the impetuous Essex, who wanted to take his ship straight into action, Howard's assault plans worked almost perfectly. Over several days of fighting, detailed descriptions of which survive, four of the largest galleons in Philip II's navy were burned or captured; over thirty merchant ships were destroyed; and the city of Cadiz was captured and sacked.[45] Both Ralegh and Essex were able to display their fighting qualities to best advantage; Ralegh by defying the harbour batteries, and Essex by scaling the walls of Cadiz at the head of his men. The city was held to ransom, as though it had been some minor Caribbean colony, and the damage to Spanish pride was incalculable. Not everyone was satisfied. The cargoes of the merchant ships were destroyed rather than captured, a potential loss of about ten million ducats; and Essex was over-ruled in council when he argued that the city should be held and fortified for the queen.[46]

Augusto Nani, the Venetian envoy in Spain, gave a dispassionate account of the operation in a despatch of 15 July.

> After the slaughter of those who opposed their landing and entry into Cadiz, the English have behaved in accordance with the customs of war. No one has been

put to death, except the governor of the castle, whose head was cut off because he would not yield at once; and three hundred soldiers of the garrison, who surrendered on terms, were set at liberty. Although the English sacked the city, they have not prophaned the churches, or permitted any violence upon women; and so, to the general surprise, they have won great commendation.[47]

To add insult to injury, not only was this Anglo-Dutch campaign carried out in a good spirit of cooperation, but the victors behaved like gentlemen, instead of heretical barbarians. On 7 July, the fleet withdrew; not this time to go plundering to the Azores, but to carry their laurels home. This was undoubtedly the right decision, because the Spaniards were belatedly mustering a formidable army in Andalusia to retake the city; and neither the English nor the Dutch could afford to commit further and larger forces to its defence. Nani's informant was right when he said that the English had a much greater ability to seize strong places than to hold on to them, and it was to Howard's credit that he refused to be carried away by the euphoria of victory, or the passionate advocacy of his fellow commander.[48]

The capture of Cadiz was probably the most successful feat of English arms of the entire war, and it is ironic that one of its principal architects should have returned home even more disgruntled and dissatisfied than he had set out. Essex felt that his contribution had been slighted by Howard, and his failure to carry the council of war with him rankled. However, it was the queen's own pusillanimous reaction which really annoyed him. The expedition had failed to cover its costs – which was not surprising as it had not been set up on a joint-stock basis – and Elizabeth was particularly annoyed that the merchant cargoes had not been recovered.[49] Instead of returning covered in glory to rapturous applause, the earl found himself subjected to a financial inquisition. Worse still, this inquisition was conducted on the queen's behalf by Sir Robert Cecil, who had been appointed to the long vacant secretaryship during his absence. 'I was more braved by your little cousin', he wrote to Anthony Bacon, 'than ever I was by any man in my life.'[50]

Essex took comfort in the familiar theory of Cecil conspiracy, and convinced himself that these plots were actually making him more agreeable to Elizabeth. But this time he seems to have been deceiving himself. Only the queen herself could have gone so far as to consider depriving him of the income from ransoms to which the law of arms entitled him.[51] It was not done, but it was a symptom of a deteriorating situation that did not need Cecil hostility to push it forward. The earl probably knew this perfectly well. He had never needed in the past to boast publicly of the queen's favour; it had been abundantly clear to all. Now it was not, and he started to absent himself from the court, sulking and feigning illness.

By March 1597 the barometer of his favour had fallen several degrees.[52] On the 5th of the month Lord Cobham, lord chamberlain and warden of the Cinque Ports, died. Essex might have had the former position, but instead he asked for the latter and was rebuffed; the position going, predictably, to Cobham's son, Henry. Soon after, Lord Hunsdon became lord chamberlain, and Essex withdrew from court, bitterly chagrined, and complaining yet again that his enemies had turned the queen against him.[53] In fact this was not the case. Elizabeth was merely doing what she had done so often before: taking the safe and obvious route. She had, after all, done the same thing in appointing Essex to succeed his stepfather as master of the horse. He had behaved very badly since returning from Cadiz, and Elizabeth had every excuse for deciding that she had had enough of him; but instead, she made him master of the ordnance. This was not a major office, but it was an important one in wartime, and reasonably remunerative.[54] Finally, he was granted what he had always craved: sole command of a major expedition against Spain.

The instructions for what was later known as 'The Islands Voyage' were issued on 15 June 1597.[55] The main objective was the destruction of the fleet that was known to be assembling at Ferrol, near La Coruña. If it had sailed, he was to pursue it; if it was successfully destroyed, he was then to proceed to the Azores for the purpose of intercepting the *flota*. To that end he was authorised to attack and capture the island of Terceira; but not to hold it for any length of time, as the expedition was to return before winter. The earl's imagination took wing. Not only would he destroy the fleet of Spain, and capture the king's treasure, he would turn the Azores into an English base for the control of the Atlantic; 'Her Majesty would be absolute Queen of the Seas', he concluded.[56] Essex's strategy was sound, but his vision was far-fetched, and his tactics showed too little attention to detail. Ferrol was a deep harbour and required an army as well as a navy to assail it. There was also a distinct danger that the two fleets would pass at sea, and each would have ended by assailing the other's undefended coast. The fleet was neither better nor worse prepared than that which had sailed against La Coruña in 1589, but that quickly became irrelevant.

Essex sailed on 10 July, accompanied as vice admirals by Ralegh and Lord Thomas Howard. By the 31st all three squadrons were back at Plymouth, battered by ferocious gales.[57] As the costs mounted, Elizabeth considered calling the whole thing off, but Essex persuaded her that an attack was still feasible, and the fleet put to sea again on 11 August. Again the weather proved to be the master. Essex never got anywhere near Ferrol, not through any fault of his own but because easterly gales blew him out into the Atlantic. He did reach Terceira, but not in sufficient strength to assault the island, or even to capture the fleet which lay under the protection of the harbour guns. The English hung about the islands for a few weeks, hoping for worthwhile prizes, but it soon became known they were there. When they were recalled in mid-October, Essex had almost nothing to show for his efforts – or the queen's expense.[58] However, it is an ill wind which blows no good, and those same gales which had frustrated the Islands Voyage similarly battered and dispersed the Spanish fleet which finally left Ferrol in October, bound for Ireland. If he had attacked Ferrol and destroyed the fleet, Essex could not have done a more effective job than the weather did for him.

Elizabeth did not blame the earl for this failure, although his extravagant optimism had driven it ahead against the odds. While he was still struggling with the elements at the end of July, she had written to him to

> remember that who doth their best shall never receive the blame that accidents may bring; neither shall you find us so rigorous a judge as to verdict enterprises by events. So the root be sound, what blasts soever wither the fruits, no condemnation shall light on their share.[59]

Essex, however, was severely shaken by the experience. He had come back from Cadiz angry and frustrated; but he came back from the Islands Voyage sour and bewildered. In 1596 he had been convinced that enemies had thwarted him, and turned the queen against him in his absence; but not even he could blame the Cecils for the weather, and the queen's attitude was one of regret rather than blame.[60]

By this time Essex was suffering from what contemporaries termed 'melancholia'. Robert Burton was to write in 1621 that melancholics 'misconstrue every word and interpret it to the worse', and 'if they be not saluted, invited, consulted with, called to council etc., or that any respect, small compliment, or ceremony be omitted, they think themselves neglected and condemned'.[61] This could stand as a good diagnosis of the earl's condition; and to it was added a subtle and tortuous preoccupation with the supposed intrigues of enemies – the country's, the queen's and his own, which was an attitude which he shared with many contemporaries. The elevation of Lord Howard of Effingham to the earldom of Nottingham on 22 October 1597 had nothing whatsoever to do with Essex, one way or the other, but he chose to regard it as a slight, particularly as Howard's patent of creation mentioned his service at Cadiz – a victory which Essex had convinced himself was his alone. When the new earl was also created lord chamberlain, which gave him ceremonial precedence over Essex, the latter again stormed out of the court in a huff, refusing to attend either parliament or council – both of which were serious misdemeanours.[62]

Elizabeth was irritated, even exasperated, by this behaviour, but not yet alienated. At Christmas 1597 she conferred upon him the office of earl marshal. This was not particularly valuable, and had no political significance, but it was rich in honour and reputation – and restored his ceremonial precedence. So delighted was Essex with this bauble that he was even prepared to bury the hatchet with Robert Cecil – for the time being. With Burghley seriously and soon terminally ill, the full weight of his power and influence had now descended to his son. Early in 1598, when a high-profile embassy was sent to France in a futile attempt to persuade Henry IV not to make peace with Spain, Cecil was chosen to lead it; and he negotiated a courtier's pact with Essex to protect his interests during his absence. Cecil himself made sure that this pact was well known. 'As the Queen's affairs must have a good portion of our minds', he wrote, 'I hope that now God has disposed us to love and kindness, we shall overcome all petty doubts about what the world may judge of our correspondency.'[63]

It may not have been 'love and kindness' which prompted Essex to busy himself about business which would normally have fallen to the secretary, but the ailing Burghley insisted that his son should take it in good part, and give him thanks – as publicly as possible. Cecil remained in France until 1 May, and for over two months Essex was in effect chief minister, a role which he discharged with more competence and responsibility than his previous record would have suggested. When he did not feel the constant need to watch his back, he could be a shrewd and effective councillor. This brief truce in the constant turf wars of domestic politics casts an interesting light on Essex, because it was almost the only time in his public career when he felt appreciated as he thought he deserved.[64] Perhaps if he had set his heart upon military glory rather than statesmanship, history would have remembered him very differently. It also suggests that his own estimate of his talents may have been more accurate than is usually allowed.

It did not last. After Henry IV concluded the treaty of Vervins in May 1598, there was increasing talk in the council of the desirability of peace. Henry had settled with his Huguenot subjects by the edict of Nantes in April, and Burghley exercised his last public influence during the summer in arguing the case for negotiation.[65] To all such talk Essex was vehemently opposed, and by July his animosity against the Cecils was as violent as ever. Lord Grey complained at one point that the earl 'has forced me to declare myself either his [friend] only or [else] friend to Mr Secretary, protesting there could be no neutrality'.[66] Grey might have been sympathetic to Essex, had such a low-key reaction been permitted, but it was not, and the earl cast him off. He also cast himself off in an even more dramatic fashion that usual.

The quarrel occurred at some time during June, over the replacement of Lord Burgh as lord deputy of Ireland. It was a job that nobody wanted. The queen favoured Sir William Knollys, and Essex favoured Sir George Carew, a partisan of the Cecils whom he wished to see banished to Dublin. When Elizabeth rejected his advice, he lost his temper and the queen boxed his ears. He then committed the unpardonable sin of laying hand on his sword in the royal presence. Having been restrained, he stormed out of the court declaring that he would not accept such indignity from anyone.[67] He should theoretically have lost his hand for such an offence, but Lord Keeper Egerton and other peacemakers persuaded him to make an apology, which Elizabeth accepted. Both had been genuinely distressed by the rupture, but of course the earl had far more to lose. By September he was back in council, his relations apparently patched up, not only with the queen but also with Robert Cecil.

Lord Burghley died on 4 August 1598, and Elizabeth's 'distraction' was probably more the result of that loss than of the behaviour of Essex.[68] Neither the lord treasurership nor his lucrative mastership of the wards was bestowed immediately, although Essex made it clear that he coveted the latter. At the same time the situation in Ireland had deteriorated markedly, with a serious defeat at the hands of the rebel forces on 14 August.[69] With the war elsewhere stalemated in the hope of peace negotiations, which were given further prominence by the death of Philip II in September, Ireland suddenly became the chief military priority.

The authority of the English crown in Ireland had ebbed and flowed since the thirteenth century. It had ebbed when the crown was weak in the fifteenth century, and recovered under Henry VII; but it remained patchy. Thomas Cromwell's attempts to increase Henry VIII's power in the 1530s ended by doing more harm than good. He succeeded in destroying the old system, whereby the country was run by a small group of Anglo-Irish magnates, in the king's name but largely in their own interests; but he had not succeeded in replacing it with effective control from London.[70] He had alienated the long established Old English of the Dublin Pale by introducing new English officials, but had made no progress in reconciling the chieftains of the 'wild Irish', who ruled about two-thirds of the island without reference to the king, or to English law. The ecclesiastical changes of Henry VIII's reign had been accepted with relatively little dispute in the Pale and the 'obedient lands', but ignored in tribal Ireland.[71] At that stage the Irish churches had not been particularly devoted to Rome, but they were very devoted to their own somewhat primitive ways of doing things.[72] Attempts to introduce Protestantism under Edward VI had had little impact, even in the Pale.

The one political initiative that might have brought stability also failed. This was the policy of 'surrender and regrant', which is associated particularly with Sir Anthony St Leger, who was lord deputy four times between 1540 and 1556. The idea was to tempt the Irish chieftains into surrendering their tribal lands (which were communal property under Irish law), and receiving them back as personal seigneuries from the English crown, along with a title, which was usually baronial.[73] Having received such a regrant, they would then become peers of the Irish parliament, to which they would be summoned by writ. The idea was to domesticate the Irish political system by translating it into a language that the English government could understand. As a part of the same policy, Ireland was raised from a lordship into a kingdom in 1541.

If this policy had been persisted with over a long period, it might have succeeded; but two factors told against it. It was taken up only very slowly, and it did not guarantee security against renewed tribal warfare, even when it was taken up. In 1556 short-term security needs triumphed over long-term vision, and the policy was abandoned. Instead it was decided to protect the Pale with plantations. These were known as the King's County and the Queen's County, and were modelled (roughly) on Roman *colonia*.[74] They were civilian settlements, but with a quasi-military purpose. The Irish landholders were dispossessed, but there were never enough English settlers to work the land, and many of the Irish peasants were allowed to remain.

These plantations were not a success, but they worked up to a point, and were much cheaper than maintaining large garrisons. This last was a critical factor, as the English government was always short of money – and desperately short during wartime. Consequently plantations were identified as the way ahead in the general aim of 'pacifying' Ireland.[75] By their very nature, however, these colonies fostered not only bitter resentment but also alienation of a very subversive nature. To those Englishmen who came fresh to the Irish scene, whether as officials or settlers, the native inhabitants were ignorant alike of the arts of peace, the rule of law, and the true worship of God.[76] The last was a particularly thorny point as the Protestant establishment began to settle down in England, and to become a part of English identity. Unlike Wales, there was no effective evangelism in the native language; and the more Protestant the English became, the more the Irish discovered their devotion to the Old Religion.[77] Religion also divided the Old English of the Pale, many of whom were already alienated by the intrusions of central government. As the English Prayer Book and the Thirty-Nine Articles became officially established after 1559, many inhabitants of the Pale began to drift into recusancy, and even into an Irish identity.

There were numerous plantation schemes in the 1570s and 1580s, some of which never came to fruition at all, and others which were only partly implemented. But every plantation caused a fresh rebellion, and every rebellion led to fresh expropriations, and further resentment.[78] By the 1570s the missionary priests were making great strides in the tribal lands, and the rebellious tribesmen regularly justified their actions in religious terms.[79] Some of their leaders were openly looking to Spain for military and financial assistance, and in 1579 Thomas Fitzmaurice actually landed with a small force which was mainly Spanish at Smerwick.

The surprising thing about these constant tribal rebellions is not that they took place, or even that they were fought with great savagery on both sides, but that they were not more successful. The English deputies could seldom deploy more than a few thousand men, and field armies were often numbered in hundreds rather than thousands. Yet the rebels were consistently defeated, with disastrous consequences for themselves.[80] One reason for this was that Irish kerns were no match for properly armed and disciplined soldiers; another was their lack of unity. Every time that there was a rebellion, the rebels' tribal enemies fought alongside the English, and often benefited largely in terms of confiscated lands. Some chieftains did this consistently, although they were not necessarily anglicised, let alone Protestant.[81] Others switched sides in accordance with priorities which are now difficult to recover. The lord deputies were therefore engaged in a constant round of small-scale negotiations, local alliances, feuds and minor wars. Irish adventurers like Thomas Stukeley were in and out of the court of Philip II, but the small landing at Smerwick was the only tangible result, and that was quickly dealt with.[82]

Two things turned this grumbling discomfort into a serious ailment. The first was the outbreak of war in 1585, which immediately increased Philip II's interest. Although he did not doubt Irish devotion to the true faith, he did doubt their ability to deliver anything in political terms. It was one thing to use Ireland as a pressure point in dealing with Elizabeth, quite another to contemplate it as a theatre of war. The second development was the alienation of Hugh O'Neill, earl of Tyrone. The first factor, by giving Ireland a higher priority on the government's agenda, acted in favour of the English. The Old English community, although it remained firmly Catholic, wished to have nothing to do with treasonable Spanish intrigues, and its loyalty was consequently strengthened.[83] In the late 1580s, thanks partly to an unusually successful plantation in Munster, and partly to the greater efforts provoked by the war, English civil government steadily advanced. The land was not pacified, but by 1590 a structure of government, modelled on the English counties, had been introduced everywhere except Ulster.[84]

The alienation of Tyrone was a very Irish crisis. He was one of that small but distinguished band who doubled as an Anglo-Irish nobleman and a Gaelic chieftain. He was a Catholic, but retained strong connections with the English court, and was putting down minor rebellions in collaboration with the lord deputy as late as 1593. He was the O'Neill as well as earl of Tyrone, however, and his power base was in Ulster, the least anglicised part of Ireland. By 1594 he was arguing that this power should be recognised, and that he should be allowed to govern Ulster, albeit in the queen's name.[85] This would have meant a return to the pre-1536 situation, and did not correspond at all with the council's intention to establish a firmer grip over this vulnerable territory. When his plan was rejected, Tyrone became an enemy. This did not happen overnight, but through a series of botched negotiations and abortive plans. By May 1595 Tyrone was in open rebellion.

Although his behaviour had so far been typical of other Irish chieftains in its deviousness, and apparent lack of coherent vision, by the summer of 1595 it had become apparent that Tyrone was a different type of antagonist.[86] For the first time since Silken Thomas in the 1530s, he set out to use ethnic hostility in an effort to overcome the chronic divisions of the Irish tribes. He also professed a crusading zeal for the Catholic Church, and a hatred of heretics. He thus sought to sweep up generations of accumulated hatred and suspicion in order to create something that began to resemble an Irish nationalism. This was extremely dangerous from the English point of view, because they had always relied upon Irish divisions to maintain their ascendancy; and it very nearly worked. Tyrone had a charisma that his predecessors had lacked, and was a man of both intelligence and cunning. So successful was he that by 1597 Philip II had become seriously interested.[87] In Ireland he could fuel a Catholic nationalism which might be as potent against England as the Protestant nationalism of the Dutch was against him. In August 1597 a major English army was destroyed at the battle of Yellow Ford, and in the succeeding weeks thousands of English settlers were killed or driven out; the programme of steady anglicisation was set back, it has been estimated, by at least fourteen years.[88]

As a result of this crisis, Essex was caught in a trap. As the acknowledged leader of the war party, and (in his own eyes at least) England's finest soldier, could he avoid the challenge of the last frontier? When neither Carew nor Knollys was sent across the Irish Sea, it began to be rumoured as early as November that Essex himself would go, with the unusually exalted title of lord lieutenant.[89] The actual circumstances in which this appointment was made are murky. The earl apparently opposed every other suggestion, and this was taken to mean that he wanted the job himself. Some saw this in a sinister light, believing that he was attempting to increase his already considerable following among the swordsmen, and 'divers feared that he was hatching some dangerous design'. He was rumoured to have boasted of his own royal descent, although these reports were probably spread by those same enemies who were eager to urge him to grasp the poisoned chalice. In fact Essex does not appear to have wanted the job, but believed that there was no way in which he could honourably avoid it. He feared being stranded in Ireland with inadequate resources (a realistic enough fear), and then blamed for failure. On the other hand, with the queen's express order, and his own military reputation on the line, how could he refuse? His commission was finally issued on 12 April 1599, by which time most of the new troops which he had been promised had already crossed over.[90]

By the time that he went on this most difficult mission, Essex was in a very peculiar and dangerous state of mind. He could have regarded the task as an opportunity that would place him beyond all challenge and doubt, or he could have regarded it as a successful ruse by Robert Cecil to shunt him off to a graveyard of reputations. In fact he seems to have blamed Elizabeth, rather as a cast-off lover might have blamed his fickle mistress.[91] The impression given is of a man thoroughly alienated. He had already begun to make surreptitious enquiries about the powers of the office of constable, to which he believed he had an hereditary claim; and more than once during his service in Ireland he spoke with apparent seriousness of returning to England with an army and putting his foes to flight.[92] Elizabeth's belief that she could use her personal hold over him, and keep him in a sort of joint harness with Robert Cecil, as she had kept Robert's father and the earl of Leicester many years before, was self-delusion.

It made matters worse that Essex's mission in Ireland was a spectacular failure. In spite of his panache he was an indifferent commander at the best of times; unfamiliar with Irish conditions, and impatient of advice. Although he had the largest English army that had ever been committed to Ireland, he had no idea how to deploy it to best advantage. In spite of boasting that he would 'beat Tyrone in the field', the first thing that he did on arrival in April 1599 was to disperse more than half his force into garrisons. He then made an eight-week progress through Munster and South Leinster, which achieved nothing but wore out his soldiers with long marches over hostile terrain.[93] While he was thus occupied, other royal forces were being defeated in detail. In the face of these setbacks, Essex's bravado rapidly diminished. In August he held a council of war, and decided that his forces were already too far depleted by disease and desertion to risk a confrontation with Tyrone that year.

When the news of this decision reached the queen, she was outraged, and ordered him to proceed to Ulster immediately with all the men available.[94] In early September he duly moved north with a force of about four thousand, and encountered Tyrone near Dundalk, on the borders of Ulster. The rebel force was much larger, and in the circumstances Essex might have done better to withdraw. Instead he allowed himself to be inveigled into a parley, and was even unwise enough to spend some time in private conversation with Tyrone. The result was an extremely unsatisfactory truce, which gave the rebels almost everything they wanted at little or no cost. There is no reason to suppose that Essex was betraying his trust, but his actions were certainly open to hostile interpretation.[95] When the queen heard the news, she simply ordered him to remain at his post and await further instructions.

Anyone other than Essex would probably have seen this for what it was – a holding order while Elizabeth decided what to do next. He, however, was immediately convinced that his enemies at court were about to execute a coup against him and did exactly the wrong thing. He rushed back to London in a bid to redeem himself and placate the royal wrath.[96] Not only had he failed to carry out his mission, and wasted his resources, he had also defied his orders not once, but twice. He had been explicitly instructed not to give any post to his friend Henry Wriothesley, earl of Southampton, who was in deep disfavour – an instruction which he ignored by appointing him general of the horse. This defiance he justified explicitly on the grounds that his commission entitled him to make such appointments as he chose (which was probably true), and implicitly on the grounds that women do not understand military matters.[97] Elizabeth responded 'it is strange that you will dare thus to value your own pleasing in things unnecessary, and think by your private arguments to carry for your own glory a matter wherein our pleasure to the contrary is made notorious.'[98] In spite of this stinging rebuke, and a series of increasingly angry exchanges during July and August, Essex persisted in the delusion that his troubles were all caused by those who were corrupting the queen's mind against him. The knowledge that Robert Cecil had secured the coveted mastership of the wards while he was flogging his way around Munster merely served as confirmation. In spite of explicit orders to the contrary, he quitted Dublin on 24 September, and proceeded straight to court.

Rumours of treason had preceded him, and it is not quite clear whether the forces that were being mobilised in the late summer of 1599 were intended for defence against Spain or against an invasion from Ireland led by the lord lieutenant.[99] There were certainly unconfirmed reports about Spanish intentions, fuelled by the failure to get any negotiations started; but quite a lot was known by the council about Essex's wild and extravagant talk, and no chances were being taken. When he arrived, with a mere handful of servants and no sign of his mutinous friends, he was immediately placed under arrest. With the benefit of hindsight, this can be seen as the end of his political career, but that was by no means obvious at the time. He was not consigned to prison, but to honourable confinement in the lord keeper's house. No charges were proffered against him, because the offences of which he was actually guilty were mainly those of incompetence and effrontery.

If there had really been a cabal intent on his destruction, much more could have been made of his rash words. He was at least as guilty as the duke of Buckingham had been in 1521 of saying irresponsible things in front of unreliable servants; and his behaviour towards the queen herself had frequently been insulting.[100] The world had moved on since 1521, however, and Elizabeth was a different person from her father. Essex had bounced back from so many crises in his public career that it would have been rash to assume that he could not do so again. For years the woman who was also the queen had been fascinated by his charm, his energy, and his sheer ability to ignore the rules. In the autumn of 1599 no one knew whether this regard had finally been killed off, or whether it was merely dormant; and it would have been dangerous to guess wrong. It also had to be considered that Essex was in some respects a representative figure. His sense of grievance was shared by all those disappointed place-hunters and under-promoted soldiers who swarmed in the wings of political life; and he was an inspiration to those who believed that the war was being prosecuted with insufficient vigour, and that total victory required just one more big effort. So Essex was left for the time being, shunted into the siding of disfavour while his rival Robert Cecil got on with the business of running the country. While under arrest, he was suspended from all his offices, except that of master of the horse; but he was not deprived of any of them, and his eventual fate remained highly uncertain.[101]

Elizabeth was not usually vindictive. Her fits of bad temper, although violent, were normally ephemeral. Consequently, when Essex was freed from his confinement in August 1600, a partial restoration at least was expected. He was a nobleman of ancient lineage and he had done, or so it was thought, good service in the past. Nor had he committed any offence for which a suitable submission would not be adequate atonement. He retired to the country and maintained a sufficiently submissive demeanour; but the expected softening of the royal heart did not take place. This was not the result of implacable enemies. Robert Cecil had no interest in destroying his rival; indeed he would have preferred to see him back at court in a suitably chastened frame of mind.

This time it was the queen herself who refused to be convinced, not because she believed her former favourite to be plotting against her, but because he had so grievously disappointed her expectations. She had intended him to be a courtier, feeding her vanity with his flattering attentions. In such a person youthful waywardness was an additional attraction, and for such she had at first taken his sulks and furious outbursts. But youthful folly palls after a decade, and he had come to take himself far too seriously. Moreover, he had become seriously disobedient. His activities in Ireland were not like that impetuous dash to join the Lisbon expedition ten years earlier. These were studied acts of defiance, for which he had also shown a disconcerting tendency to justify himself.[102] She remembered also that he was a nobleman of ancient lineage, who may well have felt that his position was not altogether dependent upon Elizabeth Tudor. It was no more her intention to destroy him than it was Robert Cecil's, but she also had no intention of encouraging him to believe that he would be received back into favour. Consequently, when his valuable sweet wine monopoly, which had been granted for ten years in 1590, came up for renewal in the autumn of 1600, she terminated it, commenting frankly 'an unruly horse must be abated of his provender, that he may be the easier and better managed'.[103] By this time he had accumulated long- and short-term debts in the region of £16,000, and the loss of that income bade fair to ruin him. Whether Elizabeth realised this at the time that she made the decision we do not know, but it seems likely that she did.

By the end of 1600 Essex was desperate. He had lost all respect for his sovereign, believing her to be the virtual prisoner of Cecil and his friends. He had also convinced himself that he stood at the head of a great following: all those who were weary of Cecil's mismanagement and monopolistic control of patronage; all those soldiers and seamen whose services had been slighted and undervalued; all the disappointed, and those who believed that the realm was being dishonoured. In other words, the countless host of the discontented. There had already been some hot-headed talk of a coup before Essex was released, but it was not known about, and the earl's professions of penitence and contrition were taken at face value. One account speaks of him 'reviving his former resolution, which was the surprising and possessing the Queen's person and the court'.[104] This 'earlier resolution' seems to have been formed in Ireland, when there had been some wild talk of returning with 'two hundred resolute gentlemen' and 'executing the surprise of her Majesty's person'.[105]

What happened in November and December 1600 was in pursuit of the same aim. There were five ringleaders (apart from Essex himself, who remained in the background): the earl of Southampton, Sir Charles Danvers, Sir Ferdinando Gorges, Sir John Davies and John Littleton.[106] Southampton was almost as deep in debt as Essex himself; the others were swordsmen, who had long been the core of the earl's following. They met secretly at Drury House, because Essex feared that his own residence would be under surveillance. Three key elements were identified: the court, the Tower and the City of London. The majority agreed that the court was the key, and detailed plans were laid to take advantage of its lax security:

> They all thought it best to seize upon the Court, and that in this manner; Sir Christopher Blount with a select number should seize upon the court gate, Davies the Hall, Danvers the Great Chamber (where the guard kept but a careless watch) and the Presence Chamber, and withall Essex himself, from the stable called the Muse, near the court, should with certain choice men (his way thus being made) come rushing in and fall upon his knees before the Queen, and pray her to remove his Adversaries from about her; whom he had determined (as some confessed afterward) to bring to their trial, and having called a parliament, to alter the form of commonwealth.[107]

There was talk of bringing forces from the Devereux estates in Wales to overawe the capital, but no serious plans seem to have been made for that purpose, and the whole plot is conspicuous for lacking the kind of magnate backing which had made Warbeck so dangerous a century before. Three earls were involved, Essex, Southampton and Rutland, but there were no private armies of retainers, and no hint of foreign intervention. The whole conspiracy is remarkable for its domestic scale, and for the apparent conviction that it could be brought to fruition with the support of no more than a few score gentlemen.[108] Essex himself seems to have been marginally more realistic, and saw the support of London as crucial to any move against the court. To that extent he was right, but he wildly overestimated the support which he enjoyed there. There was a big difference between the citizens applauding his military exploits, or sympathising with his grievances against Robert Cecil, and backing a treasonable plot against the queen.

Meanwhile, it had become obvious that something was afoot at Essex House.

> Suspicions of him grew stronger and stronger, both by reason of a more frequent resort than usual of the multitude, under pretence of hearing sermons, as also some words which had dropt from the preachers mouths, as of the superior magistrates had power to restrain kings themselves.[109]

This was a familiar notion among the radical Protestants, but quite unconnected with the private grievances of malcontent noblemen, and suggests that Essex and his supporters were making eclectic use of whatever arguments they could find. It was also an extremely dangerous note to strike in Elizabeth's hearing. How much the council knew is not quite clear, because the initial reaction was restrained. Essex was summoned to the lord treasurer's house 'that he might be admonished to use the liberty which was granted to him soberly'.[110] He was becoming a nuisance but there was no disposition to take him too seriously. The earl's reaction, however, dug him further into the mire. An anonymous person, perhaps a well-wisher, sent him a note warning him to look out for himself. Whether it was this note or his own guilty conscience, or a combination of the two, we do not know; but he pleaded illness and declined to meet the council.[111]

He now had to act quickly or not at all, for his subterfuge would soon be discovered. On the evening of 7 February, hearing that the guard at court had been strengthened, and drawing his own conclusions, he decided to act the next day by raising London to his cause. According to Camden this decision was precipitated by the arrival of a messenger,

> who as if he had been sent from the citizens made large promises of assistance from them against all his adversaries. Herewith the Earl being somewhat animated, he began to discourse on how much he was favoured throughout the city; and persuaded himself by the former acclamations of the people, and their mutterings and murmurings against his adversaries, that many of them were devoted to him, to maintain his credit and fortune.[112]

The following morning, Essex caused it to be put about in London that he had refused the summons to the council because Lord Cobham and Sir Walter Ralegh had laid an ambush to kill him as he passed by. Whether anyone believed this is not clear, but news of it reached the queen by 10 o'clock in the morning, and she sent four senior councillors headed by the Lord Keeper Egerton to Essex House to inform the earl that, if he thought he had a grievance, there was a proper remedy by way of petition.

This was not so much a conciliatory gesture as a final warning shot. Mary had done the same thing to Sir Thomas Wyatt in 1554.[113] Essex, however, was by this time committed beyond wit or discretion. When the councillors arrived, he used the mob that had assembled to intimidate them, and imprisoned them in an inner room. He then set off to raise the City, proclaiming not only that there was a plot against his life but that the country was sold to the Spaniard. At almost exactly the same time, Thomas, Lord Burghley (Sir Robert Cecil's brother) and Garter king of arms, also entered proclaiming Essex and all his adherents traitors.[114] It was no contest. Hardly anyone joined in to support Essex's furious protests, and as news of his proscription spread even his own swordsmen began to melt away.

Eventually, 'his face moulten with sweat', he retreated with the remnant of his band to Essex House, intending to use his prisoners as hostages for his own safety. When he got there he found that one of his own men,

Fernando Gorges, who had a slightly nimbler sense of self-preservation, had gone before him and secured the release of the prisoners.[115] There was now nothing left but to surrender or die fighting. Essex tried to make terms, but he had nothing to bargain with and eventually surrendered unconditionally to the earl of Nottingham. The ladies of the household having been allowed to leave unharmed, the earl and his remaining followers gave up their swords. Essex requested only a fair trial, and the company of his chaplain, Abdy Ashton, in prison. However long it may have been in gestation, the action had lasted less than twenty-four hours, and had cost no lives.

The earl of Essex had finally fallen from grace. Had he been cunningly pushed by his enemies, or was he entirely the agent of his own destruction? Robert Cecil almost certainly knew far more about what was going on in Drury House and Essex House than he ever felt the need to disclose. Where had those crucial and misleading messages come from? Given the earl's record of wild, near treasonable utterances, and the virtual certainty that he had plotted open treason in Ireland, it would have been irresponsible not to set spies in his household. Cecil may not have known all the details of the discussions going on, but he would have known about the intentions to attack the court and subvert the city.[116] The real problem was how seriously to take this extraordinary maverick. A few hundred determined men might possibly have seized the queen, but what would they have done then? The idea that Elizabeth still privately favoured Essex, and that her hostile demeanour was induced by the lies and cajolery of Robert Cecil, was pure self-deception. The queen had been angry with her former favourite, and forgiven his behaviour more times than anyone could remember. By 1599 she had had enough. Ireland was the Earl's last chance, and he blew it spectacularly, revealing that as a man of thirty-three he had learned nothing of the realities of the world.

In many ways he was still the same self-obsessed boy that he had been in 1584; only his looks had faded and his charm had been reduced to fitful flashes. There also has to be a question mark over his mental stability. The 1590s were a paranoid decade, when Spaniards lurked around every corner, and there were papal agents behind every bush.[117] It was also a period which loved intellectual subtlety, and complex allusive literature. But Essex was not an intellectual and his paranoia was entirely personal. Elizabeth was both beguiled and infuriated by him, but the balance between these two reactions changed with time, and by 1600 the susceptible old lady had been entirely overcome by the alienated and outraged monarch. Elizabeth was deeply saddened by Essex's folly, and by the course which she was compelled to take with him, but this was largely because it held up a mirror to her own weaknesses, and that kind of self-knowledge was not comfortable. If she had not been so foolish as to encourage him, his Icarus-like career need never have happened.

By contrast the Cecils, both father and son, were examples of diligent responsibility. They were not innocent of promoting their own fortunes and careers, nor of building up their clientage, but they were first and foremost the queen's servants. Lord Burghley was one of the great statesmen of the age, whom William Camden described as

> a singular man for honesty, gravity, temperance, industry and justice, seasoned with exceeding moderation and most approved fidelity; but above all singular piety towards God. The Queen was most happy in so great a councillor, and to his wholesome counsels the state of England for ever shall be beholden.[118]

In his last years he became taciturn and devious, and Essex was right to fear his hostility. The earl, however, characteristically misinterpreted his motives: Burghley did not only want to protect his son's career against this wild and seductive man; he also wanted to protect the country. Burghley knew Elizabeth well enough to have seen these emotional aberrations before, and suspected that time was on his side. In the event he did not live to see the débâcle, but he would no doubt have felt that his position had been vindicated. Robert Cecil was a man of equal ability, both as an administrator and as a politician, but he lacked his father's outstanding integrity.[119] He was not corrupt, but he could be unscrupulous, and he did not have the advantage of his father's long knowledge of the queen. He and his agents probably did play a part in his enemy's destruction, but then he was the principal target of Essex's hatred; not to defend himself would have been simply foolhardy. In retrospect Essex's treason looks insubstantial, even trivial, but given Elizabeth's record of response to his behaviour, it was prudent of Cecil to countermine his intrigues by all means available.

The day after the earl's arrest, that is on Monday, 9 February 1601, a lengthy proclamation set out the details of his treason. The official pretext for doing this was that the ramifications of the conspiracy were still unknown, and it warned the queen's subjects to be on their guard against any like attempts. The real reason, however, seems to have been a perceived need to put the whole affair so far into the public domain that there could be no chance that the queen would change her mind and pardon the whole episode as another act of folly. It was also a way of expressing gratitude to the Londoners, in case they should feel that their loyalty was not appreciated:

> notwithstanding (God be thanked) they have found themselves deceived of their expectations, being now all apprehended and within our Tower of London, as well the three principal traiterous Earls of Essex, Rutland and Southampton,

as divers others of the principal gentlemen their confederates, our good subjects of our City, and elsewhere, having showed themselves so constant and unmoveable from their duties towards us, as not any one of them of any note (that we can yet hear of) did offer to assist the said Earl and his associates.[120]

In spite of his alleged prominence, the earl of Rutland was not indicted. Essex and Southampton were tried by their peers on 19 February in a trial remarkable for the furious onslaught of the crown lawyers, whose denunciations strike the modern observer as singularly distasteful and unnecessary. Francis Bacon, now struggling to redeem a career doubly tainted, was among them.[121] Southampton threw himself on the queen's mercy but Essex defended himself with dignity, protesting to the last that his only intention had been to abase himself at the queen's feet and beg redress of his many grievances. He seems to have convinced himself that he had never intended any harm to Elizabeth, but some of his associates were less self-deceived. Sir Christopher Blount confessed that, whereas no harm was intended to her person, he was uncertain 'whether the matter could have been accomplished without blood drawn from herself'.[122]

Southampton was eventually pardoned, but Essex went to the block just six days later, on 25 February 1601, having declined to sue for pardon and reaffirming the rectitude of his intentions. Perhaps the council was determined that Elizabeth should not change her mind; but there is no sign that she had any such intention. Blount, Henry Cuff, Essex's secretary and many people's scapegoat for the whole business, Charles Danvers and Gelly Meyrick, were tried separately by commission of oyer and terminer, and suffered the death of traitors a few days later. In a sense, the episode was closed, but Elizabeth was painfully aware that she had brought it upon herself, and was not without responsibility for the earl's reckless behaviour. As one of Essex's erstwhile secretaries, Sir Henry Wotton, wrote many years later:

He had to wrestle with a queen's declining, or rather with her very setting age, which besides other respects is commonly even of itself the more umbratious and apprehensive, as for the most part all horizons are charged with certain vapours towards their evenings.[123]

Elizabeth did not like to be reminded of advancing age or diminishing faculties, but it was precisely this vulnerability which the earl of Essex had sought to exploit for his own advantage. It is not surprising that she was little disposed to forgive him. At the same time, his tragic departure left Sir Robert Cecil in a kind of isolated splendour that his father had never enjoyed.

12

The Final Years

The 1590s were hard years. There were no crises to compare with the Armada, or even with the Northern Rebellion of 1569; but for both Elizabeth and her subjects they were years of unremitting toil. Several harvests were disastrous, and prices soared at a rate not seen since the 1550s.[1] The war continued, at a heavy cost in both lives and money, and all foreign policy was fitted into that context. By 1591 the military emphasis had shifted from the Low Countries to France, and that change was confirmed by the death of the duke of Parma in March 1592. His last victory had been to raise the siege that Henry IV had laid around Paris in January 1592, and his departure signified a shift in the balance of power. The generals who followed him were competent, particularly the Genoese Ambrogio Spinola, but they were not the equal of Maurice of Nassau, who retook the eastern and northern provinces over the next few years, and had begun to make inroads into the south by the time that Philip II died in August 1598.[2] A token English force continued to serve under Maurice, but it was useful mainly as a symbol of the continuing alliance rather than for its military effectiveness.

Meanwhile, Henry IV had to extricate himself from an impasse. Although he was no longer threatened by intervention from the Low Countries, it had become clear that he could not muster enough support within France to win a decisive victory at home. Although Elizabeth's support had its uses, it was never going to be enough to tip the scales. By September 1592 he was under heavy pressure from his Catholic followers to attend mass, and shortly after sought instruction in the Catholic faith. In April 1593 Sir Thomas Edmondes warned Burghley from the French court, 'I fear your Lordship shall shortly hear he is forced to make that metamorphosis'.[3] In the summer he was received into the Roman Church.

This was not quite as straightforward as it might appear, because Henry had been this way before and was technically an apostate who could not be reconciled a second time.[4] However, a new pope, Clement VIII, had been elected in January 1592 on what might be described as an 'independent ticket', following the pontificates of several Spanish clients. He was not inclined to oblige Philip by refusing the French king's submission, because he was anxious to see the resurrection of France as a major Catholic power.

He therefore rejected Spanish representations and allowed the ceremony at St-Denis to go ahead.

Elizabeth was, or professed to be, horrified. On receiving the news in July 1593, she wrote to Henry:

> Ah what griefs, O what regrets, O what groanings felt I in my soul at the sound of such news as Morlains had told me! My God is it possible that any worldly respect should efface the terror with which the fear of God threatens us? Can we with any reason expect a good sequel from an act so iniquitous.[5]

At a personal level, her reaction was no doubt genuine enough. She could have saved herself a lot of trouble by doing the same thing in 1559; but as a political reaction it was a sham. She knew perfectly well what circumstances had prompted it, and had no intention of breaking off relations, whatever she might threaten.

As moderate Catholics began to rally to his cause, and the League could find no plausible replacement for 'Charles X', the Cardinal of Bourbon, who had sustained the ultra-Catholic claim, but who had died in 1591, Henry's need of Elizabeth's support diminished. But as long as d'Aguila and his Spaniards remained in Brittany, her need of him remained. Norris had been defeated by d'Aguila at Craon in May 1592, and that necessitated a fresh English effort, which could not possibly succeed without French cooperation.[6] Even a Catholic Henry was no more enthusiastic about a Spanish military presence in his realm than Elizabeth was. While the news of Henry's conversion was fresh, neither side was certain of its next move. Norris's force had dwindled to no more that a quarter of its notional strength, and he was evading orders from London.[7] The queen considered withdrawing him and fortifying the Channel Islands instead. Henry was still professing support that never materialised. The council advised Elizabeth, however, that the defence of the Channel Islands would be vastly more expensive than reinforcing Norris, and, in the nick of time, in August 1593 Henry offerred Norris the use of Paimpol as a secure and accessible base.[8]

Although the queen did not immediately make up her mind, events between August and November moved steadily in her favour. Several important Breton noblemen abandoned the League for the king, and the Leaguers themselves began to be uneasy about their Spanish allies, who continued to grow in strength. Around Paimpol the English began to be more favourably regarded, and this greatly eased Norris's problems with victuals, fodder and winter accommodation. Moreover, a short truce between Henry and the League expired in December, renewing fears of cooperation between the League and Spain.[9] In spite of this, Elizabeth was apparently again planning to withdraw Norris when the rumours in Britanny were suddenly focused into a Spanish intention to seize the major port of Brest.

In early March 1594 d'Aguila, with twelve ships and four thousand men, landed on the Crozon Peninsula just south of the port, and commenced the building of a strong fortress. It quickly became apparent that this stronghold, christened 'El Leon', would close down the port of Brest if it was not removed. This drove the English council into effective action, which the queen herself did not attempt to hamper. Norris was reinforced, first with pioneers and then with veteran soldiers from the Low Countries.[10] There was talk of a much larger expedition, but Norris himself did not favour that, perhaps because he wanted to concentrate upon the limited task of reducing El Leon, or perhaps because he saw himself being upstaged by some noble amateur, like the earl of Essex. In early August he got what he wanted: a fresh commission to destroy El Leon and clear the Brest Roads.[11]

By early September Martin Frobisher was blockading the Spanish fort from the sea, while Norris, with French support, was investing it from the land. Relations between the allies were not easy. Although the French Leaguer forces withdrew and played virtually no part, disputes between Norris and Aumâle, the royalist commander, repeatedly endangered the operation. Nevertheless,

> the French and English made their approach on the first of November to the fort of the Spaniards at Crodon, where Sir Martin Frobisher with ten English men of war rode at anchor expecting their coming. This fort is encompassed on two sides with water; to landward there stand two large and high Forts between which there runneth a wall thirty-seven feet wide , and within that a thick earthwork; the forts were defended on each sides with rocks whereupon pieces of Ordnance were planted.[12]

D'Aguila had been given plenty of time to strengthen his position, but he was not actually in command of the fortress when the siege was laid. Instead, he began to mobilise his forces to come to its relief. He was too late. On 7 November the allied bombardment made a breech, and Crozon was carried by storm in a bloody battle which cost many lives on both sides. According to Camden, 'the Queen, out of her innate tenderness and pity commanded him [Norris] by her letters to have more respect to the safety of his men than to his own honour, and not to expose their lives to manifest danger in a war undertaken for the assistance of others'.[13] Such letters, if they were ever written, also came too late. Virtually the whole garrison of some four hundred men was put to the sword, and English and French casualties also numbered several hundred. Norris himself was wounded, and Frobisher died a few days later of gangrene.

Although small-scale, this victory was decisive, and marked the effective end of the English presence in Brittany. It did not, of course, end the threat of Spanish attack, because d'Aguila hung on at Blavet until 1596, but it did end any possibility that he might use Brest as a base.[14] It also ended serious English involvement in France as a whole. As the last of the Leaguer nobles made their peace with the king, and the Leaguer towns opened their gates, Henry became strong enough to declare his own war on Spain:

> The Spaniards (having now their hope of getting the French sceptre and of the marriage of the Infanta with the Duke of Guise quite dashed, through the emulation of the Duke of Mayne against his nephew) were dismissed from thence with bag and baggage, and not without taunts and scoffs of the French.[15]

For a while Henry would be an ally, but not one in any way dependent upon Elizabeth's aid, and she was able to move such military resources as she had to another theatre of war that was becoming more urgent by the day: Ireland.

Tyrone had made a fool of the earl of Essex, and caused him to dissipate a major English effort with relatively little fighting. Thereafter, however, one of two things had got to happen for the Irish to consolidate their success. Either Elizabeth had to give up, believing that the endless effort and expense was not worthwhile, and accept some return to the status quo of a much earlier period, which would leave the chieftains pretty much to their own devices; or Philip II had to intervene in strength and establish a protectorate over Ireland that would transform it from an English dependency into a Spanish one. Neither of these developments was likely. English investment in Ireland, both moral and financial, was far too great to contemplate such a retreat, except in the face of irredeemable defeat; and as long as war with Spain continued, such an open back door would be unthinkable.[16] Philip made significant efforts, in 1596 and 1597, but on both occasions his fleets were dispersed by storms, and he died in 1598, with whatever intention he may have had unfulfilled. Philip III did eventually send a force to Kinsale in 1601, but it was too small and in the wrong place.[17]

By that time, Tyrone was in a cleft stick. His very success in mobilising a kind of Gaelic nationalism militated against too great a dependence upon Spain, but without outside help he simply did not have the resources for a complete victory. Neither Philip II nor Philip III had any use for an independent Ireland, however Catholic; and although the latter was willing to do a little to keep the rebellion alive, he was not going to commit major (and scarce) resources except in return for an Irish submission to himself.

Charles Blount, Lord Mountjoy, who succeeded Essex as lord deputy, and Sir George Carew, the new president of Munster, steadily took the war to Tyrone between 1600 and 1603. Although they were not always successful, persistence paid off.[18] As it became apparent that the English were not going to go away, Gaelic unity, which had been at its strongest in 1599, steadily disintegrated.

The Kinsale campaign was decisive. D'Aguila landed on 21 September 1601 with about 3500 hundred men. Tyrone was far away in the north, but had little option but to come south to link up with his allies. Mountjoy had to scrape around for troops, but by the end of October had about seven thousand men around the town. He was in serious danger of being caught between the Spaniards and the advancing Tyrone, but the latter's inexperience in formal warfare was his undoing, and on 24 November Mountjoy caught the confederate army, as it tried inexpertly to deploy for a field engagement, and routed it completely.[19] D'Aguila surrendered on terms on 2 January.

The rebellion both began and ended in Ulster. A report to the council in 1597 had declared:

> All the late rebellions in Ireland have had their beginning in Ulster. The bad estate of Ulster is like to grow worse by the late frequent practices of the two great Lords of Kantyre in Scotland, Angus McDonnell and McAlane, both labouring vehemently to come into Ulster and bring with them two thousand or three thousand Scots; under pretence to make offer to serve her Majesty, they will bend themselves against her, and convert their forces to serve the traitor [Tyrone] with whom it is to be doubted they have contracted underhand.[20]

By June 1602 Mountjoy was advancing into the province, wasting the land and receiving the submission of Tyrone's former allies, whom he was allowed to receive into favour at his discretion. This was an important concession on Elizabeth's part, because it enabled the lord deputy to deal with situations on the spot, instead of the long delays which would have been occasioned by reference to London.[21] It was also an unusual concession, in that the queen normally liked to maintain personal control of all such matters. Because of this flexibility, Mountjoy was also able to negotiate with Tyrone, who, even as a fugitive, retained the capacity to make a considerable nuisance of himself. The lord deputy offered him a pardon, and confirmation in his lands and title, in return for a full and unconditional submission to the queen's authority. These terms were accepted.

Tyrone submitted in a highly theatrical and symbolic manner, which was no doubt aimed at his erstwhile following:

> Being admitted to to the Presence Chamber (where the Lord Deputy sat in his

Chair of State, with a great number of swordsmen about him) he fell on his knees at the very threshold with a dejected countenance, being clad in sordid and careless habit. After he had been in that posture a while, the Lord Deputy beckoned him to come nearer him. He arose, and having come forward some few steps, prostrated himself again upon his knees and said: I acknowledge my sin against God, and my fault against my most gracious Queen and Sovereign Lady, to whose royal clemency as to a sacred Anchor I betake myself, offering up my life and estate to be at her disposing; whose former bounty and present power I have felt, so I most humbly beseech her, that I may now taste of her mercy. The Lord Deputy interrupted him [and] commanded him to depart, and the next day brought him with him to Dublin, intending to bring him thence into England to the Queen, that she might dispose of him at her Pleasure.[22]

Ireland was subdued for the time being, if not pacified. It had not been turned into England's Low Countries, and Spain's failure in that respect meant that the war had reached virtual stalemate. Since the Armada most of the initiative, at sea at least, had come from the English, and success and failure had been in rough equilibrium. On the credit side had been the capture of the *Madre de Dios* in 1592,[23] the destruction of Crozon in 1594, and above all the sack of Cadiz in 1596. On the debit side were the Lisbon expedition of 1589, the West Indies voyage of 1595, upon which both Drake and Hawkins died,[24] and the 'Islands Voyage' of 1597. The quixotic self-sacrifice of the *Revenge* in 1591 had not been a defeat in the ordinary sense, and the failure of the Armadas of 1596 and 1597 to achieve anything at all had not been victories.[25] The Spaniards had scarcely laid so much as a finger on England throughout the decade, but the English as consistently failed to take the American treasure fleet. On a wider front, Spain suffered far more severely than England. While the trade of London flourished, that of Seville and Barcelona was virtually stifled. Many privateers persisted, more in hope than expectation, but there was no living to be made by 'going upon' the coasts of Spain after 1595. The earl of Cumberland captured San Juan, and devastated the colony of Puerto Rico, in 1598 in what was to be last successful English incursion into New Spain. His reputation soared in Europe, and the queen was delighted; but financially the expedition was a disaster that undermined the Clifford estates for decades.[26] The earl learned his lesson, and devoted himself thereafter to mercantile promotion.

The navy continued to be active, and the earl of Nottingham continued as lord admiral, but he did not go to sea again after 1596 and the new generation of commanders, such as Richard Leveson and William Monson, although competent, lacked the flair of Drake or Hawkins. Nevertheless Leveson played an important part in the capture of Kinsale in 1601, and in June 1602 entered the Portuguese port of Cezimbra and seized a carrack worth almost a million ducats.[27] As this was a naval prize, the proceeds went almost entirely to the crown. In September of the same year Sir Robert Mansell destroyed eight out of nine Spanish galleys heading up the Channel to the Netherlands. It was not altogether a one-way traffic, however. When Spanish naval forces were deployed in strength, they won more than one bruising encounter.

By 1600 there was little to chose between the fleets in terms of seamanship, quality of ships or even gunnery, but the English did continue to have one big advantage. The dockyards at Woolwich, Chatham and Portsmouth could fit out or turn around a warship in half the time that it took the private dockyards of Portugal or Guipuzcoa. When there was a sudden alarm in 1599, eighteen warships were fitted out, victualled and rigged in twelve days. 'The Queen', as William Monson later observed, 'was never more dreaded abroad for anything she ever did'.[28] In fact all was not well in the dockyards, and the corruption there, which was to reach scandalous proportions in the next reign, was already present. Sir John Trevor, who became surveyor in 1598, lacked the integrity of his predecessors; and after 1604 he and Sir Robert Mansell, the treasurer, turned the admiralty into a private milch cow, with a resultant decline in both efficiency and morale.[29] This did not much affect the efficiency of operations as long as the war lasted, but it sprang from defects in Elizabethan policy and indeed in the queen's own personality.

Elizabeth had always been careful with money. By 1580 she was parsimonious to a fault, and by 1590 positively paranoid. In 1600–1 the navy cost approximately £54,000. This was remarkably little for war time; much less than had been spent in the last year of Henry VIII's final war (1545–46), in spite of inflation.[30] This economy was achieved at a price. Much of the cost of what was really naval warfare fell on individuals like the earl of Cumberland. A seaman's pay had been raised only once since 1545, when it was increased to ten shillings a month in 1582, and the fees of the admiralty officials had not been increased at all.[31] Shipbuilding, maintenance work and victualling were all at one time or another on a contract basis, and the contractors cut every conceivable corner in order to achieve a profit margin. Medical and other support services for pressed seamen were cut to the bone, and it is not surprising that mariners went to endless lengths to avoid naval service. In the next reign it was alleged that seamen were saying that they would sooner be hanged than serve in the king's ships.[32]

What was true of the navy was equally true of the army, the court and every other aspect of royal service. Even Sir John Norris's soldiers in Brittany, or Lord Mountjoy's in Ireland, were paid late, in short measure or not at all. The captains, whether at sea or on land, did not necessarily suffer, because they inflated their muster rolls and claimed well beyond the 10 per cent of 'dead pays' to which they were by custom entitled; but the rank and file suffered severely, so that desertion, and even mutiny, became a common hazard.[33] This was partly a question of getting cash to where it was needed when it was needed. Sixteenth-century logistics were notoriously inefficient. But it also sprang from the queen's underlying theory of government.

It was Elizabeth's business (under God, and having taken proper counsel), to make such decisions as might be necessary for the security and wellbeing of the realm. No subject had the right to do that for her, unless authority was specifically delegated; and no one had the right to offer her unsolicited advice.[34] It was also her business to reward her subjects adequately, in accordance with her perception of their worth. Patronage might also be delegated, but the ultimate control remained with her. All government was conducted, not only in her name but under her direction, either personal or through her council; and no one had the right to exercise autonomous authority in the public sphere. On the other hand, it was not her business to make law, except in partnership with her parliament. The law was not the mere will of the ruler, it was something ancient and sacrosanct, only to be amended by due process and after careful thought.[35] Nor was it her business to pay for all this. She paid for her household and domestic servants; and the public officers of the realm were given traditional fees. But there was no professional bureaucracy in the modern sense. It was the duty of noblemen and gentlemen to serve the monarch according to their status and capacity. Good service was rewarded with appropriate patronage, but it was not paid, and the rewards were at the monarch's discretion. She had set this out at the very beginning of her reign:

> so I shall desire you all, my lords (chiefly you of the nobility, everyone in his degree and power), to be assistant to me, that I with my ruling and you with your service may make a good account to almighty God and leave some comfort to our posterity in earth.[36]

It was, in a sense, a very old-fashioned notion of partnership; but in another sense it was nothing of the kind. Elizabeth did not see herself as *prima inter pares*, and the authority which her noblemen and gentlemen exercised was entirely delegated.[37] This was not a partnership that John of Gaunt or Humphrey of Gloucester would have recognised. It was a situation that required a delicate sense of balance, and a sensitive control mechanism. This was partly achieved by baffling displays of femininity, but it was also achieved by an unspoken financial concordat. By 1559 direct taxation was no longer simply a wartime expedient, and calls for the monarch to 'live of his own' were obsolete.[38] That did not mean that taxation was welcome, or conceded willingly. Unlike their continental counterparts, the English nobility had few fiscal privileges, and the gentry none at all; all alike were taxpayers, and liable to assessment as such. By allowing assessments to ossify, however, and by refraining from excessive demands, a kind of equilibrium was reached.[39] The queen's government was conducted, and her laws administered, at very little cost to the exchequer. On the other hand, by using the authority that their offices conferred, her servants were able to reward themselves with preferential deals, lucrative bargains, and the fruits of minor offices that added to their 'worship' rather than their wealth.[40]

Similar tactics were employed in commerce, and in that dubious grey area between legitimate trade and piracy. The queen lent her authority, and made modest investments, in return for a large share of the profits of what were in no sense royal or public enterprises. She had a unique partnership with the merchants of London, and in return they provided valuable credit and good financial advice. War, however, was a different matter, which was one reason why Elizabeth dreaded it so much. It was not just that war was expensive; it was also unpredictably expensive. An expert could estimate the mobilisation costs for a fleet of thirty ships, and how much it would cost to keep it at sea for a month.[41] But no one knew how long a campaign might last, or how many losses might need to be made good. On the other hand, revenue was all too predictable; in fact there were only three points of flexibility. Crown lands could be sold, which meant diminishing capital; loans could be contracted, but they had to be serviced and eventually repaid; and parliament could be asked for direct taxation.[42] Each of these meant sacrificing an element of the queen's independence. Thanks to the policy of strict economy which had been pursued during the previous decade, there was no immediate financial crisis in 1585, in spite of the fact that the Low Countries alone absorbed over £300,000 by 1589.[43] Parliament voted a subsidy, tenth and fifteenth in both 1586 and 1587, which was generous by previous standards but inadequate in the circumstances.

By 1590 the treasury was empty, and hand-to-mouth methods had to be employed. Thereafter the problem was made worse by Elizabeth's secretiveness. There was, of course, no public scrutiny of accounts, and it is possible that Lord Burghley alone understood how difficult the situation really was. Nevertheless, although Elizabeth's behaviour made it obvious that she believed herself to be very hard up, she never confessed to the House of Commons, or to anyone else, just how hard up she really was.[44] To have done so, she no doubt felt, would have made her unacceptably vulnerable; and to have asked for the kind of money which she really needed would have meant endangering the partnership understanding upon which her whole regime rested. Parliament was therefore always to some extent in the dark about the scale of the problem it was dealing with. The preamble to the 1587 Subsidy Act had commenced:

> Considering with ourselves (most gracious sovereign) what infinite charges your highness hath been driven to sustain, besides your continual princely care to prevent and withstand the sundry most dangerous practices and enterprises of long time devised, We therefore, your Majesty's most loyal and obedient subjects, having in all duty, for God's honour and your Majesty's safety and our own surety and liberty as it behoveth us, do with all humility present unto your highness a subsidy.[45]

There was no mention of the war, nor of the exceptional charges which it inevitably brought. Between 1585 and the end of the reign, parliament delivered some £1,600,000, going as far as double and even treble subsidies on occasion; but that was less than half what the war cost, and nobody had access to that extremely sensitive information.[46] Clerical subsidies produced over £200,000 of the balance, and Elizabeth died some £300,000 in debt; but it is not difficult to see why she strove by all means possible to protect her freedom of action.

The price of that freedom was high. Had the queen been more willing, or able, to be liberal with her money, it would have greatly eased relations with her allies, both in France and the Low Countries.[47] It might also have reduced the interminable struggle in Ireland to more manageable dimensions. Having said that, no English military enterprise failed simply for lack of money. Both the Lisbon expedition and the Islands Voyage might have done better if they had been funded and controlled entirely by the admiralty, but that is speculation. The disgraceful scenes at the end of the Armada campaign, and the riots which followed demobilisation in 1589, could have been avoided if ready supplies of cash had been available, but Elizabeth never suffered the embarrassment of a major army mutinying for lack of pay, as happened to Philip II at Antwerp in 1576. The price of Elizabeth's extreme parsimony was not paid in the field but at home. On the one hand, parliament was allowed to believe that the war at sea against Spain virtually paid for itself. As anyone with first-hand experience knew, that was far from the case; but it was a comfortable myth, which enabled the House of Commons to be restrained in its offers of financial support.[48] It was also a delusion that persisted well into the following century, with perilous consequences.

At the same time the well of royal bounty virtually dried up. Between 1598 and 1603 the household, including the chamber, cost about £360,000, or £72,000 a year. For the following five years, when James had relaxed the purse strings, the comparable figures are £500,000 and £100,000.[49] The comparison is not entirely fair, because James had a consort and two sons to provide for, but it serves to demonstrate how extremely tight the court budget was at the end of Elizabeth's reign. She was herself keenly aware of this, and lamented the fact that she was not able to reward her servants in accordance with their deserving – or expectation. Because she still needed to sell land to meet her own costs, there were neither land grants nor cash annuities and pensions to be had, beyond what were paid by custom for specific duties.[50] Consequently the queen sought other means to gratify what she accepted were legitimate desires.

One such method was to sell trading concessions at preferential rates, or to give licences to export so many dickers of leather, or tons of coal. These were unglamorous, but could be extremely lucrative. Another method was the grant of monopolies. These might be exclusive rights either to trade in, or to manufacture, a given commodity. The earl of Essex's sweet wine monopoly had been of that kind.[51] All sorts of things, from soap to playing cards, might be the subject of these grants. The holder usually had no intention of making such items himself or through agents; what he did was to sell licences to the actual craftsmen and traders, who continued to conduct their business as before but had to carry an additional overhead in the cost of the licence. This cost they naturally passed on to their customers, with the result that the price of the commodity went up.[52] Such monopolies were effectively taxes levied on the consumer for the benefit of the recipient, usually a courtier or official. In principle they were no different from the trading monopolies which had long been granted to companies such as the Merchant Adventurers; but there was not even a pretence of protecting the public interest. As the queen's resources became more constricted, the use of these grants grew, and resentment grew in proportion. By 1600 a crisis was approaching, and Elizabeth found herself subjected to the nearest approach to public criticism which she ever had to endure.

The 'monopolies debate' took place in the House of Commons between 20 and 25 November 1601, and the strength of the grievances presented left no room for doubt.[53] Robert Cecil executed a tactical withdrawal on the queen's behalf, and with her approval. On 28 November, while the parliament was still in session, a proclamation was issued:

> Whereas her most excellent majesty, having granted divers privileges and licenses, upon many suggestions made unto her highness that the same should tend to the common good and profit of her subjects, hath since the time of those grants received divers informations of sundry grievances lighting upon many of the poorer sort of her people (by force thereof) contrary to her majesty's expectation.[54]

The queen expressed alarm and concern that her well-intentioned grants should have been so abused, and 'doth straightly charge and command that no letters of assistance that have been granted by her council for execution of those grants shall at any time hereafter be put in execution'. It was not exactly a surrender, because the grants were not cancelled. Theoretically abuses had been checked, and the effect of monopolies was to be monitored by the council, which was no longer to enforce them automatically. How much difference this would make remained to be seen.

When the parliamentary session ended two days later, the Speaker was careful to refer to her as

> most zealous, most careful to provide all good things for us, most gracious, most tender to remove all grievances from us, which your princely actions have ever showed. And even now your most gracious published proclamation, of your own mere motion and special grace for the good of all your people.[55]

He knew, however, and so did his colleagues, that all they had really succeeded in doing was to fire a warning shot, indicating that the queen might be about to lose some of the love and affection, which she so cherished, if she did not mend her ways. Elizabeth's response to the Speaker's oration demonstrated that she had taken the point, but also that her gift for theatrical self-presentation had not diminished with the years.

> Mr Speaker, we have heard your declaration and perceive your care of our estate by falling into the consideration of a grateful acknowledgement of such benefits as you have received, and that your coming is to present thanks unto us, which I accept with no less joy than your loves can have desire to offer such a present. I do assure you there is no prince which loveth his subjects better, or whose love can countervail our love, and though God hath raised me high, yet this I count the glory of my Crown, that I have reigned with your loves.[56]

This so-called 'Golden Speech' was a masterpiece of rhetoric. It was deeply sincere, even emotional, but it went nowhere near addressing the practical problems that were on the minds of the members. Instead, it demonstrated Elizabeth's unique capacity to interpret love in her own way, and to use it as a smokescreen, under cover of which to escape an unpalatable account-ability. Instead of any real concession to their pressing concerns, they were graciously permitted to kiss her hand.[57]

How much Elizabeth really cared about the well-being of her subjects, as distinct from earning their plaudits, is difficult to fathom. She made many general statements to that effect; and they were honest up to a point. She certainly believed that she was accountable to God for the good conduct of the affairs of the realm, but that meant the enforcement of law and order, and a proper respect for the Almighty rather than any kind of welfare provision.[58] The social and economic legislation of her parliaments was usually aimed at protecting established interests, and capping wages rather than safeguarding the vulnerable; and in any case it is very unlikely that the queen had much personal involvement in any of that.[59] Until the last decade of the reign so-called poor law legislation was more concerned with curbing unruly vagabonds than it was with providing either work or relief. At the same time it has to be remembered that, whereas social discipline had always been regarded as a responsibility of the crown, welfare had traditionally been the business of the church and the local community. That continued to be the case, but the balance shifted once the crown had accepted a responsibility to make sure that the communities did their duty.[60] A statute of 1597 required the churchwardens of every parish to appoint overseers of the poor, and every parishioner who was not himself in receipt of relief to contribute to a fund administered by such overseers. The funds so established were to provide relief for the aged, sick and impotent, and work for such able-bodied persons as might require it. The recalcitrant were to be reported to the justices of the peace, and punished as before.[61]

These were not new ideas, and many cities, such as London and Norwich, already had schemes that were more comprehensive.[62] Nor were these statutory provisions intended to take the place of private charitable initiatives. They were intended to ensure a minimum basic provision, and of course they were not to be paid for by the crown, but by rates which were both locally assessed and locally collected. These provisions were completed and tidied up by another Act in 1601, which was to remain on the statute book until the nineteenth century.[63] In a way the queen's acceptance of this responsibility was an aspect of her role as Supreme Governor of the church; but apart from the use of the parish as the unit of administration, it was an entirely secular provision.

Similar arrangements had been made a few years earlier for discharged soldiers and seamen. In spite of Burghley's apparent callousness at the time, the plight of those discharged in 1588 and 1589 had awoken consciences in high places. A man discharged from active service was supposed to surrender any weapons or equipment with which he had been issued, and return to his civilian employment. In theory there should have been no problem, since there were fewer men returning than had set out. In practice, however, many experienced difficulties for two reasons: they had often not been paid; and some of them were ill or maimed. The impecunious retained their equipment, which they then sold surreptitiously to get enough money to get home. It was easy to prohibit this, which was done in 1589, but less easy to provide a constructive remedy.[64] Pay was nearly always late, and often incomplete; but whether this was a cynical lack of compassion or sheer administrative inefficiency is not clear.

The preamble to an Act 'for the relief of soldiers' of 1593 declared punctiliously:

> Forasmuch as it is agreeable with Christian charity, policy and the honour of our nation, that such as have since the 25th day of March Anno 1588 adventured their lives and lost their limbs or disabled their bodies, or shall hereafter adventure their lives, lose their limbs or disable their bodies in the defence of her Majesty and the State, should at their return be relieved and rewarded, to the end that they may reap the fruits of their good deserving, and others may be encouraged to perform the like endeavours.[65]

The statute then proceeded to set up a disability pension scheme, providing for payments of ten, fifteen or twenty pounds a year according to the former rank of the recipient. As with the civil provision, however, this scheme was not to be a burden on the exchequer. Instead, the justices of every county were to set up and administer funds for this purpose, raised by an assessment on every parish. How effective this may have been is not clear; but at least it can be attributed to a genuine sense of responsibility, or even compassion, since the capacity of the sick and maimed to cause serious disciplinary problems in their communities (if they ever reached them) was not great.[66]

Elizabeth had little scope for the kind of symbolic compassion which rulers of an earlier generation had sometimes displayed in ritual almsgiving or the washing of feet. She did not touch for the King's Evil (scrofula), or even bless cramp rings as her sister had done; all such gestures would have smacked of superstition, not only to her puritanical subjects, but also to the queen herself. Her subjects were in her keeping, both body and soul, but it was not her business to do God's work for him. Both she, and all those to whom God had given grace and capability, however, had a duty to the poor, and she discharged her conscience with the kind of legislation mentioned above. To the modern mind it may not have been generous, but it was more socially relevant than religious foundations – as well as being less taxing on the capital assets.

As Elizabeth grew old, the question of the succession again rose in the order of political priorities. It had never gone away, although the deaths of the countess of Hertford in 1569 and the queen of Scots in 1587 had removed both the main contenders and changed the whole terms of the debate. By 1590 Mary's son, James, was the most obvious candidate, but he was not the only one. A few, who found James an unpalatable prospect, favoured Arabella Stewart, Lady Beauchamp, daughter of the sixth earl of Lennox and niece to Lord Darnley.[67] More seriously, Catholics who believed the king of Scots to be ruled out by heresy, looked favourably upon the real (but extremely remote) claim of Philip II's daughter, the Infanta Isabella

Clara Eugenia. In 1594 the Jesuit missionary and political activist Robert Parsons, maquerading as 'R. Doleman', published *A Conference about the Next Succession to the Crowne of England*, in which he examined in detail every conceivable claim going back to the time of the Norman Conquest, and came up (not surprisingly) with the verdict that the infanta's was best.[68] The strongest argument against James was that the Scottish line had been ignored in Henry VIII's last Succession Act; but Parsons had no interest in that sort of reasoning, and everyone else was trying to forget it.

It has been argued that James valued the prospect of the English succession more than his existing power in Scotland, and knew that Elizabeth had the power to make or break that ambition.[69] If that was the case, he did not always take sufficient precautions against upsetting his 'good sister'. In early 1592 the earl of Moray was murdered at the instigation of his personal enemy, the Catholic earl of Huntly. The kirk was outraged, and so was Elizabeth when she discovered that Huntly was also in contact with England's Spanish enemies.[70] James, however, liked Huntly, and probably lacked the power to move decisively against him. He was also sceptical about the capacity of the Scottish Catholics to inflict any meaningful harm on England; so he gave fair words to Elizabeth's representations, but did nothing.

Over the next year or so the factional politics of the Scottish court wavered erratically, with the king now apparently taking one side, now another.[71] Elizabeth's aim was to settle the Scottish feuds in such a way as to make plain the king's dependence upon her advice and support. Not surprisingly, he was unwilling to go down that road, and the queen bombarded him with reproachful letters. On 22 December 1593, she wrote:

> My dear brother, To see so much, I rue my sight that views the evident spectacle of a seduced king, abusing council, and wry-guided kingdom. My love to your good and hate of your ruin breeds my heedful regard of your surest saftey. I doubt whether shame or sorrow have the upper hand when I read you last lines to me.[72]

He could not afford to dance to her tune, and even if he had been so inclined the realities of Scottish politics would have made it impossible. On the other hand, if she became convinced that he was useless at running his own kingdom, she might well have looked elsewhere for her successor. Fortunately, the queen's envoys in Edinburgh were unwise enough to become involved in the in-fighting, instead of standing apart as they were supposed to do, and this gave James legitimate grievances of his own, which enabled him to turn some of the reproaches back.[73]

It may have been that the king had been playing a canny game from the beginning, and that his apparent ineffectiveness was simply a device to escape from a temporary crisis without giving too many hostages to fortune. By 1596 he was certainly in firmer control than at any time since achieving his majority, while the kirk was becoming weakened by internal disputes. Ironically, these arose partly from the hostility of some of the more zealous ministers to Elizabeth, whom they denounced as a timeserver and an atheist. By suppressing these inconvenient voices, the king was not only able to increase his authority over the kirk, but to improve his credentials in the eyes of the queen of England.[74]

By 1600, when there was no longer any prospect of Philip III being interested in their far-fetched plots, the Catholic lords of Scotland had also become a shadow of their former selves. James tidied up the current border disputes, and asked for another loan, as he had done periodically for years.[75] As has been seen, the lords of Kintyre were dabbling in Ulster between 1595 and 1597. The earl of Tyrone also at one point asked James to become the protector of Ireland. However, it was not in the king's interest to allow the western lords too much freedom of action, and Tyrone's value as a bargaining counter was highly suspect, even in 1599. He did not rise to the Irish bait, and by the end of 1602 was sufficiently in control of the whole of his kingdom as to allay even the most persistent English fears. In one of her last surviving letters, written to James on 4 July 1602, the queen declared:

> this I vow, that without you list I will not willingly call you in question for such warnings [of conspiracies against her] if the greatness of the cause may not compel me thereunto. And do entreat you think that if any accident so befall you as either secrecy or speed shall be necessary; suppose yourself to be sure of such a one as shall neglect to perform so good a work. Let others promise, and I will do as much with truth as others with wiles. Your most loving and affectionate sister.[76]

It was as warm an endorsement as he was likely to get.

Inevitably, some of Elizabeth's leading subjects had been this way before her. The earl of Essex had established contact with James through Anthony Bacon and David Foulis as early as 1593. By 1594 the king was corresponding directly with the earl in terms of some warmth, and Essex responded that he and his fellow countrymen 'jointly united their hope in your Majesty's noble person as the only centre whereof our rest or happiness consists'.[77] This was a trifle premature, and it was just as well that his royal mistress did not find out. In 1598 the French ambassador described the earl as the king's trusted intermediary with the English court. Essex's principal aim was clearly to ingratiate himself with the heir to the throne, but there was also a more sinister side to his negotiations. The two men began to exchange complaints and suspicions about the Cecils. James blamed the lord treasurer for holding up his English loans, and Robert Cecil dabbled rather pointlessly in the feuds of the Scottish court. In 1594 one observer wrote that 'I find a violent impression in his Majesty of the professed evil will of Burghley and Robert Cecil towards him'.[78] Robert Cecil had indeed met the earl of Bothwell in 1598, although it is not clear that anything came of the encounter; and when Burghley died there were expressions of pleasure and relief in Edinburgh. By 1599 Robert Cecil was seriously out of favour with the Scottish king. Although this may be partly ascribed to things which he had actually done, it was mainly the result of Essex's continual representations. If Elizabeth had died in 1599, the future of the Cecils would have looked bleak.

In the event, Elizabeth did not die. Instead the earl of Essex went to the block as a traitor; and whatever may be thought of his state of mind, his deed was clear enough. King James did not know quite how to respond. He knew that, with the earl's fall, Cecil was 'king' in England; and he had been led to believe that Cecil favoured the Infanta for the succession.[79] This was a typical piece of Essex misinformation. There was no truth in it, beyond the fact that the secretary had not yet foreclosed his options. An anonymous informant told Cecil: 'The king passeth with a fair outward countenance this matter of my Lord of Essex over, but inwardly he is one way sorry for it and another pleased with it'.[80] This somewhat cryptic observation probably alludes to the fact that James was well enough aware that if the earl of Essex had survived, he would have attempted to place the new king under an obligation.

As it was, he had to decide how to deal with Cecil, and his first move was inept. Believing the secretary to be hostile to him, he instructed his ambassador in England, John Erskine, earl of Mar, to issue a threat: 'Ye shall plainly declare to Mr Secretary and his followers that since now they will thus misknow me, when the chance shall turn, I shall cast a deaf ear to their requests'.[81] Cecil, however, was too wise and too experienced to take this at face value. The time had now come, in April 1601, to make his decisions; but he would do so in his own way and in his own time. The Scottish ambassadors visited him at Duchy Chambers in the Strand, and a careful understanding was reached.

As long as Elizabeth was alive, Cecil's loyalty was to her, and nothing could be allowed to detract from that; when she died, he would bring James to the throne.[82] The agreement was to remain secret, only two or three trusted familiars on each side being party to it, and it was enshrined in skilfully ciphered letters.[83] Cecil assured the king of his future loyalty, and James assured the secretary of his loving favour. With the benefit of hindsight this may all seem rather safe and obvious; but it was not necessarily so at the time. By 1602 everyone was very nervous; not least because the queen herself had not shown her hand. It was realised that her word, if and when she uttered it, would be decisive, but it was hard to predict. Both Parsons and Essex were in different ways responsible for increasing this tension, by suggesting that there might be serious support for the Infanta.

It was largely to counter that fear that Sir John Harrington published *A Tract on the Succession to the Crown* (1602). In a specific attack on the *Conference*, he objected to 'some secret Aspirers that broach lies to her Majestie, to serve either their own ambition, or others'. And he continued:

> I add thus much, that nothwithstanding all their lyes and false fyers, I mean their false fears, either in my Lord of Leycester's time or since, yet to this power they could never perswade her Majestie in aught I could ever learne to goe from that princely worde that she gave at the beginning of her raigne, as is before recited concerning the succession; and although indeed few dare ask her such a question, as who shall be her heire, yet a vertuous and discreet Ladye as any as hath place about hir hath told me voluntarily some tyme when few are present, shee hath taken occasion to speake of it herself, and then hath not stuck plainely to say that they were fooles that did not knowe that the lyne of Scotland must needes be next heires, but for all that no bodie dares ever sooth her when she saith it.[84]

Harrington's testimony is scarcely evidence, but he did have the *entrée* to the court, and his report is quite likely to be correct. It was reassuring as far as it went, but until Elizabeth spoke such words in public, a gnawing uncertainty remained.

By 1602, two deaths had struck the queen particularly hard. Her friends and servants had been dying steadily throughout the reign, and some of them, such as Kate Ashley and Robert Dudley, had been very close to her; but these two were rather different. William Cecil had been a model servant as well as an outstanding statesman. She had known him for fifty years, since she had been a vulnerable adolescent in trouble with Thomas Seymour. For forty years they had worked closely together, and, although they had not always agreed, they had enjoyed a special understanding. His death on 4 August 1598 deprived her of a unique relationship, and one which was literally irreplaceable.[85] He had died by the course of nature, and in the fullness of years. Much as Elizabeth may have missed him, she had no responsibility for his going.

It was quite otherwise with the earl of Essex. Although Essex had destroyed himself by an act of folly bordering on insanity, Elizabeth knew perfectly well that she was responsible for his fate in more than a formal sense. She had played with him to gratify her own vanity; and by being indulgent towards his extravagances had encouraged them. He was not like Robert

Dudley. Dudley could be provoked, bullied and teased, without his affection for her diminishing. His occasional anger and distress were all part of the game; and, although he had not always seen it that way, he had never objected. Essex was different. For all his charm and brilliance, he had no self-control, and his mental stability had always been questionable. She had known that; yet she had continued to make him dance attendance, to put up with her whims and her impenetrable changes of mood. This had been a game to her, but a life and death struggle to him. When she had finally had enough, and tried to discard him, she had instead driven him to desperation. It had been a dramatic tragedy, and when it was over, Elizabeth was quite shrewd and self-knowing enough to understand her true part in it. In executing him, she had been doing no more than her unavoidable duty as queen; but in driving him to such an extremity, she was guilty of abusing both her power and her womanhood; and she knew it perfectly well.

The queen's health had been generally robust. She had suffered from occasional agues, which can probably be identified as influenza, and had notoriously come close to death in 1562. But she had been famous for rigorous exercise and abstemious diet; and in her younger days she had hunted and hawked enthusiastically.[86] However, in the winter of 1602/3 a change began to be perceptible. In September she had entered what Camden called 'her Climacterical year, to wit the seventieth year of her age'. Whether she took her Bible literally enough to believe that her allotted span was now over, or whether she was suffering from some undiagnosed illness, is not clear. It was a foul winter, and she was depressed over her role in the Essex fiasco. She 'began to be sensible of some weakness and indisposition'; and her courtiers noticed that was becoming melancholy, and multiplying her religious devotions.[87] She had a ring filed from her finger, because it was so grown into the flesh that it could not be drawn off. There was nothing particularly sinister about that except that it was her symbolic 'wedding ring' with which she claimed to have espoused her realm. Some saw, or claimed later to have seen, in this act a symbolic dissolution.

By the beginning of March 1603 her appetite was failing, and she became convinced that her end was approaching. In the circumstances it was a self-fulfilling prophecy; but the queen had still not spoken the crucial words which were necessary to identify her successor, and the council began to fear that she would never do so. Consequently,

> They all thought good that he [the Lord Admiral] with the Lord Keeper [Thomas Egerton, Lord Ellesmere] and the Secretary should wait upon her, and put her in mind thereof, and acquaint her that they were come in the name of the rest of the Council to understand her pleasure touching her successor. The Queen

made answer with a gasping breath; I said that my throne was the throne of
Kings, and I would not have any mean person to succeed me. The Secretary
asked what she meant by these words. I will (said she) that a king succeed me,
and who should that be but my nearest kinsman, the King of Scots? [88]

So her final duty was discharged. Cecil's secret compact was secured, and
his future guaranteed. In Ireland the earl of Tyrone was kneeling at the
lord deputy's feet, and committing his fate to her judgement. In England,
at St James's Palace,

> On the 24th of March, being the eve of the Annunciation of the Blessed Virgin
> she (who was born on the eve of the Nativity of the same Blessed Virgin) was
> called out of the Prison of her earthly body to enjoy an everlasting Countrey in
> Heaven, peacefully and quietly leaving this life after that happy manner of De-
> parture which Augustus wished for, having reigned forty-four years, four months,
> and in the seventieth year of her age. [89]

In a sense, she had eventually willed herself to death, refusing conversation,
food and medicine. She even refused to go to bed, and expired at last on
a pile of cushions upon the floor of her chamber. Whether she really died
with a quiet conscience we do not know, her faith requiring neither confession nor last rites. She had, however, kept that faith in every sense of
the phrase, preserving both her realm and her church. A period of theatrical
mourning was appropriate to so theatrical a ruler; but the bonfires were
also lit in London, in honour of the new king, and Robert Carey set off to
bear the news to Edinburgh. After forty years of struggle and painful anxiety,
the succession was peaceful and undisputed.

13

The Great Queen

At the end of a recent, and exhaustive, study of Elizabeth's reign, the author concluded that she merited the title, not of 'the Great', but of 'the Fortunate'.[1] This prompts two immediate thoughts; if by 'fortunate' is meant lucky, then no one is consistently lucky for nearly fifty years; secondly, she had lived over a third of her life before she became queen. Was she equally fortunate during her formative years? Fortune is also not quite the same as luck. Luck is random, but fortune can be earned. It can be interpreted as divine favour, or as an instinctive capacity to judge situations and people correctly. In the latter sense it is distinct from rational calculation, or even the exercise of conscious will, and can also be described as wisdom. Elizabeth was fortunate in the sense of being wise. She was not always right, and her mistakes sometimes had serious consequences, but she had every reason to feel, at the end of her life, that she could render a good account of her stewardship.

Her sister Mary spoke with unwonted shrewdness when she declared that there were certain respects in which Elizabeth resembled her mother.[2] What the queen probably had in mind was a proclivity for heresy, but there was a lot more to it than that. Anne Boleyn had made a career out of her sexual allure. It had brought both triumph and disaster, and her daughter had inherited much of that appeal. What Elizabeth knew of her mother's history, or which version of it, we do not know. She must, however, have realised that Edward believed his stepmother to have been a witch and a whore; otherwise he would have had no cause to exclude his younger half-sister from the succession in 1553 on the grounds of bastardy. Anne's marriage to Henry had not been dissolved on the grounds of adultery, or even incest, which was alleged to have been committed after Elizabeth was born, but on a technical pretext arising from the fact that the king was convinced that he had been deceived (or even bewitched) into the union in the first place.[3] To believe that both Mary and Elizabeth were illegitimate, as Edward clearly did, was to follow the strict line of his father's reasoning, who had rejected both his first two marriages and their offspring. On securing the throne, Mary immediately corrected the record in respect of herself. This was easy to do, because the canon law had supported her throughout, and all that was necessary was to rescind judgements in the same way in which

they had been made, and by the same authority. She had claimed the crown
as Henry's legitimate daughter, and to her the Succession Act of 1543 was
irrelevant. No such straightforward solution was available to Elizabeth. She
also had herself declared legitimate on coming to the throne, and as she
was the last of Henry's children there was little point in challenging that.
As, however, she never tried to invalidate Mary's reign retrospectively (and
did not allow anyone else to do so), her claim had to rest on the statute.
It was that Act, and that alone, which provided legal protection against the
Scottish line.[4]

Consequently, although we are told that Elizabeth 'gloried' in her father,
she was equally aware of her mother. Whichever version of the story she
accepted, it had many implications for herself. In 1547, when it was rumoured
that she was with child by the lord admiral, it was also whispered that she
was behaving exactly like her mother. Elizabeth was far too sharp not to
have heard those voices. She learned, almost as soon as it was possible to
do so, that sex was a dangerous game. It was also both exhilarating and
useful. To be reassured of her physical attractiveness did as much for her
confidence as it would for any young woman. Unfortunately for her, her
early twenties, when these instincts were at their strongest, and the skills
most highly developed, were years of acute danger and psychological pressure. She kept herself under tight control, affecting a puritanical simplicity,
and survived.[5] The slightest relaxation in that austere demeanour would
certainly have been exploited by those who were only too anxious to discredit
her, if more direct attacks were frustrated.

When she came to the throne, that sort of constraint disappeared; but
it was replaced by others. It was then that she discovered, or first displayed,
those arts of coquetry for which her mother had been famous. Courtly love
was essentially the art of man-management, and that was above all what a
ruling queen needed. Anne had succeeded brilliantly while she was playing
to a sympathetic audience, but not when she had only a husband to please.
Husbands were tricky creatures to manage, not least because of the overwhelming strength of their position in law and custom. When that husband
was also a king the difficulties were compounded. Anne had failed to adjust,
with fatal consequences.[6]

All this Elizabeth knew, but there is no evidence to suggest how it affected
her behaviour. Many years later, probably in the 1580s, she wrote:

> When I was fair and young, favour graced me,
> Of many was I sought their mistress for to be,
> But I did scorn them all, and answered them therefore,
> Go, go, go, seek some otherwhere,
> Importune me no more ...

> Then spake fair Venus' son, that proud victorious boy,
> And said Fine Dame, since that you be so coy,
> I will so pluck your plumes that you shall say no more
> Go, go, go, seek some otherwhere,
> Importune me no more.[7]

Perhaps it was a voice of poignant regret for lost love; but more likely it was a conventional trope. Neither during the dangerous years of her sister's reign, nor after she had ascended the throne herself, did Elizabeth enjoy the freedom to be a 'mistress', even in the conventional courtly sense. This caused her great personal distress and frustration, because she was by nature an emotional, even a passionate woman; but it had its compensations. Above all, by remaining unattainable, she was able to stay in control. The 'belle dame sans merci' is a dominant figure, whose lovers serve her without reward, and who is untouched by their service and devotion.

The need to stay in control was indeed the key to most of Elizabeth's behaviour, both as a queen and as a woman. It was contrary to nature, even, as some thought, to the will of God, that a woman should exercise rule over men.[8] But the Fairie Queen, by whatever name she went, was an image of power. Moreover no man denied, except at his peril, that a woman unwed had the disposition of her own body, and to intrude upon that sovereignty was both a sin and a crime. So the queen's virginity became a symbol not only of her integrity but also of her power.[9] Marriage meant compromise and a surrender of autonomy. Elizabeth did not know how to resolve that problem, and her uncertainty undermined every negotiation. It was not simply that she was acting the part of a reluctant bride, whilst manoeuvring for political advantage. Always there was an instinctive calculation as to whether the political and personal advantages would outweigh the price to be paid. That issue was never prejudged, and the balance might change from day to day, resulting in exchanges of bewildering complexity.[10]

Eventually, as each courtship developed, the queen concluded that she did not wish to compromise her independence. As long as a negotiation continued, she was a woman who had to be wooed; had a conclusion ever been reached, that freedom would have disappeared, and her position would have become defined and constrained. Her half-sister Mary had pursued marriage with a single-minded determination, not because she knew how to resolve these contradictions, but because she believed them to be less important that the securing of the succession.[11] Elizabeth lacked that singleness of purpose, and remained famously a *femme seule*. Eventually this was put to political advantage, not because the Virgin Queen could take the place of the Virgin Mary, but because the integrity of the queen's body became a symbol for the integrity of her realm. When in 1588 she rhetorically juxtaposed the body of a weak and feeble woman with her 'foul scorn' that the prince of Parma should seek to invade her realm, the imagery was quite deliberate.[12] Whether (or when) Elizabeth herself chose to use her body in this metaphorical fashion we do not know; it was always quite consistent with the imagery of marriage to the kingdom, which she had adopted from the beginning.

The queen rejected anything that smacked of submission, whether sexual or political. She had, no less than Mary, a powerful sense of vocation. Just as Mary had believed that God had called her to her high office in order to restore His own honour and true worship, Elizabeth also believed in her divine calling. The two women differed, however, in one fundamental respect. Mary remained unswerving in her conviction that God intended her to fulfil His will by becoming a wife and mother, and by acting as a channel and vehicle for her husband and son. Elizabeth believed her calling to be personal and unique. Whether she chose to marry or not, it was she and she alone who was responsible for the rule of her kingdom. In a sense, by choosing her God had absolved her from the limitations of womanhood. This did not make her, in human terms, any less a woman; but it did mean that to surrender any aspect of the responsibilities which had been given her would mean failing in her duty. Mary had no difficulty in accepting conventional gender limitations, but could not come to terms with the bitter disappointments of childlessness and a failed marriage. Elizabeth rejected gender limitation and then had to struggle, not only with a sense of personal deprivation but also with the endless problems created by dealing with men who did not see the world with her eyes.

Her constant prevarication and changes of mind have to be seen in this light. She could have simply made a decision, after proper consultation, and then left it to her ministers or other servants to carry it out. That was what her council (at first) expected her to do. In their own minds they would have glossed that expectation with the thought that women did not really understand the details of diplomacy, or ecclesiastical administration, or military deployment, or whatever was in question. Elizabeth had no time for such thoughts; so she intervened constantly. She stopped voyages that were on the point of sailing, and even tried to call them back; she authorised agreements with the Dutch or with Henry IV, and then went back on them because she thought an extra ounce of advantage could be extracted.[13] She sent clear signals to the duke of Anjou that she would marry him, then changed her mind, and left him fuming about women's inconstancy. By acting in this apparently irresponsible manner she not only kept everyone on their toes, she also made it abundantly clear that she could not be bypassed or taken for granted. Her political grasp was formidable. Although that did not make her prevarication any easier to bear, it did mean that they were never gratuitous.

Elizabeth's whole style of rule was pragmatic and free from preconceptions. It was not that she had no strategic aims, but they were broad and simple. God had entrusted her with three things: a realm to defend; a church to lead in the true way; and a people to protect, both against foreign enemies and against themselves. The second of these aims was pursued in a manner very different from the other two; and anyone tempted to believe that Elizabeth was congenitally incapable of decisive action or long-term consistency should consider her ecclesiastical policy. At the beginning of her reign, and against the best worldly advice, she created a Protestant establishment, which she then defended with tenacity and ingenuity for over forty years. It was her church, her thank offering to God, and she was utterly determined to keep it that way, against both papist assault and radical subversion. Her notoriously low opinion of the clergy who staffed that church was not caused (usually) by contempt for their learning or diligence, but by suspicion that, given the chance, they would reimpose a sacerdotal regime.[14] Protestant clergy did not claim the *potestas ordinis*, but they were set apart by their ordination and given a function which she, as a woman, could not share. It was therefore essential to keep them under firm control and to assert her authority over bishops and archbishops, such as Grindal, whose own sense of duty made them too independent, or even defiant. How dare they! She would decide what their duty was, because God had given that authority to her.[15] It was an issue of control.

By contrast, neither her foreign nor her secular domestic policies were so determined. There the queen was not predisposed to any particular strategy. Whereas Mary had been quite clear that England's best interests would be served by a Habsburg alliance, or even dependency, Elizabeth was uncommitted. She inherited a war with France, and in those circumstances the continuation of the Habsburg alliance was mere common sense: hence good relations with Philip II, and the Austrian marriage negotiations. Yet any hint of dependecy was ruled out, and the war was quickly concluded. Thereafter Elizabeth's priority was clear. England's interests, including her own, took precedence over every other consideration. This led directly to the endless convolutions and short-term shifts that every historian of Elizabethan foreign policy has charted. As the storms of ideological conflict rose in Europe, engulfing England's nearest neighbours, France and the Netherlands, the queen struggled to keep her realm in peace, and to avoid commitment. She disliked rebels on principle, fearing that such ideas could prove infectious, yet self-interest dictated that she should support them; first in Scotland, then in France and finally in the Low Countries. In every case the negotiations were a complicated dance as the queen, her advisers, and the potential allies advanced, retreated, spun, disengaged and re-engaged. Elizabeth's aim was always to do as little as possible for as long as possible; and she took advantage of every shift in the circumstances to achieve this, with baffling displays of indecisiveness and inconsistency.

The trouble with examining these negotiations in detail is that the wood cannot be seen for the trees. The observer inevitably becomes bogged down in short-term shifts, and in the anger and frustration that they caused.[16] Walsingham, Norris, Sadler, even Cecil, regularly threw up their hands in despair at having to deal with such displays of feminine inconstancy. Yet it is worth noticing how often these negotiations succeeded in achieving the desired objectives, and usually at minimal cost. The queen empowered her delegates, but frequently intervened herself. In a case like the treaty of Edinburgh (1560), where the chief credit is always given to Cecil, he knew perfectly well that he could not conclude an agreement against her wishes, or independent of them.[17]

Elizabeth, however, often had her own reasons for not wanting to make her control obvious; and she regularly reserved a position from which it was possible to disown mistakes. The growth of English piracy, particularly at the expense of Spain, between 1565 and 1580 is an obvious case in point. Elizabeth could, and occasionally did, forbid these adventurers to set out, which suggests that those who did go went with her explicit or implicit approval. Foreign complaints, however, were regularly met with bland surprise or assumed concern, and referred to the admiralty court, as not being political issues.[18] Even when the queen's own ships were involved, she could point out that the voyages had no official status, because instructions had not been issued. Even when a commitment had been made, she was at pains to limit it. It was because the earl of Leicester exceeded his orders in accepting the governorship of the Low Countries that she became so angry with him. Leicester himself appears to have believed that his commission entitled him to use his own discretion in such matters, but that was never Elizabeth's intention. She could not tell him how to fight a battle, but she could keep him on a short political lead, and that she had every intention of doing. She may have wished it to appear that he had freedom to act, so that she could disown him if made an error; but woe betide him if he made any major decision on that assumption.[19]

Norris in Brittany and Mountjoy in Ireland were given more freedom, precisely because they were not major political figures but professional soldiers doing a job which even Elizabeth did not profess to understand.[20]

Essex, however, fell into the same category as Leicester; and it was his cavalier treatment of his instructions, rather than his failure in the field, which brought him into disfavour. It was Essex who inadvertently exposed the weakness in this carefully crafted system of management. Angered and baffled as they often were, Elizabeth's servants usually accepted that it was not their business to penetrate her arcane ways. William Davison was deeply distressed when he was made a scapegoat for the execution of Mary Queen of Scots; a case in which the queen, having been forced to make a decision, was anxious to evade the responsibility. He did not run away to Spain, however, or conspire with the queen's enemies. Essex, on the other hand, could not accept that it was his function to be picked up and dropped at the whim of a woman, even one old enough to be his mother. He glossed his disaffection with hatred of Robert Cecil, but he knew perfectly well that it was Elizabeth who was responsible for his disgrace.[21] She misjudged his proud and volatile disposition, and it was the bid to escape from her control that brought him to the block.

Essex was an extreme case; but we can see in many aspects of her government how suspicious Elizabeth was of those who might, or might think that they could, act independently or upon the basis of some authority other than her own. Woe betide the preacher who told her that she was misinterpreting the will of God. Woe betide also that nobleman or great gentleman who believed that his status entitled him to flout the law. As Lord Buckhurst told the earl of Salisbury in 1592:

> Your Lordship must remember that in the policy of this Common wealth, we are not over ready to add encrease of power and countenance to such great personages as you are. And when in the country you dwell in you will needes enter in a warr with the inferiors therein, we thinke it both justice, equity and wisdom to take care that the weaker part be not put down by the mightier.[22]

Neither Elizabeth nor her council was particularly concerned by the constant aristocratic feuds over land or honour, which occasionally erupted into violence.[23] Homicide was not tolerated, but even then pardons could be obtained at a price. These feuds might be a threat to local order, but they were not a challenge to the queen's authority. The intimidation of juries, or the bullying of those unable to protect themselves, were challenges, however, and the court of Star Chamber was quick to call such offenders to account.[24] It might not always be clear to those on the receiving end when a sheriff or a justice of the peace was acting in an official capacity and when in a private one, but a degree of latitude in that respect was part of his bargain with the crown, and the line between acceptable and unacceptable behaviour was often a fine one. Nevertheless, as Buckhurst's observation makes clear, every man was expected to be accountable for the authority that he exercised. There was nothing particularly new about this; both Henry VIII and Mary had called noblemen to account for committing common felonies;[25] but Elizabeth's attitude to her nobility resembled that of her grandfather more closely than either her father or her sister. She created no dukes or marquises, and very few earls; most of her new creations were barons, and she got very upset if her field commanders dubbed too many knights, as Essex did in France. Nor, with the exception of Leicester and Essex, were noblemen used any longer as field commanders; and the days when they were expected to go to war at the head of their own retinues were over.[26] Typically, noblemen were lords lieutenant, commanding men raised and armed by public authority – that is, the authority of the queen.

By the same token, parliament was supposed to provide a service; useful, indeed essential, but not expected to show initiative. Elizabeth was quite happy for noblemen to exercise their patronage in the House of Commons, but not at all happy if they tried to put pressure upon her by that means. Similarly, she was happy to receive petitions from the House of Commons, but not to bargain with the members over issues of policy. Debates over her marriage, the succession, the government of the church and the fate of Mary Queen of Scots, were all ruled out of order at one time or another. Elizabeth nevertheless knew that the Commons, like the gentry that it represented, could be led but not driven; and it was because she knew this that she refused to put issues of principle to the test. Her prerogatives were *arcana imperii*, to be neither questioned nor defined. It was a balancing act. She knew perfectly well that she could not govern effectively without what she chose to describe as the 'love' of her subjects; but she also knew that that love constrained her own freedom of action.[27] She never admitted this publicly, but she developed political antennae that enabled her to avoid most of these obstacles without apparently noticing their existence.

Elizabeth had no grand ambitions, as her father had done, either for 'honour' in the military sense or for territorial expansion. It was a lack of such ambition that made her intervention in Scotland at the beginning of her reign acceptable.[28] It was a lapse from that principle which brought her to grief in France in 1563. She had no desire to be the leader of Protestant Europe, but she had no option but to accept the pope as a declared enemy after 1570. She did not make alliances with Protestants such as the Huguenots or the Dutch because they were Protestants (although some of her council took that view), but because they were curbs upon the power of Spain. Elizabeth would happily have avoided conflict with Philip II if she could have done so, and wriggled like an eel for years to preserve the peace; but the logic of both their positions made that eventually impossible. She was innocent of any ambition to convert Spaniards to the truth of the gospel, but perfectly well aware that they did not share a similar restraint. Unless she defended her kingdom by all the means at her disposal, both its religion and its independence would be destroyed. The fact that her subjects also knew that, and entirely supported her efforts, was one of the great bonds between them. Any enemy of Philip thus became, actively or passively, an ally. Much as she may have deplored Henry IV's conversion, he was still an ally where it mattered. The same was true of the sultan. After years of privileged and profitable trading with the Ottoman empire, she wrote to Mohammed III in 1601:

> Most high and most puissant prince; It is no small contentment to us that the amity we have with so high and renowned a prince as you, is by our neighbour princes and their subjects so well known that when they have need to ask any favour or kindness from you, they implore our mediation as the readiest way to obtain their desires.[29]

The French believed that Elizabeth had incited the sultan to war against the emperor, and Philip II had similarly supported the Persians against the Turks.

The queen was not directly involved with Frobisher's explorations, or with the Roanoake venture, although she was interested in both, but she was an active participant in many of the ventures and expeditions which brought about the diversification of English trade during her reign, and created the springboard for the great expansion of the following century.[30] Her role in this promotion was one of the most positive features of her reign, as well as one of the most neglected in conventional assessments. Elizabeth did not share John Dee's vision of a British empire, but she was impressed by it; and convinced to the point of believing that England's future strength and prosperity lay in its commerce. Both Hawkins and Drake should be counted among her favourites. Good relations with the sultan, and with the tsar of all the Russias, to say nothing of Drake's circumnavigation of the world, spelled out a global ambition which the queen herself had neither the time nor the resources to realise; but it was a legacy to her successors.

Elizabeth was not easily frightened, but her early experiences had made her apprehensive of danger. The traumatic experiences of 1547 and 1554 were never entirely erased from her mind. Then she had feared dishonour more than death, and that remained with her, although the nature of the dishonour changed. Her physical courage was perfect. When James I feared assassination, he took refuge in padded mattresses and other undignified expedients.[31] Elizabeth was similarly threatened for years, but would allow no additional precautions, and never curtailed her exposure to her people. Greatly as they feared for her safety, her people found her courage an inspiration. The dishonour which she feared as queen was not sexual assault in the common sense, but a theft of her authority which was also related to gender. If a king was weak, his male subordinates would exploit him, but a woman might be exploited simply because she was a woman. The language and imagery of power were profoundly masculine.[32] A woman's honour was sexual and private; a man's honour was military and public. So Elizabeth faced two problems: she had to lead and dominate men who were accustomed to think of women as inferior creatures and she had to find an imagery of power that was both effective and feminine. Her father had been an imposing figure, and her brother had made a somewhat feeble attempt to imitate his pose, but that was not a road open to Elizabeth.[33] At first she was the aloof, mysterious beauty of the courtly love tradition, later the magnificent unattainable Virgin, Gloriana.

In a sense this imagery was brilliantly successful, and it dictated the language of courtly discourse throughout the reign. But it was only half the battle, because practical men were quite accustomed to humouring their women with such language, while leaving them virtually no control over their own lives. Her councillors might also play the courtier, but when it came to business they were hardheaded. It was in council, not in public display, that Elizabeth faced her longest and toughest battles. Fortunately she was extremely intelligent and had a barrister's ability to grasp a brief. She could not be outfaced in debate, and her knowledge was often superior to that of her advisers. Like other women in managerial situations, she felt vulnerable; vulnerable when confronted by male bonding, and vulnerable to that patronising attitude which was instinctive to men in such a position. When Mary had felt similarly threatened she had yelled at her council; to no effect, as she admitted.[34] Elizabeth shouted at her courtiers and ladies, and occasionally boxed their ears, but she did not shout at her council. Instead she delayed decisions, recycled ideas, reopened closed issues, changed her mind, and indulged in irrelevant rhetoric. No doubt her indecisiveness was often genuine, but it was also a control mechanism. Except in routine matters, her council could not act until she had made up her mind; so she kept them waiting, dancing with frustration and impatience. She did the same thing with foreign envoys, particularly if they wanted some favour from her. Sometimes these tactics worked in an objective fashion: they won valuable time, or allowed contentious issues to resolve themselves. Sometimes they did not work, and valuable opportunities were allowed to slip away. They were only ever partly aimed at the substantive issues; partly they were aimed at the councillors themselves, and some of them probably realised this. Other than Essex, no one who worked closely with the queen was ever alienated by this behaviour, however cross it made them in the short term. Of course they attributed it to her gender, and they were right; but they never found a way to circumvent it, and eventually it just became an accepted fact of political life.

As a young woman Elizabeth had been thought beautiful; she was also an intellectual, and brilliantly educated. Apart from a Welsh great grandfather, she was entirely and self-consciously English. The first propaganda piece of the reign, published within days of her accession, had made that very point, describing the new queen as a

> Prince (as ye wot all) of no mingled blood, of Spaniard or stranger, but borne mere Englishe here amongst us, and therefore most natural unto us. Of education brought up and induct in all vertuous qualities and Godlye learnynge, specially (that may be the most comfort and ioy to us all) in the sincere knowledge and following of God's holy word.[35]

The author was, of course, a Protestant, and concerned to condemn Mary at least as much as to praise Elizabeth, but his description of the queen as 'mere Englishe' struck a responsive chord in all sections of society. Mary had been half Spanish by blood, and her husband was wholly Spanish; so that, although she never set foot outside England, she was vulnerable to the criticism that both her antecedents and her priorities were alien.[36] Elizabeth was quick to seize the opportunity that this perception created. In responding to the first of many petitions for her to marry, in February 1559, she said:

> Reproach me no more that I have no children; for every one of you, and as many as are English, are my children and kinsfolk, of whom, so long as I am not deprived and God shall preserve me, you cannot charge me, without offence, to be destitute.[37]

It was a consistent theme, and it was well judged to catch the mood of her people. As Feria observed even before her coronation, Elizabeth loved the plaudits of the crowd, and it was a characteristic that stayed with her to the end. Up to a point this was sheer vanity; she loved flattery, and did not mind much who provided it. It was also partly a consequence of her lurking insecurity. Flattery was a form of reassurance; even if she did not merit it, she was able to exact it like a kind of tribute. In later life, when she was no longer beautiful, she was no less English, and the adulation of her subjects could persuade her that God was in His heaven and all was right with the world. As parliament constantly reminded her after 1570, her life had become synonymous with her kingdom's welfare – and even its very survival. She not only knew how to talk to her subjects, she knew what gestures to make and which symbols to invoke. Richard Mulcaster's *The Passage of our most dread Sovereign Lady* is the only source for her famous coronation entry, so we cannot be sure that it is an accurate description; but we can be sure at least that it represented what the queen wanted to be believed – and that is almost the same thing for this purpose.[38]

Whether Elizabeth was equally good at listening is another matter. It would be hard to point to any aspect of her policy which was clearly influenced by public opinion; and when her subjects spoke through their representatives in the House of Commons, she was quick to tell them to mind their own business. Her policies became more obviously popular as the reign progressed. In 1560 her church settlement pleased very few, but, as Catholicism became increasingly associated with foreign interference and plots against her life, Protestantism gradually became part of the fabric of national identity. The war with Spain was popular, as was the execution of Mary Queen of Scots, while the failure of the Armada convinced all but the most sceptical that God approved of the queen of England.[39]

Elizabeth herself did little to improve the lives of most of her subjects, but there were no disturbances to equal those of 1549 or 1536. Justice was well administered in the sense that it was not widely perverted by private interests; and the council's tight control over the commissions of the peace was largely responsible for that. The crisis of her brother's reign had demonstrated the danger of ignoring what might be called the 'yeoman officers' in the interests of the gentry. Elizabethan England was a 'gentry commonwealth', and that was by the queen's deliberate choice, but enough was done to protect the interests of constables and churchwardens to prevent them from becoming disaffected as a group – either from the justices or from the crown. Consequently, although real wages continued to decline until almost the end of the reign, disaffection was successfully contained to local agrarian riots of the kind that were endemic in early modern Europe.[40]

Elizabeth's regular progresses were, and were designed to be, occasions for loyal demonstrations. Although these could be orchestrated up to a point, large-scale popular enthusiasm could not be simulated, and was recorded by disinterested observers as well as royal propagandists.[41] The courtly literature of flattery was large, subtle and frequently replicated. Some of the finest 'courtly makers' of Renaissance Europe attended upon Elizabeth and the whole image which she bequeathed to posterity reflected that fact.[42] There was also a more homely version of the same thing:

> Her faithful soldiers great and small
> as each one stood within his place,

upon their knees began to fall
desiring God to 'save her Grace!'
for joy whereof, her eyes were filled
that water down distilled,
'LORD bless you all, my friends!' she said,
'but do not kneel so much to me!' [43]

Her public utterances may have been calculated, but she had a charisma that transcended the court, and indeed was probably stronger among those who were not regularly exposed to her uncertain temper. It is hard to say whether this had any tangible effect upon her government; but the combination of a country at war with a great enemy, discovering its identity and fired by loyalty to such a ruler, certainly conferred a sense of purpose. That in turn helped to keep the peace during years of plague, harvest failure and high inflation which could easily have destabilised a less popular regime.

Intellect, image and sexuality are the three defining words that come to mind when attempting any assessment of Elizabeth; but she possessed other qualities. She was a fine scholar and linguist, and a competent poet. Many of her letters are elaborate and latinate to the point of incomprehensibility, but her style was much admired and imitated at the time. She had a good ear for music, and was a capable performer upon the virginals, although she does not appear to have inherited either her father's singing voice or his talent for composition. The fact that she protected Catholic musicians such as Byrd and Tallis tells its own story. She danced with enthusiasm, was a good horsewoman, and hunted and hawked with the best. Unlike Mary Queen of Scots, she seems not to have been a needlewoman, except as a child; but then she did not have the advantage of Mary's enforced leisure. She also had that endearing characteristic, a sense of humour, and often addressed her familiars by affectionate nicknames. The best known is 'Eyes' for Robert Dudley, but when she wrote to her old friend and servant Margery Norris to condole with her on the death of her son, she scribbled at the head of an otherwise somewhat formal letter 'Mine own Crow, harm not yourself for bootless help, but show a good example to comfort your dolorous yokefellow'.[44] More intriguingly, when writing to Lord Mountjoy about the affairs of Ireland in December 1600, she started her letter 'Mistress Kitchemaid', and proceeded to observe 'that you with your frying pan and other kitchen stuff have brought to their last home more rebels, and passed greater breakneck places than those that promised more and did less'.[45] Clearly she was in a good mood that day, and had picked up a reference in one of Mountjoy's own letters to his task in Ireland being like that of a kitchen wench.

Elizabeth also kept jesters. There was nothing surprising in that, because it was an old custom, and her father's elderly retainer Will Somers was still in her service at the very beginning of her reign.[46] He was succeeded by one Jack Greene, and then by Richard Tarlton. These were clowns and mimics, whose repertoire was probably not very sophisticated. Of the latter it was written:

> When Tarlton clowned it in a pleasant vaine
> With conceits did good opinions gaine,
> Upon the stage his merry humours shop.
> Clownes knew the Clowne by his great clownish slop.[47]

This suggests comic capers and outlandish costume rather than sharp verbal sallies; the rustic rather than the courtier. This may have been because more pointed humour frequently sailed too close to the wind. Elizabeth enjoyed a romp and a coarse joke or innuendo, but any witticism designed to deflate her dignity was not well taken; and John Pace, the earl of Leicester's fool, was banned from her presence for his 'bitter' jibes.[48] It would appear that while the queen enjoyed laughing at other people, she was not particularly good at laughing at herself. She did not, apparently, indulge in the common contemporary practice of keeping 'innocents', or freaks, although two mysterious young women feature in the records who may have been something of the kind. The first was known as Ippolyta the Tartarian, described in 1564 as 'oure deare and wellbeloved woman', and the second was Tomasina de Paris. Both were made clothing allowances over a number of years, and Tomasina appears to have been a dwarf; but the nature of the service they provided is nowhere described.[49] They are unlikely to have been jesters in the ordinary sense, and whether they were supposed to be a source of humour is not known. Tarlton, in contrast was a famous comedian who also appeared on the public stage, and was remembered with affection years after his death. But just what he did that contributed so much to Elizabeth's sense of well-being is nowhere recorded.

In spite of her occasional tantrums, the queen was a loyal friend, and the turnover of her servants, both at court and council, was very slow and almost entirely natural. Her fatal break with the earl of Essex was altogether exceptional. The fact that she never married does not mean that she either was, or felt herself to be, lonely or unloved. She may have felt frustrated as a woman, but she was devoid of self-pity, and as a monarch felt confident that she had discharged the trust that God had bestowed upon her.

Elizabeth was that rare creature, a genuinely independent woman. However gratifying an orthodox sexual relationship might have been, it would have meant sacrificing that independence; and probably the independence of her kingdom by which both she and her subjects set such store. It is unlikely that she ever made a decision of principle not to marry; but every time that a particular decision about a courtship had to be made, the price of consummation was always too great. We do not know when she passed the menopause, although she must have known herself and her physicians would have had a pretty shrewd idea. As long as marriage was on the political agenda, it was a state secret of great delicacy; then quite suddenly it no longer mattered. She was a woman forced by genetic accident (or the will of God) to do a man's job, and to manage men. No other woman in England held a public office above the parochial level. Mary had set some useful legal precedents, but her whole style of government had been a warning rather than an example.[50] Consequently Elizabeth was forced to improvise, to make up the rules as she went along. She used her sexuality, her acute brain and her sense of theatre to develop a unique method of management. She never ceased to feel vulnerable, however, which was why her control could be more than a little obsessive, and her tactics for maintaining it so devious. The motto attributed to Philip II, 'Time and I against the World', could well have been applied to Elizabeth, whose instinct was always to avoid both action and commitment for as long as possible. She also knew when her options had run out, as the treaties of Edinburgh and Nonsuch demonstrate.

In no issue of foreign policy could her prevarication and indecisiveness be said to have led to disastrous consequences for her country. On the international stage there was no better survivor. At home her achievement can only be judged with hindsight. A combination of good sense and longevity settled the church, and it was no fault of hers that confessional issues became so divisive forty years after her death. She gave her country pride, and set its commercial development on a course that was eventually to be spectacularly successful; for that she deserves more credit than she is usually given.

She failed to deal with two issues of crucial importance which were to derail the regimes of her successors. Having encouraged the gentry to adopt a higher and higher profile in government, she failed to find a satisfactory definition of the constitutional relationship between crown, lords and commons, although several models were offered to her by William Cecil in the course of the reign. By refusing to define it she protected her prerogative from formal limitation, but left it vulnerable to attack, as was already becoming apparent before she died. Secondly, she conspicuously failed to tackle the problem of inadequate revenue. By muddling along, and improvising from hand to mouth, she managed to survive; but the consequence was that nobody faced the fact that the crown needed a regular and substantial taxation income, even to conduct its normal peacetime operations, never mind to wage war. It was as much ignorance as extravagance or ill-will that caused the financial crises of the early Stuarts; and for that ignorance Elizabeth was to blame. Her inability to act promptly and decisively was thus more damaging at home than it was abroad. It was caused directly by her fear that parliament, and particularly the House of Commons, would be empowered to exercise a measure of control which she believed should belong to herself alone.

Elizabeth chose for herself the motto *Semper Eadem* ('Always the Same') and in most respects that consistency served her well, both as a person and as a ruler. It also meant an unwillingness, even an inability, to embrace change. It could be said that she was so concerned to remain in charge of the ship, and to avoid the icebergs of Spanish and papal hostility, that she failed to spot the other unobtrusive rocks lying in her path. She was not on the bridge when the ship went down. When she died, the theatrical displays of mourning were accompanied by audible sighs of relief. It would be good to have a king again after fifty years of female rule. Kings were creatures defined by ancient custom; but queens, however loved and admired, were unpredictable.

James I was a foreigner, but he spoke the same language and shared the same religion. He was also an experienced ruler with two healthy sons to guarantee the succession. As he began to make mistakes, however, the more the subtle virtues of the old queen began to be appreciated. The new king did not know how to talk to his subjects, and he misunderstood their prejudices, being in a sense too intellectual to be intelligent. He overestimated both the wealth of his new kingdom (or at least the accessibility of that wealth) and the powers of his office. As a stranger, he had no sense for the obstacles that might lie in his path, and blundered into them repeatedly. His foreign policy particularly baffled and offended those who, for over a generation, had regarded Spain as an evil enemy. By comparison 'Good Queen Bess' seemed a model of straightforward patriotism.

Charles I was a great deal worse. If James had not known how to talk to his subjects, at least he had tried. Charles never felt called upon to make any such effort. Where Elizabeth's court had been dignified but accessible, and James's had been scandalous and turbulent, Charles's was refined and esoteric. Handicapped by a speech impediment and by natural reticence, he could communicate effectively only with a small and narrow circle of friends. His belief in the divine nature of his office was probably not very different from Elizabeth's, but he completely lacked her pragmatism. Because of her dubious legitimacy, she could not appeal to the simple certainties of Divine Right. Charles, on the other hand, saw no reason to equivocate, or even to watch where he was putting his feet. Elizabeth may not have appeared to listen, but she knew her way around. Charles was like a man steering by compass, but without the benefit of either a map or a knowledge of the ground. It is not surprising that nostalgia had created a powerful myth by 1640.

Elizabeth was unique. Her myth depended less upon substantive success than upon her gender. Samuel Johnson observed that a woman preaching was like a dog walking on its hind legs, remarkable for the feat rather than its quality. Similarly what was surprising about Elizabeth as a ruler was not that she was always a brilliant success, but that she was a success at all. Those who followed her also contributed to her reputation, both directly and indirectly: directly by making mistakes that she had avoided, and indirectly by treating her memory with respect. Her reputation was also partly fortuitous, in that it depended upon developments for which she was only partly responsible. There is a good case for crediting her with the diversification and expansion of trade, and also with the growth of London as a financial centre; but her responsibility for the great flowering of English literature, drama and music was less direct. She was a discriminating patron, but not a hugely generous one, and it is difficult to say how much her courtiers owed in this respect to her example. In culture as in politics, history has credited her with other people's achievements. But it was because she caught the English imagination that this happened. As Lytton Strachey observed:

> While the Spanish ambassador declared that ten thousand devils possessed her, the ordinary Englishmen saw in King Hal's full blooded daughter a queen after their own heart. She swore, she spat, she struck with her fist when she was angry; she roared with laughter when she was amused.

An exaggeration, of course, but a testimony to a durable achievement, as well as to what the English appreciated in a ruler.

Notes

Notes to Introduction

1. G. R. Elton, *The Practice of History* (Cambridge, 1967), passim.
2. Roy Strong, *The Cult of Elizabeth* (London, 1977), pp. 14–16, 'The Last Pageant'.
3. Roy Strong, *Gloriana. The Portraits of Elizabeth* (London, 1987), pp. 9–48.
4. Wallace MacCaffrey, *Elizabeth I* (London, 1993) is the result of a lifetime spent studying the queen, her actions and her policies, but less than thirty pages (out of 450) are devoted to her formative years. Christopher Haigh's book with the same title, *Elizabeth I* (2nd edn, London, 2000), does not pretend to be a full study, of either the queen or the reign, but is rather a deliberate (and successful) attempt to demythologise the period.
5. David Starkey, *Elizabeth* (London, 2000) is probably the most attractively written study to date, and is carefully researched, but mainly from published sources.
6. For example, her letter to Queen Mary, of 2 August 1556, professing her loyalty. *Elizabeth I: Collected Works*, ed. L. S. Marcus, J. Mueller, and M. B. Rose (Chicago, 2000), pp. 43–44.
7. Anne was famous for her skill as a coquette, a skill to which she brought the gloss of a French training. Inevitably this caused her to be described (quite unjustifiably) as a whore – particularly by less successful women. E. W. Ives, *Anne Boleyn* (Oxford, 1986).
8. 1 Mary, st. 3, c. 1 . J. Loach, *Parliament and the Crown in the Reign of Mary Tudor* (Oxford, 1986), pp. 96–97.
9. Philip had been the object of vituperation in England, which extended far beyond the ranks of the Protestants. D. Loades, *The Reign of Mary Tudor*. (London, 1991), pp. 185–86.
10. Susan Doran, *Monarchy and Matrimony: The Courtships of Elizabeth I* (London, 1996).
11. Ibid., pp. 10–11; P. Berry, *Of Chastity and Power: Elizabethan Literature and the Unmarried Queen* (London, 1989).
12. J. G. Nichols, *The Progresses of Queen Elizabeth* (London, 1823), iii, p. 652.
13. P. L. Hughes and J. F. Larkin, *Tudor Royal Proclamations* (New Haven, 1964–69), ii, p. 240.
14. For the extremely delicate balancing act performed by Sir Philip Sidney in this connection, see Blair Worden, *The Sound of Virtue: Philip Sidney's Arcadia and Elizabethan Politics* (New Haven, 1996), pp. 40–57.

15. Strong, *The Cult of Elizabeth*, pp. 17–22.
16. Timothy Bright, *An Abridgement of the Booke of Acts and Monumentes* (2 vols, London, 1589) ii, sig. 8b.
17. On this theme, see particularly Haigh, *Queen Elizabeth I*, and S. Adams, 'Favourites and Factions at the Elizabethan Court', in R. G. Asche and A. M. Birke, eds, *Princes, Patronage and the Nobility: The Court at the Beginning of the Modern Age* (London, 1991), pp. 265–87.
18. William Cecil in particular had constant difficulties with a mistress who often rejected his advice, while expressing the highest confidence in his judgement. Conyers Read, *Mr Secretary Cecil and Queen Elizabeth* (London, 1955) and *Lord Burghley and Queen Elizabeth* (London, 1960).
19. The surviving manuscript of this speech, BL, Harley MS 6798, ar. 18, fol. 87, is subscribed 'Gathered by one that heard it and was commanded to utter it to the whole army the next day …'; so exactly how, to whom, and even whether, it was originally delivered is uncertain. *Elizabeth I: Collected Works*, pp. 325–26.
20. D. Loades, *Mary Tudor: A Life* (Oxford, 1989), pp. 248–51.
21. J. B. Black, *The Reign of Elizabeth, 1558–1603* (Oxford, 1959), pp. 2–5.
22. Starkey, *Elizabeth*, pp. 118–22.
23. John Foxe, *Acts and Monuments* (1563).
24. *Elizabeth I: Collected Works*, p. 137.
25. Patrick Collinson, *Archbishop Grindal, 1519–1583: The Struggle for a Reformed Church* (Berkeley, California, 1979), pp. 97–99.
26. Starkey, *Elizabeth*, pp. 65–75; G. W. Bernard, 'The Downfall of Sir Thomas Seymour', in Bernard, ed., *The Tudor Nobility* (London, 1992), pp. 212–40.
27. See below, pp. 96–99.
28. Doran, *Monarchy and Matrimony*, pp. 40–72; Derek Wilson, *Sweet Robin: A Biography of Robert Dudley, Earl of Leicester, 1533–1588* (London, 1981).
29. Read, *Mr Secretary Cecil*, pp. 117–34.
30. J. E. Neale, *Elizabeth I and her Parliaments*, 2 vols (London, 1957), ii, pp. 434–39.
31. Paul Slack, *The English Poor Law, 1531–1782* (Basingstoke, 1990).

Notes to Chapter 1: The King's Marriage

1. *Grafton's Chronicle or History of England* (1809), ii, p. 449.
2. There has been considerable debate about the date of Anne's birth, and whether she was older or younger than her sister Mary. I am following Eric Ives, *Anne Boleyn* (1986), pp. 18–19, in dating her birth to 1501, and assuming that she was the younger.
3. *Calendar of State Papers, Spanish*, i, p. 267. Garrett Mattingly, *Catherine of Aragon* (1963), pp. 46–48.
4. A treaty for the new marriage had been signed on 23 June 1503, but it was nearly eighteen months before the dispensation was issued. Mattingly, *Catherine of Aragon*, p. 56. D. Loades, *Henry VIII and his Queens* (1994), pp. 13–14.
5. The heir to Castile on her mother's death was her eldest surviving daughter,

Juana, who was in the Low Countries and married to Philip of Burgundy. By the terms of Isabella's will, Ferdinand could only have claimed the regency if Juana had refused to return to Spain. Juana and her husband did come in 1506, when Ferdinand was ousted. Philip then died and Juana became mentally unstable, enabling her father to return. Catherine, however, might have been preferred as regent by some of the nobility, if she had been available.

6. Mattingly, *Catherine of Aragon*, pp. 57–64.

7. *Letters and Papers of the Reign of Henry VIII*, i, no. 5 (ii); J. Scarisbrick, *Henry VIII* (1968), p. 24.

8. Scarisbrick, *Henry VIII*, pp. 51–52.

9. There was a circumstantial story that Henry propositioned Anne Hastings, a married sister of the duke of Buckingham. There were certainly rumours to that effect, but the main source is Don Luis Caroz, who was not close to the action. Mattingly, *Catherine of Aragon*, pp. 110–11; Loades, *Henry VIII and his Queens*, pp. 21–22.

10. For a full discussion of this affair, and the birth of Henry Fitzroy, see B. Murphy, *Bastard Prince: Henry VIII's Lost Son* (2001).

11. Mary had been betrothed to Charles by a treaty of September 1521. The initiative had come from the emperor himself, and Henry had not been sanguine about the outcome. *Letters and Papers*, iii, nos 1152, 1160; D. Loades, *Mary Tudor: A Life* (1989), pp. 20–21.

12. Murphy, *Bastard Prince*, pp. 41–68.

13. There is a common illusion that Mary was princess of Wales, but in fact there was no creation between 18 February 1504 and 4 June 1610.

14. For a plausible reconstruction of the timetable of events, see Ives, *Anne Boleyn*, pp. 108–9.

15. The relevant text is Leviticus 20:21: 'If a man shall take his brother's wife, it is an unclean thing they shall be childless'. Against this could have been set the so-called 'levirate', decreed in the Book of Deuteronomy, which required a man to take his brother's widow if the first union had been childless. The Hebraist Robert Wakefield conveniently informed the king that the Vulgate was defective, because the original Hebrew said 'they shall be without sons'.

16. Ives, *Anne Boleyn*.

17. This opportunity was created by Thomas Boleyn's diplomatic mission to the Archduchess Margaret in 1512. He made such a good impression upon the regent that she agreed to give his daughter a place as one of her eighteen *filles d'honneur*. Ives, *Anne Boleyn*, pp. 22–23.

18. Lancelot de Carles, 'De la royne d'Angleterre', lines 62–68, in G. Ascoli, *La Grande-Bretagne devant l'opinion française* (Paris, 1927).

19. The source for this story, which is questionable in detail but probably accurate in outline, is George Cavendish, *The Life and Death of Cardinal Wolsey*, ed. R. S. Sylvester, Early English Text Society, 243 (1959), pp. 29–34.

20. One of these was apparently the king's former tutor, John Skelton. Greg Walker, *John Skelton and the Politics of the 1520s* (1988).

21. Ives, *Anne Boleyn*, pp. 108–9. See also Retha Warnicke, *The Rise and Fall of Anne Boleyn* (1989).
22. Mattingly, *Catherine of Aragon*, pp. 183–84.
23. Charles's reaction may have been prompted by the political calculation that Henry's real intention was to enter into a matrimonial alliance with France (which was Wolsey's idea); but the fact that his attitude did not relax when he discovered this to be unfounded suggests that it was the affront to his family which rankled. Scarisbrick, *Henry VIII*, p. 157.
24. The best account is still that of Scarisbrick, *Henry VIII*; but see also Guy Bedouelle and Patrick Le Gal, *Le 'divorce' du roi Henry VIII* (Geneva, 1987) and Edward Surtz and Virginia Murphy, *The Divorce Tracts of Henry VIII* (Angers, 1988).
25. In Clement's mind the decisive factor seems to have been the dispensation which his predecessor Julius II had granted; it would have been damaging to have gone back on that precedent. However, he could only have afforded to offend the emperor if Charles had been very preoccupied elsewhere – which he was not.
26. Scarisbrick, *Henry VIII*, pp. 208–9.
27. By far the fullest account of the twists and manoeuvres of these year is given by Ives, *Anne Boleyn*, pp. 113–234.
28. *Grafton's Chronicle*, p. 415.
29. Ibid., pp. 416–19, Scarisbrick, *Henry VIII*, pp. 220–23.
30. 'And farther, the xvii day of November, he sent the two Dukes of Norfolk and Suffolk, to his place at Westminster, to fetch away the Great Seal of England, which he was loth to deliver, if there had been any remedy', *Grafton's Chronicle*, p. 420. Peter Gwyn, *The King's Cardinal* (1990), pp. 616–17.
31. The circumstantial detail behind this version is derived from Cavendish, but he was writing years after the event, and was not objective. Until his efforts finally collapsed in 1529, Wolsey offered Anne her best chance of a solution. After the Blackfriars fiasco her attitude became irrelevant. Ives, *Anne Boleyn*, pp. 128–30.
32. *Correspondence du Cardinal Jean du Bellay*, ed. R. Scheurer (Paris, 1969), pp. 44, 113.
33. *Calendar of State Papers, Venetian, 1527–33*, p. 241. Who the ambassador's informant may have been is not apparent.
34. Ives, *Anne Boleyn*, passim.
35. *The Papers of George Wyatt*, ed. D. Loades, Camden Society, 4th series, 5 (1968), p. 22. This passage was not written until about 1605.
36. Notably Hugh Latimer, Edward Baynton and Nicholas Shaxton. Ives, *Anne Boleyn*, pp. 310–12.
37. Diarmaid MacCulloch, *Thomas Cranmer* (1996), pp. 45–46.
38. J. G. Nichols, *Narratives of the Days of the Reformation*, Camden Society, 77 (1860), pp. 241–42.
39. Graham Nicholson, 'The Act of Appeals and the English Reformation', in *Law*

and Government under the Tudors, ed. C. Cross, D. Loades and J. Scarisbrick (1988), pp. 19–30.

40. *Calendar of State Papers, Spanish, 1531–33*, p. 33.
41. H. A. Kelly, *The Matrimonial Trials of Henry VIII* (1976), pp. 192–95.
42. Christopher St German, *Doctor and Student*, ed. T. F. T. Plucknett and J. J. Barton, Selden Society, 91 (1974), p. 327.
43. Scarisbrick, *Henry VIII*, pp. 297–300.
44. Margaret Pole had been created countess of Salisbury in her own right in 1513, although that had been technically a restoration.
45. MacCulloch, *Thomas Cranmer*, pp. 75–76.
46. Grafton says 25 April, but that is almost certainly a mistake. Hall, with an eye on Elizabeth's standing, says 14 November 1532, which is too early. Ives, *Anne Boleyn*, p. 202.
47. Nicholas Udall, 'English Verses and Ditties at the Coronation Procession of Queen Anne Boleyn', in A. F. Pollard, *Tudor Tracts* (1903), p. 21.
48. *The Noble Triumphant Coronation of Queen Anne, Wife unto the Most Noble King Henry the VIIIth* (Wynkyn de Worde for John Gough, 1533), in Pollard, *Tudor Tracts*, pp. 11–19.
49. *Calendar of State Papers, Milan*, p. 911; Ives, *Anne Boleyn*, p. 226.
50. *Letters and Papers*, vi, no. 1009; *Calendar of State Papers, Spanish, 1531–33*, p. 756.
51. Examination of Mary Baynton, before Nicholas Robson, Robert Browne and Thomas Pulvertoft, September 1533, *Letters and Papers*, vi, no. 1193.
52. Chapuys to Charles V, 16 October 1533, *Letters and Papers*, vi, no. 1296.
53. D. Loades, *Mary Tudor: A Life* (1989), p. 78.
54. *Letters and Papers*, vii, no. 1208. Catherine was undoubtedly bullied, and moved arbitarily from place to place, but Henry scrupulously provided a level of maintenance deemed appropriate for a dowager princess.
55. Ives, *Anne Boleyn*, pp. 240–41.
56. Loades, *Henry VIII and his Queens*, pp. 63–89.
57. Loades, *Mary Tudor*, pp. 82–83. When Henry was planning another trip to Calais, Anne apparently declared that she would take advantage of his absence to do away with Mary, no matter what the consequences. As usual, the source of this story is Chapuys.
58. BL, Cotton MS Otho C. x, *Letters and Papers*, x, no. 968; Loades, *Mary Tudor*, pp. 99–101.
59. For a discussion of the significance of these Acts, see G. R. Elton, *The Tudor Constitution* (1982), pp. 2–3, 59–61.
60. Ives, *Anne Boleyn*, pp. 355–57.
61. Ibid., pp. 253–55.
62. *Calendar of State Papers, Spanish, 1534–35*, p. 484. Cromwell apparently told Chapuys that if Anne found out how much he favoured the emperor, she would have his head.
63. Rethan Warnicke, 'The Fall of Anne Boleyn: A Reassessment', *History*, 70 (1985), pp. 4–6.

64. Ives, *Anne Boleyn*, pp. 335–56.
65. *Letters and Papers*, x, nos 141, 199.
66. *Calendar of State Papers, Spanish, 1534–35*, pp. 595.
67. Retha Warnicke, 'Sexual Heresy at the Court of Henry VIII', *Historical Journal*, 30 (1987), pp. 247–68. The main evidence comes from accusations made by Nicholas Sander over thirty years later.
68. *Calendar of State Papers, Spanish, 1536–38*, pp. 39–40. Again these stories were picked up by Chapuys.
69. Ives, *Anne Boleyn*, pp. 357–58.
70. This can be demonstrated particularly by the patronage which the family was continuing to receive. Stanford Lehmberg, *The Reformation Parliament* (1970) p. 230.
71. *Letters and Papers*, ix, no. 674.
72. Loades, *Mary Tudor*, p. 96.
73. Warnicke, *The Rise and Fall of Anne Boleyn*.
74. Ives, *Anne Boleyn*, pp. 375–76. Inevitably none of this extremely dubious evidence was advanced at the trial.
75. Warnicke, 'Sexual Heresy at the Court of Henry VIII'.
76. MacCulloch, *Thomas Cranmer*, pp. 154–60.
77. Ibid.

Notes to Chapter 2: The Infant Princess

1. *Grafton's Chronicle or History of England* (London 1809), ii, p. 449; BL, Harley MS 543 fol. 28; *Letters and Papers*, vi, no. 1111.
2. *Letters and Papers*, vi, no. 1112.
3. Robert, abbot of St Albans to Cromwell; *Letters and Papers*, vi, no. 1122.
4. *Grafton's Chronicle*, p. 449.
5. Chapuys to Charles V, 15 September 1533, *Letters and Papers*, vi, no. 1125.
6. *Grafton's Chronicle*, p. 449. A number of courtiers known to be sympathetic to Mary, such as the marquis and marchioness of Exeter, were deliberately given prominent roles. The Lady Mary of Norfolk was the duke's daughter, the future duchess of Richmond.
7. Chapuys to Charles V, 15 September 1533. *Letters and Papers*, vi, no. 1125.
8. Provision must have been made before the child was born, but there is no nominal roll, and no account, which suggests that the women concerned were already employed within the household.
9. 'Acts of the Privy Council', 2 December, *Letters and Papers*, vi, no. 1486.
10. Chapuys to Charles V, 9 December 1533, *Letters and Papers*, vi, no. 1509.
11. Neither of these ladies is given an official title in the surviving documents. Chapuys always refers to Lady Shelton as being in charge, and she was corresponding with Cromwell in September 1534. It is not know exactly when Lady Bryan was appointed.
12. *Letters and Papers*, vii, no. 372.

13. When the next account was rendered, on 25 March 1535, it showed a half yearly receipt of £1110 13s. 4d. *Letters and Papers*, viii, no. 440.
14. David Loades, *Mary Tudor: A Life* (Oxford, 1989), appendix 1.
15. A total of £148 8s. od. was credited to Cholmely from these sources.
16. Chapuys to Charles V, 23 December 1533. *Letters and Papers*, vi, no. 1558.
17. Randall Dodd, formerly a groom of her chamber, remained with Mary and was her messenger to the Carews. *Letters and Papers*, vii, no. 1172.
18. Cholmely had been Mary's cofferer before her establishment had been dissolved. He had survived the intended reduction of her establishment in October (when she ceased to be 'princess'); but it seems that this reorganisation never took effect, and he had been transferred directly to Elizabeth's household instead. Loades, *Mary Tudor*, p. 74.
19. *Letters and Papers*, vii, no. 1208.
20. This sentence, which was provisional rather than definitive, had been given in July, before Elizabeth's birth. It is not known exactly when Catherine learned of it. When it was being discussed by her supporters in England during October, it was realised that the repudiation of the new heir would be a consequence. J. Scarisbrick, *Henry VIII*, pp. 318–20. *Letters and Papers*, vi, nos 807, 1311.
21. PRO, E101/421/13
22. The stay at Hertford had been only brief, and Elizabeth had probably reached Hatfield about 16 December. *Letters and Papers*, vi, no. 1528. On Hatfield House, see H. M. Colvin, *The History of the King's Works*, iv, *1485–1660* (Oxford, 1982), pt 2.
23. *Letters and Papers*, vii, nos 83, 230.
24. Ibid., no. 296. Chapuys to Charles V, *Letters and Papers*, viii, no. 568.
25. Chapuys to Charles V, 21 February 1534, *Calendar of State Papers, Spanish*, v, p. 57. Loades, *Mary Tudor*, pp. 82–83.
26. Ibid., pp. 83–84.
27. *Calendar of State Papers, Spanish*, v, p. 12.
28. Eric Ives, *Anne Boleyn* (London, 1986), pp. 371, 393, *Letters and Papers*, x, nos 908, 909.
29. *Letters and Papers*, vii, no. 509; also Chapuys to Charles V 22 April, ibid., no. 530.
30. Chapuys to Charles V, 12 April 1534, *Letters and Papers*, vii, no. 469.
31. Ibid., no. 1095; Loades, *Mary Tudor*, p. 84.
32. *Letters and Papers*, vii, no. 1171.
33. *Letters and Papers*, viii, no. 438. Hunsdon, rather than Hatfield, seems to have been the household's main base at this time.
34. *Letters and Papers*, ix, no. 568.
35. J. J. Scarisbrick, *Henry VIII* (London, 1968), pp. 318–20; Ives, *Anne Boleyn*, pp. 252–54. Henry ineptly chose to send Edmund Bonner with a defiant message to Clement VII in the middle of his interview with Francis in November 1534. *Letters and Papers*, vi, no. 427.

36. *Letters and Papers*, vii, no. 1348. This was a draft, drawn up in Francis's name, which remains in the Public Record Office. It is unlikely that the French king ever saw it, although he would have been aware of what Henry wanted him to do.
37. Charles had been born in 1522 and was to die in 1545.
38. *Letters and Papers*, vii, no. 1482.
39. Gontier to Chabot, *Letters and Papers*, viii, no. 174.
40. Ibid.
41. Chapuys to Charles V, 9 February 1535, ibid., no. 189.
42. Henry VIII to de Brion (Chabot), March 1535, *Letters and Papers*, viii, no. 339.
43. Ibid., no. 343.
44. Bishop of Faenza to M. Ambrosio, *Letters and Papers*, viii, no. 399.
45. Bishop of Faenza to M. Ambrosio, 12 April 1535, ibid, no. 537.
46. Ibid., no. 557.
47. Ibid., no. 793.
48. Bishop of Faenza to M. Ambrosio, 22 June 1535, *Letters and Papers*, viii, no. 909.
49. Ibid.
50. Bishop of Faenza to M. Ambrosio, 6 June 1535, *Letters and Papers*, viii, no. 537.
51. Ibid., no. 909.
52. Chapuys to Charles V, ibid., no. 355. In the circumstances this would have been an extremely optimistic kite to fly, but Chapuys would have had no incentive to misrepresent the conversation.
53. He had been replaced at Calais by Lord Rochford. Chapuys thought that he was trying to evade responsibility for a failure which he foresaw. *Calendar of State Papers, Spanish*, v, p. 452; Ives, *Anne Boleyn*, pp. 254–55.
54. Chapuys to Charles V, 13 October 1535, *Letters and Papers*, ix, no. 597.
55. Chapuys to Charles V, 21 January 1536, *Letters and Papers*, x, no. 141.
56. There are somewhat conflicting reports of her reaction, but Chapuys wrote to Granvelle on 25 February, 'I am credibly informed that the Concubine, after her miscarriage, consoled her maids who wept, telling them it was for the best, because she would the sooner be with child again, and that the son she bore would not be doubtful, like this one, which had been conceived during the life of the Queen'. *Letters and Papers*, x, no. 352.
57. Chapuys to Granvelle, 10 February 1536 'I must not forget to tell you that there are innumerable persons who consider'. etc. *Letters and Papers*, x, no. 283.
58. Bibliothèque Nationale, MS 5045, fol. 9; *Letters and Papers*, x, no. 410.
59. BL, MS Cotton Otho C. x, fol. 278; *Letters and Papers*, x, no. 808.
60. Ibid., nos 908, 909.
61. *Letters and Papers*, x, nos 1044, 1107. No papers recording this judgement survive, and his latest biographer has described it as 'the unacceptable face of his loyalty to Henry VIII'. D. MacCulloch, *Thomas Cranmer* (London, 1996), pp. 158–59.
62. Scarisbrick, *Henry VIII*, p. 335.
63. Loades, *Henry VIII and his Queens*, pp. 90–91.

64. M. St Clare Byrne, ed., *The Lisle Letters* (Chicago, 1981), iii, p. 713.

65. *Letters and Papers*, xi, no. 41. The statute was 28 Henry VIII, c. 7.

66. The examination of Sir Anthony Browne, 14 June 1536, *Letters and Papers*, x, no. 1134; Loades, *Mary Tudor*, p. 101.

67. Chapuys to Charles V, 1 July 1536, *Letters and Papers*, xi, no. 7.

68. Loades, *Mary Tudor*, p. 103.

69. BL, Cotton MS Vespasian C. xiv, fol. 274.

70. BL, Additional Charter 67534.

71. More significantly perhaps, the first list is headed by 'Lady Troy' (Lady Herbert of Troy), who does not feature in the second. She was of higher status than those who served later. BL, Cotton MS Vespasian C. xiv, fol. 274; *Letters and Papers*, x, no. 1187.

72. These may well have been 'servants of servants', as they are allocated to the listed offices.

73. Some of these women can be only tentatively identified. Catherine Champernowne was a daughter of Sir Philip Chapernowne of Modbury, Devon; she was the sister of Sir Arthur Champernowne, and the sister-in-law of Anthony Denny. She is better known by her married name of Catherine Ashley. Elizabeth Garnet (or Garnysshe) was probably a daughter of Sir Christopher Garnet, the knight porter of Calais, and Alice Huntercombe the daughter of Sir Walter Huntercombe. Ralph Taylor may have been related to George Taylor, the (late) queen's receiver general, but the name was not uncommon.

74. Ives, *Anne Boleyn*, pp. 406–7.

75. BL, Cotton MS Otho C. x, fol. 230; *Letters and Papers*, xi, no. 203.

76. *Letters and Papers*, xi, no. 312, 'I shall provide for her as I did for my Lady Mary when she kept her chamber'.

77. Account of William Lok, 'mercer to the Quenes Maiestie', 20 January to 27 April 1536, *Philobiblion Society*, 7 (1862–63) p. 11. There was also a bill for boat hire 'from Greenwich to London and back to take the measure of caps for my Lady Princess, and again to fetch the princess's purple cap to mend it £68 4s. 1½d.' *Letters and Papers*, x, no. 913.

78. BL, Cotton MS Otho C. x, fol. 284. *Letters and Papers*, xi, no. 132.

Notes to Chapter 3: The King's Daughter

1. *Letters and Papers*, xi, no. 639. Starkey, *Elizabeth* (London, 2001), pp. 25–26. Some doubt has been cast on this identity, but no plausible alternative has been suggested. A. J. Collins, *Jewels and Plate of Queen Elizabeth* (London, 1955), p. 200.

2. Catherine is nowhere officially described as 'Lady Governess', and in the absence of detailed accounts it is not possible to say what her formal position was; but it is clear that she was responsible for Elizabeth's early education and that therefore the title is an appropriate one.

3. Starkey, *Elizabeth*, pp. 26–27. Elizabeth's commendation of Catherine was in

the context of a plea to Protector Somerset for her release from confinement in March 1549. BL, Lansdowne MS 1236, fol. 35. See also below, p. 69.

4. *Letters and Papers*, xi, no. 240. On 27 September 1536 a memorandum of business refers to one 'Rule, of the Chaundry in the Lady Mary and Lady Elizabeth's house' on a hunting trip. Ibid., p. 500.

5. Brian Tuke to Thomas Cromwell, 28 May 1537, *Letters and Papers*, xii, no. 1297.

6. *Letters and Papers*, xi, no. 860.

7. BL, MS Cotton Titus B. i, fol. 481; *Letters and Papers*, xii, no. 815.

8. BL, Royal MS 17 B, fol. xxviii; printed by Frederick Madden as *The Privy Purse Expenses of Princess Mary* (London, 1831).

9. BL, MS Cotton Titus B. i, fol. 489; *Letters and Papers*, xii, no. 816.

10. Loades, *Mary Tudor* (Oxford, 1989), pp. 107–8.

11. *Letters and Papers*, x, no. 384. David Loades, *Henry VIII and his Queens* (Stroud, 1994), p. 91.

12. Apparently he told her that she should concentrate upon making children of her own, not concern herself with others. *Historical Manuscripts Commission, Twelfth Report*; Rutland MSS, pt iv, i, pp. 309–11.

13. John Strype, *Ecclesiastical Memorials* (London, 1721), i, pt 2, p. 304.

14. Loades, *Henry VIII and his Queens*, p. 99.

15. This was essentially the same jointure which had been settled on Queen Anne, and confirmed by the statute of 25 Henry VIII, c. 25. BL, Harley MS 303, fos 16–24; Eric Ives, *Anne Boleyn* (London, 1986) p. 256.

16. *Letters and Papers*, xii, pt 1, no. 600.

17. *State Papers of Henry VIII*, i, pt 2, p. 551.

18. *Grafton's Chronicle or History of England* (London, 1809), ii, p. 462.

19. *Letters and Papers*, xii, pt 2, no. 911.

20. *Grafton's Chronicle*, ii, p. 462.

21. *Letters and Papers*, xii, pt 2, no. 973.

22. Ibid.

23. Castillon to Francis I, 14 February 1538, *Letters and Papers*, xiii, no. 273.

24. Ibid., no. 402.

25. Loades, *Mary Tudor*, p. 126; Retha M. Warnicke, *The Marrying of Anne of Cleves* (Cambridge, 1999), p. 67. Henry was keeping his options wide open at this stage, because it was at this time that he made his famous proposal that Francis I should arrange a parade of eligible French beauties for his benefit.

26. Loades, *Mary Tudor*, p. 126.

27. Marillac to Francis I, 27 December 1539, *Letters and Papers*, xiv, no. 744.

28. Warnicke, *The Marrying of Anne of Cleves*, pp. 12–93.

29. M. St Clare Byrne, *The Lisle Letters* (Chicago, 1981), v, p. 79; J. Loach, *Edward VI* (London, 1999), pp. 9–10; W. K. Jordan, *Edward VI: The Young King* (London, 1968), pp. 38–39.

30. Jordan, *Edward VI: The Young King*, p. 38.

31. *Letters and Papers*, xii, pt 1, no. 1101.

32. *Letters and Papers*, xiv, no. 1120.

33. *Letters and Papers*, xiv, no. 655.
34. Jordan, *Edward VI: The Young King*, pp. 38, 40; *Letters and Papers*, xix, no. 864.
35. Loades, *Mary Tudor*, p. 116; Chapuys to Mary of Hungary, 5 December 1540 and 6 February 1541. *Calendar of State Papers, Spanish*, vi, pp. 143, 151.
36. Chapuys to Charles V, 13 August 1543; *Letters and Papers*, xviii, pt 2, no. 39.
37. *Letters and Papers*, xiv, pt 1, no. 5.
38. Starkey, *Elizabeth*, p. 26.
39. *Letters and Papers*, xiv, pt 2, no. 697.
40. Jordan, *Edward VI; the Young King*, pp. 40–41.
41. M. Dowling, *Humanism in the Age of Henry VIII* (Beckenham, 1986), pp. 212–13; L. V. Ryan, *Roger Ascham* (Oxford, 1963), p. 303; John Strype, *The Life of Sir John Cheke* (Oxford, 1821), pp. 25–27.
42. Jane was almost exactly the same age as Edward, and both her parents were frequently at court. He knew and liked her well (there was talk of marriage at one point). It is unlikely that she could have obtained her formidable learning in the relative seclusion of Bradgate Hall.
43. *Elizabeth I: Collected Works*, ed. L. Marcus, J. Mueller and M. Rose (Chicago, 2000), pp. 5–6. (Translation.) The original is among the Cotton manuscripts in the British Library.
44. M. Dowling, *Humanism in the Age of Henry VIII*; S. James, *Katheryn Parr: The Making of a Queen* (Stroud, 1999).
45. *Elizabeth I: Collected Works*, pp. 6–7.
46. Marc Shell, *Elizabeth's Glass* (Lincoln, Nebraska, 1993), p. 4; Bodleian Library, MS Cherry 36; *A Godly Medytacyon of the Christen Sowle* (Marburg, 1548).
47. *Letters and Papers*, xiv, pt 2, nos 494, 572.
48. *Letters and Papers*, xv, nos 136, 248, 543. There is no concrete evidence that Henry ever seriously intended settling the succession on the King of Scots.
49. R. J. Knecht, *Francis I* (Cambridge, 1982), pp. 297–99.
50. *Letters and Papers*, xvi, nos 204, 306.
51. Charles, duke of Orleans, was nineteen at this point, having been born in 1522. When Francis, the Dauphin, died in 1536, Henry became dauphin and Charles, previously duke of Angoulême, inherited the Orleans title. In 1541 Mary was twenty-five and Elizabeth eight, so it was probably Mary he was interested in. *Letters and Papers*, xvi, no. 885.
52. Ibid., nos 1090, 1208. See also Chapuys's intelligences of November 1541; ibid., no. 1390.
53. Council to William Paget, 3 March 1542, William Paget to Henry VIII, 25 March; *Letters and Papers*, xvii, nos 143, 200.
54. *Grafton's Chronicle*, pp. 477–79; *Letters and Papers*, xvii, nos 818, 852–53; Scarisbrick, *Henry VIII*, p. 435.
55. *Letters and Papers*, xvi, no. 804; ibid., no. 380; ibid., no. 1389.
56. *Letters and Papers*, xvii, no. 468.
57. James's death was unconnected with the battle, as he had been ill for some time; it was later alleged that he died of chagrin.

58. Henry VIII to Sadler, 4 April 1543; *Letters and Papers*, xviii, pt 1, no. 364.

59. *Letters and Papers*, xviii, pt 1, no. 509; pt 2, nos 9, 111.

60. *Letters and Papers*, xix, no. 470.

61. *Grafton's Chronicle*, p. 492; Scarisbrick, *Henry VIII*, pp. 450–51; instructions to Christopher Mont, January 1545; *Letters and Papers*, xx, no. 90.

62. This was on the 6 November 1546, but appears to relate to the same negotiation; *Letters and Papers*, xxi, pt 2, no. 359.

63. *Letters and Papers*, xviii, pt 2, nos 128, 132.

64. *Letters and Papers*, xx, nos 639, 764.

65. *Grafton's Chronicle*, p. 497; David Loades, *John Dudley, Duke of Northumberland* (Oxford, 1996), pp. 78–79.

66. 35 Henry VIII, c. 1. *Statutes of the Realm*, iii, p. 955.

67. Loades, *Reign of Mary*, pp. 18–19.

68. P. W. Hasler, ed., *The History of Parliament: The Commons, 1558–1603* (London, 1981), where he is called Astley.

69. *Elizabeth I: Collected Works*, preface.

70. Ibid., pp. 10–13. The original MS is NAS RH 13/78 (fos 1–7) in the Scottish Record Office.

71. Ibid., pp. 9–10. The MS is BL, Royal 7 D. X.

72. Ibid., p. 9, n. 1.

73. They are included as witnesses in the notarial instrument, *Letters and Papers*, xviii, pt 1, no. 873.

74. *Letters and Papers*, xix, pt 1, no. 780. There is a similar arrangement noted for 17 September.

75. *Letters and Papers*, xix, pt 2, no. 688. The errand is described as being 'at her grace's commandment', but whether this refers to the queen or Elizabeth is not clear.

76. *Letters and Papers*, xx, pt 2, no. 909. At the same time Elizabeth is noted as having petitioned for the provision of one John Huddlestone to a fellowship at King's Hall, Cambridge, which was granted 'upon the next vacation'.

77. *Letters and Papers*, xxi, pt 2, nos 963, 969.

78. Ibid., nos 502, 571; 5 and 18 December 1546.

79. Ibid. no. 555. Scarisbrick, *Henry VIII*, pp. 482–83.

80. Loades, *Mary Tudor*, pp. 135–36.

81. W. K. Jordan, *The Chronicle of Edward VI* (London, 1966), p. 4, refers to 'great lamentation and weeping', but not in the first person.

Notes to Chapter 4: The King's Sister

1. J. Strype, *Ecclesiastical Memorials* (London, 1721), ii, 2, pp. 289–311.

2. David Loades, *Mary Tudor: A Life* (Oxford, 1989), p. 135.

3. PRO, LC2/2, fos 5v, 49r–52v.

4. Ibid., 49r–50r

5. 'The Household accounts of the Princess Elizabeth, 1551–52', ed. Viscount

Stranford, *Camden Miscellany*, ii (1853). The note records the gift being taken to her, so she was clearly not in the household at that time.

6. T. Rymer, *Foedera, conventiones etc.* (London, 1704–35), xv, p. 117.

7. *Acts of the Privy Council*, ii, pp. 83–84.

8. Ibid., 86, 92, 100, 120.

9. Ibid., 196.

10. David Starkey, *Elizabeth* (London, 2001), p. 78. Denny died in September 1549.

11. *Calendar of the Patent Rolls, Edward VI*, iii, p. 238. Thomas Seymour's enquiries about the signing of the patent before Christmas 1548 indicate that the decisions had already been made by then.

12. J. Maclean, *The Life of Sir Thomas Seymour* (London, 1869), pp. 36–41. He had had considerable experience of naval command in Henry's last French war, but neglect and abuse of this office were to feature largely in the charges against him.

13. *Calendar of State Papers, Domestic, Edward VI*, no. 185.

14. David Loades, *John Dudley, Duke of Northumberland* (Oxford, 1996), p. 113. Sir Michael was the brother of his wife, originally Anne Stanhope.

15. Loades, *Mary Tudor*, pp. 138–39.

16. Deposition by the marquis of Dorset, P. F. Tytler, *The Reigns of Edward VI and Mary* (London, 1839), i, pp. 137–41.

17. *Calendar of State Papers, Domestic*, nos 185, 189, 220; Maclean, *Thomas Seymour*, pp. 56–58.

18. Confessions of Catherine Ashley and Thomas Parry, *Historical Manuscript Commission Reports, Salisbury MSS*, i, pp. 72–73.

19. Sir Robert Tyrwhyt to the Protector, 22 and 23 January 1549. *Salisbury MSS*, pp. 61–64.

20. Deposition by Catherine Ashley, 4 February 1549. *Calendar of State Papers, Domestic*. no. 197.

21. Confession of Thomas Parry, *Salisbury MSS*, p. 73.

22. Sir Robert Tyrwhyt, who had been Catherine's master of the horse, seems to have accompanied Elizabeth as chamberlain. He is nowhere specifically mentioned as holding this office; but he was in the Protector's confidence, and was the first person to communicate with Somerset when the investigations began in January 1549. He was certainly an officer by April 1549, and his wife Elizabeth a lady of the privy chamber. The name of Sir Walter Bucler is also mentioned in a context which suggests office.

23. *Elizabeth I: Collected Works*, pp. 17–19.

24. Samuel Haynes and William Murdin, *Collection of State Papers Left by William Cecil, Lord Burghley*, i, p. 103; Maclean, *Thomas Seymour*, pp. 68–69.

25. G. W. Bernard, 'The Downfall of Sir Thomas Seymour', in *The Tudor Nobility* (Manchester, 1992), pp. 212–40. This is the best modern account of the whole saga.

26. 'Articles objected against Sir Thomas Seymour, Lord Seymour, 23 February 1549', *Acts of the Privy Council*, ii, p. 251.

27. Depositions of Lord Clinton and the earl of Rutland. *Calendar of State Papers, Domestic*, nos 186, 187; Bernard, 'The Downfall of Sir Thomas Seymour'.

28. To judge from the reactions of those who testified against him, he had wildly overestimated his chances of success. Bernard, 'The Downfall of Sir Thomas Seymour'.

29. These depositions are printed variously by Haynes, and in *Historical Manuscripts Commission Reports* and *Calendar of State Papers, Domestic*, see above, pp. 64–65.

30. See particularly Tyrwhyt's letters of 22 and 23 January, which also testified 'the princess has a very good wit, and nothing is gotten of her but by very great policy'. Haynes and Murdin, *Collection of State Papers*, p. 71.

31. She threatened to inform the council of his goings on, but Seymour appears to have taken this as a joke.

32. *Elizabeth I: Collected Works*, pp. 29–30. Copies of these depositions were sent to Elizabeth, and also to Mary Cheke, who may have been temporarily in charge of her chamber.

33. Ibid.

34. *Calendar of State Papers, Domestic*, no. 195.

35. Ibid., no. 196.

36. *Acts of the Privy Council*, ii, p. 240.

37. *Salisbury MSS*, pp. 61–62.

38. *Acts of the Privy Council*, ii, p. 251.

39. 'The Lord Admiral questioned him closely as to the quality and tenure of Elizabeth's lands, and whether she had got her Letters Patent, and offered to procure for her a certain piece of land in Gloucestershire, as part of the lands which she wished to have in exchange, saying he wished she had her lands westward, or in Wales', *Salisbury MSS*, p. 73.

40. Bernard, 'The Downfall of Sir Thomas Seymour'. It was alleged at the time that the Act of Attainder was to spare the Protector's feelings in executing his brother.

41. *Elizabeth I: Collected Works*, pp. 22–24.

42. Starkey, *Elizabeth*, pp. 74–75. Elizabeth's indignation at the slur on her reputation was a measure of her awareness of how dangerous they could be.

43. *Salisbury MSS*, p. 72. Kate Ashley had clearly been an eye witness of many of these familiarities.

44. *Calendar of State Papers, Domestic*, no. 198.

45. BL, Lansdowne MS 1236, fol. 35; Collins, *Jewels and Plate*, p. 201.

46. Robert Tyrwhyt to the Protector, 19 February 1549; *Salisbury MSS*, p. 69. The council had already (17 February) 'thought it good to speak somewhat roundly' to the unfortunate Elizabeth Tyrwhyt for not doing her duty with sufficient diligence in the face of this opposition. Ibid.

47. See below, p. 117.

48. *Elizabeth I: Collected Works*, pp. 33–35.

49. Starkey, *Elizabeth*, p. 75.
50. *Calendar of State Papers, Domestic*, no. 207.
51. *Acts of the Privy Council*, ii, p. 266.
52. *Calendar of the Patent Rolls*, iv, p. 88.
53. PRO, E179/69/68
54. Starkey, *Elizabeth*, pp. 81–83; *Elizabeth I: Collected Works*, p. 15n. Ascham was taxed as a member of the household in 1549.
55. L. V. Ryan, *Roger Ascham* (Oxford, 1963), p. 303. L. Weisener, *The Youth of Queen Elizabeth*, trans. C. M. Yonge (London, 1879), i, pp. 89–90.
56. Ibid., p. 90, from Ascham, *Letters*, i, pt 1, pp. 191–92.
57. *Original Letters relative to the English Reformation*, Parker Society (1846), i, p. 76.
58. Starkey, *Elizabeth*, pp. 82–83.
59. Weisener, *The Youth of Queen Elizabeth*, pp. 94–95.
60. This contrast becomes clear from examining the letters written at different stages of her life, and published in *Elizabeth I: Collected Works*.
61. Henry Ellis, *Original Letters Illustrative of English History* (11 vols, London, 1824–46), i, p. 156. BL, Cotton MS Vespasian F. iii, fol. 48; *Elizabeth I: Collected Works*, pp. 35–36. Whether this portrait survives is not clear. Elizabeth seems to have made a practice of having her portrait painted. On 2 October 1551 George Tarling was paid a reward of £10 'being sent with his wife to the Lady Elizabeth's Grace to drawe out her portrait'. His wife was Lavina, better known as Lavina Teerlinc, later Mary's court painter.
62. Weisener, *The Youth of Queen Elizabeth*, pp. 97–99. Ascham respected the science of mathematics but had no skill in it.
63. Starkey, *Elizabeth*, pp. 87–88, who discusses the possibility that this sobriety was a calculated act.
64. *Acts of the Privy Council*, ii, p. 342.
65. *Calendar of State Papers, Spanish*, ix, p. 489.
66. *Acts of the Privy Council*, ii, p. 392.
67. Ibid., iii, p. 52.
68. *Calendar of State Papers, Spanish*, x, p. 186.
69. BL, Harleian MS 353, fos 38–39. Nichols, *Literary Remains of Edward VI*, ii, pp. 297–99; Jordan, *Chronicle and Political Papers of Edward VI*, p. 50 and n.
70. *Calendar of State Papers, Spanish*, x, p. 214.
71. Scheyfve's Advices, June and July 1551; *Calendar of State Papers Spanish*, x, pp. 299, 325.
72. Jordan, *Chronicle*, p. 78. This was linked to an order 'to see that there should be no conveyance overseas of the Lady Mary secretly done'. Commentators were agreed that Edward showed affection towards Elizabeth, although that could not be gathered from the chronicle.
73. *Calendar of the Patent Rolls*, iv, p. 88.
74. PRO, E179/69/69

75. *Acts of the Privy Ccouncil,* iv, p. 174.

76. *Camden Miscellany,* 2 (1853).

77. Starkey, *Elizabeth,* pp. 96–97.

78. John Foxe, *Acts and Monuments* (1576), pp. 1870–71.

79. Reconstructing a list of Elizabeth's servants, or even her officers, from these certificates presents a number of difficulties. Parker probably followed Tyrwhyt, and was commissioned, along with Parry and Robert Oxenbridge, to collect subsidy payments in December 1550. The commission was so issued, but the names on the certificate are illegible. A similar commission in October 1552 was addressed to Bucler and Parry, but the certificate has not survived. In May 1552 one Richard le Strange, appointed collector of customs for Kings Lynn, was licensed to act by deputy because he was in Elizabeth's service; and on another occasion the princess wrote on behalf of Sir Anthony Wingfield as her servant. No specific offices are attached to either le Strange or Wingfield, although the latter was controller of the royal household from 1550 to 1552. There is a biography of Parker in S. T. Bindoff, *The House of Commons, 1509–1558* (London, 1982). About thirty names can be identified between 1549 and 1552, most of them gentlemen and yeomen.

80. PRO, E179/69/70

81. *Acts of the Privy Council,* iv, p. 240.

82. *Elizabeth I: Collected Works,* pp. 35–38. Elizabeth's health seems to have been generally good; there are two or three references to sickness, but no suggestion that any of these attacks was serious.

83. *Acts of the Privy Council,* iii, p. 397. A list of those who did attend, including the marchioness of Northampton and the countess of Pembroke, appears in Edward's *Chronicle,* pp. 93–94.

84. *Calendar of State Papers, Spanish,* x, p. 493. For Robert Dudley's wedding, see *Chronicle,* p. 33.

85. *Calendar of State Papers, Spanish,* xi, p. 38.

86. Ibid. p. 46.

87. There are a number of discussions of Edward's intentions at this time; most recently in Loades, *John Dudley,* pp. 231–73, and Loach, *Edward VI,* pp. 159–69.

88. In 1566 William Maitland of Lethington wrote at length to Cecil to argue that Henry's will was invalid because it had been stamped and not signed, a point nobody had raised in 1553. Gilbert Burnet, *The History of the Reformation of the Church of England* (3 vols, London 1679–1715), i, pt 2, pp. 267–70.

89. BL, MS Harleian 35, fol. 364; printed by J. G. Nichols as an appendix to *The Chronicle of Queen Jane,* Camden Society, 48 (1850).

90. Henry's will had introduced the 'Suffolk line' into the succession if Edward, Mary and Elizabeth all deceased without direct heirs.

Notes to Chapter 5: In Danger

1. William Camden, *Annales anglicarum et hibernicarum regnante Elizabetha* (London, 1615); apparatus, no. x. Cited L. Weisener, *The Youth of Queen Elizabeth* (London 1879) i, p. 141.

2. See above, p. 75.

3. Popular stories to that effect circulated later, which Weisener declared to be 'without foundation', Weisener, *The Youth of Queen Elizabeth*, i, p. 142). There is no contemporary evidence, although Sir John Williams, who proclaimed Mary in Oxfordshire, was one of those who accompanied Elizabeth to London.

4. *The Diary of Henry Machyn*, ed. J. G. Nichols, Camden Society (1848), p. 37.

5. *The Chronicle of Queen Jane*, ed. J. G. Nichols, Camden Society (1850), says 'the whole number of the horsemen were esteemed to be 10,000', p. 14; Machyn, *Diary*, says 3000, p. 39.

6. 'Vita Mariae Reginae', ed. D. MacCulloch, Camden Miscellany, 28 (1984), p. 271. Ambassadors to Charles V, 6 August 1553; *Calendar of State Papers, Spanish*, xi, p. 151.

7. Ambassadors to Charles V, 16 August 1553; *Calendar of State Papers, Spanish*, xi, p. 169.

8. P. L. Hughes and J. F. Larkin, *Tudor Royal Proclamations* (Cambridge, Massachusetts, 1964–69), ii, no. 390.

9. Ambassadors to the Emperor, 16 August 1553, *Calendar of State Papers, Spanish*, xi, p. 169.

10. Antoine de Noailles to the king of France, 9 August 1553, *Ambassades des Messieurs de Noailles*, ed. R. A. de Vertot (Leyden, 1743), ii, p. 199; Renard to Charles V, 21 October 1553, *Calendar of State Papers, Spanish*, xi, p. 310. Weisener, *Youth of Elizabeth*, i, p. 149.

11. Ambassadors to Charles V, 9 and 19 September 1553, *Calendar of State Papers, Spanish*, xi, pp. 217, 220. 'Perceiving that the queen did not show her as kindly a countenance as she would wish, and judging the reason was her obstinacy in error, she besought the queen to grant her a private audience. Two days later they met, and Elizabeth knelt, weeping she said she saw only too clearly that the queen was not well disposed towards her, and she knew of no other cause except religion. She had been brought up in the new faith, and knew no other, so she asked for instruction. The queen was very glad and granted her request.'

12. Weisener, *Youth of Elizabeth*, i, pp. 151–52.

13. Renard to Charles V, 4 November 1553. *Calendar of State Papers, Spanish*, xi, p. 334; E. H. Harbison, *Rival Ambassadors at the Court of Queen Mary* (Princeton, 1940), pp. 94, 96; J. Loach, *Parliament and the Crown in the Reign of Mary Tudor*, pp. 77–90.

14. Renard to Charles V, 21 October 1553, *Calendar of State Papers, Spanish*, xi, p. 310. Renard's deep suspicion of Mary's council was largely the result of their reluctance to do his master's bidding, Harbison, *Rival Ambassadors*, passim.

15. Edward Courtenay was the son of Henry Courtenay, earl of Devon and marquis of Exeter, who had been executed in January 1539. His paternal grandmother was Katherine, daughter of Edward IV.

16. David Loades, *Mary Tudor* (Oxford, 1989) p. 187; *Calendar of State Papers, Spanish*, xi, pp. 117–19.

17. M.-J. Rodriquez Salgado, *The Changing Face of Empire* (Cambridge, 1988), pp. 37–39.

18. *Calendar of State Papers, Spanish*, xi, pp. 126–27, 177–78; Harbison, *Rival Ambassadors*, pp. 71–72.

19. *Calendar of State Papers, Spanish*, xi, pp. 288–93, 300–2.

20. Noailles to Montmorency, 7 September 1553, Archives du Ministère des Affaires Etrangères, ix, fol. 69; Harbison, *Rival Ambassadors*, p. 78.

21. 1 Mary, st. 2 c. 1; Loach, *Parliament and the Crown*, pp. 79–80.

22. Renard to Charles V, 21 October, *Calendar of State Papers, Spanish*, xi, p. 310.

23. *Calendar of State Papers, Spanish*, xi, pp. 319, 327; Loades, *Mary Tudor*, p. 204.

24. E. H. Harbison, 'French Intrigue at the Court of Queen Mary', *American Historical Review*, 45 (1940), pp. 533–51.

25. *Calendar of State Papers, Spanish*, xi, pp. 363–64; Loach, *Parliament and the Crown*, pp. 79–80.

26. Loades, *Mary Tudor*, p. 270n.

27. Renard to Charles V, 31 October, 4 November 1553, *Calendar of State Papers, Spanish*, xi, pp. 328, 334.

28. Ibid., p. 334. There appears to have been no substance in the report of a pre-contract.

29. Renard to the Charles V, 28 November 1553, *Calendar of State Papers, Spanish*, xi, p. 393.

30. Ibid.

31. Charles V to Philip, 24 December 1553, *Calendar of Sate Papers, Spanish*, xi, p. 453.

32. PRO, SP11/1/20; Rymer, *Foedera*, xv, p. 377. The whole text was included in the proclamation, *Tudor Royal Proclamations*, ii, no. 398.

33. A document *ad cautelem* to this effect is enclosed with the copy of the marriage treaty preserved at Simancas. Secretaria de Estado, 807/36/2; *Calendar of State Papers, Spanish*, xii, p. 4.

34. Harbison, *Rival Ambassadors*, pp. 107–13; Vertot, *Ambassades*, ii, p. 246.

35. Renard to Charles V, 29 November 1553, *Calendar of State Papers, Spanish*, xi, p. 400.

36. *Calendar of State Papers, Spanish*, xi, p. 411.

37. Renard to Charles V, 8 December 1553, *Calendar of State Papers, Spanish*, xi, p. 418; Vertot, *Ambassades*, ii, pp. 289–90, 310; Harbison, pp. 113–119.

38. Renard to Charles V, 9 December 1553, *Calendar of State Papers, Spanish*, xi, p. 426. Henry Carey, later Lord Hunsdon, was the son of Elizabeth's aunt, Mary Boleyn.

39. Ibid. It seems likely that on this occasion the scheme was killed on the imperial side, by imposing unacceptable conditions upon the duke in return for supporting his suit. David Starkey, *Elizabeth* (London 2000), pp. 206–7.

40. For the careers of all these men, see S. T. Bindoff, *The House of Commons, 1509–1558* (London, 1982); Loades, *Two Tudor Conspiracies* (Cambridge, 1965), pp. 18–19.

41. Ibid., pp. 15–16. For Winter, see also David Loades, *The Tudor Navy* (Aldershot, 1992), pp. 151 et seq.

42. Loades, *Two Tudor Conspiracies*, took the view that the rising was mainly secular, but a number of critics have argued for the religious interpretation. See particularly M. R. Thorp, 'Religion and the Rebellion of Sir Thomas Wyatt', *Church History*, 47 (1978), pp. 363–80.

43. Harbison, *Rival Ambassadors* p. 112.

44. John Proctor, *The Historie of Wiats Rebellion* (London, 1554), p. 48.

45. G. Redworth, *In Defence of the Church Catholic; The Life of Stephen Gardiner* (Oxford, 1990), pp. 311–15.

46. This was the version officially given to Philip on the 16 February. *Calendar of State Papers, Spanish*, xii, p. 100.

47. *Calendar of State Papers, Spanish*, xi, pp. 408, 453.

48. Loades, *Two Tudor Conspiracies*, pp. 22–24; Harbison, *Rival Ambassadors*, pp. 126–27.

49. Renard to Charles V, 18 January 1554, *Calendar of State Papers, Spanish*, xii, p. 34. The significant event turned out to be the assembling of a French fishing fleet off the Breton coast.

50. *The Chronicle of Queen Jane*, p. 35.

51. Ibid., p. 36. This report was slightly exaggerated. Neither Lord Cobham nor the lord warden (Sir Thomas Cheney) joined the rebels.

52. *Calendar of State Papers, Spanish*, xii, p. 50.

53. Ambassadors to Charles V, 29 January 1554, *Calendar of State Papers, Spanish*, xii, p. 55.

54. *The Chronicle of Queen Jane*, pp. 62–63.

55. John Foxe, *Actes and Monuments of Matters Most Speciall and Memorable* (London, 1583), p. 2091.

56. Howard, Hastings and Cornwallis to the queen, 11 February 1554 from Ashridge, PRO, SP11/3/21.

57. Foxe, *Actes and Monuments*, p. 2092.

58. *The Chronicle of Queen Jane*, pp. 37–39.

59. *The Historie of Wiats Rebellion*, ed. A. F. Pollard, *Tudor Tracts* (London, 1903), pp. 239, 241–42.

60. *The Chronicle of Queen Jane*, pp. 49–50.

61. Proctor, ed. Pollard, pp. 251–52.

62. *The Chronicle of Queen Jane*, p. 59.

63. Ibid., p. 69.

64. Ibid., pp. 73–74; *Two Tudor Conspiracies*, p. 92 and notes.

65. Renard to Charles V, 29 January 1554, *Calendar of State Papers, Spanish*, xii, p. 56; Harbison, *Rival Ambassadors* p. 130 and notes. It is thought that Gardiner deliberately lost this letter because it incriminated Courtenay. He blamed the rebel incursion into his house in Southwark.

66. *Calendar of State Papers, Spanish*, xii, p. 140; *Two Tudor Conspiracies*, p. 93.

67. Queen Elizabeth's reply to a parliamentary petition for the execution of Mary Queen of Scots, 12 November 1586, *Elizabeth I: Collected Works*, ed. L. S. Marcus et al. (Chicago, 2001), pp. 186–190.

68. Renard to Charles V, 14 March 1554, *Calendar of State Papers, Spanish*, xii, p. 151.

69. Foxe, *Actes and Monuments*, p. 2092.

70. Renard to Charles V, 22 March 1554, *Calendar of State Papers, Spanish*, xii, p. 166.

71. *Elizabeth I: Collected Works*, pp. 41–42.

72. *Chronicle of Queen Jane*, pp. 70–71; Foxe, *Acts and Monuments*, p. 2092.

73. Ibid.

74. Renard to Philip, 19 February 1554, *Calendar of State Papers, Spanish*, xii, p. 120.

75. Renard to Charles V, 14 March 1554, ibid., p. 151.

76. *Calendar of State Papers, Spanish*, xii, pp. 150, 218, 221.

77. *Chronicle of Queen Jane*, p. 71; Foxe, *Acts and Monuments*, p. 2092.

78. Renard to Charles V, 22 March, *Calendar of State Papers, Spanish*, xii, p. 166.

79. Charles V to Renard, 19 March 1554, ibid., p. 160.

80. Foxe, *Acts and Monuments*, pp. 2093–94.

81. Renard to Charles V, 17 April 1554, *Calendar of State Papers, Spanish*, xii, p. 218. Renard suspected, correctly, that Paget and his supporters in the council were shielding Elizabeth, just as Gardiner was shielding Courtenay. Harbison, *Rival Ambassadors* pp. 146–47.

82. *Calendar of State Paper, Spanish*, xii, p. 218.

83. Foxe, *Acts and Monuments*, p. 2095.

84. Ibid., p. 2093.

85. Ibid. Foxe leaves his story unfinished and does not name any of the servants or officers involved.

86. 'Bedingfield Papers', *Norfolk Archaeological Society Transactions*, 4 (1855), p. 133. Bedingfield had been one of the first in Norfolk to declare for Mary in July 1553. She never forgot that support.

87. *Chronicle of Queen Jane*, p. 76.

88. 'Bedingfield Papers', pp. 143 etc. Elizabeth was accompanied by sixteen of her own servants, although it is not certain that the number stayed the same at Woodstock.

89. 'Bedingfield Papers', p. 145.

90. Ibid., p. 154.

91. The council instructed him that Elizabeth was to receive no messages, and to see no one 'out of his hearing'. Bedingfield, who seems to have had no

particular education, believed that these books (which were Latin works of history and philosophy) contained coded messages. 'Bedingfield Papers', pp. 160 etc.

92. Ibid., pp. 172 etc.

93. Elizabeth Sandes was apparently replaced by Elizabeth Marbury, the wife of one of her gentleman ushers. Anne Grey is also mentioned as being replaced by Mrs Thomas, and a Mrs Broughton recalled to court, to be replaced by Mrs Morton. Several male servants are also mentioned by name, usually because of sickness or misbehaviour. Bedingfield Papers, various; *Acts of the Privy Council*, v, p. 29.

94. 'Bedingfield Papers', p. 143; *Acts of the Privy Council*, v, p. 38.

95. 'Bedingfield Papers', p. 175.

96. Ibid., p. 173.

97. For example, in John Bradford's *Copye of a Letter* (1556), which accused the Spaniards of a plot to do away with her in Philip's interest. Loades, *Two Tudor Conspiracies*, pp. 239–41.

98. Weisener, *Youth of Elizabeth*, ii, pp. 146–47. As Savoy was allocated Elizabeth's lodgings at court for his stay, she was probably not there; although she may have visited from Somerset House.

99. Foxe, *Acts and Monuments*, pp. 2092–96. It should be remembered that Bedingfield was still alive, although living in semi-retirement, when Foxe was writing. He died in 1583.

100. Ibid., p. 2095. Gardiner certainly had a confidential secretary named James Bassett, who also served the queen in that capacity. Redworth, *In Defence of the Church Catholic*, p. 323n.

101. Foxe, *Acts and Monuments*, p. 2096.

102. *Chronicle of Queen Jane*, p. 76.

103. *Calendar of State Papers, Spanish*, xii, p. 94; Harbison, *Rival Ambassadors*, pp. 89–108.

104. Loades, *Reign of Mary*, pp. 90–92. Renard was even convinced that the lord admiral, Lord William Howard, might raise the fleet on her behalf. *Calendar of State Papers, Spanish*, xii, p. 251.

105. Renard to the Charles V, 1 May, 14 June, 29 July 1554, *Calendar of State Papers, Spanish*, xii, pp. 231, 276; xiii, p. 4.

106. Ibid., pp. 90, 92.

107. Weisener, *Youth of Elizabeth*, ii, pp. 134–50; *Calendar of State Papers, Spanish*, xiii, p. 113.

108. *Calendar of State Papers, Spanish*, xiii, p. 143.

109. Ibid., p. 145. Renard writes of 'a certain Lord William', who could not have been William Howard, whom he knew well. It was therefore probably Lord Williams of Thame.

110. Ibid.

111. Licenciate Games to the king of the Romans, 29 September 1555, *Calendar of State Papers, Spanish*, xiii, p. 251.

112. Loades, *Reign of Mary*, pp. 166–69. The main concession had been the inclusion of the papal dispensation in the statute of repeal, an action (unnecessary to Pole and Mary) which gave it the force of law in England.

113. Foxe, *Acts and Monuments*, passim; J. A. Muller, *Stephen Gardiner and the Tudor Reaction* (Cambridge, 1926), pp. 247–77; David Loades, *Oxford Martyrs* (London, 1970), pp. 148–49.

114.   'Marie the mirrour of mercifulnesse
        God of his Goodness hath lent to this land
        Our Iewell oure ioye, our Judith doutless
        The great Holofernes of hell to withstand, etc.'
    Leonard Stokes, *An Ave Maria in Commendation of Oure Most Vertuous Queen* (London, 1553) [*STC* 23292]. There were a number of other writings of a similar nature.

115. Machyn, *Diary*, p. 93.

116. Redworth, *In Defence of the Church Catholic*, passim.

117. Loades, *Mary Tudor*, pp. 308–9. The contemporary opinion was that she died of a 'dropsy', which probably means cancer of the womb. Alternatively, she may have been a victim of the influenza epidemic (as Pole was).

118. Weisener, The *Youth of Elizabeth*, ii, pp. 151–69; Loades, 'Philip II and the Government of England', in *Law and Government under the Tudors*, ed. C. Cross, D. Loades and J. Scarisbrick (Cambridge, 1988), pp. 177–194.

119. *Calendar of State Papers, Spanish*, xiii, p. 227.

120. Michieli to the doge and senate, *Calendar of State Papers, Venetian*, vi, p. 137. The cousins were the sons of John Sutton, Lord Dudley, who had died in 1553. They were always known by the surname Dudley.

121. Montmorency to Noailles, 27 July 1555, Ministère des Affaires Etrangères, ix, fol. 498–99; Harbison, *Rival Ambassadors*, pp. 271–72.

122. PRO, SP11/16–21, 82, 83; BL, Cotton MS Titus B. ii, fos 114–16; Badoer to the doge and senate, 13, 27 October 1555. *Calendar of State Papers, Venetian*, vi, pp. 212, 227.

123. Michieli to the doge and senate, 16 September 1555. *Calendar of State Papers, Venetian*, vi, p. 188.

124. Harbison, *Rival Ambassadors*, pp. 270–296.

125. For a full discussion of the divisions in this parliament, and their significance, see Loach, *Crown and Parliament*, pp. 128–58.

126. *Acts of the Privy Council*, v, pp. 202–3; Loades, *Two Tudor Conspiracies*, pp. 183–84.

127. Ibid., pp. 186–90. Perhaps their most telling achievement was to recruit Richard Uvedale, the captain of the Isle of Wight.

128. *Letters and Papers of the Verney Family*, ed. John Bruce, Camden Society, 56 (1853), p. 64; Examination of Peter Killigrew, PRO, SP11/9/25.

129. PRO, SP11/7/39, third examination of White, 30 March 1556, *Verney Papers*, p. 64.

130. Weisener, *The Youth of Elizabeth*, ii, pp. 203–12.

131. PRO, SP11/9/22. Kenneth Bartlett, '"The Misfortune that is Wished for Him"; The Exile and Death of Edward Courtenay, Eighth Earl of Devon', *Canadian Journal of History*, 14 (1979), pp. 1–28.

132. PRO, SP11/9/22 (i).

133. Starkey, *Elizabeth*, pp. 192–93. This represents Ashton as infatuated with Elizabeth, and by implication devoted to her service. He was an eccentric man with a chequered history, and deeply involved in the plot, but there is no evidence of direct contact.

134. Indictment of John, Lord Bray, *Calendar of the Patent Rolls, Philip and Mary*, iii, p. 396; *Verney Papers*.

135. Vertot, *Ambassades*, v, pp. 298–99.

136. Their interrogations are preserved with those of the other suspects; PRO, SP11/8/54, SP11/8/80.

137. Michieli to the doge and senate, 2 June 1556, *Calendar of State Papers, Venetian*, vi, p. 474.

138. Starkey, *Elizabeth*, p. 203.

139. Foxe, *Acts and Monuments*, p. 2097; Starkey, *Elizabeth*, p. 201.

140. Ibid., p. 203.

141. *Acts of the Privy Council*, v, p. 316, 29 July 1556; John Strype, *Ecclesiastical Memorials*, iii, p. 336; J. Gage, *Antiquities of Hengrave* (London, 1822), p. 158; *Elizabeth I: Collected Works*, p. 44.

142. Simon Renard to Philip II, 12 January 1557, *Calendar of State Papers, Spanish*, xiii, p. 285; Weisener, *The Youth of Elizabeth*, ii, pp. 213–33; Memoir by Don Bernardino de Mendoza, *Calendar of State Papers, Spanish*, xiii, p. 293.

143. Ibid., p. 221; Machyn, *Diary*, p. 120.

144. Ibid. Machyn gives no hint of rejection or disgrace.

145. Bishop of Dacq to Montmorency, 4 December 1556, and to the king, 15 December 1556, Vertot, *Ambassades*, iv, pp. 193, 206.

146. Francois de Noailles to Henry II, 15 December 1556. Archives du ministère des affaires étrangères, Correspondance Politique, Angleterre (CPA) xiii, fol. 112; Harbison, *Rival Ambassadors*, pp. 312–13.

147. Harbison, *Rival Ambassadors*, p. 313n., where he says 'I have been unable to discover the original of Francois' letter of 2 December 1570, quoted by Vertot (i, p. 334) which is the basis of the story for Elizabeth's intended flight.

148. *Acts of the Privy Council*, vi, pp. 76–77.

149. Loades, *Reign of Mary*, p. 193.

150. Starkey, *Elizabeth*, pp. 210–11.

151. Ibid.

152. Advis au roi, 26 March 1557, Ministère des Affaires Etrangères, CPA, xiii, fol. 176. Harbison, *Rival Ambassadors*, p. 323.

153. She had been divorced from the marquis after a difficult and protracted case, a decision which she refused to recognise, and was consequently in limbo. Having no recognised status, she seems to have been living on her wits.

154. *Calendar of State Papers, Venetian*, vi, p. 1057, 13 May 1557.

155. *Calendar of State Papers, Spanish*, xiii, p. 372. This letter is misdated in the calendar, because it refers to Thomas Stafford as still alive, and therefore can have been written no later than May 1557.
156. D. L. Potter, 'The Duc de Guise and the Fall of Calais', *English Historical Review*, 98 (1983), pp. 481–512.
157. Loades, *Reign of Mary*, pp. 363–89.
158. Machyn, *Diary*, pp. 166–67.
159. Surian to the doge and senate, 15 January 1558, *Calendar of State Papers, Venetian*, vi, p. 1427; Philip II to Cardinal Pole, 21 January 1558, *Calendar of State Papers, Spanish*, xiii, p. 340. The text of the will is printed as appendix 3 to *Mary Tudor; A Life*.
160. Feria to Philip, 1 May 1558, *Calendar of State Papers, Spanish*, xiii, p. 379.
161. Feria to Philip, 23 June 1558, ibid., pp. 399–400.
162. Loades, *Mary Tudor: A Life*, pp. 380–83.

Notes to Chapter 6: The New Queen

1. The *Diary of Henry Machyn*, ed. J. G. Nichols, Camden Society (1848), p. 37.
2. Both Anne Grey and Charles Smyth, 'groom of the pantry', appear to have been dismissed by Bedingfield for that reason. Bedingfield Letters, pp. 165, 167.
3. 'The like also may be testified and recorded of Mistres Sandes, nowe wyfe to Syr Morice Bartlet, then Gentlewoman wayter to the sayde Ladye Elizabeth, which Mistres Sandes denyed in lyke maner to come to Masse, and therefore [was] put out of the house. But the Lorde who disposeth for every one as he seeth best, wrought her way out of her enemyes handes by flying over the Seas'. John Foxe, *Acts and Monuments* (1583), p. 2082.
4. BL, Lansdowne MS 3, fol. 88.
5. Hubert Languet to the duke of Saxony, 16 July 1561: 'The queen replied that she never thought of contracting a marriage with my Lord Robert, but she was more attached to him than to any of the others, because when she was deserted by everybody in the reign of her sister, not only did he never lessen in any degree his kindness and humble attention to her, but he even sold his possessions that he might assist her with money.' Cited by Derek Wilson, *Sweet Robin: A Biography of Robert Dudley, Earl of Leicester, 1533–1588* (London, 1981), p. 73.
6. Feria wrote 'The Queen seems not to have favoured him as he expected, and this, no doubt, has increased his malady'. *Calendar of State Papers, Spanish, Elizabeth*, i, pp. 7–13. Cecil continued to consult him, but his identification as an arch-enemy by the godly persuaded the secretary to keep him at an arm's length.
7. 'The Count of Feria's dispatch to Philip II of 14th November 1558', ed. M.-J. Rodriquez Salgado and Simon Adams, *Camden Miscellany*, 28 (1984), p. 331.
8. Ibid.
9. Ibid., p 332.

10. 'The xix day of november ded be-twyne v and vi in the morning my lord cardenall Polle at Lambeth', Machyn, *Diary*, p. 178.

11. Including Susan Clarencius, Mary's closest servant. For an assessment of the role of the Feria household, see H. Clifford, *The Life of Jane Dormer, Duchess of Feria*, ed. J. Stevenson (London, 1887).

12. Heath was retained on the council on a sort of probation. When he led the opposition to the Bill of Supremacy in the House of Lords, there was clearly no way back into office.

13. Sidney was reappointed after Mary's death, but in July 1559 moved to Wales as lord president of the council in the Marches. His place in Ireland was taken by the earl of Sussex as lord deputy.

14. D. E. Hoak, *The King's Council in the Reign of Edward VI* (Cambridge, 1976), p. 83.

15. Francis Peck, *Desiderata Curiosa* (1732), i, p. 9.

16. C. H. Garrett, *The Marian Exiles* (Cambridge, 1938), p. 16. For the information relating to Day in Lincolnshire, I am indebted to Dr Elizabeth Evenden.

17. Elizabeth was free to chose her councillors in a way which Mary had not been, because there had been no disputed succession, and she also had a pool of talent available which Mary had discarded for religious reasons. MacCaffrey, *The Shaping of the Elizabethan Regime* (London, 1969), pp. 27–40.

18. Garrett, *Marian Exiles*.

19. MacCaffrey, *The Shaping of the Elizabethan Regime*, pp. 31, 32.

20. *Elizabeth I: Collected Works*, p. 51.

21. BL, Lansdowne MS 3, fos 193, 199–200.

22. Ibid., fol. 193.

23. PRO, LC2/4/2.

24. BL, Lansdowne MS 3, fol. 193.

25. PRO, LC2/4/3.

26. The only surviving account was drawn up on Tamworth's death in 1569. It is not known when he was appointed, as he is not on the 1558 list. BL, Harley Roll AA23; Pam Wright, 'A Change of Direction', in D. Starkey (ed.), *The English Court* (London, 1987), p. 153.

27. A 'short table' of Cecil's disbursements in this capacity, May to August 1561, remains among the Hatfield MSS; *HMC Hatfield MSS*, i, p. 261.

28. Cited by Simon Adams in 'Eliza Enthroned' in C. Haigh (ed.), *The Reign of Elizabeth I* (London, 1984). Vaughn was Blanche Parry's nephew.

29. Susan Doran, *Monarchy and Matrimony: The Courtships of Elizabeth I* (London, 1996), p. 6; citing the example of her striking Mary Shelton, on discovering the latter's secret marriage to James Scudamore.

30. Loades, *Mary Tudor* (Oxford, 1989), pp. 223–73. Glyn Redworth, '"Matters Impertinent to Women"; Male and Female Monarchy under Philip and Mary', *English Historical Review*, 112 (1997), pp. 597–613.

31. 'Queen Elizabeth's Conversations with William Maitland, Laird of Lethington, September and October 1561', *Elizabeth I: Collected Works*, pp. 60–70. Also

S. Adams, 'Queen Elizabeth's Eyes at Court', *Leicester and the Court* (London, 2002).

32. This knowledge is reflected in her first recorded speech to her peers, delivered at Hatfield on 20 November 1558, wherein she famously described herself as 'but one body naturally considered, though by [God's] permission a body politic to govern'. *Elizabeth I: Collected Works*, p. 52.

33. *Annals of the First Four Years of the Reign of Queen Elizabeth, by Sir John Hayward, Knt*, ed. John Bruce, Camden Society, 7 (1840), p. 6.

34. *The Passage of Our Most Dread Sovereign Lady Queen Elizabeth through the City of London to Westminster the Day before her Coronation* (1559), A. F. Pollard, *Tudor Tracts* (London, 1903), pp. 367–400.

35. PRO, SP12/1/9.

36. MacCaffrey, *The Shaping of the Elizabethan Regime*, p. 43.

37. Foxe, *Acts and Monuments* (1583), pp. 2001–200; J. Strype, *Annals of the Reformation*, i, pp. 38–39.

38. Proclamation prohibiting unlicensed preaching and regulating ceremonies, 27 December 1558; *Tudor Royal Proclamations* (Cambridge, Massachusetts, 1964–69), ii, no. 451; Strype, *Annals*, p. 41.

39. Ibid.

40. J. Fines, *A Biographical Register of Early English Protestants, 1525–1558* (Sutton Courtenay, 1981), i, p. 140.

41. C. G. Bayne, 'The Coronation of Queen Elizabeth', *English Historical Review*, 22 (1907), pp. 650–73; A. L. Rowse, 'The Coronation of Queen Elizabeth I', *History Today*, 3 (1953), pp. 301–10.

42. See particularly Carl S. Meyer, *Elizabeth I and the Religious Settlement of 1559* (St Louis, Missouri, 1959); J. E. Neale, 'The Elizabethan Acts of Supremacy and Uniformity', *English Historical Review*, 65 (1950), pp. 304–24; N. L. Jones, *Faith by Statute* (London, 1982).

43. *The Passage of Our Most Dread Sovereign Lady*, p. 395.

44. *Elizabeth I: Collected Works*, p. 137.

45. PRO, SP12/1.

46. For Nicholas Heath's speech of 18 March, see *Proceedings in the Parliaments of Elizabeth I*, ed. T. E. Hartley (London, 1983), pp. 12–17.

47. Strype, *Annals*, i, pp. 73–81.

48. *The Passage of Our Most Dread Sovereign Lady*, pp. 375–389; C. G. Bayne, 'The Coronation of Queen Elizabeth', *English Historical Review*, 22 (1907), pp. 650–73.

49. C. Haigh, 'The Continuity of Catholicism in the English Reformation' in Haigh (ed.), *The English Reformation Revised* (Cambridge, 1987), pp. 176–209; Haigh, *English Reformations*, pp. 251–67.

50. Vacant were Canterbury, Hereford, Norwich, Oxford, Salisbury, Sodor and Man, and Bangor. Nominations had been made to Hereford (Reynolds) and Salisbury (Mallett). The three who died were Griffin of Rochester (20 November 1558), Holyman of Bristol (20 December 1558), and Christopherson of Chichester (28 December 1558).

51. Kitchen of Llandaff accepted; Goldwell of St Asaph resigned. Tunstall of Durham and Morgan of St Davids died during 1559.

52. R. O'Day, 'Thomas Bentham: A Case Study in the Problems of the Early Elizabethan Episcopate', *Journal of Ecclesiastical History*, 23 (1972); Scott A. Wenig, *Straightening the Altars: The Ecclesiastical Vision and Pastoral Achievements of the Progressive Bishops under Elizabeth I, 1559–1579* (New York, 2000).

53. W. P. Haugaard, *Elizabeth and the English Reformation* (London, 1970), pp. 233–290.

54. Foxe was careful not to blame Mary directly, because he did not wish to give protestant radicals the chance to claim that her authority was unlawful because of the way in which it had been used, an approach to which Elizabeth was entirely sympathetic. J. Norskov Olsen, *John Foxe and the Elizabethan Church* (Los Angeles, 1973).

55. *The Correspondence of Matthew Parker, DD, Archbishop of Canterbury*, ed. J. Bruce and T. T. Perowne (Cambridge, 1853), pp. 49–53; J. Strype, *The Life and Acts of Matthew Parker, the First Archbishop of Canterbury in the Reign of Elizabeth* (Oxford, 1821), iii, p. 278.

56. Haugaard, *Elizabeth and the English Reformation*, p. 33.

57. The fourteen who had been abroad were: Barlow (Chichester), Bentham (Coventry and Lichfield), Berkeley (Bath and Wells), Bullingham (Lincoln), Cox (Ely), Davies (St Asaph), Grindal (London), Horne (Winchester), Jewel (Salisbury), Parkhurst (Norwich), Pilkington (Durham), Sandys (Worcester), Scory (Hereford) and Young (St Davids).

58. Elizabeth was uncompromising in her insistence upon her own authority to run the church, and it may have been to avoid muddying the waters in that connection that she at first excluded all clergy from the council. A comprehensive proclamation announced the royal injunctions for religion in July 1559, *Tudor Royal Proclamations*, ii, no. 460.

59. Henry Gee, *The Elizabethan Clergy and the Settlement of Religion, 1558–1564* (Oxford, 1898); Conyers Read, *Mr Secretary Cecil and Queen Elizabeth* (London, 1954), pp. 126–29.

60. J. Strype, *Annals*, i, appendix, 16.

61. 'Royal Articles of Queen Elizabeth', in *Visitation Articles and Injunctions of the Period of the Reformation*, ed. W. H. Frere (Alcuin Club, 1910), iii, pp. 1–29; *The Royal Visitation of 1559: Act Book for the Northern Province*, ed. and trans. C. J. Kitching, Surtees Society, 187 (1975).

62. D. Marcombe, 'The Dean and Chapter of Durham, 1558–1603', unpublished Durham University Ph.D thesis (1973).

63. Haugaard, *Elizabeth and the English Reformation*, pp. 67–73.

64. E. C. S. Gibson, *The Thirty-Nine Articles of the Church of England* (London, 1910).

65. Haugaard, *Elizabeth and the English Reformation*, pp. 128–30.

66. Doran, *Monarchy and Matrimony*, pp. 21–22.

67. *Calendar of State Papers, Spanish, 1558–67*, pp. 1–4.

68. For example, in letters of Feria, 21 November and 14 December 1558, ibid., pp. 2, 9.

69. Archivo de la Casa de Medinaceli, caja 7, legajo 249, 11–12. Cited and translated in G. Parker and C. Martin, *The Spanish Armada* (London, 1988), p. 281.

70. 20 February 1559, *Calendar of State Papers, Spanish, 1558–67*, p. 31.

71. Doran, *Monarchy and Matrimony*, pp. 25–26.

72. Feria to Philip II, 18 April 1559, *Calendar of State Papers, Spanish, 1558–67*, pp. 56–58.

73. Ibid.

74. Conyers Read, *Mr Secretary Cecil* (London, 1955), pp. 198–217. Cecil frequently disagreed with Elizabeth, and even organised opinion against her in council, leaving detailed memoranda of his thinking. Her confidence in him seems to have been enhanced rather than diminished by this activity. Stephen Alford, *The Early Elizabethan Polity: William Cecil and the British Succession Crisis, 1558–1569* (Cambridge, 1998).

75. AGS, Estado Inglaterra, 650, fol. 7; *Calendar of State Papers, Spanish, 1558–67*, p. 83; Doran, *Monarchy and Matrimony*, pp. 27–28.

76. 2 October 1559, *Calendar of State Papers, Spanish, 1558–67*, p. 104.

77. Doran, *Monarchy and Matrimony*, pp. 28–29.

78. Ibid.

79. *Calendar of State Papers, Spanish, 1558–67*, p. 51.

80. As these are de Quadra's accounts; they may not be altogether impartial. AGS, Estado Inglaterra, 812, fos 100, 101; *Calendar of State Papers, Spanish, 1558–67*, pp. 91, 93.

81. Doran, *Monarchy and Matrimony*, pp. 30–31.

82. 'Proposals of the King of Sweden Presented through the Duke of Finland', 11 December 1559, *Calendar of State Papers, Foreign, 1559–60*, p. 190.

83. *Calendar of State Papers, Foreign, 1560–61*, pp. 443, 556–57; *1561–62*, pp. 49, 73.

84. Ian Aird, 'The Death of Amy Robsart', *English Historical Review*, 71 (1956), pp. 69–79; BL, Add. MS 48023, fol. 353.

85. Throgmorton to Chamberlain, 29 October 1560; PRO, SP70/19/132.

86. Bruener to Emperor Ferdinand, 6 August 1559, cited Doran, *Monarchy and Matrimony*, pp. 41–42.

87. Read, *Mr Secretary Cecil*, p. 203.

88. *Coleccion de documentos ineditos para la historia de España*, ed. M. F. Navarete et al. (Madrid, 1842–95), pp. 87, 317–19; K. Bartlett, 'Papal Policy and the English Crown, 1563–5: The Bertano correspondence', *Sixteenth Century Journal*, 23 (1992), pp. 643–59.

89. Francis II was succeeded by his brother, Charles IX, who was nine years old. This required a regency, and the queen mother, Catherine de Medici, was appointed. As one of her objectives was to reduce the influence of the Guise connection, Mary's return to Scotland was likely to be sooner rather than later.

90. Doran, *Monarchy and Matrimony*, pp. 33–34.

91. Both Catherine Ashley and Dorothy Broadbelt seem to have been involved in promoting the Swedish match, probably because they were so much opposed to Dudley. Dymock to Cecil, 20 February 1561, *Calendar of State Papers, Foreign, 1560–61*, pp. 556–57; Machyn, *Diary*, p. 127; Ashley and Broadbelt to Guildenstern, 22 July 1562, PRO, SP70/39/119.

92. The Scots pursued this marriage with some enthusiasm, and moved the French to promote it. Peronet to Chantonnay, AGS, Estado Francia, K1493 B11, fol. 112; Doran, *Monarchy and Matrimony*, pp. 36–37.

93. De Quadra to Philip II, 31 January 1562, *Calendar of State Papers, Spanish, 1558–67*, p. 225.

94. De Quadra to Philip II, 25 October 1562, ibid., p. 263.

95. Ibid.

96. Dudley to Maitland, cited by Adams 'Queen Elizabeth's Eyes', p. 137; *Tudor Royal Proclamations*, ii, no. 516.

97. Mortimer Levine, *The Early Elizabethan Succession Question* (Stanford, California, 1966), and Stephen Alford, *The Early Elizabethan Polity*, provide the fullest discussions of the succession options. For Elizabeth's responses to the various petitions, see *Elizabeth I; Collected Works*, pp. 58–86.

98. Simon Adams, 'Favourites and Factions at the Elizabethan Court', in *Princes, Patronage and the Nobility: The Court at the Beginning of the Modern Age*, ed. R. G. Asch and A. M. Birke (Oxford, 1991), pp. 265–87.

99. George Adlard, *The Sutton Dudleys of England* (London, 1842), p. xv; Simon Adams, 'The Dudley Clientele, 1553–1563', in *The Tudor Nobility*, ed. G. Bernard (Manchester 1992), pp. 241–55.

100. Holinshed, *Chronicle*, p. 205; Read, *Mr Secretary Cecil*, pp. 259–60.

101. Ibid., pp. 142–43; PRO, SP52/1/77.

102. *The State Papers and Letters of Sir Ralph Sadler*, ed. A. Clifford (Edinburgh, 1809), ii, p. 126.

103. *The Egerton Papers*, ed. J. Payne Collier, Camden Society, 12 (1840), pp. 30–32.

104. PRO, SP12/7/169–71. T. Glasgow, 'The Navy in the First Undeclared Elizabethan War', *Mariners' Mirror*, 54 (1968), pp. 23–37.

105. BL, MS Cotton Caligula B. ix, fos 34, 38; *Calendar of State Papers Relating to Scotland, 1559–60*, pp. 413–15.

106. The French commanders in Scotland were already negotiating, but it would have been impossible to conclude an agreement without Mary of Guise's participation, had she still been alive.

107. *Calendar of State Papers Relating to Scotland, 1560–61*, pp. 172–74. These negotiations were conducted by Cecil himself, who travelled north for the purpose.

108. In spite of periodic alarms over the revival of Guise influence, the peace between England and Scotland until 1587 was kept intact by the shared problem of Mary Stuart, and thereafter by the succession prospects of her son James in England.

109. C. G. Bayne, *Anglo-Roman Relations, 1558–1565* (Oxford, 1913), pp. 62–116.

110. Levine, *Early Elizabethan Succession Question*, passim.

Notes to Chapter 7: Threats

1. Wallace MacCaffrey, *The Shaping of the Elizabethan Regime* (London, 1969), pp. 63–66, makes much of Cecil's difficulties in council. At the same time the secretary's own comment 'I have had such a torment herein with the Queen's Majesty as an ague hath not in five so much abated' makes it clear that he knew who he had to persuade. When he went north in person to negotiate the treaty, many expected that his absence from court would prove fatal to him. This tells us more about conventional attitudes to court politics than it does about Elizabeth's real intentions. Once she had made up her mind, she trusted Cecil to see the policy through. For a fresh and original examination of Cecil's relations with the queen, see Stephen Alford, *The Early Elizabethan Polity, 1558–1569* (Cambridge, 1998).

2. *Calendar of State Papers, Spanish, 1558–67*, p. 199. MacCaffrey, *The Shaping of the Elizabethan Regime*, p. 79.

3. Loades, 'Relations between the Anglican and Roman Catholic Churches in the Sixteenth and Seventeenth centuries', in *Rome and the Anglicans* (Berlin, 1982), pp. 22–23. C. G. Bayne, *Anglo-Roman Relations, 1558–65* (Oxford, 1913), pp. 40–61.

4. William Camden, *Annales rerum anglicarum et hibernicarum*, trans. H. Norton (London, 1635), p. 61.

5. *Calendar of State Papers, Spanish, 1558–67*, p. 194; Bayne, *Anglo-Roman Relations*, pp. 270–71

6. *Calendar of State Papers, Spanish, 1558–67*, pp. 193, 195.

7. *Relations politiques des Pays-Bas et de l'Angleterre sous le règne de Philippe II*, ed. J. M. B. C. Kervyn de Lettenhoven (Brussels, 1882–1900), ii, pp. 557, 559–60.

8. PRO, SP70/26; SP12/16/ fos 55, 66–68.

9. Bayne, *Anglo-Roman Relations*, pp. 179, 297, 298.

10. MacCaffrey, *The Shaping of the Elizabethan Regime*, pp. 114–15

11. *Elizabeth I: Collected Works*, p. 66. 'The Discourse of the Laird of Lethington's Negotiation with the Queen of England'.

12. *Calendar of State Papers, Spanish, 1558–67*, pp. 308–15.

13. Instruction to Thomas Randolf, 16 November 1563, *Calendar of State Papers, Scottish, 1563–69*, p. 27.

14. Thomas Randolf to William Cecil, 21 February 1564, ibid., pp. 43–44.

15. Thomas Randolf to William Cecil, 30 March 1564, ibid., pp. 56–57.

16. Elizabeth to Mary, 16 June 1563, ibid., p. 14.

17. Whatever Elizabeth's intentions may have been, the countess had been intriguing for a marriage between Mary and her son since 1561. Cecil knew this, and had placed the whole family under arrest in the winter of 1561–62. Margaret had also delivered herself of some very undiplomatic remarks about the queen. They had made their peace at court, however, and returned to Yorkshire by November 1562. *Calendar of State Papers Relating to Scotland, 1563–1569*, p. 77; proceedings of the Scottish parliament, 25 September 1564.

18. Thomas Randolf to William Cecil, 15 April 1565, *Calendar of State Papers Relating to Scotland, 1563–1569*, pp. 142–43. 'the queen has already such a good liking of him that she can be content to forsake all other offers'.

19. MacCaffrey, *The Shaping of the Elizabethan Regime*, pp. 121–22; Moray to Cecil, 7 December 1565, *Calendar of State Papers Relating to Scotland, 1563–1569*, p. 244.

20. Captain Cockburn to Cecil, 2 October 1565, *Calendar of State Papers Relating to Scotland, 1563–1569*, p. 216; 'Circular on the murder of Rizzio', ibid., pp, 268–69.

21. David Loades, *England's Maritime Empire* (London, 2000), pp. 81–82.

22. 'His Majesty findeth this to be the trewe way wholy to deverte the said traphique from his said lowe countries and to transport it into some other place and to separate the subjects of both partes from al mutual traphique'. Articles presented to the English Council by Charles Quarrentyne, councillor of the Council of Brabant, 'by commandement of the kinges Maiestie', 17 October 1556, BL, Lansdowne MS 170, fol. 129.

23. Derek Wilson, *Sweet Robin* (London, 1981), pp. 16, 20, 85, 151.

24. Robert Brenner, *Merchants and Revolution* (Cambridge, 1993), pp. 4–20.

25. Ibid., pp. 56–57; G. D. Ramsay, *The City of London in International Politics at the Accession of Elizabeth* (London, 1975), p. 50.

26. A. Pettegree, *Foreign Protestant Communities in Sixteenth Century London* (Oxford, 1986), pp. 133–81.

27. Brett Usher, 'Backing Protestantism: The London Godly, the Exchequer and the Foxe Circle', in *John Foxe: An Historical Perspective*, ed. D. Loades (Aldershot, 1999), pp. 105–34.

28. *The Naval Tracts of Sir William Monson*, ed. M. Oppenheim, Navy Records Society (1902–14), i, p. 7.

29. K. R. Andrews, *The Spanish Caribbean: Trade and Plunder, 1530–1630* (London, 1978).

30. Michael Lewis, *The Hawkins Dynasty* (London, 1969), pp. 41–49; Richard Hakluyt, *Principall Navigations and Voiages* (London, 1589), p. 520.

31. Lewis, *The Hawkins Dynasty*, pp. 76–78. For a good reason why he was deceiving himself, see Lorenzo Bernaldez to Philip II, August 1563, AGI, Santo Domingo 71, tomo 2, fos 280–82; cited H. Kelsey, *Sir Francis Drake: The Queen's Pirate* (New Haven, Connecticut, 1998), p. 16.

32. Lewis, *The Hawkins Dynasty*, p. 84.

33. Ibid., pp. 85–86.

34. Hakluyt, *Principall Navigations*, pp. 523–43; K. R. Andrews, *Drake's Voyages* (London, 1967), pp. 16–17.

35. The pretext for this inhibition was an outbreak of plague, but the ban was not lifted when the plague abated. BL, Lansdowne MS 16, fol. 134; PRO, SP12/33/42.

36. Memorandum by Sir William Cecil, 1564, PRO, SP12/35/33.

37. Cited Black, *The Reign of Elizabeth*, p. 53.

38. Diego Herero to Philip II, 8 January 1568, AGI, Santo Domingo 202, ramo 1, no. 15; cited Kelsey, *Sir Francis Drake*, pp. 21–24.

39. There was a story about a search for a mysterious silver mine in Africa, and an almost equally mysterious incursion by Flemish warships into Plymouth Sound, which provoked Hawkins to open fire. There were mutual recriminations, but no explanation of how this happened. Lewis, *The Hawkins Dynasty*, pp. 98–99.

40. Hakluyt, *Principall Navigations*, p. 553.

41. Conyers Read, 'Queen Elizabeth's Seizure of Alba's Pay Ships', *Journal of Modern History*, 5 (1933), pp. 443–64; MacCaffrey, *The Shaping of the Elizabethan Regime*, p. 189.

42. Extract from a statement made by the English ambassador resident in France to Don Frances de Alava, January 1569, *Calendar of State Papers, Spanish, 1568–79*, p. 114.

43. Ibid., pp. 90, 91, 101, 102.

44. Camden, *Annales*, p. 195.

45. Ibid.

46. MacCaffrey, *The Shaping of the Elizabethan Regime*, pp. 202–05. There is a dramatic, but unsubstantiated story of the council, under Leicester's leadership, seeking to humiliate Cecil on 22 February, and of the secretary's being rescued by the entrance of the queen, saying 'I pardon thee that and more', Cuthbert Sharp, *Memorials of the 1569 Rebellion* (1840; reprint 1975), p. xiv. The difficulty with this story is that anti-Cecil plotting seems to have continued after that date.

47. Elizabeth is alleged to have described herself as 'a barren stock' on hearing the news, but 'the queenes Maiestie of England was the godmother, who gave a font of gold curiously wrought and inamelled, weighing three hundred and thirtie three ounces', Holinshed, *Chronicle*, p. 231.

48. J. B. Black, *The Reign of Elizabeth* (Oxford, 1959), pp. 100–1.

49. Bedford to William Cecil, 9 January 1567, *Calendar of State Papers Relating to Scotland, 1563–1569*, pp. 309–10.

50. Depositions of the king's murder, 11 February 1567, BL, Add. MS 33531, fol. 37. *Calendar of State Papers Relating to Scotland, 1563–1569*, pp. 312–13.

51. G. Adlard, *Amye Robsart and the Earl of Leicester* (London, 1870), p. 41; I. Aird, 'The Death of Amy Rosart', *English Historical Review*, 71 (1956), pp. 69–79.

52. Cited Black, *The Reign of Elizabeth*, p. 105.

53. Kirkaldy to Bedford, 8 May 1567, *Calendar of State Papers Relating to Scotland, 1563–1569*, pp. 327–28.

54. Camden, *Annales*, p. 148.

55. Ibid.

56. Ibid.; Throgmorton to Elizabeth, 26 July 1567, *Calendar of State Papers Relating to Scotland, 1563–1569*, pp. 362–64.

57. Camden, *Annales*, p. 148; *Calendar of State Papers Relating to Scotland, 1563–1569*, pp. 405–7.

58. Cited Black, *The Reign of Elizabeth*, pp. 109–10; *Calendar of State Papers Relating to Scotland, 1563–1569*, p. 408.
59. Memorial by William Cecil, 30 May 1568, BL, Cotton MS Caligula C. i, fol. 97; *Calendar of State Papers Relating to Scotland, 1563–1569*, pp. 418–19.
60. Camden, *Annales*, p. 148.
61. *Calendar of State Papers Relating to Scotland, 1563–1569*, pp. 438–40; MacCaffrey, *The Shaping of the Elizabethan Regime*, pp. 172–74.
62. Knollys to Norfolk, 14 October 1568, Knollys to Cecil, 20 October, *Calendar of State Papers Relating to Scotland, 1563–1569*, pp. 530, 534–35.
63. Conyers Read, *Mr Secretary Cecil* (London, 1955), pp. 440–43. Camden, *Annales*, p. 122.
64. *Calendar of State Papers, Spanish, 1568–79*, p. 111.
65. Ibid., pp. 186, 217, 224.
66. *Correspondance diplomatique de B. Salaignac de la Mothe Fenelon* (Paris, 1838–40), ii, p. 194.
67. Camden, *Annales*, p. 212.
68. 'When he found no comfort among his owne, and Heidon, Cornwallis and others of his traine perswaded him that if he were guilty, should flye to the Queenes mercy, he was almost distracted with sorrow.' Ibid.
69. MacCaffrey, *The Shaping of the Elizabethan Regime*, p. 219.
70. Sharp, *Memorials*, pp. xviii–xix. For the resurrection of the Percy earldom in 1557, see P. S. Boscher, 'Politics, Administration and Diplomacy: The Anglo-Scottish Border, 1550–1560', unpublished Durham University Ph.D thesis (1985).
71. A. Fletcher and D. MacCulloch, *Tudor Rebellions* (4th edn, London, 1997); *Calendar of State Papers, Domestic, Addenda, 1566–79*, p. 402; *Calendar of State Papers, Spanish, 1568–79*, p. 96. Sharp, *Memorials*, pp. 191–92, 194.
72. Camden, *Annales*, p. 212.
73. *Calendar of State Papers, Domestic, Addenda, 1566–79*, p. 89.
74. Ibid., p. 104.
75. Holinshed, *Chronicle*, p. 235.
76. Sharp, *Memorials*, p. 185.
77. Sussex, Hunsdon and Sir Ralph Sadler to Elizabeth, 22 December 1569; Sharp, *Memorials*, pp. 113–14.
78. *Elizabeth I: Collected Works*, p. 126.
79. Sharp, *Memorials*, pp. 133–34.
80. *Calendar of State Papers, Spanish, 1568–79*, pp. 186, 217, 224; MacCaffrey, *The Shaping of the Elizabethan Regime*, pp. 232–33.
81. Loades, *Rome and the Anglicans*, p. 26.
82. Ibid. On Sander, see J. K. McConica, 'The Catholic Experience in Tudor Oxford', in *The Reckoned Expense: Edmund Campion and the Early English Jesuits*, ed. T. M. McCoog (Woodbridge, 1996), pp. 39–66.
83. Sharp, *Memorials*, p. 179.
84. J. Strype, *Annals of the Reformation*, ii, p. 17. The Latin text and translation are transcribed in Holinshed, *Chronicle*, p. 252.

85. Memorandum by Antonio de Guaras, 22 June 1570, *Calendar of State Papers, Spanish, 1568–79*, p. 249.

86. In 1563 the administration of the oath of Supremacy was extended to all lay office holders, including members of parliament. The exclusion of Catholics from the council was *de facto* rather than by prescription. Membership of the House of Lords was unaffected, as peerage was not deemed to be an office. MacCaffrey, *The Shaping of the Elizabethan Regime*, pp. 112, 153.

87. Whether the story of the council session is true or not, Elizabeth had made it clear by the summer of 1570 that she would entertain no motion against her secretary. Camden, *Annales*, p. 104. For a full account of this episode, drawn from various sources, see Conyers Read, *Mr Secretary Cecil*, pp. 440–43.

88. *Elizabeth I: Collected Works*, pp. 122–23.

89. Holinshed, *Chronicle*, p. 252.

90. Memorandum by de Guaras, *Calendar of State Papers, Spanish, 1568–79*, p. 249.

91. Maximilian II to Elizabeth, 27 November 1565, *Calendar of State Papers, Foreign, 1564–65*, pp. 526–27; AGS, Estado Inglaterra, legajo 819, fol. 66, cited by Susan Doran, *Monarchy and Matrimony: The Courtships of Elizabeth I* (London, 1996), p. 83.

92. Ibid.

93. Thomas Wright, *Queen Elizabeth and her Times* (London, 1838), i, pp. 107–08.

94. *Elizabeth I: Collected Works*, p. 99.

95. Doran, *Monarchy and Matrimony*, pp. 88–89.

96. Sussex to Elizabeth, 24 October 1567, PRO, SP70/94, fos 161–62; BL, Add. MS 4149, fol. 89.

97. Doran, *Monarchy and Matrimony*, pp. 99–100.

98. *Calendar of State Papers, Foreign, 1569–71*, pp. 372–73; N. M. Sutherland, *The Huguenot Struggle for Recognition* (London, 1980), pp. 83–84.

99. Fenelon, *Correspondance diplomatique*, iv, p. 225.

100. 'A Discourse of the Queenes Mariage with the Duke of Anjou, Drawen out by the Lord Keeper', *Egerton Papers*, ed. J. P. Collier (1840), p. 51–55.

101. Doran, *Monarchy and Matrimony*, p. 105.

102. Sir Dudley Digges, *The Compleat Ambassador* (1655), pp. 67, 85–86.

103. Dispatch from Sir Thomas Smith and Sir Henry Killigrew, 8 January 1572; *Calendar of State Papers, Foreign, 1572–79*, pp. 8–10.

104. Camden, *Annales*, p. 311.

105. Moray had died in January 1570 and been succeeded as regent by James Douglas, earl of Morton. The agreement with France meant that Elizabeth could reduce her backing for the regent, without any risk that he would be defeated. *Calendar of State Papers Relating to Scotland, 1569–71*, pp. 182, 183, 191, 204.

106. *Calendar of State Papers, Rome, 1558–71*, pp. 338, 349.

107. BL, Cotton MS Caligula C. ii, fol. 518.

108. *Calendar of State Papers, Rome, 1558–71*, pp. 393–400.

109. MacCaffrey, *The Shaping of the Elizabethan Regime*, p. 274.

110. But that was in the context of having been told that the queen would not countenance the match in 1569. Ibid., p. 219. Camden, *Annales*, p. 212.
111. MacCaffrey, *The Shaping of the Elizabethan Regime*, pp. 278–79.
112. Ibid., pp. 277–78.
113. Count Lamarque, the leader of the Dutch 'Sea Beggars', was expelled from England in February 1572. Taking advantage of the fact that Alba had deployed his main force in the south to confront the expected French invasion, Lamarque seized the port of Brill. By the time that Alba was able to disengage in the south, the rebels were too entrenched to be dislodged, and the duke, having been undermined by his enemies in Madrid, was recalled.
114. *A Complete Collection of State Trials*, ed. William Cobbett et al. (1816–98), i, p. 978.
115. MacCaffrey, *The Shaping of the Elizabethan Regime*, pp. 281–82.
116. Ibid., pp. 284–85; BL, Cotton MS Caligula B. viii, fols 240–46; Digges, *Compleat Ambassador*, p. 218.
117. BL, Cotton MS Caligula C. iii, fol. 145; *Elizabeth I: Collected Works*, p. 130.
118. *Collection of State Papers Left by William Cecil, Lord Burghley*, ed. S. Haynes and W. Murdin (1740–59), ii, pp. 194, 208–10.
119. There is abundant evidence for the competition and emulation between Elizabeth's courtiers, which could take rather childish forms. But groupings and alliances changed according to the issues; there were no stable parties or factions.
120. *Elizabeth I: Collected Works*, p. 110.

Notes to Chapter 8: France and the Netherlands

1. Raphael Holinshed, *Chronicles*, ed. John Hooker et al. (London, 1587), iii, p. 252.
2. 13 Elizabeth I, c. 1, 13 Elizabeth I, c. 2, *Statutes of the Realm*, iv, pp. 526–28; ibid., pp. 528–31.
3. Peter Milward, *Religious Controversies of the Elizabethan Age* (Aldershot, 1977), pp. 29–30. A controversial storm surrounded these writings, and several supporting tracts were also produced.
4. M. B. Pulman, *The Elizabeth Privy Council in the 1570s* (Berkeley, California, 1971), pp. 62–66.
5. Minutes of a council meeting, 30 October 1568, Hatfield MS 155, fol. 128.
6. Francis Knollys to William Cecil, 15 June 1568, BL, Cotton MS Caligula B. ix, fol. 291.
7. William Cecil to Francis Walsingham, 27 July 1572, BL, Harley MS 260, fol. 277.
8. For Cecil's manner of conducting this campaign, see particularly M. A. R. Graves, *Thomas Norton: The Parliament Man* (Oxford, 1994), pp. 346–50.
9. BL, Cotton MS Titus B. ii, fol. 233.
10. *Collection of State Papers Left by William Cecil, Lord Burghley*, ed. S. Haynes and W. Murdin (1740–59), i, pp. 498–99.

11. Susan Doran, *Monarchy and Matrimony: The Courtships of Queen Elizabeth* (London, 1996) pp. 130–35.

12. Burghley to Walsingham, 27 July 1572, BL, Harley MS 260, fol. 278.

13. Commission of Charles IX to the duke of Montmorency and other deputies, 25 April 1572, Bibliothèque Nationale, FF 3253, fos 368–70; cited Doran, *Monarchy and Matrimony*, p. 133.

14. BL, Cotton MS Vespasian F. vi, fol. 88, 6 June 1572.

15. Sir Dudley Digges, *The Compleat Ambassador* (London, 1655) pp. 226–28.

16. Doran, *Monarchy and Matrimony*, pp. 138–39.

17. Alençon to Elizabeth, 22 April 1573, Valentine Dale to Burghley, 27 April; PRO, SP70/127, fos 44, 56.

18. Address of the lords of the council to La Mothe-Fenelon, 2 June 1573, Fenelon, *Correspondance diplomatique*, vii, pp. 424–27.

19. R. M. Kingdon, *Myths about the St Bartholomew's Day Massacre, 1572–76* (Cambridge, Massachusetts, 1988), p. 68. Doran, *Monarchy and Matrimony*, p. 141.

20. Ibid., pp. 142–43.

21. PRO, SP70/135, fos 78–79, 89–90.

22. Instructions for Thomas Randolph, 2 April 1576, *Calendar of State Papers, Foreign, 1575–7*, pp. 302–4.

23. Kervyn de Lettenhove, *Les Huguenots et les Gueux* (Bruges, 1883–85, iv, pp. 633, 638; Doran, *Monarchy and Matrimony*, p. 144.

24. On learning of Elizabeth's infatuation with Dudley in 1560, she had observed contemptuously that the queen of England was proposing to 'marry her horsemaster'.

25. Geoffrey Parker, *The Dutch Revolt* (London, 1977), pp. 69–74; L. P. Gachard, ed., *Correspondance de Guillaume le Taciturne, prince d'Orange* (Brussels, 1847–66), vi, pp. ii–iv; trans. H. H. Rowen, *The Low Countries in Early Modern Times* (London, 1972), pp. 37–39.

26. Parker, *Dutch Revolt*, pp. 176–77. For some indication of the fierceness of the religious passions aroused, see *The Bee Hive of the Romish Church*, by Philip de Marnix, trans. George Gilpin the elder (London, 1623), and cited in Rowen, *The Low Countries*, pp. 49–54.

27. Parker, *Dutch Revolt*, pp. 169–79.

28. Ibid., p. 178.

29. Ibid., p. 191.

30. *Calendar of State Papers, Spanish, 1568–79*, pp. 413–15.

31. Wallace MacCaffrey, *Queen Elizabeth and the Making of Policy, 1572–1588* (Princeton, New Jersey, 1981), pp. 217–21.

32. Ibid., pp. 180–85,

33. Parker, *The Dutch Revolt*, p. 191.

34. Doran, *Monarchy and Matrimony*, pp. 147–48.

35. Lettenhove, *Relations Politiques*, x, p. 697.

36. MacCaffrey, *Queen Elizabeth and the Making of Policy*, pp. 65–67. The

Admonitions are published in a modern edition, by W. H. Frere, *Puritan Manifestos: A Study of the Origin of the Puritan Revolt* (1907; reprint, London, 1954), pp. 1–39, 79–134.

37. Patrick Collinson, *The Elizabethan Puritan Movement* (London, 1967), pp. 121–22.
38. Patrick Collinson, *The Religion of Protestants* (Oxford, 1982), pp. 92–140.
39. *Elizabeth I: Collected Works*, pp. 168–72.
40. R. Usher, *The Rise and Fall of High Commission* (Oxford, 1913), p. 90.
41. A. O. Meyer, *England and the Catholic Church under Queen Elizabeth* (London, 1916); Nancy Brown, 'Robert Southwell: The Mission of the Written Word', in McCoog, *The Reckoned Expense* (Woodbridge, 1996), pp. 193–213.
42. For a full discussion of this aspect, see Alexandra Walsham, *Church Papists* (Woodbridge, 1993).
43. Petition by the House of Commons, 2 and 9 March 1576, BL, Add. MS 33271; *Proceedings in the Parliaments of Elizabeth I, 1, 1558–81*, ed. T. E. Hartley (London, 1981), pp. 445–47.
44. Collinson, *Elizabethan Puritan Movement*; MacCaffrey, *Queen Elizabeth and the Making of Policy*, pp. 87–88.
45. The queen's letter to Thomas Cooper, bishop of Lincoln (1577), Strype, *Annals of the Reformation*, ii, p. 111.
46. 'I am forced with all humility and yet plainly to profess that I cannot with safe conscience and without the offence of the majesty of God, give my assent to the suppressing of the said exercises', J. Strype, *A History of the Life and Acts of Edmund Grindal* (Oxford, 1821), pp. 569–70.
47. Collinson, *The Elizabethan Puritan Movement*, passim.
48. A. J. Loomie, *The Spanish Elizabethans* (New York, 1963), pp. 14–52; M.-J. Rodriguez-Salgado, *The Changing Face of Empire* (Cambridge, 1988), pp. 332–35.
49. *Dialogi sex contra summi pontificatus, nunc primum ad Dei Optimi Maximi gloriam, et Catholicae religionis confirmationem ab Alano Copo Anglo editi* [1566]; Milward. *Religious Controversies*, p. 21.
50. MacCaffrey, *Queen Elizabeth and the Making of Policy*, pp. 119–53.
51. Walsham, *Church Papists*; J. Bossy, *The English Catholic Community, 1570–1850* (London, 1976); C. Haigh, *English Reformations* (Oxford, 1993), pp. 251–68.
52. G. Anstruther, *The Seminary Priests*, 4 vols (1968–77), a biographical dictionary; E. Duffy, 'William, Cardinal Allen, 1532–1594', *Recusant History*, 22 (1995), pp. 265–90; Peter Holmes, *Resistance and Compromise: The Political Thought of the Elizabethan Catholics* (Cambridge, 1982).
53. C. Haigh, 'From Monopoly to Minority: Catholicism in Early Modern England', *Transactions of the Royal Historical Society*, fifth series, 31 (1981), pp. 129–47; P. McGrath, 'Elizabethan Catholicism: A Reconsideration', *Journal of Ecclesiastical History*, 35 (1984), pp. 414–28.
54. Bossy, *Catholic Community*; C. Haigh, 'The Continuity of Catholicism in the English Reformation', in Haigh, ed., *The English Reformation Revised* (Cambridge, 1987), pp. 176–208.

55. 13 Elizabeth I, c. 1; 13 Elizabeth I, c. 2.

56. M. E. Williams, 'Campion and the English Continental Seminaries', in *The Reckoned Expense*, pp. 285–99.

57. F. X. Walker, 'The Implementation of the Elizabethan Statutes against Recusants, 1581–1603' (unpublished London University Ph.D. thesis, 1961), p. 37, citing John Morris, *The Troubles of our Catholic Forefathers* (1877).

58. McCaffrey, *Queen Elizabeth and the Making of Policy*, pp. 127–28.

59. *The Annals of the Kingdom of Ireland by the Four Masters*, ed. J. O'Donovan (Dublin, 1998), vols 4–6; M. O'Dowd, *Power, Politics and Land: Early Modern Sligo, 1568–1688* (Belfast, 1991); Ciaran Brady, 'England's Defence and Ireland's Reform: The Dilemma of the Irish Viceroys, 1541–1641', in *The British Problem, 1534–1707*, ed. B. Bradshaw and J. Morrill (London, 1996), pp. 89–117; Susan Brigden, *New Worlds, Lost Worlds* (London, 2000), pp. 149–71.

60. *Calendar of State Papers Relating to Ireland (1571–1575)*, ed. M. O'Dowd (London, 2000), pp. 16–17.

61. Ibid., pp. 18–19.

62. Brigden, *New Worlds*, pp. 149–71.

63. *Calendar of State Papers Relating to Scotland*, iv, pp. 160–62, 183–84.

64. McCaffrey, *Queen Elizabeth and the Making of Policy*, pp. 404–5.

65. J. B. Black, *The Reign of Elizabeth* (Oxford, 1959) pp. 372–74; Graves, *Thomas Norton* (Oxford, 1994) pp. 347–50.

66. Black, *Reign of Elizabeth*, pp. 372–74.

67. *Elizabeth I: Collected Works*, pp. 212–13.

68. McCaffrey, *Elizabeth I* (London, 1993), pp. 343–54.

69. Black, *The Reign of Elizabeth*, p. 164.

70. Ibid.

71. H. Kelsey, *Sir Francis Drake* (New Haven, Connecticut, 1998) pp. 40–67.

72. A full, and not particularly complimentary account of this expedition, written by 'one Lopez, a Spaniard', was printed by Hakluyt in *Principall Navigations*, pp. 594 et seq. For a more complimentary narrative, see Philip Nichols, *Sir Francis Drake Revived* (London, 1626), pp. 8–10.

73. Kelsey, *Sir Francis Drake*, pp. 82–83.

74. Camden, *Annals* (London, 1635), p. 426.

75. Ibid.

76. Thomas H. Symonds, ed., *Meta Incognita: A Discourse of Discovery* (Hull, Quebec, Canada, 1999), p. xx.

77. Loades, *England's Maritime Empire* (London, 2000) pp. 111–12.

78. Michael Lewis, *The Hawkins Dynasty* (London, 1969), p. 17.

79. N. A. M. Rodgers, *The Safeguard of the Sea: A Naval History of Britain, 660–1648* (London, 1997), pp. 238–53; K. R. Andrews, *Elizabethan Privateering, 1585–1603* (London, 1962), pp. 3–52.

80. Kelsey, *Sir Francis Drake*, p. 217. Burghley was one of those who rejected Drake's gifts after his circumnavigation.

81. Lewis, *The Hawkins Dynasty*, pp. 127–44; S. Adams, 'New Light on the

"Reformation" of John Hawkins: The Ellesmere Naval Survey of 1584', *English Historical Review*, 105 (1991), pp. 97–111.

82. Pulman, *Elizabethan Privy Council*, p. 24.

83. Ibid., pp. 17–51.

84. *Acts of the Privy Council*, ix, p. 11.

85. Ibid., x, pp. 85, 89.

86. D. Loades, *The Tudor Court* (Bangor, 1992), appendix 2.

87. BL, Lansdowne MS 34, fol. 23.

88. *The Progresses of Queen Elizabeth*, ed. J. Nichols, Society of Antiquaries, 4 vols (London, 1788–1821), vol. 2.

89. Ibid.

Notes to Chapter 9: The Gathering Storm

1. Susan Doran, *Monarchy and Matrimony: The Courtships of Elizabeth I* (London, 1996) pp. 150–52.

2. Churchyard was a gentleman of the Chapel Royal, and frequently prepared masques and other entertainments for the court. For a full discussion of the Norwich entertainments, see Zillah Dovey, *An Elizabethan Progress: The Queen's Journey into East Anglia, 1578* (Stroud, 1995), which draws heavily on Churchyard's own account.

3. Quotations from John Nichols, *The Progresses and Public Processions of Queen Elizabeth* (London, 1823), ii, pp. 115–210.

4. Ibid. On the role which the image of chastity played in later Elizabethan politics, see Philippa Berry, *Of Chastity and Power* (London, 1989), pp. 83–110.

5. I. Cloulas, *Correspondance du nonce en France, Anselmo Dandino (1578–1581)*, Acta Nuntiaturae Gallicae, 8 (1970), p. 238.

6. Henry Kamen, *Philip II* (London, 1997) pp. 168–69.

7. In spite of its name, the Catholic League was at least as much about restoring the power of the nobility as it was about defending the church. Henry III quickly became conscious of this threat to his authority, which was manifested at the estates general at Blois in 1576. In January 1577 he displaced the duke of Guise as head of the League, and declared himself its leader; causing its (temporary) disintegration.

8. This move was partly in response to the increasingly aggressive Calvinism of Holland and Zeeland. The original union at Arras was signed by the estates of Hainault and Artois on 6 January. The northern estates immediately responded with the Union of Utrecht on 22 January. This drove the Walloon provinces into the Union of Arras, which came to terms with Parma in May. Geoffrey Parker, *The Dutch Revolt* (London, 1977) pp. 194–95.

9. William Camden, *The History of the Most Renowned Princess Elizabeth, Late Queen of England* (London, 1688), p. 227.

10. J. M. B. C. Kervyn de Lettenhove, *Relations Politiques des Pays-Bas et de*

l'Angleterre sous le règne de Philippe II (Brussels, 1882–1900) xi, pp. 304–5; Doran, *Monarchy and Matrimony*, p. 155.

11. Ibid., pp. 155–57.

12. Anjou was still refusing to reconsider his position at this stage, as is shown in his letter of 8 March, *Historical Manuscripts Commission Report*, 58, *Salisbury MSS*, pp. 234–35.

13. PRO, 31/3 (Baschet's Transcripts), 27, fos 259, 262, 266, 273.

14. Ibid., fos 266, 273–74.

15. Doran, *Monarchy and Matrimony*, p. 157. The full set of Burghley's memoranda of these discussions are in Hatfield, MS 148. Sir Walter Mildmay's views are given in BL, Harley MS 6265, fos 104–110.

16. 'Objections Made against the Queen's Marriage, with the Answers of Cecil', March 1579, *HMC*, 9, *Salisbury MSS*, ii, p. 240.

17. Bernardino de Mendoza to Philip II, 13 January 1580, *Calendar of State Papers, Spanish, Elizabeth, 1579–90*, p. 1.

18. Camden, *History of Elizabeth*, p. 95. Leicester did not attend council meetings between 15 June and 6 July, so his rustication appears to have been brief.

19. Cited by Doran, *Monarchy and Matrimony*, p. 162; from a letter of Mary, Queen of Scots.

20. *STC*, 23400. For a fuller discussion of Stubbs and his work, see Wallace MacCaffrey, *Elizabeth I* (London, 1993) pp. 202–5.

21. Hughes and Larkin, *Tudor Royal Proclamations*, ii, pp. 445–49.

22. Hugh Singleton was also found guilty of assisting in the production of the book but was pardoned on account of his age. K. Barnes, 'John Stubbe, 1579: The French Ambassador's Account', *Historical Research*, 64 (1991), pp. 421–26.

23. Norfolk and Norwich Record Office, Mayors Court Book 10, fol. 469

24. Berry, *Chastity and Power*, pp. 120–25.

25. Samuel Haynes and William Murdin, *A Collection of State Papers left by William Cecil, Lord Burghley* (London, 1740–59) p. 331; Doran, *Monarchy and Matrimony*, pp. 172–73.

26. Of the five commissioners, only Hunsdon opposed the match; PRO, SP78/3, fos 133–36.

27. Bibliothèque Nationale, FF3307, fol. 5; cited Doran, *Monarchy and Matrimony*, p. 175.

28. Parker, *Dutch Revolt*, pp. 196–97; Doran, *Monarchy and Matrimony*, p. 177.

29. *Calendar of State Papers, Foreign, 1579–80*, p. 503.

30. BL, Harley MS 6265, fol. 285; *Calendar of State Papers, Foreign, 1581–82*, pp. 175–76.

31. There are a number of drafts of Walsingham's instructions concerning this support, which were finalised on 22 July; Digges, *Compleat Ambassador*, pp. 352–56; *Calendar of State Papers, Foreign, 1581–82*, pp. 271–82.

32. Digges, *Compleat Ambassador*, p. 374.

33. Ibid., p. 397.

34. *Calendar of State Papers, Foreign, 1581–82*, pp. 368–69.

35. Camden, *Annals*, iii, p. 12; *Calendar of State Papers, Spanish, 1568–79*, p. 227.

36. Camden, *Annals*, iii, p. 12.

37. Ibid. Mendoza, on the other hand, was informed at the time that he took the situation 'very mildly'; *Calendar of State Papers, Spanish, 1580–86*, p. 229. Camden may well have been guilty of embroidery.

38. By far the most thorough investigation into Elizabeth's shifting moods and purposes is Doran, *Monarchy and Matrimony*, pp. 154–94. There were nearly always political explanations for the twists and turns of the queen's attitude, but her main concern appears to have been to keep her options open for as long as possible, and not to be constrained by pressure, from the French, her council, or her people.

39. C. Piot, *Correspondance de Granvelle* (Brussels, 1878–96), i, p. 631.

40. Berry, *Chastity and Power*, passim.

41. H. Kelsey, *Sir Francis Drake: The Queen's Pirate* (New Haven, Connecticut, 1998), pp. 207–8. Most of these complaints were routed via Mendoza.

42. Camden, *Annals* (London, 1635), p. 426.

43. Ibid. The sequestration apparently involved leaving the cargo in the hands of his friend John Blitheman, the mayor of Plymouth. Elizabeth instructed him to bring some samples of his gold and silver to London, where she received him in a long audience. The whole complex episode is examined in detail by Kelsey, *Sir Francis Drake*, pp. 211–17.

44. Camden, *Annals*, p. 426. Mendoza's account of his fruitless efforts to recover this property is printed in the *Coleccion de documentos ineditos para la historia de España*, ed. Jose Sancho Rayon and Francisco de Zabalbura (Madrid, 1887–89), pp. 91, 434.

45. Kelsey, *Sir Francis Drake*, pp. 210–11.

46. Parker, *Dutch Revolt*, pp. 194–95.

47. Ibid., pp. 196–97; L. P. Gachard, *Correspondance de Guillaume le Taciturne* (Brussels, 1851), vi, pp. xxxvii–xxxix. The formal renunciation is translated and printed by H. H. Rowen, *The Low Countries in Early Modern Times* (London, 1972), pp. 92–105.

48. Wallace MacCaffrey, *Queen Elizabeth and the Making of Policy 1572–1588* (London, 1981), pp. 272–74.

49. Ibid., p. 279.

50. Parker, *Dutch Revolt*, p. 206.

51. Ibid.; *Calendar of State Papers, Foreign*, xvii, pp. 19–22.

52. Ibid., pp. 144–45; J. S. Nolan, *Sir John Norreys and the Elizabethan Military World* (Exeter, 1997), pp. 59–64.

53. *Elizabeth I: Collected Works*, pp. 259–60.

54. Anjou's death left Henry of Navarre, the Huguenot leader, as the next heir in blood. The former leaders of the Catholic League immediately declared this to be unacceptable, and resurrected their organisation, again under the leadership of the duke of Guise.

55. MacCaffrey, *Queen Elizabeth and the Making of Policy*, pp. 303–5.

56. Parker, *Dutch Revolt*, p. 217.

57. *Calendar of State Papers, Foreign*, xviii, pp. 628–29, 653–55.

58. *Calendar of State Papers, Foreign*, xix, pp. 318, 354–55.

59. *The Naval Tracts of Sir William Monson*, ed. M. Oppenheim, Navy Records Society (1902–14) i, pp. 125–26. The admiralty court in London was immediately besieged with claims for compensation.

60. MacCaffrey, *Queen Elizabeth and the Making of Policy*, pp. 311–12.

61. Camden, *Annals*, ed. by W. MacCaffrey (London, 1970), p. 206.

62. *Calendar of State Papers, Foreign*, xix, pp. 655, 666, 668–69.

63. R. B. Wernham, *After the Armada* (Oxford, 1984). Elizabeth became increasingly obsessed with economy after 1585; but she also refused to commit any major forces for fear of conceding power to those who led them. Her experience with the earl of Leicester in the Low Countries between 1585 and 1587 reinforced that fear.

64. *Calendar of State Papers, Spanish, Elizabeth*, iii, pp. 45, 49, 126, 142.

65. C. Martin and G. Parker, *The Spanish Armada* (London, 1988), pp. 95–96.

66. *Calendar of State Papers, Spanish, Elizabeth*, iii, p. 60, MacCaffrey, *Queen Elizabeth and the Making of Policy*, p. 320.

67. *Calendar of State Papers, Spanish, Elizabeth*, iii, pp. 132–36, 140–42.

68. Ibid., pp. 185–90.

69. It is clear that agents of either Cecil or Walsingham were tapping Mary's correspondence from the beginning. This was probably done with Shrewsbury's knowledge, which would explain his apparent lack of diligence in this respect.

70. Camden, *Annals* (1635), pp. 229–30; *Calendar of State Papers Relating to Scotland*, v, pp. 316–20; *Calendar of State Papers, Spanish, Elizabeth*, iii, pp. 121–25.

71. MacCaffrey, *Queen Elizabeth and the Making of Policy*, pp. 408–412.

72. *Calendar of State Papers Relating to Scotland*, vi, pp. 184–85; PRO, 31/1, 13 and 14 September 1582.

73. *Calendar of State Papers, Spanish*, iii, pp. 463–64, 475–76.

74. Ibid., pp. 33–34.

75. MacCaffrey, *Queen Elizabeth and the Making of Policy*, pp. 325–28.

76. J. B. Black, *The Reign of Elizabeth* (Oxford, 1959), pp. 375–76.

77. Ibid.

78. *A Discoverie of the Treasons Practised and Attempted against the Queenes Maiestie and her Realme*, by Francis Throckmorton (1584), *Harleian Miscellany*, 3 (1809), pp. 190–200.

79. Raphael Holinshed, *Chronicle* (London, 1807–8), iv, p. 536.

80. Ibid.

81. For an oblique look at these intrigues, see D. M. Lockie, 'The Political Career of the Bishop of Ross, 1568–80', *University of Birmingham Historical Journal*, 4 (1953), pp. 98–145.

82. There was a keen awareness of just how essential Elizabeth was to the political stability of the country, expressed both in execration of Throgmorton and in loyal demontrations. Black, *Reign of Elizabeth*, pp. 376–77.

83. Confession of faith written for the magistrates of London, 19th July 1580. *Letters and Memorials of Robert Parsons*, i, *1578–88*, ed. Leo Hicks, Catholic Record Society, 39 (1942).

84. MacCaffrey, *Queen Elizabeth and the Making of Policy*, pp. 479–80.

85. 23 Elizabeth I, c. 1; *Statutes of the Realm*, iv, pp. 657–58.

86. T. M. McCoog, ed., *The Reckoned Expense: Edmund Campion and the Early English Jesuits* (Woodbridge, 1996), pp. xxi–xxii.

87. 'A Letter of Information Sent to Lord Burleigh Concerning the Activities of Englishmen in Rome, 1583', Strype, *Annals of the Reformation*, iii, appendix 1, no. xxxv.

88. J. E. Neale, *Queen Elizabeth and her Parliaments*, ii, *1584–1601* (London, 1957), pp. 44–54.

89. Black, *Reign of Elizabeth*, pp. 377–78. A copy of this Bond of Association is printed in *Elizabeth I: Collected Works*, pp. 183–85, from BL, Cotton MS Caligula C. ix, art. 41, fol. 122. A number of other original copies survive, some with signatures.

90. MacCaffrey, *Queen Elizabeth and the Making of Policy*, p. 479. There is no reason to suppose that Cecil adopted this strategy unwillingly, as he had proposed a rather similar scheme himself in 1567–68. Stephen Alford, *The Early Elizabethan Polity* (Cambridge, 1998), pp. 158–81.

91. Ibid.

92. 35 Henry VIII, c. 1. Henry's will is PRO, E23/4/1, which was printed in T. Rymer, *Foedera* (London, 1741), vi, pt 3, pp. 142–45.

93. *Statutes of the Realm*, iv, pp. 704–5; 27 Elizabeth I, c. 1.

94. Ibid.

95. *Calendar of State Papers Relating to Scotland*, vii, pp. 596–98, 602; *The Letter Book of Sir Amyas Paulet, Keeper of Mary, Queen of Scots*, ed. John Morris (London, 1874).

96. Black, *Reign of Elizabeth*, pp. 379–80.

97. J. H. Pollen, *Mary Queen of Scots and the Babington Plot*, Scottish Historical Society, third series, 3 (1922).

98. Ibid.; Conyers Read, *Mr Secretary Walsingham and the Policy of Queen Elizabeth* (London, 1925), ii, p. 44.

99. Pollen, *Mary Queen of Scots and the Babington Plot*, pp. 63–66.

100. *Calendar of State Papers, Venetian*, vii, p. 202.

101. G. C. Cruickshank, *Elizabeth's Army* (Oxford, 1966).

102. *Calendar of State Papers, Domestic, 1547–80*, p. 648; *Tudor Royal Proclamations*, ii, pp. 463–64; Conyers Read, *Mr Secretary Walsingham and the Policy of Queen Elizabeth* (Oxford, 1925) ii, pp. 364 et seq.

103. *Tudor Royal Proclamations*, ii, pp. 350–52.

104. The shift was slow, and the interpretation of it controversial. On different aspects and opinions see S. J. Gunn, *Early Tudor Government, 1485–1558* (London, 1995), Helen Miller, *Henry VIII and the Nobility* (Oxford, 1986), D. Loades, *Politics and the Nation, 1450–1660* (Oxford, 1999), Penry Williams, *The Tudor*

Regime (Oxford, 1979), and G. W. Bernard, ed., *The Tudor Nobility* (Manchester, 1992).

105. D. Loades, *The Tudor Navy* (Aldershot, 1992) passim; M. Oppenheim, *The History of the Administration of the Royal Navy, 1509–1660* (London, 1896; reprint 1988).

106. Loades, *Tudor Navy*, pp. 184–85; Oppenheim, *Administration*, pp. 162–63; S. Adams, 'New Light on the "Reformation" of John Hawkins: The Ellesmere Naval Survey of January 1584', *English Historical Review*, 105 (1991), pp. 97–111. PRO, SP12/132/88–91.

107. PRO, SP12/156, fos 88–90.

108. MacCaffrey, *Elizabeth I*, pp. 323–24.

Notes to Chapter 10: War with Spain

1. In 1578 two London merchants, Sir Edward Osborne and Richard Staper, set out to revive the long-defunct Levant trade by sending an envoy, William Harborne, to the court of Murad III. This led to the grant of a *firman* in June 1580 and the establishment of the Levant Company. Diplomatic relations were established in the following year. Sir William Foster, *England's Quest of Eastern Trade* (London, 1933), pp. 69–72.

2. MacCaffrey, *Queen Elizabeth and the Making of Policy*, pp. 475–78; Giovanni Dolfini to the doge and senate, 12 September 1586, *Calendar of State Papers, Venetian*, vii, p. 202.

3. No existing law covered Mary's circumstances. An ordinary person was subject to the laws of the country in which they were dwelling, irrespective of whether they were citizens or not. This did not apply to Mary, because as an anointed queen she was subject to no other monarch. I am not aware of any full discussion of this issue, which appears to lie behind a lot of Elizabeth's ambivalence.

4. To John Foxe it was a mark of the False Church to kill anyone for erroneous belief. He argued that the penalty for heresy in the early church had been (eventually) banishment. *Acts and Monuments* (1563), passim. Elizabeth appears to have shared that view.

5. P. Hughes, *Rome and the Counter Reformation in England* (London, 1942), p. 214.

6. BL, Cotton MS Caligula C. ix, fol. 459; *Elizabeth I: Collected Works*, pp. 287–88.

7. Read, *Mr Secretary Walsingham*, ii, p. 44.

8. *Tudor Royal Proclamations*, ii, pp. 528–32.

9. Cambridge University Library, MS Gg. III. 34, fos 304–8. *Elizabeth I: Collected Works*, pp. 186–89.

10. J. B. Black, *The Reign of Elizabeth* (Oxford, 1959), p. 386.

11. See above, p. 224.

12. Camden, *Annals* (1688), iii, p. 202.

13. Ibid.

14. The effect of this was particularly clear in the writings of the Jesuit Robert Southwell, who professed the allegiance of Catholics in all temporal matters; *A Consolatory Letter to All the Afflicted Catholikes in England* (1588) (*STC*, 1032), and *An Humble Supplication to Her Maiestie* (1600) (*STC*, 7586).

15. J. Strype, *Annals of the Reformation*, iii, appendix 2, no. 13.

16. The total sum raised from fines and compositions in 1589 was in the region of £8000. F. C. Dietz, *English Government Finance, 1558–1640* (New York, 1932), p. 63.

17. For the queen's responses to these petitions, see *Elizabeth I: Collected Works*, pp. 167–204.

18. Strype, *Annals*, iii, appendix 1, p. 68.

19. PRO, SP12/176/68, fol. 215; *Elizabeth I: Collected Works*, pp. 177–81.

20. Ibid., p. 180.

21. For her application of this doctrine in the case of the prophesyings, see P. Collinson, *Edmund Grindal, 1519–1583* (Berkeley, California, 1979).

22. Elizabeth herself was keenly aware of these divisions. In discussion with her bishops she reported having received a letter 'from beyond the seas', in which the writer had declared 'that the papists were in great hope to prevail again in England for that her protestants themselves misliked her, and indeed so they do, quod she, for I have heard that some of them of late have said that I was of no religion'. *Elizabeth I: Collected Works*, p. 179.

23. *O Read Over Dr Bridges, for it is a Worthy Worke* (*STC*, 17454); *Certaine Minerall and Metaphisicall Schoolpoints* (*STC*, 17455); *Hay Any Worke for Cooper* (*STC*, 17456); *Theses Martinianae* (*STC*, 17457); *The Iust Censure and Reproofe of Martin Iunior* (*STC*, 17458); *The Protestatyon of Martin Marprelat* (*STC*, 17459).

24. Cited D. Loades, *Chronicles of the Tudor Queens* (Stroud, 2002), p. 212.

25. C. Read, *Lord Burghley and Queen Elizabeth*, p. 470.

26. P. Collinson, *The Religion of Protestants: the Church in English Society, 1559–1625* (Oxford, 1982). For the kind of effect which this could have at the local level, see John Craig, *Reformation, Politics and Polemics* (Cambridge, 2002), pp. 64–133.

27. Collinson, *The Elizabethan Puritan Movement*; P. McGrath, *Papists and Puritans under Elizabeth I* (London, 1967).

28. *Elizabeth I: Collected Works*, pp. 319–20.

29. MacCaffrey, *Queen Elizabeth and The Making of Policy*, pp. 349–50.

30. Simon Adams, *Leicester and the Court* (London, 2002), pp. 133–50.

31. Dudley Papers, Longleat House, box iii, fol. 63; *Calendar of State Papers, Foreign*, xxi, pt 2, p. 110; BL, Cotton MS Galba D. iii, fos 211–25. MacCaffrey, *Queen Elizabeth and the Making of Policy*, p. 352.

32. *Calendar of State Papers, Foreign*, xx, pp. 322–24; John Bruce, ed., *The Correspondence of Robert Dudley, Earl of Leicester, 1585 and 1586*, Camden Society, 27 (1844), pp. 105–6.

33. MacCaffrey, *Queen Elizabeth and the Making of Policy*, pp. 354–56.

34. Adams, *Leicester and the Court*, pp. 46–67. Elizabeth liked her successful soldiers, and sailors, to be of relatively humble rank. By 1590 there were no soldiers on the council, and only Essex (1593) subsequently joined.

35. *Calendar of State Papers, Foreign*, xx, pp. 277, 287, 303, 311, 326; Bruce, *Correspondence of Dudley*, pp. 57–63, 95–98.

36. *A Collection of Scarce and Valuable Tracts of the Late Lord Somers*, ed. Walter Scott (1809), i, pp. 420–21.

37. *Calendar of State Papers, Foreign*, xx, pp. 322–24.

38. Bruce, *Correspondence of Dudley*, p. 112.

39. Ibid.

40. MacCaffrey, *Queen Elizabeth and the Making of Policy*, pp. 358–59.

41. G. Parker, *The Dutch Revolt*, pp. 218–21.

42. BL, Harleian MS 6993, fol. 129; Cotton MS Galba C. xi, fos 143–44.

43. G. Parker and C. Martin, *The Spanish Armada* (London, 1988), pp. 113–116, discusses these preparations.

44. J. E. Neale, 'Elizabeth and the Netherlands, 1586–7', *English Historical Review*, 45 (1930), pp. 373–96; *Calendar of State Papers, Foreign*, xix, p. 635; BL, Cotton MS Galba D. i, fol. 120.

45. MacCaffrey, *Queen Elizabeth and the Making of Policy*, pp. 362–64.

46. D. Wilson, *Sweet Robin: A Biography of Robert Dudley, Earl of Leicester, 1533–1588* (London, 1981), p. 282.

47. Neale, 'Elizabeth and the Netherlands'; MacCaffrey, *Queen Elizabeth and the Making of Policy*, pp. 363–64.

48. Ibid., p. 367.

49. Wilson, *Sweet Robin*, pp. 284–85.

50. PRO, SP84/9/38, fos 85–86; *Elizabeth I: Collected Works*, pp. 282–83.

51. J. S. Nolan, *Sir John Norreys and the Elizabethan Military World*, pp. 94–107.

52. H. Kelsey, *Sir Francis Drake: The Queen's Pirate* (New Haven, Connecticut, 1998), p. 240.

53. Devon Record Office, Drake Papers, 346M/F551, 1–2, testimony of Thomas Drake, October 1605; M. F. Keeler, *Sir Francis Drake's West Indian Voyage*, Hakluyt Society (1981), p. 53n.

54. *Calendar of State Papers, Spanish, Elizabeth*, iii, pp. 531–32.

55. PRO, AO1/1685/20A; Keeler, *West Indian Voyage*, pp. 52–53.

56. PRO, SP12/180, fol. 22; J. S. Corbett, ed., *Papers Relating to the Navy during the Spanish War, 1585–7*, Navy Records Society (1898), pp. 36–38.

57. R. N. Worth, *Calendar of the Plymouth Municipal Records* (1893), p. 18.

58. Walter Bigges, *Summarie and True Discourse*, was published in 1589; a journal by Carliell, or kept on his behalf, survives as BL, Cotton MS Otho E. viii, published in Keeler, *Drake's West Indian Voyage*, pp. 71–73. Drake appears to have intended to keep his own record, but if he did it has not survived.

59. Kelsey, *Sir Francis Drake*, p. 245. Drake deliberately underprovisioned on other voyages, on the grounds that food regularly went rotten before it could be consumed.

60. Kelsey, *Sir Francis Drake*, p. 249; Vincenzo Gradinego to the doge and senate, 25 October 1585, *Calendar of State Papers, Venetian*, viii, p. 123.
61. BL, Harley MS 2202, fos 57–58; Keeler, *Drake's West Indian Voyage*, pp. 130–31.
62. Ibid.
63. 'The Discourse and Description of the Voyage of Sir Francis Drake', BL, Royal MS 7 C. xvi, fos 167–68; Keeler, *Drake's West Indian Voyage*, pp. 186–90.
64. Kelsey, *Sir Francis Drake*, p. 255.
65. Cristobal de Ovalle to Philip II, 24 February, 1586, AGI, Santo Domingo 51 ramo 9, no. 87, fol. 3; Kelsey, *Sir Francis Drake*, pp. 260–61.
66. 'Relacion de lo que declaro Pedro yndio natural de la provincia de la Margarita, que esta preso en la cuidad de Cartagena', 16 February 1587, AGI, Santa Fe 89, ramo 3, no. 35, fos 1–3; Kelsey, *Sir Francis Drake*, pp. 263–64.
67. *Papers Relating to the Spanish War, 1585–87*, ed. J. S. Corbett, Navy Records Society (1898), pp. 18–20.
68. The Spaniards believed that the English had taken far more casualties at Cartagena than they would admit. See a report to the Audiencia, made on 12 March 1586, AGI, Patronato 266, ramo 50, no. 13, fol. 2; Kelsey, *Sir Francis Drake*, p. 268.
69. Bigges, *Summarie and True Discourse*, pp. 30–34.
70. Keeler, *Drake's West Indian Voyage*, pp. 301–9.
71. Kelsey, *Sir Francis Drake*, pp. 277–83.
72. Parker and Martin, *The Spanish Armada*, pp. 109–13, 282.
73. Thomas Fenner to Walsingham, 1 April 1587, PRO, SP12/200/1; Corbett, *Papers Relating to the Navy*, pp. 99–100.
74. BL, Lansdowne MS 56, no. 52, fol. 175, Corbett, *Papers Relating to the Navy*, pp. 105–6.
75. Kelsey, *Sir Francis Drake*, p. 287.
76. Parker and Martin, *The Spanish Armada*, pp. 129–30.
77. Fenner to Walsingham, 17 May 1587, PRO, SP12/201/34; Corbett, *Papers Relating to the Navy*, pp. 136–37. See also Augustin de Horosco, 'Discurso de la fundación y antiguedades de Cadiz y los demas subcesos que por ella an passado', BL, Royal MS 14 A. iii, fol. 157.
78. Kelsey, *Sir Francis Drake*, p. 299; PRO, SP12/202/53; Corbett, *Papers Relating to the Navy*, pp. 200–1.
79. Kelsey, *Sir Francis Drake*, pp. 294, 299.
80. Drake to Walsingham, 27 April 1587, PRO, SP12/200/46; Corbett, *Papers Relating to the Navy*, pp. 108–9.
81. Parker and Martin, *The Spanish Armada*, pp. 112–119.
82. The main method was by a version of ship service, and some ports were still sending in excuses for non-fulfilment long after the Armada had failed. M.-J. Rodriguez Salgado, *Armada* (Greenwich, 1988), pp. 173–75.
83. Ibid.
84. Sluys, which had been recently captured, was not large enough for the purpose. Parker and Martin, *The Spanish Armada*, pp. 117–18; Kelsey, *Sir Francis Drake*, p. 308.

85. Mendoza to Philip II, 27 December 1587; *Calendar of State Papers, Spanish, Elizabeth*, iv, pp. 179-80, 183-84.
86. BL, Royal MS 14 B. xiii; J. Charnock, *History of Marine Architecture* (London, 1802), pp. 59-72.
87. Drake to Elizabeth I, 13 April 1588; PRO, SP12/209/89, fol. 135.
88. Kelsey, *Sir Francis Drake*, p. 318.
89. The Spaniards were working on the new Gregorian calendar. The English had refused to accept this papal innovation and were still working on the old Julian calendar. There is consequently a ten-day dating difference in documents emanating from the two countries.
90. There are several contemporary accounts of the battle of the Channel, printed in J. K. Laughton, ed., *State Papers Relating to the Defeat of the Spanish Armada, Anno 1588* Navy Records Society (1894), and G. P. B. Naish 'Documents Illustrating the History of the Spanish Armada', *Naval Miscellany*, 4 (1952), pp. 1-84. These narratives are summarised in Parker and Martin, *The Spanish Armada*, pp. 157-78.
91. Ibid., pp. 187-8.
92. Winter to Walsingham, 1 August 1588, Laughton, *State Papers*, ii, pp. 8-10.
93. Parker and Martin, *The Spanish Armada*, pp. 191-92. The large number of ships wrecked on the Scottish and Irish coasts can be largely attributed to this battle damage.
94. Ibid., 253-54.
95. BL, Harley MS 6798, art. 18, fol. 87; *Elizabeth I: Collected Works*, pp. 325-26, which also discusses the various versions of the speech which remain, and their provenance.
96. The delivery of this speech on 9 August would have allowed time for the news to reach her, as the fleet had disengaged on the 2nd. On the other hand, the full significance of the victory may well not have been clear.
97. For a full discussion of official attitudes to morbidity and mortality in the fleet, and the customary rights of seamen, see Cheryl A. Fury, *Tides in the Affairs of Men: The Social History of Elizabethan Seamen, 1580-1603* (Westport, Connectict, 2002), pp. 137-97.
98. BL, Add. MS 23240, art. 24, fol. 77; *Elizabeth I: Collected Works*, pp. 357-58.
99. R. B. Wernham, *The Expedition of Sir John Norris and Sir Francis Drake to Spain and Portugal, 1589*, Navy Records Society (1988), pp. 12-14.
100. Ibid., pp. 21-26.
101. Ibid., pp. 42-43.
102. Ibid., pp. 57-62, 82. The emperor's message was sent verbally 'by his servant Muschac Reyz' and there is no indication that any reliance was placed on it.
103. Ibid., pp. 82-88.
104. It is also possible that decision arose from an undisclosed understanding which the commanders had with Dom Antonio. 'Avisos de Inglaterra de 5 de Noviembre 1588 traduizos de Ingles', AGS, Estado K 1568, B 61, no. 127B; Kelsey, *Sir Francis Drake*, p. 343.

105. Wernham, *The Expedition of Sir John Norris*, pp. 164–68.

106. Ibid., p. 181.

107. Elizabeth I to Norris and Drake, 7 July 1589; privy council to the same, 7 July; Wernham, *Expedition*, pp. 200–2.

108. Ibid., pp. 291–94, which prints both the charges and the replies.

109. Henry of Navarre was the grandson of Francis I's sister, Margaret; but because of the Salic Law his claim actually derived from his father, Anthony, duke of Vendôme, descended in the seventh generation from Louis IX. His rival 'Charles X' was his uncle, the cardinal of Bourbon, whose claim was similarly derived.

110. MacCaffrey, *Elizabeth I; War and Politics, 1588–1603* (London, 1992), p. 142.

111. Henry Radcliffe, who succeeded his brother, had no political career, and Ambrose Dudley died without issue.

112. Simon Adams, *Leicester and the Court* (London, 2002) pp. 148–50. It is not clear whether Elizabeth ever replied to his 'last letter'.

113. On the age, antecedents and composition of the privy council in 1590, see Wallace MacCaffrey, *Elizabeth I: War and Politics, 1588–1603* (London, 1992), pp. 468–70.

Notes to Chapter 11: The Earl of Essex

1. He was appointed master at the coronation, and held the position until his death; PRO, LC2/4(3), fol. 104; Pam Wright, 'A Change of Direction: The Ramifications of a Female Household, 1558–1603', in D. Starkey, *The English Court* (London, 1987), p. 155.

2. Hatfield House, Salisbury MS. 32, fol. 50, Wright, 'A Change of Direction', pp. 156–57.

3. PRO, E351/1795, fos 12–63; BL Lansdowne MS 3, fol. 88; MS 29, fol. 68; MS 34, fol. 30; MS 59, fol. 72; MS 104, fol. 17.

4. Wright, 'A Change of Direction'.

5. On the issue of control in Elizabeth's various courtships, see Susan Doran, *Monarchy and Matrimony* (London, 1996) and Philippa Berry, *Of Chastity and Power* (London, 1989), pp. 83–110.

6. Walter Devereux, *Lives and Letters of the Devereux Earls of Essex*, 2 vols (London, 1853), i, p. 90. L. B. Smith, *Treason in Tudor England: Politics and Paranoia* (London, 1986), pp. 193–94.

7. W. W. R. Ball and J. A. Venn, *Admissions to Trinity College, Cambridge* (Cambridge, 1913), ii, p. 125. There is some dispute about Robert's actual age on admission.

8. L. B. Smith, *Treason in Tudor England: Politics and Paranoia* (London, 1986), p. 195. Burghley regularly ensured a first-class education for all the wards in his care, believing that this was essential for any life of public service.

9. Ibid., p. 200.

10. Ibid.

11. Camden, *Elizabeth* (1688), pp. 623–24.
12. W. B. Devereux, *Lives and Letters of the Devereux Earls of Essex, 1540–1646* (London, 1853), i, p. 185.
13. Essex was perfectly well aware of this aspect of his personality, and indeed flaunted it as a trademark of his style. After one early quarrel with the queen, he wrote 'an honourable death is better than a disquiet life. My friends will make the best of it; mine enemies cannot say it is dishonest; the danger is mine, and I am content to abide the worst.' Devereux, *Earls of Essex*, i, pp. 186–89.
14. Ibid., p. 184.
15. Smith, *Treason in Tudor England*, p. 203. The quarrel was over the earl's sister, Dorothy Perrot, to whom Elizabeth had taken an irrational dislike – apparently for her mother's sake.
16. R. B. Wernham, *The Expedition of Sir John Norris and Sir Francis Drake to Spain and Portugal, 1589*, Navy Records Society (1988), pp. 133–38.
17. Ibid., p. 133.
18. Norris and Drake to the council, 7 April 1589; Wernham, *The Expedition to Spain and Portugal*, p. 134.
19. This can be deduced from his failure to communicate with either Norris or Drake, and from his apparent assumption that he had the right to commandeer ships on demand.
20. Smith, *Treason in Tudor England*, p. 204.
21. PRO, SP12/231, fos 70, 103.
22. Thomas Birch, *Memoirs of the Reign of Queen Elizabeth from the Year 1581 till her Death*, 2 vols (London, 1754), i, p. 155.
23. Camden, *Elizabeth*, p. 524.
24. 2 August 1591; *Acts of the Privy Council*, xxi, p. 358.
25. W. MacCaffrey, *Elizabeth I: War and Politics, 1588–1603*, pp. 152–62. The League operated all over France, and the king's strategy had to be constantly adapted to meet the threat.
26. Camden, *Elizabeth* p. 442; J. S. Nolan, *Sir John Norreys and the Elizabethan Military World* (Exeter, 1997) pp. 172–73.
27. MacCaffrey, *Elizabeth I*, p. 465.
28. Conyers Read, *Lord Burghley and Queen Elizabeth* (London, 1960), pp. 477–79.
29. MacCaffrey, *Elizabeth I*, pp. 469–71.
30. *The List and Analysis of State Papers, Foreign Series, 1591–92*, ed. R. B. Wernham, pp. 588, 591.
31. MacCaffrey, *Elizabeth I*, pp. 165–67.
32. Devereux, *Earls of Essex*, i, p. 234.
33. Smith, *Treason in Tudor England*, pp. 204–6.
34. Ibid., p. 206.
35. *Acts of the Privy Council*, xxiv, p. 78; Read, *Lord Burghley*, pp. 478–87.
36. Francis Bacon, 'Letters', in *Works* (London, 1861–74), iii, pp. 226–31; L. B. Smith, *Elizabeth Tudor: Portrait of a Queen* (London, 1976), p. 206. More generally,

George Puttenham, *The Arte of English Poesie* (1589), ed., G. D. Willock and A. Walke (Cambridge, 1936).

37. Thomas Birch, *Memoirs of the Reign of Queen Elizabeth from the Year 1581 till her Death* (London, 1754) i, pp. 150, 152.

38. Smith, *Treason in Tudor England*, pp. 210–11.

39. Ibid., p. 211.

40. Birch, *Memoirs of Elizabeth*, i, p. 153.

41. Ibid. For other moves in Essex's campaign, see Birch, *Memoirs of Elizabeth I*, pp. 121, 123, 166–67, 172.

42. PRO, SP78/37/110, fos 150–53, 180, 182.

43. For Drake's last voyage, see Kelsey, *Sir Francis Drake*, pp. 367–91; S. and E. Usherwood, *The Counter Armada, 1596* (London, 1983), pp. 18–19. His instructions remain in BL, Cotton MS Otho E. ix.

44. Usherwood, *The Counter Armada*, pp. 20–23.

45. 'The Journal of the Mary Rose'; Lambeth Palace, Codex 250, fos 344–62; printed as appendix 1 to Usherwood, *The Counter Armada*.

46. Lambeth Palace, Codex 250, fol. 260.

47. *Calendar of State Papers, Venetian*, ix, no. 470.

48. Usherwood, *The Counter Armada*, pp. 91–94.

49. Smith, *Treason in Tudor England*, p. 214.

50. Birch, *Memoirs of Elizabeth*, ii, p. 131.

51. Smith, *Treason in Tudor England*, p. 214.

52. Birch, *Memoirs of Elizabeth*, ii, p. 289; Henry Sidney, *Letters and Memorials of State from the Originals at Penshurst Place in Kent*, ed. A. Collins, 2 vols (London, 1746), ii, pp. 22–24.

53. Ibid.

54. Birch, *Memoirs of Elizabeth*, ii, p. 296. The office was worth about £150 a year, but varied according to the number of guns in store.

55. *Calendar of State Papers, Domestic, 1595–97*, p. 439.

56. MacCaffrey, *Elizabeth I*, p. 127.

57. Ibid., p. 128.

58. Samuel Purchas, *Hakluytus Posthumus: or Purchas His Pilgrims* (1625, reprint Glasgow, 1905–7), xx, pp. 27, 71–72.

59. *Elizabeth I: Collected Works*, p. 388.

60. HMC, *Hatfield MSS*, 7, pp. 433–34.

61. Robert Burton, *The Anatomy of Melancholy*, ed. F. Dell and P. Jordan-Smith (New York 1938), p. 333.

62. Smith, *Treason in Tudor England*, p. 218.

63. *Calendar of State Papers, Domestic, 1598–1601*, p. 71.

64. MacCaffrey, *Elizabeth I*, pp. 512–13.

65. Read, *Lord Burghley*, pp. 540–42. Burghley's health seems to have recovered in the early summer, and he attended every council during June.

66. Camden, *Elizabeth*, p. 555.

67. MacCaffrey, *Elizabeth I*, pp. 516–17.

68. The queen was deeply distressed by the last illness and death of her old servant. Francis Peck, *Desiderata Curiosa*, 2 vols (London 1732–35), i; anonymous life of Burghley.

69. MacCaffrey, *Elizabeth I*, p. 410.

70. For general discussions of the impact of Cromwell's policies on Ireland, see S. G. Ellis, *Tudor Ireland* (London, 1985), pp. 132–37; and Brendan Bradshaw, *The Irish Constitutional Revolution of the Sixteenth Century* (Cambridge, 1979), pp. 132–64.

71. Bradshaw, *The Dissolution of the Religious Orders in Ireland under Henry VIII* (Cambridge, 1974); R. D. Edwards, *Church and State in Tudor Ireland* (Dublin, 1934).

72. Bradshaw, 'Sword, Word and Strategy in the Reformation in Ireland', *Historical Journal*, 21 (1978), pp. 475–502; J. Watt, *The Church in Medieval Ireland* (Dublin, 1972).

73. Bradshaw, 'The Edwardian Reformation in Ireland', *Archivum Hibernicum*, 34 (1976–77), pp. 83–99; Ciaran Brady, 'England's Defence and Ireland's Reform: The Dilemma of the Irish Viceroys, 1541–1641', in *The British Problem, c. 1534–1707*, ed. B. Bradshaw and J. Morrill (London, 1996), pp. 89–117.

74. J. G. Crawford, *Anglicising the Government of Ireland: The Irish Privy Council and the Expansion of Tudor Rule, 1556–1579* (Dublin, 1993); C. Brady, *The Chief Governors: The Rise and Fall of Reform Government in Tudor Ireland, 1536–1588* (Cambridge, 1994).

75. N. Canny, *The Elizabethan Conquest of Ireland: A Pattern Established, 1565–1576* (Hassocks, 1976); D. B. Quinn, 'Sir Thomas Smith (1513–1577), and the Beginnings of English Colonial Theory', *Proceedings of the American Philosophical Society*, 79 (1945).

76. Edmund Spenser, *A View of the Present State of Ireland* (1598), ed. W. L. Renwick (Oxford, 1970).

77. Colm Lennon, 'Edmund Campion's *Histories of Ireland*, and Reform in Tudor Ireland', in T. M. McCoog, *The Reckoned Expense* (Woodbridge, 1996), pp. 67–84.

78. Ellis, *Tudor Ireland*, pp. 228–77.

79. 'Notes of the Irish Confederates by William Herlle, April 1571', *Calendar of State Papers Relating to Ireland, 1571–1575* (London, 2000), pp. 16–17.

80. Canny, *Elizabethan Conquest of Ireland*.

81. Ellis, *Tudor Ireland*, pp. 278–88.

82. 'Relation of Thomas Stukeley's Proceedings' (*c.* 1573); *Calendar of State Papers Relating to Ireland, 1571–1575*, pp. 18–19; C. Falls, *Elizabeth's Irish Wars* (London, 1950), pp. 123–26.

83. N. Canny, *The Formation of the Old English Elite in Ireland* (Dublin, 1975); Hiram Morgan, *Tyrone's rebellion: The Origin of the Nine Years War in Ulster* (Woodbridge, 1993).

84. Crawford, *Anglicising the Government of Ireland*.

85. MacCaffrey, *War and Politics*, pp. 377–79; Fynes Moryson, *An History of Ireland from 1599 to 1603*, 2 vols (Dublin, 1735), i, p. 28.

86. Morgan, *Tyrone's Rebellion*; B. Bradshaw, 'Native Reaction to the Westward Enterprise: A Case Study in Gaelic Ideology', in K. Andrews, N. Canny and P. Hair, *The Westward Enterprise* (Liverpool, 1978), pp. 66–80.

87. *Calendar of State Papers Relating to Ireland*, vi, p. 50.

88. Ellis, *Tudor Ireland*, p. 305.

89. Birch, *Memoirs of Queen Elizabeth*, ii, p. 426.

90. The army which Essex led to Ireland consisted of 16,000 foot and 1300 horse, and its projected annual cost was £290,000. This made it more than twice the size of the force committed to the Netherlands by the treaty of Nonsuch. It was by far the largest land army committed anywhere during the war. S. G. Ellis, *Tudor Ireland*, p. 306.

91. According to Smith, *Treason in Tudor England*, p. 225, it was Elizabeth's refusal to grant him the mastership of the wards which tipped Essex over the edge.

92. He had already uttered the fateful words 'what, cannot princes err?' and this was known to the queen. She seems to have regarded the Irish command as a last chance to redeem himself; he also saw it as a chance to re-establish his position, but he was not quite certain in what way. Smith, *Treason in Tudor England*, pp. 224–27.

93. Ellis, *Tudor Ireland*, p. 306. The choice of this strategy was not entirely Essex's. The Irish council advised against an Ulster campaign so early in the season, and the queen gave her specific assent to the Leinster move. *Calendar of State Papers Relating to Ireland, 1599–1600*, p. 28; L. W. Henry, 'The Earl of Essex in Ireland, 1599', *Bulletin of the Institute of Historical Research*, 32 (1959), p. 12.

94. *Calendar of State Papers Relating to Ireland, 1598–99*, pp. 426, 451; *1599–1600*, pp. 7, 19, 28, 92, 114–16, 117–18. The problem had been compounded by the lack of shipping for reinforcements, but Elizabeth brushed that aside.

95. *Calendar of State Papers Relating to Ireland, 1599–1600*, pp. 138–39, 144–47, 154–55; Smith, *Treason in Tudor England*, pp. 233–34.

96. *Calendar of State Papers Relating to Ireland, 1599–1600*, pp. 156–58; MacCaffrey, *Elizabeth I*, pp. 425–26.

97. Devereux, *Earls of Essex*, ii, p. 44.

98. Ibid., p. 43.

99. Smith, *Treason in Tudor England*, pp. 236–38.

100. Ibid. Buckingham had made more of an issue of the hereditary constableship, and was closer to the throne than Essex; but he was similarly betrayed by servants reporting his irresponsible words. Barbara Harris, *Edward Stafford, Third Duke of Buckingham, 1478–1521* (Stanford, California, 1986), pp. 180–202.

101. Smith, *Treason in Tudor England*, p. 242. At this stage Essex was judged to have been guilty of contempt only, not of disloyalty.

102. His standard line of argument in letters to the queen, was that he was merely protecting himself against his enemies. 'I meant that I lay open to the malice and practice of mine enemies in England, who first procured a cloud of disgrace to overshadow me, and now in the dark give me wound upon wound.' The implication, of course, was that she was failing to protect him

against his traducers. *Calendar of State Papers Relating to Ireland, 1599–1600,* pp. 95–96.

103. Camden, *Elizabeth,* pp. 602–3.
104. Smith, *Treason in Tudor England,* pp. 240–41.
105. Ibid., p. 242.
106. Francis Bacon, 'A Declaration of the Practices and Treasons Attempted and Committed by Robert, Late Earl of Essex', in *Works,* iii, pp. 136–65.
107. Camden, *Elizabeth,* p. 606.
108. Mervyn James, 'At a Crossroads of the Political Culture; the Essex Revolt, 1601', in *Society, Politics and Culture* (Cambridge 1986).
109. Camden, *Elizabeth,* p. 606.
110. Ibid.
111. Bacon, 'A Declaration of the Practices and Treasons'.
112. Camden, *Elizabeth,* p. 607.
113. PRO, SP11/2/9.
114. Camden, *Elizabeth,* p. 607.
115. Bacon, 'A Declaration of the Practices and Treasons'; Smith, *Treason in Tudor England,* p. 246.
116. Cecil had been in direct correspondence with Essex's officers while he was still in Ireland, and had a good insight into his uncertain state of mind. *Calendar of State Papers Relating to Ireland, 1599–1600,* pp. 402, 440–47. It is clear from the speed of his reaction on the 7 February, and the fact that troops could be deployed at Essex House within hours of the outbreak, that he had a very good idea of what to expect.
117. One of the earl's more implausible claims was that Cecil was intriguing with Spain; 'England is sold to the Spaniard'. William Cobbett, *State Trials,* i, p. 1353; Camden, *Elizabeth,* p. 610. This was probably a distortion of the fact that the secretary was seeking to open peace negotiations.
118. Camden, *Annals,* p. 494.
119. Algernon Cecil, *A Life of Robert Cecil, First Earl of Salisbury* (London, 1915); P. M. Handover, *The Second Cecil: The Rise to Power, 1563–1604, of Sir Robert Cecil, Later First Earl of Salisbury* (London, 1959); Joel Hurstfield, 'Robert Cecil, Earl of Salisbury: Minister of Elizabeth and James I', *History Today,* 7 (1957), pp. 279–89.
120. Hughes and Larkin, *Tudor Royal Proclamations,* iii, p. 230.
121. Smith, *Treason in Tudor England,* pp. 268–69; Camden, *Elizabeth,* p. 616.
122. Bacon, 'A Declaration of the Practices and Treasons'.
123. Sir Henry Wotton, *Reliquiae Wottonianae: or A Collection of Lives, Letters, Poems* (London, 1651), pp. 31–32.

Notes to Chapter 12: The Final Years

1. The index of a composite unit of foodstuffs rose from 217 to 315 between 1550 and 1560, and from 389 to 530 between 1590 and 1600 (taking the price from

1451–1475 as 100). R. B. Outhwaite, *Inflation in Tudor and Early Stuart England* (London, 1969), p. 10. The harvests of 1594, 1595 and 1596 were all bad, and the last was one of the worst of the century. A. G. R. Smith, *The Emergence of a Nation State, 1529–1660* (London, 1984), pp. 433–34.

2. G. Parker, *The Dutch Revolt* (London,1977), pp. 225–40.

3. *The Edmondes Papers*, ed. C. G. Butler (London 1913), pp. 70–73.

4. He had been reconciled originally while imprisoned at court following the massacre of St Bartholomew's Day (1572), and had renounced that conversion on his escape. He claimed that this did not count, as it had been enforced.

5. *Elizabeth I: Collected Works*, pp. 370–71.

6. *List and Analysis of the State Papers, Foreign, Reign of Elizabeth*, ed. R. B. Wernham (London, 1964–1993), iv, p. 222; J. S. Nolan, *Sir John Norreys and the Elizabethan Military World* (Exeter, 1997), p. 194.

7. PRO, SP78/30/15, fos 241–44, 246. There were frequent changes of mind by all those principally engaged. Nolan, *Norreys*, pp. 204–5.

8. *List and Analysis of State Papers*, ed. Wernham, iv, pp. 247–48.

9. Wallace MacCaffrey, *Elizabeth I: War and Politics, 1588–1603* (London, 1992), pp. 185–86.

10. Jean Moreau, *Mémoires de Chanoine Jean Moreau sur les Guerres de la Ligue en Brétagne*, ed. H. Waquet (Quimper, 1960), p. 130; Nolan, *Norreys*, pp. 209–10.

11. *List and Analysis of State Papers*, ed. Wernham, v, p. 298.

12. Camden, *Elizabeth* (1688).

13. Ibid.

14. MacCaffrey, *War and Politcs*, pp. 200–2.

15. Camden, *Elizabeth*.

16. G. A. Hays-McCoy, 'The Army of Ulster, 1593–1601', *Irish Sword*, 1 (1950–51), pp. 105–27; J. J. Silke, *Ireland and Europe, 1559–1607* (Dublin 1966).

17. Silke, *Kinsale: The Spanish Intervention in Ireland at the End of the Elizabethan Wars* (Liverpool, 1970), pp. 108–22.

18. MacCaffrey, *War and Politics*, pp. 433–55; Cyril Falls, *Mountjoy: Elizabethan General* (London, 1955).

19. Silke, *Kinsale*, pp. 140–47.

20. 'A Summary Report Made of the Estate of Ireland, 5th November 1597', *Calendar of the Carew Manuscripts*, ed. T. D. Hardy and J. S. Brewer (London, 1864), pp. 271–73.

21. Camden, *Elizabeth*, p. 657.

22. Ibid. Mountjoy knew, and Tyrone did not, that Elizabeth had died at St James on 24 March, just six days earlier. Whether this would have made any difference, except to the rhetoric, seems doubtful.

23. A Portuguese carrack taken off the Azores, by a composite fleet of royal and private ships, in August 1592. The cargo was valued at over £250,000. C. L. Kingsford, 'The Taking of the *Madre de Dios*, Anno 1592', *Naval Miscellany*, 2 (1912), pp. 85–122.

24. H. Kelsey, *Sir Francis Drake: The Queen's Pirate* (New Haven, Connecticut, 1998), pp. 367–391.

25. The heroic end of the *Revenge* should not conceal the fact that it was both unnecessary and pointless. Grenville had been given plenty of notice to get his ship out of danger. Michael Barrington, 'The Most High Spirited Man on Earth: Sir Richard Grenville's Last Fight, September 1591; New Evidence', *Mariners' Mirror*, 36 (1950), pp. 350–53.

26. R. T. Spence, *The Privateering Earl: George Clifford, 3rd Earl of Cumberland, 1558–1605* (Stroud, 1995), pp. 157–75.

27. W. L. Clowes, *The Royal Navy: A History from the Earliest Times to the Present Day*, 7 vols (London 1897–1903), i, p. 533.

28. Ibid., p. 528.

29. A. P. McGowan, *The Jacobean Commissions of Enquiry, 1608, 1618*, Navy Records Society (1971).

30. Bodleian, MS Rawlinson A 206, fol. 41, gives a figure of £36,370, but that is incomplete.

31. PRO, SP12/186/43.

32. N. A. M. Rodger, *The Safeguard of the Sea* (London, 1997), pp. 364–68.

33. Ibid.

34. It was the assumption by certain members of the House of Commons that they had the right to offer this kind of advice, upon any topic they chose, which provoked the free speech debate. G. R. Elton, *The Tudor Constitution* (Cambridge, 1982), pp. 12–14, 260–68.

35. J. H. Baker, *An Introduction to English Legal History* (London, 1979)

36. *Elizabeth I: Collected Works*, p. 52.

37. D. Loades, *Tudor Government* (Oxford, 1997), pp. 1–17.

38. J. D. Alsop, 'Innovation in Tudor Taxation', *English Historical Review*, 99 (1984), pp. 83–93.

39. F. C. Dietz, *English Public Finance, 1558–1640* (New York, 1932).

40. L. Stone, *The Crisis of the Aristocracy, 1558–1641* (Oxford, 1965), pp. 424–45; 'the creation of sixty two new borough seats [in the House of Commons] by Elizabeth between 1558 and 1586 was the result of pressure from courtiers seeking new forms of patronage'.

41. 'A Book for Sea Causes, 1559', PRO, SP12/3, fos 131–34.

42. R. S. Schofield, 'Taxation and the Political Limits of the Tudor State', in C. Cross, D. Loades and J. Scarisbrick, ed., *Law and Government under the Tudors* (Cambridge, 1988), pp. 227–57.

43. PRO, SP12/244/72.

44. J. E. Neale, *Elizabeth I and her Parliaments*, ii, *1584–1601* (London, 1957), pp. 298–312.

45. *Statutes of the Realm*, iv, pt 2, pp. 778–79, 29 Elizabeth, c. 8.

46. F. C. Dietz, *English Public Finance, 1558–1641* (New York, 1932), pp. 91–96.

47. For full discussions of the subsidy needs of both these allies, see MacCaffrey, *War and Politics*, pp. 61–62.

48. Dietz, *Public Finance*, pp. 96–99.

49. Ibid., pp. 407–20; S. Adams, 'Eliza Enthroned?', in Adams, *Leicester and the Court*, pp. 25–26.

50. Stone, *Crisis of the Aristocracy*, makes this point in appendix 19, and pp. 488–99.

51. Walter Devereux, *Lives and letters of the Devereux Earls of Essex*, 2 vols (London, 1853), ii, pp. 98–99.

52. J. A. Chartres, *Internal Trade in England, 1500–1700* (1977); W. H. Price, *The English Patents of Monopoly* (Cambridge, Massachusetts, 1906).

53. 'The Commons Journal of Hayward Townshend, 1601', Bodleian, MS Rawlinson A 100, fos 97–101; J. E. Neale, *Elizabeth and her Parliaments*, ii (London, 1957), pp. 352–56.

54. Hughes and Larkin, *Tudor Royal Proclamations*, iii, pp. 235–37.

55. *Elizabeth I: Collected Works*, p. 336.

56. Ibid., p. 343.

57. 'Townshend's Journal', fos 67–75; *Elizabeth I: Collected Works*, pp. 342, 344–46.

58. Her speeches, letters and prayers throughout her reign reflect these priorities, but see particularly her final speech to parliament on 19 December 1601; *Elizabeth I: Collected Works*, pp. 346–54.

59. The queen seldom intervened directly in the preparation of legislation, which was done by her council, and principally by the secretary. The councillors in the Commons sometimes managed the debates themselves, and sometimes through their 'men of business'. For a study of one such man, see M. A. R. Graves, *Thomas Norton: The Parliament Man* (Oxford, 1994).

60. There are many studies of this development, but see particularly Paul Slack, *Poverty and Policy in Tudor and Stuart England* (London, 1988).

61. 39 Elizabeth, c. 3; *Statutes of the Realm*, iv, pt 2, p. 896.

62. Valerie Pearl, 'Social Policy in Early Modern London', in H. Lloyd Jones, *History and Imagination* (London, 1979), pp. 115–31; P. Clark and P. Slack, *English Towns in Transition, 1500–1700* (London, 1976).

63. 43 Elizabeth I, c. 2.

64. 'An Act against Embezzling of Armour Habiliaments of War and Victual', 31 Elizabeth I, c. 4, *Statutes of the Realm*, iv, pt 2, p. 801.

65. 'An Act for the Relief of Soldiers', 35 Elizabeth I, c. 4, *Statutes of the Realm*, iv, pt 2, p. 847.

66. Slack, *Poverty and Policy*.

67. Emily Bradley, *The Life of Arabella Stewart*, 2 vols (London, 1889); P. M. Handover, *The Second Cecil* (London, 1959), discusses the support for her claim.

68. *A Conference about the Next Succession* (Antwerp? 1594), p. 141.

69. Handover, *The Second Cecil*, pp. 234–37.

70. MacCaffrey, *War and Politics*, pp. 306–8.

71. Ibid., pp. 308–9.

72. *Elizabeth I: Collected Works*, pp. 372–77.

73. MacCaffrey, *War and Politics*, pp. 313–14.

74. *Calendar of State Papers Relating to Scotland*, xii, pp. 404–7.

75. Ibid., pp. 123–24, 216–18, 220–21, 233–36, 238–41, 265–66, 299–300.

76. *Elizabeth I: Collected Works*, pp. 402–3.

77. Handover, *The Second Cecil*, pp. 183–84; Thomas Birch, *Memoirs of the Reign of Queen Elizabeth, from the Year 1581 till her Death*, 2 vols (London, 1754), i, p. 176.
78. MacCaffrey, *War and Politics*, p. 533.
79. Handover, *The Second Cecil*, pp. 232–34.
80. Ibid., p. 234.
81. Ibid.
82. Francis Bacon, *Apology*, in James Spedding, *The Life and Letters of Francis Bacon*, 14 vols (London, 1857), iii, p. 148.
83. Handover, *The Second Cecil*, pp. 235–36.
84. Ed. C. R. Markham, Roxburgh Club (1880), p. 45.
85. Conyers Read, *Mr Secretary Cecil and Queen Elizabeth* and *Lord Burghley and Queen Elizabeth* (London, 1955, 1960).
86. She had been famous in her youth for dancing the men's steps of the volta in order to keep fit (in strict privacy, of course.)
87. Camden, *Elizabeth*, p. 658.
88. Ibid.
89. Ibid.

Notes to Chapter 13: The Great Queen

1. Wallace MacCaffrey, *Elizabeth I: War and Politics, 1588–1603* (London, 1992), p. 574.
2. *Calendar of State Papers, Spanish*, xi, p. 393. This had been in the context of a discussion on excluding her from the succession.
3. E. W. Ives, *Anne Boleyn* (London, 1986), pp. 393–95.
4. Mary was undoubtedly the legitimate granddaughter of Margaret Tudor, and had been excluded only on the dubious grounds that she had been born outside the realm. On the other hand the statute which had passed her over was both valid and lawful.
5. A number of observers commented upon her simple style of dress; a marked contrast with her image as queen.
6. Ives, *Anne Boleyn*, pp. 358–82.
7. There are a number of versions of this poem, which are discussed in *Elizabeth I: Collected Works*, pp. 303–4.
8. The most extreme expression of this view was in John Knox, *The First Blast of the Trumpet against the Monstrous Regiment of Women* (Geneva, 1558). This had been aimed at Mary Tudor and Mary of Guise, the queen regent of Scotland, but Knox became *persona non grata* in England as a consequence.
9. On this point see particularly Philippa Berry, *Of Chastity and Power* (London, 1989), esp. pp. 111–33.
10. For a detailed exposition of all these shifts and changes, see Susan Doran, *Monarchy and Matrimony: The Courtships of Elizabeth I* (London, 1996) passim.

11. The imperial ambassadors reported this as her opinion on 2 August 1553, *Calendar of State Papers, Spanish*, xi, pp. 129–34.
12. In her Tilbury speech, *Elizabeth I: Collected Works*, pp. 325–26.
13. For one typical example of such tactics, see MacCaffrey, *War and Politics*, pp. 156–62.
14. She was particularly suspicious of convocation for that reason; W. P. Haugaard, *Elizabeth and the English Reformation: The Struggle for a Stable Settlement of Religion* (Cambridge, 1970).
15. So, of course, had the Act of Supremacy, which had declared 'that it be established and enacted by the authority aforesaid that such jurisdictions, privileges [etc] for reformation, order and correction of all manner of errors, heresies, schisms abuses, offences, contempts and enormities, shall forever by authority of this present parliament be united and annexed to the Imperial Crown of this realm.' *Statutes of the Realm*, iv, pt 2, pp. 350–55.
16. Cecil's frustration over the Scottish situation in 1560 even prompted him to offer his resignation; Conyers Read, *Mr Secretary Cecil and Queen Elizabeth* (London, 1955), p. 161.
17. Ibid., 135–72.
18. N. A. M. Rodger, *The Safeguard of the Sea* (London, 1997), pp. 199–200.
19. MacCaffrey, *Making of Policy*, pp. 348–53.
20. E.g., J. S. Nolan, *Sir John Norreys and the Elizabethan Military World* (Exeter, 1997), pp. 177–79.
21. L. B. Smith, *Treason in Tudor England: Politics and Paranoia* (London, 1986), pp. 235–36.
22. Longleat, MS 114 A, iv, fol. 66; Lawrence Stone, *Crisis of the Aristocracy* (Oxford, 1965), p. 237.
23. Ibid., pp. 234–40.
24. Ibid.
25. Lord Dacre of the South was hanged in 1541 for murdering a witness to a poaching expedition; and Lord Stourton was hanged in 1556 for imprisoning and murdering two private enemies.
26. For a discussion of the way in which the musters were organised, see L. O. Boynton, *The Elizabethan Militia* (London, 1967).
27. Judith Richards, 'Love and a Female Monarch: The Case of Elizabeth Tudor', *Journal of British Studies*, 38 (1999), pp. 133–60.
28. Cecil was very careful to renounce any territorial or jurisdictional ambition in respect of Scotland, in spite of his conviction that England possessed an imperial authority over its neighbour.
29. *Elizabeth I: Collected Works*, pp. 400–2.
30. D. Loades, *England's Maritime Empire: Seapower, Commerce and Policy, 1490–1690* (London, 2000), pp. 79–108.
31. Or is alleged to have done so, his horror of violence arising, it was claimed, from his mother having witnessed the murder of David Rizzio while carrying him. D. H. Willson, *King James the VI and I* (London, 1956).

32. J. N. King, *Tudor Royal Iconography: Literature and Art in an Age of Religious Crisis* (Princeton, New Jersey, 1989); Sydney Anglo, *Images of Tudor Kingship* (London, 1992).

33. There is a well-known portrait of Edward, imitating his father's hand-on-hip posture, by Willem Scrots. Jennifer Loach, *Edward VI* (London, 1999), plate 7.

34. D. Loades, *The Reign of Mary Tudor* (London, 1991), pp. 196–202.

35. *A Speciall Grace Appointed to Have Been Said after a Banket at York*, November 1558 (*STC*, 7599), sigs Aiii verso–Aiv.

36. 'The Queen is a Spaniard at heart. She loves another realm better than this' etc.; Loades, *Reign of Mary*, pp. 186–88.

37. *Elizabeth I: Collected Works*, pp. 56–58.

38. *The Passage of Our Most Dread Sovereign Lady, Queen Elizabeth, through the City of London* (1559), in A. F. Pollard, *Tudor Tracts* (London, 1903), pp. 365–95; Richards, 'Love and a Female Monarch'.

39. MacCaffrey, *War and Politics*, p. 3.

40. Peter Clark, *English Provincial Society from the Reformation to the Revolution* (Brighton, 1977).

41. 'The great rejoycing of the said parish and the country thereabouts' is recorded in the Lewshall parish register in the Bury St Edmunds Record Office; Zillah Dovey, *An Elizabethan Progress* (Stroud, 1996), p. 47.

42. Blair Worden, *The Sound of Virtue: Philip Sidney's Arcadia and Elizabethan Politics* (New Haven, 1996).

43. 'The Queens Visiting of the Camp at Tilbury', T. Delony, 10 August 1588; A. F. Pollard, *Tudor Tracts* (London, 1903), p. 494.

44. Lady Norris was apparently dark complexioned; *Elizabeth I: Collected Works*, p. 389.

45. Ibid., p. 399.

46. John Southworth, *Fools and Jesters at the English Court* (Stroud, 1998), p. 107.

47. *The Letting of Humours Blood in the Head-Vaine* (1600), epigram 30, sig. C 2 verso.

48. Southworth, *Fools and Jesters*, p. 110.

49. Janet Arnold, *Queen Elizabeth's Wardrobe Unlock'd* (London, 1988), pp. 107–8.

50. On Mary's legal definitions of female rule, see above, p. 86. She was generally felt to have surrendered her kingdom's interests to her husband – particularly in going to war with France in 1557.

Bibliography

PRIMARY SOURCES

Manuscripts

Bodleian Library, Oxford

Rawlinson	A. 100
Rawlinson	A. 206

British Library, London

Additional MSS	4149
	33531
Additional Charter	67534
Cotton MSS	Caligula B. viii
	Caligula B. ix
	Caligula C. i
	Caligula C. ii
	Caligula C. iii
	Galba C. xi
	Otho C. x
	Otho E. ix
	Titus B. i
	Titus B. ii
	Vespasian C. xiv
	Vespasian F. vi
Harley MSS	260
	2202
	6265
	6993
Lansdowne MSS	3
	29
	34
	56
	59

Lansdowne MSS	104
(*continued*)	170
	1236
Royal MSS	7 C. xvi
	14 A. iii
	17 B. xxviii

Public Record Office, London

Exchequer	E101	Accounts various
	E179	Lay subsidy rolls
	E351	Pipe Office declared accounts
Lord Chamberlain's Office, LC2		Records of special events
State Papers	SP1	Henry VIII, general series
	SP10	Edward VI, domestic
	SP11	Mary and Philip and Mary, domestic
	SP12	Elizabeth, domestic
	SP52	Elizabeth, Scotland
	SP70	Elizabeth, foreign
	SP78	Foreign policy, France
	SP84	
PRO 31/3		Baschet's transcripts

Contemporary Printed Works

Ascham, Roger, *The English Works (1545–1570)*, ed., W. A. Wright (London, 1904).

Bacon, Francis, *Works*, ed. J. Spedding et al., 14 vols (London, 1857–74).

Camden, William, *Annales Anglicarum regnante Elizabeth* (London, 1615); trans. H. Norton (1635), as *The History of the Most Renowned Princess Elizabeth, Late Queen of England* (London, 1688).

Digges, Sir Dudley, *The Compleat Ambassador* (London, 1655).

Doleman, R. [Robert Parsons], *A Conference about the Next Succession* (Antwerp, 1594).

A Discourse of Treasons Practiced and Attempted against the Queenes Maiestie and her Realme by Francis Throgmorton (London, 1584); Harleian Miscellany, 3 (1809).

Foxe, John, *The Acts and Monuments of these Latter and Perillous Days* (London, 1563, 1576, 1583).

Grafton, Richard, *The Chronicle or History of England* (London, 1569; 1809 edn).

Hakluyt, Richard, *Principall Navigations, Voiages and Discoveries of the English Nation* (London, 1589).

Hay Any Work for Cooper? (anon, 1588)

Holinshed, Raphael, *Chronicles etc.* (London, 1577, 1587), ed. H. Ellis, 6 vols (1807–8).

Knox, John, *The First Blast of the Trumpet against the Monstrous Regiment of Women* (Geneva, 1558), in *Works*, ed. D. Laing, 6 vols (1846–64).

Nichols, Philip, *Sir Francis Drake Revived* (London, 1626).

Proctor, John, *The Historie of Wiats Rebellion* (London, 1554), in Pollard, *Tudor Tracts* (1903).

Purchas, Samuel, *Hakluytus Posthumus: or Purchas his Pilgrims* (London, 1625), 20 vols, Hakluyt Society (1905–7).

Puttenham, George, *The Arte of English Poesie*, ed. G. D. Willocke and A. Walke (Oxford, 1936).

Saint German, Christopher, *A Dialogue betwene a Doctour and a Student* (London, 1533), ed. T. F. T. Plucknett and J. Barton, Selden Society, 91 (1974).

A Speciall Grace to be Said after a Banket at York (London?, 1558).

Southwell, Robert, *A Consolatory Letter to the Afflicted Catholics in England* (Douai?, 1588).

Southwell, Robert, *An Humble Supplication to Her Maiestie* (Douai?, 1600).

Spenser, Edmund, *A View of the Present State of Ireland in 1596* (London, 1633), ed. W. L. Renwick (1970).

Stokes, Leonard, *An Ave Maria in Commendation of our Most Vertuous Queene* (London, 1554).

Surtz, E., and Virginia Murphy eds, *The Divorce Tracts of Henry VIII (1529–35)* (Angers, 1988).

The Noble Triumphant Coronation of Queen Anne (London, 1533), in A. F. Pollard, *Tudor Tracts* (1903).

The Passage of our Most Dread Sovereign Lady Queene Elizabeth … the Day before her Coronation (London, 1559), in Pollard, *Tudor Tracts* (1903).

Wotton, Sir Henry, *Reliquae Wottonianae: or a Collection of Lives, Letters, Poems* (London, 1651).

Calendars and Printed Sources

Accounts of William Lok, 1536. Philobiblion Society, 7 (London, 1862–63).

A Collection of Scarce and Valuable Tracts of the Late Lord Somers, ed. Walter Scott (London, 1809).

Acts of the Privy Council, ed. J. Dasent et al. (London, 1890–1907).

Annals of the First Four Years of the Reign of Queen Elizabeth by Sir John Hayward, Knight, ed. J. Bruce, Camden Society, 7 (London, 1840).

Birch, Thomas, *Memoirs of the Reign of Elizabeth from the Year 1581 till her Death*, 2 vols (London, 1754).

Bedouëlle, Guy, and P. Le Gal, eds, *Le 'divorce' du Roi Henry VIII* (Geneva, 1987).

Bull, W. W. R., and J. A. Venn, *Admissions to Trinity College, Cambridge* (Cambridge, 1913).

Burton, Robert, *The Anatomy of Melancholy* (London, 1621), ed. F. Dell and P. Jordan Smith (London, 1938).

Calendar of the Carew MSS, ed. T. D. Hardy and J. S. Bremer (London, 1864).

Calendar of the Patent Rolls, 1547–53, ed. R. H. Brodie (London, 1924–29); *1553–1558* (London, 1936–39); *1558–* (London, 1939–).

Calendar of the Plymouth Municipal Records, ed. R. N. Worth (Plymouth, 1893).

Calendar of State Papers, Domestic, ed. C. S. Knighton: *Edward VI* (London, 1992); *Mary and Philip and Mary* (London, 1998).

Calendar of State Papers, Domestic; 1547–1603, ed. R. Lemon; *Addenda, 1566–1625* (London, 1856–72).

Calendar of State Papers, Foreign, 1547–53, ed. W. Turnbull (London, 1861); *1558–89,* ed. J. Stevenson et al. (London, 1863–1950).

Calendar of State Papers Relating to Ireland, 1596–1601, ed. E. G. Atkinson (London, 1893–1905).

Calendar of State Papers Relating to Ireland, 1571–75; ed. M. O'Dowd (London, 2000).

Calendar of State Papers, Milan, 1385–1618, ed. A. B. Hinds (London, 1912).

Calendar of State Papers, Rome, 1558–78, ed. J. M. Rigg (London, 1916–26).

Calendar of State Papers Relating to Scotland, 1547–1603, ed. J. Bain et al. (London, 1898–1952).

Calendar of State Papers, Spanish, 1485–1558, ed. by Royall Tyler et al. (London, 1862–1954); *1558–1603,* ed. M. A. S. Hume (London, 1892–99).

Calendar of State Papers, Venetian, 1202–1603, ed. Rawdon Brown et al. (London, 1864–98).

Cavendish, George, *The Life and Death of Cardinal Wolsey,* ed. R. S. Sylvester, Early English Text Society, new series, 243 (London, 1959).

Cobbett, William, et al., eds, *A Complete Collection of State Trials* (London, 1816–98).

Colleccion de documentos ineditos para la historia de España, ed. M. F. Navarrete (Madrid, 1842–95).

Correspondance du Cardinal Jean du Bellay, ed. R. Scheurer (Paris, 1969).

Correspondance diplomatique de B. Salaignac de la Mothe Fénelon, ed. A. Teulet, 7 vols (Paris, 1838–40).

Correspondance du nonce en France; Anselmo Dandino, 1578–81; ed. I. Cloulas. Acta Nuntiaturae Gallicae, 8 (Paris, 1970).

Correspondance de Granvelle, ed. C. Piot; 9 vols (Brussels, 1878–96).

Desiderata curiosa, ed. Francis Peck, 2 vols (London, 1732–35).

Devereux, Walter, ed., *Lives and Letters of the Devereux Earls of Essex,* 2 vols (London, 1853).

'Documents Illustrating the History of the Spanish Armada, Anno 1588', ed. G. P. B. Naish, *Naval Miscellany,* 4 (1952).

Elton, G. R., *The Tudor Constitution* (Cambridge, 1982).

Foedera, conventiones, etc., ed. T. Rymer (London, 1704–35).

Haynes, Samuel, and William Murdin, eds., *A Collection of State Papers, Left by William Cecil, Lord Burghley* (London, 1740–59).

Historical Manuscripts Commission Reports: Duke of Rutland (12th Report); *Marquis of Salisbury (Hatfield MSS)* (3rd, 4th, 5th, 6th, 7th, 12th, 13th, 14th, 15th, 16th, 17th reports; vols 1–15).

Jordan, W. K., *The Chronicle and Political Papers of Edward VI* (London, 1970).

Kingsford, C. L., 'The Taking of the Madre de Dios, 1592', *Naval Miscellany,* 2 (1912).

Letters and Memorials of Robert Parsons, ed., Leo Hicks, Catholic Records Society, 39 (London, 1942).

Letters and Papers, Foreign and Domestic, of the Reign of Henry VIII, ed. J. S. Brewer et al. (London, 1862–1910).

Letters and Papers of the Verney Family, ed. John Bruce, Camden Society, 66 (London, 1853).

Madden, Sir Frederick, *The Privy Purse Expenses of the Princess Mary* (London, 1831).

Marcus, L. S., J. Mueller and M. B. Rose, eds, *Elizabeth I: Collected Works* (Chicago, 2000).

Mémoires de la Chanoine Jean Moreau sur les Guerres de la Ligue en Brétagne, ed. W. Waquet (Paris, 1960).

Narratives of the Days of the Reformation, ed. J. G. Nichols, Camden Society, 77 (London, 1860).

Nichols, J. G., ed., *Literary Remains of Edward VI*, Roxburghe Club (London, 1857).

Original Letters Illustrative of English History, ed. Henry Ellis, 11 vols (London, 1824–46).

Original Letters Relative to the English Reformation, ed. H. Robinson, Parker Society (London, 1846, 1859).

Papers Relating to the Navy during the Spanish War, 1585–7, ed. J. S. Corbett, Navy Records Society, 11 (London, 1898).

Relations politiques des Pays Bas et de L'Angleterre sous le règne de Philippe II, ed. J. M. B. C. Kervyn de Lettenhove (Brussels, 1882–1900).

Sharp, Cuthbert, *Memorials of the 1569 Rebellion* (London, 1840).

Sidney, Henry, *Letters and Memorials of State, from the Originals at Penshurst Place in Kent*, ed. A. Collins, 2 vols (London, 1746).

Sir Francis Drake's West Indian Voyage, ed. M. F. Keeler, Hakluyt Society (London, 1981).

State Papers of King Henry VIII, 11 vols (London, 1830–52).

State Papers Relating to the Defeat of the Spanish Armada, Anno 1588, ed. J. K. Laughton, Navy Records Society, 1, 2 (1894).

Statutes of the Realm, ed. A Luder et al. (London, 1810–28).

The Annals of the Kingdom of Ireland by the Four Masters, ed. J. O'Donovan (Dublin, 1998).

'The Bedingfield Papers', *Norfolk Archaeological Society Transactions*, 4 (1855).

The Chronicle of Queen Jane, ed. J. G. Nichols, Camden Society, 48 (London, 1850).

The Correspondence of Matthew Parker, ed. J. Bruce and T. T. Perowne, Parker Society (London, 1853).

The Correspondence of Robert Dudley, Earl of Leicester, 1585 and 1586; ed. John Bruce, Camden Society, 27 (London, 1844).

'The Count of Feria's Dispatch to Philip II of 14th November 1558', ed. M.-J. Rodgriguez Salgado and S. Adams; *Camden Miscellany*, 28 (London, 1984).

The Diary of Henry Machyn, ed. J. G. Nichols, Camden Society, 42 (London, 1848).

The Edmondes Papers, ed. G. G. Butler, Roxburghe Club (London, 1913).

The Egerton Papers, ed. J. Payne Collier; Camden Society, 12 (1840).

'The Household Accounts of the Princess Elizabeth', ed. Viscount Stratford, *Camden Miscellany*, 2 (1853).

The Jacobean Commissions of Enquiry, 1608, 1618, ed. A. P. McGowan, Navy Records Society, 116 (London, 1971).

The Letter Book of Sir Amyas Poulet, Keeper of Mary, Queen of Scots, ed. J. Morris (London, 1874).

The Lisle Letters, ed. M. St Clare Byrne, 6 vols (Chicago, 1981).

The List and Analysis of State Papers, Foreign Series, 1591–97, ed. R. B. Wernham, 5 vols (London, 1964–89).

The Naval Tracts of Sir William Monson, ed. M. Oppenheimer, Navy Records Society, 22, 23 (London, 1902–14).

The Papers of George Wyatt, ed. D. Loades, Camden Society, 4th series, 5 (London, 1968).

The Royal Visitation of 1559: The Act Book for the Northern Province, ed. C. J. Kitching, Surtees Society, 187 (Durham, 1975).

The State Papers and Letters of Sir Ralph Sadler, ed. A. Clifford (London, 1809).

'The Vita Mariae Angliae of Robert Wingfield of Brantham', ed. D. MacCulloch, *Camden Miscellany*, 28 (1984).

Tudor Royal Proclamations, ed. P. L. Hughes and J. F. Larkin, 3 vols (New Haven, Connecticut, 1964–69).

Vertot, R. A. de, ed., *Ambassades de Messieurs de Noailles* (Louvain, 1743).

Visitation Articles and Injunctions of the Period of the Reformation, ed. W. H. Frere and W. M. Kennedy, Alcuin Club (London, 1910).

Wernham, R. B., ed., *The Expedition of Sir John Norris and Sir Francis Drake to Spain and Portugal, 1589*, Navy Records Society, 127 (London, 1988).

SECONDARY WORKS

Books

Adams, S., *Leicester and the Court: Essays on Elizabethan Politics* (London, 2002).

Adlard, George, *Amy Robsart and the Earl of Leicester* (London, 1870).

Adlard, George, *The Sutton Dudleys of England* (London, 1842).

Alford, S., *Kingship and Politics in the Reign of Edward VI* (Cambridge, 2002).

Alford, S., *The Early Elizabethan Polity: Sir William Cecil and the British Succession Crisis, 1558–1569* (Cambridge, 1998).

Andrews, K. R., *Drake's Voyages* (London, 1967).

Andrews, K. R., *Elizabethan Privateering, 1585–1603* (Cambridge, 1964).

Andrews, K. R., *The Spanish Caribbean: Trade and Plunder, 1530–1630* (New Haven, Connecticut, 1978).

Anglo, Sydney, *Images of Tudor Kingship* (London, 1992).

Anstruther, G., *The Seminary Priests*, 4 vols (Ware, Durham, 1968–77).

Arnold, Janet, *Queen Elizabeth's Wardrobe Unlock'd* (Leeds, 1988).

Ascoli, G., *La Grande Brétagne devant l'opinion française* (Paris, 1927).

Baker, J. H., *An Introduction to English Legal History* (London, 1979).

Bayne, C. G., *Anglo-Roman Relations, 1558–1565* (Oxford, 1913; 1968).

Berry, Philippa, *Of Chastity and Power: Elizabethan Literature and the Virgin Queen* (London, 1989).

Bindoff, S. T., *The History of Parliament: The House of Commons, 1509–1558* (London, 1982).

Birke, A. M., and R. G. Asche, *Patronage and Nobility; the Court at the Beginning of the Modern Age* (Cambridge, 1991).

Black, J. B., *The Reign of Elizabeth, 1558–1603* (Oxford, 1959).

Bossy, J., *The English Catholic Community, 1570–1850* (London, 1976).

Boynton, L. O., *The Elizabethan Militia* (Oxford, 1967).

Bradley, Emily, *The Life of Arabella Stuart*, 2 vols (London, 1889).

Bradshaw, Brendan, *The Dissolution of the Religious Orders in Ireland under Henry VIII* (Cambridge, 1974).

Bradshaw, Brendan, *The Irish Constitutional Crisis of the Sixteenth Century* (Cambridge, 1979).

Brady, Ciaran, *The Chief Governors: The Rise and Fall of Reform Government in Tudor Ireland, 1536–1588* (Cambridge, 1994).

Bremmer, Robert, *Merchants and Revolution* (Cambridge, 1993).

Brigden, Susan, *New Worlds, Lost Worlds* (London, 2000).

Burnet, Gilbert, *The History of the Reformation of the Church of England*, 3 vols (London, 1679–1715).

Canny, N., *The Elizabethan Conquest of Ireland: A Position Established, 1565–1576* (Hassocks, 1976).

Canny, N., *The Formation of an Old English Elite in Ireland* (Dublin, 1975).

Charnock, J., *A History of Marine Architecture* (London, 1802).

Clark, P., *English Provincial Society from the Reformation to the Revolution* (Hassocks, 1977).

Clark, P., and P. Slack, *English Towns in Transition, 1500–1700* (Oxford, 1976).

Clifford, Henry, *The Life of Jane Dormer, Duchess of Feria*, ed., J. Stevenson (London, 1887).

Clowes, W. L., *The Royal Navy: A History from the Earliest Times to the Present Day*, 7 vols (London, 1897–1903).

Collins, A. J., *The Jewels and Plate of Queen Elizabeth* (London, 1956).

Collinson, Patrick, *Edmund Grindal, 1519–1583: The Struggle for a Reformed Church* (Berkeley, California, 1979).

Collinson, Patrick, *The Elizabethan Puritan Movement* (London, 1967).

Collinson, Patrick, *The Religion of Protestants: The Church in English Society, 1559–1625* (Oxford, 1982).

Colvin, H. M., *The History of the King's Works*, iv (Oxford, 1982).

Craig, John, *Reformation, Politics and Polemics* (Cambridge, 2002).

Crawford, J. G., *Anglicising the Government of Ireland: The Irish Privy Council and the Expansion of Tudor Rule, 1556–1579* (Dublin, 1993).

Cruickshank, G. C., *Elizabeth's Army* (London, 1966).

Dawson, J. E. A., *The Politics of Religion in the Age of Mary Queen of Scots: The Earl of Argyll and the Struggle for Britain and Ireland* (Cambridge, 2002).

Dietz, F. C., *English Public Finance, 1558–1641* (New York, 1932).

Doran, Susan, *Monarchy and Matrimony: The Courtships of Elizabeth I* (London, 1996).

Dovey, Zillah, *An Elizabethan Progress: The Queen's Journey into East Anglia, 1578* (Stroud, 1995).

Dowling, Maria, *Humanism in the Reign of Henry VIII* (London, 1986).

Edwards, R. D., *Church and State in Ireland* (Dublin, 1935).

Ellis, S. E., *Tudor Ireland, 1470–1603* (London, 1985).

Elton, G. R., *The Practice of History* (Cambridge, 1967).

Falls, Cyril, *Elizabeth's Irish Wars* (London, 1950).

Falls, Cyril, *Mountjoy: Elizabethan General* (London, 1955).

Fines, John, *A Biographical Register of Early English Protestants, 1525–1558* (Sutton Courtenay, 1981).

Ford, A., *The Protestant Reformation in Ireland* (Frankfurt, 1985).

Foster, Sir William, *England's Quest of Eastern Trade* (London, 1933; 1966).

Frere, W. H., *Puritan Manifestos: A Study in the Origin of the Puritan Revolt* (London, 1907; 1954).

Fury, Cheryl A., *Tides in the Affairs of Men: The Social History of Elizabethan Seamen, 1580–1603* (Westport, Connecticut, 2002).

Gage, John, *The Antiquities of Hengrave* (London, 1822).

Garrett, C. H., *The Marian Exiles* (Cambridge, 1938).

Gee, Henry, *The Elizabethan Clergy and the Settlement of Religion, 1558–1564* (London, 1898).

Gibson, E. C. S., *The Thirty-Nine Articles of the Church of England* (London, 1910).

Graves, M. A. R., *Thomas Norton: The Parliament Man* (Cambridge, 1994).

Gunn, S. J., *Early Tudor Government, 1485–1558* (London, 1995).

Gwyn, Peter, *The King's Cardinal* (London, 1990).

Haigh, Christopher, *Elizabeth I* (2nd edn, London, 2000).

Haigh, Christopher, *English Reformations* (Oxford, 1993).

Hammer, P. E. J., *The Polarisation of Elizabethan Politics: The Career of Robert Devereux, 2nd Earl of Essex* (Cambridge, 1999).

Handover, P. M., *The Second Cecil: The Rise to Power, 1563–1604, of Sir Robert Cecil, Later First Earl of Salisbury* (London, 1959).

Harbison, E. H., *Rival Ambassadors at the Court of Queen Mary* (Princeton, 1940).

Harris, Barbara, *Edward Stafford, 3rd Duke of Buckingham, 1478–1521* (London, 1986).

Hartley, T. E., *Proceedings in the Parliament of Elizabeth I, 1559–1581, 1983; 1584–1601* (Leicester, 1989).

Hasler, P. W., *The History of Parliament: The House of Commons, 1558–1603* (London, 1981).

Haugaard, W. P., *Elizabeth and the English Reformation* (Cambridge, 1968).

Hoak, D. E., *The King's Council in the Reign of Edward VI* (Cambridge, 1976).

Holmes, Peter, *Resistance and Compromise: The Political Thought of the Elizabethan Catholics* (Cambridge, 1982).

Hughes, Philip, *Rome and the Counter Reformation in England* (London, 1942).

Ives, E. W., *Anne Boleyn* (Oxford, 1986).

James, Susan, *Katheryn Parr: The Making of a Queen* (Stroud, 1999).

Jones, N. L., *Faith by Statute* (Cambridge, 1982).

Jones, N. L., *The Birth of the Elizabethan Age: England in the 1560s* (Oxford, 1993).

Jordan, W. K., *Edward VI: The Threshold of Power* (London, 1970).

Jordan, W. K., *Edward VI: The Young King* (London, 1968).

Kamen, Henry, *Philip II* (New Haven, Connecticut, 1997).

Kelly, H. A., *The Matrimonial Trials of Henry VIII* (Hassocks, 1976).

Kelsey, H., *Sir Francis Drake: The Queen's Pirate* (New Haven, Connecticut, 1998).

Kervyn de Lettenhove, *Les Huguenots et les Gueux* (Brussels, 1883–85).

King, J. N., *Tudor Royal Iconography: Literature and Art in an Age of Religious Crisis* (Princeton, New Jersey, 1989).

Kingdom, R. M., *Myths about the St Bartholomew's Day Massacre, 1573–4* (Cambridge, Massachusetts, 1988).

Knecht, R. J., *Francis I* (London, 1982).

Lehmberg, S. E., *The Reformation Parliament* (Cambridge, 1970).

Levine, Mortimer, *The Early Elizabethan Succession Question* (Stanford, California, 1966).

Lewis, M., *The Hawkins Dynasty* (London, 1969).

Loach, J., *Parliament and the Crown in the Reign of Mary Tudor* (Oxford, 1986).

Loach, J., *Edward VI* (London, 1999).

Loades, D. M., *England's Maritime Empire* (London, 2000).

Loades, D. M., *Henry VIII and his Queens* (Stroud, 1994).

Loades, D. M., *John Dudley, Duke of Northumberland* (Oxford, 1996).

Loades, D. M., *Mary Tudor: A Life* (Oxford, 1989).

Loades, D. M., *Relations between the Anglican and Roman Catholic Churches in the Sixteenth and Seventeenth Centuries* (Oxford, 2002)

Loades, D. M., *The Chronicles of the Tudor Queens* (Stroud, 2002)

Loades, D. M., *The Dudley Conspiracy* (Oxford, 2001).

Loades, D. M., *The Oxford Martyrs* (London, 1970; Bangor, 1992).

Loades, D. M, *The Reign of Mary Tudor* (London, 1991).

Loades, D. M., *The Tudor Court* (London, 1986; Bangor, 1992).

Loades, D. M., *The Tudor Navy: An Administrative, Political and Military History* (Aldershot, 1992).

Loades, D. M., *The Wyatt Rebellion* (Oxford, 2001).

Loomie, A. J., *The Spanish Elizabethans* (London, 1963).

MacCaffrey, Wallace, *Elizabeth I* (London, 1993).

MacCaffrey, Wallace, *Elizabeth I: War and Politics, 1588–1603* (London, 1992).

MacCaffrey, Wallace, *Queen Elizabeth and the Making of Policy, 1572–1588* (Princeton, New Jersey, 1981).

MacCaffrey, Wallace, *The Shaping of the Elizabethan Regime, 1558–1572* (Princeton, New Jersey, 1968).

MacCulloch, Diarmaid, *Thomas Cranmer* (New Haven, Connecticut, 1996).

Maclean, J., *The Life of Sir Thomas Seymour* (London, 1848).

McGrath, P., *Papists and Puritans under Elizabeth I* (London, 1967).

Mattingly, Garrett, *Catherine of Aragon* (London, 1963).

Meyer, A. O., *England and the Catholic Church under Queen Elizabeth*, trans. J. R. McKee (London, 1916).

Meyer, C. S., *Elizabeth I and the Religious Settlement of 1559* (St Louis, Missouri, 1959).

Miller, Helen, *Henry VIII and the English Nobility* (Oxford, 1986).

Milward, Peter, *Religious Controversies of the Elizabethan Age* (London, 1977).

Morgan, Hiram, *Tyrone's Rebellion: The Origin of the Nine Years War in Ulster* (Woodbridge, 1993).

Morison, Fynes, *An History of Ireland from 1599 to 1603*, 2 vols (Dublin, 1735).

Murphy, B., *Bastard Prince: Henry VIII's Lost Son* (Stroud, 2001).

Muller. J. A., *Stephen Gardiner and the Tudor Reaction* (New York, 1926).

Neale, J. E., *Queen Elizabeth and her Parliaments*, 2 vols (London, 1953, 1957).

Nichols, J. G., *The Progresses of Queen Elizabeth*, 4 vols (London, 1788–1821).

Nolan, J. S., *Sir John Norreys and the Elizabethan Military World* (Exeter, 1997).

O'Dowd, M., *Power, Politics and Land: Early Modern Sligo, 1568–1688* (Dublin, 1991).

Olsen, V. Norskov, *John Foxe and the Elizabethan Church* (Berkeley, California, 1973).

Oppenheim, M., *The History of the Administration of the Royal Navy, 1509–1660* (London, 1896, 1988).

Outhwaite, R. B., *Inflation in Tudor and Early Stuart England* (London, 1969).

Parker, Geoffrey, *The Dutch Revolt* (London, 1977).

Parker, Geoffrey, and Colin Martin, *The Spanish Armada* (London, 1988).

Pettegree, A., *Foreign Protestant Communities in Sixteenth-Century London* (Oxford, 1986).

Price, W. H., *The English Patents of Monopoly* (New Haven, Connecticut, 1906).

Pulman, M. B., *The Elizabethan Privy Council in the 1570s* (Berkeley, California, 1971).

Ramsey, G. D., *The City of London in International Politics at the Accession of Elizabeth* (London, 1975).

Read, Conyers, *Lord Burghley and Queen Elizabeth* (London, 1960).

Read, Conyers, *Mr Secretary Cecil and Queen Elizabeth* (London, 1955).

Read, Conyers, *Mr Secretary Walsingham and the Policy of Queen Elizabeth* (London, 1925).

Redworth, G., *In Defence of the Church Catholic: A Life of Stephen Gardiner* (Oxford, 1990).

Rodgers, Nicholas, *The Safeguard of the Sea: A Naval History of Britain, 660–1648* (London, 1997).

Rodriquez Salgado, M.-J., *Armada* (London, 1988).

Rodriguez Salgado, M.-J., *The Changing Face of Empire, 1551–1559* (Cambridge, 1988).

Rowen, H. H., *The Low Countries in Early Modern Times* (London, 1972).

Scarisbrick, J. J., *Henry VIII* (London, 1968; 1997).

Shell, Marc, *Elizabeth's Glass* (Lincoln, Nebraska, 1993).

Sidney, Algernon, *A Life of Robert Cecil, 1st Earl of Salisbury* (London, 1915).

Silke, J. J., *Ireland and Europe, 1559–1607* (Dublin, 1966).

Silke, J. J., *Kinsale: The Spanish Intervention in Ireland at the End of the Elizabethan Wars* (Liverpool, 1970).

Slack, Paul, *Poverty and Policy in Tudor and Stuart England* (London, 1988).

Slack, Paul, *The English Poor Law, 1531–1782* (Basingstoke, 1990).

Smith, L. B., *Elizabeth Tudor: Portrait of a Queen* (Boston, New Jersey, 1975).

Smith, L. B., *Treason in Tudor England: Politics and Paranoia* (London, 1986).

Southworth, John, *Fools and Jesters at the English Court* (Stroud, 1998).

Spence, R. T., *The Privateering Earl: George Clifford, 3rd Earl of Cumberland, 1558–1605* (Stroud, 1995).

Starkey, David, *Elizabeth* (London, 2000).

Stone, L., *The Crisis of the Aristocracy, 1558–1641* (Oxford, 1965).

Strong, Roy, *Gloriana: The Portraits of Elizabeth* (London, 1987).

Strong, Roy, *The Cult of Elizabeth* (London, 1977).

Strype, John, *A History of the Life and Acts of Edmund Grindal* (London, 1710; 1821).

Strype, John, *Annals of the Reformation*, 4 vols (London, 1725).

Strype, John, *Ecclesiastical Memorials*, 3 vols (London, 1721).

Strype, John, *The Life and Acts of Matthew Parker*, 1711; 3 vols (London, 1821).

Strype, John, *The Life of Sir John Cheke* (London, 1705).

Sutherland, N. M., *The Huguenot Struggle for Recognition* (London, 1980).

Symonds, T. H., ed., *Meta Incognita: A Discourse of Discovery* (Hull, Quebec, 1999).

Tytler, P. F., *The Reigns of Edward VI and Mary* (London, 1839).

Usher, R., *The Rise and Fall of High Commission* (Oxford, 1913).

Usherwood, S. and E., *The Counter Armada, 1596* (London, 1983).

Walker, Greg, *John Skelton and the Politics of the 1520s* (Cambridge, 1988).

Walsham, Alexandra, *Church Papists: Catholicism, Conformity and Confessional Polemics in Early Modern England* (Woodbridge, 1993).

Warnicke, Retha, *The Marrying of Anne of Cleves* (Cambridge, 2000).

Warnicke, Retha, *The Rise and Fall of Anne Boleyn* (Cambridge, 1989).

Watt, J., *The Church in Medieval Ireland* (Dublin, 1972).

Weissener, L., *The Youth of Queen Elizabeth*, trans. C. Yonge (London, 1879).

Wenig, Scott A., *Straightening the Altars: The Ecclesiastical Vision and Pastoral Achievements of the Progressive Bishops under Elizabeth I, 1559–1575* (New York, 2000).

Wernham, R. B., *After the Armada* (Oxford, 1984).

Williams, Penry, *The Later Tudors, 1547–1603* (Oxford, 1995).

Williams, Penry, *The Tudor Regime* (Oxford, 1979).

Wilson, Derek, *Sweet Robin: A Biography of Robert Dudley, Earl of Leicester, 1533–1588* (London, 1981).

Willson, D. H., *King James the VI and I* (London, 1956).

Worden, Blair, *The Sound of Virtue: Philip Sidney's Arcadia and Elizabethan Politics* (New Haven, Connecticut, 1996).

Wright, Thomas, *Queen Elizabeth and her Times* (London, 1838).

Articles

Adams, Simon, 'Eliza Enthroned? The Court and its Politics', in Simon Adams, ed., *Leicester and the Court. Leicester and the Court: Essays on Elizabethan Politics* (London, 2002).

Adams, Simon, 'Faction, Clientage and Party: English Politics, 1550–1603', in Simon Adams, ed., *Leicester and the Court. Leicester and the Court: Essays on Elizabethan Politics* (London, 2002).

Adams, Simon, 'Favourites and Factions at the Elizabethan Court', in Simon Adams, ed., *Leicester and the Court. Leicester and the Court: Essays on Elizabethan Politics* (London, 2002).

Adams, Simon, 'New Light on the "Reformation" of John Hawkins: The Ellesmere Naval Survey of 1584', *English Historical Review*, 105 (1991), pp. 97–111.

Adams, Simon, 'The Dudley Clientele, 1553–1563', in G. Bernard, ed., *The Tudor Nobility* (London, 1992).

Adams, Simon, 'The Patronage of the Crown in Elizabethan Politics: The 1590s in Perspective', in Simon Adams, ed., *Leicester and the Court. Leicester and the Court: Essays on Elizabethan Politics* (London, 2002).

Aird, Ian, 'The Death of Amy Robsart', *English Historical Review*, 71 (1956), pp. 69–79.

Alsop, J. D., 'Innovation in Tudor Taxation', *English Historical Review*, 99 (1984), pp. 83–93.

Barnes, K., 'John Stubbe, 1579: The French Ambassador's Account', *Historical Research*, 64 (1991), pp. 421–26.

Barrington, Michael, 'The Most High Spirited Man on Earth: Sir Richard Grenville's Last Fight, September 1591. New Evidence', *Mariners' Mirror*, 36 (1950), pp. 350–53.

Bartlett, Kenneth, 'Papal Policy and the English Crown, 1563–5: The Bertano Correspondence', *Sixteenth Century Journal*, 23 (1992), pp. 643–59.

Bartlett, Kenneth, ' "The Misfortune that is Wished for Him": The Exile and Death of Edward Courtenay, Eighth Earl of Devon', *Canadian Journal of History*, 14 (1979), pp. 1–28.

Bayne, C. G., 'The Coronation of Queen Elizabeth', *English Historical Review*, 22 (1907), pp. 650–73.

Bernard, G., 'The Downfall of Sir Thomas Seymour', in G. Bernard, ed., *The Tudor Nobility* (London, 1992).

Bradshaw, B., 'Native Reaction to the Westward Enterprise: A Case Study in Gaelic Ideology', in K. Andrews, N. Canny and P. Hair, eds, *The Westward Enterprise* (1978).

Bradshaw, B., 'Sword, Word and Strategy in the Reformation in Ireland', *Historical Journal*, 21 (1978), pp. 475–502.

Bradshaw, B., 'The Edwardian Reformation in Ireland', *Archivum Hibernicum*, 34 (1976–77), pp. 83–99.

Brady, Ciaran, 'England's Defence and Ireland's Reform: The Dilemma of the Irish Viceroys, 1541–1641', in B. Bradshaw and J. Morrill, eds, *The British Problem, 1534–1707* (1996).

Brown, Nancy, 'Robert Southwell: The Mission of the Written Word', in McCoog, ed., *The Reckoned Expense*.

Dawson, J. E. A., 'Mary Queen of Scots, Lord Darnley and Anglo-Scottish Relations in 1565', *International History Review*, 8 (1986), pp. 1–24.

Dawson, J. E. A., 'William Cecil and the British Dimension of Early Elizabethan Foreign Policy', *History*, 74 (1989), pp. 196–216.

Duffy, E., 'William, Cardinal Allen, 1532–94', *Recusant History*, 22 (1995), pp. 265–90.

Glasgow, T., jnr, 'The Navy in the First Undeclared Elizabethan War', *Mariners' Mirror*, 54 (1968), pp. 23–37.

Haigh, Christopher, 'From Monopoly to Minority: Catholicism in Early Modern England', *Transactions of the Royal Historical Society*, 5th series, 31 (1981), pp. 129–47.

Haigh, Christopher, 'The Continuity of Catholicism in the English Reformation', in Haigh, ed., *The English Reformation Revised* (1987).

Haugaard, W. P., 'Elizabeth Tudor's Book of Devotions: A Neglected Clue to the Queen's Life and Character', *Sixteenth Century Journal*, 12 (1981), pp. 79–105.

Harbison, E. H., 'French Intrigue at the Court of Queen Mary', *American Historical Review*, 45 (1940), pp. 533–51.

Hays McCoy, G. H., 'The Army of Ulster, 1593–1601', *Irish Sword*, 1 (1950–51), pp. 105–27.

Henry, L. W., 'The Earl of Essex as Strategist and Military Organiser, 1596–7', *English Historical Review*, 68 (1953), pp. 363–93.

Henry, L. W., 'The Earl of Essex in Ireland, 1599', *Bulletin of the Institute of Historical Research*, 32 (1959)

Hurstfield, Joel, 'Robert Cecil, Earl of Salisbury; Minister of Elizabeth and James I', *History Today*, 7 (1957), pp. 279–89.

James, Mervyn, 'At a Crossroads of Political Culture: The Essex Revolt of 1601', in James, *Society, Politics and Culture* (1986).

Loades, D. M., 'Philip II and the Government of England', in *Law and Government under the Tudors*.

Lockie, D. M., 'The Political Career of the Bishop of Ross, 1568–1580', *University of Birmingham Historical Journal*, 4 (1953), pp. 98–145.

McConica, J. K., 'The Catholic Experience in Tudor Oxford', in *The Reckoned Expense*.

McGrath, P., 'Elizabethan Catholicism: A Reconsideration', *Journal of Ecclesiastical History*, 35 (1984), pp. 414–28.

Mears, Natalie, 'Love Making and Diplomacy: Elizabeth I and the Anjou Marriage Negotiations, 1578–1582', *History*, 86 (2001), pp. 442–66.

Mears, Natalie, 'Counsel, Public Debate and Queenship: John Stubb's *The Discoverie of a Gaping Gulf*', *Historical Journal*, 44 (2001), pp. 629–50.

Morgan, Hiram, 'The Colonial Venture of Sir Thomas Smith in Ulster, 1571–1575', *Historical Journal*, 28 (1985), pp. 261–78.

Neale, J. E., 'Elizabeth and the Netherlands, 1586–7', *English Historical Review*, 45 (1930), pp. 373–96.

Neale, J. E., 'The Elizabethan Acts of Supremacy and Uniformity', *English Historical Review*, 65 (1950), pp. 304–24.

Nicholson, G., 'The Act of Appeals and the English Reformation', in C. Cross, D. Loades, J. Scarisbrick, eds, *Law and Government under the Tudors* (1988).

O'Day, R., 'Thomas Bentham: A Case Study in the Problems of the Early Elizabethan Episcopate', *Journal of Ecclesiastical History*, 23 (1972).

Pearl, Valerie, 'Social Policy in Early Modern London', in H. Lloyd Jones et al., eds, *History and Imagination* (1979).

Pollen, J. H., 'Mary Queen of Scots and the Babington Plot', *Scottish Historical Society*, 3rd series, 3 (1922).

Potter, D. L., 'The Duc de Guise and the Fall of Calais', *English Historical Review*, 98 (1983), pp. 481–512.

Quinn, D. B., 'Sir Thomas Smith and the Beginnings of English Colonial Theory', *Proceedings of the American Philosophical Society*, 79 (1945).

Read, Conyers, 'Queen Elizabeth's Seizure of Alba's Pay Ships', *Journal of Modern History*, 5 (1933), pp. 443–64.

Redworth, G., '"Matters Impertinent to Women": Male and Female Monarchy under Philip and Mary', *English Historical Review*, 112 91997), pp. 597–613.

Richards, Judith, 'Love and a Female Monarch: The Case of Elizabeth Tudor', *Journal of British Studies*, 28 (1999), pp. 133–60.

Rowse, A. L., 'The Coronation of Queen Elizabeth I', *History Today*, 3 (1953), pp. 301–10.

Schofield, R. S., 'Taxation and the Political Limits of the Tudor State', in *Law and Government under the Tudors*.

Thorpe, M. R., 'Religion and the Rebellion of Sir Thomas Wyatt', *Church History*, 47 (1978), pp. 363–80.

Usher, Brett, 'Building Protestantism: The London Godly, the Exchequer and the Foxe Circle', in D. Loades, ed., *John Foxe: An Historical Perspective* (1999).

Walker, Greg, 'Rethinking the Fall of Anne Boleyn', *Historical Journal*, 45 (2002), pp. 1–30.

Warnicke, Retha, 'Sexual Heresy at the Court of Henry VIII', *Historical Journal*, 30 (1987), pp. 247–68.

Warnicke, Retha, 'The Fall of Anne Boleyn: A Reassessment', *History*, 70 (1985), pp. 1–15.

Williams, M. E., 'Campion and the English Continental Seminaries', in *The Reckoned Expense*.

Wright, P., 'A Change of Direction: The Ramifications of a Female Household', in D. Starkey, ed., *The English Court from the Wars of the Roses to the Civil War* (1987).

Index

Lightning Source UK Ltd.
Milton Keynes UK
UKOW04n0618250816

281439UK00011B/76/P